Understanding Computers and Information Processing:
Today and Tomorrow

Understanding Computers
and Information Processing:
Today and Tomorrow

with
BASIC

Charles S. Parker

The University of New Mexico, Albuquerque, New Mexico
The College of Santa Fé, Santa Fé, New Mexico

THE DRYDEN PRESS   Chicago Fort Worth San Francisco Philadelphia Montreal Toronto London Sydney Tokyo

To Mom and Dad

Acquisitions Editor: DeVilla Williams
Developmental Editor: Joanne Smith
Project Editor: Karen Hill
Design Supervisor: Alan Wendt
Production Manager: Barb Bahnsen
Permissions Editor: Doris Milligan
Director of Editing, Design, and Production: Jane Perkins

Text and Cover Designer: Barbara Gibson
Copy Editor: Nancy Maybloom
Indexer: Lois Oster
Compositor: The Clarinda Company
Text Type: 10/12 ITC Cheltenham Book

Library of Congress Cataloging-in-Publication Data

Parker, Charles S., 1945–
  Understanding computers and information processing : today and
tomorrow, with BASIC / Charles S. Parker. — 3rd ed.
    p. cm.
  Rev. ed. of: Understanding computers and data processing.
  Includes index.
  ISBN 0-03-030909-3
  1. Electronic digital computers.
I. Parker, Charles S., 1945–   Understanding computers and data
processing.   II. Title.
QA76.5.P318   1990
004–dc20   89-7753
                                                                  CIP

Printed in the United States of America
901-036-987654321

Address orders:
The Dryden Press
Orlando, FL 32887

Address editorial correspondence:
The Dryden Press
908 N. Elm Street
Hinsdale, IL 60521

The Dryden Press
Holt, Rinehart and Winston
Saunders College Publishing

Frontispiece: Image by James Dowlen; © Vision Technologies, Fremont, CA.

Preface Photos: (1) Cathrine Colgan/Wasatch Computer Technology. (2) "Beach Scene" by Jim Thompson. Produced with Lumena/16 software. Image courtesy Time Arts Inc. (3) Cathrine Colgan/Wasatch Computer Technology. (4) "Jade Cat" by James Dowlen. Courtesy Vision Technologies.

See the "Credits" section in the back matter for all other photo credits.

Preface

We are living at a time when the key to success in virtually every profession or career depends on the skillful use of information. Whether one is a teacher, lawyer, doctor, politician, manager, or corporate president, the main ingredient in the work involved is information—knowing how to get it, how to use it, where to keep it, and how to disseminate it to others.

At the root of all of these information-based work activities are computers and the systems that support them. Currently there are millions of computer systems in the world, and collectively, they are capable of doing thousands of different tasks. Some of the tasks that computer systems can now handle—such as making movies and creating art, or "speaking," "seeing," and "listening"—were thought impossible not too long ago. Few professions remain untouched by computers today or will remain so in tomorrow's world. No matter who you are or what you do for a living, it is highly likely that computers somehow affect the way you work.

The importance of computers in virtually every profession brings us to the purpose of this book. *Understanding Computers and Information Processing: Today and Tomorrow,* third edition, has been written with the end user of computers in mind. This nontechnical, introductory text explains in straightforward terms the importance of learning about computers, the types of computer systems and their components, the principles by which computer systems work, practical applications of computers and related technologies, and the ways in which the world is being and will be changed by computers. The goal of the text is both to provide knowledge of computer basics and to impart a perspective for using this knowledge effectively in the workplace.

The textbook is available in two versions—one with an appendix on BASIC programming and one without. However, the textbook is but one component of a complete and flexible instructional package—one that can easily be adapted to virtually any teaching format. Supplementing the textbook is a comprehensive set of student and teacher support materials.

THE TEXTBOOK

Understanding Computers and Information Processing: Today and Tomorrow, third edition, is designed for students taking a first course in computers and information processing. The text meets the requirements proposed for the first course in computing by both the Data Processing Management Association (DPMA) and the Association for Computing Machinery (ACM). Although it provides a comprehensive introduction to the world of computers, the text is not overly technical. Coverage is given to both commercial and personal applications of computers and large and small computer systems.

Key Features

Like previous editions, the third edition of *Understanding Computers and Information Processing: Today and Tomorrow* is current and comprehensive. It offers a flexible teaching organization and a readable and engaging presentation. Learning tools in each chapter help students master important concepts. Tomorrow boxes and Feature boxes provide insight on current issues of interest. The nine thematic "Windows," each of which highlights a major aspect of information processing, bring the world of computers to life. A glossary at the end of the book gives concise definitions of important terms. The appendix on BASIC, for those who adopt the version of the text that contains it, provides a comprehensive introduction to BASIC in a style students will find easy to use.

Currency. Perhaps more than textbooks in any other field, computer texts must reflect current technologies, trends, and classroom needs. The state-of-the-art content of this book and its support package reflects these considerations. Before the third edition was started, reviews were commissioned and meetings were held to identify key areas of change for the text and support package. Also, throughout the writing and production stages, enhancements and new developments were continually being made to ensure that the final product would be as state-of-the-art as possible throughout its life. A glance at the Windows, Tomorrow boxes, Feature boxes, and chapter outlines should illustrate why this text has been and will continue to remain a market leader.

Comprehensiveness and Depth. In planning for the third edition of this book, the publisher conducted several extensive research studies to determine the selection of topics, degree of depth, and other features that instructors of introductory information processing courses most want to see in their texts. As the manuscript evolved, instructors at a variety of institutions around the country were asked for their comments. The resulting textbook accommodates a wide range of teaching preferences. It not only covers traditional topics thoroughly but also includes the facts every student should know about today's "hot" topics, such as telecommunications, microcomputers, database processing, desktop publishing packages, decision support and expert systems, fourth-generation-language products, user and programmer productivity tools, office automation, computer graphics, and nontraditional approaches to systems development.

Flexible Organization. A textbook locked into a rigid organization, no matter how thorough, will inevitably find its uses limited. To appeal to a wide audience, this book is designed to be flexible. Its nineteen chapters are grouped into five modules: Introduction (Chapters 1–3), Hardware (Chapters 4–7), Software (Chapters 8–14), Computer Systems (Chapters 15–17), and Computers in Society (Chapters 18 and 19). Every effort was made to have each chapter as self-contained as possible, making it easy for one to skip chapters or learn them in a sequence other than the one in the book. And each chapter is organized into well-defined sections, so you can assign parts of a chapter if the whole provides more depth than you need.

Readability. We remember more about a subject if it is presented in a straightforward way and made interesting and exciting. This book is written

in a conversational, down-to-earth style—one designed to be accurate without being intimidating. Concepts are explained clearly and simply, without use of overly technical terminology. Where technical points are presented, they are made understandable with realistic examples from everyday life.

Chapter Learning Tools. Each chapter contains a number of learning tools to help students master the materials.

1. **Outline** An outline of the headings in the chapter shows the major topics to be covered.

2. **Objectives** A list of learning objectives is provided to serve as a guide while students read the chapter.

3. **Overview** Each chapter starts with an overview that puts the subject matter of the chapter in perspective and lets students know what they will be reading about.

4. **Boldfaced Key Terms** Important terms appear in boldface type as they are introduced in the chapter. These terms are also defined in the glossary.

5. **Tomorrow Boxes** These special elements, one in each chapter, provide students with a look at possible future developments in the world of computers and serve as a focus for class discussion.

6. **Feature Boxes** Each chapter contains one or more Feature boxes designed to stimulate interest and discussion about today's uses of information processing technology.

7. **Photographs and Diagrams** Instructive, full-color photographs and diagrams appear throughout the book to help illustrate important concepts. The use of color in the diagrams is a functional part of the book.

8. **Summary and Key Terms** This is a concise summary of the main points in the chapter. Every boldfaced key term in the chapter also appears in boldface type in the summary. Students will find the summary a valuable tool for study and review.

9. **Review Exercises** Every chapter ends with a set of fill-in, matching, discussion, and critical thinking questions.

Windows. The book contains nine spectacular photoessays. Each of these "Windows" on the world of computers is organized around a major text theme and vividly illustrates state-of-the-art uses of computer technology.

Glossary. The glossary at the end of the book defines approximately 500 important computer terms mentioned in the text, including all boldfaced key terms. Each glossary item has a page reference indicating where it is boldfaced or where it first appears in the text.

Appendix A: Number Systems. At the end of the book is an appendix that covers number systems. Contained in it are explanations of the binary, octal, decimal, and hexadecimal numbering systems, as well as rules for converting numbers from one system into another.

Appendix B: A Beginner's Guide to BASIC. The version of this book that contains an appendix on BASIC provides a comprehensive introduction to that language. Much more than a list of rules and procedures, it is an engaging, easy-to-read tutorial that encourages students to begin creating programs immediately. Systematic program development techniques and the honing of debugging skills are also an integral part of the presentation.

Changes from the Second Edition

Although the second edition of this text was one of the most successful textbooks ever published, the pace of technological advances has necessitated a number of key changes. Among the noteworthy differences between the second and third editions of *Understanding Computers* are the following:

1. There are now three full chapters dedicated to the most widely used types of end-user, business-oriented productivity software. Chapter 12 covers word processing and desktop publishing; Chapter 13, spreadsheets and presentation graphics; and Chapter 14, file managers, database management systems, and integrated software packages.

2. Chapter 5, on secondary storage, has been reorganized and now includes an introduction to properties of secondary storage systems, coverage of disk before tape, and new topics such as disk cartridge devices, hard cards, cache disk, and helical-scan tapes.

3. Chapter 16 has been substantially revised with expanded coverage on expert systems, management information systems, and office automation.

4. Coverage has been expanded on topics such as fourth-generation languages (4GLs), CASE tools, optical disks, end-user development, local area networks (LANs), microcomputer-based processing, and user interfaces. The text also includes a variety of new topics, including workgroup computing, hypermedia, computer viruses, object-oriented languages, superconductors, "smart" materials, reduced instruction set computing (RISC), executive support systems, high-definition television, action diagrams, reusable code, grey-scale and multifunction monitors, cellular phones, electronic data interchange (EDI), and biometric security devices.

5. The microcomputing emphasis has been thoroughly updated to include new IBM PS/2 and Macintosh computers, Intel 80486- and Motorola 68040-based processing, multitasking operating systems, and bus designs such as those conforming to Micro Channel Architecture, NuBus, and EISA standards.

6. Windows, Tomorrow boxes, and Feature boxes have been completely revised with new text materials, photographs, and line art. Among the new window topics are hypermedia, desktop publishing, and laptop computers.

7. New to the exercises at the end of each chapter are critical thinking questions, which challenge students' problem-solving skills.

8. The BASIC appendix now includes coverage of both pseudocode and flowcharts.

STUDENT AND TEACHER SUPPORT MATERIALS

Understanding Computers and Information Processing: Today and Tomorrow is available with a complete package of support materials for instruc-

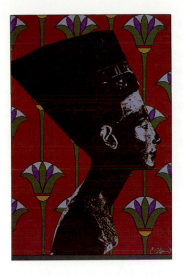

tors and students: Included in the package are a student *Study Guide,* an *Instructor's Manual* with transparency masters, *Transparency Acetates,* a *Test Bank* in hard-copy and computerized form, videotapes from Dryden's new Information Processing Video Library, selected abstracts, and a variety of productivity software manuals and supporting documentation to meet lab needs.

Study Guide

The *Study Guide* is designed to help students master the material in the text through self-testing. For each of the nineteen chapters in the text, the *Study Guide* provides

1. An **Outline** and list of **Objectives.**
2. A **Pretest** that lets students test their knowledge of the chapter before they begin to study it intensively.
3. An **Overview** that puts the subject matter of the chapter in perspective.
4. A **Learning Outline** that summarizes the main points in the chapter and that corresponds to the instructor's Teaching Outline.
5. A list of the chapter **Key Terms,** with space for filling in the proper definition. Provided with each key term is the text page number on which it is boldfaced.
6. **Study Exercises** that require recall of chapter material.
7. A **Crossword Puzzle,** using many chapter key terms to reinforce vocabulary.
8. Five types of **self-test questions:** matching, true/false, multiple-choice, fill-in, and short answer.
9. An **Answer Key.**

The *Study Guide* also covers the number systems appendix and the appendix on BASIC programming. For each section of the BASIC appendix, the *Study Guide* provides a brief summary, a review of BASIC commands, multiple-choice questions, and new programming problems.

Instructor's Manual

In the *Instuctor's Manual* I draw on my own teaching experience to provide instructors with practical suggestions for enhancing classroom presentation. The *Instructor's Manual* contains suggestions for adapting this textbook to various course schedules, including one-quarter, two-quarter, one-semester, two-semester, and night courses. For each of the nineteen chapters of the text the *Instructor's Manual* provides

1. A list of **Objectives**.
2. A **Summary,** oriented to the instructor, with teaching suggestions.
3. A list of the **Key Terms** in the chapter, their definitions, and references indicating the text page on which each is boldfaced.
4. A **Teaching Outline** that gives a detailed breakdown of the chapter, with all major headings and subheadings, as well as points to cover under each. References to the Transparency Acetates and Transparency Masters are keyed in to this outline. In addition, the Learning Outline in the *Study Guide* corresponds to this outline.

5. **Teaching Tips,** with recommended topics for class discussion, important points to cover on the transparency acetates, and mention of additional instructor resources.

6. **Notes for Windows and Boxes,** which include both capsule summaries of these materials and points to raise in class.

7. **Lecture Anecdotes** providing additional stories, news items, and information specific to chapter content to liven up lectures.

8. **Transparency Scripts** for each transparency acetate and transparency master in the instructional package.

9. **Answers to Discussion Questions** that appear at the end of the chapter.

10. **Additional Discussion Questions,** for in-class discussion or testing, and their answers.

11. **Answers to Critical Thinking Questions** that appear at the end of the chapter.

12. **Transparency Masters** covering the chapter objectives and other key topics for classroom discussion.

The *Instructor's Manual* also covers the number systems appendix and the appendix on BASIC programming. A brief teaching summary and suggested solutions to the Programming Exercises and Programming Problems are included for each section of the BASIC appendix. A BASIC program, a flowchart, and pseudocode are provided for each programming problem.

Transparency Acetates

A set of approximately 100 *Transparency Acetates* for use with an overhead projector is available to help explain key points. Included among the acetates are outlines for every chapter, figures derived from selected text diagrams, and new pieces of art. The Teaching Outlines in the *Instructor's Manual* indicate when to show each of the acetates (as well as the Transparency Masters), and the Transparency Scripts in the *Instructor's Manual* list points to make about each.

Test Bank

The *Test Bank* contains over 3,200 test items in various formats, including true/false, multiple-choice, matching, fill-in, and short-answer questions. Answers are provided for all but the short-answer questions. The *Test Bank* is available in both hard-copy and computerized forms. The electronic versions—available for use with IBM and Apple microcomputers—allow instructors to preview, edit, or delete questions as well as to add their own questions, print scrambled forms of tests, and print answer keys.

A new feature of the *Test Bank* in the third edition is a key indicating the chapter section from which each question was taken. Keys are included with each question, except for the matching questions. Also new to this edition is a ten-question, ready-to-copy-and-distribute multiple-choice quiz for every chapter, which enables testing students on a representative sample of important topics.

Videotapes

Videotapes from Dryden's new Information Processing Video Library will be available to adopters of *Understanding Computers and Information Process-*

ing: *Today and Tomorrow,* third edition. Videos focus on applications and cutting-edge technology involving computers, and illustrate concepts such as hardware, software, and systems; database management; graphics; and telecommunications. Adopters will have immediate access to two professional-quality videotapes, which explore the role of computers at Florida's Sea World theme park and at Andersen Consulting, Arthur Andersen & Co., one of the worldwide leaders in information systems consulting.

Selected Abstracts

Selected abstracts are available free to adopters of *Understanding Computers and Information Processing: Today and Tomorrow,* third edition. Since 1987, The Dryden Press has published an annual volume of *Selected Abstracts in Data Processing and Management Information Systems,* which consists of abstracts of recent articles from leading journals that are useful for lecture material and classroom handouts.

Productivity Software Options

Understanding Computers and Information Processing: Today and Tomorrow is available shrink-wrapped with the *Microcomputer Applications Workbook,* by Wilson T. Price of Merritt College. An ideal lab supplement to *Understanding Computers,* the workbook provides complete proficiency-based software instruction and abundant exercises for using WordPerfect, dBASE, and Lotus 1-2-3 (or Joe Spreadsheet). It includes a data disk and is available with or without software.

In addition to the Parker/Price shrink-wrapping option, Dryden also publishes a variety of other successful texts for the lab component of the first computer course. Any of the following texts can be used in conjunction with *Understanding Computers:*

1. *Productivity Software Guide,* by Charles S. Parker
2. *The Integrated Solution: Problem Solving with PC Software,* by Kenneth C. Laudon and Jane P. Laudon
3. *Microsoft® Works: A Window to Computing,* by Jan L. Harrington
4. *Using Productivity Software,* by Wilson T. Price

Check with your Holt/Dryden/Saunders sales representative about any of these options.

ACKNOWLEDGMENTS

I could never have completed a project of this scope alone. I owe a special word of thanks to the many people who reviewed the text—those whose extensive suggestions on the first two editions helped define the third, those whose comments on drafts of the third helped mold it into its final form, and those who reviewed the instructional package.

Third Edition. Virginia T. Anderson, *University of North Dakota;* Gary E. Baker, *Marshalltown Community College;* Luverne Bierle, *Iowa Central Community College;* Curtis Bring, *Moorhead State University;* Carl Clavadetscher, *California State Polytechnic University;* J. Patrick Fenton, *West Valley Community College;* William Fink, *Lewis and Clark Community College;* Kay H.

Gray, *Jacksonville State University;* Rosemary C. Gross, *Creighton University;* Stanley P. Honacki, *Moraine Valley Community College;* L. Wayne Horn, *Pensacola Junior College;* Joan Krone, *Ohio State University;* Liang Chee Wee, *University of Arizona;* Richard W. Manthei, *Joliet Junior College;* Donavan J. Nielsen, *Golden West College;* Kenneth R. Ruhrup, *St. Petersburg Junior College;* Larry Schwartzman, *Trident Technical College;* Sue Traynor, *Clarion University of Pennsylvania;* James R. Walters, *Pikes Peak Community College;* James D. Woolever, *Cerritos College.*

Second Edition. Richard Batt, *Saint Louis Community College at Meremec;* James Buxton, *Tidewater Community College, Virginia;* Vernon Clodfelter, *Rowan Technical College, North Carolina;* Robert H. Dependahl, Jr., *Santa Barbara City College, California;* Eugene T. Dolan, *University of the District of Columbia;* J. Patrick Fenton, *West Valley Community College, California;* William C. Fink, *Lewis and Clark Community College, Illinois;* George P. Grill, *University of North Carolina, Greensboro;* David W. Green, *Nashville State Technical Institute, Tennessee;* Dennis Guster, *Saint Louis Community College at Meremec;* L. D. Harber, *Volunteer State Community College, Tennessee;* Sharon A. Hill, *Prince Georges Community College, Maryland;* J. William Howorth, *Seneca College, Ontario, Canada;* Richard Kerns, *East Carolina University, North Carolina;* Gordon C. Kimbell, *Everett Community College, Washington;* James G. Kriz, *Cuyahoga Community College, Ohio;* Alden Lorents, *Northern Arizona University;* James McMahon, *Community College of Rhode Island;* Don B. Medley, *California State Polytechnic University;* Marilyn D. Moore, *Indiana University Northwest;* Kenneth R. Ruhrup, *Saint Petersburg Junior College, Florida;* Sandra Swanson, *Lewis and Clark Community College, Illinois;* Joyce V. Walton, *Seneca College, Ontario, Canada.*

First Edition. James Ambroise, Jr., *Southern University, Louisiana;* Richard Batt, *St. Louis Community College;* James Bradley, *University of Calgary;* Laura Cooper, *College of the Mainland, Texas;* John DiElsi, *Mercy College, New York;* William Hightower, *Elon College, North Carolina;* Peter L. Irwin, *Richland College, Texas;* Richard Kerns, *East Carolina University, North Carolina;* Glenn Kersnick, *Sinclair Community College, Ohio;* Wayne Madison, *Clemson University, South Carolina;* Gary Marks, *Austin Community College, Texas;* Robert Ralph, *Fayetteville Technical Institute, North Carolina;* Alfred C. St. Onge, *Springfield Technical Community College, Massachusetts;* John J. Shuler, *San Antonio College, Texas;* Michael L. Stratford, *Charles County Community College, Maryland;* Joseph Waters, *Santa Rosa Junior College, California;* Charles M. Williams, *Georgia State University;* A. James Wynne, *Virginia Commonwealth University.*

At The Dryden Press, a special word of thanks to my acquisitions editor, DeVilla Williams, for the many suggestions she made that produced a better manuscript, for weathering the many shouting matches we had in the name of quality, and for being a wonderful and inspirational human being. Also at Dryden I would like to thank Joanne Smith, Karen Hill, Alan Wendt, Patti Arneson, Cate Rzasa, Jane Perkins, Elizabeth Allebach, Doris Milligan, Barb Bahnsen, Thomas Hoffa, Bill Schoof, and the many others who worked hard on behalf of the book.

Charles S. Parker
September 1989

Brief Contents

Windows

Contents

MODULE C   251   SOFTWARE

MODULE E 563 COMPUTERS IN SOCIETY

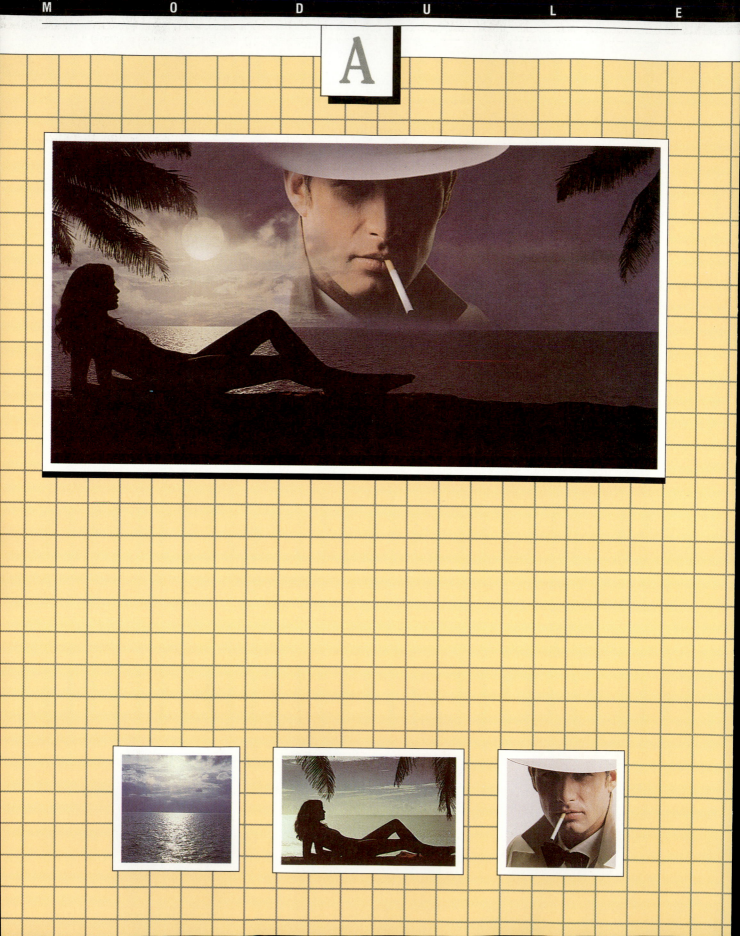

Introduction

We are living in an age of computers. Businesses, government agencies, and other organizations use computers and related technologies to handle tedious paperwork, provide better service to customers, and assist managers in making better decisions. As the costs of computers and computer resources continue to decrease relative to the price of everything else, computer technology will become even more widespread in our society. It is therefore essential to know something about it.

The chapters in this module introduce you to computers and some of their uses. Chapters 1 and 2 orient you to what computer systems are, how they work, and how they're used. These chapters also present some key terminology that you will see repeatedly throughout the text. Chapter 3 describes how the fast-paced world of computers has evolved.

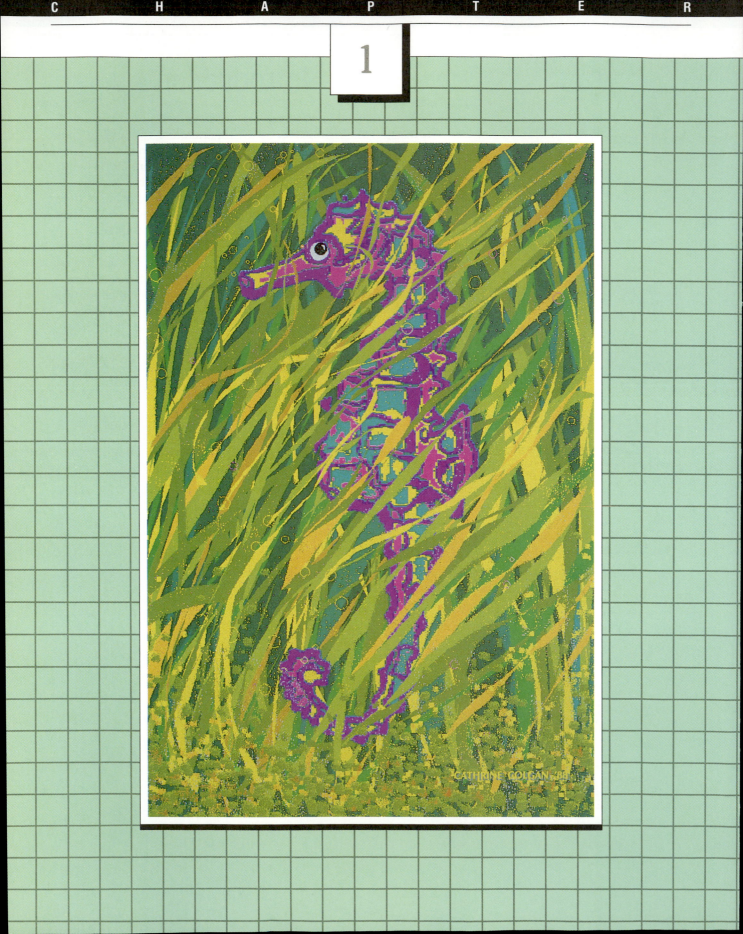

CATHRINE COLGAN '88

Introduction to the World of Computers

Objectives

After completing this chapter, you will be able to:

1. Understand why it's important to learn about computers.
2. Identify some of the major components in a computing environment and their relationships to one another.
3. Describe several applications in business and other areas of society in which computers play an important role.
4. Define several terms that are useful to know when reading about or discussing computers.
5. Appreciate the social impact of computers.

OVERVIEW

Unless you plan to spend your life living off the land in the upper reaches of the Yukon, computers and other forms of high technology will probably have an important impact on your life. Whether that makes you glad, sad, or mad doesn't matter. Computers are here to stay, and it's getting ever more difficult to get along, much less get ahead, without some knowledge of what they are and what they do.

Computer systems keep track of our bank accounts and credit card purchases. They, along with sophisticated communications systems, are the cornerstones of the airlines' massive reservations systems. Computers perform the millions upon millions of computations needed to send astronauts into outer space and bring them back safely. Computers also direct production in our factories and provide executives with the up-to-date information they need to make decisions. They are embedded in watches, microwave ovens, television sets, phones, automobiles, and probably even the stationary workout bike at your local spa. The applications are almost endless. Fifty short years ago, computers were part of an obscure technology of interest to only a handful of scientists. Today they are part of almost everyone's daily life.

Many people are intimidated by computers and think they need an advanced degree to understand them. In fact, computers are very much like cars—you don't need to know everything about them to use them effectively. You can learn to drive a car without knowing about internal combustion engines, and you can learn to use a computer without knowing about technical details such as logic circuits.

Still, with both cars and computers, a little knowledge can give you a big advantage. Knowing something about cars can help you make wise purchases and save money on repairs. Likewise, knowing something about computers can help you use them for maximum benefit.

This book is about computers—what they are, how they work, and what they do. It is intended to give you the knowledge you need to use them effectively today and, through the Tomorrow boxes, give you a look into the future. Other boxed features throughout the text provide additional insights into the dynamic world of computers.

This book is not designed to make you a computer expert. It's a beginner's guide. If you're considering a career as a computer professional in business, this book will give you a comprehensive introduction to the field. If you're not, it will give you the basic knowledge you need to understand and use computers in school and on the job.

In this chapter, we'll first take a look at what computers are and how they work. Then, we'll look at the various sizes in which computers come. Finally, we'll examine several examples of computer systems in action. Window 1, which follows Chapter 1, gives you a glimpse of the myriad applications of computers in today's world.

WHAT'S A COMPUTER AND WHAT DOES IT DO?

Four words sum up the operation of a computer system: **input, processing, output,** and **storage.** To see what these words mean, let's look at something you probably have in your own home—a stereo system.

A simple stereo system consists of a turntable, an amplifier, and a pair of speakers. To use the system you place a record on the turntable, turn the system on, and place the tone arm on the record. The needle in the tone arm converts the patterns in the grooves of the record into vibrations and transmits them to the amplifier as electronic signals. The amplifier takes the signals, strengthens them, and transmits them to the speakers. The result is music. In computer terms, the turntable sends signals as *input* to the amplifier. The amplifier *processes* the signals and sends them to the speakers, which produce a musical *output.* The turntable is an **input device,** the amplifier is a *processing unit,* and the speakers are **output devices.** The amplifier is the heart of the system, and the turntable and speakers are examples of **support equipment.**

Most stereo systems have a variety of other support equipment. An antenna, for example, is another kind of input device. Headphones are another form of output device. A tape recorder is both an input and output device—you can use it to send signals to the amplifier or to receive signals from it. The tapes and records in your collection are, in computer terms, **input/output (I/O) media.** They *store* music in a **machine-readable** form—a form that the associated input device (tape recorder or turntable) can recognize (that is, "read") and convert into signals for the amplifier to process.

Computer Systems

All the elements in a stereo system have their counterparts in a computer system. A **computer system** consists of the computer itself, all the support equipment, and the machine-readable instructions and facts it processes, as well as operating manuals, procedures, and the people who use the system. In other words, all the components that contribute to making the computer a useful tool can be said to be parts of a computer system.

At the heart of any computer system is the **computer** itself, or **central processing unit (CPU).** The CPU is the equivalent of the stereo amplifier. Like its counterpart, the CPU can't do anything useful without support equipment for input and output and I/O media for storage. Computer input and output devices include, to name just a few, keyboards, display devices, disk units, tape units, and printers. I/O media include disks, tapes, and paper. We will discuss these and many other items in Chapters 2, 5, and 6.

A computer system, of course, is not a stereo system, and a computer is much more versatile than a stereo amplifier. For example, a computer system can perform an enormous variety of processing tasks and a stereo system only a few. Also, a computer can support a much greater variety of input and output devices than can a stereo amplifier.

What gives a computer its flexibility? The answer, in a word, is *memory*. A computer has access to a memory, or "workspace," that allows it to retain whatever inputs it receives and the results it produces from these inputs. An ordinary stereo amplifier has no such memory; what's playing on the turntable or tape recorder passes directly through the amplifier to the speakers. Because computers can hold materials in such a workspace, they can be directed by *programs* to rearrange or recombine those materials in an amazing variety of ways before sending them along as output. Thus, if you could hook up a full-fledged computer and a good chunk of electronic workspace to your home stereo, you'd be able to do things like play the selections on a record in any order you wished, create your own music, or combine and manipulate music from many different sources in any way that struck your fancy.

Most stereo equipment sold today is in fact built with inexpensive computer and memory chips. These chips have made possible such conveniences as quartz tuning and assignment of your favorite radio frequencies to push buttons. Still other technological breakthroughs such as compact disk and digital television are pushing consumer products further and further into the computer age. Even the car you drive probably contains several independent computer systems (see Tomorrow box).

Data and Programs

The material that a computer receives as input is of two kinds: data and programs. **Data** are, essentially, facts. **Programs** are instructions that tell the computer how to process those facts to produce the results that you, the computer system user, want. Returning to our example of a computer-driven music system, we could say that the tunes inputted to the system by the turntable or tape deck are data (facts) and the instructions that tell the music system the order in which to play those tunes are a program. Now let's discuss these important terms in a little more detail.

Data. Almost any kind of fact can become computer data—facts about a company's employees, facts about airline flight schedules, or facts about a satellite's orbit. Even picture images and sounds can be used as data. When we input data into a computer system, we usually aren't interested in getting them back just as we entered them. We want the system to process the data and give us new, useful *information*. (**Information,** in the language of computers, refers to data that have been processed into a meaningful form.) We might want to know, for example, how many employees earn over $15,000, how many seats are available on flight 495 from Los Angeles to San Francisco, or the moment when a damaged satellite might plunge back into the earth's atmosphere.

Of course, you don't necessarily need a computer system to get this kind of information from a set of facts. For example, anyone can go through an employee file and make a list of people earning a certain salary. But to do so would take a lot of time, especially for a company with thousands of employees. In contrast, computers, with their electronically fast speeds, can do such jobs almost instantly. The processing of data on computers is called by a variety of terms, one of which, as the title of this book attests, is **information processing.**

Programs. Like many other machines, the amplifier in your home stereo system is a *special-purpose* device. It is designed to support only a few specific tasks—play a record, make a recording on tape, play music into speakers or headphones, and so forth. These functions are built into its circuitry. To put it another way, it is "hardwired" to perform a very limited number of specific tasks.

Most computers, in contrast, are *general-purpose* devices. They must perform an enormous variety of tasks, any one of which may involve extremely complex processing. For example, in a small company, one person may want the computer system to scan a list of customer accounts and print a report of all customers who owe more than $300. Another person may want a report, in a different format, of all customers with good credit references. A secretary may need the computer to help prepare a series of letters to clients.

Because most computers must be flexible, they can't be hardwired to do all the tasks they need to do. Instead, they rely on programs for guidance. As we said before, a program is a list of *instructions.* Often a program is read into the computer system and followed by the data it is to process. The program then directs the circuits in the computer to open and close in the manner needed to do whatever task needs doing with these data.

Programs cannot be written in ordinary English. They must be written in a **programming language**—a language the computer system can read and translate into the electronic pulses that make it work. Programming languages come in many varieties. In the early days of computers, they consisted of strings of numbers that only experts could comprehend. Over the years, they have become easier for ordinary mortals to understand and use. Programming languages are not universal; any given computer system will understand some languages but not others. Most computer systems, however, are capable of understanding several different languages. We will discuss programs and programming languages in detail in Module C.

A Look at Computer Storage

So far we've seen that if you want to get something done on a computer system, you must supply it with both facts (data) and instructions (a program) specifying how to process those facts. For example, if you want the system to write payroll checks, you must supply such data as employees' names, social security numbers, and salaries. The program instructions must "tell" the system how to compute taxes, how to take deductions, where and how to print the checks, and so forth. Also, the computer relies on a memory (storage) to remember all these details as it is doing the work.

Actually, computer systems contain two types of storage. A **primary memory** (sometimes called **main memory** or **internal memory**), which is often contained in the unit that houses the computer, holds the data and

T   O   M   O   R   R   O   W

Smart Cars

How Computers Are Revolutionizing Cars and Driving

You are heading out to work one morning when a voice deep within the bowels of your dashboard blurts, "Traffic jam with delays of up to 20 minutes six miles ahead; better to take route 495." As you take the next available exit, a sensor by your front left wheel senses a pothole and adjusts the suspension at the proper time to soften any impact.

If these events sound like something out of a James Bond movie, be prepared for a shock: They may be here—and rather widespread—sooner than you think.

Today the average car carries anywhere from one to three dozen on-board computer chips. These computers are vital components of fuel-injection systems, cruise control, antilock brake systems, voltage regulation, air and heat control, speedometer systems, door-locking devices, and burglar alarms. Not only can electronic systems perform many tasks that mechanical devices cannot; their superb precision has enhanced many tasks, such as deliver-

ing fuel to your engine, that traditionally were wholly mechanical.

Today the average car may contain about $300 worth of computers. But many ex-

> By the year 2000, electronic systems may amount to as much as a third of the cost of producing a car.

perts predict that by the year 2000, electronic systems may amount to as much as a third of the cost of producing a car. Currently many higher-priced models feature the more exotic applications of computers, often in the form of options. However, many of these uses are expected to trickle down into lower-priced cars in the next few years.

Auto manufacturers say the trend in on-board computers is toward safety rather than gimmickry. Some of the innovations coming down the pike that are currently in the drawing-board or test stage are:

- ☐ A collision avoidance feature that warns drivers about upcoming hazards

- ☐ A sight-improvement feature that digitally enhances the view from the front window when driving in conditions such as dense fog or a heavy snowstorm or rainstorm
- ☐ A series of diagnostic systems that check virtually every potential hazard or expensive headache on your car—low tire pressure, bald tires, poor fuel economy, malfunctioning lights, and so on—and flash a warning on the dashboard display
- ☐ A navigation system consisting of a video screen that maps a car's current location and the best route to a given destination
- ☐ A specialized computer system that picks up bothersome noises in the vehicle by sensors, analyzes them, and develops soothing "antinoises" that cancel out the unwanted sounds
- ☐ A system that detects actual and potential pollution problems—a feature that many predict will someday be required by California law on all cars sold in that state
- ☐ A feature that displays in the air, around the windshield area, such important driving information as car speed, abnormal oil pres-

sure, a low level of gas left in the tank, and so forth

Drivers on many parts of the globe are beginning to see "smart roads," which assist a car in its duties of getting passengers safely to a destination in the least possible time. For instance, in West Berlin, Siemens AG, one of Europe's largest computer firms, has established a project called Autoguide, which currently involves about 1,000 cars and over 500 miles of city roads. Infrared beacons on selected traffic lights monitor traffic flows and communicate these data to a central computer control center. The control center processes the data into a meaningful form and beams information out to the test vehicles. One user of the system claims that his commuting time has been halved as a result of the information he gets.

And there are many other applications for smart roads, as well. Imagine programming an on-board computer with your tastes. As you are driving along a highway, the computer apprises you of local radio stations in which you might be interested, hotels and restaurants that appear to match your needs, and upcoming activities in the area that may be worthwhile seeing.

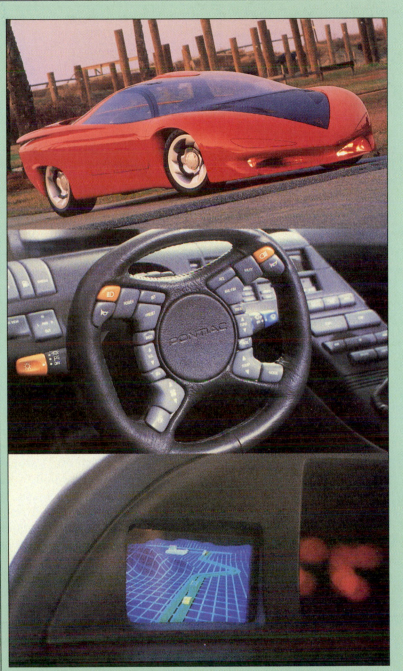

The car of the future. A concept car with its keyboardlike steering wheel and computerized navigation system.

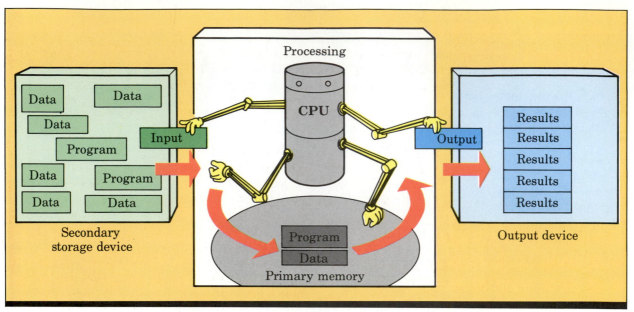

FIGURE 1-1

Doing work in a computer system. The computer system above is obtaining the programs and data it needs from secondary storage, putting them in its primary memory, and processing them according to the instructions in the program. The results are then delivered to an output device.

programs the computer is currently processing. When data are "captured" in the computer's primary memory or "workspace," they can be rearranged or recombined by the instructions in the program.

Data and programs the computer doesn't need for the job at hand are stored in **secondary (external) storage.** In large computer systems, secondary storage is usually located in a device separate from the computer itself. In smaller computer systems, secondary storage is usually implemented by a device that is fitted into the unit containing the computer. Whatever the case, this piece of equipment is called a *secondary storage device.* It enables us to conveniently save large quantities of data and programs in machine-readable form so that we need not rekey them into the system every time we use them. Some secondary storage devices are capable of storing thousands of programs and billions of pieces of data.

When the CPU needs a certain program and set of data, it requests them from the secondary storage device—much as you might request a particular song from a jukebox—and reads them into its primary memory for processing. Unlike the turntable, however, which puts the original record in play, the CPU puts a copy of the original program or data into primary memory for use. It is often useful to think of secondary storage as a large "library" of programs and data resources on full-time call to the CPU.

Figure 1-1 illustrates the relationships among input, processing, output, primary memory, and secondary storage. We will discuss secondary storage devices and their associated media in Chapter 5.

Hardware and Software

In the world of computers, it is common to distinguish between hardware and software. The word **hardware** refers to the actual machinery that makes up a computer system—for example, the CPU, I/O devices, and storage devices. The word **software** refers to computer programs.

Users and the Experts

In the early days of computing, there was a clear distinction between the people who made computers work and those who used the results computers produced. This distinction still exists, but as computers become more available and easier to use, it is breaking down.

End users, or *users,* are the people who need the output computer systems produce. They include the accountant who needs a report on a client's taxes, the engineer who needs to know whether a bridge will be structurally sound, the shop-floor supervisor who needs to know whether the day's quotas were met, and the company president who needs a report on the firm's profitability over the last ten years.

Programmers, on the other hand, are the people who write the programs that produce such information. Programming is their primary job responsibility. Thus, although end users may do modest amounts of programming as part of their jobs, the distinction between an ordinary end user and a professional programmer is based on what the person has actually been hired to do.

There are many other types of computer professionals whom organizations employ. For instance, *systems analysts* are hired to build large computer systems within a company. *Computer operations personnel,* on the other hand, are people responsible for the day-to-day operation of large computer systems.

Most large companies have thousands of programs to carry out well-defined companywide tasks—doing the payroll, writing checks, preparing accounting reports, and so forth. Such organizations usually employ a staff of specialists to develop new programs as they are needed, to make changes in existing programs, and to keep their systems running efficiently. However, with smaller, desktop-sized computer systems becoming cheaper as well as easier to learn and use, many users are acquiring their own compact systems to meet personal information needs that other, larger company systems cannot satisfy.

COMPUTER SYSTEMS TO FIT EVERY NEED AND POCKETBOOK

A great variety of computer systems are available commercially to serve computer users' needs. In Module D, you will learn how computers fit into settings ranging from the living room to the office of a giant corporation.

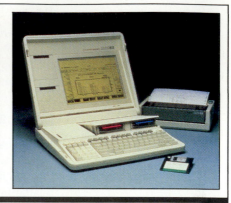

FIGURE 1-2

Three popular microcomputer systems. (a, left) IBM PS/2 Model 25. (b, middle) Apple Macintosh IIX. (c, right) Hewlett-Packard Portable Vectra CS.

Here we'll consider one important way in which computers differ from one another: size.

Computers are generally classified in one of four size categories: small, or microcomputers; medium-size, or minicomputers; large, or mainframe computers; and super-large, or supercomputers. In practice, the distinction among these different sizes is not always clear-cut. Large minicomputers, for example, often are bigger than small mainframes.

In general, the larger the computer, the greater its processing power. For example, big computers can process data at faster speeds than small computers. Big computers can also accommodate larger and more powerful support devices. Naturally, the larger the computer and its support equipment, the greater the price. A computer system can cost anywhere from a couple of hundred dollars to many millions.

Microcomputers

A technological breakthrough in the early 1970s made it possible to produce an entire CPU on a single silicon chip smaller than a dime. These "computers-on-a-chip," or *microprocessors,* could be mass produced at very low cost. Microprocessors were quickly integrated into all types of products, making possible powerful hand-held calculators, digital watches, a variety of electronic toys, and sophisticated controls for household appliances such as microwave ovens and automatic coffee makers. Microprocessors also made it possible to build inexpensive computer systems, such as those in Figure 1-2, small enough to fit on a desktop or even in a briefcase. These small computer systems have informally come to be called **microcomputers** (or *micros*). Because they are inexpensive and small enough for one person to use at home or work for personal needs, they are also commonly called **personal computers,** or *PCs*.

Microcomputers appear in homes, classrooms, and offices. At home they help families keep track of their finances, help students write term papers,

FIGURE 1-3

DEC VAX minicomputer. Digital Equipment Corporation's VAX 897X series is one of today's most widely used lines of minicomputers.

regulate heating systems to lower fuel bills, and challenge players of games like PAC-MAN and chess. Universities, high schools, and elementary schools, attracted by these machines' low cost and ease of mastery and use relative to larger computers, frequently purchase micros for courses in computing. In fact, several universities now require incoming students to buy or rent their own microcomputers.

Micros are also widely used in businesses, both small and large. Small businesses use them to keep track of merchandise, prepare correspondence, bill customers, and do routine accounting. Large businesses use them for purposes such as word processing and filing systems for secretaries and analysis tools for decision makers, to name just two important applications. Also, salespeople often tote briefcase-sized micros to make presentations at client sites. Microcomputers are increasingly being networked into large communications systems, where they are used as data-entry devices or as general-purpose workstations.

Minicomputers

Minicomputers, or *minis,* generally are regarded as "medium-sized" computers (see Figure 1-3). Most of them fall between microcomputers and mainframes in their processing power. The very smallest minicomputers, however, are virtually indistinguishable from the largest microcomputers, and the largest (sometimes called *superminis*) closely resemble small mainframes. Minicomputers usually are far more expensive than microcomputers and are unaffordable for most individuals.

Any of several factors might lead an organization to choose a minicomputer over a micro or mainframe. A small or medium-sized company may simply find microcomputer systems too slow to handle its current volume of processing. Or, a company may need a computer system that can do several jobs at once and interact with multiple users at the same time. Many microcomputer systems lack sufficient power for such applications. Mainframes, of course, have these capabilities, but they are much larger and more expensive than minis.

Mainframes

The **mainframe** (see Figure 1-4) is the standard for almost all large organizations. It often operates 24 hours a day, serving hundreds of users on display devices during regular business hours and processing large jobs such as payroll and billing late at night. Many large organizations need several mainframes to complete their computing workloads. Typically these organizations own or lease a variety of computer types—say, mainframes, minis, and micros—to meet all their processing needs.

Most mainframes are employed to handle high-volume processing of business transactions and routine paperwork. For most businesses, this includes tasks such as keeping track of customer purchases and payments, sending out bills and reminder notices, paying employees, and maintaining detailed tax records. These operations were some of the earliest applications of computers in business and have been the responsibility of mainframes from day one.

Supercomputers

Some organizations, such as large scientific and research laboratories, have extraordinary information processing needs. Applications such as sending astronauts into outer space and weather forecasting, for example, require extreme degrees of accuracy and a wealth of computations. High-quality animation, which produces the special effects you see in computer-generated movies and commercials, also demands enormous amounts of high-speed computation. To meet such needs, a few vendors offer very large, sophisticated machines called **supercomputers** (see Figure 1-5). These machines are very expensive, often costing several millions of dollars.

FIGURE 1-5

Cray-2 supercomputer.
Supercomputers are faster than conventional computers because they pack circuits much tighter. Cray accounts for over half of the supercomputers sold worldwide.

USING COMPUTERS: SOME EXAMPLES

Now that we've briefly seen how a computer system works, let's "walk through" a few applications within a typical organization to put many of the concepts you've just read about into sharper focus.

Large System. Paradise Beach Resort is a large hotel on the Florida coast. It uses a *mainframe* computer system to keep track of such things as guest reservations, bills, and employees. Without the mainframe, the hotel would never be able to accommodate the number of guests it handles with its current staff, nor would it be able to provide the high level of service its guests expect.

In the precomputer days, operations were far less efficient. For instance, it was quite common for bills to be incorrect, misplaced, or mismanaged. Frequently, if a reservation was improperly recorded, the guest was detained in the lobby. In fact, often two desk clerks would be in the process of booking different guests for the same room—an embarrassing mishap for the hotel and one that sometimes resulted in lost business.

Today, with a computer keeping track of guests, these types of problems occur very infrequently. The mainframe also handles various other types of accounting tasks—paying employees and preparing comprehensive reports for management and taxing agencies, for instance—and does so much more quickly and accurately than was possible in the precomputer days. Some of the information that management now routinely receives was impossible to obtain before the computer arrived.

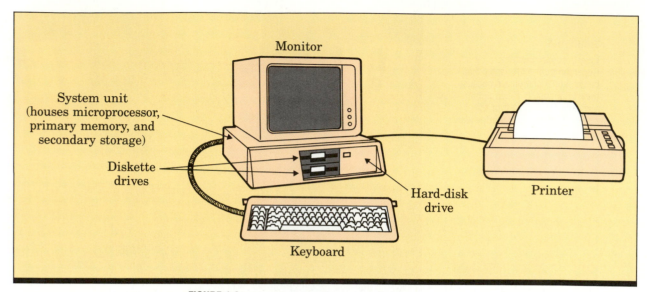

FIGURE 1-6

The catering manager's microcomputer system. The system unit contains the microprocessor, primary memory, and secondary storage devices—two diskette drives and a hard-disk drive.

The hotel's mainframe is run by a staff of just four people. A *director* of computing oversees all planning in computer-related areas. A *systems analyst* decides which new software and hardware must be bought and which programs must be custom written to meet the evolving needs of the hotel. A resident *programmer* attends to the latter need, coding programs from specific guidelines provided by the systems analyst. An *operations person* ensures that the mainframe runs smoothly on a daily basis and troubleshoots potential technical problems when the computer system malfunctions.

User 1. Lydia Maxwell is the catering manager at Paradise Beach Resort. She has no need for the mainframe but finds a desktop *microcomputer system* a useful tool in her work. The hardware in Lydia's microcomputer system consists of four pieces of equipment: a keyboard, a display device, a printer, and a system unit (see Figure 1-6). Within the *system unit* are the microprocessor, primary memory, and secondary storage devices—two diskette drives and a hard-disk drive—as well as a lot of circuitry that we'll talk about later in the book.

The *keyboard,* which resembles that of an ordinary typewriter, enables Lydia to direct the microcomputer system to do what she wants. Everything she inputs at the keyboard and the computer system's responses to these inputs are shown on the *display device,* which resembles a television screen. When she wants something printed out, she directs the computer system to send the output to her *printer.*

The *diskette unit* on Lydia's microcomputer system consists of two *drives.* On the drives, Lydia can mount *diskettes,* or *floppy disks*—small platters capable of storing, say, 100 or more pages of data or programs. Often users

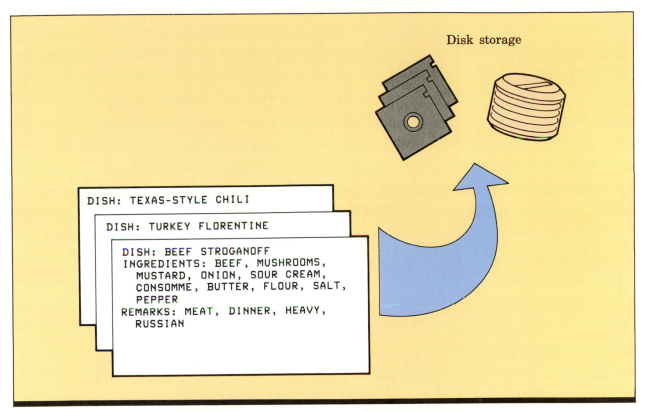

Disk storage

DISH: TEXAS-STYLE CHILI

DISH: TURKEY FLORENTINE

DISH: BEEF STROGANOFF
INGREDIENTS: BEEF, MUSHROOMS,
  MUSTARD, ONION, SOUR CREAM,
  CONSOMME, BUTTER, FLOUR, SALT,
  PEPPER
REMARKS: MEAT, DINNER, HEAVY,
  RUSSIAN

FIGURE 1-7

Meal planning data stored on disk. Each set of data consists of several "filled-in forms." Several *hundred* such forms can be stored on a single diskette and several *thousand* on hard disk.

such as Lydia keep their *data* and *programs* on separate diskettes. The diskettes must be properly inserted into the computer system's disk drives if the system is to access the programs and data on them. Diskettes make it convenient to transport data to and from the computer system in machine-readable form.

The *hard-disk unit* on Lydia's system, on the other hand, has almost 50 times the capacity of a single diskette and permits much quicker accessing of both programs and data. Three years ago, Lydia acquired the hard-disk unit for her system because her collection of programs and data was expanding rapidly and she was getting tired of mounting and dismounting diskettes every time she wanted to use a particular program or set of data.

Once a program and its data are loaded into primary memory from any of the disk devices, the computer is transformed into a powerful calculating tool. One application in which Lydia finds her computer system useful is meal planning. Here she uses it to search through descriptions of food dishes to find ones that will fit a particular client's needs. On her hard disk are stored thousands of filled-in "forms," one form for each food dish Lydia can offer to guests (see Figure 1-7). Each form contains three separate types, or *fields,* of data—the name of the dish, its ingredients, and a few remarks.

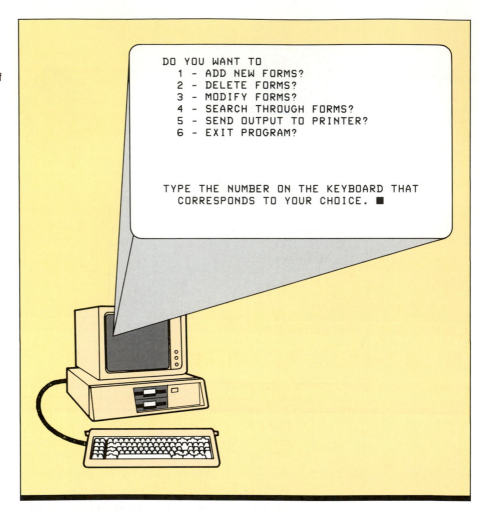

FIGURE 1-8

A computer menu. Menus beckon a user to choose a specific course of action. Using them effectively requires neither typing skills nor an extensive knowledge of computers.

```
DO YOU WANT TO
    1 - ADD NEW FORMS?
    2 - DELETE FORMS?
    3 - MODIFY FORMS?
    4 - SEARCH THROUGH FORMS?
    5 - SEND OUTPUT TO PRINTER?
    6 - EXIT PROGRAM?



TYPE THE NUMBER ON THE KEYBOARD THAT
CORRESPONDS TO YOUR CHOICE. ■
```

Therefore, if Lydia is helping a client plan a Saturday night banquet over the phone, and the client wants a beef dish with mushrooms, Lydia can summon a program stored on her hard disk called a *database management system* to search for all forms on her entrées disk file in which "ingredients" contains "beef" and "mushrooms" and "remarks" contains "dinner." Then she can have the names of these dishes directed to her display screen.

Sure, Lydia can rely on her memory, but having the computer system make the search for her often turns up good alternatives that didn't cross her mind. Also, she can save a lot of phone time by having her computer system do the searching in the background while she attends to other matters with the client. Lydia's database manager lets her add new forms to the file when she wants them, delete forms, and modify forms. She does this with a *menu* of processing alternatives (not to be confused with a food menu) that the database manager sends to her display screen, asking her what she wants to do (see Figure 1-8).

User 2. Don Kawashima is the convention manager at Paradise Beach Resort and also a very heavy computer user. His job responsibilities are many.

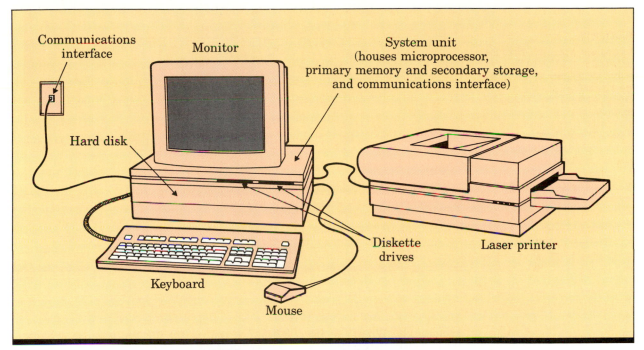

FIGURE 1-9

The convention manager's microcomputer system. The system depicted here is more sophisticated than the one shown in Figure 1-6, demonstrating how microcomputer systems can be configured to virtually any specific set of needs.

He promotes the hotel to convention groups, arranges for groups to reserve hotel facilities, and performs a variety of other tasks. There's a lot of paperwork involved—sending letters back and forth, booking facilities, establishing budgets, filing reports, and so on. Also, Don finds that success in his job involves lots of little things that aren't in his job description, such as preparing an immediate thank-you letter to an important client when the secretary is swamped with other tasks.

To assist him in his work, Don has a microcomputer system on his desk (see Figure 1-9). Don's system is more sophisticated than Lydia's because he often needs to interact with the hotel's mainframe and frequently must prepare correspondence to clients.

For instance, Don's system has a *communications interface,* which enables him to interact with the hotel's mainframe. It gives him the option of using his own computer or the mainframe to do his work. For secondary storage, his system, like Lydia's, has both diskette units and a hard-disk unit. Of course, since Don can tap into the mainframe, he can also use the secondary storage on that system, which may be 100 or so times greater than that of his own.

Don also has a *laser printer,* which enables him to prepare crisp-looking correspondence and newsletters to clients, and a *mouse,* which he uses to select commands or menu choices from the screen. As the user moves the mouse along a desktop, an onscreen arrow, called a *cursor,* moves corre-

FIGURE 1-10

Pointing with a mouse. When the user ''clicks'' a button on the mouse, the selection to which the arrow is currently pointing is invoked. Here the ''System Disk'' selection—which will provide a set of computer system options—is chosen. On many systems, a symbol (icon) darkens when selected, as shown here.

spondingly. When the user "clicks" a button on the mouse, the selection (usually in the form of a graphic symbol, or *icon*) to which the arrow currently points is invoked (see Figure 1-10). Although the mouse cannot directly be used for such things as typing letters or keying in numbers, it is very helpful for making screen selections—especially for a person such as Don, who considers himself a relatively poor typist.

Don interacts with the hotel's mainframe daily to get reservations information necessary for his job. If an important client phones to request a particular set of dates for a conference, Don must be able to get to up-to-date reservations data stored on the mainframe while talking to the client. Or, if an angry client complains about a bill, Don must quickly retrieve billing data from the mainframe to sort out the problem. Don performs these types of tasks with a database management system stored on the mainframe. This system is much more sophisticated than the one Lydia uses because it must handle bigger tasks.

One reason for Don's success at his job is his skill at getting to key information quickly when dealing with clients, thereby allowing him to give them first-class service. Hotel management realizes fully that a $50,000 booking can easily be won or lost on service to clients, so they are more than happy that Don is hooked up to the mainframe with his own system.

Don also does a lot of computing work that doesn't involve communicating with the mainframe. For instance, when a letter must be quickly prepared and sent to a client to confirm a booking date or to thank the client for his or her patronage, Don uses a *word processing* software package and a form letter (called a "boilerplate"), both of which are stored on his hard disk. To prepare the client letter, he first summons the word processor by selecting an appropriate menu choice or icon on the screen with his mouse. Next, also via the mouse, he may select a file-folder-shaped icon corresponding to the boilerplate letter. In doing this, he asks the word processor to find the boilerplate letter in storage. When the letter is retrieved and displayed onscreen, Don uses the keyboard to type in certain parts of the letter to make it appear personalized. When he finishes typing, he will use the mouse to select an icon that will store a copy of the letter on his hard disk and then to choose another icon that will output the letter on his printer.

Don also frequently uses his microcomputer system to prepare budgets, a task that requires him to use a *spreadsheet* software package. He may summon this package with a special icon similar to the one he uses to summon the word processor. The spreadsheet package also has a facility that enables Don to manage the enormous number of budgets he prepares. And, of course, he can send completed budgets to his printer when he requires them in printed form.

Computer systems, such as those used by Lydia and Don, are making a profound impact in today's workplace. Not only do such systems improve the types of information people need to do their jobs, but also they are fundamentally changing the way work is done (see Feature 1A).

COMPUTERS AND SOCIETY

The examples we've just presented should give you some idea of why computer systems have become such an important part of modern life. Their ability to sort through massive amounts of data and quickly produce useful information for almost any kind of user—from payroll clerk to president—makes them indispensable in a society like ours. Without computers, neither the catering manager nor the convention manager in our example could possibly provide the level of service they now extend to clients. The government would be unable to tabulate all the data it collects for the census every ten years. Banks would be overwhelmed by the job of tracking all the transactions they must process. The efficient telephone service we are used to would be impossible. Moon exploration and the space shuttle would still be science fiction fantasies. The list is virtually endless.

But along with the benefits computers bring to society have come some troubling problems, ranging from health to personal security and privacy. The catering manager in our example, for instance, spends many hours in front of a display screen. Do the radiation and glare emanating from the screen impair her health? Banks keep data on customers' accounts on external storage devices. Can they prevent clever "computer criminals" from using their computer systems to steal from those accounts? The Internal Revenue Service has confidential information about every American taxpayer. Can it protect that information from unauthorized use?

These are serious issues, but we can only mention them briefly in this chapter. In Chapter 19, we will discuss the costs and benefits of computers at length.

Computers Change the Way People Work

Today's Best Reason for Learning about Computers

A student sidles into his chair on the first day of his Intro to Computers class, pops his hand up, and asks, "Why do we need to take this course?" The instructor reflects for a few seconds and responds, "Because when you get a job, computers will likely influence how you do your work."

This, in fact, is probably the best reason to learn about computers. Furthermore, if you plan to blow off learning about computers and how to use them, you can almost certainly expect to be upstaged in your job by computer-savvy colleagues. In fact, for many jobs, you may not even be employable.

Computers abound in today's workplace because we are living in an era when most jobs heavily depend on the collection, use, creation, and dissemination of information. Whether you become a teacher, lawyer, doctor, professional athlete, or executive, your performance will largely depend on information and your use of it. Because computer systems can handle tons of information at

> A distinct trend in workplace decentralization is evolving worldwide.

dizzying speeds, their availability may be equivalent to having an army of clerks at your disposal.

Picture these examples of computers in the work force if you are a born doubter:

☐ Managers and professionals at all levels of the business world use software products called electronic *spreadsheets*—which in essence are powerful calculators—to perform analytical tasks in minutes that once took hours or days to do by hand. Not only can these people assemble information faster than they did before; they can do tasks that once were impossible to perform manually. By being able to study "all the angles" of strategies or propositions, these individuals often find that they make better decisions.

☐ Executives are relying increasingly on *database management systems*—tools that provide instant access to local or remote banks of information—to learn about business conditions. Many of these systems are so easy to use that even the most computer-shy executives are being won over to their use, knowing that failure to keep up will give competitors an edge. Worker groups such as lawyers, doctors, and

COMPUTERS IN ACTION

Where would you expect to find computers? In our discussion so far, we've seen some of the amazing variety of ways in which computers have become part of our lives. As you read through this book, you should get a good idea of what computer systems can and cannot do and where they do and do not belong. Window 1 presents an extensive picture essay of computers in action in just a few of the many settings in which you are likely to encounter them.

stockbrokers, who need to search through mounds of data to draw conclusions, have also found that database technology has improved their performance.

☐ Many companies have given thousands of *laptop computers* to their field sales forces. These devices often give salespeople an advantage when dealing with clients, because the salesperson can analyze a client proposal on the spot, while the client is in a receptive mood. The laptop can also be used to access remote data—possibly supplying information that will help close the sale. In one reported case, for instance, a salesperson was able to access damaging information about a competitive product from a government database—and keep a client he was about to lose.

☐ At all levels of business, computers are helping workers put *presentation materials* together by creating stunning charts and slides to help sell a live audience and by enhancing written materials. Researchers have found that people who use computers in this manner often are considered by others as being more "professional."

☐ In fields such as design and publishing, computers have completely revolutionized the way people work. Products such as cars, packages, buildings, shoes, and fabrics are all widely computer designed today. The rise of powerful *desktop publishing systems* that enable the average person to create printshop-quality documents on his or her own has altered the structure of the entire publishing industry.

☐ People in most types of businesses are now using some form of *electronic mail* system to improve communications. For instance, facsimile (fax) machines can transmit documents between sites almost instantaneously. This allows people to complete within a few hours a task that could stretch out over days or even weeks with just a physical delivery system at hand. Also, electronic mailbox and messaging systems enable people to more easily work in groups, even though they may be at different locations.

And these applications only scratch the surface in demonstrating how computers are impacting the workplace. Many users now have microcomputer systems at home, making it possible for them to leave the office early and to shift part of their workload to the evening. This not only helps the worker but also it leaves highways less congested at rush hour. Because microcomputers and sophisticated communications systems have placed "computer power" virtually everywhere, a distinct trend in workplace decentralization is evolving worldwide.

SUMMARY AND KEY TERMS

Computers appear almost everywhere in today's world. They're embedded in consumer products, used to run businesses, and employed to direct production in our factories, to name just a few applications.

Four words summarize the operation of a **computer system: input, processing, output,** and **storage.** The processing function is performed by the

computer itself, which is sometimes called the **central processing unit, or CPU.**

The input and output functions are performed by **support equipment,** such as **input devices** and **output devices.** Just as your stereo amplifier would be useless if it had no speakers, headphones, or turntable to supplement it, the computer would be helpless without this support equipment.

On most of the support equipment are mounted **input/output (I/O) media.** Many of these media *store* materials in **machine-readable** form, which the computer system can recognize and process.

The material that a computer receives as input is of two kinds: data and programs. **Data** are facts the computer has at its disposal; **programs** are instructions that explain to the computer what to do with these facts. Programs must be written in a **programming language** that the computer can understand.

Data that have been processed into a useful form are called **information.** The processing of data into information on computers is called **information processing.**

Computer systems have two types of memory, or storage. **Primary memory** (sometimes called **main memory** or **internal memory**) is often built into the unit housing the computer itself; it holds the programs and data that the system is currently processing. **Secondary (external) storage** holds other programs and data. In many systems, secondary storage is located in a separate hardware device.

In the world of computers, it is common to distinguish between hardware and software. **Hardware** refers to the actual machinery that makes up the computer system, such as the CPU, input and output devices, and secondary storage devices. **Software** refers to computer programs.

End users are the people who need the output computer systems produce. In a computing environment, there are many types of "experts" who help users meet their computing needs—for example, **programmers** are responsible for writing programs.

Small computers are often called **microcomputers** or **personal computers**; medium-size computers **minicomputers;** and large computers **mainframes.** The very largest computers, which are used for applications that demand the most in terms of speed in memory, are called **supercomputers.** Although categorizing computers by size can be helpful in practice, it is sometimes difficult to classify computers that fall on the borders of these categories.

Although computer systems have become an indispensable part of modern life, their growing use often creates troubling problems ranging from health to personal security and privacy.

REVIEW EXERCISES

Fill-in Questions

1. Four words sum up the operation of a computer system: input, output, _____ , and storage.

2. When programs and data are being processed, they are stored in _____ memory.

3. Processed data that are in a useful form are called _____ .

4. Another name for computer programs is _____ .

5. When programs and data are not being processed but need to be "at the fingertips" of the computer, they are stored in _____ storage.

6. A term used for the equipment in a computing environment is _____ .

7. A series of instructions that direct a computer system is known as a(n) _____ .

8. The hardware, software, data, procedures, and personnel needed to process data successfully are called a(n) _____ .

Matching Questions

Match each term with the description that best fits.

a. minicomputer   d. supercomputer
b. input device   e. hardware
c. mainframe   f. microcomputer

_____ 1. The equipment that makes up a computer system.
_____ 2. Another name for personal computer.
_____ 3. A medium-sized computer.
_____ 4. A large computer used to process business transactions in high volume.
_____ 5. Any piece of equipment that supplies programs and data to a computer.
_____ 6. The most powerful type of computer.

Discussion Questions

1. Provide some examples of input devices, output devices, processing devices, and input/output media that are found in the average household and are not necessarily computer related.

2. What is the difference between a computer and a computer system?

3. Name as many computer support devices as you can. What is the purpose of each?

4. What are the major differences between primary memory and secondary storage?

5. What is the difference between programs and data?

6. Define and give some examples of end users of a computer system.

7. Identify some social problems created by the existence of computer systems.

Critical Thinking Questions

1. Should everyone getting a degree from a college or university today be required to take an introductory computer course? Defend your response.

2. Feature 1A provides several examples describing how computers are changing the way ordinary people work. Can you think of three additional examples not mentioned in the box?

3. The term "computer literacy"—knowing something about computers—is widely used today. In your opinion, what types of things about computers should people be literate about?

1

Computers in
Our World

A Visual Portfolio of the
Widespread Use of Computers

Computers rapidly have become an important force in almost every segment of our society. This first "window to the world of computers" presents a small sample of the many tasks to which these machines may be applied. Included are examples from the art/advertising, television, publishing, design, and business/finance fields.

ART/ADVERTISING

1 A computer-created brochure cover. The sunset image was read into the computer, which created the head profiles and mirrorlike reflections.

TELEVISION GRAPHICS

If you've watched television recently, you've probably noticed a number of flashy graphics that are used for advertising, sports, news, and weather segments. Many such graphics, including those on this two-page spread, were created using sophisticated computer hardware and software geared to creating art images and animation.

2, 3 Computer-created stills from a short animated sequence used in ABC's fall 1988 "Something's Happening" promotional campaign.

4 A still used in a television ad promoting the Los Angeles Marathon.

28

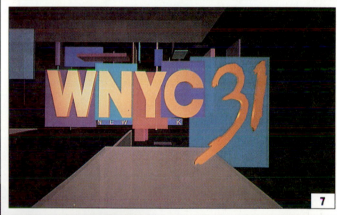

5–8 Computer graphics are commonly used to create logos for specific shows and for local-network identification packages.

PUBLISHING

Only 25 years ago computers were first applied, in the form of word processors, to manipulate words. Today computer systems are being used for an increasing variety of publishing-related tasks—from preparing newsletters for local distribution to creating complex, attention-getting magazine covers that feature optical illusion.

9 Desktop publishing hardware and software, which have made it possible to lay out pages electronically, have completely revolutionized the creation of newspapers and books. Today, with an investment of only a few thousand dollars and moderate training, virtually anyone can do respectable desktop publishing on his or her own.

10 Sophisticated art and illustration packages enable art and typeface elements to be either read into the computer or created extemporaneously. Once stored, they can be manipulated at very high computational speeds to produce almost any type of new image imaginable.

11 Art and text can be combined to form the seemingly impossible page image. Today computer technology is widely used to both retouch images and "cut and paste" images together from a variety of other images, thereby making fantasy look real.

DESIGN

Computers routinely support a nearly endless variety of design functions, such as the design of consumer products, product packages, building and floor plans, cars and planes, and corporate logos. Shown below are a few of these types of applications.

12 Computers enable marketing personnel to experiment with the creation of an ever greater number of packaging design alternatives before making a final selection.

13, 14 Computers often are used to create striking, three-dimensional logos for organizations. The logo or sign images can also be "mapped" onto surfaces to show how they might appear to others when implemented in real life.

15 Today fabrics and clothing are commonly designed with computer assistance. When manufacturers and buyers can view simulated woven cloth patterns on a color display screen, there is no need to develop large numbers of costly preproduction samples. Also, production requests can be filled more promptly.

BUSINESS/FINANCE

Businesses and financial institutions first called on computer systems about 40 years ago to tackle their mounting paperwork problems. Today they also use computers extensively to provide better customer service and assist managers with decision making.

16 Computers are used on all major financial exchanges throughout the world to record securities prices. Thousands of companies and individuals use these prices to electronically identify promising and troublesome stocks and to trigger buy and sell orders.

17 Automatic teller machines (ATMs) have brought computer technology face to face with virtually anyone who has a bank account. Today banking is one of the most computer-intensive industries.

18 The supermarket industry is one of the heaviest users of recognition systems, which identify machine-readable codes on packaging and perform automatic price lookups. Such systems provide fast and accurate data entry and often make data instantly available for management analysis.

19 Computers are widely used in the airlines industry to keep track of flights and passengers, perform ticketing and billing tasks, and schedule and optimize air routes.

32

20 The kiosk, pioneered by banks and their automatic teller machines, is becoming a familiar fixture in stores, in hotels, in museums, in airports, on ski slopes, and in other places where machines can replace clerical personnel. The Sears Home Lighting Center shown here provides information to customers and enables them to complete orders on hundreds of lighting products.

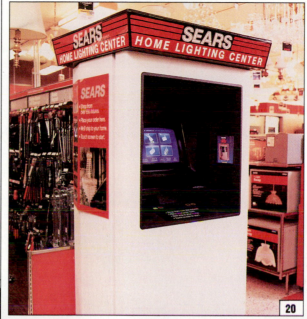

21 Laptops help salespeople close orders while on the road. These compact machines can hook into the telephone system to quickly gather key data stored on mainframes, and they can help sell customers with sophisticated, on-the-spot analyses of proposals.

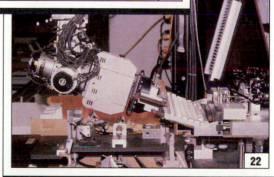

22 Robots, which are simply computers with humanlike motor capabilities, are widely used by manufacturing firms to perform tasks considered too monotonous, time consuming, or dangerous for humans.

23, 24 Microcomputer systems are rapidly becoming a "must-have" for small businesses. They help these enterprises handle their transaction workloads and enable professionals such as managers, lawyers, doctors, and architects to better perform their jobs.

C H A P T E R

2

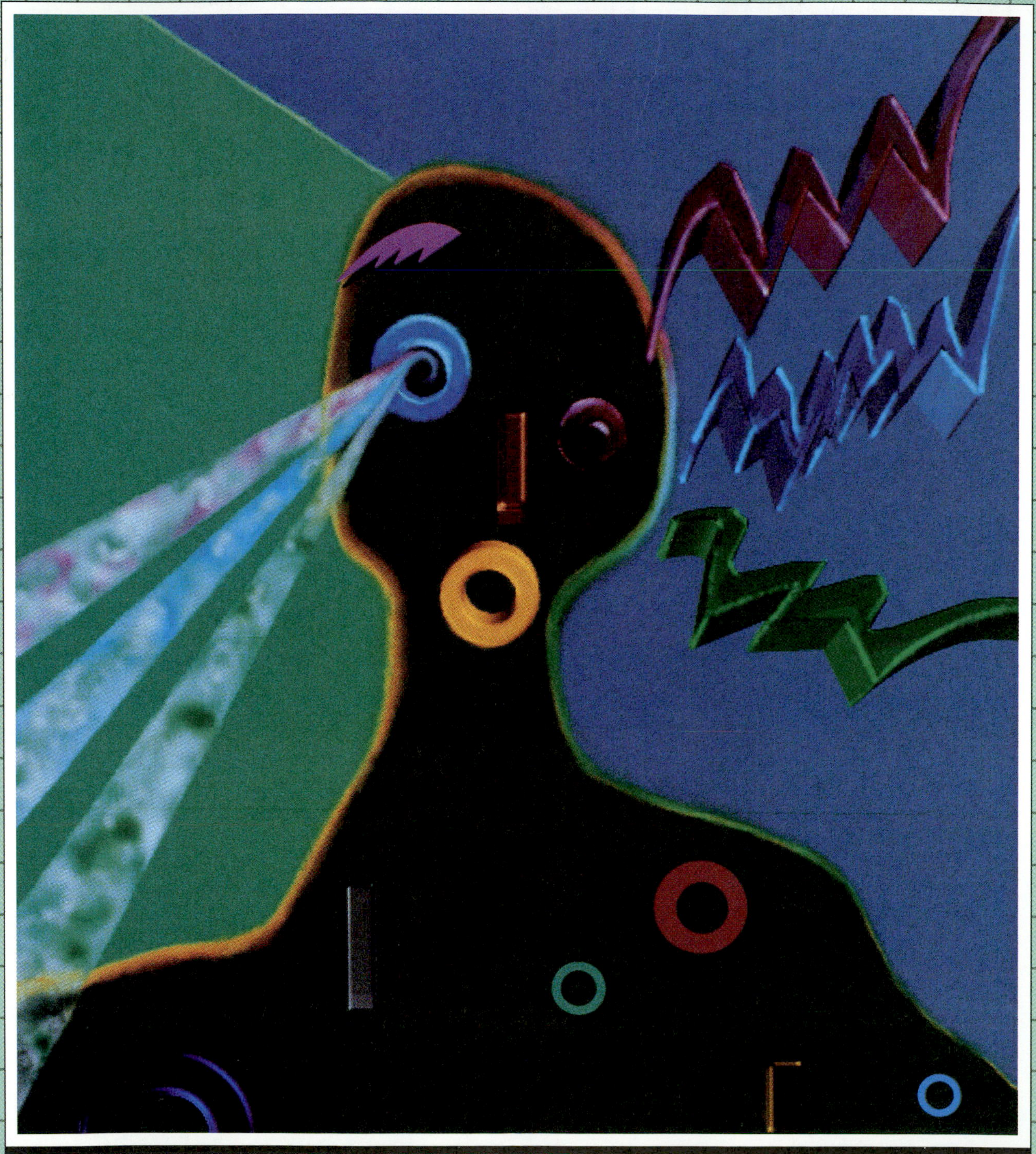

Computer Systems and Information Processing

Objectives

After completing this chapter, you will be able to:

1. Identify several major classes of input, output, processing, and storage hardware.

2. Explain how data are organized in a computing environment.

3. Distinguish between applications and systems software.

4. Describe some of the ways in which computer systems process data into useful information.

5. Define several more key terms that are useful to know when reading about or discussing computers.

OVERVIEW

As you learned in Chapter 1, input, processing, and output, together with storage, are the major components of any computer system. In this chapter, you will see how they work together in more detail.

First, we'll take a look at computer system hardware. We'll cover some basic hardware concepts and discuss some of the most important kinds of input, output, and storage equipment. Then we'll see how these can be linked, first in a small computer system and then in a large one. This section will introduce you to the detailed discussion of hardware in Module B.

Next, we'll take up the subject of data, specifically how data must be organized for processing on a computer system. Study the terms introduced in this section carefully, because you will encounter them frequently throughout the rest of the book.

Then we'll go on to a discussion of program software to introduce you to a subject we cover extensively in Module C.

Finally, we'll discuss information processing on computer systems. We'll examine representative examples of some of the most common types of processing to see how hardware, data, software, procedures, and users interact to do useful work.

COMPUTER HARDWARE

All computer systems consist of some combination of computers and support equipment. The main **computer,** often called the *central processing unit,* or *CPU,* is the heart of the system; it controls the actual processing of data and programs. Closely tied to the CPU is its *primary memory,* which is almost always housed in the same hardware device, called the **system unit.** Many people, in fact, refer to the system unit as the computer, but strictly speaking it is merely the "box" that contains the computer.

Support equipment consists of all the machines that make it possible to get data and programs into the CPU, retrieve processed information, and store data and programs for ready access to the CPU. Figure 2-1 summarizes the relationships among these hardware elements and lists some of the most important examples of each.

Support Equipment

There are a number of ways to classify support equipment for computer systems. One of the most basic is by function: Is the device predominantly for input, output, or storage? Another is by medium: Does it use tapes or disks? A third is by relation to the CPU: Is it peripheral or auxiliary? Online or offline? Let's consider each of these in turn.

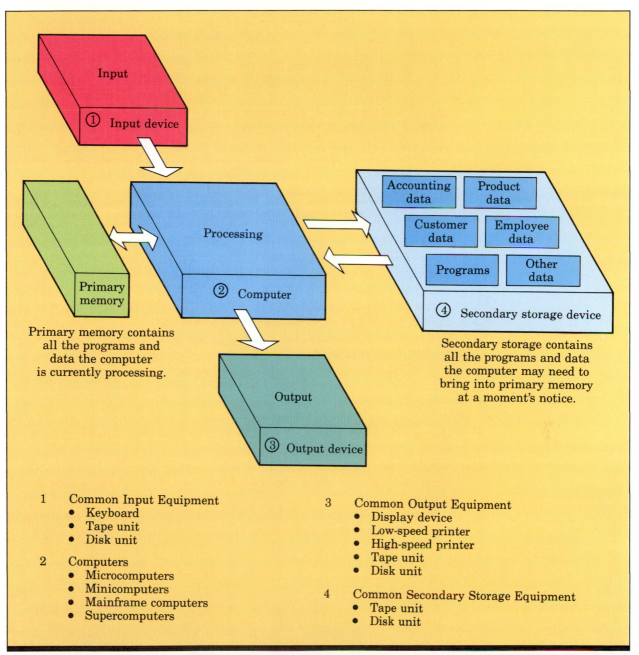

FIGURE 2-1
The four major aspects of computing: input, output, processing, and storage.

Input, Output, or Storage?

Input devices are machines that convert data and programs into a form that the CPU can understand and process. **Output devices** are machines that convert processed data into a form that users can understand. **Secondary storage devices** are machines that make frequently used data and pro-

FIGURE 2-2

Input devices. (a, left) The keyboard is the most widely used input device for entering instructions and data into a computer system. (b, right) The mouse is useful for rapidly moving the cursor around the display screen and for pointing to onscreen selections.

grams readily available to the CPU. These functions often overlap in a single machine. Some machines, for example, work as both input and output devices, and all secondary storage devices also function as both input and output devices. Now let's discuss some of the most common kinds of support equipment in terms of these three functions.

Computer *keyboards* (see Figure 2-2) are input devices that closely resemble typewriter keyboards. They are used to type in programs and data and to interactively issue instructions to the computer system. As Figure 2-2 shows, people are increasingly using a pointing device called a *mouse* to supplement computer keyboard operations.

Display devices (see Figure 2-3) appear in almost all computer systems. Many of these devices use a televisionlike picture unit called a cathode ray tube, or CRT. Display devices are used for output. The operator enters commands to the computer system through a keyboard or mouse; then both the input the operator enters and the output the CPU produces appear on the screen.

A *display terminal* is a display device and a keyboard that are packaged together and used as a communications workstation to a large computer.

FIGURE 2-3

Display devices. (a, left) A display terminal consists of a screen and a keyboard. (b, right) A monitor consists of only a screen.

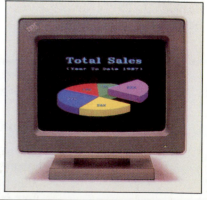

FIGURE 2-4

A low-speed printer. Low-speed printers, such as this Canon model, are commonly used with microcomputer systems.

On the other hand, the local display devices commonly found with micro-computers are generally referred to as *monitors.*

Printers produce output. *Low-speed printers* (Figure 2-4) are designed to output small amounts of printed information. Because of their low cost, they are very popular devices for microcomputer systems. Many low-speed print-ers that are configured to larger computer systems also contain keyboards, which enable operators to use them to send data to the computer. These devices are called *teleprinters.*

High-speed printers (Figure 2-5) are used to produce extensive printed reports. They may operate at speeds 10 to 30 times faster than those of low-speed devices. Some types of high-speed printers, such as those based on laser technology, are especially oriented toward graphical output, such as drawings, photographic images, and fancy typefaces.

Secondary storage devices hold frequently used data and programs for ready access to the CPU. They also function as both input and output de-vices; that is, they contain stored data and programs that are sent to the CPU as input and the CPU transmits new data and programs to them as output. The most common types of secondary storage devices are *magnetic disk units* and *magnetic tape units.*

Disk units store data and programs on magnetized platters called disks. *Hard-disk units* (Figure 2-6), which work with fast-spinning, rigid disks, are designed to make relatively large volumes of material immediately available to the CPU. *Diskette units* (Figure 2-7), which work with small, plastic disks coated with a magnetizable material, are slower than hard-disk units and have much less data-carrying capacity. However, they are far cheaper. Hard-disk units play an important role in both large and small computer systems, while diskette units generally are associated with smaller systems.

Tape units are designed to use tapes, either those in detachable-reel form or those packaged in cartridges. Traditionally, the tape units on large com-puters have used detachable tape reels. Many of the newer tape units, such

FIGURE 2-5

A high-speed printer. Line printers, such as this IBM 4248, which is rated at 4,000 lines per minute, are commonly used with mainframes and minicomputers.

FIGURE 2-6

A hard-disk unit. Devices such as the IBM disk storage unit shown here are ideal for storing large amounts of data online and gaining fast access to them.

FIGURE 2-7

A diskette unit. Diskettes come in a variety of sizes, as do the units that contain the drives on which they are mounted. The drive shown here can read 5¼-inch-diameter diskettes that can store up to 175 double-spaced, typewritten pages of data.

as the IBM 3480 tape storage system (see Figure 2-8), use tape cartridges—tapes that are enclosed in a plastic case. Cartridge tape units are also the most common type of tape unit found on smaller computer systems.

Input/Output Media

Input and output devices are machines for getting data and programs into a computer and getting the results out in a usable form, respectively. Often, however, data and programs are not permanently stored in a particular device. Instead they are recorded on **input/output (I/O) media** in a form the associated device can read and transmit to the CPU. In other words, just as the record player on your home stereo system works with vinyl records, input/output devices work with specific input/output media. Four of the most common input/output media in use today are *hard magnetic disks, diskettes, detachable-reel magnetic tapes,* and *magnetic tape cartridges.* These are illustrated in Figure 2-9 and will be discussed in detail in Chapter 5.

Peripheral and Auxiliary; Online and Offline

Support equipment is either peripheral or auxiliary and online or offline.

    Peripheral equipment consists of machines that can be "plugged into" the CPU to allow them to communicate with it directly. All of the machines we have discussed so far—keyboards, display devices, printers, and secondary storage devices—fall into the peripheral-equipment category.

FIGURE 2-8

A tape unit. Each of the small tape cartridges this unit reads can store a couple of thousand pages of data at a very low cost.

FIGURE 2-9

Common types of input/output media. (a, top left) Magnetic tape on reels. (b, top right) Cartridge tape. (c, bottom left) Hard magnetic disks. (d, bottom right) Diskettes.

Auxiliary equipment consists of machines that always work independently of the CPU in what is called the *standalone mode.* Examples are *key-to-disk units* and *key-to-tape units.* These two machines are also examples of **data preparation devices,** because their purpose is to get input material onto a particular input/output medium—a disk for a key-to-disk machine and tape for a key-to-tape unit. After the data have been entered onto the input/output medium, the medium is loaded onto the appropriate peripheral device—a disk unit or tape unit—for the CPU to process the data.

Any device that is ready for or in communication with the computer at a given time is said to be **online** at that time. If a device isn't online, it's **offline.** When peripheral equipment is plugged into the computer, it's considered online. Some peripherals also have standalone capability. Thus, when we "pull the plug," detaching them from the computer, they're offline. Auxiliary equipment, since it functions independently of the CPU, is always offline.

Getting It Together: Combining Hardware into a System

Now that we've covered some basic hardware concepts and discussed some particular machines in terms of them, let's see how hardware is linked in a computer system. We'll consider both a small and a large computer system.

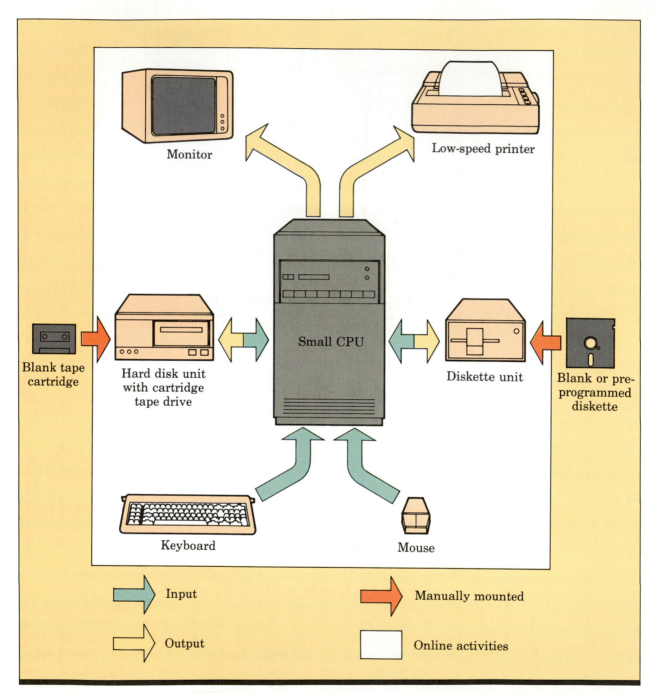

FIGURE 2-10

Components of a small computer system run by a microcomputer or small minicomputer. In some microcomputer systems, the monitor, keyboard, CPU, disk devices, and even printer may all be physically housed in the same unit.

Figure 2-10 illustrates a system run by a small computer, such as a microcomputer or small minicomputer. The system includes a

□ CPU/system unit   □ Mouse   □ Hard-disk unit
□ Keyboard   □ Diskette unit   □ Cartridge tape unit
□ Monitor   □ Low-speed printer

Of course, not every microcomputer or minicomputer system looks like the one in the figure. In many portable (laptop) microcomputer systems, for instance, a monitor, keyboard, diskette unit, hard-disk unit, and system unit are packaged together as a single unit. As unbelievable as it may seem, it is now even possible to fit a complete computer system onto a credit card (see Tomorrow box). In most minicomputer systems, all of the devices depicted in Figure 2-10 usually exist as separate hardware units, and there will also likely be a high-speed printer available. In fact, there may be several monitor-keyboard workstations (i.e., display terminals) hooked into the CPU. Many top-of-the-line microcomputer systems also allow several workstations.

Figure 2-11 illustrates a large computer system. Such a system might be run by a mainframe computer or a large minicomputer, either of which is capable of running the most powerful types of support equipment. The simple system shown here includes a

□ CPU/system unit   □ High-speed printer   □ Key-to-disk unit
□ Display terminal   □ Key-to-tape unit   □ Hard-disk units
□ Teleprinter   □ Tape unit

A system run by a large computer can contain hundreds of terminals, several tape and disk units, numerous printers, and many other types of equipment.

Computer systems, both small and large, are often linked together in a variety of ways to perform work—and often with other devices that one wouldn't normally think of as being part of an information processing system. Feature 2A describes how "smart materials" are being incorporated into computer systems to provide ever more accurate inputs.

ORGANIZING DATA FOR COMPUTER SYSTEMS

Data, as we said before, are essentially facts. But you can't just randomly input a collection of facts into a computer system and expect to get results. Data to be processed in a computer system must be organized in a systematic way. A common procedure is to organize data into fields, records, files, and databases. Each of these words has a precise meaning in a computing environment, and you should use them with care.

A **field** is a collection of characters (such as a single digit, letter of the alphabet, or special symbol like a decimal point) that represents a single type of data. A **record** is a collection of related fields. A **file** is a collection of related records. Files, records, and fields normally are stored on an input/

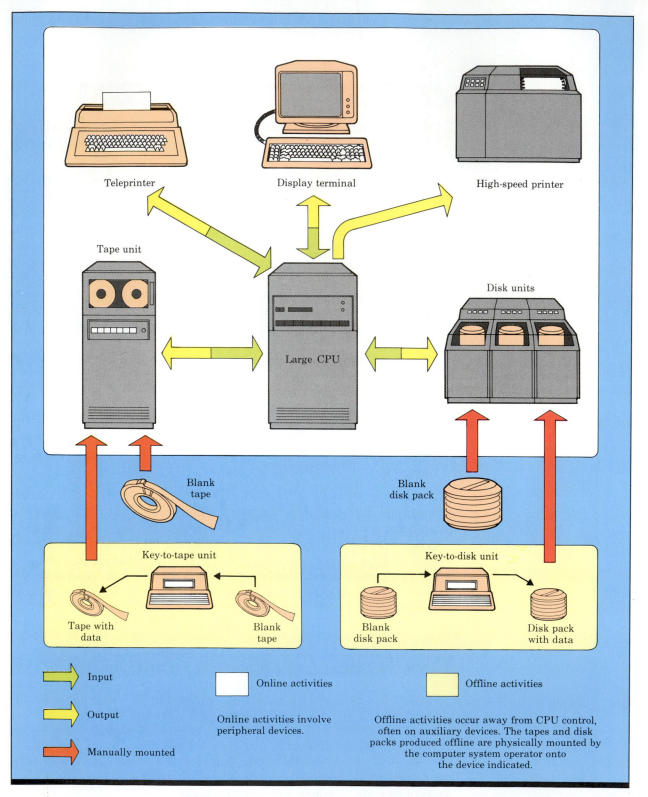

Teleprinter

Display terminal

High-speed printer

Tape unit

Large CPU

Disk units

Blank tape

Blank disk pack

Key-to-tape unit

Tape with data

Blank tape

Key-to-disk unit

Blank disk pack

Disk pack with data

Input

Output

Manually mounted

Online activities

Online activities involve peripheral devices.

Offline activities

Offline activities occur away from CPU control, often on auxiliary devices. The tapes and disk packs produced offline are physically mounted by the computer system operator onto the device indicated.

FIGURE 2-11

Components of a large computer system run by a mainframe or large minicomputer. Note the relationship of input/output media to online and offline activities and to peripheral and auxiliary devices.

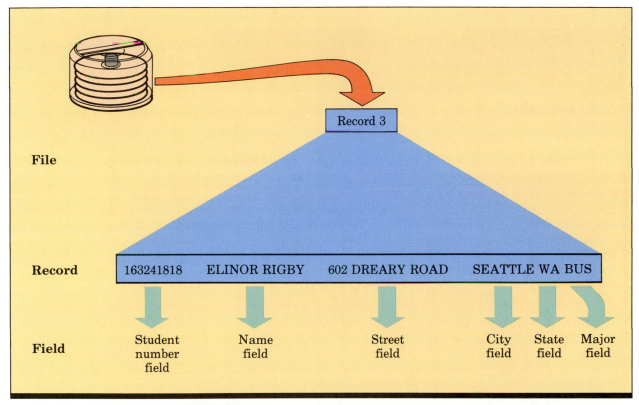

FIGURE 2-12

Differences among a file, a record, and a field. The file shown here contains name and address data on students enrolled at a college. If there were 2,000 active students at the college, this file would contain 2,000 records. Each record in the file has six data fields—student's ID number, name, street, city, state, and major.

output medium such as a disk or a tape. Your school, for example, probably has a *file,* perhaps stored on disk, of all students currently enrolled (see Figure 2-12). The file likely contains a *record* for each student. Each record has several *fields* containing various types of data about each student: ID number, name, street, city, state, major subject area, and the like.

The concept of a **database** is a bit more complicated to explain at this point, but you can safely consider it a collection of data that contains the contents of several files. For example, a student database may contain the contents of a student address file (such as the one in Figure 2-12), a student history file (courses completed and grades earned by each student), and perhaps other data. In other words, most of the information regarding students would be found in the student database. We'll discuss the concept of a database more formally in Chapter 14.

In most large computer systems, many data files are kept on disk storage for rapid access. These files often contain operational data. For example, most businesses (such as your local department store) have files storing data such as the following:

Super Smart Cards

A Microcomputer System for Every Pocket

When most of us think about the smallest computer systems, the image of a laptop computer may come to mind. But what about a computer system—complete with a processor, storage, a keyboard, and a display—that you can fit inside your wallet? Sounds impossible? Then consider the super smart card.

Physically speaking, *smart cards* are credit-card-sized pieces of plastic that contain, at a minimum, a microprocessor chip and a memory. The memory capacity may be as small as a few thousand characters or as large as a few million (the equivalent of several hundred pages of text).

Smart cards, which were pioneered in France and are still in the pilot stage in many places, are most often used to make electronic purchases or to transfer funds between accounts—say, between the cardholder's account and the account at a bank or credit card company. They can also be used for a variety of other purposes.

To use the card to make a purchase, the user or clerk inserts it into a machine. Then the user types in a "secret" personal identification number on the machine's keyboard. Next, the user or clerk completes typing in the transaction. If the purchase is acceptable, the card's microprocessor inscribes a record of the transaction into the card's

memory. This memory can be used to update the user's account at the bank and also serve as an electronic checkbook register.

Super smart cards, which contain a keyboard and display, provide even greater capability. For instance, the user types in the personal identification number on the card itself, making it difficult for anyone to see the value entered. Since the keyboard can also be used to enter a short program, the card issuer can set up special routines to effectively disable the card if it is ever lost or stolen. Also, special keys on the keyboard ensure that proprietary control information required by the card issuer's system is always present. The display, on the other hand, enables a merchant to obtain an authorization code for each transaction locally rather

---

☐ Key customer data, such as names, addresses, and credit standings (called a *customer master file*). A **master file** is a file containing relatively permanent data

☐ Daily customer transactions, such as purchases and payments (called a *customer transaction file*). A **transaction file** is a file containing data that are used to update, or modify, data in a master file

☐ Amounts owed by credit customers (called a *receivables file*)

☐ The organization's own outstanding debts (called a *payables file*)

As mentioned previously, data from related files often are stored in databases. For example, data that normally would appear in the customer transaction file, customer master file, and receivables file described previously might be collectively stored in a customer database.

Whatever the medium on which they are stored, entities such as files and databases always have names. The computer system uses these names to

than having to call up a credit bureau. On a new VISA card now in pilot testing (see photo), cardholders will be able to output on the 16-character display previous transactions and current balances of up to four accounts.

The uses for smart cards and super smart cards abound. In the health care industry, such cards could be used to store a patient's identity and address, insurance data, next of kin, allergies, and a brief medical history. If the card carrier were disabled in an accident, the card could immediately be put into use to assist with treatment. A university issuing such cards could use them to allow students access to grade or financial data. Smart cards also could be useful for making phone calls; a cardholder would have an electronic record of all phone calls made—

useful for tax and billing purposes—right on the card. In security applications, such a card could carry a digitized version of a fingerprint or voice and thereby serve as an electronic passkey, allowing an authorized user into restricted areas or access to a sensitive computer network.

In Norway, smart cards are now being tried out at toll booths. The card is mounted in a specific place on the front window of the booth and scanned electronically by a transmitter as the cardholder cruises by. Then the cardholder's account is debited for the toll. A future version of this system, now under development, will eliminate the traditional tollbooth and record the toll at a station as the cardholder zooms past at normal speed.

The possibility of interfacing the smart card with per-

sonal computers, which would allow access to a larger video display and a wider variety of hardware and software tools, has also been a subject of much discussion.

Around the corner. The VISA Super-Smart Card, with built-in display and keyboard.

identify the files or databases when it needs to access them. For example, "AR-D200" may be the name of a receivables data file and "AR-P201" the name of a program that produces a list of customers with overdue balances from this file. Each organization has its own naming convention. In the above example, "AR" stands for accounts receivable, "P" for program file, and "D" for data file. All 100-numbered program files may be related to billing, 200-level files to overdue balances, and so forth.

A BRIEF INTRODUCTION TO SOFTWARE

As mentioned earlier, the word *software* refers to computer programs. Programs direct the computer system to do specific tasks, just as your thoughts direct your body to speak or move in certain ways. There are two classes of software: applications software and systems software.

Smart Materials

Information-Age Materials Extend the Reach of Computers

How many times have you watched a sporting event and witnessed a questionable call? Was the tennis ball in or out? Did the player fumble the football before hitting the turf? Was the pitch a ball or a strike? Was there an offensive foul or an illegal block? In our information age, technology may indeed eventually become the ultimate referee or umpire to these disputes.

Okay, so the National Football League's videotape replay system hasn't been the panacea that many hoped it would be. A major problem with the replay system is that cameras, like referees, can be positioned at the wrong angle so that what gets recorded on tape looks just as muddled as what spectators saw live. Another problem, of course, is that human interpretation of taped action causes an annoying delay to both the stadium audience, which might be braving 10 degree weather to watch the game, and the

couch-potato-cum-armchair-quarterback, who is ready to zap the channel with the remote control. But let's not give up on technology yet, especially with smart materials now available.

Smart materials are thin, skinlike materials containing small fibers that serve as sensors. When the sensors are disturbed by something happening around them, they generate signals to computers, which interpret the results. In some cases, the computers consist of microprocessor chips that are themselves embedded in the smart materials.

In the world of tennis, for instance, a system called Accu-Call has been developed to prevent outbursts and umpire harassment like those doled out by players who get carried away. Sensors are embedded into a fine metal mesh woven around the outside edge of the critical inbounds lines on the court. Also, tiny metallic fibers are woven into the tennis ball. Whenever a ball touches the mesh, a signal goes to a

nearby laptop computer indicating that the ball is out. The system is accurate enough to pinpoint to a hundredth of an inch where the ball struck the court.

The military and the airlines industry also are looking into smart materials to assist pilots and to make aircraft safer. For instance, an airplane's wings may have an outer layer that consists of a "skin" composed of sensitive, hair-thin optical fibers that are laid out in a grid (see figure). These fibers are so sensitive that virtually any type of pressure, strain, or temperature change will distort the light that normally passes through them. The distortion is picked up by flexible circuit boards, patched onto the skin, that contain embedded microprocessors.

On conventional airplanes, such a fiber-and-microprocessor skin would be able to detect cracks on the surface of a plane and sense if the wings had too much ice on them to enable a safe takeoff. For military applications, the skins would be able to do these and other chores. For instance, the skins would be able to tell whether a plane was being scanned by radar and also to activate systems to confuse ground-based radar. The U.S. Air Force is bullish enough on smart skins to rank them among their top-priority new-technology initiatives.

While the Air Force may rank at the top of the list of groups interested in smart materials, entrepreneurs in other areas have their own ideas. A professor at Michigan State, for instance, envisions smart materials being used in golf clubs. The club's shaft would be hollowed to accommodate a fluid containing smart materials. The materials would allow the club to deliver more whip during the initial stage of the golfer's swing, but when sensors in the head sensed the ball was about to be struck, the material would stiffen the shaft to deliver a greater impact. Who knows—maybe this will do for the budding Lee Trevinos of the world what the fiberglass pole did for vaulters in the 1960s. The professor also sees fishing poles using the same principle as golf clubs, with the smart materials sensing the weight of the fish and flexing the pole for maximum play.

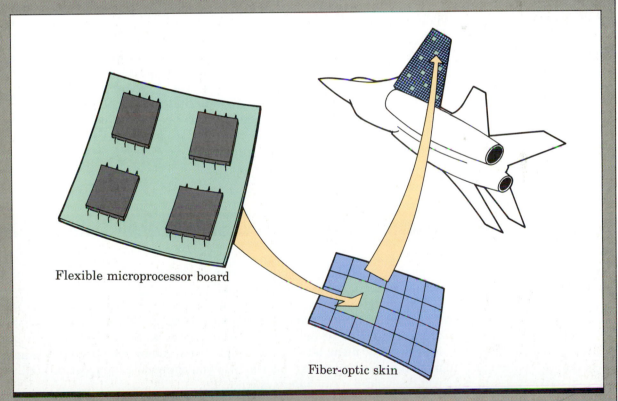

Flexible microprocessor board

Fiber-optic skin

Smart skins. Putting safety under wraps.

Applications Software. **Applications software** is written by users or programmers to perform tasks such as computing the interest or balance in bank accounts, preparing bills, playing games, scheduling airline flights, diagnosing hospital patients' illnesses, and so forth. In other words, applications software makes possible the "computer work" users have in mind when they acquire computer systems.

You can buy applications software prewritten (e.g., word processing programs, spreadsheet programs, payroll programs, and video games) or write it yourself. If you write it yourself, you must know a specific programming language. The trade-offs involved in buying or creating software are covered in Chapter 9. Some of the more popular programming languages are discussed in Chapter 11, and prewritten software is covered in Chapters 12 through 14.

Systems Software. **Systems software** consists of "background" programs that enable applications software to run smoothly. One of the most important pieces of systems software is the *operating system,* a set of control programs that supervise the computer system's work. Viewed another way, the operating system enables applications software to interface with a specific set of hardware. Many recent Hollywood movies have portrayed the role of the operating system in some overly exaggerated manner—for example, a demon master control program that tries to take over the world. Fortunately, operating systems don't control people; rather, people control operating systems. We'll address these and other types of systems software in more depth in Chapter 8.

INFORMATION PROCESSING

Computer systems process data into information. When we talk about information processing, however, what kinds of processing do we have in mind?

The number of ways in which a full-fledged computer system can turn data into useful information is truly staggering and defies a simple, systematic enumeration at this early stage in the book. So rather than trying to look at all of them, let's focus on just a few commonly encountered information processing tasks. This will help you appreciate the types of work you will likely need a computer system to do.

Some common information processing tasks are

- ☐ Selection
- ☐ Summarizing
- ☐ Issuance
- ☐ Sorting
- ☐ Information retrieval
- ☐ Updating

We will discuss each of these in turn and illustrate each with an example. All of our examples will use the personnel file in Figure 2-13. This file is housed in a secondary storage device, such as the hard-disk unit shown in the figure. We've used a small, five-record file here to simplify the examples (in reality, many personnel files contain thousands of such records). Also, each record shown contains only five fields. The sixth column, "Other Data," indicates that we could have added many more fields had we wanted to.

Each of the information processing operations we'll describe should be located in a program somewhere in secondary storage. For example, if we want to sort our data file, we will need a program that will enable us to sort data records.

In each of our examples, output can be directed to one or more output devices in the system—the display device, the printer, or secondary storage. Again, to make things straightforward, we've shown output directed to only one device in each of the six example applications in Figure 2-13.

Selection. **Selection** involves going through a set of data and picking out only those items that meet certain criteria. Figure 2-13a illustrates a selection problem and how a computer system could handle it. The problem illustrated here is selecting the names of all employees in department A and printing out those names. Naturally, if we wished, we could have directed the names to the display screen instead (and saved paper, too).

Selection criteria can be either simple or complex. For example, we could have asked the computer system to extract and display the names of all department A employees who were hired either last year or before 1970. And remember our example in Chapter 1 where the catering manager used her file to select recipes that were dinner dishes containing beef and mushrooms. All of the types of applications software packages we'll be discussing in Chapters 12, 13, and 14 have some kind of easy-to-use selection feature.

Summarizing. **Summarizing** involves reducing a mass of data to a manageable form. This could require making a tally of items, determining sums for items in a particular class, and so forth. For example, in Figure 2-13b we have had the computer system output to the printer the number of people in each department and in the personnel file. Still another possible summarizing application would be to have the computer system output the number of people hired in each of several years, such as 1989, 1990, 1991, and so on. Software packages such as spreadsheets, file managers, and database management systems have strong facilities for summarizing data.

Issuance. Computer systems are also widely used to input records, perform a series of calculations on each record, and prepare a document for each record based on these computations. This process is sometimes called **issuance,** since the end result is the issuing of documents. In billing operations, for example, the computer system reads a record of payments and purchases for each customer, computes the amount due, and prepares a bill. Payroll processing, illustrated in Figure 2-13c, is another example.

Checks such as those shown in Figure 2-13c cannot be generated from the personnel file alone. After all, how is the computer system to know how much to pay each employee? Therefore, to produce paychecks, the payroll program may consult two other files, one with the hours worked by each employee and another consisting of employee pay rates. Then, for each employee the computer multiplies hours worked by a corresponding pay rate to produce the earnings due.

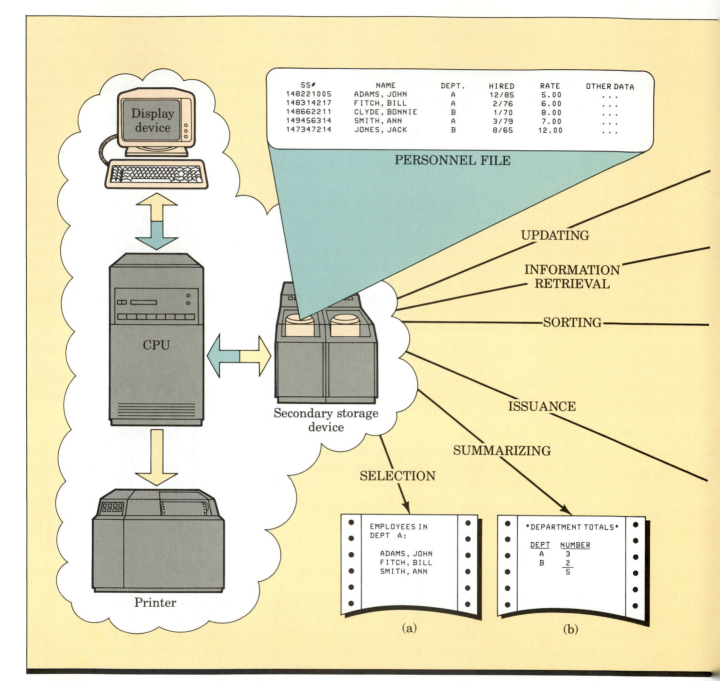

SS#	NAME	DEPT.	HIRED	RATE	OTHER DATA
148221005	ADAMS, JOHN	A	12/85	5.00	...
148314217	FITCH, BILL	A	2/76	6.00	...
148662211	CLYDE, BONNIE	B	1/70	8.00	...
149456314	SMITH, ANN	A	3/79	7.00	...
147347214	JONES, JACK	B	8/65	12.00	...

PERSONNEL FILE

Display device

CPU

Secondary storage device

Printer

UPDATING

INFORMATION RETRIEVAL

SORTING

ISSUANCE

SUMMARIZING

SELECTION

EMPLOYEES IN
DEPT A:

ADAMS, JOHN
FITCH, BILL
SMITH, ANN

(a)

DEPARTMENT TOTALS

DEPT	NUMBER
A	3
B	2
	5

(b)

FIGURE 2-13

Information processing. Depicted are six fundamental ways in which computers are capable of processing data into useful information.

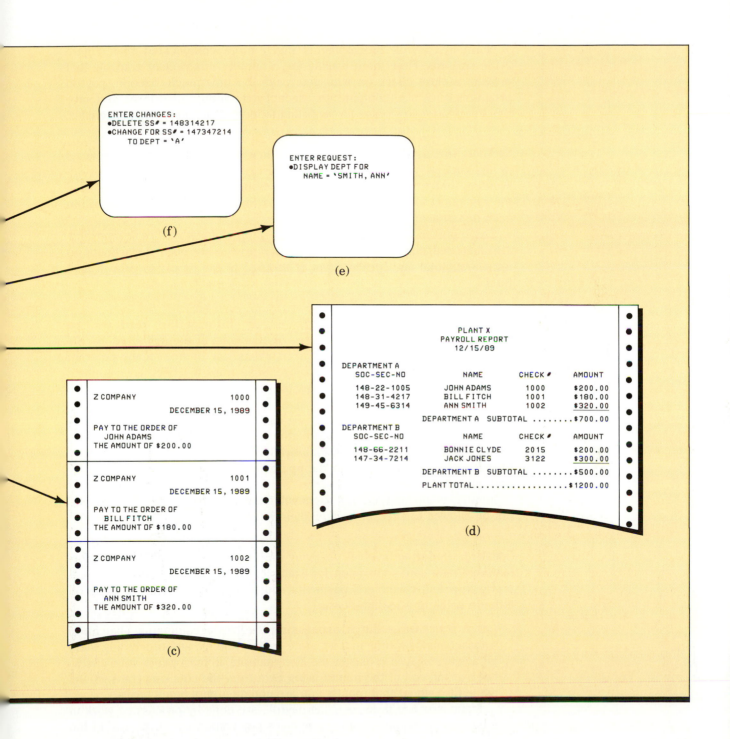

ENTER CHANGES:
●DELETE SS# = 148314217
●CHANGE FOR SS# = 147347214
    TO DEPT = 'A'

(f)

ENTER REQUEST:
●DISPLAY DEPT FOR
    NAME = 'SMITH, ANN'

(e)

PLANT X
PAYROLL REPORT
12/15/89

DEPARTMENT A
  SOC-SEC-NO   NAME   CHECK #   AMOUNT
  148-22-1005   JOHN ADAMS   1000 $200.00
  148-31-4217   BILL FITCH   1001 $180.00
  149-45-6314   ANN SMITH   1002 $320.00
  DEPARTMENT A SUBTOTAL $700.00
DEPARTMENT B
  SOC-SEC-NO   NAME   CHECK #   AMOUNT
  148-66-2211   BONNIE CLYDE   2015 $200.00
  147-34-7214   JACK JONES   3122 $300.00

  DEPARTMENT B SUBTOTAL $500.00

  PLANT TOTAL $1200.00

(d)

Z COMPANY   1000
                       DECEMBER 15, 1989

PAY TO THE ORDER OF
  JOHN ADAMS
THE AMOUNT OF $200.00

Z COMPANY   1001
                       DECEMBER 15, 1989

PAY TO THE ORDER OF
  BILL FITCH
THE AMOUNT OF $180.00

Z COMPANY   1002
                       DECEMBER 15, 1989

PAY TO THE ORDER OF
  ANN SMITH
THE AMOUNT OF $320.00

(c)

Normally, payroll processing is much more complicated than Figure 2-13c suggests. First, there usually are a number of stringent controls that provide a close check on who gets paid and how much. Second, payroll programs must also compute and deduct federal and local taxes and save this information in storage for reporting to federal and state taxing agencies.

Sorting. **Sorting** involves arranging data in a specific order—a list of names in alphabetical order, for example, or a list of numbers in ascending or descending order. Figure 2-13d shows a computer report in which data from the personnel file are sorted first by department and then by name within each department.

The report in Figure 2-13d is also an example of *control-break reporting.* As illustrated, the computer breaks after processing each department to print a subtotal and breaks again at the end of the report to print a final total.

Information Retrieval. Programs created for **information retrieval,** or *query,* enable users to enter a series of questions at the keyboard for the purpose of extracting information from a database or from many different data files. For example, a bank manager may want to check a customer's credit rating. The checking, savings, trust, and loan data needed to determine credit ratings are contained in a customer database. An information retrieval program that responds to the manager's request for a credit check could extract all the needed information from the database and calculate the customer's credit rating automatically. Figure 2-13e illustrates a query to the personnel file, in which the operator is trying to determine the department in which Ann Smith works.

In many companies, certain users will be allowed to retrieve data but will not be allowed to alter, or *update,* them in any way.

Updating. **Updating** involves changing the data in a file to reflect new information. Credit card companies, for example, update their customer files regularly to reflect customers' payments and purchases. Updating is done on either a batch or a realtime basis.

☐ *Batch processing* **Batch processing** involves accumulating (batching) transactions over time in a separate transaction file and processing them all at once against a master file. For example, if you update your checkbook at the end of the month using data from the checking transactions made throughout that month, you are updating on a batch basis.

Many issuance tasks, such as payroll, are done by processing work in a batch. For example, many companies pay employees at the end of the month. Billing is another operation that is often done in the batch mode. A company may maintain a file of customer transactions, which include purchases and payments. At a certain time of the month, this transaction file is processed against a master file of all customer balances. The computer system updates the balance in each account and issues statements that are sent to the customers.

☐ ***Realtime processing*** The airline industry updates flight reservations on a realtime basis. Every time an agent sells a seat, everyone else using the system needs to get the most up-to-date information on seat availability. **Realtime processing** involves entering transaction data immediately into a computer system and updating master files as each individual transaction takes place. All realtime processing is performed online.

Another example of realtime processing occurs in banking, where tellers with terminals can update an account as soon as a customer makes a withdrawal. If the customer makes a withdrawal at an automatic teller machine, the machine updates the account immediately. The ability to check and update accounts on the spot protects the bank from overwithdrawals. Deposits, however, usually are not recorded in a customer's balance until the end of the day, when all deposits made by all customers that day are processed together. In other words, deposits typically are processed in the batch mode.

Figure 2-13f illustrates updating of the personnel file to show that Bill Fitch has left the company and Jack Jones has moved to department A. If changes such as these are immediately reflected in the computer system, realtime processing is in effect; if they are done at the end of a day or week, batch processing is taking place. Feature 2B discusses vote processing, which largely takes place in the batch mode today.

SUMMARY AND KEY TERMS

All computer systems consist of some combination of **computers,** their primary memories, and **support equipment.** The computer and its primary memory often are housed in the same hardware device, called the **system unit.** The most common types of support equipment are **input devices, output devices,** and **secondary storage devices.**

Input and output devices include keyboards, display devices such as display terminals and monitors, low-speed printers, and high-speed printers.

Secondary storage devices include hard-disk units, diskette units, detachable-reel tape units, and cartridge tape units. These devices use, respectively, hard disks, diskettes, detachable tape reels, and cartridge tapes as their **input/output (I/O) media.**

Support equipment that can be plugged into the computer is considered **peripheral equipment;** if not, it's **auxiliary equipment.** Peripheral devices may be either **online** or **offline** to the CPU at any point in time. Auxiliary equipment, such as **data preparation devices,** is always offline.

Data are commonly organized into fields, records, files, and databases. A **field** is a collection of individual characters, such as digits and letters of the alphabet. A **record** is a collection of related fields. A **file** is a collection of

Vote Processing

Still a Long Way for Computers to Go

If anything, the 1948 U.S. presidential election certainly underscored the need for better information. That's the election in which many midwesterners saw the banner "Dewey defeats Truman" boldly emblazoned across the front page of the *Chicago Tribune* only hours after the votes were in and a Dewey victory seemed a shoo-in. The next morning, however, newspaper readers across the country were treated to a photo of the smiling president-elect, Harry S. Truman, holding aloft a newspaper with the premature scoop.

When 1952 rolled around, it appeared that things would be different. A computer called UNIVAC I was ready to assist with the vote processing—and it would soon become the first computer used by the media to predict a winner in a U.S. presidential election. CBS had decided to pi-

oneer this event, placing one UNIVAC in Philadelphia to perform the computations and another as a prop in its New York television studio. A third machine was ready to serve as a backup. But a funny thing happened along the way: With only 7 percent of the vote in, UNIVAC had awarded 438 electoral votes to Eisenhower and only 93 to Stevenson. This couldn't be right, thought the staff supervising the returns; everyone had predicted the election to be much closer. Could such a machine actually be trusted? Consequently, these results were withheld and UNIVAC was reprogrammed to forecast a closer election. Guess what. The final vote count was 442 votes to Eisenhower and 89 for Stevenson! Edward R. Murrow, the legendary newscaster, remarked about this event, "The trouble with machines is people."

We've come a long way since then. During the 1988 U.S. presidential election, the

major TV networks (ABC, NBC, and CBS) and wire services (United Press International [UPI] and the Associated Press [AP]) formed a consortium called the News Election Service (NES) to tally votes. NES hired a one-night army of 100,000 people and distributed them among all the precincts at which votes were being counted. Many of these temporary reporters came from civic groups, such as the League of Women Voters, who traded volunteers for contributions to their organization.

As each reporter had something interesting to report, he or she phoned in to a regional reporting center in Dallas, Chicago, or Cincinnati. Operators at these centers transcribed the voice-transmitted data into machine-readable form at their display terminals, which were hooked up into one of several IBM Series 1 minicomputers located at their sites. The minis, in turn, sent the data to two IBM 4381 mainframes in NES's Manhattan-based offices. There was also a backup site in nearby northern New Jersey, ready and waiting

related records. As transaction data are generated, they are stored as records in a **transaction file;** a **master file** contains more permanent types of data. A **database** contains the contents of several files.

Software falls into one of two categories: applications software and systems software. **Applications software** is the "computer work" most people have in mind when they buy a computer system. **Systems software** consists of support programs that keep the applications software running smoothly.

in the event of a glitch in one of the Manhattan mainframes.

As NES collected the data, it distributed them to each of its member networks and news associations. What each of the networks did with the data it received and how it interpreted them were its own business. For instance, each network had its own computers and statistical algorithms for interpreting these data and projecting winners in national and state races. Also, each network presented these data differently to its audience. Each had its own staff of graphics designers or design consultants who worked months prior to election night with computer art software. This software was used to create exciting graphic elements to depict races in visually interesting and unusual ways.

While the use of computers in elections has come quite far in the past 40 years, there is still a long way to go. Recently a computerized voting machine that uses a touch screen was developed by Nixdorf, a West German firm. Now all voters need to do is point to their choices on the display screen, and their votes are automatically recorded and tallied. It appears that these machines ultimately will be hooked up to a service such as NES, providing realtime assessment of races and eliminating the expensive 100,000-member force that forays out into the districts and manually reports vote counts. And beyond that, people might even be able to vote by pointing to choices on their television sets or by keying in the right codes on their touch-tone phones—a convenience that could get almost everyone "out" to the polls.

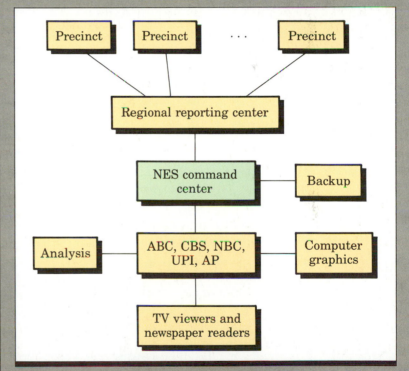

Vote tabulation. From the precinct count to the TV watcher, automation can still make big improvements.

Six common information processing tasks are selection, summarizing, issuance, sorting, information retrieval, and updating. **Selection** involves extracting from files only those fields or records that meet certain criteria. **Summarizing** consists of reducing a mass of data to a manageable form. **Issuance** involves inputting records, performing a series of calculations on each record, and preparing a document for each record based on the computations. **Sorting** means arranging data in some specified sequence, such as alphabetical order or numeric order. Summarizing, sorting, and issuance often are combined to do *control-break reporting*. **Information retrieval,** or *query,* enables users to extract information from data files. **Updating,** which involves changing data in a file to reflect new information, can be done on a periodic or immediate basis. These types of updating are called **batch processing** and **realtime processing,** respectively.

REVIEW EXERCISES

Fill-in Questions

1. To be read by a computer system, data must be recorded in machine-readable form on some type of _____ .

2. Machines that always work in a standalone mode are referred to as _____ equipment.

3. Any device that is in communication with the CPU at any given time is said to be _____ at that time.

4. _____ software is written by users or programmers to perform tasks such as computing the interest or balance in bank accounts.

5. _____ software consists of "background" programs that enable other programs to run smoothly on a computer system.

6. A(n) _____ is a collection of characters that represents a single type of data.

7. A(n) _____ is a collection of related records.

8. The method of updating that the airline industry uses for passenger reservations is called _____ processing.

Matching Questions

Match each term with the description that best fits.

a. information retrieval   d. realtime processing
b. issuance   e. control-break reporting
c. batch processing   f. sorting

_____ 1. A company prepares a reminder notice for a customer whose payment deadline has passed.

_____ 2. A company produces an employee phone book with names in alphabetical order.

_____ 3. A bank records all deposits made to customer accounts at the end of each day.

_____ 4. A report shows information on the sales of a single product, with three subtotals and a grand total.

_____ 5. A librarian keys in the title of a book on a display terminal to see whether it has been checked out.

_____   **6.**   Jane Williams withdraws $100 from her checking account, and that amount is immediately subtracted from her account balance.

Discussion Questions

1. Name some common types of computer support equipment, and state whether each is used for input, output, storage, or some combination of these functions.

2. Name some common types of secondary storage devices and the I/O media each uses.

3. Create a small file of data. Can you identify the records and fields?

4. What is the difference between applications software and systems software?

5. What is the difference between a master file and a transaction file?

6. Identify and define the types of information processing discussed in this chapter. Can you think of any other examples of information processing?

Critical Thinking Questions

1. Identify several uses for computers in a videocassette rental store.

2. The Tomorrow box on page 46 describes several applications for super smart cards, in which a keyboard, display, processor, and storage is contained on a credit-card-sized card. Can you think of any additional applications for such cards that are not covered in this box?

3. Feature 2A covers vote processing, which today largely takes place in the batch mode. Can you foresee any implementation problems as technology makes possible realtime tabulation of races in national elections?

4. Feature 2B covers smart materials, which contain tiny built-in sensors that relay data to a computer system. If such materials were embedded into highways, what types of benefits may be realized?

5. You have joined a small computer club on your campus. The club has about 20 members. At a recent meeting, you agreed to conduct a survey to find out how members feel about tours the club may make of local businesses next semester. You've designed a two-page questionnaire that consists of seven to eight questions. Answers to most of the questions will be in the form of ideas or opinions that will likely run about two or three sentences. The thought has crossed your mind that the computer might be of some help in tabulating the results of the questionnaire. Will it?

Doubling Univac's Speed!

The famous Univac of Remington Rand has widened still further its lead over other electronic business computing systems. Univac is still the *only* completely self-checked system . . . the only one which can read, write, and compute simultaneously without extra equipment. And now, the Univac II adds to these superior features the speed of a magnetic-core memory.

The Remington Rand magnetic-core mem-

ory is more than a laboratory promise. It has been in actual customer use for over a year, passing all tests with flying colors in the first commercially available electronic computer to use core storage successfully.

The *size* of the internal memory of Univac has also been doubled, giving instantaneous access to 24,000 alphabetic or numeric characters. If needed, this capacity can be further increased to 120,000 characters.

Univac's external memory—magnetic tape—now has greater capacity, too, increasing input and output to 20,000 characters per second . . . the equivalent of reading or writing every character on this page more than 1,000 times a minute.

These new Remington Rand developments can be incorporated into any existing Univac installation to double its speed of operation and to increase its economy still further.

ELECTRONIC COMPUTER DEPARTMENT **Remington Rand** ROOM 2009, 315 FOURTH AVENUE, NEW YORK 10, NEW YORK
DIVISION OF SPERRY RAND CORPORATION

Computers Past and Present

Objectives

After completing this chapter, you will be able to:

1. Describe some of the key pioneers and events that have influenced today's computers.

2. Understand how hardware and software have evolved over the past half-century.

3. Explain the differences among the first, second, third, and fourth generations of computers.

4. Appreciate how fast the "computer revolution" is progressing and speculate intelligently what might evolve during your lifetime.

5. Identify the major segments of today's computer industry.

OVERVIEW

Many people tend to dismiss the need to learn about our technological heritage. But a subject's history gives us insight into why things are the way they are today and sharpens our ability to predict future events.

Electronic computers as we know them were invented about 50 years ago. But the history of computers actually goes back much further than that. Since the beginning of civilization, merchants and government officials have used computing devices to help them with calculations and recordkeeping. The abacus, invented thousands of years ago, is an example of such a device.

In the first part of this chapter, we will discuss the early advances that gave birth to today's electronic computer, beginning with the invention of the first mechanical calculating machines in the 1600s. In the remainder of the chapter, we will cover the development of commercial computer systems from the 1950s to the present.

FROM GEARS AND LEVERS TO CIRCUITS AND TUBES

Pascal and Leibniz

Blaise Pascal, the French mathematician, is credited with inventing the first **mechanical calculating machine** around 1642. Pascal got the inspiration for his invention at age 19, after spending many hours poring over columns of figures and painstakingly adding them up. Pascal realized that this tedious chore could be done faster and more accurately with a machine. After much effort, he built a mechanical device that was powered by levers and gears. This machine was named the **pascaline** after its inventor. The pascaline could add and subtract automatically. But it never caught on. Clerks and bookkeepers, fearing for their jobs, refused to use it.

Later in the 1600s, Gottfried von Leibniz, the German philosopher and mathematician, went one step beyond Pascal and devised a machine that could multiply and divide as well as add and subtract. Like Pascal's, this device was run by levers and gears.

Jacquard's Loom

One important event in the development of the computer might seem unrelated at first glance. In the early 1800s, a weaver named Joseph Jacquard invented a loom that produced patterned cloth automatically. The remarkable thing about this loom was that it used punched cardboard cards to control the pattern in the cloth. The holes in the cards determined which rods in the loom were engaged at any given time.

Jacquard's loom introduced two concepts that proved important to the future development of the computer. The first concept was that information could be coded on *punched cards*. Punched cards, as we'll see, were to become the main input/output medium for the first "modern" computers. The second concept was that the information stored in the cards could serve as a series of instructions—in effect, a *program*—when the cards were activated.

Babbage and His Engines

One of the most noteworthy figures in the history of computers was the nineteenth-century English mathematician Charles Babbage. About 150 years ago, he designed a machine with an amazing similarity to the first modern computers.

Babbage first became interested in mechanical computing devices while studying mathematical tables. These tables contained many errors because they had been hand-set into print. Babbage realized that a machine that could automatically calculate the numbers and print the results would produce much more reliable tables.

Babbage was able to get funds from the British government to build such a machine, which he called the **difference engine.** He succeeded in building a small prototype (Figure 3-1). His attempts to build a larger version failed, however, because the technology for creating the parts he needed did not yet exist.

While working on the difference engine, Babbage conceived another, much more powerful machine, which he called the **analytical engine.** Like the difference engine, it would consist of gears and shafts run by a steam engine. It is this machine that is so similar in concept to the modern computer. It was to be a general-purpose machine, capable of many kinds of computing work. It would be directed by instructions on punched cards, contain a memory for storing instructions and the intermediate results of calculations, and automatically print results.

Babbage became obsessed with the analytical engine and devoted all of his energy and resources to creating it. But he was never able to complete a working model, and he died without knowing how his vision would shape the future.

Much of what we know about Charles Babbage's analytical engine comes not from Babbage himself but from the work of his close friend and associate Ada Augusta, Countess of Lovelace, the daughter of the poet Byron. She has been called "the first programmer" because of her work on the kinds of instructions that would have been fed into the analytical engine to make it work.

Hollerith, the Census, and Punched Cards

Another milestone on the way to the modern computer was passed during the tabulation of the 1890 U.S. census. Until 1890, census figures had been tabulated manually. The 1880 census took seven years to complete, and of-

ficials worried that if something weren't done, the results of the 1890 census would not be completed before it was time to begin the 1900 census.

The government commissioned a man named Herman Hollerith to build a machine to aid in the tabulation of the 1890 census. The machine Hollerith built (Figure 3-2) used punched cards and was powered by electricity. With its help, the results of the census were finished in three years.

Hollerith did not rest on his laurels, however. He founded the Tabulating Machine Company to develop punched-card equipment to sell to business and government. Hollerith's company merged with several others in 1911 to become the Computer-Tabulating-Recording Company. In 1924, this company changed its name to International Business Machines (IBM) Corporation.

IBM rapidly became the leader in the manufacture of punched-card equipment and had an 80 percent market share by the mid-1930s. By this time, the mechanical machines of the nineteenth century had been replaced by electromechanical devices such as the one Hollerith pioneered. Simply put, **electromechanical machines** are mechanical machines driven by electricity. But while these devices were a vast improvement over their hand-cranked ancestors, they had some serious drawbacks. For example, the moving parts were slow to align themselves, which limited their speed. Also, the repeated movement of those parts caused wear, making the machines failure prone.

FIGURE 3-2

The Hollerith census tabulator.
Trained as an engineer, Hollerith began work with the U.S. Bureau of the Census in 1879. Shortly thereafter, Hollerith later recalled, the head of the division of vital statistics remarked to him, " . . . there ought to be a machine for doing the purely mechanical work of tabulating population and similar statistics." The rest is history.

Aiken, IBM, and the Mark I

The age of electromechanical computing devices reached its zenith in the early 1940s with the work of Howard Aiken of Harvard University. Aiken had long been interested in developing ways to use these machines for scientific calculations. IBM and other manufacturers had designed machines with business users in mind, but during the late 1920s and early 1930s, many scientists began to use them for their work as well. Aiken had the important insight that the technology of these machines could be adapted to create a *general-purpose computer*—one that could be programmed to do a variety of computing tasks.

With the support of a $500,000 grant from IBM and the help of four of IBM's top engineers, Aiken started work on his machine in 1939. Its official name was the "Automatic Sequence Controlled Calculator," but it came to be called simply the **Mark I.** It was completed in 1944 and was gargantuan. It contained 500 miles of wire and 3 million electrical connections. It could do a multiplication in about 6 seconds and a division in about 12 seconds.

The ABC

While Aiken and IBM were still at work on the Mark I, others were exploring the use of a new technology in computer design—electronics—that would make the Mark I obsolete almost as soon as it was turned on. Computers with electronic components, unlike electromechanical machines, have no

FIGURE 3-3
ENIAC. Programming ENIAC often was a two-day undertaking. Each time a new program was run operators had to manually reset thousands of electrical switches and replug hundreds of cables.

moving parts. In **electronic machines,** the main elements change from one state to another depending on, for example, the presence or absence of current flowing through them. Because they have no moving parts, electronic machines are much faster and more reliable than electromechanical devices.

The first person to design and build an electronic computing machine was John Atanasoff at Iowa State University. In the late 1930s, Atanasoff needed a machine that could help his graduate students with the tedious job of solving simultaneous linear equations. None of the machines available at the time met his needs, so he began designing his own.

In early 1939, Atanasoff received a $650 grant from Iowa State University. This sum was enough to buy the part-time services of a graduate student, Clifford Berry, and some materials. Atanasoff and Berry built a machine that they called the **ABC,** for **Atanasoff-Berry Computer.** The main electronic components in the ABC were 300 vacuum tubes. The machine could solve a set of 29 simultaneous equations with 29 variables. Although small and limited in what it could do, the ABC was the first electronic digital computer.

ENIAC

World War II created a sudden demand for computing power. The U.S. Army, for example, desperately needed accurate tables that would tell gunners how to aim their weapons. These tables required vast numbers of arduous calculations. As a result, when J. Presper Eckert, an electrical engineer, and John Mauchly, a physicist, presented a proposal to the army for an electronic computer that could do these calculations in seconds, they received enthusiastic backing.

Eckert and Mauchly's computer, called **ENIAC** (Electronic Numerical Integrator and Calculator), was unveiled in 1946. It was the world's first *large-scale, general-purpose* electronic computer. As Figure 3-3 shows, the ENIAC was enormous compared with today's computers. It was 100 feet long, 10 feet high, and 3 feet deep. It contained 18,000 vacuum tubes and consumed 140 kilowatts of electricity when in operation.

Von Neumann and the Stored-Program Concept

A major problem with ENIAC was that every time its operators wanted to do a new series of computations, they had to rewire it and reset switches, a process that often took several hours. John Von Neumann, a mathematician, conceived a way around this shortcoming. He visualized a computer in which processing instructions could be fed in together with the data to be processed. Both the program and the data could be stored in the computer's memory. In such a *stored-program* computer, operators would feed in a new set of instructions when they wanted the computer to execute a new program; thus, they would not have to rewire the machine. With this stored-program concept, the idea of software was born.

The first stored-program computer, called **EDSAC** (Electronic Delay Storage Automatic Calculator), was completed in England in 1949. Von Neumann's machine, **EDVAC** (Electronic Discrete Variable Automatic Computer), was started in 1946 and completed in the United States in 1950. With these devices, the stage was set for the computer revolution and the explosive growth of the commercial computer industry.

THE COMPUTER AGE

Until the early 1950s, electronic computers were the exclusive tool of scientists, engineers, and the military. The early machines had been built in military and academic settings with massive support from the government. No electronic computer had yet served a role in commerce. With the success of machines such as ENIAC, EDSAC, and EDVAC, however, big business was ready to enter the field as both a producer and a user of computers.

The history of commercial computing often is separated into four distinct *generations*. What primarily distinguishes each generation is the main electronic logic element in use at the time. The term *logic element* refers to the principal electronic components used to facilitate the circuit functions within the computer. The four generations and their logic elements are as follows:

☐ First generation (1951–1958): vacuum tube
☐ Second generation (1959–1964): transistor
☐ Third generation (1965–1970): integrated circuit
☐ Fourth generation (1971–?): microminiaturized integrated circuit

Each new logic element led to improvements that made computers significantly faster, smaller, cheaper, more flexible, and capable of more storage than those of past generations.

FIGURE 3-4
UNIVAC I. This was the first machine used to tabulate returns in a U.S. presidential election. In 1952, it declared Dwight Eisenhower the victor over Adlai Stevenson only 45 minutes after the polls closed.

THE FIRST GENERATION (1951–1958): UNIVAC I

The **first generation** and the era of commercial computing began in earnest in June 1951, when the U.S. Bureau of the Census purchased a computer called **UNIVAC I.** This machine was the brainchild of the pioneers of ENIAC, J. Presper Eckert and John Mauchly. Having seen the great commercial potential of computers, they had formed their own company. In order to secure operating capital, they became a subsidiary of Remington-Rand (currently known as Unisys Corporation), which successfully marketed the computer under its own name.

The UNIVAC I differed from its predecessors in a very important respect: It was the first electronic computer manufactured by a business machine company specifically for business applications. Now a general-purpose machine was available for payroll processing and other routine, labor-intensive accounting work. Figure 3-4 shows an early UNIVAC I.

Attributes of the First Generation

Vacuum Tubes. The most important attribute of first-generation computers was the use of **vacuum tubes,** like those found in old radios and television sets, as the main logic element. Though tubes were a vast improvement over electromechanical parts, like those in the Mark I, they created many problems. They generated excessive heat, were large, and were prone to frequent failure. Because of the heat the tubes generated, first-generation computers

FIGURE 3-5

Punched-card processing. Punched cards were the dominant input/output medium of the first generation and were widely used as late as the 1970s. Today they are found primarily in specialized applications. Shown here is a keypunch machine, used to punch holes representing character codes onto cards.

had to be cooled by extensive air-conditioning units. And because the tubes were large, first-generation computers were colossal.

Punched-Card Orientation. The punched card (see Figure 3-5 and Feature 3A), used to process data since the 1800s, continued as the primary input/output medium for computer systems. Processing speeds for punched cards are notoriously slow compared with those for disk and tape, but the latter technologies did not mature until later generations.

Magnetic Drum Internal Memory. Many computers of the first generation used rotating magnetic drums for internal memory. Programs and data could be read from punched cards and stored on the drum, along with intermediate computations and final results. Because drums contain moving parts, they are relatively slow by today's standards.

Limited Applications. The typical commercial applications of the first generation were payroll, billing, and other accounting tasks. These applications—known as *transaction processing applications,* since they involve mainly the processing of business transactions—were very easy to "cost justify." For example, if a computer system could do the work of 20 clerks, each of whom earned $5,000 annually, a cost of $100,000 was a bargain. The system could pay back its purchase price in one year.

The Punched Card

A Closer Look at Yesterday's Premier I/O Medium

One of the earliest media used for entering data into electronic computers was the punched card. First developed by Herman Hollerith in the 1880s for use with tabulating machines, punched cards were widely employed on first-, second-, and third-generation computer systems. In the present fourth generation, they are no longer used as a major input medium, but they are still viable for certain applications, such as warranty records packed with stereos and microwaves.

Punched cards are rectangular pieces of thin cardboard. In their heyday as a major input medium for computers, they were usually cut to a standard 3¼ by 7⅜ inches and contained 80 columns and 12 rows (see figure). Today they come in a variety of sizes to suit specialized applications. Characters are represented by columns of holes punched into fixed positions on the card in varying configurations. Each character has its own unique pattern of holes. The letter *A*, for example, is represented on the standard punched card by a hole in row 12 and a hole in row 1, as shown in the figure.

When punched cards are in use, a program or a data file normally consists of a stack of cards. For instance, a program containing 39 statements usually requires 39 cards, with a single statement per card. It is also possible to continue a long statement on a second card. In most languages, program statements must start in a certain column of the card—say, column 7 if you are coding a FORTRAN program.

A variety of machines can be used to process punched cards. A *keypunch machine* (see Figure 3-5 in the chapter for an early model of a keypunch machine), for example, punches holes in the card. When enough cards are generated to form a complete computer program or data file, they are manually transported to the hopper of a *card reader,* which communicates their contents to the computer. A *verifier* enables an operator to rekey data on a card to ensure that they are correct before they are sent to the card reader. A *sorter* allows cards to be arranged in a certain order before being processed. All of these devices, however, are large, noisy, and notoriously slow compared with the computing equipment used today.

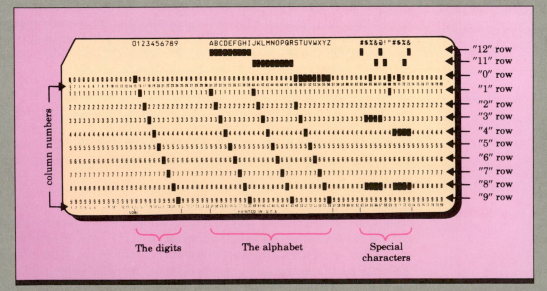

The standard punched card. Today's high-capacity diskette, which can fit in a shirt pocket, can store the equivalent of more than 17,000 punched cards.

Programming in Machine and Assembly Languages. The first programmers had to work in something called machine language. **Machine-language** instructions consist entirely of strings of 0s and 1s (called *bits*). A machine-language statement might look like this:

0 1 0 1 1 0 0 0 0 1 1 1 0 0 0 0 0 0 0 0 0 0 0 0 1 0 0 0 0 0 1 0

Since a program might consist of hundreds of lines like this one, you can see that programming in machine language was difficult and that errors were frequent.

Fortunately, other languages have since become available to spare people the awesome task of machine-language programming. Dr. Grace Hopper at the University of Pennsylvania made the first breakthrough in 1952 when she produced an assembly language. **Assembly languages** made it possible to write instructions in shorthand form. Although assembly-language programming represented a large improvement over machine-language coding, it is tedious by today's standards and is best left to programming experts.

THE SECOND GENERATION (1959–1964): THE TRANSISTOR

In **second-generation** computers, transistors replaced vacuum tubes as the main logic element. **Transistors** perform the same function as tubes, but they are faster, smaller, and more reliable. They also generate less heat and require less power than tubes.

Attributes of the Second Generation

The transistor was only one of several improvements in the second generation. Other noteworthy developments included magnetic tape and disk storage, magnetic-core internal memory, modular hardware design, high-level programming languages, and new applications for computers.

Tape and Disk Secondary Storage. Although the potential of magnetic tape as a storage medium was perceived in the first generation, it was not until the second generation that tape technology developed sufficiently to make it competitive with punched cards. Not only is magnetic tape a faster input/output medium than cards, it also packs much more data into far less space. Today tape is still going strong, whereas punched cards have virtually disappeared.

Disk storage was first introduced during the second generation, although its full potential was not realized until a generation later. The advantage of disk over tape is that it often allows faster access to data. Some commercial applications couldn't exist today in the form we've grown used to if fast disk processing weren't available. Making airline reservations, which involves millions of transactions daily, is one of them.

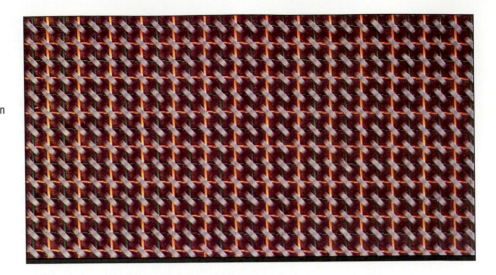

FIGURE 3-6

Magnetic-core memory. Ring-shaped cores were strung onto tiered racks inside the computer unit. Data were stored by magnetizing blocks of these cores in a certain way.

Magnetic-Core Internal Memory. Small, doughnut-shaped **magnetic cores,** which were strung on racks within a computer unit, began to replace magnetic drums as internal memory devices on many second-generation machines. Core planes (see Figure 3-6) offer much higher storage access speeds than first-generation drums. They have no moving parts, so they are not subject to the time-consuming rotation required of mechanically driven drums.

Modular Hardware Elements. A big headache with early computers was maintenance. When components failed they had to be replaced individually, which was very time consuming. Manufacturers countered this problem in the second generation by introducing modular design. In modular design, related components are grouped together onto portable boards. If a component on a board fails, the entire board is replaced. Although this may seem wasteful, modular design makes it easier to diagnose and correct malfunctions.

High-Level Programming Languages. Software and programming took an important step forward during the second generation with the emergence of **high-level programming languages.** In machine and assembly languages, the programmer must spell out every step the computer takes in an operation. Getting the computer to add two numbers, for example, might take three separate instructions. In high-level languages, a single simple statement like

$$A = B + C$$

can accomplish the same result.

Another important feature of high-level languages is their use of simple words and mathematical expressions. This characteristic makes them less intimidating and easier to learn than machine and assembly languages.

Among the first high-level languages were *FORTRAN* (FORmula TRANslator) and *COBOL* (COmmon Business-Oriented Language). FORTRAN, developed at IBM, was designed for scientific applications. COBOL, developed with government support, was designed for business use. Both these languages are still widely used today.

As high-level languages gained in popularity, users often found that programs they had written for one computer system wouldn't work on equipment made by another manufacturer. This was because manufacturers often developed radically different versions of the same language. Often, when a company changed from one kind of equipment to another, it had to completely rewrite all its programs. Consequently, the American National Standards Institute (ANSI) began to establish rules, called *standards,* to enable common approaches to the more popular languages.

New Computer Applications. Three noteworthy events that occurred during the second generation were the development of airline passenger reservation systems, the launching of Telstar, and the rise of management information systems.

The first airlines passenger reservation system, Sabre, was developed jointly in 1962 by IBM and American Airlines. Sabre, still very much in use today, was the first large-scale application of computer and communications technologies.

Telstar, launched in 1962, was the first communications satellite. Communications satellites enable data to be transmitted through the air, and today they are a critical component of communications networks used by business and government.

Management information systems (MISs) slowly evolved throughout the second generation as a by-product of the computerized transaction processing systems businesses had in place. While the role of transaction processing systems is to process the day-to-day paperwork burden, the purpose of MISs is to provide managers with information concerning critical organizational activities on a routine basis, thereby improving the quality of managerial decisions throughout the organization.

THE THIRD GENERATION (1965–1970): THE FAMILY CONCEPT AND THE INTEGRATED CIRCUIT

The **third generation** began in mid-1964, when IBM made one of the most important product announcements in the history of computers: It had designed a *family* of six upward-compatible computers, the System/360 line. A machine at the "high end" of the line, such as the 360/Model 195, would be bigger and more powerful than one at the "low end," such as the 360/Model 10. *Upward compatibility* meant that programs written for a low-end machine would work on a larger machine in the series. A company with grow-

FIGURE 3-7

The IBM System/360. The revolutionary 360 line, in which IBM risked its very existence, caused *Fortune* magazine to report: "It was roughly as though General Motors had decided to scrap its existing makes and models and offer in their place one new line of cars, covering the entire spectrum of demand, with a radically redesigned engine and exotic fuel." Interestingly, many of today's mainframes are designed much like the popular 360 line.

ing processing needs and a low-end machine could buy a larger machine in the series without having to completely rewrite its applications software. Until the advent of the System/360 line, conversion from one computer to another normally was a big headache, requiring massive amounts of reprogramming and staff retraining. Figure 3-7 shows a member of the 360 family.

The main logic element of the System/360 was a device called an **integrated circuit (IC).** The IC, which replaced the second-generation transistor, consists of thousands of small circuits etched onto a tiny silicon chip. These chips are so small that several of them can fit into a thimble.

After IBM introduced the System/360, the family concept became widespread in the computer industry. Other major manufacturers quickly followed suit with their own families of machines. With the family concept, users began to feel that they had a solution to the massive conversion problems they had encountered in the transition from the first to the second generation and later from the second to the third.

Attributes of the Third Generation

Besides the integrated circuit and family concept, several other noteworthy developments characterized the third generation. Perhaps the most important of these were the operating system, continued improvements in programming languages, the minicomputer, and word processing.

Operating Systems. An **operating system,** which Chapter 8 covers in detail, is a set of control programs that supervises the work of the computer system. Most first- and second-generation computers did not use operating systems. Programs were entered one by one and monitored individually by the computer operator. Also, automatic communication between the CPU and devices such as the printer was not yet possible; these elements had to be coordinated manually. With operating systems, however, these tasks could be performed automatically under program control.

Also, computers in the first and second generations were *serial* processors; that is, they would do all their work in a one-program-at-a-time fashion. For example, job 1 would be started and completed, then job 2 would be processed, and so forth. Many modern operating systems enable computer systems to speed up processing by working on several programs *concurrently*.

Improvements in Software. The development of new high-level programming languages flourished in the third generation. Each new language was created in response to the needs of an important market of users. *BASIC* (Beginners All-purpose Symbolic Instruction Code), for example, was developed to address the need for a programming language that was easy to learn and use. It is still one of the most popular languages for microcomputer systems.

The development of *RPG* (Report Program Generator) in the mid-1960s signaled a new trend in programming languages. With RPG, a user or programmer merely describes to the computer system *what* a report is to look like, not *how* to produce it. Once given the input/output formats and formulas for calculations, the computer system automatically generates its own computer program to produce the report. These report-generator languages have proven to be incredibly time saving, and companies use them extensively.

An additional boost to the quality of software came in 1969, when IBM—which was rapidly becoming a virtual monopoly—was forced through government pressures to "unbundle" pricing on software and hardware. Roughly speaking, this meant that organizations would be billed separately for hardware and software. Users of IBM equipment were no longer locked into acquiring their programs from IBM. Almost immediately, dozens of companies went into the business of designing better and cheaper software for IBM machines, which dominated the marketplace at that time. Many succeeded, and the software industry soon mushroomed.

The Rise of the Minicomputer. In the mid-1960s, the first successful *minicomputer* was built. The mini—a scaled-down version of larger computers of the day—was largely the brainchild of an electrical engineer named Kenneth Olsen. Olsen saw early on the need for a small, rugged, inexpensive computer, one that didn't need to be housed in a computing center and tended to by a staff of trained operators. Together with his brother and another engineer, Olsen founded Digital Equipment Corporation (DEC) in an old brick wool mill in Maynard, Massachusetts (see Figure 3-8). Their first successful mini, a refrigerator-sized computer called the PDP-8, cost about $18,000. It became widely used in both small and large companies.

Following DEC's success, other companies soon started to manufacture minis. Data General, founded by four engineers (three of whom had worked for DEC), was another early entrant into the minicomputer market. In 1969 Data General introduced its Nova minicomputer, which sold for a mere $8,000. The race for inexpensive computers was on.

FIGURE 3-8

Digital Equipment Corporation (DEC). Started in an old wool mill in Maynard, Massachusetts, DEC is one of today's leading producers of minicomputers and the world's second-largest computer company.

Word Processing. *Word processing* refers to using computer technology to assist in the typing of documents. IBM coined the term in 1964, when it first marketed the magnetic tape selectric typewriter (MT/ST). This machine enabled secretaries to store "canned" portions of documents on a tape unit connected to the typewriter and to interweave fresh text with preprepared materials. Today, of course, the tape units are gone and word processing has been enhanced by disk units, display screens, and large electronic memories.

Word processing initiated the widespread use of computers in office settings, a phenomenon that many people refer to today as *office automation (OA)*. Later, in the 1970s and 1980s, innovations such as desktop microcomputer systems, electronic mail, desktop publishing systems, facsimile (fax) machines, and intelligent copiers would further fuel the rise of OA in organizations.

THE FOURTH GENERATION (1971–?): ENTER THE MICROCOMPUTER

The earliest electronic computers reached fruition largely through the creative efforts of established scholars and the sponsorship of blue-chip corporations, prestigious academic institutions, and the federal government. In

FIGURE 3-9

The Intel 4004. On November 15, 1971, *Electronic News* carried the first advertisement for the Intel 4004. With only 2,250 transistors—which is less than 1 percent of the elements on some of today's microprocessors—the 4004 was an adequate processor for simple electronic devices such as calculators and cash registers. Only a year later Intel introduced the 8080 microprocessor, the first device capable of supporting a complete microcomputer system.

stark contrast, the beginning of the microcomputer industry—perhaps the singular most important event of the **fourth generation**—is absolutely grass roots. The history of microcomputers is a collage of interesting stories about bright teenagers, high-school dropouts, after-hours hobbyists tinkering in their garages or basements, shoestring budgets, speculative venture capital, and rags-to-riches enterprises.

The Microcomputer Revolution

A good place to begin the story of microcomputers is in 1969, when an ambitious, though now defunct, Japanese company contracted with Intel, a small California firm, to build programming logic into an ordinary calculator. The project was assigned to Marcian E. ("Ted") Hoff, whom many called an "engineer's engineer." Hoff developed a general-purpose logic chip, the Intel 4004 (see Figure 3-9), that became known as the first microprocessor, or

FIGURE 3-10

Bill Gates. The ultimate entrepreneur, Gates rode the crest of the microcomputer revolution and became a billionaire in the process.

"computer on a chip." Intel later became the world's leading producer of microprocessor chips.

Now that a computer on a chip was available, the next logical step was to develop it into a complete microcomputer system that the average person could use. One of the first noteworthy efforts in this direction came from a small group of Air Force personnel operating out of an Albuquerque garage in their off-hours. The name of their firm was Micro Instrumentation and Telemetry Systems (MITS). MITS initially made electronic calculators. In the early 1970s, when the bottom fell out of the calculator market, MITS turned its attention to making a kit computer to keep itself afloat. This machine was called the **Altair 8800,** and it became the world's first microcomputer system.

Most firsts in the history of computing were crude devices, and the 8800 was no exception. Users had to be knowledgeable enough to build it themselves from a kit. Moreover, it required users to code their own programs—in machine language, no less. MITS subsequently hired Bill Gates, a Harvard freshman, to install the BASIC programming language on the 8800. This attempt was successful, but MITS went bankrupt a few years later. Gates (see Figure 3-10) subsequently dropped out of Harvard and formed Microsoft Corporation, today one of the largest software producers in the world.

The Rise of Apple. Enter Stephen G. Wozniak, or Woz, as he was known to his friends. A talented California computer enthusiast, he had dropped out of college. Fortunately for the history of microcomputing, Woz liked to build computers.

Now enter Steven Jobs, another brilliant college dropout. Jobs saw the potential in Wozniak's work and was able to raise thousands of dollars of venture capital to support it. Thus, Apple Computer, one of the biggest success stories in modern corporate history, was born (see Figure 3-11). But Apple, which introduced its first computer in kit form in 1977, wasn't an immediate success. It needed another verse to take its place in computer history before it would see its biggest triumphs.

On the East Coast, Harvard Business School student Dan Bricklin studiously watched his accounting professor erase large chunks of blackboard every time a single number changed in an interdependent series of calculations. Astonished by the labor involved in the recalculations, Bricklin and Bob Frankston, a programming friend from MIT, went to work developing *VisiCalc* (VISIble CALCulator). Introduced in 1978, VisiCalc was the first spreadsheet package. It was easy to use and could do repetitive, accounting-type calculations in a snap.

With the availability of spreadsheets, businesspeople (who routinely prepare time-consuming budgets and profit-and-loss-statements) suddenly had a very compelling reason to buy microcomputers. The first computer manufacturer to adopt VisiCalc was Apple, which just recently had introduced its first preassembled computer, the Apple II. Apple II computers started selling wildly. Meanwhile, back in Armonk, New York, IBM, the behemoth of computing corporations, was taking careful note of all these grass-roots happenings.

FIGURE 3-11

Steve Wozniak and Steve Jobs.
These two jeans-clad founders of Apple Computer, the largest company evolving from the microcomputer revolution, are shown here holding a board from the Apple I.

Enter IBM. In 1981, IBM entered the microcomputing market with the IBM Personal Computer (IBM PC). This highly successful product immediately cut into sales of the Apple II as well as those of the other two premier microcomputer systems of the day—the Tandy/Radio Shack TRS-80 Model I and the Commodore Pet. Although the IBM PC was a widely hailed product and was more powerful than its competitors, many people attribute the PC's success largely to the fact that many businesspeople suddenly took microcomputers seriously when IBM, one of the world's largest corporations, became a player. Meanwhile, another new firm, Lotus Development Corporation, which today is one of the world's biggest software producers, created a spreadsheet product, 1-2-3, which became widely used on the IBM PC. Just as VisiCalc had helped sales of the Apple II, 1-2-3 helped sell the IBM PC.

During the early 1980s, a spate of firms entered the burgeoning microcomputer marketplace. So-called *clone manufacturers* came along to nip at the heels of IBM and Lotus, offering nearly identical products at bargain-basement prices. *Aftermarket vendors* sprouted up like weeds, offering add-in or add-on products that would enhance existing major products with new features. *Niche vendors* also entered the picture, providing specialized products targeted to narrow ranges of needs. The grass-roots era had suddenly vanished, and an age of aggressive competition and marketing suddenly loomed on the horizon. Today microcomputers compose the major market segment in the computer industry, outpacing all other types of computers.

Attributes of the Fourth Generation

Many other developments characterize the fourth generation, which is still very much in progress. These include microminiaturization, semiconductor

FIGURE 3-12

Microminiaturization. An IBM 3090 VSLI memory chip, capable of holding over 1 million characters of data.

internal memory, further improvements in software, decision support systems, and information resource management (IRM).

Microminiaturization. The technological hallmark of the fourth generation is **microminiaturization** (see Figure 3-12). Over the years, more and more circuits have been packed into less and less space, and integrated circuits have become increasingly smaller, faster, and cheaper. The terms *large-scale integration (LSI)* and later *very-large-scale integration (VLSI)* have been coined to describe this process. Now a single silicon chip smaller than the size of a fingernail can contain over a million circuit elements. Future systems, experts predict, will contain billions of circuits in the same space, perhaps leading to "ultra-large-scale integration (ULSI)." The end result has been computer systems that are both smaller and more powerful than their predecessors.

Semiconductor Internal Memory. Over the course of the third generation, core memory slowly gave way to MOS (metal oxide semiconductor) memory. By the fourth generation, MOS memory, which is faster, smaller, and cheaper than core planes, had become a common fixture. **Semiconductor memories,** as MOS devices are usually called, are similar to microprocessors in that the memory is etched onto a small silicon chip. Also like microprocessors, these chips are commonly mounted onto metal carriers, which plug into boards that reside in the computer's system unit.

Further Improvements in Software. Many people are intimidated by computers and especially by programming languages. Yet computer technology is a powerful tool in the hands of the right users, and many people would be more productive in their jobs if the right computer tools were available. In response to such demands, a number of software vendors have developed over the last several years *fourth-generation-language (4GL)* software products that are specifically targeted to the on-the-job needs of people in virtually every field. These products, which include database retrieval languages, report generation languages, spreadsheets, modeling packages, application generators, and the like, are much easier to work with than BASIC, FORTRAN, COBOL, RPG, and other third-generation languages.

Decision Support Systems. The 1970s and 1980s gave rise to a new type of information system—the *decision support system (DSS)*. While the MISs of the 1960s provided managers with information in the form of preplanned, hard-copy reports, the DSSs that later evolved offered managers a set of hardware and software tools. These tools gave managers the power to interact directly and easily with the computer, and to satisfy their own information needs in the manner they desired.

Information Resources Management (IRM). The importance of computers and other information-related technologies has skyrocketed in many organizations. Rather than seeing computers as merely a means of mechanically processing transactions, such organizations perceive information technology as a *strategic force* that will largely determine their survival in the 1990s. For instance, firms such as banks, brokerage firms, and insurance companies sell products and services that depend critically on how information is collected, packaged, and disseminated. Today even the major airlines make more money from their computerized reservations systems than they do from selling seats on their own planes. The growing philosophy that information is a critical asset that must be properly planned for and managed rather than just a necessary cost to be controlled is known as *information resources management (IRM)*.

THE COMPUTER INDUSTRY TODAY

During the first generation, the computer industry consisted of a handful of vendors. Each company produced its own line of hardware and software and provided services to its clientele. Multiply the number of computer product vendors that existed 30 years ago by several thousand, and you have an idea of how large the computer industry is today.

The computer industry is commonly broken down into three distinct segments: hardware, software, and services. Some firms within the industry specialize in only a single segment; others compete in two or three.

Figure 3-13 lists the top 25 firms in the worldwide computer market, along with a number of other interesting statistics.

FIGURE 3-13

The top 25 worldwide firms in the information processing industry. Also shown in the figure is the country in which each firm is headquartered and the revenues deriving from information technology products.

1987 Rank	Company	Country	1987 Revenue*
1	IBM	United States	$50,485.7
2	Digital Equipment Corp.	United States	10,391.3
3	Unisys Corp.	United States	8,742.0
4	Fujitsu Ltd.	Japan	8,740.0
5	NEC Corp.	Japan	8,230.5
6	Hitachi Ltd.	Japan	6,273.7
7	Siemens AG	West Germany	5,703.0
8	NCR Corp.	United States	5,075.7
9	Hewlett-Packard Co.	United States	5,000.0
10	Ing. C. Olivetti & Co. SpA	Italy	4,637.2
11	Toshiba Corp.	Japan	3,441.3
12	Wang Laboratories Inc.	United States	3,045.7
13	Apple Computer Inc.	United States	3,041.2
14	Groupe Bull	France	3,007.5
15	Control Data Corp.	United States	3,000.9
16	Nixdorf Computer AG	West Germany	2,821.5
17	Matsushita Electric Indust. Co.	Japan	2,628.5
18	NV Philips Gloeilampenfabrieken	Netherlands	2,601.6
19	Xerox Corp.	United States	2,415.0
20	STC plc	England	2,123.9
21	Honeywell Bull Inc.	United States	2,059.0
22	Alcatel NV	Belgium	2,052.1
23	AT&T Corp.	United States	2,000.0
24	TRW Inc.	United States	1,960.0
25	Tandy Corp.	United States	1,692.4

Source: Adapted from *Datamation,* June 15, 1988, p. 29.
*Revenue figures, which are in millions of dollars, represent funds deriving from information technology products only.

Hardware. Today well over 100 firms manufacture computer system units. Some are particularly strong in mainframes, others in minis, and still others in microcomputers. Only a few large firms offer products in more than one of these areas. Many companies that produce their own system units also make supporting hardware. However, not all firms that make peripheral devices also make system units.

Because the computer market is so big, virtually every company specializes in certain areas. For example, Apple and Compaq concentrate on microcomputing products. Digital Equipment Corporation (DEC) and Data General are prominent vendors of minicomputer products. Qume is a major manufacturer of printers and display devices. Other companies specialize in certain industries. For instance, Diebold concentrates on technology products for banking, and Quotron specializes in products that relate to providing stock market quotations. IBM is in a class by itself as a major force in mainframes, small-business systems, microcomputers, peripheral equipment, and software. The Japanese firms, on the other hand, have become especially formidable players in the peripheral hardware markets (see related Tomorrow box).

With so many products made by companies other than the ones that sell them today, it's sometimes hard to tell who does what. In fact, some products bear the logo of one company even though they are manufactured by another. Companies that buy equipment made by other firms and "manufacture" their own systems out of it (or merely affix their logos) are sometimes referred to as *original-equipment manufacturers (OEMs), turnkey vendors,* or *value-added resellers (VARs).*

Software. In recent years, there has been a virtual stampede into the software business. Entrepreneurs have been attracted to the field because the amount of capital required for starting a software firm is relatively low. All one really needs is time, access to a computer system, and some good ideas.

Most software is produced by independent software firms rather than by companies that also produce hardware. Among the most prominent software-only firms (most of which derive their major revenues from microcomputer software) are Microsoft Corporation, Lotus Development Corporation, Computer Associates International, and Borland International. Naturally, there are few hard-and-fast rules in the software industry; companies often expand into new areas based on the talent they have available and the opportunities that lie ahead. Like firms in the hardware sector of the computer industry, software firms usually specialize in a particular "niche" area, such as database systems, word processing packages, or accounting packages.

In addition to applications software, organizations must buy systems software. In the case of larger computers, such software traditionally has been produced by the computer manufacturers. But after IBM unbundled its hardware and software pricing in the late 1960s and computer usage burgeoned, independent software houses popped up to satisfy unmet needs. In the case of microcomputers, virtually all systems software is produced by independent software firms.

Services. Although advances in microcircuitry have made it easier than ever for a firm to buy its own computer, this is not always the best course of action. In some cases, it's still better to do work manually, "share time" on someone else's computer system, or even use outside expertise. A small company may have no equipment or computer knowledge on hand, or a large company may run out of capacity on its own computer system and need to use a piece of someone else's system temporarily. Firms that are in business to sell expertise or computer-related services are called *computer services companies.*

T   O   M   O   R   R   O   W

Waiting for the Fifth Generation

Will It Be Here in the 1990s?

It won't be accompanied by a preplanned, timed announcement claiming "We have just now entered the fifth generation." Nor will it happen on a certain predetermined date. The long-awaited arrival of the fifth generation of computing will be very subtle. In fact, when it comes, some will argue that we are still in the fourth generation and others will say that we've been in the fifth generation for years.

At least most people agree, however, on what the fifth generation of computing will look like. Back in October 1981, Japan first announced to the world its plans for the fifth generation: to develop so-called "intelligent" computers for the 1990s and beyond—computers that could understand human speech, carry on a conversation with a human using the latter's natural language, decipher picture information it received as input, move about similarly to humans, and make inferences and decisions with humanlike skill. What the Japanese were saying, in essence, was that they expected to produce computers that possessed *artificial intelligence*—the ability to perform tasks once considered the exclusive domain of humans.

One can only be awed by what Japan, a tiny island in the Pacific, has done within the last half-century. In the mid-1940s, the Japanese were in the throes of devastation. They had just lost a war, and two of their major cities were in ruins. Moreover, they faced an acute shortage of land, a population density close to 40 times that of the United

> The goal is to make the interface between computers and humans as seamless as possible.

States, and severely depleted energy and oil resources. But they had one ace to play: human resources. Then, as now, the Japanese population was well educated, hard working, and diligent.

Within a few decades after the war, Japan became the world's leading producer of automobiles and consumer electronics products. Executives from around the globe started visiting the Japanese to find out what "made them tick." So when the Japanese made known their ambitious computing goals, everyone else, as in the E. F. Hutton commercials, listened. Although many people in other parts of the world had been planning the same types of projects, and critics were citing Japan's track record in refining rather than inventing products, it still appeared that a superstar on a blistering roll had just stepped up to the plate and pointed prophetically over the center-field fence.

As you will see in this book, a lot of things are now possible with computers that hint that we are well on our way to a fifth generation. In the Tomorrow box in Chapter 1, you read about smart cars—cars equipped with vision sensors that can detect approaching danger. In Chapter 16, you will read about expert systems—computer systems that can beat skilled masters in chess and assist doctors with patient diagnosis. In time, these systems will be helping executives run major corporations. Also, speech recognition systems have come into use, and many say that by the turn of the century people will be using their voices rather than keyboards to enter documents into computers. In these fifth-generation computer systems, the goal is to make the interface between computers and humans as seamless as possible. Instead of people awkwardly trying to fit into the computer's environment, computers will have to fit into the human environment.

These companies work in a variety of ways. For instance, a computer services company might provide printing and graphics services to other firms. Such a company might be able to create high-quality brochures and slides for firms that can't afford to produce such outputs in-house. Other computer services companies sell only educational services, such as training a firm's accounting staff in the use of auditing software or its programmers in the use of a new programming language. Still others may offer an online service, such as providing information over the phone lines about securities prices, news items, and so forth. The variations are almost endless.

SUMMARY AND KEY TERMS

The world's oldest computing device, the abacus, dates back thousands of years. The first **mechanical calculating machine,** the **pascaline,** was developed by Blaise Pascal in the early 1600s. This device could only add and subtract. Later in the 1600s, Gottfried von Leibniz devised a calculator that could also multiply and divide.

In the early 1800s, weaver Joseph Jacquard invented an automated loom that introduced two concepts important to the development of the computer: *Data* could be recorded on punched cards, and a sequence of cards could act as a *program.*

The first computing device bearing a resemblance to today's computers was proposed by Charles Babbage in the 1800s. He initially conceived a machine called the **difference engine,** which would both compute and print results. Later he developed a more ambitious machine called the **analytical engine,** which embodied the principles of input, processing, output, and storage found in today's modern computers. Unfortunately, Babbage died without seeing either machine completed.

The first **electromechanical machine** to perform computing was built by Herman Hollerith to aid in tabulating the 1890 census. Hollerith went on to become a pioneer in the development of business-oriented electromechanical tabulating machines.

Howard Aiken, with the help of IBM, designed and built the first large-scale, general-purpose electromechanical computer. It was completed in 1944 and called the **Mark I.**

While Aiken was constructing his machine, John Atanasoff was at work in the Midwest with a technology that would make the Mark I obsolete almost as soon as it was completed. With the assistance of Clifford Berry, Atanasoff created the **ABC (Atanasoff-Berry Computer),** the first **electronic machine** to do computing. In 1946, J. Presper Eckert and John Mauchly created the world's first large-scale, general-purpose electronic computer, the **EN-IAC.** Later in the 1940s, mathematician John Von Neumann developed the concept of *stored programs.* This concept was originally implemented on two computers, the **EDSAC** and **EDVAC.**

The era of commercial computing, which began when the **UNIVAC I** computer was completed and delivered to the U.S. Bureau of the Census in 1951, is commonly divided into four distinct generations.

First-generation (1951–1958) computers used **vacuum tubes** as the main logic element. They also relied heavily on the use of punched cards and magnetic-drum internal memory. Programs were written in either **machine language** or, later, **assembly language.** Most first-generation commercial computers were limited to transaction processing applications, because these were relatively easy to justify in terms of labor savings.

In **second-generation** (1959–1964) computers, **transistors** replaced vacuum tubes as the main logic element. Other noteworthy developments included the rise of magnetic tapes and disks for secondary storage, **magnetic-core** internal memory, modular hardware design, **high-level programming languages** (such as FORTRAN and COBOL), airline passenger reservations systems, communications satellites, and management information systems.

In **third-generation** (1965–1970) computers, **integrated circuits (ICs)** replaced transistors as the main logic element. Other major developments were the family concept of computers, **operating systems,** improvements in language software (such as BASIC and RPG), minicomputers, and word processing.

Three terms sum up the **fourth generation** (1971–?): "small," "smaller," and "even smaller." This generation has been a period of **microminiaturization,** perhaps the singular most important event being the development and acceptance of microcomputer systems. From such crude devices as the **Altair 8800,** circa 1970, the microcomputer industry has boldly surged forward to become the major market segment of the entire computer industry. Other major developments through which people will remember the fourth generation are tiny but powerful microprocessors and **semiconductor memories,** fourth-generation languages, decision support systems (DSSs), and information resources management (IRM).

The computer industry consists of firms that sell hardware, software, and services. Most firms in the industry specialize in specific product areas.

REVIEW EXERCISES

Fill-in Questions

1. The world's first large-scale, general-purpose electronic computer was called the _____ .

2. The device Pascal developed in the 1600s that could add and subtract was called the _____ .

3. The first calculating machine to be developed by Charles Babbage was called the _____ .

4. The electromechanical computer that was developed jointly in the 1940s by Harvard and IBM was called the _____ .

5. The first electronic computer was called by the initials _____ .

6. The name of the first electronic computer to be widely used in business was the _____ I.

7. The name of the company that produced the first minicomputer was (is) _____ Corporation.

8. The first widely used microcomputer system, developed in an Albuquerque garage, was called the _____ .

Matching Questions

Match each term with the description that best fits.

a. Herman Hollerith   e. Blaise Pascal
b. Steven Jobs   f. Charles Babbage
c. John Atanasoff   g. Ted Hoff
d. John Von Neumann   h. Grace Hopper

_____ 1. A pioneer in the development of assembly language.

_____ 2. Invented the first device that could automatically add numbers.

_____ 3. Nineteenth-century British mathematician who anticipated many of the principles of modern computers.

_____ 4. Developed the first microprocessor.

_____ 5. Used punched cards to record census data.

_____ 6. Starting with $650, developed an electronic computer with 300 vacuum tubes in 1939.

_____ 7. The mathematician who pioneered the stored-program concept.

_____ 8. A cofounder of Apple Computer.

Discussion Questions

1. Identify the major technological development associated with each of the four generations of commercial computing.

2. Every important technological development in computers has occurred in response to some critical problem. Identify the problem each of the following developments attempted to solve: assembly languages, operating systems, high-level programming languages, tape and disk secondary storage, management information systems, and fourth-generation languages.

3. What was the significance of the "family concept" of computers?

4. Why did minicomputers become so popular in the early 1970s? Why are microcomputers becoming so popular today?

5. Name three major trends that have existed throughout the evolution of computers.

6. What development in the history of personal computers was instrumental in getting businesspeople to see personal computers as valuable in their jobs?

Critical Thinking Questions

1. Many observers have pointed out that the availability of microcomputer systems since the early 1980s has led to a proliferation of high-quality software products. They claim that in just the decade that microcomputers have been available, progress in software that has made end users more productive has far exceeded the progress that took place from 1950 through 1980, when virtually the only computers around were mainframes, minicomputers, and supercomputers. Do you think this is true? Why or why not?

2. The earliest users of computers were from government and academia. Why, do you think, did it take so long for the business sector of the economy to become involved?

3. The Japanese have fared well in the worldwide hardware market but have made very little impact in software. Why do you think this is so?

B

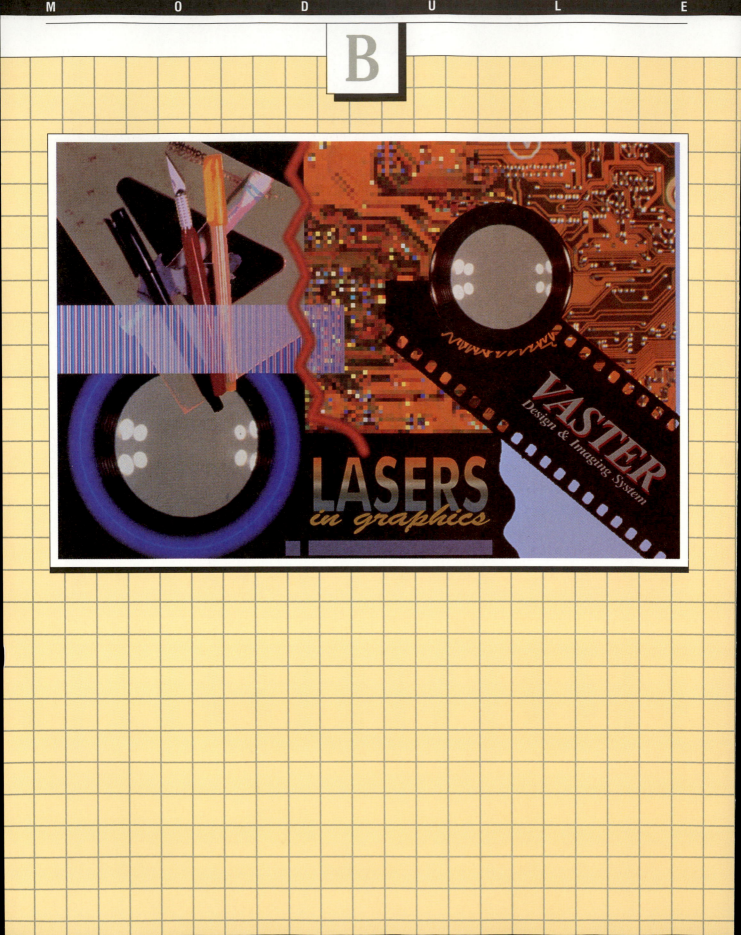

Hardware

When most people think of computers or computer systems today, hardware most readily comes to mind. Hardware is the exciting pieces of equipment delivered in crates or boxes when you buy a computer system. As you'll learn in this module, a rich variety of computer hardware is available in today's marketplace. But as you'll see later in this book, hardware needs a guiding force—namely software—to be of any use. Hardware without software is like a human without the ability to reason and manipulate thoughts.

The hardware discussed in this module is divided into four areas. Chapter 4 describes the role of the CPU—the computer itself. Chapter 5 discusses the class of hardware that provides an indispensable library of resources for the CPU—secondary storage devices. Chapter 6 delves into input and output equipment. Module B closes, in Chapter 7, with a discussion of the various types of telecommunications hardware that make it possible to transmit data and programs between the types of hardware devices covered in Chapters 4 through 6.

The Central Processing Unit and Primary Memory

Objectives

After completing this chapter, you will be able to:

1. Describe the differences among computers.

2. Describe how the CPU and its primary memory process instructions and data.

3. Identify several binary-based codes used in a computing environment.

4. Explain the function of the various pieces of hardware commonly found under the cover of the system unit.

OVERVIEW

So far we've considered the system unit, which houses the CPU and its primary memory, as a mysterious "black box." In this chapter, we'll demystify that notion by flipping the lid off the box and closely examining the functions of the parts inside. In doing so, we'll try to get a feel for how the CPU, primary memory, and other devices commonly found in the system unit work together.

To start, we'll consider the types of computers available today and the features that differentiate general-purpose CPUs from other computing devices. Then we'll examine how a CPU is organized and how it interacts with primary memory to carry out processing tasks. Next, we'll discuss how data and programs must be represented in the computer system. Here we'll talk about the codes developed for translating back and forth from symbols the CPU can understand to symbols people find meaningful. These topics will finally lead us into a discussion of how the CPU and its primary memory are packaged with other computing and memory devices inside the system unit.

Window 2, at the end of the chapter, visually tells the interesting story of how today's silicon-backed computer chips are currently produced. The Tomorrow box in the chapter addresses the search for materials that will enable ever faster processors.

TYPES OF COMPUTERS

There are many ways to classify computers. In Chapter 3, we touched on one such classification—electronic versus nonelectronic computers. Virtually all "modern" computers are electronic. Three other ways to classify computers are according to whether they are digital or analog, central or specialized processors, or full-instruction-set or reduced-instruction-set processors.

Digital versus Analog. A **digital computer** is one that *counts;* an **analog computer** is one that *measures.* Counting and measuring, which are the most basic types of computation, were with us long before computers existed. When we observe that there are 15 people in a room, for example, we are counting. Entities such as people, books, and dollars are capable of being counted. When we estimate that there are 10 gallons of fuel in a gas tank, on the other hand, we are measuring; there may actually be 10.0001, 9.872, or some other quantity of fuel. Entities such as speed, height, and length can only be measured, because they don't exist naturally as indivisible units.

When most of us discuss computers today, we are referring to digital computers. Digital computers are the ones that help run businesses, manage family budgets, and perform most of the tasks we generally think of as "computer work." In fact, digital computers are really what this chapter, and indeed this book, is about. As you'll see later, digital computers convert all programs and their data to strings of 0s and 1s that can be manipulated at electronically fast speeds.

Nonetheless, you'll probably encounter several analog computers, devices that measure physical phenomena and convert them to numbers, in your lifetime. For example, a gasoline pump contains an analog computer that measures the amount of gas pumped and converts it into gallon and price amounts that appear on the pump's register. A car has an analog computer that measures drive shaft rotation and converts it into a speedometer reading. A thermometer is an analog computer that measures temperature and converts it into degrees.

Central versus Specialized Processors. Another way to classify computers is according to whether they are the *central* processors (that is, the CPUs) of their computer systems or *specialized* processors relegated to dedicated tasks. Since the circuitry for today's computers can fit on a tiny silicon chip that costs only a few dollars, all sorts of specialized computers are now liberally embedded into peripheral devices such as keyboards and printers. In fact, you'll likely find several specialized computers under the cover of your computer's system unit. Thus, many computer systems today consist of a hierarchy of processors, with a CPU at the top followed by a set of "slave" chips that perform such chores as helping with keyboard communications or speedily crunching out arithmetic computations. This chapter focuses primarily on the CPU.

Full versus Reduced Instruction Set Processors. Computers must be equipped with a variety of instructions in order to process data effectively. These instructions are called the computer's *instruction set*. Studies have shown that many computers can be given only a limited number of instructions—a fraction of those traditionally provided—and still be able to process data more efficiently. The remainder of the instructions, while useful, create a certain degree of "overhead" and often only get in the way.

In the mid-1980s, CPUs with limited instruction sets became available. These machines have been aptly named **reduced instruction set computers (RISC).** Their advocates claim that RISC machines are much faster than their conventional counterparts. Motorola's 88000 family of RISC chips, for instance, can process instructions 10 times faster than the 68020 microprocessor, the chip used to power the Macintosh II. Many traditionalists feel, on the other hand, that machines based on RISC technology have a long way to go to prove themselves in the "real" world of business computing.

HOW THE CPU WORKS

Every CPU is basically a collection of electronic circuits. Electronic impulses enter the CPU from an input device. Within the CPU, these impulses are sent under program control through circuits to create a series of new impulses.

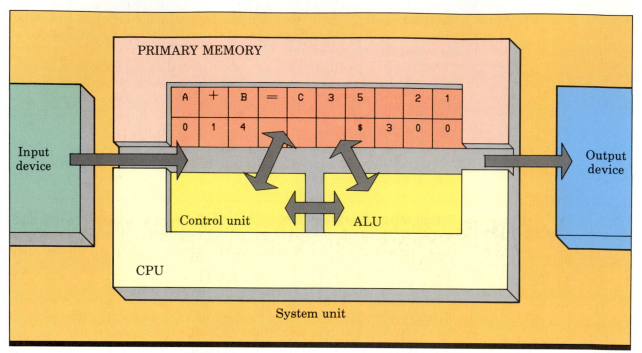

FIGURE 4-1

The CPU and its primary memory. Primary memory temporarily stores a program on which the computer is currently working, as well as its input data, intermediate computations, and output. Each location in the memory has an address, and often a single address can store a single character. Although only 20 locations are shown, primary memories typically contain from a few thousand addresses to several billion. All "figuring" done by the computer is accomplished in the arithmetic/logic unit (ALU). Data are transferred between primary memory and the ALU under supervision of the control unit.

Eventually a set of impulses leaves the CPU, headed for an output device. What happens in those circuits? To begin to understand this process, we need to know first how the CPU is organized—what its parts are—and then how electronic impulses move from one part to another to process data.

The CPU and Its Primary Memory

The CPU works closely with its primary memory to carry out processing inside the system unit. This relationship is described below and illustrated in Figure 4-1.

The CPU. The CPU has two principal sections: an arithmetic/logic unit and a control unit.

The **arithmetic/logic unit (ALU)** is the section of the CPU that performs arithmetic and logical operations on data. In other words, it is the part of the computer that does the computing. *Arithmetic* operations include tasks such as addition, subtraction, multiplication, and division. *Logical* operations involve comparing two items of data to determine whether they are equal and, if not, which is larger. As we'll see, all data coming into the CPU, including nonnumeric data such as letters of the alphabet, are coded in digital (numeric) form. As a result, the ALU can perform logical operations on letters and words as well as on numbers.

The basic arithmetic and logical operations just described are the only ones the computer can perform. That might not seem very impressive. But when combined in various ways at great speeds, these operations enable the computer to perform immensely complex tasks.

The **control unit** is the section of the CPU that directs the flow of electronic traffic between primary memory and the ALU and between the CPU and input and output devices. In other words, it is the mechanism that coordinates or manages the computer's operation.

Primary Memory. **Primary memory**—also called **main memory** or **internal memory**—holds

☐ The programs and data that have been passed to the computer for processing

☐ Intermediate processing results

☐ Output that is ready to be transmitted to secondary storage or to an output device

Once programs, data, intermediate results, and output are stored in primary memory, the CPU must be able to find them again. Thus, each location in primary memory has an *address*. In many computer systems, a single address will store a single character of data.

The size of primary memory varies among computer systems. The smallest computers can accommodate a memory of only a few thousand characters and the largest a few billion. Whenever an item of data, an instruction, or the result of a calculation is stored in memory, it is assigned an address so that the CPU can locate it again when it is needed.

Primary memory is relatively expensive and limited in size. For this reason, it is used only temporarily. Once the computer has finished processing one program and set of data, another program and data set are written over them in the storage space they occupy. Thus, the contents of each storage location are constantly changing. The address of each location, however, never changes. This process can be compared with what happens to the mailboxes in a post office: The number on each box remains the same, but the contents change as patrons remove their mail and new mail arrives.

Registers

To enhance the computer's performance, the control unit and ALU contain special storage locations that act as high-speed staging areas. These areas are called **registers.** Since registers are actually a part of the CPU, their contents can be handled much more rapidly than can those of primary memory. Program instructions and data are normally loaded (that is, staged) into the registers from primary memory just before processing. These devices play a crucial role in making computer speeds extremely fast.

There are several types of registers, including the following:

□ *Instruction register and address register* Before each instruction in a program is processed, the control unit breaks it into two parts. The part that indicates what the ALU is to do next (for example, add, multiply, compare) is placed in the **instruction register.** The part that gives the address of the data to be used in the operation is placed in the **address register.**

□ *Storage register* The **storage register** temporarily stores data that have been retrieved from primary memory prior to processing.

□ *Accumulator* The **accumulator** temporarily stores the results of ongoing arithmetic and logic operations.

The instruction and address registers are often located in the control unit, while the storage register and accumulator are frequently found in the ALU.

Machine Cycles

Now that we've described the CPU, primary memory, and registers, let's see how these elements work together to process an instruction. The processing of a single instruction is called a **machine cycle.** We touched on machine language instructions in Chapter 3 and will discuss them further in this chapter.

A machine cycle has two parts: an *instruction* cycle (I-cycle) and an *execution* cycle (E-cycle). During the **I-cycle,** the control unit fetches a program instruction from primary memory and prepares for subsequent processing. During the **E-cycle,** the data are located and the instruction is executed. Let's see how this works in a little more detail, using a simple addition as an example.

I-cycle

1. The control unit fetches from primary memory the next instruction to be executed.
2. The control unit decodes the instruction.
3. The control unit puts the part of the instruction that shows what to do into the instruction register.
4. The control unit puts the part of the instruction that shows where the associated data are located into the address register.

E-cycle

5. Using the information in the address register, the control unit retrieves data from primary memory and places them into the storage register.
6. Using the information in the instruction register, the control unit commands the ALU to perform the required operation.
7. The ALU performs the specified operation, adding together the values found in the storage register and in the accumulator.
8. The result of the operation is placed back into the accumulator, destroying the value that was there previously.

FIGURE 4-2

The machine cycle. Each statement that you code in languages such as BASIC or Pascal actually requires several machine instructions, or cycles.

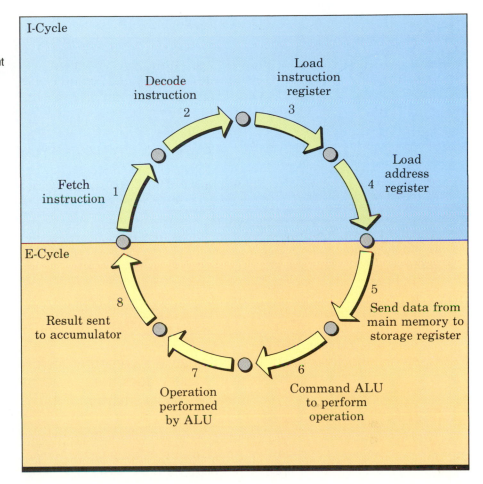

Figure 4-2 depicts how the machine cycle works.

All this may seem like an extremely tedious process, especially when a computer must go through thousands, millions, or even billions of machine cycles to process a single program fully. But computers are *very* fast. In the slowest of them, cycle times are measured in **milliseconds** (thousandths of a second). In others, they are measured in **microseconds** (millionths of a second). In the fastest computers, they are measured in **nanoseconds** (billionths of a second) or in **picoseconds** (trillionths of a second). Feature 4A describes how speeds are measured on specific sizes of computers.

BINARY-BASED DATA AND PROGRAM REPRESENTATION

The electronic components of digital computer systems work in two states. For example, a circuit is either open or closed; a magnetic spot is either present or absent; and so on. This two-state, or **binary,** nature of electron-

Hertz, Mips, and Flops

Three Common Measures of Processor Speed

Hertz, mips, and *flops* are information-age terms used to represent computer speeds. Hertz is used to represent microcomputer speeds, mips to describe mainframe and minicomputer speeds, and flops to measure supercomputer speeds.

One hertz equals one cycle per second. Microcomputers work with internal "clocks" (no relation to clocks that keep the time of day). During one tick (cycle) of these clocks, a single piece of a machine-language instruction is processed. The portion of an instruction that is operated on during a clock cycle is called a *microinstruction,* or *microcode.* Because microcomputers can process microinstructions very quickly, most microcomputers are rated in megahertz (MHz)—millions of cycles per second. The clock speeds of many microcomputer systems today are in the 16–20 MHz range. New computer chips such as the Intel 80486 and Motorola 68040 are making possible clock speeds of 50 MHz and higher.

Mips—millions of (machine-language) instructions per second—are the most common benchmark for rating the speeds of mainframes and minicomputers. Many DEC VAX minicomputers run at speeds of between 1 and 12 mips, while most IBM 3090 mainframes run in the range of 30 to 60 mips.

Just because a computer works faster does not mean it works smarter.

Flops—floating-point instructions per second—are the most common gauge of supercomputer speeds. Today's largest supercomputers are measured in megaflops or gigaflops—millions or billions of operations per second, respectively. The Honeywell-NEC SX2-100 is rated at about 330 megaflops; the larger, more expensive Cray-2, in contrast, is rated at nearly 2 gigaflops. Future supercomputers will be able to execute trillions of operations per second—that is, in the teraflops range—which is equivalent to the power of 10 million of today's microcomputers.

While measures such as hertz, mips, and flops have been used for years to impress would-be buyers of computer systems, critics have pointed out that such measures can be misleading. For instance, reduced instruction set computer (RISC) chips have enabled systems possessing such an architecture to take much better advantage of instruction sets. Thus, for certain types of applications, an 8-MHz RISC processor may be able to run circles around a conventional processor that runs at 16 MHz. Also, some operating systems on larger computers consume an inordinate number of mips, making fewer mips available for applications programs.

The moral to this story? Just because a computer works faster does not mean it works smarter and will get a job done more quickly. While computer speeds can be impressive, they can also be somewhat misleading in figuring out how effectively a particular application can be performed.

FIGURE 4-3

The binary nature of electronics.
Circuits are either open or closed, a current runs one way or the opposite way, a charge is either present or absent, and so forth. Whatever, the two possible states of an electronic component are referred to as *bits* and represented by computer systems as 0s and 1s.

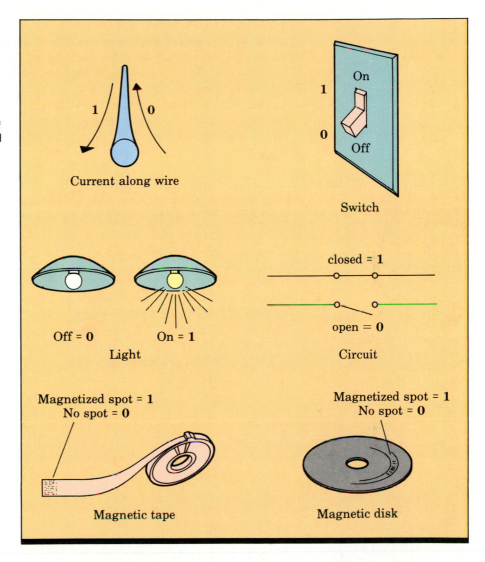

ics is illustrated in Figure 4-3. It is convenient to think of these binary states as the *0-state* and the *1-state.* Computer people refer to such zeros and ones as **bits,** which is a contraction of the words *BInary digiTS.* Being primarily electronic, computers do all their processing and communicating by representing programs and data in bit form. Binary, then, is the computer's "native tongue."

People, of course, don't talk binary. You're not likely to go up to a friend and say,

$$1 1 0 0 1 0 0 0 1 1 0 0 1 0 0 1$$

which in one binary-based coding system translates as "HI." People communicate with one another in *natural languages,* such as English, Chinese, and Spanish. In our part of the world, we speak English. Also, we write with a 26-character alphabet, and we use a number system with 10 rather than just 2 digits. Computers, however, understand only 0 and 1. So in order for us to interact with a computer, our messages to it must be translated into binary form and its messages to us must be translated from binary into a natural language.

The programming languages most people use to interact with computer systems consist of a wide variety of natural-language symbols. When we type a message such as

```
RUN FA-287
```

at a keyboard, the computer system must translate all the natural-language symbols in the message into 0s and 1s. After processing is finished, the computer system must translate the 0s and 1s it has used to represent the program's results into natural language. This conversion process is illustrated in Figure 4-4.

Computer systems use a variety of binary-based codes to represent programs and data. For example, when data and programs are being sent to or from the CPU (steps 2 and 4 in Figure 4-4), a fixed-length, binary-based code such as EBCDIC or ASCII is often used to represent each character transmitted. We will cover these two codes shortly.

Once data and programs are inside the CPU (step 3 of Figure 4-4), other types of binary-based codes typically handle them. For example, when a program is about to be executed, it is represented by a binary code known as *machine language*. Data, on the other hand, may be represented by several different binary-based codes when being manipulated by the computer. One such code, which everyone learning how computers store numbers should know, is *true binary representation*. This code, as well as some fundamentals of number systems, is covered in Appendix A.

EBCDIC and ASCII

As mentioned earlier, when data or programs are being sent between the computer and its support equipment, a *fixed-length* binary-based code is commonly used. With a fixed-length code, the transmitting machines can easily tell where one character ends and another begins. Such codes can be used to represent digits, alphabet characters, and other symbols.

Among the most popular of these fixed-length codes are **EBCDIC** (Extended Binary-Coded Decimal Interchange Code) and **ASCII** (American Standard Code for Information Interchange). IBM developed EBCDIC, and this code is used heavily on IBM mainframes. ASCII, jointly developed by the American National Standards Institute and a number of non-IBM computer vendors, is used on many other CPUs. Virtually all microcomputers, including those manufactured by IBM, use ASCII.

Both EBCDIC and ASCII represent each printable character as a unique combination of a fixed number of bits (see Figure 4-5). EBCDIC uses eight bits to represent a character. A group of 8 bits has 256 (2^8) different combinations; therefore, EBCDIC can represent up to 256 characters. This is

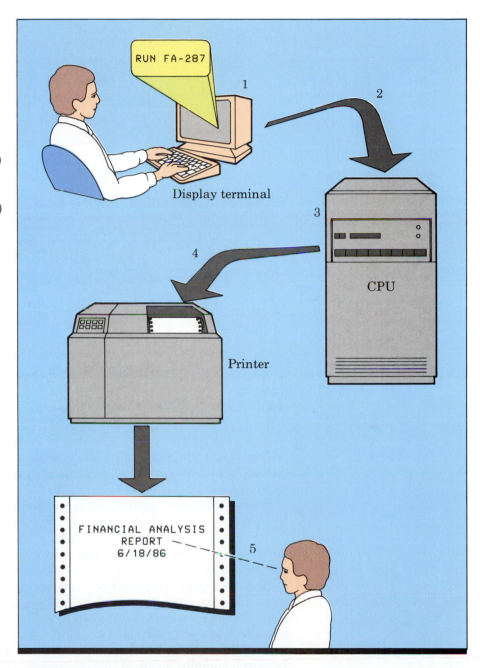

FIGURE 4-4

Conversion to and from binary-based form. (1) The user types in a message in natural-language symbols. (2) The computer system translates the message into binary-based form (this conversion often takes place in the input device). (3) The CPU does all the required processing in binary-based form. (4) The computer system translates the output back into natural-language symbols (this conversion usually takes place in the output device). (5) The user can now read the output.

RUN FA-287

Display terminal

CPU

Printer

FINANCIAL ANALYSIS
REPORT
6/18/86

more than enough to account for the 26 uppercase and 26 lowercase characters, the 10 decimal digits, and several special characters.

ASCII originally was designed as a 7-bit code that could represent 128 (2^7) characters. Several 8-bit versions of ASCII (called ASCII-8) have been developed because computers are designed to handle data in chunks of 8 bits (see Feature 4B). Many computer systems can accept data in either

Character	EBCDIC Bit Representation	ASCII Bit Representation	Character	EBCDIC Bit Representation	ASCII Bit Representation
0	11110000	0110000	I	11001001	1001001
1	11110001	0110001	J	11010001	1001010
2	11110010	0110010	K	11010010	1001011
3	11110011	0110011	L	11010011	1001100
4	11110100	0110100	M	11010100	1001101
5	11110101	0110101	N	11010101	1001110
6	11110110	0110110	O	11010110	1001111
7	11110111	0110111	P	11010111	1010000
8	11111000	0111000	Q	11011000	1010001
9	11111001	0111001	R	11011001	1010010
A	11000001	1000001	S	11100010	1010011
B	11000010	1000010	T	11100011	1010100
C	11000011	1000011	U	11100100	1010101
D	11000100	1000100	V	11100101	1010110
E	11000101	1000101	W	11100110	1010111
F	11000110	1000110	X	11100111	1011000
G	11000111	1000111	Y	11101000	1011001
H	11001000	1001000	Z	11101001	1011010

FIGURE 4-5

EBCDIC and ASCII. These two common fixed-length codes represent characters in byte form. In EBCDIC, a byte consists of 8 bits; in ASCII, 7 bits.

coding system and perform the conversion to their native code. The eight (seven) bits used to represent a character in EBCDIC (ASCII) are collectively referred to as a **byte.**

In many computer systems, one byte represents a single *addressable* storage location. For this reason, computer manufacturers use the byte measure to define their machines' storage capacity. As you may have noticed, computer advertisements are filled with references to kilobytes, megabytes, gigabytes, and terabytes. One **kilobyte** (**K-byte** or **KB**) is equal to a little over 1,000 bytes (1,024, to be precise), one **megabyte** (**M-byte** or **MB**) equals about 1 million bytes, one **gigabyte** (**G-byte** or **GB**) equals about 1 billion bytes, and one **terabyte** (**T-byte** or **TB**) equals about 1 trillion bytes. So, for example, when you read about a system with a 512 K-byte system unit and a 40 M-byte hard disk storage unit, it means that the computer's primary memory can store about 512,000 characters of data and the disk unit an additional 40 million.

The conversion from natural-language words and numbers to their EBCDIC or ASCII equivalents and back again usually takes place on an input/output device. For example, when a user types in a message such as

RUN

at a keyboard, a specialized processor inside the keyboard usually translates it into EBCDIC (or ASCII) and sends it as a series of bytes to the CPU. The

ASCII Files

How ASCII Files Work on Your Computer System

Virtually everyone working with computers will, at some point, need to create a data file. Such files may consist of items such as a word-processed document, an accounting worksheet, or data for a BASIC program. On many computer systems, files fall into one of two categories: program-dependent files and ASCII files.

Both types of files consist of sequences of 0s and 1s. The difference is that the strings of 0s and 1s in a *standard ASCII file* represent text that theoretically any program can process, while the strings in a *program-dependent file* represent text that usually only a particular computer program can understand. Most program packages are not able to read and translate program-dependent files created by another package, unless, say, the latter is so popular that it represents a standard unto itself. On the other hand, many software packages can read and understand standard ASCII files. So, if you can find a way to get your file into ASCII, you can probably get most program packages to read it.

The seven-bit ASCII code runs from 0 to 127 and is called the *standard ASCII character set.* Codes 0 through 32 are control codes and represent functions such as carriage return, line feed, and form feed. One control code is even assigned to generate a beep or ring a bell. Codes 33 through 127 cover the set of printable characters; for example, code 33 is the exclamation point and 76 is the uppercase *L.* If all software and hardware manufacturers used only these 128 standard codes, we'd have a lot fewer interfacing problems with programs.

But because most computers handle 8 bits, it is possible to generate 128 additional ASCII codes. These are collectively known as the *extended ASCII character set.* Each software manufacturer uses the additional codes in its own way and, consequently, it's these eight-bit forms of ASCII (i.e., ASCII-8) that cause the interfacing problems. For example, some programs use the extra codes to store data more compactly, while others use them to generate special graphics characters and printer sequences. Fortunately, a number of solutions are available for making files cre-

> A number of solutions are available for making files created by one package acceptable to another.

ated by one package acceptable to another.

One common solution is using a software routine that strips away the eighth ASCII bit, thereby turning a program-dependent file into standard ASCII. Many software packages will create ASCII files if commanded, and many will accept ASCII files. But translating a file into ASCII may be only half the battle. The other half concerns the formatting differences among packages. If one program marks the end of each data record with a carriage return character (ASCII 13) while another uses a line feed (ASCII 10), the user may be forced to write a short program to strip away one of these delimiters and replace it with the other.

Fortunately, a more straightforward solution often exists. Many packages offer routines that will automatically translate their files into other program-dependent forms. For example, Lotus 1-2-3 has a "transport option" that translates a 1-2-3 spreadsheet into a file that can be employed with Ashton-Tate's dBASE (a database management system).

Still another approach software manufacturers use to make files compatible is to produce output that conforms to a common file interchange standard, such as the Data Interchange Format (DIF) or Microsoft's SYmbolic LinK (SYLK) format. Any program that supports one of these formats can accept files from any other programs that use the same format.

output the CPU sends back to the display or some other output device is also in EBCDIC (or ASCII), which the output device—usually with the aid of another imbedded specialized processor—translates into understandable words and numbers. So, if the CPU sent the EBCDIC message

1 1 0 0 1 0 0 0 1 1 0 0 1 0 0 1

to your display device, the word "HI" would appear on your screen.

The Parity Bit. Suppose you are at a keyboard and press the *B* key. If the keyboard processor supports EBCDIC coding, it will transmit the byte "11000010" to the CPU. Sometimes, however, something happens during transmission and the CPU receives a garbled message. Interference on the line, for example, might cause the third bit to change from 0 to 1 so that the CPU receives the message "11100010." Unless the CPU had some way of knowing that a mistake was made, it would wrongly interpret this byte as the letter *S*.

To enable the CPU to detect such transmission errors, EBCDIC and ASCII have an additional bit position. This bit, called the **parity bit,** is automatically set to either 0 or 1 to make all the bits in a byte add up to either an even or an odd number. Computer systems support either an even or an odd parity. In *odd-parity* systems, the parity bit makes all the 1-bits in a byte add up to an odd number. In *even-parity* systems, it makes them add up to an even number. Figure 4-6 shows how the parity bit works for the EBCDIC representation of the word "HELLO" on an even-parity system.

The parity bit is automatically generated by the keyboard's processor. Thus, if you typed the *B* character on an even-parity system, "110000101" would be sent up the line to the CPU. If the message were garbled so that the even-parity computer received "111000101" (an odd number of 1-bits), the CPU would sense the error immediately.

The parity check is not foolproof. For example, if two bits are incorrectly transmitted in a byte, they will self-cancel. A two-bit error, however, will rarely occur.

Machine Language

Before a program can be executed by a computer, it must be converted into a binary-based code known as **machine language.** An example of a typical machine-language instruction appears in Figure 4-7. As you can see, what looks like a meaningless string of 0s and 1s actually consists of groups of bits that represent specific locations, operations, and characters. Each computer has its own machine language. A code that is used on an IBM computer will be totally foreign to a Unisys computer.

Machine language instructions are what the CPU works on during the machine cycles we talked about earlier in the chapter. Because it is most closely patterned to the computer's actual behavior, machine language is often called a *low-level language. Assembly languages,* developed in the 1950s, are symbolic counterparts of machine languages; they replace binary code with understandable symbols composed of numbers and letters. But

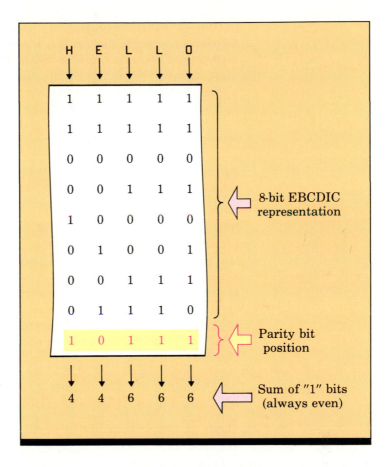

FIGURE 4-6

The parity bit. If the system used supports even parity, as shown here, the 1-bits in every byte must always add up to an even number. The parity bit is set to either 0 or 1 in each byte to force an even number of 1-bits in the byte.

because they so closely resemble machine language and are tedious for the average programmer to work with, assembly languages are also considered low-level languages.

With the first computers, all programs were written in machine language. Today, although it is still possible to write in machine language, hardly any-

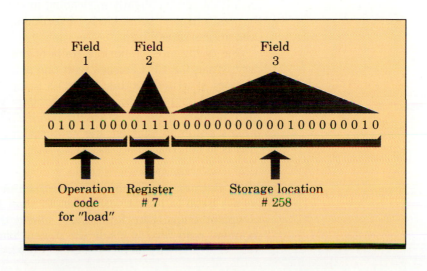

FIGURE 4-7

A 32-bit machine language instruction. The instruction commands the computer to load the contents of primary memory location 258 into register 7. In the example, the numbers 7 and 258 are represented in the instruction by their true binary counterparts.

body does. As we mentioned in Chapter 3, programmers now can work in *high-level languages* that are much easier to comprehend. Programs written in high-level languages, such as BASIC or Pascal, or in an assembly language must, however, be translated into machine language before they can be executed. This takes place automatically under the control of special systems software called a *language translator* (discussed in Chapter 8).

THE SYSTEM UNIT

Now that we've talked conceptually about how the CPU and primary memory work, let's consider how they're realized in hardware and how they relate to other devices inside a system unit of, say, a typical microcomputer. Almost all computers sold today use a modular hardware approach; for example, related circuitry is etched onto memory or processor chips, the chips are mounted onto carrier packages that are plugged into boards, and the boards are fitted into slots inside the **system unit.** Let's now look in more detail at the individual hardware components that are involved in this process.

Memory Chips: RAM and ROM

There are two principal types of chips: memory chips and processor chips. The most common types of memory chips are RAM and ROM.

RAM. Primary memory is commonly referred to by the acronym **RAM,** which stands for **random access memory.** *Random access* means that the storage has addresses and, therefore, the computer system can go to the programs and data it wants directly. This is in contrast to *sequential access,* where the computer system must check each storage location in turn. The term RAM can be slightly misleading in studying computers. As we'll see in the next chapter, some kinds of secondary storage devices also have random access capabilities.

One of the most important traits of primary memory is that it is *temporary.* When the CPU finishes with one set of data and programs in primary memory, it writes another set in its place. In order to be used again, programs and data must be kept in secondary storage, which is relatively slow. Also, primary memory is usually *volatile.* This means that when the computer's power is shut off, the contents of primary memory are destroyed. This is in contrast to secondary storage, which is nonvolatile.

ROM. Because of advances in small semiconductor memories, there has been a trend in recent years to build some software functions directly into computer chips. Like RAM, these all-electronic random-access chips are mounted onto boards inside the system unit. Once placed on these chips, programs can be accessed very rapidly. On many microcomputer systems, for example, certain operating-system routines are built onto a chip rather than stored on disk.

This kind of software-within-hardware is called **firmware.** Several kinds of firmware are available:

☐ **Read-only memory (ROM)** is by far the most common form of firmware. A ROM module contains a prewritten program supplied by the firmware manufacturer. The program can be read from the module, but it is impossible for a user to destroy the module's contents by accidentally or purposely writing over them (hence the term *read-only*).

☐ **Programmable read-only memory (PROM)** is identical to ROM except that the buyer writes the program. In other words, a PROM module is like a blank ROM module. Special equipment is needed to write a program onto a PROM module, and once the program is on it can't be erased.

☐ **Erasable programmable read-only memory (EPROM)** is like PROM except that its contents can be erased by exposure to ultraviolet light and a new program written on. The newest type of EPROM, which is *electrically erasable,* is called *EEPROM.* EEPROM modules are commonly used in supermarket cash registers to store product prices.

Firmware is usually supplied with the computer system purchased. It can also be bought separately.

Computer Chips: The CPU and Specialized Processors

Virtually every microcomputer system sold today runs under the control of a single native CPU, that is, a chip that acts as the central processor for the entire system. Some of the more widely used chips and several computer systems that use them are shown in Figure 4-8. These chips differ in many respects, one of the most important of which is the word size used.

Word Size. A computer **word** is a group of bits or bytes that may be manipulated and stored as a unit. It is a critical concept, because the internal circuitry of virtually every computer system is designed around a certain word size. The Apple Macintosh IIX and IBM PS/2 Model 80 computers, for example, use the Motorola 68030 and Intel 80386 chips, respectively. Both the 68030 and 80386 chips have a 32-bit-word internal architecture, which means that data are transferred within each CPU chip itself in 32-bit chunks. Both chips also have a 32-bit-word I/O *bus,* meaning that there is a 32-bit-wide data path from each CPU to external devices.

Besides speed, there are many other important reasons to consider word size when buying a computer. For one thing, the longer the word size, the greater the RAM capacity. A 32-bit machine theoretically can address about 4 gigabytes of memory, although most operating systems designed around them use at most several megabytes. A 16-bit machine, in contrast, often is practically limited to several hundred thousand addresses.

Longer word sizes also generally make for greater precision. A big number that occupies one word in a large computer may occupy two words in

Vendor	Chip	Size (Bits)*	Computer Systems
Intel	8086	16	IBM PS/2—Models 25 and 30 Wang Professional Computer AT&T 6300 Compaq Deskpro Model 2
	8088	16	IBM PC (and XT model) TI Professional Tandy 1000 SX PC's Limited Turbo Leading Edge Model D Compaq Portable Zenith Z-150 and Z-159
	80286	16	IBM PC AT IBM PS/2—Models 50 and 60 Compaq Deskpro 286 Hewlett-Packard Vectra PC PC's Limited 286 Tandy 3000 HL Zenith Z-286 Leading Edge Model D2
	80386	32	IBM PS/2—Models 70 and 80 Compaq Deskpro 386 Tandy 4000 Zenith Z-386 PC's Limited 386
Motorola	68000	32	Apple Macintosh Apple Macintosh Plus Apple Macintosh SE
	68020	32	Apple Macintosh II
	68030	32	The NeXT Computer System Apple Macintosh IIX and IICX Apple Macintosh SE/30

*Size indicates the width of the path along which data are transferred on the CPU chip.

FIGURE 4-8

Some common computer chips and the computer systems that use them. Two companies dominate the CPU chip marketplace—Intel and Motorola. Intel chips are used on IBM microcomputers and similar devices; Motorola chips, on the Apple Macintosh line of computers.

a smaller machine, resulting in some loss in accuracy, not to mention reduced speed. On very large, scientific computers, where speed and accuracy are extremely important, word sizes as great as 60 or more bits are not unusual.

The greater the size of the word the machine manipulates, the greater the number of bits available to represent machine language instructions. For example, most 32-bit machines are designed such that the first 8 bits are reserved for the instruction type. This permits a total of 2^8, or 256, different instructions. Sixteen-bit machines, on the other hand, have a smaller number of bits available for this purpose. Typically these computers reserve 6 bits for instructions, which permits only 2^6, or 64, different instructions. Thus, the bigger the word size, the larger the set of possible instructions available to the computer.

T O M O R R O W

Superconductors

What They Mean to the Future of Computing

Relatively speaking, today's computers are pretty darn slow. Relative to what? Superconductors, of course. If and when they eventually emerge from the laboratories and are implemented into actual products, superconductive circuits are expected to be at least 100 times faster than conventional integrated circuits, which form the backbone of today's fast-access memories.

The significance of superconductivity to the computing world is obvious. As Window 2 shows, computer chips are formed by packing thousands of circuits into an area smaller than a human fingerprint. Unfortunately, one of the problems chip designers face is that electricity causes heat, and if circuits are packed much more densely than they are now, they would melt. Moreover, all matter, including circuits, consists of atoms that are constantly in motion. Thus, any current flowing through circuits is impeded by the prevailing atom movement, losing some energy as a re-

sult. Electrical engineers call this property resistance.

Superconductive materials, however, mitigate both of these problems. Cooling combats the heat problem, enabling circuits to be placed closer together. Also, when superconductive materials are cooled, the atoms they contain are rendered less active, thereby reducing electrical resistance.

> Superconductive circuits are expected to be at least 100 times faster than conventional integrated circuits.

Superconductivity is not a new phenomenon. Dutch physicist Kamerlingh Onnes studied and documented superconductivity shortly after the turn of the century. Onnes found that mercury loses all resistance to the flow of electricity when it is sufficiently cooled. Shortly thereafter, Onnes also discovered the cooling properties of helium gas. Interestingly, manufac-

turers of many of today's supercomputers immerse conventional circuitry, which is made from nonsuperconductive materials, in a cool helium bath to achieve the machines' high speeds.

Today one of the biggest areas of superconductivity research involves discovering a conductive material with the highest possible "transition temperature"—the temperature that will destroy electrical resistance. The holy grail in the search, of course, is a material that is superconductive at room temperature. When used in computer circuits, such a material would eliminate the need to ensconce the entire processor unit in some type of expensive cooling environment. Of course, the material must also be abundant, stable, and sufficiently manufacturable to be mass-produced inexpensively and with no loss in reliability.

Today, despite the voluminous press coverage devoted to superconductivity, we are still far from realizing this goal. Even the most promising superconductors can hold their superconductivity for only a short time, are brittle, and require a special cooling agent such as helium or nitrogen gas to achieve high performance.

FIGURE 4-9

A board. Processor chips, as well as RAM and ROM modules, are placed into carrier packages that fit into specific sockets on the board. Pictured here is a system board for a computer in the IBM PS/2 line.

Specialized Processors. As mentioned earlier, many computer systems today have specialized processor chips that supplement the CPU. The purpose of these chips is to either take on part of the burden the CPU normally handles or enhance system performance by providing features not normally found in the CPU.

For instance, specialized processors are built into most computer keyboards today. Such processors determine which keys are being depressed, determine the ASCII equivalent of each of these keys, and check to see that the keyboard is communicating properly with the CPU. Another example of a specialized chip is the Motorola 68882 floating-point *numeric coprocessor,* which is a standard item on the Macintosh IIX. This chip performs arithmetic calculations hundreds of times faster than the Mac's Motorola 68030 CPU. On the IBM PS/2, the (optional) Intel 80387 coprocessor chip performs similar duties. Many computer systems built today also contain *graphic coprocessors*—chips that assist with computational chores associated with providing sophisticated graphical output on display devices.

Putting It All Together

Once manufactured, each processor or memory chip is mounted onto a carrier package. The carrier packages are fitted into specific locations on boards, which are placed inside the system unit.

FIGURE 4-10

Add-in boards. Add-in boards fit into slots within the system unit. The unit shown here has four boards—two "long boards" and two "short boards." Every system unit has different specifications with respect to the number and type of boards it will accommodate.

Boards. A **board** (see Figure 4-9) is a card that contains the circuitry for performing one or more specific functions. The most important board in the microcomputer's system unit is the **system board** (sometimes called the *motherboard*). This board often contains the CPU and a limited amount of primary memory. On larger computers, the CPU and its primary memory may require several such boards.

Many microcomputer-system vendors enable you to customize your system by choosing your own **add-in boards** (see Figure 4-10). These boards, which plug into expansion slots within the computer's system unit, enable you to either interface with specific types of peripheral devices or add new capabilities. For example, if you want a certain model of display unit attached to your computer, you may need a special *display adapter board* that contains the proper interfacing routine for establishing the connection. Similarly, you can sometimes increase the RAM on your system board by getting a *memory expansion board* with enough memory chips to bring your total RAM up to the desired level. An *emulator board,* on the other hand, enables your computer system to behave like another device; for instance, it may allow a PS/2 to function as a communications terminal to a remote mini or mainframe. With so many types of devices now available in the microcomputer marketplace, and with both processor speed and memory approaching mainframe-level heights, add-in boards are an especially hot topic, and we'll address it in more depth in Chapter 15.

Because system units that allow add-in boards have a finite number of slots to accommodate such boards, many board manufacturers squeeze as many functions onto a board as practicable. Such products are commonly

FIGURE 4-11

How devices are linked. A set of wires or circuits called a *bus* allows the CPU to communicate with RAM, with ROM, and with peripheral devices connected through either boards or ports.

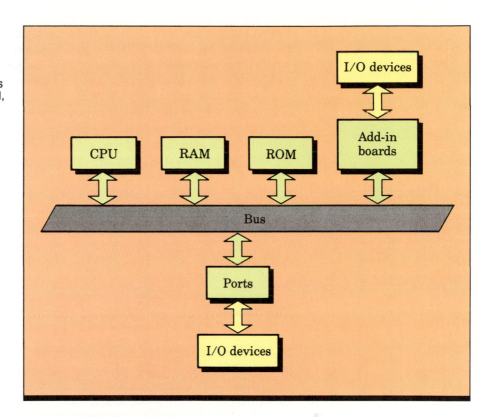

called *multifunction boards*. A single multifunction board might contain enough memory chips to give your system, say, an additional several hundred kilobytes of RAM as well as a clock/calendar feature and special software routines to optimize the performance of your hard disk.

System units that allow you to customize with add-in boards are said to possess an *open architecture. Closed-architecture* machines generally are faster and easier to deal with, but they lack the flexibility you get from being able to configure a wide variety of devices to your computer. Virtually all of the leading computers made today, whether microcomputers, minicomputers, mainframes, or supercomputers, are open-architecture devices.

Ports. Most system units, regardless of whether they have closed or open architectures, contain sockets that enable you to plug in other devices. These sockets, which often are found on the back of the system unit, are known as **ports.** Printers, for instance, generally hook up to microcomputers through either *parallel ports* or *serial ports.* IBM microcomputers and similar devices typically interface printers with parallel ports; Apple computers interface printers with serial ports. Most computers also use serial ports to permit connection to remote devices over phone lines. We'll look more closely at serial and parallel connections in Chapter 7.

System Unit. Figure 4-11 shows an example of how many of the devices we've talked about in this chapter may be connected inside the system unit.

Coded information travels through the system unit on an input/output (I/O) **bus**—a set of wires that acts as a data highway between the CPU and other devices. Large computers usually contain several I/O buses.

The type of I/O bus the CPU uses is extremely important. On many microcomputer systems, for instance, there is a 32-bit bus that allows other CPU chips, on add-in boards, to gain control of the computer system. This feature can effectively turn one type of computer system into another type. Alternatively, such a feature lets you operate several CPUs concurrently. Thus, for example, the system's native CPU can be dedicated to a high-priority application while another CPU on an add-in board is dedicated to a low-priority function in the background. This feature, called *Micro Channel Architecture* in the IBM world and *NuBus* in the Apple Macintosh world, will be explored more fully in Chapter 15.

SUMMARY AND KEY TERMS

There are many ways to classify computers. **Digital computers,** for example, are devices that *count,* while **analog computers** are devices that *measure.* Also, some computers are *central* processors while others are *specialized* processors. And, some machines are *full instruction set computers* and others are **reduced instruction set computers (RISC)**.

The CPU has two major sections. The **arithmetic/logic unit (ALU)** performs arithmetic and logical operations on data. The **control unit** directs the flow of electronic traffic between primary memory and the ALU and between the CPU and input and output devices. Both of these units work closely with primary memory to carry out processing tasks inside the system unit.

Primary memory, also called **main memory** or **internal memory,** holds the programs and data that have been passed to the computer, the results of intermediate processing, and output that is ready to be transmitted to secondary storage or an output device.

Registers are high-speed staging areas within the CPU that hold program instructions and data immediately before they are processed. The part of a program instruction that indicates what the ALU is to do next is placed in the **instruction register;** the part showing the address of the data to be used in the operation is placed in the **address register.** Before data are processed, they are taken from primary memory and placed in the **storage register.** The **accumulator** is a register that temporarily stores the results of ongoing operations.

The processing of a single instruction is called a **machine cycle**. A machine cycle has two parts: an **I-cycle** (instruction cycle), in which the control unit fetches and examines an instruction, and an **E-cycle** (execution cycle), in which the instruction is actually executed by the ALU under control unit supervision. A computer may need to go through thousands, millions, or even billions of machine cycles to fully process a single program. Computer cycle times generally are measured in **milliseconds** (thousandths of a second), **microseconds** (millionths of a second), **nanoseconds** (billionths of a second), or **picoseconds** (trillionths of a second).

The electronic components of digital computers work in a two-state, or **binary,** fashion. It is convenient to think of these binary states as the 0-state and the 1-state. Computer people refer to such 0s and 1s as **bits.**

The computer uses several binary-based codes to process data. Two popular codes are **EBCDIC** and **ASCII.** These fixed-length codes can represent any single character of data—a digit, alphabet character, or special symbol—as a string of seven or eight bits. This string of bits is called a **byte.** EBCDIC and ASCII allow for an additional bit position, called a **parity bit,** to enable computer systems to check for transmission errors.

The storage capacity of computers often is expressed in **kilobytes** (**K-bytes** or **KB**), or thousands of bytes; **megabytes** (**M-bytes** or **MB**), or millions of bytes; **gigabytes** (**G-bytes** or **GB**), or billions of bytes; and **terabytes** (**T-bytes** or **TB**), or trillions of bytes.

Machine language is the binary-based code used to represent programs. A program must be translated into machine language before the computer can execute it.

Almost all computer systems sold today use a modular hardware approach; that is, related circuitry is etched onto *processor chips* or *memory chips,* the chips are mounted onto carrier packages that are later fitted into boards, and the boards are positioned into slots inside the **system unit.**

The most popular types of memory chips are RAM and ROM. Primary storage is commonly referred to by the acronym **RAM,** which stands for **random access memory.** This memory is used to *temporarily* store programs and data with which the computer is currently working. *Permanent* storage of important programs is commonly provided through **firmware,** which is software-within-hardware modules. There are several types of firmware, including **ROM (read-only memory), PROM (programmable read-only memory),** and **EPROM (erasable programmable read-only memory).**

Processor chips differ in many respects; one example is word size. A computer **word** is a group of bits or bytes that can be manipulated as a unit. Often the larger the word size, the more powerful the processor.

Boards contain the circuitry needed to perform one or more specific functions. The **system board,** for example, contains the CPU and a limited amount of primary memory. Many microcomputer-system vendors enable buyers to customize their systems by choosing their own **add-in boards.**

In addition to chips and boards, many system units have external **ports** that enable users to plug in support devices. Also, there must be circuitry to connect everything together within the system unit. A set of wires called an I/O **bus,** for example, connects the CPU to other devices.

REVIEW EXERCISES

Fill-in Questions

1. A thousandth of a second is called a(n) _millisecond_.
2. A millionth of a second is called a(n) _microsecond_.
3. A billionth of a second is called a(n) _nanosecond_.
4. A trillionth of a second is called a(n) _picosecond_.
5. A(n) _kilobyte_ is approximately 1 thousand bytes.
6. A(n) _mega_ " is approximately 1 million bytes.
7. A(n) _giga_ " is approximately 1 billion bytes.
8. A(n) _tera_ " is approximately 1 trillion bytes.

Matching Questions

Match each term with the description that best fits.

a. ALU   e. ASCII
b. binary   f. word
c. bit   g. EPROM
d. EBCDIC   h. parity bit

_b_ 1. The base-2 numbering system.
_D_ 2. The fixed-length code most associated with IBM mainframes.
_g_ 3. A type of firmware that is erasable.
_e_ 4. A fixed-length code developed by the American National Standards Institute.
_h_ 5. Used to check for transmission errors.
_a_ 6. The section of the CPU in which computations are performed.
_f_ 7. A group of bits or bytes that may be manipulated and stored as a unit.
_c_ 8. A binary digit.

Discussion Questions

1. What is the principle advantage of a reduced instruction set computer (RISC)?
2. Describe the various sections of the CPU and their roles.
3. Explain how a program instruction is executed.

4. Why is the binary system used to represent data and programs?

5. What is the purpose of the parity bit, and how does it work?

6. What are the differences among a bit, a byte, a kilobyte, a megabyte, and a word?

7. How does RAM differ from ROM?

8. What devices are located under the cover of the system unit? What functions do these devices perform?

Critical Thinking Questions

1. The chapter mentions the continuing quest for faster computers. Aren't computers fast enough now? What difference could it make to have mainframe power on the desk of ordinary end users or computers that are, say, hundreds or thousands of times faster than those we have today?

2. The earliest computers were decimal rather than digital machines. In other words, they broke down each piece of data into ten states instead of just two. Why, would you guess, were decimal computers slower than digital (binary) computers?

3. Comment on this statement: "Computers are now so easy to work with that it's no longer necessary for the average user to know any of the technical details about how they work." In making your comments, be sure to state how much technical knowledge you feel the average business student should have about computers.

How Computer Chips Are Made

From Design to Assembly

Computer chips are found in a multitude of products, including toys, phones, digital watches, scales, audio and video equipment, washers and dryers, microwave ovens, and personal computers. The story of how these chips are produced is fascinating. First, a drawing of the chip is created in computer memory using special hardware and software. Then a series of computer programs test the chip design and modify it as needed. Next, the final chip design is converted into physical form. The design is replicated dozens of times on the surface of a circular silcon wafer. Incredibly, many thousands of circuits are fitted onto a single chip, which is smaller than a human fingerprint. Finally, the individual chips are cut from the wafer, mounted in carrier packages, and sold for just a few dollars apiece. Look through this Window for more details on this process.

1 Chips are designed with the help of a computer-aided design (CAD) system. Such systems are equipped with standard electronic symbols that represent each of the circuit elements and with software that automatically sizes and tests each element. Thus, engineers can tell whether the design will work before a chip is built.

2 A CPU chip mounted in its carrier package with a pencil alongside for comparison purposes.

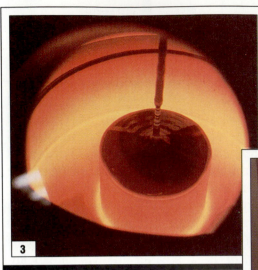

3

4

3, 4 The material most often used to form the body of a chip is silicon, which is extracted from rocks and sand and put through a purification process. After purification, molten silicon (photo 3) is formed into cylindrical ingots. Then a diamond saw slices each ingot into thin, circular wafers (photo 4). These are polished to a mirrorlike finish and given an oxide coating.

5, 6 A single wafer is large enough to produce several dozen chips, which are laid out on the wafer's surface like a sheet of postage stamps. Circuits are formed onto the wafer in layers by masks (photo 5) that carry circuit patterns. A light-sensitive emulsion called photoresist is applied to the wafer, and the wafer and mask are mounted on a special machine (photo 6). When ultraviolet light passes from the machine through the mask, it hardens the photoresist in the places that will not have circuits. The photoresist lying along the circuit paths remains soft.

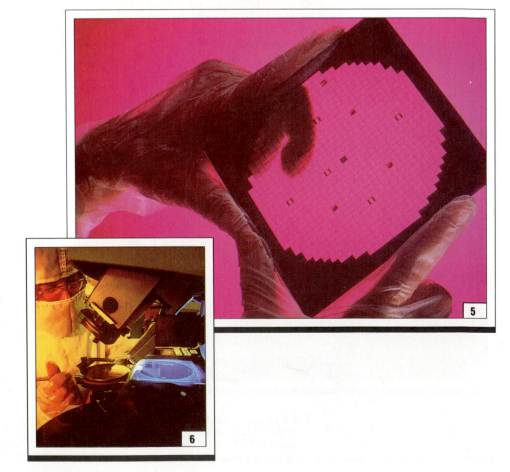

5

6

7, 8 Wafers are next placed into a holder and dropped into an acid bath (photo 7) to remove all the soft photoresist. The oxide layer is exposed wherever the photoresist is removed. Wafers are then placed into a diffusion furnace (photo 8), which changes their atomic structure and forms the conductive circuit paths. Because a single wafer may have over a dozen circuit layers, each one represented by its own mask, the process depicted in photos 5 through 8 must be repeated for each circuit layer.

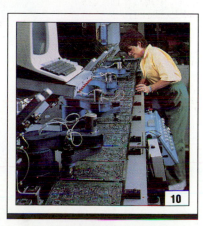

9 Once the wafers are finished being treated, the individual chips are cut out and each is mounted onto a carrier package. The pins on the package plug into a board that fits inside the computer's system unit. Pictured in the photo is the Intel 80486 chip, which is used on many IBM microcomputers and similar devices and can address up to four gigabytes of main memory.

10 Robots are commonly used to mount the carrier packages and other electronic components onto boards. The robots shown here are capable of placing on boards up to 150,000 components per day.

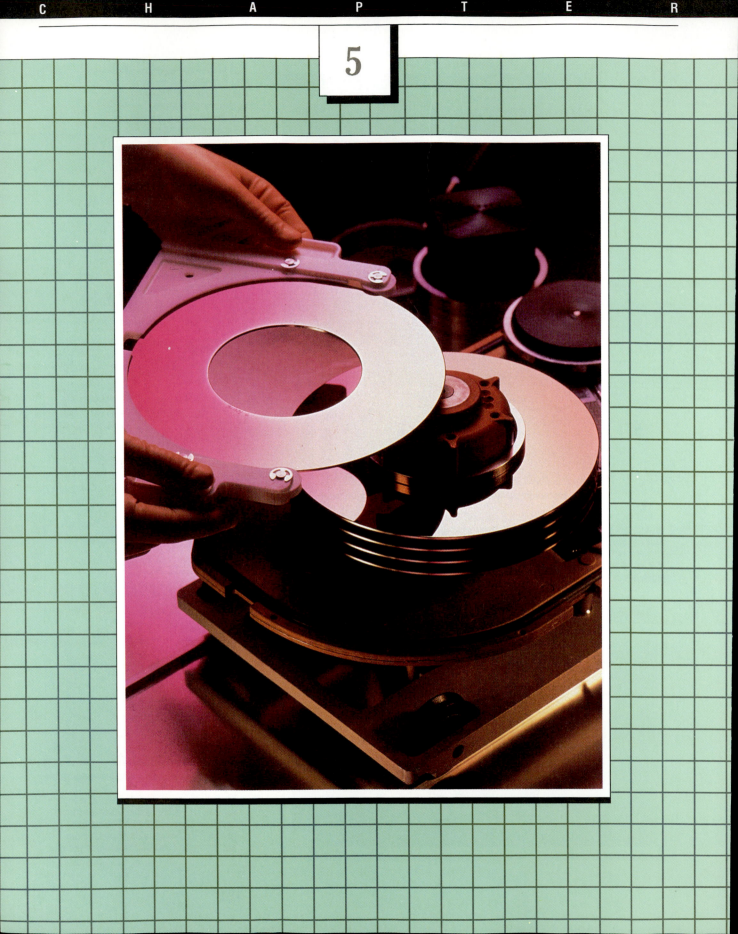

Secondary Storage

Objectives

After completing this chapter, you will be able to:

1. Name several general properties of secondary storage systems.

2. Identify a number of disk and tape storage systems as well as describe how they work and where they are particularly useful.

3. Describe the roles of other secondary storage media and equipment.

4. Explain several types of data access and organization strategies and identify situations where each is appropriate.

OVERVIEW

In Chapter 4, we discussed the role of primary (internal) memory. Primary memory is designed to provide immediate access to stored items. It is here that programs, data, intermediate results, and output are temporarily stored. However, as soon as a program has been executed, new data and programs are written over the existing ones. Thus, if data, programs, and processing results are to be preserved for repeated use, additional storage capacity must be made available. Secondary (external) storage serves this purpose. Although slower than primary memory, secondary storage is less expensive and provides greater storage capacity.

We will begin this chapter with a discussion of certain common characteristics of secondary storage systems. One of the most important is data access—the way in which data are retrieved from secondary storage. Then we'll cover the two most important kinds of secondary storage systems in use today: those that use magnetic disk and those that use magnetic tape. Next we'll look at some less common secondary storage systems, such as those that use optical disk or magnetic bubbles. Finally, we'll cover data organization—methods of storing data on a medium for efficient access.

PROPERTIES OF SECONDARY STORAGE SYSTEMS

In this section, we'll look at several important properties of secondary storage systems. We will consider in turn (1) the two physical parts of a secondary storage system, (2) the nonvolatility property of secondary storage, (3) the removability of media from the secondary storage unit, and (4) sequential versus direct access.

Physical Parts. Any secondary storage system involves two physical parts: a *peripheral device* and an *input/output medium*. A disk unit and a tape unit are examples of peripheral devices; magnetic disk platters and magnetic tape cartridges are types of media. Data and programs are written onto and read from some type of medium. The medium must be situated on a peripheral device in order for the CPU to process its contents.

In most secondary storage systems, media must pass by a **read/write head** in the peripheral device to be read from or written to. For instance, when you play or record to a music tape on your home stereo system, the tape passes by a head on the tape recorder, which will either play or record music. Magnetic tapes on computer systems work by an identical principle. Magnetic disks also use read/write heads that perform similar types of reading and writing tasks.

Nonvolatility Property. Secondary storage media are **nonvolatile.** This means that when the power on the peripheral device is shut off, the data stored on the medium remain there. This is in contrast to most types of primary memory, which are **volatile.** With volatile storage, the data on the medium disappear once the power is shut off.

Removable versus Nonremovable Media. In many secondary storage systems, although the peripheral device is online to the computer, the associated medium must be loaded into the device before the computer can read from it or write to it. These are called *removable-media* secondary storage systems. Diskettes, many types of hard disks, magnetic tape cartridges, and magnetic tape reels are examples of removable media used on such systems. Other secondary storage systems, such as those that use Winchester disks (discussed later in this chapter), are *fixed-media* secondary storage systems. In Winchester disk systems, the disk is encased in a sealed unit, within the peripheral device, and it cannot be conveniently removed.

Removability of media provides virtually unlimited storage capacity, because the medium can be replaced when it is filling up. Removability also particularly facilitates backup (see Feature 5A). For instance, a duplicate set of data or programs can be written onto a disk or tape and later stored offline. Security is also enhanced, because programs or data do not have to stay on the disk unit. Finally, removability makes it possible to assign a specific application to a specific medium—say, assigning all customer accounts to one disk and all vendor accounts to another. Fixed media, in contrast, generally offer the advantages of higher speed, greater storage capacity, and better reliability.

Sequential versus Direct Access. When the computer system is instructed to use data or programs residing in secondary storage, it must be able to find the materials first. The process of retrieving data and programs in storage is called *access.*

There are two basic types of access methods: sequential and direct. With **sequential access,** the records in a file can be retrieved only in the same sequence in which they are physically stored. With **direct access,** also called **random access,** records can be retrieved in any sequence.

The distinction between sequential and direct access is observable on a typical home stereo system. Suppose you have both a cassette tape and a phonograph record of the same album of music. Now assume that you want to hear the fifth song on side one of the record and this song is also the fifth selection on the tape. With the tape, you must pass sequentially through the first four songs to hear the fifth one. With the phonograph record, however, you can place the needle directly on the fifth song and listen to it immediately.

The phonograph record is also an effective sequential-access device. If you want to listen to the entire first side of the album, you simply place the needle at the beginning of the record and play the tunes in sequence. Thus, the phonograph record is really both a sequential- and direct-access me-

Backup

It's Not Fun, but It Can Avert Disaster

Virtually everyone who has logged months or years of his or her life away on a computer system will swear to you that at one time or another you will lose some critical files. Maybe lightning will strike nearby, zapping your RAM. Or maybe a small brownout will cause the heads on your hard disk to drop out of orbit and crash onto the disk surface, carving a miniature canyon through the electronic version of a 45-page term paper that's due tomorrow. Most computer veterans will also tell you that these file losses always seem to happen at the worst possible times.

Fortunately, there is a solution to most of these problems—backup. *Backup* is defined as making a duplicate of any file you can't afford to lose so that when the fickle fingers of fate cause inadvertent erasure, you're confronted with only a minor nuisance rather than an outright catastrophe. Theoretically you can back up any file on your computer system. The

> File losses always seem to happen at the worst possible time.

backups you create through, say, a file-copy or disk-copy command can reside on diskette, hard disk, optical disk, streaming tape, or virtually any other storage medium.

One common form of backup involves duplicating a long file that is being developed in RAM. For instance, suppose you are word processing a paper for a class. About every half-hour or hour, you should make sure that you save the current version of the file onto disk. This way, if the power on your system somehow goes out, you will lose only what you typed in since your last save command. Many commercial packages provide certain types of automatic file backup, but unless you know for sure what is being backed up and when, it's safer to do it yourself.

But having a file stored on a diskette or a hard disk, both of which are less vulnerable to power surges than RAM, does not completely let you out of the woods. Suppose, for instance, that you erase the wrong file from secondary storage. Worse yet, suppose you think you're issuing a format command—a command that erases everything on a secondary storage medium and sets up a new file directory for it—to your diskette drive when, in fact, the system is pointed at your hard-disk drive. Or what if someone comes near your computer system with a magnetic device, causing the bits

dium in that you can play a series of songs sequentially or pick individual ones in random order.

Now let's apply this distinction to computer systems. Machine-readable magnetic tape has the sequential properties of music tape, and magnetic disk has both the sequential and direct properties of the phonograph record.

Some information processing applications are essentially sequential in nature, while others are direct. For example, the preparation of mailing labels is often a sequential operation. If you want to send Christmas cards to all employees in a company, you can process the computerized employee

stored on your magnetic tracks to repolarize, or you bump your hard disk when moving your system unit around your desktop, making the sensitive heads crash? Any of these events can make you want to jump off the Golden Gate bridge if backup isn't part of your game plan.

There are many strategies for backing up files on a hard disk or diskette. One is to perform a *global backup* (see photo), in which you back up *all* the files on disk several times throughout the day or at the end of a day or a session. The advantage of a global backup is that it is relatively straightforward and, because it employs a "shotgun" approach, sometimes backs up "treasures" that you neglected to copy previously. On the other hand, a global backup takes longer than a backup targeted at selected files. Also, you need more storage space to contain the files copied.

An alternative to the global backup is an *incremental backup*, in which only files created since the last backup are copied. While an incremental backup is faster than a global backup, it requires a special software routine, and there is always a chance that something you neglected to copy before will somehow "fall between the cracks." Many people with hard disks perform an incremental backup daily and a global backup weekly.

Whenever you back up on disk, make sure the backup files are not stored on the same disk as the originals. In theory, they shouldn't even be in the same room or building. That way, if a serious accident, such as a fire or flood, occurs at one location, the files at the other location will be safe—unless, of course, you're *really* unlucky.

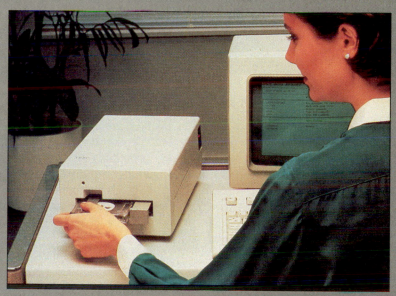

Global backup. Streaming tape systems can back up an entire hard disk in minutes.

file sequentially, that is, from the beginning of the list to the end. As names and addresses are extracted from the file, they are printed on the mailing labels. Obtaining the latest inventory information about products, on the other hand, often involves direct processing, because requests are made to the inventory file in random order. For example, suppose a salesperson wants to find out how many units of item number 6402 are on hand. A minute later, a customer calls to get the price of item number 36. Then a question comes up regarding deliveries of item number 988. In this case, you move back and forth randomly through the records to obtain information from this file.

MAGNETIC DISK

Today **magnetic disks** are undoubtedly the most widely used secondary storage medium for information processing. Because they allow direct access to data, disks permit much faster retrieval of information than do tapes, and at a reasonable cost as well. Without disk storage, many of the computer applications we see around us would not be possible. Banking with automatic teller machines and making airline reservations are just two of the many activities that depend on the rapid access to data that magnetic disks provide.

Two common types of magnetic disk are hard disks and diskettes. **Hard disks** are round, rigid platters. Because of their large storage capacities and fast data-retrieval capabilities, hard disks are by far the preferred medium on minicomputer and mainframe systems. A growing number of microcomputer users are also finding hard disks helpful in their work. There are many types of hard-disk systems in use today; the most common are those that use either a removable-pack or sealed-pack design.

The advantages of hard disks notwithstanding, inexpensive **diskettes,** which are packaged in small plastic cases, are still the medium of choice on many microcomputer systems today. Diskettes also are used occasionally with minicomputers and mainframes as a medium for transferring small amounts of data from one system to another and for small amounts of backup.

In this section, we'll discuss disk systems for large computers first. Since mainframes were commercially available before any other type of computer, many of the principles guiding their disk systems influenced disk systems on other types of computers. Next we'll turn to smaller computers, focusing primarily on diskettes and hard-disk systems and, secondarily, on hard cards and cartridge disks. Finally, we'll look at some methods for optimizing disk processing. The chapter Tomorrow box addresses the future of magnetic disks.

Disk Systems for Large Computers

The disks used by large computers—mainframes, superminis, and supercomputers—are commonly 14-inch-diameter aluminum platters that are coated on both sides with a magnetizable substance such as ferrous oxide. Records are stored in concentric rings, or **tracks** (see Figure 5-1). Characters are represented by binary bits, which appear as magnetic fields on the tracks. Each track may consist of several records.

On most disk systems that serve large computers, each track is designed to carry the same total amount of data even though the tracks near the outer edge are much longer than those nearer the center and move past the read/write heads faster. This design constraint keeps the data transfer rate constant throughout the system, independent of the location of the track being accessed. The number of tracks per disk varies among manufacturers, but it is typically several hundred. Data are read or written by a read/write

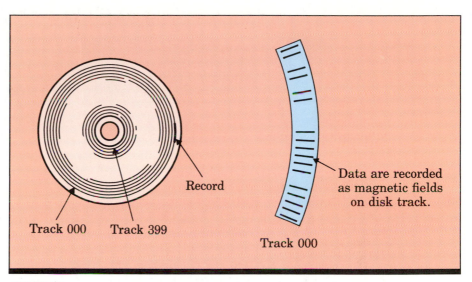

FIGURE 5-1

Surface of a disk. Unlike a phonograph record, which bears a single spiral groove, a disk is composed of concentric tracks. The number of tracks per surface varies among manufacturers. The hard disk shown here has 400 tracks. Diskettes commonly have only 40 or 80 tracks.

head, which moves above or below the spinning disk to access the disk tracks.

Disks on disk systems designed for large computers often are assembled into groups of six, eight, ten, twelve, or some other number, depending on the manufacturer, and mounted on a shaft that spins all the disks at the same rate of speed. The disks are spaced far enough apart to permit the read/write heads to move in and out between the disks. Such an assembly is called a **disk pack.** Depending upon the disk system in use, packs may be removable or nonremovable.

Figure 5-2 shows a removable disk pack. The pack is encased in a plastic shell, similar to a cake cover, to protect the recording surfaces from foreign objects. On removable-pack systems, the top and bottom surfaces of the pack aren't used, because they are the ones most exposed to dust. Nonremovable-pack disk systems use hermetically sealed packs and are much less vulnerable to exposure to foreign matter.

Disk packs function on a device called a **disk unit.** Figure 5-3 shows a removable-pack disk unit, onto which packs are manually mounted by operators. These units are plugged into the computer, enabling it to access any of the data recorded on the disks. A disk pack bears the same relation to a disk unit as a row of phonograph records does to a jukebox. Figure 5-3 also illustrates the relationship among a disk, disk pack, and disk unit.

Reading and Writing Data. Most disk systems have at least one read/write head for each recording surface. These heads are mounted on a device called an **access mechanism.** Figure 5-4 shows how access is accomplished with a *movable access mechanism.* The rotating shaft spins at high speeds (3,600 revolutions per minute are common), and the mechanism

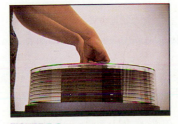

FIGURE 5-2

A disk pack. A disk pack such as the removable one depicted here must be mounted on a disk unit like the one in Figure 5-3 in order for data on any of the disk surfaces to be processed.

T   O   M   O   R   R   O   W

The Future of Magnetic Disks

A Technology Doomed to Get Caught in a Product Squeeze

Since their introduction in the mid-1950s, magnetic disks have become the workhorse secondary storage device on most computer systems. Punched cards have virtually vanished from the scene. Magnetic tape, once used widely for various types of processing, is increasingly being relegated to backup tasks. Will magnetic disk too follow the road to oblivion?

While magnetic disks are unlikely to disappear overnight, they appear to be slowly getting caught in a classic product squeeze. Currently magnetic disk enjoys a comfortable niche between semiconductor RAM and optical disk. RAM is much faster and much more reliable than magnetic disk, but it is more expensive and harder to implement in a portable form. Optical disk is more capa-cious but slower and more costly. Also, write-and-erase capabilities for optical disks still present a number of problems.

But what happens if, as many predict, integrated circuitry gets so compact and inexpensive that it makes more sense to have solid-state secondary storage than

> A "chipdisk" . . . will be available before the middle of the decade.

to have mechanically driven disks? And what if at the same time optical media improve in price and speed and people start demanding to be able to cart around byte-thirsty visual or graphical images on disks?

While the aforementioned events are unlikely to occur immediately, most experts agree that magnetic media currently are relatively limited with respect to how much more data they can pack in. While tremendous improvements in chip and optical disk technology are likely to take place, advances in magnetic disks are expected to be slower. The basic problem is that data can't be moved much closer together without causing magnetized bits to interfere with one another. Nevertheless, magnetic disks continue to be improved. Three current frontiers in magnetic disk manufacturing are thin-film recording, vertical (perpendicular) recording, and magnetoresistive heads.

Thin-Film Recording. Traditionally hard disks have been made with an iron oxide film on each surface. Iron oxide allows about 900 tracks per inch to be put onto a disk surface. *Thin-film recording* (see photo) involves replacing the iron oxide with a thinner film of cobalt or chromium. Because the disks can be machined to finer tolerances, they allow a smaller

moves the heads in and out *together* between the disk surfaces to access the required data. Movable devices are by far the most popular type of access mechanism.

A head never touches the surface of a disk at any time, even during reading and writing. Head and disk are very close, however. The IBM 3350 disk heads, for example, glide 17 millionths of an inch above the recording surfaces. If present on a surface, a human hair or even a smoke particle (about 2,500 and 100 millionths of an inch, respectively), will damage the disks and heads—an event known as a *head crash.* As Figure 5-5 shows, the results

distance between the surface of the disk and the read/write heads. As a result, the heads can exert a stronger magnetic field on a given area, allowing more data to be packed into the same amount of space. Thin-film disks make it possible to pack 1,500 or more tracks per inch.

Vertical Recording. The principle behind *vertical recording* is relatively simple. Suppose you are laying bricks on a patio. A friend claims you bought far too many bricks and to prove it promises to give you $1,000 if you wind up with fewer than twice the number of bricks you need. You later realize your friend is right, so to win the bet you decide to arrange the bricks standing up instead of on their side. Vertical recording on disks works the same way: Instead of laying each bit representation lengthwise across the track, the manufacturer writes each bit down into the track's surface.

Magnetoresistive Heads. The closer together tracks get on the disk's surface, the harder it becomes to po-

sition heads correctly on the right track. A *magnetoresistive head,* however, contains a strip of material that keeps adjacent tracks from interfering with it. This allows the head to be directed to the right track and stay there when reading or writing takes place.

How far will magnetic disks improve in the future? Many say by just a few orders of magnitude. This is in contrast to other storage products,

in which a hundredfold or thousandfold performance increase may not be unusual. In fact, at this writing, a large Japanese firm has announced such a product—a "chipdisk." They claim that this semiconductor alternative to the venerable magnetic disk will be available before the middle of the decade. When such a product becomes economically feasible, the days of magnetic-disk processing will truly be numbered.

Thin-film technology. Horizontally recorded bits along the tracks of a thin-film surface can be packed 22 million per square inch.

will be like placing a pebble on your favorite phonograph album while playing it.

Disk Cylinders. In disk systems that use disk packs, an important principle for understanding disk storage and access strategies is the concept of **disk cylinders.** Again consider the disk system in Figure 5-4. In the disk pack shown, there are 8 possible recording surfaces with 400 tracks per surface. One might envision the disk pack as being composed of 400 imaginary con-

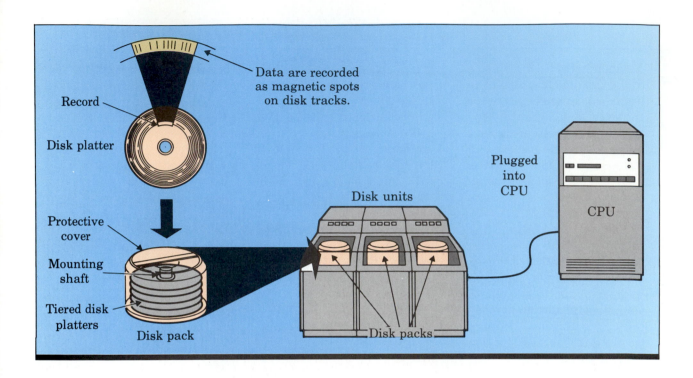

FIGURE 5-3

A removable-pack disk system. Disks are assembled into disk packs, which are mounted in the disk unit.

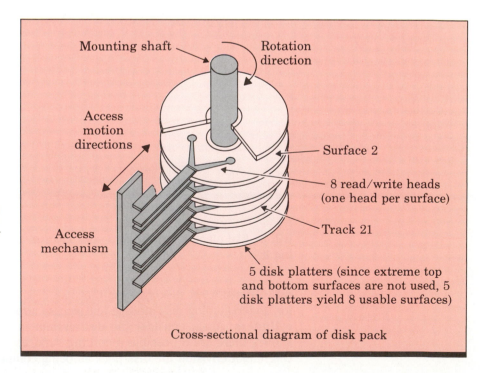

FIGURE 5-4

A movable access mechanism. Each read/write head is assigned to a particular disk surface. As the mounting shaft spins the disks, the comblike access mechanism moves the heads in or out between the disks to read or write data on the tracks. On most systems, all the heads move together. Thus, if you need to retrieve data from track 21 on surface 2, all the read/write heads must move together to track 21. At that point, the head assigned to surface 2 will read the data. Only one head may be actively reading or writing at any given time.

Mounting shaft

Rotation direction

Access motion directions

Access mechanism

Surface 2

8 read/write heads (one head per surface)

Track 21

5 disk platters (since extreme top and bottom surfaces are not used, 5 disk platters yield 8 usable surfaces)

Cross-sectional diagram of disk pack

FIGURE 5-5

The space between a disk and a read/write head compared with a smoke particle and a human hair. A human hair or even a smoke particle, if present on a fast-spinning hard-disk surface, can damage both the surface and the read/write head.

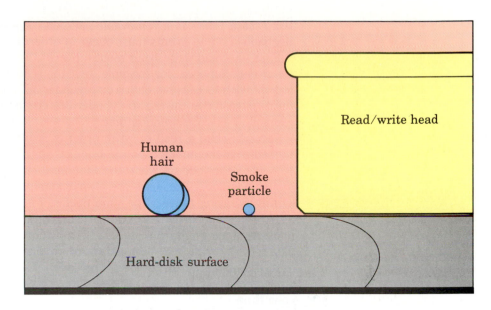

centric cylinders, each consisting of 8 tracks, as illustrated in Figure 5-6. Outer cylinders fit over the inner ones like sleeves. Each cylinder is equivalent to a track position to which the heads on the access mechanism can move. With a movable access mechanism, all the read/write heads are positioned on the same cylinder when data are read from or written to one of the tracks on that cylinder.

FIGURE 5-6

The cylinder concept. To envision a particular cylinder, think of pushing an actual cylinder such as a tin can downward through the same track in each disk in the pack. In this example, cylinder 357 is made up of track 357 on surfaces 1 through 8.

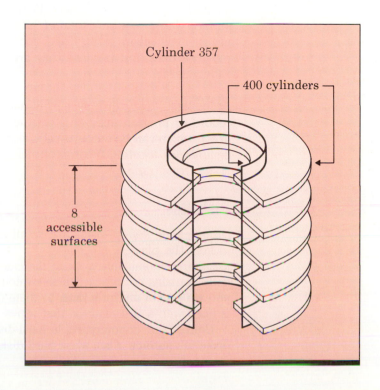

Disk Access Time. In a removable-pack disk system with a movable access mechanism, three events must occur in order to access data.

First, the read/write head must move to the cylinder on which the data are stored. Suppose, for example, that the read/write head is on cylinder 5 and we wish to retrieve data from cylinder 36. For us to do this, the mechanism must move inward to cylinder 36. The time required for this task is referred to as *access motion time*.

Second, when a read or write order is issued, the heads usually are not aligned over the position on the track on which the desired data are stored. So some delay occurs while the mounting shaft rotates the disks into the proper position. (The disks are always spinning whether or not reading or writing is taking place.) The time needed for completing this alignment is called *rotational delay*.

Third, once the read/write head is positioned over the correct data, the data must be read from disk and transferred to the computer (or transferred from the computer and written onto disk). This last step is known as *data movement time*. The sum of these three components is known as **disk access time.**

To minimize disk access time on a system such as the one depicted in Figure 5-4, related data should be stored on the same cylinder. This strategy sharply reduces access motion time. For example, if we need to store 500 records, and we can place 100 records on a track (requiring 5 tracks), we will do better to select 5 tracks on the same cylinder rather than on different ones. Thus, if we store the 500 records on cylinder 235, we need only one movement of the access mechanism to reach all 500 records.

Access motion time can be eliminated entirely by acquiring a disk system with a *fixed access mechanism*. These mechanisms have a read/write head for each track on every surface. Eight accessible surfaces and 400 tracks per surface would require a total of 3,200 read/write heads mounted onto the 8 access-mechanism arms. Fixed access mechanisms are much faster than movable ones, but because they are much more expensive, they are less widely used.

Addressing. Every disk system is *addressable*. This means that each data record or program may be stored and later accessed at a unique *disk address,* which can be automatically determined by the computer system. Procedures for locating records on disk are discussed in the section entitled "Data Organization."

Diskettes

Diskettes, or *floppy disks,* are small, round platters encased in a plastic jacket. The platters are made of a tough Mylar plastic and coated with a magnetizable substance. As in the case of hard disks, each side of the diskette contains concentric tracks, which are encoded with 0- and 1-bits when you write data and programs to them (refer back to Figure 5-1). The jacket is lined with a soft material that wipes the disk clean as it spins.

Unlike their counterparts in hard-disk systems, read/write heads touch a diskette's surface. Also, while hard disks often spin continuously even when

FIGURE 5-7

Diskettes. Despite the fact that 3½-inch diskettes have become today's preferred standard on microcomputer systems, 5¼-inch diskettes continue to enjoy wide use.

not in use, a diskette spins only when a read or write command is issued to its drive. Both of these facts, as well as their removability and flexible surface, account for the diskette's relatively slow rate of speed (400 to 600 rpm) and lengthy access time.

Types of Diskettes. There are dozens of types of diskettes commercially available. If one were to cite a single property, however, that most distinguishes one of these products from another, that property would likely be *size.*

Diskettes are widely available in three sizes (diameters)—3½ inches, 5¼ inches, and 8 inches—as shown in Figure 5-7. Historically, the 8-inch diskettes came along first, then, respectively, their 5¼-inch and 3½-inch counterparts. The 8-inch and 5¼-inch diskettes are encased in flexible, plastic-coated, cardboard jackets, whereas the 3½-inch diskettes are contained in rugged plastic cases that can fit into a shirt pocket. Eight-inch diskettes are more commonly used with small minicomputers and 5¼-inch and 3½-inch sizes with microcomputer systems. Strange as it may seem, 3½-inch diskettes can store more data than 5¼-inch ones.

Despite their small size, diskettes can store a respectable amount of data. Common capacities are 360 kilobytes for 5¼-inch diskettes and 720 kilobytes, 800 kilobytes, or 1.44 megabytes for 3½-inch diskettes. A 360-kilobyte diskette can store over 100 typewritten pages of information; thus, 3½-inch diskettes can store about 400 pages. *Megafloppies*—diskettes that can carry 2, 4, or 10 megabytes of data—are also available, although not commonly found in practice. It is highly possible that the next generation of microcomputers will use a megafloppy format.

To protect data, diskettes also contain a write-protect notch or square (see Figure 5-8). This prevents the user from accidentally writing on the disk. Covering the notch on 5¼-inch diskettes makes it impossible to write on the surface. The convention on 3½-inch and 8-inch diskettes is the opposite: Exposing the notch or square makes writing impossible.

Other Features. Besides their availability in several diameters, diskettes have many other important, distinguishing characteristics.

First, a diskette can be soft-sectored or hard-sectored. As you will see later, **sectors** divide a diskette into manageable, pie-shaped pieces. If you buy a *soft-sectored* diskette, you can use your computer system to sector (that is, *format*) the diskette for you. A *hard-sectored* diskette is already presectored for a specific computer system. Hard-sectored diskettes are faster but more expensive. Most diskettes sold today offer the flexibility of soft-sectoring, because computers and their operating systems differ widely with respect to sectoring requirements.

Second, diskettes differ with respect to the maximum number of bits they can store. For instance, *double-sided* diskettes, which can store data on both sides, obviously can hold twice as much data as *single-sided* ones. Most diskettes sold today are double-sided. Also, some diskettes have 40 tracks per side and others 80. Furthermore, some diskettes pack data more tightly than do others. For example, 5¼-inch diskettes are sold as *single-density*

FIGURE 5-8

5¼-inch and 3½-inch diskettes compared. (a) In a 5¼-inch diskette, the recording window is always open, meaning the disk surface is constantly exposed. (b) In a 3½-inch diskette, the recording window exposes the disk surface only when the shutter mechanism is slid to the left, which happens during reading and writing operations. In addition to offering this improved design feature, having a more rugged cover, and being a more compact size, 3½-inch diskettes can store more data than can 5¼-inch diskettes.

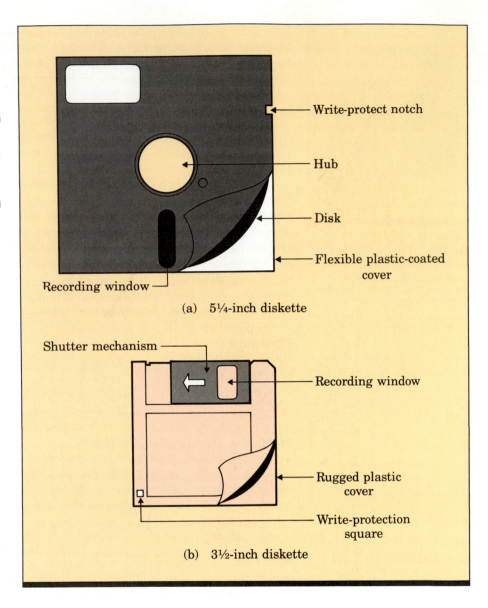

(a)   5¼-inch diskette

(b)   3½-inch diskette

(3,200 bits per inch as measured along the innermost track), *double-density* (6,400 bits per inch), and *quad-density* (12,800 bits per inch).

The most important fact to keep in mind with respect to data densities is that diskette drives are built to accommodate specific types of diskettes. Thus, a 40-track drive is designed for 40-track diskettes, a single-sided drive for single-sided diskettes, and so on. Also, more recent diskette drives usually can accommodate certain earlier diskette designs. For example, the 80-track IBM PC AT drives can read both 80-track diskettes and the older, 40-track diskettes used with the earlier IBM PC. Conversely, however, the older IBM PC drives cannot read the newer 80-track diskettes.

Sectoring on Diskettes. Computer systems differ in the number of sectors into which they divide, or format, a disk. For example, diskettes formatted with IBM and similar computer systems commonly are formatted into 8, 9, 15, or 18 sectors depending on the type of diskette and operating system used. Typically there are 512 bytes per sector. On the Apple Macintosh line of computers, which use 3½-inch diskettes, the number of sectors varies on a single disk. The outermost 16 tracks have 12 sectors each, the next 16 tracks have 11 sectors, the next 16 have 10 sectors, and so forth (see Figure 5-9).

Formatting a diskette organizes it into addressable storage locations, as Figure 5-9 illustrates. For instance, let's assume the diskette in Figure 5-9a has 40 tracks, as do most disks used with the IBM PC, and the computer system divides the diskette into 9 sectors, as shown. Formatting the diskette causes it to be divided into nine pie-shaped sectors, 0 through 8. Because the diskette has 40 tracks, this results in $9 \times 40 = 360$ addressable storage locations per side.

A **file directory** on the diskette, which the computer system automatically maintains, keeps track of the contents of each location. This directory shows the name of each diskette file, its size, and the sector in which it begins. On many microcomputer systems, a FORMAT command is used to format the diskette and a diskette is not usable for storage unless it has been formatted.

Using Diskettes. To use a diskette, the operator inserts it into a device called a *diskette drive* (see Figure 5-10). When using 5¼-inch diskette drives, the operator must manually shut the drive door before the diskette can be accessed. Drives for 3½-inch diskettes do not contain a door as such; instead, the operator just inserts the diskette into the appropriate slot. In both cases, there is only one correct way to insert the diskette into the drive.

While the diskette is rotating, the read/write heads access tracks through the recording window. While the indicator light for a drive is on, meaning that the read/write heads are accessing the diskette in the drive, you must not try to remove the diskette.

Caring for Diskettes. Diskettes may look like inert slabs of plastic, but they are extremely sensitive items and must be cared for accordingly. For instance, never touch an exposed diskette surface or bend the diskette in any way. Also, keep the diskette away from magnetic objects, motors, stereo speakers, and extreme temperatures. Furthermore, never subject the diskette to pressure, say, by using a ballpoint pen to write something on an attached label.

Hard Disks for Small Computers

Small computers—such as microcomputers and low-end minicomputers—often employ nonremovable Winchester disks. **Winchester disk** systems consist of rigid metal platters that are tiered on a mounting shaft in the

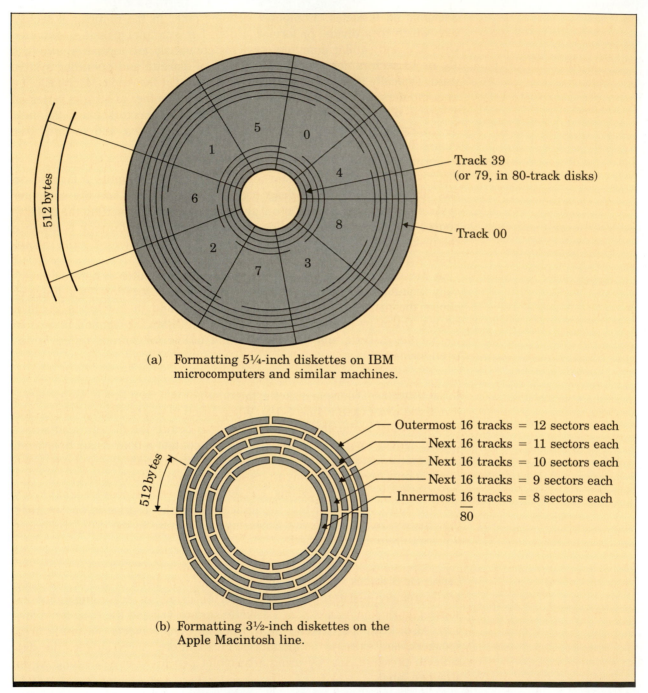

(a) Formatting 5¼-inch diskettes on IBM microcomputers and similar machines.

Track 39 (or 79, in 80-track disks)

Track 00

512 bytes

(b) Formatting 3½-inch diskettes on the Apple Macintosh line.

512 bytes

Outermost 16 tracks = 12 sectors each
Next 16 tracks = 11 sectors each
Next 16 tracks = 10 sectors each
Next 16 tracks = 9 sectors each
Innermost 16 tracks = 8 sectors each
80

FIGURE 5-9

Formatting (sectoring) a diskette. (a) IBM microcomputers and similar machines use the same number of sectors on every track with both 3½- and 5¼-inch diskettes. (b) The Apple Macintosh line of computers uses a variable sectoring scheme, packing more data onto the longer, outer tracks.

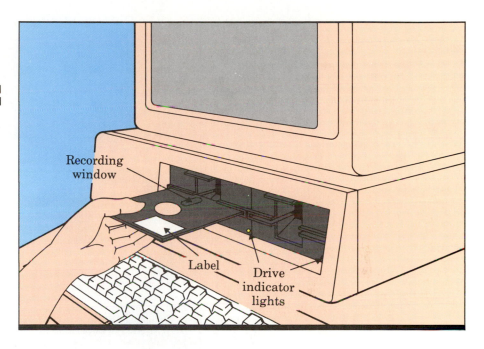

FIGURE 5-10

Inserting a diskette into a drive.
Diskettes correctly fit into the drive
only one way—usually with the label
up and the recording window toward
the drive door, as shown.

Recording
window

Label

Drive
indicator
lights

same way as disks accompanying larger computers, discussed earlier. However, these disks are hermetically sealed in the storage unit along with the
access mechanism containing the read/write heads. Because the storage unit
is completely sealed and free from the air contamination that plagues removable-pack hard-disk systems, Winchester disks need not go through an
air filtration procedure before they are brought online. Also, they result in
fewer head crashes if maintained properly.

Winchester disks are used on both small and large computer systems. On
larger computer systems—where Winchesters are often referred to as *fixed
disks* or *sealed-pack disks*—the disks are commonly 14 or 8 inches in diameter. Companies that don't want to handle removable packs find these systems attractive, but they face buying additional disk units if they need more
storage. Also, they must have room in their data centers for the additional
disk cabinets.

Although many microcomputer systems still use diskettes heavily, Winchester disk systems are rapidly gaining in popularity and, in most organizations, becoming a necessity. In the microcomputing world, Winchesters
are commonly referred to as *hard disks*. They are especially appropriate
when an organization needs greater amounts of online storage and faster
access to programs and data than diskettes can provide. So if you have a
40-megabyte Winchester unit, you have the storage equivalent of about 100
double-sided/double-density 5¼-inch diskettes online the minute you turn
on the power. Also, you don't have to constantly shuffle diskettes in and out
of disk drives.

FIGURE 5-11

An internal Winchester disk unit. Winchester (hard-disk) systems for microcomputers are most commonly found in capacities of 10 to 40 megabytes. Capacities of 100 megabytes or more are also available.

Winchester units for microcomputers are most commonly found in capacities of roughly 10, 20, 30, and 40 megabytes. Devices that store 100 megabytes or more are also available. For microcomputers, Winchesters are most widely available in 8-, 5¼-, and 3½-inch diameters. The IBM PS/2 Model 50, to give just one example, uses a 20-megabyte Winchester disk unit consisting of two 5¼-inch disks.

Winchester disk units on microcomputer systems can be internal or external. An *internal* Winchester system is fitted into your computer's system unit in the space normally occupied by one of the diskette drives (see Figure 5-11). An *external* system is a detached hardware unit that has its own power supply. Many external systems also have a built-in slot for a tape cartridge, which can be used to back up important programs and data. On larger computer systems, Winchester disk units are always external.

Sectoring. Winchester disk systems, like those that accompany the IBM PC AT, PS/2, and similar computers, use a sectoring scheme similar to that for diskettes to store data. On the 44MB Winchesters available with some PS/2 models, for instance, tracks are broken into 17 sectors. On each of the 4 recordable surfaces, there is a total of 732 tracks. In the language of hard disks, the tracks on these surfaces trace out 732 cylinders.

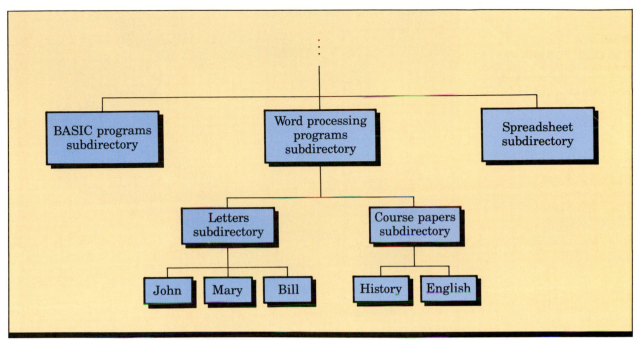

FIGURE 5-12
Organizing files into subdirectories.

Subdirectories. Because hard disks have large storage capacities, files commonly are organized hierarchically into *subdirectories*. For example, as Figure 5-12 shows, you can store all of your BASIC programs in one subdirectory, word-processed documents in another subdirectory, and so forth. Moreover, you can further divide these subdirectories. As shown in Figure 5-12, you can organize your word processing subdirectory by putting letters and school papers into two lower subdirectories. If you so wish, you can add several additional levels of subdirectories.

Later, when you want to access a file in any subdirectory, you must specify the path through the subdirectories to get to the file, for example,

C:\WORD\LETTER\MARY

Here the hard disk is the *C* drive and WORD and LETTER are the names of the two subdirectories on the path to a letter named MARY. On most microcomputer systems, the *A* and *B* drive designations are reserved for floppy drives.

Partitioning. *Partitioning* a hard disk enables you to divide a hard disk into separate disk drives, such as *D, E, F,* and so forth. You can also change the number and size of the partitions at any time, although doing so will destroy any data in the partitions. Thus, you have to download any affected data onto diskettes or tape first and then load the data back onto the repartitioned hard disk.

FIGURE 5-13

A hard card. Hard cards are popular with users who are looking for a compact alternative to the conventional hard disk.

One reason for partitioning a hard disk is to enable you to use different operating systems on it, say, PC-DOS, OS/2, and UNIX. Each operating system has its own method of formatting and managing disk space. By assigning each operating system to a different partition, you avoid the problem of having an operating system deal with a partition that works in a manner foreign to it.

Other Types of Magnetic Disks

Although Winchester disks dominate the hard-disk scene for small computers, there are alternatives. Two of these are the hard card and the cartridge disk.

Hard Cards. An increasingly popular alternative to the Winchester disk in the microcomputer hard-disk marketplace is the hard card (see Figure 5-13). **Hard cards** are hard disks that are configured onto an add-in board. As with any other board, the hard card fits into a slot in the computer's system unit. The card contains both the disk and the interface circuitry necessary for dealing with the CPU. Although relatively expensive, this type of hard-disk alternative is ideal for people who need hard-disk speed and capacity in a limited space.

Cartridge Disk. Cartridge disk devices are commonly found on microcomputer and minicomputer systems. **Cartridge disk** devices used on microcomputer systems are external hardware units that accept small, removable high-capacity disk cartridges (see Figure 5-14). The high-capacity disk is

FIGURE 5-14

Microcomputer cartridge disk. Cartridge disk provides a storage alternative with the capacity of a conventional hard disk and the removability of a diskette.

packaged into a square case (i.e., the cartridge) to protect the disk's contents. The operator inserts a cartridge into a cartridge drive in a manner similar to inserting a diskette into a diskette drive. Cartridge disks are commonly 3½ inches in diameter and have a capacity of about 10 to 40 megabytes. Their biggest pluses are large storage capacity and, due to their removability, backup and security. The biggest negative is cost—the disk unit can cost $2,000 to $3,000 and the cartridges about $100 apiece.

Cartridge disks also exist for minicomputers. The "removable pack," or disk cartridge, usually consists of a single 14-inch platter encased in an opaque plastic shell (see Figure 5-15). Because cartridge disks have only one platter they have less data-carrying capacity than do multiplatter packs.

RAM Disk and Cache Disk

RAM disk and cache disk are two strategies for creatively using RAM to compensate for the access-speed differences between primary memory and secondary storage. Both methods overcome the slow speeds involved with fetching instructions or data from disk, and both can be implemented inexpensively under certain conditions.

RAM Disk. **RAM disk,** sometimes referred to as *electronic disk, E-disk,* or *disk emulation,* is a storage alternative in which the computer's operating system is "tricked" into thinking it is dealing with secondary storage when in fact it is dealing with primary memory.

When computer systems process programs or data files, typically only a limited number of program instructions or data records are in primary memory at any given time. When more instructions or data are needed, the

FIGURE 5-15

Minicomputer cartridge disk. Most cartridge disks for minis consist of a single hard-disk platter in a plastic casing.

operating system must fetch them from disk. However, if your system has enough RAM to store the entire program or data file, you can use an emulation package to load it into RAM and point the system to this part of RAM every time it would go to the disk to fetch additional program commands or data. Thus, the emulation software essentially tricks the system into thinking it's dealing with the disk drive when it actually is dealing with RAM. Such a technique can boost the speed of applications processing considerably.

RAM disk is implemented in a number of ways. For instance, a vendor selling such a product might offer it as a plain-vanilla software routine, available through coded instructions on a multifunction board or through a disk-based program. The routine enables you to "tell" your computer system how many bytes of primary memory you want to set aside as RAM disk. This inexpensive approach to RAM disk is commonly used on microcomputer systems.

Another vendor selling a RAM-disk product might offer it as a dedicated add-in board with a built-in, RAM-like static memory that can be established as RAM disk. Although this second approach is more expensive than the first, it affords the luxury of not using up primary memory and can provide access speeds 50 to 200 times faster than that of rotating disks.

Cache Disk. **Cache disk** refers to a strategy whereby, during any disk access, program or data contents in neighboring disk areas are also fetched and transported to RAM. For instance, if only a single data record needs to be read, a cache-disk feature may read the entire track on which the record is located. The theory behind cache disk is that neighboring program commands and data will likely have to be read later anyway, so one can save disk accesses by bringing those commands or data into RAM early so that they can be accessed more quickly. Thus, caching saves time and wear and tear on the disk unit. In portable computers, it can also extend battery life.

Cache disk, like RAM disk, can be implemented in several ways. One method is to buy an add-in board called a cache card, which contains a semiconductor memory. Some of these memories are five to ten times faster than conventional RAM while costing a fraction of the price of registers. Another method is to acquire a disk controller (the board that manages a hard-disk or diskette unit) that contains a cache-disk feature. Still another possibility is to buy a software routine (say, as part of an operating system) that will set up a portion of RAM into a cache area. Whichever option one chooses, the cache-disk feature will intercept and process every disk-access command the operating system issues.

MAGNETIC TAPE

For years, **magnetic tape** has been one of the most prominent secondary storage alternatives. Although less popular than disk, it is still widely used on all sizes of computer systems. The tapes often are stored either on detachable reels or in cartridges.

FIGURE 5-16

Magnetic tape. Shown here is an IBM 3480 tape cartridge and, underneath, a conventional IBM 3420 10½-inch tape reel.

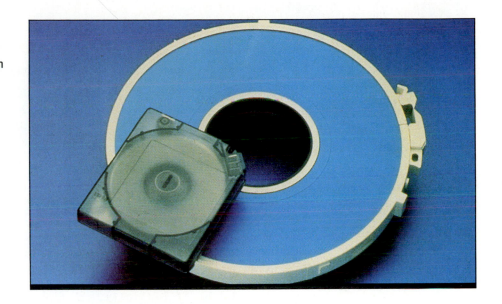

Detachable-reel tapes are commonly ½-inch wide, made of plastic Mylar, and coated with a magnetizable substance. A standard reel diameter is 10½ inches, although smaller "minireels" are also quite common. A typical 2,400-foot-reel can pack data at densities as high as 6,250 bytes per inch. When such a tape is read, it can transfer more data in one second than many secretaries could type in a month—and error free.

Cartridge tapes are housed in a small plastic casing. On microcomputer systems, cartridges are commonly used to back up the contents of a hard disk. These tapes can have huge capacities and work very fast. A ¼-inch tape up to 1,000 feet long can hold 10, 20, 40, or 60 megabytes of data and copy the contents of a disk in a matter of minutes. Recently cartridges using *helical-scan* recording methods, which store data at an angle to the edge of the tape rather than perpendicular to it, have permitted storage capacities in the 2GB range. These super-high-capacity tapes can take an hour or longer to back up a hard disk. Cartridge tapes designed specifically for disk backup are sometimes referred to as *streaming tapes*.

The IBM 3480 tape storage system, which is used with the IBM 3090 series of mainframe computers, also uses cartridge tapes. These tapes have twice the number of tracks as traditional detachable-reel tapes and a storage capacity of 200 megabytes. In contrast to streaming tapes, which are intended solely for backup, the IBM 3480 cartridges are designed for general use, including both regular input/output processing operations and backup.

The discussion that follows in this section is based principally on the nine-track, detachable-reel tapes that have been used with mainframes and minicomputers for years. These tape systems are still the most prevalent in the marketplace. Nonetheless, many of the principles described here apply to cartridge tapes as well.

Figure 5-16 shows a tape cartridge compared with a conventional, detachable-reel tape.

FIGURE 5-17

Magnetic tape units. This photo compares the sizes of IBM 3480 tape units (foreground), which use cartridges, and 3420 tape units (background), which use detachable reels.

Processing Tapes

A tape must be mounted onto an online **tape unit** (see Figure 5-17) to be processed. Detachable-reel tape units are about the size of a common household refrigerator. The *supply reel* on the unit contains the tape that is to be read from or written to by the computer system. The *take-up reel* collects the tape as it unwinds from the supply reel. As it is processed, the tape passes by a read/write head, which reads data from the tape or records data on it. On many devices, the tape is allowed to droop in a vacuum chamber so that it will not break if the two reels move at different speeds. After processing, the tape is rewound onto the supply reel and removed from the unit. The take-up reel never leaves the unit.

Storing Data on Tape

Figure 5-18 shows how data are stored on nine-track magnetic tape. Data may be coded using the eight-bit byte of either EBCDIC or ASCII-8 depending on the equipment used. Magnetized spots of iron oxide represent 1s; non-magnetized spots represent 0s. The tape contains a track for each bit of information in a character, plus an additional parity track to allow the computer system to check for transmission errors. The tape unit reads across the nine tracks to identify the character represented in each column. Recall

FIGURE 5-18

Storing data on nine-track magnetic tape. Shown here is the number 6 represented in EBCDIC (11110110, or 111110110 with the odd-parity track). In the shaded cross-section of the tape, the magnetized spot representing the 1-bit is shown by a vertical mark in the appropriate track. The 0-bit is characterized by the absence of a mark.

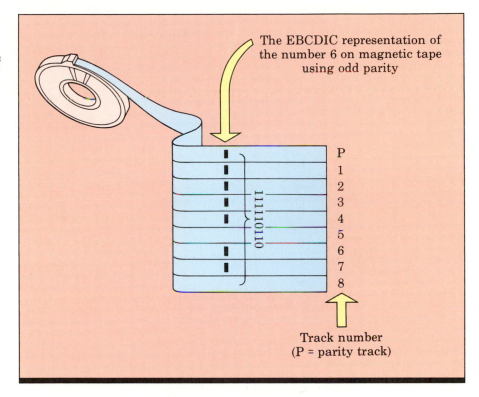

The EBCDIC representation of the number 6 on magnetic tape using odd parity

Track number
(P = parity track)

from Chapter 4 that in odd-parity machines, all 1-bits add up to an odd number and in even-parity machines to an even number. An incorrect sum indicates an error. The parity bit is included with the byte representation of each character when it is placed onto tape.

A magnetic tape is basically a long, narrow strip. Thus, when the records in a data file are stored on it, they must be alongside one another in sequence. The sequence often is determined by a **key field,** such as customer ID number, which can be ordered numerically. Every record's key field generally has a different value.

If you want to read a particular record from a tape, you can't go directly to it. Instead, you must pass through all the records that precede it. In a sense, this is similar to the fast forwarding you do on a music tape when the tune you want to hear is in the middle of it. Retrieving records in the order in which they are stored is called *sequential access,* and organizing data in sequence by a key field is called *sequential organization.* We will talk more about data access and organization later in the chapter.

Blocking Records

Tape units are not purely electronic like the CPU. They have moving parts that must stop and start. Because all records read from tape must pass by the read/write heads at the same speed, some "dead space" must exist be-

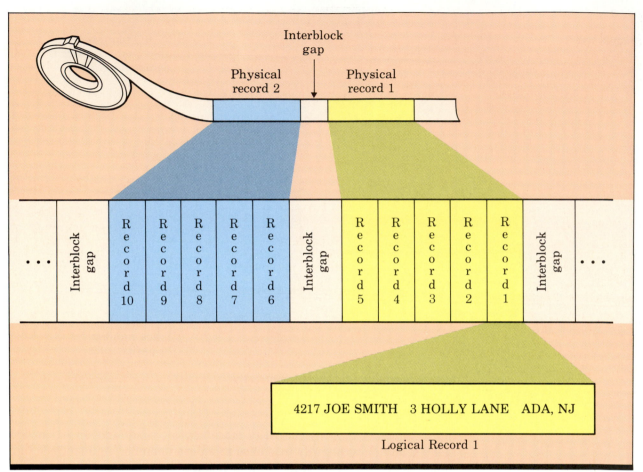

FIGURE 5-19

Blocking records on magnetic tape. Logical records are blocked into physical records. The diagram illustrates a blocking factor of 5. In other words, five logical records form a single physical record. Usually much larger blocking factors are employed to save space.

fore and after each record to allow the tape to speed up and slow down between starts and stops. These spaces are called **interblock gaps,** or *interrecord gaps.* Unfortunately, each interblock gap occupies about ½ inch of tape, while a single record may use only ¹⁄₂₀ inch. This means that a tape conceivably could consist of about 10 percent data and 90 percent dead space.

To correct this problem, a solution called **blocking** is often employed. Individual records, called **logical records,** are grouped into larger units of fixed size, called **physical records.** The number of logical records in each physical record is the *blocking factor.* If each physical record contains 10 logical records, the blocking factor is 10. An interblock gap is then placed between each physical record. This technique is illustrated in Figure 5-19.

Besides saving space, blocking permits faster processing. Computer systems that allow blocking contain special high-speed memory areas within the computer unit called **buffers.** Buffers used for blocking data function

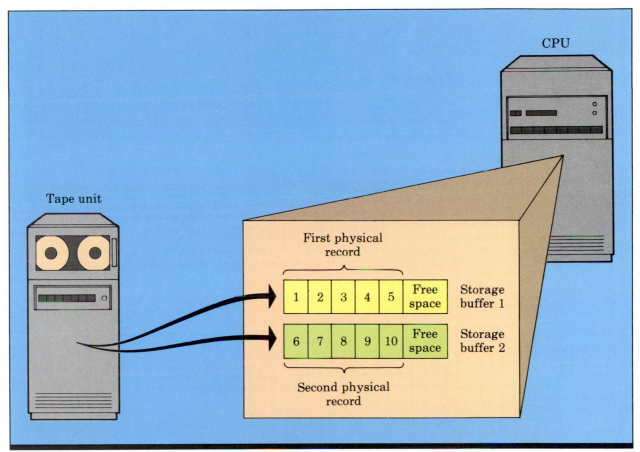

FIGURE 5-20

Buffering of physical records in storage. Suppose records are blocked in the manner suggested in Figure 5-19. The computer's systems software initially places the first physical record in buffer 1 and the second in buffer 2. All READ instructions in an applications program retrieve data from these buffers, where the computer can retrieve logical records faster than if they were in secondary storage. When the first buffer has been exhausted, reading shifts to the physical record in the second buffer. Meanwhile, the third physical record is loaded into the first buffer.

much like the registers in the CPU: They stage data in a fast-access (or "waiting") area just before processing. As the tape is processed, physical records are placed into the buffers, as shown in Figure 5-20. Often there are two buffers. Whenever a program issues a READ instruction, the logical record can be retrieved directly from the buffer rather than from the remote tape unit, which must spin and read the tape in response to each request. Because the buffers are entirely electronic like the rest of the computer unit, data can be retrieved much more rapidly than they could be from the mechanical tape unit. When all the logical records in one buffer have been processed, reading continues in the other buffer. In the meantime, the next physical record on the tape is loaded into the first buffer, writing over the physical record that was stored there before. This process of alternating between the buffers continues until the file is exhausted. Buffers are also

FIGURE 5-21

A magnetic tape with a rubber file-protection ring. When the ring is off the reel, you can read from the tape but you can't write onto it. When the ring is on, you can both read from and write onto the tape.

commonly used for output, batching logical output records before they are written to tape as a physical record.

Protecting Tapes

Tape reels are equipped with safety features that prevent operators from accidentally destroying the contents of the tape. One such device is the *file-protection ring* (see Figure 5-21). When tapes are stored offline, these rings are not mounted on the reel. To write onto any part of the tape, thereby destroying any data already stored there, the operator must insert this ring into the center of the reel. The tapes can be read, however, whether or not the ring is present.

Another device designed to protect tapes is the *internal header label*. This label appears at the beginning of the tape and identifies it. The identifying information in the label is usually generated automatically by the computer system or data-entry device. Thus, if you commanded the computer system to process tape AP-601 and the operator accidentally mounted tape AR-601 instead, no processing would occur. Also, the operator would receive a warning message.

OTHER SECONDARY STORAGE ALTERNATIVES

Magnetic tape and disk systems are by far the most common form of secondary storage. However, a number of other alternatives are possible. In this section, we will discuss the mass storage unit, optical disk storage, and magnetic bubble storage.

Mass Storage Unit

Disk storage units can make large amounts of data available online, but they have limitations. In many systems, disk packs must be manually loaded onto the disk unit, which takes time. Disk systems with nonremovable packs avoid this problem but are limited in the amount of data they can store. For most applications, these drawbacks are not serious. But because the capacity of the largest disk units is only a few billion characters, organizations that must keep massive amounts of data online to the computer have found **mass storage units** extremely useful. A device such as the IBM 3850 mass storage unit can store 472 billion bytes of data, the equivalent of almost 50,000 reels of magnetic tape.

The IBM 3850 consists of 9,440 cylindrical data cells, each capable of storing 50 million bytes of data. Each cell contains a spool of 770 feet of 3-inch magnetic tape. The cells reside in a honeycomb-shaped rack, as Figure 5-22 shows. When the data in a cell must be retrieved, a mechanical arm pulls the correct cell from its container. Next, the tape is unwound, the data are transferred to disk, and processing is performed. All this takes place automatically, without the aid of human operators.

FIGURE 5-22

FIGURE 5-22

Mass storage unit. The honeycombed device shown in the photo stores small, cylindrical cartridges containing magnetic tape. The device shown here, the IBM 3850, has enough memory capacity to store a 100-character record for every person in the world, or, alternatively, as many words as exist in 27 million pages of a typical daily newspaper.

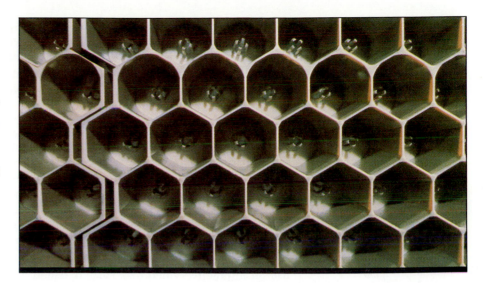

With mass storage, the user sacrifices speed to gain storage capacity. Retrieval of the data cell and transfer of the data to disk may take as long as 15 seconds. Compared with the fraction of a second that elapses during access to disk, 15 seconds is a long time. Therefore, mass storage is feasible only for applications that require enormous online storage and do not need extremely high speed.

Optical Disk Storage

An emerging technology that many expect will have a profound impact on mass storage strategies in the 1990s is the **optical disk.** With this technology, laser beams write and read data at incredible densities, thousands of times finer than the density of a typical magnetic disk. Data are placed onto optical disks with high-intensity laser beams that burn tiny holes into the disks' surface. Then a lower-intensity laser beam reads the data inscribed.

Optical disk systems have recently started to become widely used on microcomputer systems, which, until recently, did not have mass storage available to them. Most optical disk units, such as the one in Figure 5-23, are of the *CD-ROM* (Compact Disk/Read-Only Memory) type; that is, you buy a prerecorded disk and "play" (read) it on the optical disk unit attached to your computer. You cannot write new data to the disk in any way.

There are also systems available that will let you write once to the disk; once written, the data cannot be erased. These are called *WORM* (Write Once, Read Many) disk systems. Since optical disks have very large storage capacities, most users can write to the disk for a year or more before using it up. Optical disk systems that allow you to erase unwanted data have also recently become available.

Today 5¼-inch optical disks can store almost 1 gigabyte of data. Roughly translated, that's close to 1 million pages of text or, alternatively, the contents of approximately 2,500 diskettes. So-called *optical jukeboxes*, which

FIGURE 5-23

Optical disk unit and disk cartridge. The optical disk cartridge shown here can contain up to 200MB of data—over 500 times the amount of data one can store on a 360KB floppy.

offer online access to hundreds of optical disks, also have become available. These devices can store close to 300 billion bytes of data.

Despite the excitement over optical disks, hard disks still have two very important advantages. First, hard disks are much faster; 10 to 15 times faster is not unusual. Second, there's a lot of software around written for hard disks that will have to be modified to work on optical disks.

Video Disk. One type of optical disk that is becoming useful for many types of applications today is the video disk. A **video disk** is a shiny platter that can store text, graphics, video images, and audio signals. These data are stored on 54,000 microscopic tracks etched onto the disk surface. Today a track on the surface of a video disk can be accessed in about three seconds. Most of the video disk systems currently marketed are of the CD-ROM type.

Video disk systems are now used in a variety of settings. At the Dayton Hudson Corporation department store chain, for example, customers can use an interactive video disk system, called a *kiosk,* to buy furniture. Using a touch screen, customers can select furniture and see it in a variety of room settings. All of the appropriate frames are stored on the video disk, and the computer searches for specific frames to display based on the customer input.

A video disk system that helps realtors conduct faster searches for homes and properties has been developed. The client describes the type of home wanted—say, three bedrooms, fireplace, five acres, and a price under $80,000. The realtor types these data into the video disk system, and presto—pictures of listed homes and facts about them are available to the display screen.

Video disk applications don't stop there. Video disk has also been used by car makers to show their lines, by travel agents to interest clients in resorts, by various makers of consumer goods to display their wares, and for training purposes (see Figure 5-24). In the future, say industry observers, many kiosks will be equipped with video disk components that will make consumers much less dependent on clerks and showrooms. When a desired item flashes on the display screen, the customer can insert a credit card and order it immediately.

Magnetic Bubble Storage

Magnetic bubble storage is a storage technology in which thousands of magnetized bubbles, each a fraction of the diameter of a human hair, are arranged on a thin film of magnetic material. The presence of a bubble in a location represents a 1-bit and its absence a 0-bit. Bubble storage often is packaged in chip form.

During the late 1970s, many experts thought magnetic bubble devices would replace disks as the major secondary storage medium in computer systems. This optimism was grounded in the fact that magnetic bubble units are static, thus requiring no moving parts. In contrast, disk units generally employ spinning platters and movable access heads. Static assemblies generally are much faster and more reliable than nonstatic ones. So far, bubble

FIGURE 5-24

A video disk kiosk. The "JeansScreen," available at several retail stores, enables customers to page through an electronic catalog of Levi's jeans, jackets, and shirts and view stories featuring jeans products. If the desired product isn't available in the store, the customer can order it from the kiosk and expect home delivery in two weeks. Kiosks such as these greatly extend a store's "inventory," and many observers expect them to eventually have a revolutionary impact on shopping.

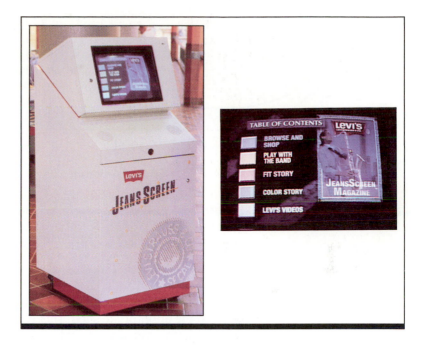

devices have failed to live up to expectations, largely because their cost is still high relative to that of disks.

Despite their apparent failure to capture the general market for secondary storage devices, magnetic bubbles are popular components in several niche markets. They are often used as memory units in terminals, desktop computers, robots, and communications devices.

DATA ORGANIZATION

When a computer system is instructed to use data or programs residing in secondary storage, it first must be able to find the materials. The process of retrieving data and programs in storage is called **data access.** Arranging data for efficient retrieval is called **data organization.**

As we have seen, a major difference between, say, tape and disk is that data on tape can be accessed only sequentially, while data on disk can be retrieved both sequentially and in a direct (random) fashion. With sequential access, the records in a file can be retrieved only in the same sequence in which they are physically stored. With direct, or random, access, the time needed to fetch a record is relatively independent of its location in secondary storage.

The need for certain data access methods necessarily dictates the choice of ways to organize data files. Let's consider a practical example. Most book libraries are organized with card indexes ordered by title, author, and subject, so you can retrieve books directly. To locate a particular book, you

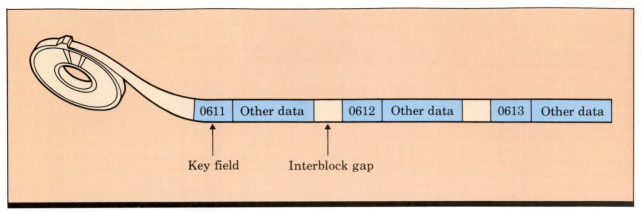

FIGURE 5-25
Sequential organization of records on tape.

simply look under the book's title in the index, find its call number, and go directly to the appropriate shelf. This type of organization is loosely referred to as an indexed organization. Indexed organization schemes facilitate direct access.

However, suppose there were no card indexes and books were organized alphabetically by title on shelves from the first shelf to the last (say, the 758th shelf). With this sequential organization of books, it would take you much longer to retrieve the title you wanted—although you would get a lot of exercise. As you can see, sequential organization does not permit straightforward access to a specific book.

Data organization on computers works in a similar fashion. First, you decide on the type of access you need—direct, sequential, or both. Then you organize the data in a way that will minimize the time needed to retrieve them with the access method selected.

There are many ways to organize data. Here we will describe three—sequential, indexed-sequential, and direct organization.

Sequential Organization. In a file having a **sequential organization,** records follow one another in a predetermined sequence. Sequentially organized files generally are ordered by a key field or fields, such as ID number. Thus, if a four-digit ID number is the key field being used to order the file, the record belonging to, say, ID number 0612 will be stored after number 0611 but before number 0613 (see Figure 5-25).

Now that you have an idea of what sequential organization is, let's see how it is used in information processing. Many companies update customer balances and prepare bills at the end of the month. Such an operation is known as a *sequential update*. Two data files are used. The *master file* normally contains the customer's ID number, the amount owed at the beginning of the month, and additional information about the customer. This file is sorted by the key field, customer ID number, and records are arranged in ascending sequence—from the lowest ID number to the highest. The *trans-*

action file contains all the transactions made during the month by old customers, who appear in the master file, and by new customers, who do not. Transactions might include purchases and payments. Like the master file, the transaction file is ordered in ascending sequence by customer ID number.

In a sequential update, the two files are processed together in the manner shown in Figure 5-26. The sequential-update program reads a record from each file. If the key fields match, the operation specified in the transaction file is performed. Note that in Figure 5-26, the key fields of the first records in each file match. Thus, record 101 is updated to the updated customer master file. For example, if the transaction file shows that customer 101 bought a toaster, data on this purchase are added to the master file. Next, both files are "rolled forward" to the next records. Here the program observes that customer 102 is not in the master file, since the next master file record after 101 is 103. Therefore, this must be a new customer, and the program will create a new record for customer 102 in the updated master file. At this point, only the transaction file will be rolled forward, to customer 103. The program now observes that this record matches the one to which it is currently pointing in the master file. However, the transaction file indicates that 103 is a new customer. Hence, there appears to be an inconsistency, since the master file contains only old customers. The program makes no entry in the updated master file but sends information about this transaction to the error report.

The processing continues in this manner until both files are exhausted. The processing is sequential because the computer processes the records in both files in the order in which they physically appear.

Indexed-Sequential Organization. Indexed-sequential organization is a way of organizing data for both sequential and direct access. This type of organization requires disk, since tapes can't provide direct access. Records are ordered on the disk by key field. Also, several indexes are created to locate these records later. These indexes work similarly to those in a phone book. For example, if the top of a phone book page reads "Alexander—Ashton," you'll know to look for the phone number of Amazon Sewer Service on that page. When implemented on a computer, as Figure 5-27 shows, such indexes permit rapid access to records.

Many computer systems have systems programs that help programmers set up indexes and indexed-sequential-organized files painlessly. As records are added to or deleted from a file, the systems software automatically adds them to or deletes them from the disk and updates the index. Since the records remain organized sequentially on the disk, the file can be processed sequentially at any time.

Direct Organization. Although indexed files are suitable for many applications, the process of finding disk addresses through index searches can be time consuming. Direct-organization schemes have been developed to provide faster direct access.

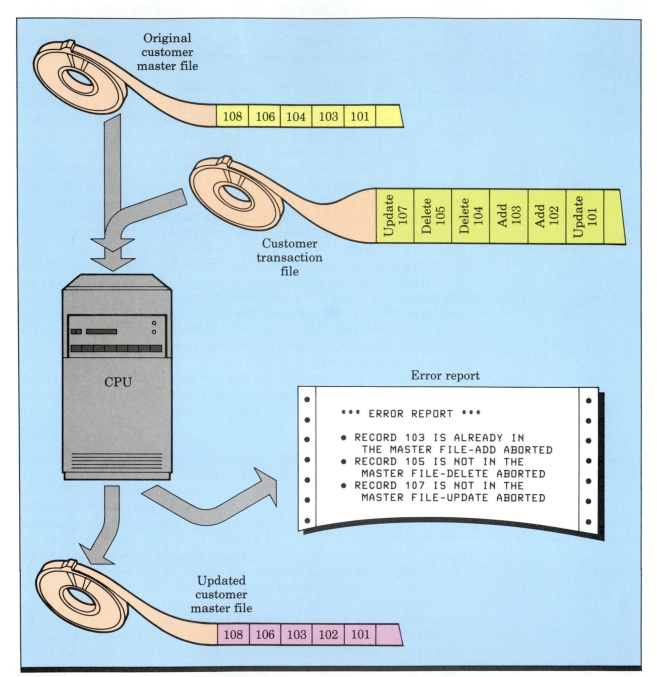

FIGURE 5-26

A sequential update of a master file. Each customer record in the original master file might contain the customer's ID number (the key field), name, address, amount owed, and credit limit. For simplicity, only the key field is shown in the illustration. The transaction file contains a record of each customer transaction. Each record in this file might contain the customer's ID number (the key field), the amount of the purchase or payment, and the type of transaction involved (update, add, or delete). Only the key field and type of transaction are shown in the illustration. As both files are processed together, an updated master file is produced, as well as a printed listing of records that couldn't be processed because of some discrepancy.

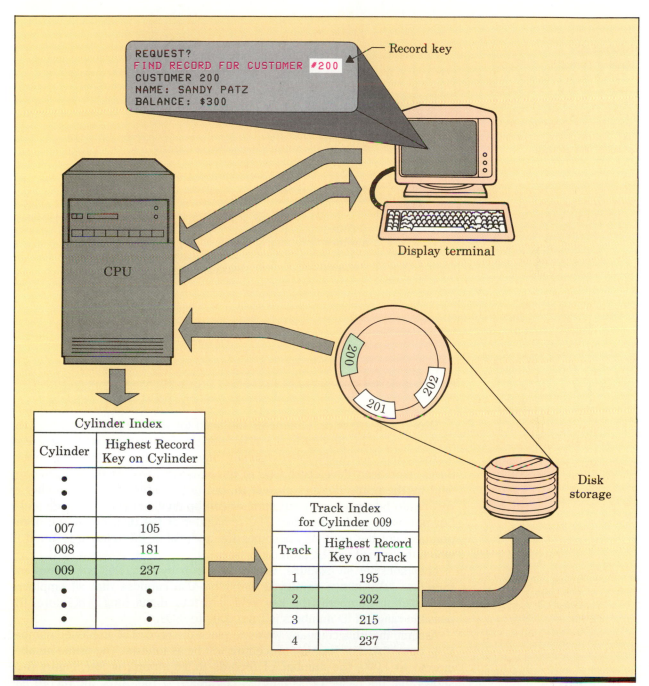

FIGURE 5-27

Indexed-sequential organization. Records are ordered on disk by key, and all record addresses are entered in an index. To process a request to find a record—say record 200—the computer system first searches a cylinder index and then a track index for the record's address. In the cylinder index, it learns that the record is on cylinder 009. The computer system then consults the track index for cylinder 009, where it observes that the record is on track 2 of that cylinder. The access mechanism then proceeds to this track to locate the record.

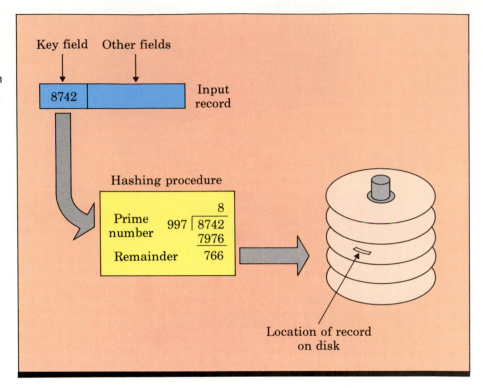

FIGURE 5-28

Hashing illustrated. The CPU follows a hashing procedure to assign a record to a disk address. In this case, the hashing procedure involves dividing the key field by the prime number closest to 1,000— 997. The remainder corresponds to an actual disk address.

Direct organization eliminates the need for an index by translating the record's key field directly into a disk address. This is done with the use of mathematical formulas called *hashing algorithms.* Several hashing procedures have been developed. One of the simplest involves dividing the key field by the prime number closest to, but not greater than, the number of records to be stored. A prime number can be divided evenly by itself and 1 but not by any other number. The remainder of the division by the prime number (not the quotient) becomes the address of the relative location in which the record will be stored.

Let's consider an example. Suppose a company has 1,000 employees and therefore 1,000 active employee numbers. Also suppose that all employee identification numbers (the key field) are four digits long. Therefore, the possible range of ID numbers is from 0000 to 9999.

Assume that this company wants to place the record of employee number 8742 onto disk. The hashing procedure will be as follows. The prime number closest to 1,000, the number of records to be stored, is 997. Figure 5-28 shows that the hashed disk address computes to 766. After the record has been placed at an address corresponding to this number, the computer can retrieve it as needed by applying the hashing procedure to the key field of the record again. Calculation of an address in this manner usually consumes much less time than would a search through one or more indexes.

Hashing procedures are difficult to develop and pose certain problems. For example, it is possible for two or more records to be hashed to the same relative disk location. This, of course, means they will "collide" at their common disk address. When this happens, one record is placed in the computed location and assigned a "pointer" that chains it to the other, which often goes in the available location closest to the hashed address. Good hashing procedures result in few collisions. A detailed discussion of hashing is well beyond the scope of this book.

The disadvantage of direct organization is that since records are not stored sequentially by key, it is impractical to process the records sequentially.

SUMMARY AND KEY TERMS

Secondary storage technologies make it economically feasible to keep large quantities of programs and data online to the CPU. The most common types of secondary storage media are magnetic disk and magnetic tape.

Any secondary storage system involves two physical parts: a peripheral device and an input/output medium. In most systems, media must pass by a **read/write head** in the peripheral device to be read from or written to.

Secondary storage media are **nonvolatile**—that is, when the power to the peripheral device is shut off, the data stored on the medium remain intact. This contrasts with most types of primary memory, which are **volatile.** Also, media on secondary storage devices can be either *removable,* meaning they must be mounted onto the peripheral device every time they are used, or *fixed,* meaning they are permanently mounted, or nonremovable.

Two basic types of access methods are used on secondary storage systems: sequential and direct. With **sequential access,** the records in a file can be retrieved only in the same sequence in which they are physically stored. With **direct,** or **random, access,** records can be retrieved in any sequence.

Magnetic disk is most commonly available in the form of hard disks and diskettes. **Hard disks** consist of rigid platters. **Diskettes,** or *floppy disks,* on the other hand, consist of flexible platters.

The disks used with large computers frequently are 14 inches in diameter. Data are represented in byte form on the concentric **tracks** of each disk surface. Often the same amount of data is stored on each track of a disk to keep the data-transfer rate constant throughout the disk system.

In the disk systems serving larger computers, several platters are usually assembled into a **disk pack.** The disk pack, in turn, is mounted either permanently or temporarily on a **disk unit,** which makes the data on the disks online to the computer. In most systems, a read/write head is assigned to each recordable disk surface. The heads are mounted onto an **access mech-**

anism, which can move them in and out among the concentric tracks to fetch data.

All tracks in the same position on the tiered platters of a disk pack form a **disk cylinder.**

Three primary factors determine the time needed to read from or write to most disks. *Access motion time* is the time required for the access mechanism to reach a particular track. The time needed for the disk to spin to a specific area of a track is known as *rotational delay*. Once located, data must be transferred to or from the disk, a process known as *data movement time*. The sum of these three time components is called **disk access time.**

Diskettes are commonly used with microcomputers and small minicomputers. Diskettes are available in a number of sizes (diameters) and data densities. They also come in double-sided and single-sided form and in soft-sectored and hard-sectored form. **Sectors** divide a floppy into addressable, pie-shaped pieces. The disk's **file directory,** which the computer system maintains automatically, keeps track of the contents at each disk address. A diskette drive works only when the appropriate type of diskette is inserted into it correctly.

Sealed hard-disk units called **Winchester disks,** for many years popular on large computers, are now commonly found on microcomputer systems. Winchesters are faster and have greater data-carrying capacity than diskettes. **Hard cards** and **cartridge disk** are two other hard-disk alternatives for microcomputer systems.

Two strategies for reducing the number of time-consuming disk accesses are RAM disk and cache disk. **RAM disk** is a storage strategy whereby the computer's operating system is "tricked" into thinking it is dealing with secondary storage when in fact it is dealing with primary memory. **Cache disk** refers to a strategy whereby during any disk access, program or data contents in neighboring disk areas are also fetched and transported to RAM.

Magnetic tape often consists of ½-inch-wide plastic Mylar, coated with a magnetizable substance and wound on a 10½-inch-diameter reel. Each character of data is represented in byte form across the tracks in the tape. Many **detachable-reel tapes** contain nine tracks—eight corresponding to the eight bits in a byte and an additional parity track to check for transmission errors. **Cartridge tapes,** in which both supply and take-up reels are enclosed in a plastic case, are also widely available.

In order to be processed by the CPU, the tape must be mounted on a hardware device called a **tape unit.** The drives on the tape unit spin the tape past a read/write head, which either reads from or writes to the tape. Often records are systematically organized on a tape with respect to a **key field,** such as customer ID numbers.

Because the tape unit requires that records pass by the read/write head at a constant speed, **interblock gaps** must be provided on the tape for acceleration and deceleration between records. To minimize the number of these gaps on the tape, a technique called **blocking** is frequently used. With this technique, conventional data records, called **logical records,** are grouped, or blocked, into **physical records.**

The size of a physical record depends largely on the size of input-record **buffers** within the computer unit. Often there are two buffers, each of which can contain a complete physical record. Because the buffers are within the all-electronic computer unit, the records they contain can be fetched quickly by active programs.

Several devices other than disk and tape may be used for secondary storage. The **mass storage unit** is particularly suitable for storing enormous quantities of data online. Although slower than magnetic disk, it is more cost effective when the CPU must have large quantities of data readily accessible. **Optical disks,** which work with laser read/write devices, are a relatively recent secondary storage technology. Most optical disk systems available today are *CD-ROM, WORM,* write-and-erase, or **video disk** systems. **Magnetic bubble storage** is frequently used for small amounts of local memory in devices such as terminals, desktop computers, robots, and communications devices.

The process of retrieving data and programs in storage is called **data access.** Systematically arranging data for efficient retrieval is called **data organization.**

There are three major methods of storing files in secondary storage: sequential, indexed-sequential, and direct organization. With **sequential organization,** records are arranged with respect to a key field. With **indexed-sequential organization,** records are arranged sequentially by key field on the disk to facilitate sequential access. In addition, one or more indexes are available to permit direct access to the records. **Direct organization** facilitates even faster direct access to data. It uses a process called *hashing* to transform the key field of each record into a disk address.

REVIEW EXERCISES

Fill-in Questions

1. A secondary storage medium is _Volatile_ if it loses its contents when the power is shut off.
2. A tiered assembly of disk platters enclosed in a protective cover is known as a(n) _disk pack_ .

3. For rapid access, related data often are stored on the same _cylinder_, a collection of disk tracks that are in the same relative position on different disk surfaces of a pack.

4. A hard disk on an add-in board is called a(n) _hard card_.

5. The number of _logical_ records per _physical_ record is known as the blocking factor.

6. Each character of data on magnetic tape is represented in byte form across parallel _tracks_ of the tape.

7. In order to write data onto a tape, a(n) _file protection ring_ must be mounted in the center of the tape.

8. A(n) _mass storage unit_ is a secondary storage device capable of storing almost 500 billion bytes of data online.

Matching Questions

Match each term with the description that best fits.

a. diskette
b. cache disk
c. removable-pack disk unit
d. Winchester disk
e. mass storage unit
f. RAM disk

_d_ 1. Used when one needs a lot of fast, random access to run a business on a microcomputer system.

_a_ 2. A storage alternative, often under one or two megabytes in capacity, that is available in a soft-sectored, double-sided, double-density format.

_c_ 3. A common storage alternative for minicomputers and mainframes.

_f_ 4. Used to "trick" the operating system into thinking it is dealing with secondary storage when it is really dealing with primary memory.

_e_ 5. Used by organizations needing extremely large amounts of data online.

_b_ 6. Used to fetch more data from disk on each access than the amount of data needed immediately.

Discussion Questions

1. What is the difference between volatile and nonvolatile storage?
2. Describe the advantages and disadvantages of removable media.
3. Identify several types of magnetic disk, and for each type describe a situation in which it may be useful.
4. Provide examples of sequential access and direct access to data.
5. What physical differences exist among diskettes?
6. What potential do optical disks offer?
7. Explain how data are stored on magnetic tape.

8. How and why are records blocked on tape?

9. How does buffering work in sequential processing?

10. How does indexed-sequential organization work?

Critical Thinking Questions

1. Does a microcomputer user with a hard-disk drive really need diskette drives, too?

2. Some people feel that magnetic tape will completely disappear early in the 21st century. What argument(s) do you feel support this contention? Do you feel that there are any types of applications for which magnetic tape will continue to hold a strong competitive edge?

3. In comparing computers to humans, many observers have pointed out the similarity of computer primary memory to human memory and the CPU chip to the human mind. Extending this analogy further, what would computer secondary storage resemble?

6

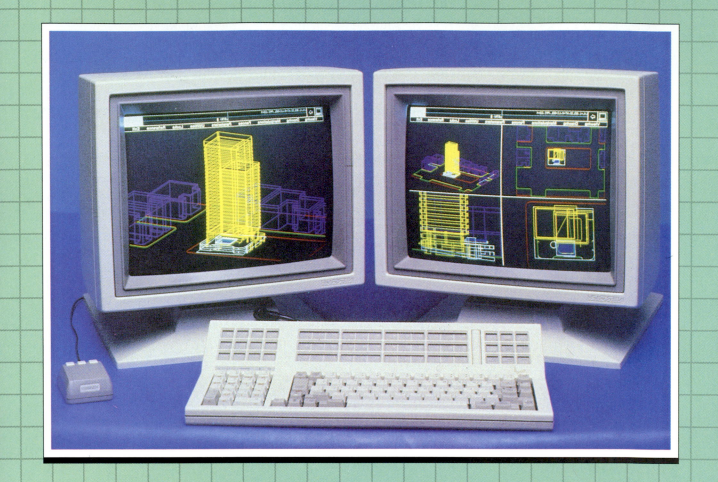

Input and
Output
Equipment

Objectives

After completing this chapter, you will be able to:

1. Identify several types of input and output devices and explain their functions.
2. Describe the differences among display devices.
3. Describe the differences among printers.
4. Explain what source data automation means and discuss several ways to accomplish it.
5. Appreciate the large variety of input and output equipment available in the marketplace.

OVERVIEW

In Chapter 5, we covered secondary storage devices. Although most of those devices perform both input and output operations for the computer, storage is their main role. In this chapter, we turn to equipment designed primarily for input of programs and data into the computer, for output, or for both. Many of these devices possess a limited amount of storage capacity as well.

We'll begin the chapter with a look at display devices. These units are ideal for applications that require considerable interaction between the operator and the computer. We'll also highlight some of the qualities that distinguish one display device from another.

Next, we will turn to printers. Printers place the results of computer processing onto paper, sometimes at incredible speeds.

Following that, we'll cover hardware designed for source data automation. This equipment provides fast and efficient input for certain kinds of applications.

Finally, we'll describe some special-purpose output equipment. Included among these devices are machines that can record output onto microfilm, machines that can speak, plotters, and film recorders.

Keep in mind that the hardware described in this chapter is only a small sample of the kinds of input/output equipment available today. There are, in fact, thousands of products in the marketplace, and these can be put together in so many ways that it is possible to create a computer system to fit almost any conceivable need.

INPUT AND OUTPUT

Input and output equipment allows people and computers to communicate. **Input devices** convert data and programs that humans can understand into a form the computer can comprehend. These devices translate the letters, numbers, and other natural-language symbols that humans conventionally use in reading and writing into the configurations of 0- and 1-bits that the computer uses to process data. **Output devices,** on the other hand, convert the strings of bits the computer uses back into natural-language form to make them understandable to humans. These devices produce output for screen display, output onto paper or film, and so forth.

The equipment we are about to discuss can be classified in a number of ways. Some of it is *peripheral equipment.* These are input or output devices that are normally under the computer's direct control. Display devices and printers are examples. Other input or output equipment, such as many electronic cash registers and computer output microfilm (COM) devices, are *auxiliary equipment.* These devices normally work independently of the main CPU. Some auxiliary devices prepare input data for later mounting onto a peripheral device. Others convert output produced on a peripheral device into a form more useful to humans.

This equipment, of course, can also be discussed in terms of its input or output functions. Teleprinters, for example, are capable of both input and output. Keyboards and optical character recognition devices are designed primarily for input. Printers, monitors, and most computer microfilm devices, on the other hand, specialize in output. Most input and output devices contain limited storage capacity as well.

Output devices produce results in either hard copy or soft copy form. The term **hard copy** generally refers to output that has been recorded onto a medium such as paper or microfilm—in other words, output that is in a permanent and highly portable form. Printed reports and program listings are among the most common examples. The term **soft copy,** on the other hand, generally refers to display output—output that is temporary and of limited portability.

DISPLAY DEVICES

Display devices are peripheral equipment that contain a televisionlike viewing screen. Most display devices fall into one of two categories: monitors and display terminals. A **monitor** is an *output* device that consists of only the viewing screen. A **display terminal** is typically an *input/output* "communications workstation" that includes the screen (for output) and an attached keyboard (for input).

In practice, one commonly finds monitors plugged into and sitting on top of the system units of microcomputers. The keyboard is usually a separate input device that also connects to the system unit. Although the monitor is strictly an output device, the user can also see keyboard input on the display because the computer routes it to the monitor as output. Display terminals, on the other hand, are generally hooked up to either mainframes, minicomputers, or supercomputers in communications networks. After all, communication is the primary function of these display devices. The keyboard unit is cabled directly to the display unit, which in turn is hooked up to the computer.

Display devices are handy when the user requires only small amounts of output and has to see what is being sent as input to the computer system. A student writing a program for a class, an airline clerk making inquiries to a flight information database, a stockbroker analyzing a security, and a bank teller checking the status of a customer account would each employ a display device. However, the display is useful only up to a point. If, for example, the student writing the program wanted to take a copy of it home, he or she would have to direct the output to a printer.

Many features differentiate the hundreds of display devices currently on the market (see Figure 6-1). A discussion of some of the more noteworthy features follows.

FIGURE 6-1

A variety of display devices.
(a, top left) Monochrome, CRT-type display terminal. (b, top right) Color, CRT-type monitor.
(c, bottom left) Monochrome, flat-panel display terminal. (d, bottom right) Two-page, grey-scale monitor.

Text versus Graphics

Many of the display devices sold today are capable of providing both text and graphics output. *Text* output consists of only letters, digits, and special characters. Two examples are program listings and letters to friends. *Graphics* output includes complex "picture images," such as maps and drawings.

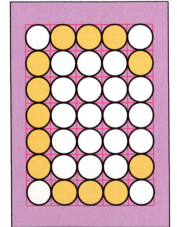

FIGURE 6-2

A *C* character as formed by a 5-by-7 dot matrix of pixels. Generally, the more dots available in the matrix to form characters, the better the character resolution.

Resolution. A key characteristic of any display device is *resolution,* or sharpness of the screen image. On many displays, images are formed by lighting up tiny dots on the screen. On such devices, resolution is measured by the number of these dots, or **pixels** (a contraction of the phrase *picture elements*). The more pixels on the screen, the higher the resolution (i.e., the clearer the picture). A display resolution of, say, 640 by 480 means that the screen consists of 640 columns by 480 rows of dots—that is, $640 \times 480 = 307,200$ pixels.

Text characters are formed on the screen in a dot-matrix configuration, as shown in Figure 6-2. Generally, several specific matrix sizes—say, 5 by 7 (= 35 pixels) or 7 by 12 (= 84 pixels)—are available for users to display text. For instance, a user may be able to display 25 rows of 65-character lines for one application and 50 rows of 132-character lines for another. The more pixels used to form characters and the more pixels packed per square inch of screen, the higher the text resolution.

Bit Mapping. The earliest display devices were strictly *character addressable;* that is, only text could be output. Every character sent to the screen

FIGURE 6-3

Computer generated presentation graphics. Presentation graphics images are useful for making dramatic and easily understood points in meetings, and they make the presenter look more professional as well. Presentation graphics can be shown to an audience through a variety of media, such as a monitor screen, printer or plotter hard copy, and slides or overhead transparencies.

was the same size and was fitted into a specific block of pixels in a predesignated grid. As demand for graphics devices grew, manufacturers developed techniques to make displays multipurpose, that is, capable of both graphics and standard text output.

Display devices that produce graphics output often use a technique called **bit mapping.** With bit-mapped graphics, each pixel on the screen (rather than simply a block of pixels) can be individually controlled by the operator. This enables the operator to create virtually any type of image on the screen.

One of the largest markets for graphics display devices today is in the engineering, science, and art fields. Powerful devices called *technical workstations,* or "diskless PCs," are used for mapping, circuit design, mechanical design, drafting, art, advertising, and other graphics-intensive tasks. Such applications collectively fall under the heading of *computer-aided design (CAD).* We will discuss CAD in greater detail in Chapter 16.

Another large market for computer graphics is in the business sector. Managers, for instance, can easily become overwhelmed as they try to make decisions from piles of raw data. A possible solution lies in the old adage "One picture is worth a thousand words." Using a graphics image, a decision maker can more easily spot problems, opportunities, and trends. Many business applications of computer graphics fall into the general category of *presentation graphics,* which we'll cover in Chapter 13 and Window 6. With presentation graphics, computer images are used to increase the effectiveness of managerial and sales presentations (Figure 6-3).

Recently, computer graphics techniques have brought many businesses squarely into the age of *electronic document handling,* where digital images of paper documents and photographs are electronically maintained by or-

FIGURE 6-4

Electronic document handling.
Graphics terminals, optical disk storage, and superfast processors have made it possible to maintain digital images of photos and paper documents and to access them at electronic speeds. Here, an insurance adjuster's handwritten report, an estimate, and an accident photo are pulled together on the same screen.

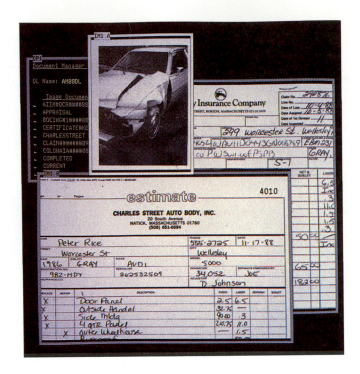

ganizations and processed by workers at their display workstations (see Figure 6-4). The paper documents and photographs are initially read into the computer system with an image scanner, a device we'll cover later in the chapter. Once in digital form, the images are stored on a high-capacity optical disk system. Workers having access to the system can summon documents to their workstations, where they can cull, sort, summarize, or repackage the information to their heart's content. Workers may also be authorized to annotate certain documents with comments or approvals and send them to other workers who are hooked into the system.

Monochrome and Color Display Devices

Most display devices in use today are classifiable as monochrome or color. *Grey-scale displays,* which provide output similar to that on a black-and-white TV screen (see Figure 6-1d), have also recently become available for specialized applications.

Monochrome. *Monochrome displays* output images using a single foreground color (see Figure 6-1a). Many of the earliest monochrome devices were of the black-and-white variety, providing white text on a black background. Through a technique known as *reverse video* (reversing the color of the pixels), black text on a white background is also possible. Over the years, a number of studies have shown that people become less fatigued when working with amber or green on a black background. Although such studies have produced conflicting results, many of the display devices now available in the marketplace are of the amber or green type.

Color. Most *color displays* (see Figure 6-1b) are of the *red-green-blue (RGB)* type. Those of the highest resolution work with beams whose intensities vary by analog rather than by digital means. Depending on such factors as the sophistication of the display unit itself and the amount of RAM available with the computer, users may be able to display from 8 to 16,000,000 colors. Business users who require presentation graphics output often need only a few colors, but people such as artists and product designers need many, many more. Display devices that meet the latter set of needs often cost several thousand dollars. Nonetheless, users who have only eight or so colors available can create the illusion of many more colors by painting alternate pixels different colors. For example, painting alternate pixels yellow and green produces a lime color.

Monochrome display devices have advantages over color ones in that they are cheaper, generally provide better resolution for text display (an important consideration if the display will be used extensively for word processing), and emit less radiation. But if you need more than a single color, only a color monitor will suffice.

CRT and Flat-Panel Display Devices

Traditionally, most display devices have used a large picture-tube element similar to the one inside a standard TV set. This type of display device is commonly called a **CRT (cathode-ray tube).** CRT technology is relatively mature. Over the years, CRTs have become very inexpensive and capable of providing excellent color output. These features notwithstanding, CRTs are bulky, fragile, and consume a great deal of power. Feature 6A describes how CRTs work.

Recently monitors and display terminals that use charged chemicals or gases sandwiched between panes of glass have become very popular alternatives to CRTs. These slim-profile devices are called **flat-panel displays.** Although they can be relatively expensive and have only recently become commercially viable for color output, flat-panel displays are compact, are lightweight, and require little power. Because of these features, they are commonly found on laptop computers.

Figure 6-1c features a flat-panel display that uses a *liquid crystal display (LCD)* technology. LCDs are by far the most common type of flat-panel display devices in use. Among the major advantages of LCD technology over CRTs are low cost, low power consumption, and compactness. However, LCDs provide less contrast, produce more glare, and have poorer screen resolution than CRTs. To overcome the contrast problem, many LCDs are back-lit.

Two other flat-panel technologies in use are *gas plasma* displays and *electroluminescent (EL)* displays. Although devices that use these technolo-

How CRTs Work

A Closer Look at the Most Popular Display Technology

Cathode ray tubes, or CRTs, are still by far the most widely used type of display device, outselling competitors such as flat-panel displays by a considerable margin. With their large flat ends and long necks, they closely resemble television tubes.

Most CRTs work through a principle called *raster graphics*. All of the air inside the tube is removed, creating a vacuum. In monochrome displays, electrons are shot out in a single narrow beam toward the flat face end of the tube (see figure). The interior of the flat face is coated with phosphorous materials that emit light when struck by electrons at high velocity. As each pixel is struck by a beam, it glows for a small fraction of a second.

Because too many electrons striking the same spot can burn the phosphors, the beam moves in a Z-like pattern (sometimes called a *raster pattern*), from pixel to pixel across the entire tube surface. A magnetic field at the neck of the tube is used to deflect the beam to each

> Most CRTs work through a principle called *raster graphics*.

pixel precisely. Since a pixel glows only for a brief moment, it must be constantly "refreshed"; therefore, the raster pattern is repeated again and again. The number of times per second that the electron gun scans the entire surface of the tube is called the CRT's *refresh rate*. Refreshing the screen pixels 30 or more times per second is common. If the refresh rate is too low, the tube will flicker because the phosphors will lose their glow momentarily.

The luminescence of each pixel on the screen also depends on the intensity of the electron beam striking it, which in turn depends on the voltage applied to the electron gun. This voltage can be controlled precisely. In *digital monitors,* the voltage is present or absent to turn pixels on and off. The more sophisticated monitors, known as *analog monitors*, can also control the brightness of the individual pixels by varying the beam intensity along a continuous scale. On monochrome CRTs, this technique allows a grey-scale effect; on color CRTs, it permits an ever

gies are more costly and less common than LCD devices, they offer better screen resolution and contrast as well as greater color potential.

The Operator Interface

Operators who interface with display devices can do their jobs more effectively if the proper input hardware and display software are available.

Hardware Interfaces. Whether they use monitors or terminals, most operators also work concurrently with some type of input device. The traditional and still most widely used input device is a keyboard, and a device called a mouse is also relatively common (Figure 6-5).

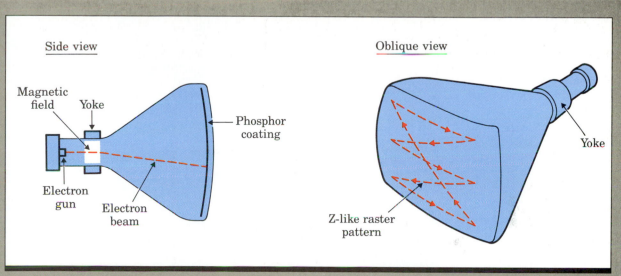

Side view

Magnetic field | Yoke

Phosphor coating

Electron gun

Electron beam

Oblique view

Yoke

Z-like raster pattern

CRTs. Phosphor pixels are constantly refreshed by an electron gun.

greater number of colors than is possible with conventional, digital devices.

In color CRTs, several other elements are added to those described above. For example, instead of one gun there are three—one each for the color red, green, and blue. Also, the phosphor coating contains trios of phosphor dots for each pixel, which glow in each of the three colors when struck by a beam. Shades and colors other than red, green, and blue are created by varying the intensities of the three electron beams. The number of colors available on a given CRT depends on how the intensities of the beams are controlled.

Not all CRTs use raster graphics. Some of the most so-phisticated graphics displays use a technique called *vector graphics*, which works by a different set of imaging principles. While raster devices are well suited to both text and graphics applications, vector devices are designed specifically for graphics and animation and work awkwardly when text output is demanded from them.

As each key is depressed on the **keyboard,** the corresponding character representation of the key appears on the display screen at the cursor position. The **cursor** is a highlighted position on the screen indicating where the next character the operator types in is to be placed. Alternatively, the cursor may point to the option the operator can select next.

Keyboards can vary dramatically with respect to touch, number and arrangement of keys, and built-in functions. Many keyboards today are *detachable,* enabling the operator to move them around independently of the display for greater comfort.

Typing on computer keyboards is often facilitated with the presence of *function keys.* These keys are often labeled F1, F2, F3, and so on and are located in a cluster on the left-hand side or at the top of the keyboard. When

FIGURE 6-5
Computer keyboard and mouse.
Both the keyboard and the mouse
(foreground) are useful tools for
interacting with display devices. The
keyboard is better for entering data,
while the mouse can move the
cursor around the display screen
more rapidly.

depressed by the operator, these keys initiate a command or even an entire computer program. Generally speaking, each software package you work with will define the function keys differently. For example, depressing the F2 key may enable you to block-indent text with your word processor but edit cells with your spreadsheet package.

Many people supplement keyboard operations with a **mouse.** When the mouse is moved along a flat surface, the cursor on the display screen moves correspondingly. Mice are very useful for moving the cursor rapidly from one location to another on a display screen. Using a mouse in this way often is much faster than pressing combinations of cursor movement (arrow) keys on a keyboard. When you use the mouse, say, to move to a choice on the display screen, you can select that choice by clicking a button on the mouse. Mice are especially handy to use when pointing to **icons** on the screen—small geometric symbols that represent commands or program options.

Keyboards and mice, although extremely popular, are not the only types of input equipment used to interface with display devices. For example, some displays are designed to respond when the operator touches a finger or light pen to a certain position on the screen. These interfacing devices are especially appropriate for graphics-oriented work, for situations in which the operator is a poor typist, and for applications that require the operator to wear gloves, such as in a factory.

A **light pen,** such as the one in Figure 6-6, contains a light-sensitive cell at its tip. When the tip of the pen is placed close to the screen, the display device can identify its position. Some pens are even equipped with a remote-control press-button feature that allows access to any page-length image on the display screen, as shown in Figure 6-6. Display devices that are

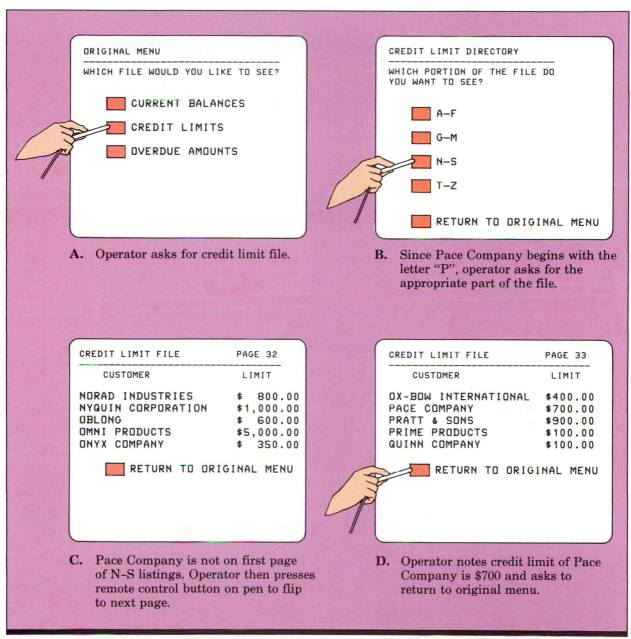

```
ORIGINAL MENU
-----------------------------------
WHICH FILE WOULD YOU LIKE TO SEE?

      ▨  CURRENT BALANCES

      ▨  CREDIT LIMITS

      ▨  OVERDUE AMOUNTS
```

A. Operator asks for credit limit file.

```
CREDIT LIMIT DIRECTORY
-----------------------------------
WHICH PORTION OF THE FILE DO
YOU WANT TO SEE?

      ▨  A-F

      ▨  G-M

      ▨  N-S

      ▨  T-Z


      ▨  RETURN TO ORIGINAL MENU
```

B. Since Pace Company begins with the letter "P", operator asks for the appropriate part of the file.

```
CREDIT LIMIT FILE          PAGE 32
-----------------------------------
    CUSTOMER            LIMIT

NORAD INDUSTRIES      $   800.00
NYQUIN CORPORATION    $1,000.00
OBLONG                $   600.00
OMNI PRODUCTS         $5,000.00
ONYX COMPANY          $   350.00

      ▨  RETURN TO ORIGINAL MENU
```

C. Pace Company is not on first page of N-S listings. Operator then presses remote control button on pen to flip to next page.

```
CREDIT LIMIT FILE          PAGE 33
-----------------------------------
    CUSTOMER            LIMIT

OX-BOW INTERNATIONAL  $400.00
PACE COMPANY          $700.00
PRATT & SONS          $900.00
PRIME PRODUCTS        $100.00
QUINN COMPANY         $100.00

      ▨  RETURN TO ORIGINAL MENU
```

D. Operator notes credit limit of Pace Company is $700 and asks to return to original menu.

FIGURE 6-6

Simple series of screens presented to a light pen operator. As the light pen is activated near the desired option, the display device automatically takes the appropriate action. In the panel of screens shown, the operator is attempting to locate the credit limit of Pace Company.

designed to allow a finger to activate the screen rather than a light pen are commonly called **touch-screen devices** (see Figure 6-7).

A variety of other input interfaces are possible with display devices. We'll discuss a number of these in the "Source Data Automation" section of this chapter.

FIGURE 6-7
FIGURE 6-7
A touch-screen display device.
This operator interface requires
neither typing skills nor a knowledge
of programming-language
commands. All one does is point to
an option and the computer system
takes the appropriate action.

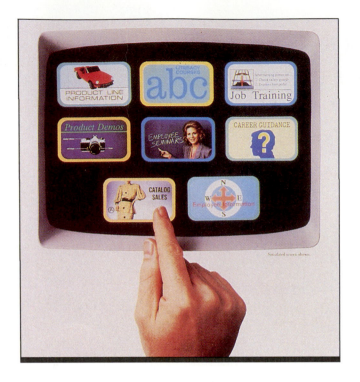

Software Interfaces. Many types of software products that make display devices easier to use are commercially available. For example, windowing software subdivides a screen into independent "boxes" of information called *windows.* A screen with, say, three windows may contain a computer program listing in the first window, the data for that program in the second, and the results from executing the program with its data in the third. Figure 6-1d illustrates how a screen with windows looks.

Menus, on the other hand, make display device interaction feasible for people who find it difficult to compose computer commands or to type. Figures 6-6a and 6-6b illustrate menus and how they work. Interfacing alternatives such as touch screens, light pens, and mice are excellent for menu-driven computer applications.

Since this chapter focuses on hardware, software interfaces such as windows and menus will be discussed more fully in Module C.

PRINTERS

Display devices have two major limitations as output devices: (1) only a small amount of data can be shown on the screen at one time, and (2) output, being in soft copy form, is not very portable. Also, you must be physically present at a display device to get any results at all. To preserve output in portable form, you virtually must take notes.

Printers overcome these limitations by producing hard copy—a permanent record of output. Hard copy is created when digital electronic signals from the computer are converted into printed material in a natural language that people can easily read and understand. A great deal of output can be placed onto computer printouts, although hard copy can become difficult to handle and store as it accumulates. In fact, many executives now complain that they are literally drowning in a sea of computer-generated paperwork.

Printers differ in a number of important respects. One involves the printing technology used, namely whether it is *impact* or *nonimpact.* Another concerns speed of operation. *Low-speed printers* are capable of outputting only one character at a time, whereas *high-speed printers* can output either a full line or a full page at a time.

Impact Printing

Impact printing is the method used by conventional typewriters. In some types of impact printing, a metal "hammer" embossed with a character strikes a print ribbon, which presses the character's image onto paper. In other types, the hammer strikes the paper and presses it into the ribbon. Characters created through impact printing can be formed by either a solid-font or dot-matrix printing mechanism.

Solid-Font Mechanisms. A **solid-font mechanism** produces fully formed characters similar to those on conventional typewriters.

A popular device for producing fully formed characters on low-speed printers is the daisywheel print element, shown in Figure 6-8. *Daisywheel printers* operate at very slow speeds—often in the neighborhood of 30 to 80 characters per second—but their output quality is very high. Thus, daisywheel printers are sometimes called *letter-quality* printers because they are often used to produce attractive correspondence to be sent outside the user's organization. *Print-thimble printers,* popularized by NEC, are another example of low-speed, solid-font, letter-quality printers. A print thimble looks like a daisywheel with its spokes bent upward in the shape of a sewing thimble.

Many high-speed printers also employ a solid-font mechanism to produce fully formed characters. In chain printers, for example, all characters are mounted on a *print chain* that revolves rapidly past the print positions, as Figure 6-9 shows. Hammers are lined up opposite each of up to 132 print positions. These hammers press the paper against a ribbon, which in turn presses against the appropriate embossed character in the chain.

Dot-Matrix Mechanisms. Most low-speed printers in use today employ a print head that's an impact, dot-matrix mechanism. Typically, an **impact dot-matrix mechanism** constructs printed characters by repeatedly activating one or more vertical rows of pins, as illustrated in Figure 6-10. Impact dot-matrix printers are usually much faster than solid-font printers; a speed of

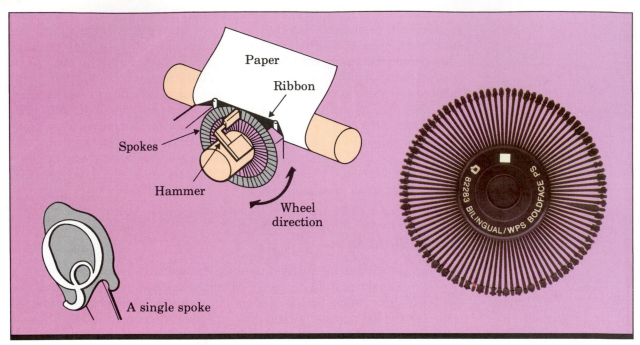

FIGURE 6-8
The daisywheel. Each spoke has an embossed character that strikes the ribbon when impacted by a hammer.

100 to 200 characters per second is common. Top-of-the-line impact dot-matrix printers are currently rated at about 700 characters per second.

The quality of output on dot-matrix devices is often lower than that on solid-font devices. Nonetheless, many relatively inexpensive impact dot-matrix printers are capable of printing very respectable-looking output.

FIGURE 6-9

The print chain. Hammers press the paper against a ribbon, which then presses against the appropriate embossed character in the chain.

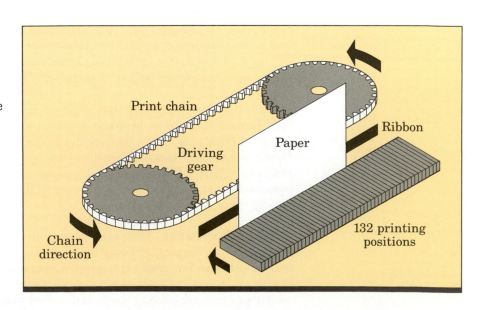

FIGURE 6-10

Impact dot-matrix printing. This character-formation technique is similar to the one used to light up electronic scoreboards at sports stadiums. The printing mechanism contains a vertical line of pins that form the characters on the paper. Depending on the character to be represented, different pins in the mechanism are activated. The characters shown are formed from a 5-by-7 dot matrix. The more dots in the matrix, naturally, the higher the quality of the printed character.

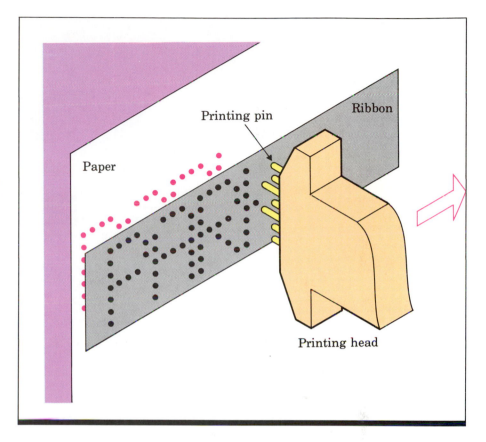

These printers use techniques such as packing as many pins as possible on the print head, overstriking by making multiple passes on a line, and blending overstrike dots into previous dots by shifting the paper very slightly (see Figure 6-11). Top-of-the-line impact dot-matrix printers have 24 pins on their print heads, configured in two 12-pin rows. Generally, these printers

FIGURE 6-11

Overstriking on a dot-matrix printer. (a) Single striking. (b) Overstriking with multiple passes produces denser characters.

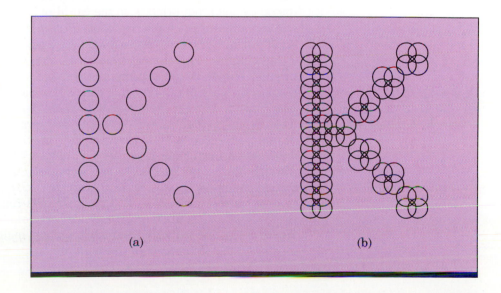

FIGURE 6-12

Dithered output. Through multiple passes, overstrikes, and so very light paper shifts, the printer "mixes" new colors right on the paper. While not ideal, dithering meets the need for inexpensive color output.

can create characters that are virtually indistinguishable from those produced by solid-font printers. In the world of impact dot-matrix printing, low-quality output is often referred to as *draft-quality* printing and presentation-quality output as *near-letter-quality (NLQ)* printing.

Many impact dot-matrix printers can also be used to produce graphical or color output. Graphical output is possible if the printer supports bit mapping. In the case of printers, this means that each individual pin on the print head may be independently software-controlled. Although producing graphical output is possible and in fact widely practiced on impact dot-matrix printers, however, it is a relatively slow process and usually causes faster wear on the print head than does text output. Color output is often possible through a process called *dithering*. Here a multicolored ribbon is used and, through multiple passes, overstrikes, and imperceptible paper shifts, the printer "mixes" new colors and blends colors right on the paper. Dithering isn't elegant, but it often meets the need for color output inexpensively (see Figure 6-12). The software used must support multicolored ribbons in order for one to take advantage of this feature.

FIGURE 6-13

Thermal-transfer printer output. Thermal-transfer printers are ideal for users who need high-quality color output as well as crisp-looking text.

Nonimpact Printing

Nonimpact printing, which most often employs dot-matrix characters, does not depend on the impact of metal on paper. In fact, no physical contact at all occurs between the printing mechanism and the paper. The most popular nonimpact methods today utilize electrothermal, thermal-transfer, ink-jet, laser, and array technologies.

In *electrothermal printing,* characters are burned onto a special paper by heated rods on a print head. Electrothermal printers are available at a very low cost, but they have the disadvantages of requiring special paper (which some people find unpleasant to touch) and being unable to produce color output.

Thermal-transfer printers, which represent a relatively new technology, thermally transfer ink from a wax-based ribbon onto plain paper. These printers can produce output that rivals a daisywheel's and, because they use a dot-matrix print head, can support high-quality graphics as well (see Figure 6-13). In addition, thermal-transfer printers can produce overheads for use at meetings.

Ink-jet printers spray small dots of electrically charged ink onto a page to form images. Many models hold several color cartridges simultaneously, so they are excellent for producing color output. Ink-jet printers are flexible enough to be used as plotters, an output device we'll discuss later in the chapter, and as transparency-making machines.

About Laser Printers

Today's Favorite Business Printer

Laser printers have been used on computer systems since the mid-1970s. The earliest models were targeted at high-volume mainframe applications. Only since the mid-1980s have inexpensive laser printers—about $3,000 and under—been available for microcomputers. Today laser printers are a favorite among hard-copy output devices for virtually all sizes of computers. They are relatively fast, and they produce comparatively high-quality text and graphic images.

Laser printers most commonly form images onto a page through a technology known as *xerography*, pioneered by the familiar Xerox machine. Xerography is a type of photography in which the film is a drum coated with a material that holds an electrical charge when exposed to light. Once the electronic image is imparted to the photosensitive drum, it is transferred to paper.

In many laser printers, a single laser beam acts as the light source that charges the drum (see figure). The beam is focused on a polygon-shaped scanning mirror. As the scanning mirror spins, the beam is deflected through focusing lenses onto another mirror, which transmits the image to the drum. The rotating scanning mirror enables the laser to reach the entire length of the drum, which accepts images line by line. The laser source never moves.

> Approximately 9 million dots are precisely transferred to each sheet of paper.

As the drum turns, it picks up toner consisting of very fine, charged particles of a specific color (e.g., black if one wants black characters on the paper). The toner particles adhere to the charged parts of the drum and are pulled off by the paper as it passes by. Then heated rollers seal the toner, making the image on the paper permanent. Approximately 9 million dots are precisely transferred to each sheet of paper at a rate of anywhere from 8 to over 100 pages per minute.

Many vendors of laser printers, including Apple and Hewlett-Packard, use the Canon LBP-CX engine. Less than a decade ago, Canon found a way to convert designs and parts from low-end photocopiers to laser printers. Because of the production economies realized in using a common basic design for several different devices, the inexpensive laser printer became a reality. So did the affordable "personal copier" (such as the one Jack Klugman plugs on TV), facsimile machine, and image scanner, all of which work by similar principles. In fact, experts predict that at some future point a single device that performs the functions of all of these separate machines will be available.

Most laser printers have their own microprocessors, RAM, and ROM. ROM is used to store both fonts (i.e., typefaces) and programs that specify how to lay out a page. The more fonts the printer has available to it, the more flexibility you have in designing a printed page. If you need more fonts than are available in ROM, you must buy them in disk form and "download" them into the laser's RAM. Fonts are available in *bit-mapped form* (meaning the entire dot-matrix pattern

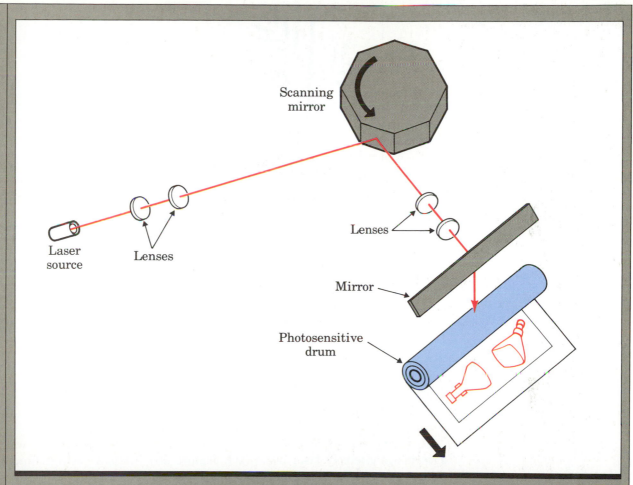

Laser printing. The principle by which laser printers work is similar to that of copying machines.

of pixels is described for each character) or *outline form* (where only the outline of each character is mathematically described and is later filled in with pixels). Outline fonts are more expensive, but they can be upscaled or downscaled to any size before they are filled. With a bit-mapped font, all the pixels are preset and you are stuck with the specific character size (called *point size*) that you buy.

While laser printers produce wonderful output in most users' opinions, their character resolution is actually inferior to that of solid-font printers, such as those that use the daisywheel and print-thimble elements. Also, most laser printers work at a resolution of 300 dots per inch (dpi), which is considered unsatisfactory for many commercial publishing applications. Commercial-quality digital printing starts at resolutions of 1,000 dpi and may even exceed 5,000 dpi.

FIGURE 6-14

Laser printer output. Laser printers are most useful when users need high-resolution, black-and-white text or graphics—and want it done quickly.

Laser printers form images by charging thousands of dots on a platen with a very-high-intensity laser beam (see Feature 6B). Then, as with photocopiers, toner is affixed to the charged positions and, when paper is pressed against the platen, an image is formed. Laser printers produce high-resolution text and graphics (see Figure 6-14) quickly, but they are usually more expensive than other types of printers.

Array printers, which first became available in 1985, have many of the same properties as laser printers. They contain fewer moving parts, however, so they are more reliable. They are also more expensive.

Impact versus Nonimpact Printers. There are many important practical differences between impact and nonimpact printers. For one, because nonimpact printers contain fewer moving parts, they generally are much faster and subject to fewer breakdowns. In addition, because they don't use hammers, nonimpact printers are quiet. But unless you require very high speeds or high-quality color, these printers are often an expensive alternative. Furthermore, because most nonimpact printers are dot-matrix devices, they generally can't match the letter-quality output produced by impact, solid-font printers. Figure 6-15 highlights some other differences between the most common types of impact and nonimpact printers.

	Device					
Criterion	**Impact Dot Matrix**	**Daisywheel and Print Thimble**	**Ink Jet**	**Electrothermal**	**Thermal Transfer**	**Laser and Array**
Type	Impact	Impact	Nonimpact	Nonimpact	Nonimpact	Nonimpact
Speed	Fast	Slow	Medium to very fast	Medium to fast	Medium to fast	Very fast
Print quality	Fair to very good	Excellent	Good to excellent	Fair to very good	Excellent	Excellent
Cost	Low	Medium	Medium to high	Low	Medium to high	High
Graphics capabilities	Fair	Very limited	Fair to excellent	Good	Good to excellent	Excellent
Color	Fair	Very limited	Excellent	Not available	Excellent	Very limited

FIGURE 6-15
Comparison of printing technologies.

Printers for Microcomputers

A rich assortment of printers is available today for microcomputers (see Figure 6-16). Most of these printers are of the low-speed variety and output a single character at a time. The most common low-speed devices are daisywheel, print-thimble, impact dot-matrix, thermal-transfer, and ink-jet printers.

Low-speed printers typically operate in the range of 30 to several hundred characters per second. The slower units print in a single direction, like a conventional typewriter. The faster ones print in two directions (i.e., *bidirectionally*) to save a time-consuming carriage return. Usually the latter devices are also *logic-seeking* in that they are always "peeking" at the next line to decide how to print it the fastest way. Many low-speed printers can output subscripts, superscripts, color, graphic material, or multilingual and scientific text.

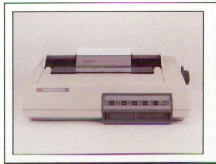  

FIGURE 6-16
A variety of printers for microcomputers. (a, left) Impact dot-matrix printer. (b, middle) Thermal-transfer printer. (c, right) Laser printer.

FIGURE 6-17

A font cartridge. Font cartridges are often used for changing typefaces on an impact dot-matrix printer. For this particular cartridge to be activated, it must be inserted into one of the ports located on the right front panel on the printer in Figure 6-16a.

Many low-speed printers offer adjustable character widths, enabling the operator to change the number of characters per line or lines per inch. On dot-matrix units, the operator can make these adjustments by setting a switch or through the use of software. With solid-font devices, however, the operator must usually change the printing element by hand.

Changing *fonts,* or typefaces, is also usually easily achievable. On dot-matrix printers, fonts are usually changed by switching font cartridges (see Figure 6-17), which contain font descriptions in ROM. On solid-font printers, fonts are changed by replacing the printing element.

Low-speed printers utilize either a friction feed or an adjustable tractor feed, and often both. A *friction feeding* mechanism controls the paper as a conventional typewriter does. Friction feeding is the cheapest type of paper-feed mechanism, but continuous-form paper often gets out of alignment after a few pages have been printed and must be readjusted. *Tractor feeding* works with a pair of sprocket mechanisms that pass through holes on the left and right sides of the paper to keep it in alignment. The sprocket mechanisms can be adjusted to fit a wide range of paper widths. On many printers, the sprocket mechanisms can be slid aside, enabling the operator to friction-feed single sheets of precut letterhead paper.

Perhaps the greatest potential for high-speed printing on microcomputer systems exists with laser printing. Only since the mid-1980s have relatively inexpensive laser devices—costing $3,000 or less and printing about eight pages per minute—become available for microcomputers. Many of these print at a resolution of 300 dots per inch (dpi), meaning that every square inch of the output image is broken down into a 300-by-300 matrix of dots. That's 90,000 dots packed into every inch! Such devices have become especially popular in business in the last few years because they can produce letter-quality output that rivals that of solid-font printers, can quickly create presentation graphics for reports and meetings, and permit performance of certain publishing functions on a desktop. Laser printing is a special case of page printing, which we shall cover shortly.

Printers for Large Computers

Most printing on large computer systems is accomplished with high-speed printers. Whereas low-speed printers top out at speeds of several hundred *characters per second,* the slowest high-speed printers operate at several hundred *lines per minute* (roughly twice the speed of the fastest low-speed printer). In many commercial settings that use both kinds of printers, you will often find the high-speed printers operating at speeds of from 10 to 30 times higher than the low-speed printers.

High-speed printers fall into two major categories: line printers and page printers. Teleprinter terminals, which are low-speed printing devices, are also commonly configured to large computers.

LIne Printers. Line printers (see Figure 6-18) are so called because they print whole lines at a time rather than just characters. Most line printers use impact printing technologies. For instance, many line printers use the

FIGURE 6-18

A line printer. Line printers are targeted to larger computers—most notably, minicomputers and mainframes—and produce output at speeds ranging from 300 to 3,000 lines per minute (lpm).

solid-font, impact chain mechanism (refer back to Figure 6–9), which IBM introduced in 1959 on its 1403 printer. This device has proven to be the most popular printer of all time and is still used today. Band printers, which use a character-embossed print band instead of a chain, are currently the most popular type of line printer. Other forms of line printers use mechanical devices such as print trains, drums, wheels, and belts. Impact line printing typically occurs at speeds ranging from 300 to 3,000 lines per minute.

Because line printers commonly produce high volumes of output on perforated, continuous-form paper, a piece of special auxiliary equipment called a *burster* is often needed to separate the printed pages. Also, if forms with carbon-paper interleaves are used with an impact printer, another auxiliary machine, called a *decollator,* removes the carbons. This operation can also be done by hand. If both operations must be performed on the same output, decollating is done before bursting.

Page Printers. As the term suggests, **page printers** (see Figure 6-19) can produce a page of output at a time. These devices, which can print up to a few hundred pages of output per minute, all employ nonimpact technology. Many of them utilize an electrophotographic process similar to that used by the copying machines found in many offices. Either lasers or light-emitting-diode arrays are used to form the printed images.

The printing commonly occurs on 8-by-11-inch paper, which is cheaper than the larger, sprocket-fed paper line printers typically use. The smaller-size paper is cheaper to file and mail as well. Also, since page printers do not use carbon paper, the decollating operation that accompanies multiple-copy impact printing is eliminated. Some page printers can print in color or on both sides of the page.

FIGURE 6-19

A page printer. Operating at peak capacity over a weekend, some page printers can produce well over a million pages of output.

A useful feature of page printers is their ability to store digital images of forms and letterheads. In fact, users of such systems often can design their own forms and letterheads if they have art or illustration software. Thus, page printers offer considerable savings over line printers, which require changing of paper and printing elements when output dictates a new form or format.

Page printers generally cost considerably more than line printers. Line printers range from $3,000 to $100,000, while page printers for large computers may cost between $100,000 and $300,000. In general, an organization that produces over a million lines of output per month should investigate the feasibility of acquiring one of these machines.

Teleprinters. **Teleprinter terminals** are low-speed printers with a keyboard for operator input. They are handy for obtaining small amounts of hard-copy output from a large computer. The operator can enter a short request from the keyboard and the output will be immediately directed back to the teleprinter terminal.

SOURCE DATA AUTOMATION

Often data must be translated from handwritten form into machine-readable form so that they can be processed, a procedure that sometimes consumes thousands of hours of duplicated effort and that can result in many mistakes and delays. Data must be hand-entered on documents or forms, keyed into machine-readable form on a data preparation device, verified, and read into the computer. Usually, several people will be involved in this process, complicating matters further.

Source data automation eliminates much of this duplicated effort, delay, extra handling, and potential for error by making data available in machine-readable form at the time they are collected. Because ready-to-process transaction data are collected by the people who know most about them, source data automation is rapidly becoming the most dominant form of data entry today.

Source data automation has been applied to a number of tasks. For example, many orders taken over the phone today are entered directly into display terminals. A microchip designer draws some circuits on a special pad, and the drawings are immediately digitized and displayed on screen. Source data automation has also been used to speed up checkout lines and inventory at supermarkets, quality control operations in factories, and processing of checks by banks.

In the next few pages, we will discuss several technologies that can be used to achieve source data automation: optical character recognition (OCR), magnetic ink character recognition (MICR), voice input, digitizing, and image scanning.

FIGURE 6-20

Exam taken on an OCR form.
When this completed exam is
optically scanned, the scanner can
recognize penciled-in areas because
light reflects from those areas.

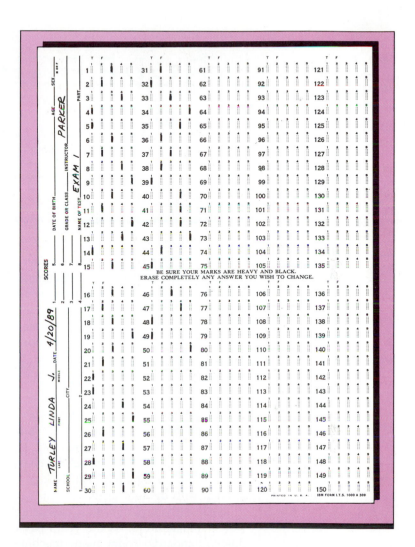

Optical Character Recognition (OCR)

Optical character recognition (OCR) refers to a wide range of optical-
scanning procedures and equipment designed for machine recognition of
marks, characters, and codes. These symbols are transformed into digital
form for storage in the computer. Most symbols designed for OCR can be
read by humans as well as by machines. Optical recognition of hand-printed
characters is also technically possible but is still in its infancy. OCR equipment is among the most varied and highly specialized in the information
processing industry. A scanner that can read one type of document may be
totally unable to read another.

Optical Marks. One of the oldest applications of OCR is the processing of
tests and questionnaires completed on special forms using *optical marks*
(see Figure 6-20). Take the case of grading a test in which the student dark-

ens the bubbles on the answer sheet to indicate the answers to multiple-choice questions. An optical document reader scans the answer sheets off-line. This machine passes a light beam across the spaces corresponding to the set of possible responses to each question. The light is reflected where a response is penciled in, and the machine tallies that choice. Some document readers can automatically score the test from a key of correct responses. Others produce a magnetic tape of all the data gathered from the test forms for subsequent grading and analysis by a computer system.

Optical Characters. *Optical characters* are characters specially designed to be identifiable by humans as well as by some type of OCR reader. Optical characters conform to a certain font, such as that shown in Figure 6-21. The optical reader reflects light off the characters and converts them into digital patterns for recognition. The reader can identify a character only if it is familiar with the font used.

In the early days of optical character reading, fonts differed widely among OCR manufacturers. As the years passed, however, a few fonts became industry standards. Today many machines are designed to read several fonts even when these fonts are mixed in a single document.

Probably the best-known use of optical characters is **point-of-sale (POS) systems,** which are employed widely in retail stores. POS systems allow a store to record a purchase at the time and place it occurs. A sale is automatically recorded from machine-readable information on a price tag attached to the product. The information on the tag is input to a special cash register. Today many cash registers are equipped with local, direct-access memories containing descriptions of stocked items, so they can print what each item is along with its price on the customer receipt (see Figure 6-22).

Another common application of optical characters is in billing operations, such as the processing of insurance and utility bills.

Optical Codes. The most widely used type of *optical code* is the *bar code,* and the most familiar bar code is the **universal product code (UPC)** commonly found on packaged goods in supermarkets (see Figure 6-23). Because

```
YURI'S FOODMART

04/02/89  11:09  2 201  48
KETCHUP                 .89*
RAISIN BRAN            1.09*
    2.34 LB @ 39/LB
PEACHES               1.59*
QT NONFAT MILK          .79*
DOZ LARGE EGGS          .98*
    SUBTOTAL           5.34
    TAX                 .27
    TOTAL              5.61
    CASH TEND          6.00
    CHANGE DUE          .39
```

FIGURE 6-22

An informative cash register receipt made possible by a local memory.

they enable immediate recording of purchases, universal product codes fall also into the category of POS systems.

The UPC consists of several vertical bars of varying widths. Information in the code describes the product and identifies the manufacturer. The UPC can be read either by passing a wand containing a scanning device over the coded label or by sending the item past a fixed scanning station (see Figure 6-24). Using the data from the code, the terminal/cash register can identify the item, look up its latest price, and print the information on a receipt such as the one in Figure 6-22. The UPC has been in use since 1973, and currently over 80 percent of the products sold in supermarkets carry it.

Many other bar codes exist besides the UPC. These are used for applications such as credit card verification, library book checkin and checkout, warehouse freight identification, and inventory (see Figure 6-25).

Magnetic Ink Character Recognition (MICR)

Magnetic ink character recognition (MICR) is a technology confined almost exclusively to the banking industry, where it is used for processing checks in high volume. Figure 6-26 shows the 14-character font adopted by the industry, and Figure 6-27 illustrates a check that has been encoded with MICR characters.

The characters are written on the check with a special magnetic ink. As with OCR readers, a machine called a MICR reader/sorter senses the identity of a MICR-encoded character on the check by recognizing its shape. But in contrast to OCR, the characters must be magnetized in order to be sensed by the reading device; no optical recognition is used. With MICR, checks can be quickly sorted, processed, and routed to the proper banks.

FIGURE 6-23

A UPC code used on supermarket goods. Because items bearing a UPC label can be identified by optical means, the supermarket industry has saved millions of dollars in localities where it is permitted to post a single price on the shelf for a product instead of marking the price on each individual item.

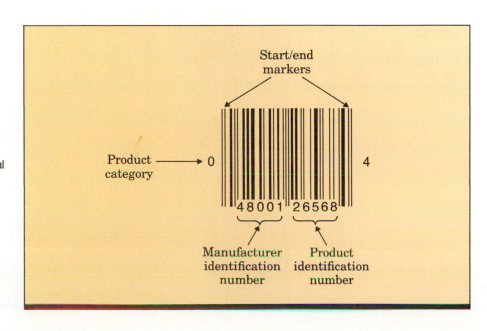

FIGURE 6-24

A UPC scanning station. If you buy peas selling at two cans for 49 cents, the system will charge you 25 cents for the first can and ''remember'' to charge you 24 cents on the next can that passes by. Some systems also use a speech synthesizer that names each item and states its price as the item passes over the scanning mechanism.

Voice-Input Devices

Machines that can convert spoken words into digital form for computer storage and processing are known as **voice-input devices.** If you stop to think about how complicated the interpretation of a spoken word can be for humans, you can realize how tricky it is to design a voice-input device to do

FIGURE 6-25

Inventory application. A wand scans optically recognizable codes or characters on labels, thereby enabling data corresponding to these codes or characters to be retrieved or entered. In inventory environments such as the one depicted here, OCR technologies result in lower labor costs, fewer errors, and data instantly available for management analysis.

FIGURE 6-26

The 14-character E-13B font. This font has been adopted as the standard for magnetic ink character recognition (MICR) by the banking industry.

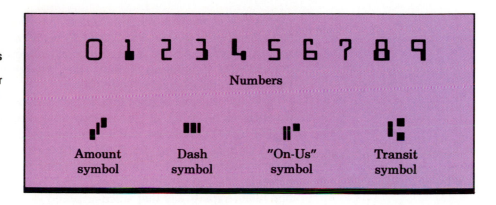

Numbers

Amount symbol   Dash symbol   "On-Us" symbol   Transit symbol

essentially the same thing. Two people may pronounce the same word differently because of accents, personal styles of speech, and the unique quality of each person's voice. Even the same person can pronounce words differently at various times depending on his or her health or level of anxiety. Moreover, in listening to others, we not only ignore irrelevant background noises but decode complex grammatical constructions as well as sentence fragments.

Equipment designers have tried to overcome these obstacles in a number of ways. Voice-input devices are designed to be "trained" by users, who

FIGURE 6-27

Check encoded with MICR characters. The characters at the bottom left of the check are preprinted and contain identifying information, including the customer's account number. The characters at the bottom right show the amount of the check and are imprinted by an operator after the check has been cashed. If there is a discrepancy in the account, the customer should note whether the amount recorded by the operator is the same as the one written on the check.

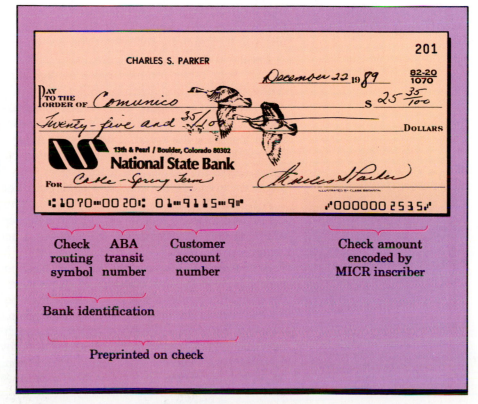

Check routing symbol   ABA transit number   Customer account number   Check amount encoded by MICR inscriber

Bank identification

Preprinted on check

repeat words until the machines know their voices. These devices can also screen out background noise. Unfortunately, most voice-input devices can recognize only a limited number of isolated words and not whole sentences composed of continuous speech. Thus, the complexity of the messages to which they can respond is quite limited.

Still, the possible applications of this technology are exciting. In fact, its potential is probably far greater than that of voice output (discussed later in this chapter), a more mature technology at this time. Imagine yourself speaking into a microphone while a printer automatically types your words. Such a system is in fact commercially available today; however, the number of words the computer can "understand" is extremely limited, typically under 1,000. Experts say that voice-actuated word processing will require recognition of at least 10,000 words.

One typical commercial application of voice input is a system installed by one chemical company to sort roughly 25,000 pieces of mail received each day. An operator speaks the recipient's first initial and the first four letters of the last name into a microphone headset. Then the recipient's corporate mail zone appears on a display device, enabling the package to be routed to the right place. The company claims that this procedure has doubled the operator's productivity.

Digitizers

A **digitizer** is a device that converts a measurement into a digital value. Digitizers determine a position, distance, or speed and move the cursor on the display screen accordingly. Digitizers facilitate source data automation because they directly collect data on events in machine-readable form.

Earlier in the chapter, we covered a familiar example of a digitizer: the mouse. Four other common types of digitizers are the joystick, trackball, crosshair cursor, and digitizing tablet.

A **joystick** (see Figure 6-28), which looks like a car's stick shift, is often used for computer games and for computer-aided design (CAD) work. With many joysticks, the speed at which they move and the distance they travel determine the speed and distance traveled by the screen cursor. Today, some electronic games are using gloves with built-in sensors in place of joysticks, to enable the computer to directly detect hand movements.

A **trackball** consists of a sphere resting on rollers, with only the top of the sphere exposed outside its case. The screen cursor travels in whatever direction the operator spins the sphere. A mouse is merely a trackball turned upside down.

A **crosshair cursor** is moved over hard-copy images of maps, survey photos, and even large drawings of microchips. The image is digitized into the computer system's memory as the cursor passes over it. Using a keypad on the cursor, the operator can enter supplementary information into the memory. With maps, for example, features such as rivers, roads, and buildings may be scanned with the crosshair and any identifying labels keyed in from the pad. Once the maps are in digital form, the operator can call them up for display on the screen and modify them at will.

FIGURE 6-28

A joystick. Resembling an automobile stick shift, the joystick is widely used in computer graphics work and computer games.

FIGURE 6-29

Digitizing tablets. Digitizing tablets often work with (a, left) a crosshair cursor or (b, right) a stylus. As either is moved along the tablet, the pattern it traces is entered into computer memory.

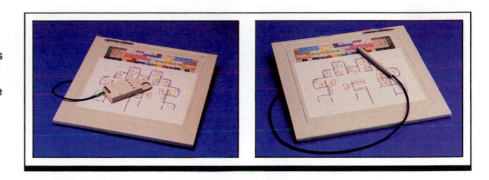

A **digitizing tablet** employs either a crosshair cursor or a penlike stylus that the operator uses to trace over the flat tablet (Figure 6-29). You can think of the tablet as a matrix of thousands of tiny dots. Each dot has a machine address. When you trace a line on the tablet, the stylus passes over some of the dots, causing their status in computer memory to change from a 0-state to a 1-state. When the drawing is complete, it is stored in digital form as a large matrix of 0s and 1s and may be recalled at any time.

Recently there have been some ambitious—and successful—efforts to push digitizing to new heights. Today there are penlike devices available that trace over a three-dimensional object so that it can be electronically reconstructed in computer memory, devices that digitize and reproduce images from a standard TV or videocassette recorder (VCR), and even "digitizing cameras" that take a picture and generate a digital image based on the intensity of the light incident upon the subject. There are also robots that "see" (that is, "recognize") objects by digitizing their shapes and other physical properties and comparing them with those stored in computer memory.

Image Scanners

Image scanners, such as the one in Figure 6-30, are used to digitize images of photographs, drawings, and documents into computer memory (see the Tomorrow box on page 198). Many image scanners sold for PCs scan at a resolution of 300 dpi. As you might expect, the more dots the computer uses to store the image, the better the resolution will be when the image is finally output. Typeset-quality imaging, available through professional print shops, generally starts at a resolution of about 1,000 dpi.

Many image scanners are "dumb," meaning that they can't recognize any of the text they read. "Intelligent" image scanners, on the other hand, are accompanied by optical character recognition (OCR) software, which enables them to recognize as well as read characters. Thus, a person with an OCR-capable image scanner can later edit any text on a standard word processor once it is read in. While such software packages allow only a limited number of fonts to be read, many of them contain routines that enable scanners to learn new fonts.

FIGURE 6-30

FIGURE 6-30

An image scanner. Image scanners, such as this Howtek color scanner, are used to digitize images of photographs, drawings, and documents into computer memory. Some scanners are also equipped with software that enables them to recognize text.

SPECIAL-PURPOSE OUTPUT EQUIPMENT

In this section, we will consider output devices that are appropriate for specialized uses. The technologies we will describe are computer output microfilm (COM), plotters, voice-output devices, and film recorders.

Computer Output Microfilm (COM)

Computer output microfilm (COM) is a way of placing computer output on microfilm media, typically either a *microfilm reel* or *microfiche card*. Microfilming can result in tremendous savings in paper costs, storage space, and handling. For example, a 4-by-6-inch microfiche card can contain the equivalent of 270 printed pages. COM is particularly useful for organizations that must keep massive files of information that do not need to be updated. It's also useful for organizations that need to manipulate large amounts of data but find fast methods of online access too costly.

The process of producing microfilm or microfiche output generally takes place offline on a special COM unit. If a report is to be generated and placed onto film, the computer system may first output it onto magnetic tape. Then the tape is mounted offline on the COM unit, which typically can produce both microfilm and microfiche. This device displays an image of each page on a screen and produces microfilmed photographs from these images. In online processes, output passes directly from the computer to the COM unit. Most COM units can work both online and offline depending on an organization's needs.

To read the microfilm or microfiche that COM produces, people either select the reels or cards by hand and mount them onto the appropriate

FIGURE 6-31

Flatbed electrostatic plotter. Electrostatic plotters, which are very similar in principle to printers, are useful for rapid production of graphic images.

reading device or use an auxiliary retrieval system driven by a minicomputer that automatically locates and mounts the desired frames. Reading usually takes place offline.

Plotters

A **plotter** is an output device that is primarily used to produce charts, drawings, maps, three-dimensional illustrations, and other forms of hard copy. The two most common types of plotters are pen plotters and electrostatic plotters.

A *pen plotter* is an output device that uses pens, which create images by moving across the paper surface. Watching these machines draw is an experience and always attracts interest among people who are seeing them for the first time. The plotter looks like a mechanical artist working in fast motion. As the machine switches colors and begins new patterns, the audience is hard put to guess what the plotter will do next. Many pen plotters can accept either standard fiber-tipped pens or, if the highest possible output quality is desired, high-precision, technical drafting pens.

Electrostatic plotters are also very popular. These devices work with a toner bed similar to that of a copying machine, but instead of light they use a matrix of tiny wires to charge the paper with electricity. When the charged paper passes over the toner, the toner adheres to it and produces an image. Electrostatic plotters are relatively fast but their output quality is lower than that of pen plotters. Nonetheless, the output quality of electrostatic devices is improving, and many industry experts expect them to eventually replace the slower, mechanically intensive pen plotters.

Whether they employ pens or electrostatic printing, plotters are of either the flatbed or drum type. A *flatbed plotter,* which resembles a drafting board, is shown in Figure 6-31. *Drum plotters,* in contrast, draw on paper that is rolled onto a drumlike mechanism. Figure 6-32 shows a drum plotter.

FIGURE 6-32

Drum pen plotter. While pen plotters produce the highest-quality hard-copy graphical output, they are relatively slow.

Voice-Output Devices

For a number of years, computers have been able to communicate with users, after a fashion, by "speaking" to them. How often have you dialed a phone number only to hear, "We're sorry, the number you are trying to reach, 774–0202, is no longer in service" or "The time is 6:15 . . . the downtown temperature is 75 degrees"? **Voice-output devices,** the machines responsible for such messages, convert digital data in storage into spoken messages. These messages may be constructed as needed from a file of prerecorded words, or they may be synthesized using other techniques.

Computerized voice output is also used extensively at airline terminals to broadcast information about flight departures and arrivals, in the securities business to quote the prices of stocks and bonds, and in the supermarket industry to announce descriptions and prices of items as they are scanned. Voice output has great potential in any company with employees who do little else all day but, say, give out balances and status reports.

Computers and Photography

The Inevitability of Digital Imagery

With high-resolution graphics now possible on computer systems, a frequent question that comes to people's minds is: Will conventional photography still be around tomorrow? The most probable answer is "yes and no." While it will likely not be within your lifetime that computer robots are running around snapping photos that compare with those of Ansel Adams and Eliot Porter, high-quality digital cameras and digital reproduction techniques are already here and encroaching on the domain of conventional photography.

The need to be able to capture, process, store, and output photographic images in digital form has long been recognized. Most of the print images professional photographers make eventually wind up in digital form. And the process of preparing a photograph for printing by conventional means is long, tedious, and characterized by much trial-and-error guesswork. If any profession could benefit from the speed and precision of computers, photography would certainly rank high.

Nonetheless, we are still far away from being able to represent a digital image in a photographic-quality form. To do justice to a 35mm negative, one would need a system that provided an image resolution of 15 million pixels. In contrast, most of the digital cameras and scanners now available provide a resolution of only a small fraction of that amount. Today electronic prints come close to many instant films in quality.

However, digital photographic techniques are improving dramatically, and for many applications digital technology works just fine. For instance, in the production of newspapers and magazines, image quality is, to a point, often less important than speed and flexibility. While most experts feel that conventional photography and digital photography will coexist for a number of years, many concede that digital photography eventually will become the predominant form.

Some of the things one can do with digital photographic images today are certainly impressive. For instance, sup-

---

Currently one of the main shortcomings of this technology is that the number of potential messages is quite limited if the system must create them extemporaneously and a high output quality is desired. Most voice-output devices have a vocabulary on the order of a few hundred words and a limited ability to combine words dynamically to form intelligible sentences. As a result, these devices are most useful when short messages are required—a telephone number, a bank balance, a price, and so on.

Film Recorders

Film recorders are cameralike devices that capture high-resolution computer-generated images directly onto 35mm slides, transparencies, and

pose you have a standard camera and want to take a picture of your' dog. Unfortunately, the telephone pole in the background looks like it is growing out of its head. But armed with an image scanner, you can digitize the photo into your PC. Using any of a number of touch-up programs, such as Letraset's Image Studio or Aldus's SnapShot, you can make the pole disappear. In fact, if you have also scanned in a photo of a beach scene taken on a recent trip to Mazatlan or St. Thomas, you can even combine the two photographs electronically—a process called *composite imaging*—making it appear as though your dog jetted down with you to enjoy the sun. While the image quality might not qualify for *National Geographic,* it certainly will be good enough to print in a newspaper or inexpensive magazine if you keep it small.

If you are curious to see just how far computers can go in helping the camera distort reality, just look at the panel of photos showing the ship in the cove, on the fifth page of Window 8. Then imagine what tomorrow's image processing might do for your future: "Hi Mom. Here I am, landing on the rooftop of Trump Towers." Or "There I was, bored silly having chateaubriand with Robin Leach in my $10,000-a-night hotel suite and wishing I was back home in Hoboken."

Digital photography. It will eventually make the conventional darkroom obsolete.

other film media (see Figure 6-33). Only a few years ago film recorders served only large computers, with which they were used for applications such as art, medical imaging, and scientific CAD work. Today they are increasingly being used with PCs for applications such as spicing up corporate business meetings or client presentations with slide shows. Some experts predict that such computer-generated slides will soon account for a large percentage of all business slides made. Since film recorders, like cameras, are "dumb" and need not recognize an image in order to record it, they can easily transfer onto film virtually any image that can be captured on a display screen. Most of the images in Window 3 were produced on film recorders, which by far provide the highest resolution of any of the output devices discussed in this chapter.

FIGURE 6-33

Film recorder. Film recorders are cameralike devices that capture display-screen images. The film is imaged in three different scans, one each for the three colors on the color wheel.

SUMMARY AND KEY TERMS

Input and output devices enable people and computers to communicate. **Input devices** convert data and programs into a form that the CPU will understand. **Output devices** convert computer-processed information into a form that people will comprehend.

Output devices produce results in either hard copy or soft copy form. The term **hard copy** generally refers to output that has been recorded into a *permanent* form onto a medium such as paper or microfilm. The term **soft copy,** in contrast, generally refers to display output, which is *temporary*.

Display devices are peripheral devices that contain a televisionlike viewing screen. Most display devices fall into one of two categories: monitors and display terminals. A **monitor** is an output device that consists of only the viewing screen. A **display terminal** is an input/output communications workstation that consists of a screen for output and a keyboard for input.

A key characteristic of any display device is *resolution,* or the sharpness of the screen image. On many display devices, resolution is measured by the number of dots, or **pixels,** on the screen. With a **bit-mapped** device, the operator can control each pixel on the screen.

One common way to classify display devices is according to whether they are monochrome or color. *Monochrome* display devices output using a single foreground color, whereas *color* display devices often are capable of outputting in eight or more colors.

Most display devices on the market today use a large picture-tube element similar to those found inside standard TV sets. These devices are called **CRTs (cathode-ray tubes).** Recently slim-profile devices called **flat-panel displays** have also become available.

Operators who interact with display devices commonly use a **keyboard** for input. As the keyboard operator depresses a key, that key's corresponding character appears on the display screen at a highlighted area called the **cursor** position. Many people supplement keyboard operations with a device known as a **mouse.** Mice are especially handy when pointing to **icons** on the screen—small geometric symbols that represent commands or program options. **Light pens** and **touch screen devices,** as well as the numerous devices discussed in the "Source Data Automation" section, are other devices commonly used to facilitate operator input.

Printers, unlike display devices, produce hard-copy output. *Low-speed printers* output one character at a time. Because of their relatively low cost, they are popular units for small computer systems. *High-speed printers,* which can output either a line or a page at a time, are popular for larger computer systems.

All printers use either an impact or a nonimpact printing technology. In **impact printing,** a hammer strikes the paper or ribbon to form characters. A **solid-font mechanism** is an impact device that produces fully formed characters such as those a typewriter creates. Most low-speed printers in use today employ a print head that's an **impact dot-matrix mechanism,** which constructs printed characters out of a series of closely packed dots. **Nonimpact printing,** which outputs dot-matrix characters, uses a variety of techniques to form printed images. The most popular nonimpact printing methods today use *electrothermal, thermal-transfer, ink-jet, laser,* and *array* technologies.

The printers most commonly available for microcomputer systems are low-speed devices that use either daisywheel, print-thimble, impact dot-matrix, thermal-transfer, or ink-jet technologies. Although impact-dot matrix printers are still the most widely used, relatively high-speed laser printers have become especially popular in business in the last few years. Laser printers produce letter-quality output that rivals that of solid-font printers, quickly generate presentation graphics for reports and meetings, and enable certain publishing functions to be performed on a desktop.

Most of the printing done on large computer systems is accomplished by high-speed printers. The most notable exception is the **teleprinter terminal,** a low-speed printer with a keyboard for small amounts of operator input. High-speed printers fall into one of two major categories: **line printers,** which produce a line of output at a time, and **page printers,** which produce a page of output at a time. Line printers often must be used with auxiliary devices such as *decollators* and *bursters*.

Source data automation refers to technologies for collecting data in machine-readable form at their point of origin. Among these technologies are optical character recognition (OCR), magnetic ink character recognition (MICR), voice input, digitizing, and image scanning.

Optical character recognition (OCR) refers to a wide range of optical-scanning procedures and equipment designed for machine recognition of marks, characters, and codes. *Optical marks* are most frequently used in test-taking situations where students pencil in responses on special forms. Probably the best-known use of *optical characters* is the **point-of-sale (POS) systems** widely used at checkout stations in stores. In many of these systems, the characters on the price tag are coded in a special font readable by both machines and humans. Some POS systems use *optical codes,* such as *bar codes.* The most widely used bar code is the **universal product code (UPC),** which appears on the labels of most packaged supermarket goods.

Magnetic ink character recognition (MICR) is a technology confined almost exclusively to the banking industry. MICR characters, preprinted on bank checks, enable the checks to be rapidly sorted, processed, and routed to the proper banks.

Voice-input devices enable computer systems to recognize the spoken word. Voice-input technologies have tremendous work-saving potential but have been slow to mature because of their relative complexity.

A **digitizer** is an input device that converts a measurement into a digital value. Besides the mouse, discussed earlier, some other widely used digitizing devices are the **joystick, trackball, crosshair cursor,** and **digitizing tablet.**

An **image scanner** is used to input images such as photographs, drawings, and documents into computer storage. In the case of text documents, some image scanners are accompanied by software that enables the scanners to recognize the inputted characters.

A number of special-purpose output devices exist for a variety of information processing applications. Among these are computer output microfilm (COM) equipment, plotters, voice-output devices, and film recorders.

Computer output microfilm (COM) is a way of placing computer output on microfilm media such as microfilm reels or microfiche cards. COM can result in tremendous savings in paper costs, storage space, and handling.

A **plotter** is an output device that is used primarily to produce graphic output such as charts, maps, and engineering drawings. The two most common types of plotters are *pen plotters,* which use drawing pens to create images, and *electrostatic plotters,* which creates images through electrostatic charges. Whether they employ pens or electrostatic charges, plotters are of either the flatbed or drum type. A *flatbed plotter* uses a drawing surface that resembles a drafting table. A *drum plotter* draws on a cylindrically backed surface.

Voice-output devices enable computer systems to compose intelligible spoken messages from digitally stored words and phrases.

Film recorders are cameralike devices that are used to capture computer-generated images directly onto 35mm slides, transparencies, and other film media. Virtually any image that can be captured on a display screen can be output onto film.

REVIEW EXERCISES

Fill-in Questions

1. The term ___hardcopy___ generally refers to output that has been recorded onto a medium such as paper or film.

2. Resolution on a display screen is measured by the number of dots, or ___pixels___ .

3. A highlighted position on a display screen indicating where the next character the operator types in will be placed is called a(n) ___cursor___ .

4. A display device that outputs images in a single foreground color is known as a(n) ___monochrome___ display.

5. High-quality dot-matrix printing is sometimes called ___Near letter quality___ (NLQ) printing.

6. A(n) ___thermal transfer___ printer heats ink from a wax-based ribbon onto paper.

7. A(n) ___ink jet___ printer sprays small droplets of electrically charged ink onto paper to form images.

8. Two types of pen plotters are ___flatbed___ and ___drum___ plotters.

9. A display device in which all screen pixels can be controlled by the operator is called ___bit mapped___ .

10. A(n) ___film recorder___ is a cameralike device used to capture computer-generated images directly onto 35mm slides.

Matching Questions

Match each term with the description that best fits.

a. crosshair cursor   e. MICR
b. OCR   f. COM
c. POS   g. plotter
d. UPC   h. mouse

_e_ 1. Used almost exclusively by the banking industry.

_f_ 2. Refers to microfilmed output.

_g_ 3. A type of output device used to produce graphical images on paper with pens.

_B_ 4. Refers to a collection of different technologies used for optical recognition of marks, characters, and codes.

_d_ 5. A code that is prominent on the packaging of most supermarket goods.

_a_ 6. A device that would be useful for digitizing a map into computer storage.

_h_ 7. A device used to move the cursor rapidly around the display screen.

_c_ 8. Refers to the use of electronic cash registers, optical scanning devices, and so forth in retail establishments.

Discussion Questions

1. List several types of input and output devices. State whether each device is used for input, output, or both.
2. Identify several ways in which display devices differ.
3. Name some hardware devices that are used in conjunction with display devices for entering data into the computer system.
4. In which major respects do printers differ?
5. What is source data automation, and why is it significant?
6. How does MICR differ from OCR?
7. What are the limitations of voice-input and voice-output devices?
8. What are the major advantages COM offers?

Critical Thinking Questions

1. A page of typed text that is created and saved with a word processor takes up a different amount of storage than a copy of that same page read by a scanner. Why do you think this is so? Which would take up more space?
2. Refer to the Tomorrow box in Chapter 2 and, also, Features 2A and 2B. List all applications mentioned in which source data automation is taking place.

3. Some people predicted years ago that there would never be a significant market for color CRTs among office workers. This prediction proved dead wrong. Why do you think this is so?

4. The president of J.C. Penney has stated that the leading retailers in the coming decade will be those who make the best use of information processing technologies. Do you agree with this point of view? Explain why or why not.

The Electronic Canvas

A Peek at the Leading Edge in Computer Output

Probably nothing exemplifies the rapid advances made in computer output over the last few years better than the field of computer art. As you examine the images on the next few pages, keep in mind that only since about 1980 has the computer emerged as a viable tool for artistic expression. All of the early computer artists were scientists with a keen knowledge of both computers and mathematical modeling, and they worked on large, general-purpose computers. As the potential and demand for computer-generated art in business-related fields such as advertising, publishing, and movie production evolved, specialized hardware and software for noncomputer professionals began to emerge. The field of computer art is truly in the pioneering stage, and one can only guess what the leading edge of computer output will look like ten years from now.

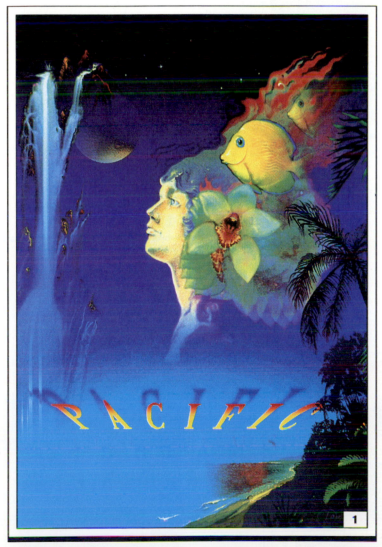

1 "California Dreams" by James Dowlen, a prominent artist in northern California famous for his surreal images.

2–4 The top three award-winning images in the fine arts division of the 1987 Truevison Art Contest—"The Pour," "Roots," and "Globe."

5 The effervescent art of Michael Lucero often features simple geometric shapes and windows floating through space, bright colors, and a Jersey cow.

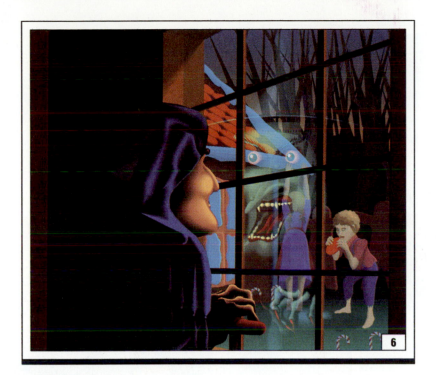

6–9 Artists frequently use computers to create images for cartoons, children's books, and movie storyboards.

10 A state-of-the-art image produced by Design Vision of Toronto. The blue glass buildings and covered walkway in the background were created with software and combined on graphics equipment with a photographic image, shown in the foreground.

11 Computers often are used to produce neorealistic images in which the sharpness of scanned-in images is softened.

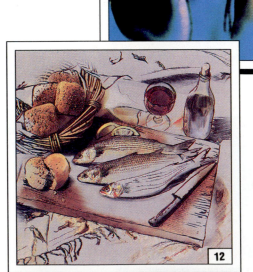

12 Working from a single scanned-in photograph, artist Julie Gibula produced this image on a Quantel Paintbox, a turnkey art system, in less than an hour. An electronic airbrush and an electronic chalk facility were used to paint over the original input image to impart a hand-drawn look.

PLOTTER OUTPUT

13

13–15 While the highest-resolution hard-copy graphic images are obtainable from film recorders, plotters and printers recently have improved to the point where they too can produce respectable-looking output. Images 13 and 14 were produced on a Tektronix Color Image Printer (a thermal-transfer printer). Image 15 was created on a Calcomp 5800 color plotter.

14

15

COMMERCIAL ART

16–18 "Old Cars," "Chardonnay," and "Eyetech" were, respectively, the three top vote-getters among hundreds in the commercial division of the 1988 Truevision Art Contest. All three images were produced with Time Arts' Lumena software, a microcomputer-based product.

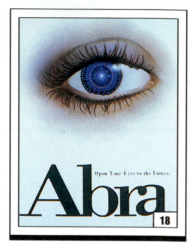

19 Computer graphics were used to create this Chicago album cover when the band specifically requested a high-tech look.

20–22 Computers are frequently used to create poster images, as exemplified here in these stunning pieces from Brian Johnson and Cathrine Colgan of Wasatch Computer Technology.

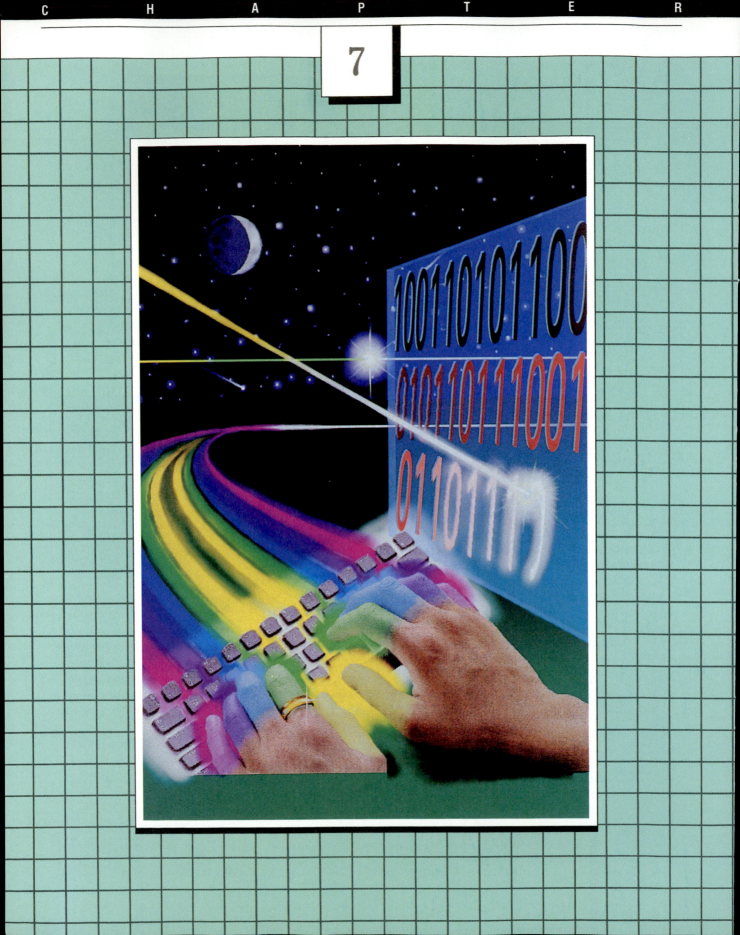

Telecommunications

Objectives

After completing this chapter, you will be able to:

1. Identify the hardware and software components of a telecommunications system.

2. Describe various types of communications media and explain how messages can be sent over them.

3. Identify some types of communications services and facilities that organizations may acquire.

4. Describe several types of telecommunications networks.

5. Explain the conventions devices use to communicate with one another.

6. Describe some of the strategies used to manage networks.

OVERVIEW

Telecommunications refers to communication over a distance—over phone lines, via privately owned cable, or by satellite, for instance. Today, telecommunications technologies are integrated in a variety of ways into many organizations' routine operations. Through telecommunications, for example, a marketing manager at company headquarters can instantly receive information on inventories from a warehouse at another location and then transmit that information to a division office across the country or even across the globe. Or, a purchasing agent on the 25th floor of an office building can use a personal computer workstation to call up the status of a purchase order stored on the mainframe system located in the building's basement. Later, the agent can use the same workstation to dial up a computer owned by a supplier, 1,000 miles away, and get a list of prices.

Telecommunications has become increasingly critical to many organizations in recent years for a number of reasons, the most important of which are the increased pace at which business is done, the globalization of economies, the distribution of data in electronic form to ever more points, and changing lifestyles that have been made possible through computers and communications (see Feature 7A).

In this chapter, we'll first look at how data are sent over distances. We'll begin by describing the media, such as phone lines and microwaves, that carry data and the types of signals that encode the data. Next, we'll discuss the various ways in which people or organizations can get the resources they need to transmit data. Finally, we'll examine several issues concerning the management of telecommunications systems. These issues include determining how to set up communications networks and dealing with the problems that arise when interfacing numerous pieces of "incompatible" equipment in a network.

TELECOMMUNICATIONS IN ACTION

To see how a telecommunications system works, let's turn immediately to an example—a small mail-order catalog firm. Figure 7-1 shows a simple telecommunications network that links the firm's North Chicago headquarters and South Chicago warehouse to a small minicomputer. Each day the firm processes nearly 1,000 phone and mail orders from its customers. At North Chicago headquarters, eight I/O devices (six display terminals and two printers) are configured to the mini. The computer's storage device contains, among other things, up-to-date data on product prices, quantity of items in stock, and the firm's customers. Authorized personnel may draw on any of these data in the course of processing an order.

When headquarters receives an order, an order clerk keys data into a display terminal. The clerk checks such things as whether the items re-

FIGURE 7-1

Telecommunications system for a mail-order catalog firm.

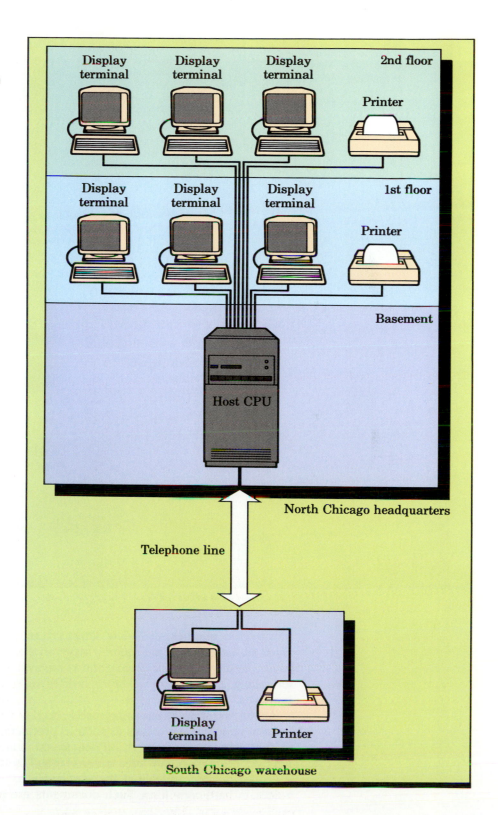

The Communications Revolution

Why Telecommunications Is Such a Hot Area

It's difficult these days to pick up a business, news, or computer journal without seeing something about how communications is changing the nature of business. We are living in an era in which information is the commodity upon which most work is based. Since telecommunications systems are the "grease" that gets information from one point to another, it's understandable why there's such a fuss. Following are four trends that are particularly important for appreciating why the word *telecommunications* is today on the lips of virtually every corporate executive.

The Pace of Business Is Accelerating. Business is being conducted faster today than ever before, largely due to the rapidity at which computers can transform data into meaningful information and the quickness with which these data or information can be transmitted over a communications medium. Al-

> Business . . . . must compete in a global economy, with a global information base.

though a decade ago weeks, days, or even hours were typically needed for information to arrive, that same amount of time is often unacceptable today. A first-rate stockbroker, for instance, must be ready to pounce on a juicy buy or a sell candidate—even if it's coming over the wires at 3:00 a.m. Similarly, many executives would not be caught dead without a mobile phone in their car, golf cart, or yacht. What if an important client needs to get in touch or an opportunity comes along that just can't wait? And, if it weren't for communications options such as facsimile machines, electronic mailboxes, and overnight mail services, work bottlenecks would slow some jobs to a pace that would put many a company out of business.

The bottom line: Telecommunications makes it possible for work to be done more quickly. Although some argue that telecommunications has contributed to making life a rat race, you must choose either to run with the rats or to be left at the starting gate.

The Reach of Business Is Expanding. At the beginning of the 20th century, most organizations conducted business within a small, local area. Later, such developments as cars, roads, planes,

quested are in stock, the items' latest prices, and customers' credit status. Once all these details are squared away, an electronic order is prepared and routed to the warehouse. Two printers are available at the headquarters site for billing, preparing out-of-stock notices to customers, and various other purposes.

At the warehouse, personnel use a display terminal to check the order log and update stock counts as soon as products are received from vendors or shipped out to customers. All data keyed in at this terminal are transmitted over ordinary phone lines and processed by the headquarters computer. A printer is also available at the warehouse to prepare packing lists or invoices in hard-copy form. Such documents are placed in a shipping enve-

phones, radio, and television contributed greatly to expanding the reach of businesses to the entire nation. Now, with high-speed computers and communications, many big businesses no longer can afford to think in terms of a national economy, especially if they are in the private sector. They must compete in a global economy, with a global information base. Virtually every large organization that hopes to make it into the 21st century is feeling the pinch to put in place some type of global information system, putting it more closely in touch with employees, customers, suppliers, and events all over the world.

Electronic-based Information Is Available Everywhere. Only a few years ago, mainframes that were clustered in a single room or in a processing center contained all of an organization's electronic data. As minicomputers and personal computers became available, a lot of these data were distributed to smaller machines. In the 1960s and 1970s, for instance, divisions and offices in many organizations were able to afford their own computers. When personal computers became available, virtually everyone wanted one. Consequently, many organizations have thousands of computers today, and telecommunications provides the potential to link these machines effectively. The buzzword in many corporations today is *connectivity*—the ability to link machines and users in networks, so as to share information.

The Technology of Telecommunications Is Changing Lifestyles. This is an area that we'll look at more closely in Chapter 16. Because telecommunications allows people to perform work at a site other than the location at which they are employed, many interesting work possibilities are emerging. People with small children can use terminals or personal computers at home, uploading and/or downloading data to or from mainframes at work. Remember that executive with the mobile phone on the yacht; where would he or she be without telecommunications? You guessed it—back in the office! Experts also say that many of the hottest college prospects in the future will want to work for companies that are heavily networked. This way, if the prospect prefers working out of a condo in Aspen, he or she can use personal computers, facsimile machines, teleconferencing, and satellite transmission to make that possible. Thus, telecommunications can be used as a bargaining chip to gain competitive advantage in the labor market. Some futurists also feel that telecommunications evenually will change the structure of many corporations.

lope to the customer that is attached to the top of the carton containing the order.

System Elements. A *telecommunications network* such as the one shown in Figure 7-1 consists of the following elements:

1. A central computer, called the *host computer* (or *host*), handles the processing.
2. Peripheral devices, called *terminals,* send data to or receive data from the host computer.

3. *Communications media* transmit the data. In this case, ordinary phone lines carry the data between the remote warehouse peripherals and the host CPU, and special cables link the peripherals at headquarters to the host.

4. Devices called *modems* convert computer signals into a form compatible with the phone lines, and vice versa.

5. *Communications management devices* optimize the flow of messages to and from the CPU.

We will see the role these elements play in such a telecommunications network throughout the chapter. We will also consider several other types of networks. For instance, there are a number of networks in use that do not contain a host computer. Also, you will see that virtually any device that is capable of input, output, processing, or storage can serve as a terminal on a network. Besides the traditional display terminal, among the most widely used types of terminals found today in communications networks are personal computer workstations, direct-access storage devices, touch-tone phones, facsimile (fax) machines, and high-speed printers and copiers.

Data. Although the system depicted in Figure 7-1 is simple, with text being the only type of data transmitted, keep in mind as you read Chapter 7 that data can exist in many forms. The four types of data that may be transmitted in a network are text, graphics, voice, and video.

Text data have been around the longest in communications networks. These data usually consist of standard alphabetic, numeric, and special characters—that is, the type of data one normally sees in a simple word-processed letter, budget, or computer program listing.

Graphics data consist of pictures such as drawings, photographs, illustrations, and the like. Graphics data often require a more sophisticated communications medium than do text because they are naturally more complicated and are often in color.

Voice data are the type of data transmitted during an ordinary telephone call. Any type of sound—including stereo music—is considered voice data.

Video data consist of motion pictures, such as a movie or a live conference. If sound is to accompany the video data, the communications medium must also be able to carry voice data.

Device Management. Even in telecommunications networks as simple as the one in Figure 7-1, difficult problems related to managing remote devices can arise. For example, if several display terminals on the system are competing for service, how will the system handle the requests? This problem can be especially knotty if the host CPU and terminals have been manufactured by a number of different vendors utilizing a variety of communication codes and data-transmission techniques. Also, if some of the terminals are used very sparingly, how can the telecommunications system be set up to minimize line costs? These are two of the problems we will address in this chapter. Solutions to such telecommunications dilemmas are particularly impor-

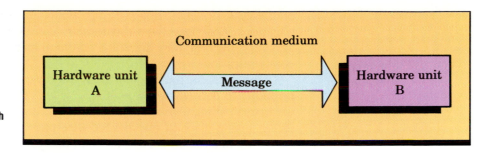

Communication medium

Hardware unit
A   Message   Hardware unit
B

FIGURE 7-2

A simple telecommunications system. As complicated as telecommunications systems may seem to the casual observer, they reduce simply to one device being able to communicate effectively with another.

tant because communications costs often constitute a major percentage of information processing expense.

COMMUNICATIONS MEDIA

Figure 7-2 shows a simple telecommunications system. Two hardware units that are distant from each other transfer messages over some type of **communications medium.** The hardware units may be a terminal and a computer, two computers, or some other combination of two devices. The medium may be privately operated or public phone lines, microwave, or some other alternative. When a message is transmitted, one of the hardware units is designated as the *sender* and the other as the *receiver*. There are several ways to send the message over the medium, as this section will demonstrate.

Types of Media

Communications media fall into one of two classes: physical lines and microwaves.

Physical Lines. Three types of physical lines are used in telecommunications systems today: twisted-wire pairs, coaxial cable, and fiber optic cable.

Twisted-wire pairs, in which strands of wire are twisted in twos, is the communications technology that has been in use the longest. The telephone system, which carries most of the data transmitted in this country and abroad, still consists heavily of twisted-wire pairs. In some cases, several thousand pairs may be placed into single cables, which might connect switching stations within a city. In contrast, only a few pairs are needed to connect a home phone to the closest telephone pole.

Generally, each twisted-wire pair in a cable can accommodate a single phone call between two people or two machines. Since the bulk of the phone system was set up many years ago for voice transmission, it is not the ideal medium for computerized telecommunications. Nonetheless, the

FIGURE 7-3
Optical fibers. A fiber optic cable the width of a pencil may contain as many as 144 optical fibers, each capable of carrying more than 1,000 telephone messages simultaneously.

phone system is fast enough to accommodate many types of computer applications. And since twisted-wire pairs can be manufactured and installed at a very low cost, they are still a common means of linking two points in a communications system.

Coaxial cable, the medium employed by cable television, was developed primarily to deal with a phenomenon called *crosstalk* that occurs in twisted-wire pairs during high-speed transmission. Crosstalk results when a conversation taking place in one twisted-wire pair interferes with a conversation occurring in another. For example, on many phone lines one can sometimes hear background conversations. With voice communication, this problem isn't serious. However, crosstalk can inhibit the high-speed transmission required for television reception and some other sophisticated types of communication. Thus, coaxial cable was developed to fill the need for a fast, relatively interference-free transmission medium. Coaxial cable is also used extensively by the phone companies, typically as a replacement for twisted-wire pairs in important links within the phone network.

One of the most promising developments in cable technology is fiber optics. An innovation whose potential is just beginning to be realized, **fiber optic cable** (see Figure 7-3) consists of thousands of clear glass fiber strands, each approximately the thickness of a human hair. Transmission is made possible by the transformation of data into light beams, which are sent through the cable by a laser device at speeds on the order of billions of bits per second. Each hairlike fiber has the capacity to carry a few television stations or a few thousand two-way voice conversations.

The principal advantages of fiber optics over wire media include speed, size, weight, resistance to tapping, and longevity. For example, it is common for a fiber optic cable to have ten times the data-carrying capacity and one-twentieth the weight of a standard coaxial cable. Fiber optic cable is especially suitable in situations involving heavy point-to-point transmission between two stations.

Microwaves. **Microwaves** are high-frequency radio signals. Text, graphics, voice, and video data can all be converted to microwave impulses. Microwave transmission works by what is known as a *line-of-sight principle*. The transmission stations need not actually be within sight of each other; however, they should have a relatively unobstructed path along which to communicate. When one microwave station receives a message from another, it amplifies it and passes it on. Because of mountains and the curvature of the earth, microwave stations often are placed on tall buildings and mountaintops to ensure an obstacle-free transmission path.

Microwave signals can be sent in two ways: via terrestrial stations or by way of satellite. Both technologies can transmit data in large quantities and at much higher speeds than can twisted-wire pairs.

Terrestrial microwave stations, illustrated in Figure 7-4, must be no more than 25 to 30 miles apart to communicate with each other directly. This limitation arises because the moisture at the earth's surface causes interference, which impedes communication between stations. As you can imagine, it is quite impractical to build all the repeater stations needed to connect distant locations.

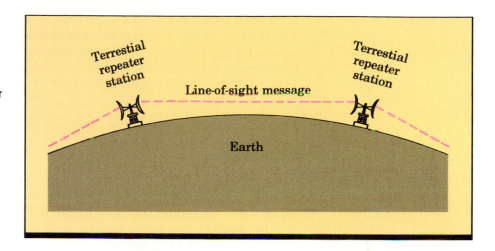

FIGURE 7-4

Terrestrial microwave station.
Stations normally are placed on
mountaintops and tall buildings
when they must transmit with other
terrestrial stations.

Communications satellites were developed to reduce the cost of long-
distance transmission via terrestrial repeater stations as well as to provide
a cheaper and better overseas communications medium than underseas cable. Communications satellites, such as the one shown in Figure 7-5, are
placed into an orbit about 22,300 miles above the earth. Because they travel
at the same speed as the earth's rotation, they appear to remain stationary
over a given spot.

Both communications satellites and terrestrial microwave stations are
most appropriate for transmitting large amounts of data one way at a time.

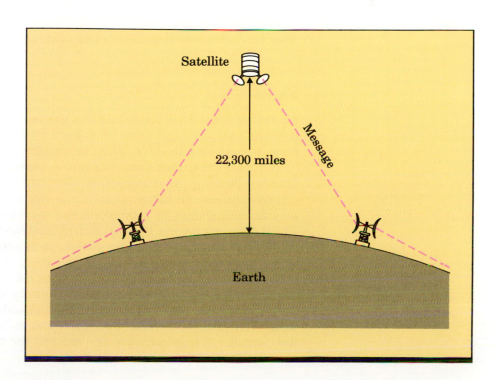

FIGURE 7-5

Satellite transmission. Satellites
move in correspondence to the
earth's rotation, so they appear
stationary to an observer on earth.

Thus, they are ideal for applications such as television and radio broadcasting. Because of the long transmission distances involved, they are not intended for rapid-response, interactive communications. Microwave networks are different than networks supporting cellular phones (see Tomorrow box), in which a radio wave is used to reach a *cell station* that ties into the public phone network.

Media Speed

The speed of a communications medium, generally measured in terms of the number of bits that can be transmitted per second (**bits per second,** or **bps**), partly determines the uses to which the medium can be put. Media can be grouped by speed into three grades, or bandwidths. The speed of transmission is proportional to the width of the frequency band.

Narrowband transmission refers to a medium with a data-carrying capacity in the range of 45 to 150 bps. These rates are suitable only for very-low-speed operations, such as telegraph and teletype communication.

Voice-grade transmission (300 to 9,600 bps) represents a medium level of speed. This kind of transmission is so called because spoken messages can be transmitted in this speed range. On regular telephone lines, the most common voice-grade lines, speeds of 300 bps are practical for transmitting data. To realize higher-than-normal speeds on voice-grade lines, a "private" line usually must be obtained and conditioned. To *condition* a line, technicians place amplifiers at given intervals along the line to clean up the interference that accompanies the higher speeds and to bolster the strength of the transmission.

Wideband transmission rates (19,200 to 500,000 or more bps) are possible only with coaxial and fiber optic cable and with microwave media.

Media Mode

Communications media also can be classified in terms of whether or not they can send messages in two directions. In the vernacular of communications, transmission mode is said to be simplex, half-duplex, or full-duplex.

In **simplex transmission,** data can be transmitted only in a single, prespecified direction. An example from everyday life is a doorbell—the signal can go only from the button to the chime. Although simplex lines are cheap, they are uncommon for computer-based telecommunications applications, which generally involve two-way communication. Even devices that are designed primarily to receive information, such as printers, communicate an acknowledgment back to the sender device.

In **half-duplex transmission,** messages can be carried in either direction, but only one way at a time. The press-to-talk radio phones used in police cars employ this mode of transmission; only one person can talk at a time. Often the line between a terminal and its host CPU is half-duplex. If the computer is transmitting to the terminal, the operator cannot send new messages until the computer is finished.

Cellular Phones

Will They Change the Way You Live or Work?

In the century or so since Alexander Graham Bell made his great discovery, the telephone has changed remarkably little. It is still basically a product with which people communicate by going to stations at predesignated locations and speaking to each other. While cellular phones are not a complete departure from the past, they do provide one very alluring advantage over conventional telephones: Because they are not wired to a wall, they theoretically can put two people into contact with each other anywhere, even if they are in motion.

Currently those who most benefit from the cellular phone boom are people who need to be in constant contact with the office or clients but must be on the move as well, such as a busy executive, salesperson, or real estate agent. Such a user might, for instance, take a cellular phone out of a briefcase and use it while waiting in line, sitting at a traffic light, or taxiing down a runway. Many executives, in fact, communicate by cellular phone with other executives in their firms on their way to work, thereby making themselves productive during the rush hour.

And the applications of cellular phones don't stop there. People who work out-doors, such as farmers and ranchers, who may need to be in contact with others but can't afford the time it takes to get to a regular phone, are also reaping the benefits of cellular phone technology. For many handicapped persons who are unable to physically get to a regular desk-bound phone, the cellular phone is a godsend. And for commercial fishers who need to talk with others about where the fish are and don't want competitors listening in, cellular phoning provides an ideal solution. You can even hook up a laptop computer to a modem on a cellular phone and gain access to huge databases of information while you are far from an office or a regular phone. This possibility enables such high-tech help as new forms of medical assistance for emergency situations that arise at remote locations.

But while cellular phones may be handy in your line of work or the envy of your friends, they are, alas, not cheap. The price of a good cellular phone often starts at about $1,000. And the expense doesn't end there. You may also wind up paying a fixed monthly service fee of $25 to $50 and up to 50 cents per minute for local calls. Further, you'll get billed for incoming calls. But while cellular phones may be considered a luxury now, their prices are expected to come down on all of these fronts if cellular products become a hit with the general public. Some industry insiders expect the cost of a cellular phone to halve within only the next few years.

Cellular phones operate by keeping in contact with transmitter stations called *cell stations,* or *cells.* These stations, which resemble tall metal telephone poles and are operated by private franchises that have successfully applied to the government for licenses to provide public communications services, are strategically placed throughout a calling area. Cells perform two essential functions: (1) They provide an interface with the regular public phone network, and (2) they enable a moving vehicle with a phone to receive uninterrupted transmitting power by passing signals off to contiguous cells located in the zone into which the vehicle is moving. Unlike many conventional mobile transmission solutions, cellular technology can maintain a quality transmission free from interference and eavesdropping.

Cellular phones. At the right price, will everybody want one?

FIGURE 7-6
Analog and digital transmission.

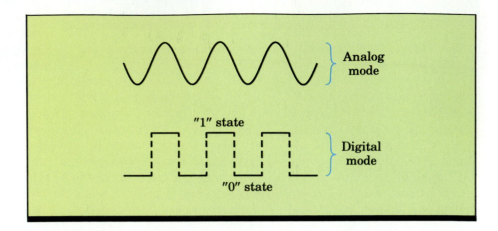

Full-duplex transmission is like traffic on a busy two-way street: The flow moves in two directions at the same time. Full-duplexing is ideal for hardware units that need to pass large amounts of data between themselves, as in computer-to-computer communication. Full-duplex channels generally are not needed for terminal-to-host links, because the terminal operator's response usually depends on the results sent back from the computer.

Media Signal

There are two possible ways to classify the signal sent along a medium: analog and digital.

The phone system, established many years ago to handle voice traffic, carries signals in an **analog** fashion, that is, by a *continuous* sine wave over a certain frequency range. The continuous wave reflects the myriad variations in the pitch of the human voice. Unfortunately, most business computing equipment is **digital;** it is built to handle data coded into two *discrete* states—that is, as 0- and 1-bits. This difference between analog and digital states is illustrated in Figure 7-6.

Modems. Because digital impulses can't be sent over analog phone lines, some means of translating each kind of signal into the other had to be developed. Conversion of signals from digital to continuous-wave form is called *modulation,* and translation from continuous waves back to digital impulses is termed *demodulation.* A single device called a **modem** (coined from the words *MOdulation* and *DEModulation*) takes care of both operations. As Figure 7-7 shows, when a terminal sends a remote CPU a message that must be carried over an analog line, a modem is needed at both the sending end (to convert from digital to analog) and the receiving end (to convert from analog to digital).

Modems are available on add-in boards, which can be fitted into an expansion slot within the computer's system unit, and as standalone hardware devices (see Figure 7-8), which are physically detached from the system unit. Common bps rates on modems targeted to microcomputer users are

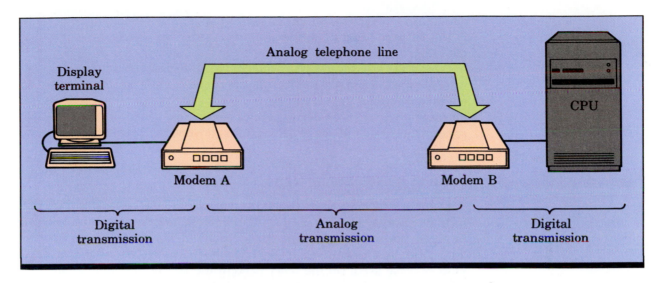

FIGURE 7-7

How modems work. An operator at a display terminal types in data that are encoded digitally and sent to modem A. Modem A converts the data to analog form and sends them over the phone lines to modem B. Modem B reconverts the data to digital form and delivers them to the CPU. When the CPU transmits back to the terminal, these steps are reversed.

300, 1,200, 2,400, 4,800, and 9,600 bps. Often modems capable of higher speeds have independent circuitry that enables them to function at the lower rates as well.

Digital Lines. Although physical lines traditionally have been analog, *digital lines* are also available. These lines can transmit data significantly faster and more accurately than their analog counterparts. Also, with digital lines several types of data (say, text, voice, and video) can be sent along the same

FIGURE 7-8

An external modem. The Hayes modem shown here is capable of transmitting at 9,600 bps.

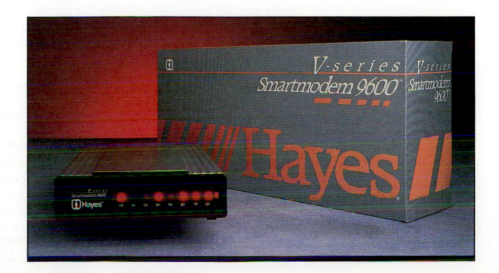

circuit. And, of course, no modem is necessary. The public phone network is still far from being all digital, but urban areas are rapidly moving in that direction.

During the last several years integrated, all-digital communications networks, called *integrated services digital networks (ISDNs),* have started to appear throughout the world. These networks are designed to carry several different types of data—text, graphics, voice, and video, for instance—at greater speeds than those realizable with conventional, analog networks.

Parallel versus Serial Transmission

Transmission devices differ in the number of channels, or tracks, they use to transmit data. The bits used to represent characters may be transmitted in parallel or in serial. If, for example, all the 8-bits needed to convey the letter *H* are sent out at once in eight separate channels, **parallel transmission** is being used. On the other hand, if the bits representing *H* are sent out one at a time over a single channel, **serial transmission** is occurring. Figure 7-9 illustrates the difference between the two.

As Figure 7-9 suggests, parallel transmission is much faster than serial transmission. However, because it requires many more channels, parallel transmission is also more expensive. Thus, parallel transmission usually is limited to short distances.

Computers and their remote terminals traditionally have communicated with each other in serial. A common serial interface, the RS-232C, was developed to standardize remote computer-to-terminal connections. Modems, for instance, use this particular interface on many computer systems. An enhanced form of this interface, the RS-422, is widely used on the Apple Macintosh line of computers to connect modems, printers, and electronic musical instruments. These ports will also accept most RS-232C devices, which operate at higher voltages, without damage to the ports.

Of course, computers must communicate with other nearby peripherals, such as disk and tape units, at high speeds. Since the distance involved is short, parallel transmission is feasible for this purpose. In many IBM microcomputer systems, nearby printers are connected in parallel to the computer's system unit with a popular standard known as the *Centronics* interface.

Asynchronous versus Synchronous Transmission

Serial transmission can be further classified in terms of whether it's asynchronous or synchronous.

In **asynchronous transmission,** one character at a time is transmitted over a line. When the operator strikes a key on the terminal, the character's byte representation is sent up the line to the computer; striking a second key sends a second character; and so forth. But because even the fastest typist can generate only a very small amount of data relative to what the line can accept, a lot of "idle time" occurs on the line.

Synchronous transmission corrects for this deficiency by dispatching data in blocks of characters rather than one at a time. Each block can con-

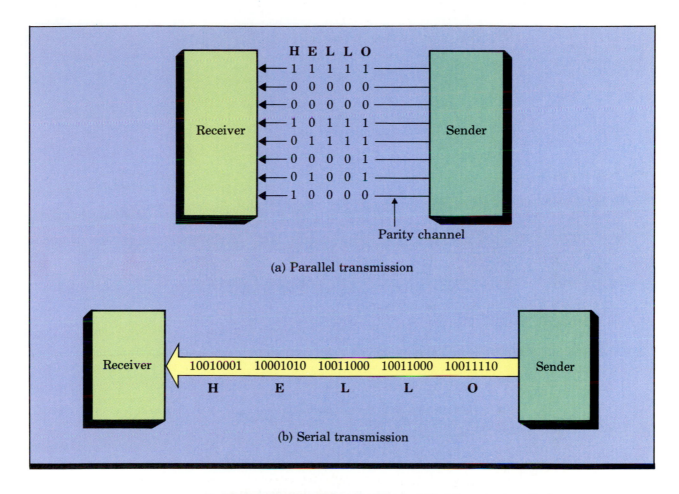

Parallel and serial transmission. Parallel transmission is faster, but the cabling it uses is more expensive. Consequently, devices in close proximity to each other often communicate in parallel, whereas those far apart communicate serially.

sist of thousands of characters. Because no idle time occurs between transmission of individual characters in the block, the utilization of the line is much more efficient. Synchronous transmission is made possible by a *buffer* in the terminal—a storage area large enough to hold a block of characters. As soon as the buffer is filled, all the characters in it are sent up the line to the computer.

Figure 7-10 illustrates the differences between asynchronous and synchronous transmission. In asynchronous transmission, a start bit precedes each byte representation of a character and a stop bit follows each character. When the sending machine has no character to send, it transmits a steady stream of stop bits. The machine at the receiving end "listens" to the line for the start bit. When it senses this bit, it counts off the regular bits used to represent the character. When it encounters the stop bit, it reverts to a "listen-to-the-line" state and waits for the next start bit.

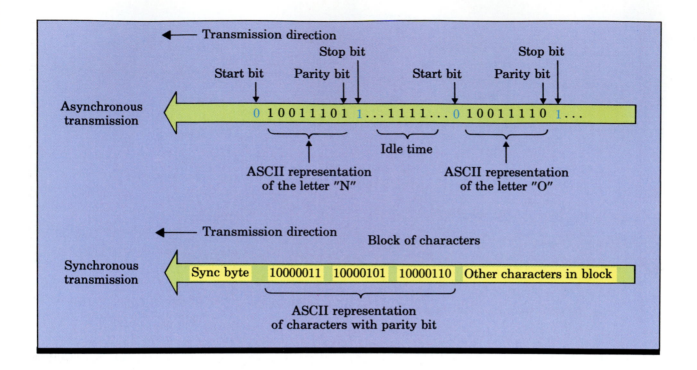

FIGURE 7-10

Asynchronous and synchronous transmission. In asynchronous transmission, each byte is preceded by a start bit and followed by a stop bit. In synchronous transmission, large blocks of bytes are preceded by a sync byte.

In synchronous transmission, each block of characters is preceded by one or more *sync* (synchronous) bytes. The machine at the receiving end listens to the line for this byte. When it's sure it has sensed it (some systems use more than one sync byte to ensure this), the receiving machine starts reading the characters in the block. Since it knows the speed of transmission and number of characters per block, it can interpret the message. After the block is finished, the receiving mechanism continues to "listen" to the line for the next sync byte. Synchronous transmission is commonly used for data speeds of 2,400 bps and higher.

Many display terminals are designed for synchronous transmission, especially those that must transfer data at high speeds. Those that are designed for low-speed data transmission and use asynchronous transmission are sometimes called *ASCII terminals*. Teleprinters, which involve a relatively slow typing operation for input and a slow mechanical printing head for output, almost always use asynchronous transmission.

Synchronous equipment is more expensive and requires a synchronous modem. The higher initial cost, however, may be offset by the greater speed and the lower cost resulting from more efficient transmission.

Figure 7-11 summarizes communications media and their properties.

FIGURE 7-11
Communications media at a glance.

Media Type
☑ Twisted-wire pairs
☑ Coaxial cable
☑ Fiber optic cable
☑ Terrestrial microwave
☑ Satellite

Media Speed
☑ Narrowband (45–150 bps)
☑ Voice grade (300–9,600 bps)
☑ Wideband (19,200–500,000 bps)

Media Mode
☑ Simplex (single fixed direction)
☑ Half duplex (one way at a time)
☑ Duplex (both ways simultaneously)

Media Signal
☑ Analog (modem necessary)
☑ Digital

Data Transmission
☑ Serial transmission
☑ Parallel transmission

Character Packaging
☑ Asynchronous
☑ Synchronous

COMMUNICATIONS SERVICES AND FACILITIES

An organization generally has three choices for services and facilities for transmitting data: common carriers, which maintain public-access facilities; value-added network (VAN) vendors, which provide incremental services upon the common carriers' facilities; and communications media vendors, which provide facilities that the organization may lease or purchase for its own use. Some large organizations, such as the federal government, are able to build their own communications networks; however, this option is often prohibitively expensive.

Common Carriers

Common carriers are companies licensed by the government to provide wide area communications services to the public. **Wide area networks (WANs)** are communications networks that encompass a relatively wide geographical area.

Among the most familiar common carriers are the Bell-system phone companies and firms such as GTE Sprint Communications Corporation, MCI Communications Corporation, and AT&T Communications. The Bell-system companies provide in-state and nearby-state communications services, and the other firms serve a wider area. Among the less familiar common carriers are the *specialized carrier companies*, such as those that provide satellite transmission facilities.

Switched Lines. Because points in the public telephone system receive calls from different locations, the phone system is designed to route calls into a huge switching network. Remember the telephone operators in the old-time movies who switched plugs in and out of a big board to connect people? Today's **switched lines** work in much the same way except that most of the switching is automated rather than manual. Users of these lines can "dial up" computers from their terminals, and the calls are routed, or switched, through paths in public or private phone networks to the proper destinations.

Switched lines are attractive because a person can dial any computer that has a phone number and gain access to it. Also, using the public phone network is often inexpensive because, as with home phones, charges are based directly on the number and length of calls. Unfortunately, switched lines can transmit data only at slow rates. As a result, switched lines often are impractical for devices such as graphics workstations, which require fast transmission speeds to communicate pictures. It is also possible to get annoying busy signals on switched lines just as on a home phone.

Three common ways of switching data in communications networks are circuit switching, message switching, and packet switching.

☐ *Circuit Switching*   *Circuit switching* is the procedure most people encounter when they dial a phone number. You place a call, and you either reach your destination or you don't. If the party doesn't answer, you don't get through.

☐ *Message Switching*   Perhaps the most familiar example of *message switching* is the answering machine. When you place a call, your message reaches its destination whether or not the person is ready to receive it.

☐ *Packet Switching*   *Packet switching* is a method whereby a message is broken up into small packets, each of which can travel along a different path en route to the ultimate destination. The routes along which packets travel to the destination are dynamically determined as they are sent. Network software selects these routes so as to optimize network traffic flow. As the packets arrive at the destination, they are reassembled into the original message.

Dedicated Lines. **Dedicated lines,** or *nonswitched lines,* can be leased or purchased from either common carriers or non-government-licensed vendors that sell communications media for private use. Dedicated lines are used to circumvent many of the problems inherent in public-access switching. They provide a constantly available, point-to-point connection between two devices. Thus, one makes immediate contact with a given computer system every time the "on" switch is activated at the terminal. In addition, because only the owner or lessee has access to the line, dedicated lines can be specially conditioned to transmit data at higher speeds. Generally the caller is not charged for every call made on the line but pays a flat rate.

Thus, users of dedicated lines get to transmit data quickly, in volume, at a fixed cost, and with no threat of busy signals. However, they lack the flexibility to dial up other computer systems over these lines.

Figure 7-12 compares the advantages and disadvantages of switched and dedicated lines.

FIGURE 7-12

Comparison of switched and dedicated lines.

Type of Line	Advantages	Disadvantages
Switched	☑ Operator can choose calling destination ☑ Inexpensive for low volume of work	☑ Slower speed ☑ Possible to get busy signal ☑ Expensive for high volume of work
Dedicated	☑ No busy signals ☑ Higher speed supports more applications ☑ Inexpensive for high volume of work	☑ No choice of calling destination ☑ Expensive for low volume of work

Value-Added Networks (VANs)

Value-added network (VAN) vendors are firms that use the facilities of a common carrier to offer the general subscribing public additional services using those facilities. These services include information processing, information retrieval, electronic mail, and the like. Organizations that use the services are billed by both the common carrier (if toll charges are involved) and the VAN company.

One of the most popular types of VAN service is information retrieval (see Feature 7B). Examples of firms that offer such services are CompuServe, Dow Jones News/Retrieval, and The Source. A subscriber to one of these services has access over the phone lines to large banks of potentially interesting information, for instance, stock and security prices, news, airline schedules, hotel information, and trade journals. There may even be electronic mall (E-mall) shopping, which allows users to browse through goods online. Many VAN companies also offer electronic mailboxes, letting subscribers send confidential messages to business associates who subscribe to the same electronic mail service.

Once users make phone contact with the VAN company, the firm's software systems generally provide easy-to-use menus of available options. After users make requests from their keyboards, the selected services become available over the phone lines for use at their remote workstations. Generally, the VAN companies bill at an hourly rate, and the fee charged depends on both the service provided and the time one is hooked up to the system. There may also be an initial subscription fee.

Local Networks

Common carriers and VANs are most closely associated with wide area networks. Although these networks certainly are useful, many firms need communications facilities that connect local resources—say, computers and terminals located on the same college campus or several microcomputer workstations located in the same office. These types of networks are known as **local networks.**

Getting Your Information Online

A Bounty of Data Are Available through Your Modem

The assortment of information you can get through your modem today is amazing. Alfred Glossbrenner, author of *How to Look It Up On-line* and a long-time observer of communications services available to microcomputer systems, recently reported that more than 3,700 public databases are currently available online. Among these are services for recreational users, shoppers, businesses, researchers, and other people or groups with specialized information needs.

Businesspeople, for instance, can summon a variety of corporate financial reports, such as those available from Moody's, Standard & Poor's, and Dun & Bradstreet. Also available is a never-ending stream of information from news wires such as those of Dow Jones and Reuters. Additionally, there is access to reports filed with the Securities and Exchange Commission, records of trademarks and patents, a variety of financial newsletters, marketing and public relations data, economic indicators and time series, securities prices, and much, much more. Because all of these data are available online, on sophisticated computer systems, one can use a number of electronic retrieval techniques to find information much more quickly than by searching through books.

For researchers and others who read a lot, virtually every major general-interest or trade magazine, newspaper, and journal published worldwide is now online. Also, many regional newspapers in dozens of U.S. cities are available in online versions that can be "delivered" to your monitor screen. And these materials are only a fraction of the things that are out there. There are even electronic clipping services that will scan publications for you and save articles in an electronic mailbox on subjects you designate.

Professionals such as lawyers and doctors also have databases targeted to their specialized needs. Mead Corporation, one of the largest electronic publishers, has been wildly successful with Lexis, a legal database. And for the medical professional, there's Medis.

Want a Brooks Brothers suit or a charge account at Hammacher Schlemmer? Database services called *electronic malls,* or *E-malls,* allow you to E-browse through the goods of any participating merchants. Certain database services let you type in a description of the item you want, along with information such as whether you are after low price or high quality. They will then automatically search inventory to come up with the deal you can't refuse. Other services will even do some analysis for you, for instance, telling you whether it's cheaper to buy or lease a car. While many database services are geared to retail buyers, some services also let

Local networks often are acquired from communications media vendors—firms that sell or lease media for private rather than public use. These media may consist of dedicated point-to-point lines, shared lines, switched lines that are unavailable for public use, or perhaps networks composed of a combination of these lines. Three common types of local networks are cable-based "local area networks" (LANs), private branch exchanges (PBXs), and hierarchical local networks.

you shop wholesale if you are buying in quantity.

And the parade of information doesn't stop there. You can get movie reviews, access to any page of Grolier's *American Experience* encyclopedia, information about the Texas job market, flight information, reservations at tens of thousands of hotels throughout the world, electronic mail and bulletin board access, news blurbs about the latest turmoils on your favorite soap opera, and much, much more. It is expected that in the future many of these services will use super-high-capacity optical disks and all-digital (ISDN) networks to provide near-photo-quality images and stereo sound to you.

Most people get their online information through a particular service company (see figure), which works similarly to a pay television network. When you subscribe to the service company and call it up, you gain access to the variety of participating databases to which it in turn subscribes. CompuServe, for instance, is targeted to information useful to the average person, including news and weather, personal investing and money management, travel, and shopping. Dialog, which perhaps can lay claim to having the world's largest collection of databases under a single roof, specializes in disseminating knowledge in a wide variety of areas, including business, science, technology, education, humanities and social sciences, law, government, agriculture, energy, and chemistry. Dialog grows at a rate of about 30 to 40 databases per year. On the other hand, if you want to read the full text of either *The New York Times* or *The Wall Street Journal,* you need look no further than Nexis and Dow Jones News/Retrieval.

Many services have a one-time fee and an hourly hookup charge. They may also impose special charges for some types of services.

Company	Product	Description
Dow Jones & Company	Dow Jones News/ Retrieval Service	Historical stock prices, business articles and information
H & R Block, Inc.	CompuServe	Historical stock prices, shopping, travel, abstracts and complete articles on a variety of subjects, bulletin boards
Knight-Ridder, Inc.	Dialog	Over 300 databases containing abstracts and complete articles on a variety of subjects
Mead Corporation	Lexis, Medis, Nexis	Abstracts and complete articles targeted to legal, medical, and general-interest readers, respectively

Services companies. North America's favorite database sources.

Local Area Networks (LANs). Cable-based **local area networks (LANs)** utilize coaxial or fiber optic cable technology. Figure 7-13 shows an LAN. Note that the network does not utilize a host computer (or switching station) as such. Instead, "transparent" processors within the network itself manage the devices as they demand the shared facilities. These processors (not shown in the figure) are commonly called **servers.** For example, a *file server* might be used to manage either hard-disk or optical-disk storage activities, ena-

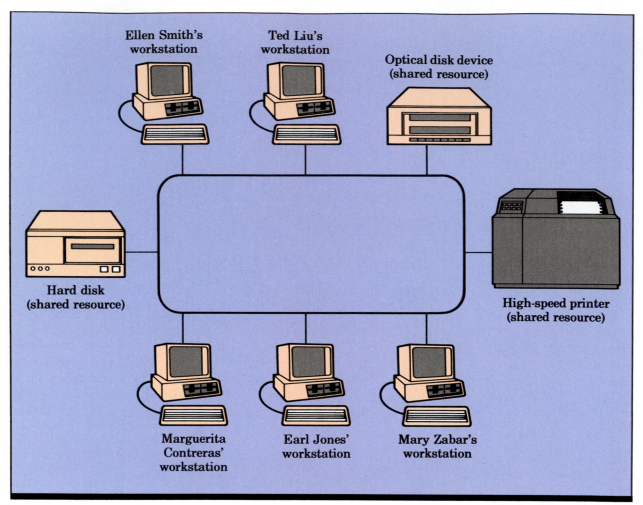

FIGURE 7-13

A local area network (LAN). The surge in microcomputer usage has made local area networking a particularly attractive solution for sharing resources.

bling workstation users to access any of several available operating systems, applications programs, or data files. Similarly, a *print server* is used to handle printing-related activities, such as managing user outputs.

LANs usually employ either a baseband or broadband cable technology. *Baseband* products consist of a single path over which text, graphics, voice, and video data can pass—but only one type of data at a time. *Broadband* networks, on the other hand, consist of several paths, thereby allowing transmission of many dissimilar types of data simultaneously. Broadband can also cover much longer distances than baseband.

Xerox's Ethernet is one of the most widely used baseband products. Wang's Wangnet is a prominent broadband product. Broadband, being more complex and powerful than baseband, is, as you might expect, more expensive as well.

Private Branch Exchanges (PBXs). The phone system consists of several switching stations that essentially are public branch exchanges. When a company leases or purchases a switching station for its own use, such a facility becomes known as a **private branch exchange (PBX).** Most PBXs are commonly referred to as "company switchboards"—you call a company's number and a private (company) operator routes you to the proper extension. But in the world of computers, many PBXs need to deal with machine-to-machine communication. Thus, such PBXs are controlled by host computers that route machine-to-machine calls automatically and let the human operator deal with many of the interpersonal communications. Sometimes these computer-based private branch exchanges are referred to as *CBXs* (*computerized branch exchanges*) or *PABXs* (*private automatic branch exchanges*).

Hierarchical Local Networks. Hierarchical local networks are the oldest type of local network. At the top of the hierarchy is often a big host computer such as a mainframe or minicomputer. At the bottom are display terminals. Between the top and bottom are devices such as communications controllers—discussed in detail later in the chapter—which manage exchanges between the host and the terminals.

In recent years, microcomputers themselves have been used in hierarchical local networks. In some cases, microcomputer workstations serve as terminals that communicate with a host mainframe or mini through *terminal emulation software.* Also, with the introduction of powerful 32-bit microcomputers, the microcomputer itself can be used as a host in a small network.

Gateways and Bridges. Local networks often must communicate with outside resources, such as those on wide area networks and on other local networks.

Let's look at an example. An executive working at a microcomputer workstation on a LAN may wish to access a financial database such as Dow Jones News/Retrieval. In this particular case, a facility known as a gateway is necessary for linking the two networks—here, the LAN and the WAN. A **gateway** is a collection of hardware and software resources that enable devices on one network to communicate with devices on another, *dissimilar* network.

When the two networks being linked—say, a LAN in one campus building and an identical LAN in another nearby campus building—are based on similar technology, a device called a bridge is used to connect them. A **bridge** is a collection of hardware and software resources that enable devices on one network to communicate with devices on another, *similar* network.

Network Topologies

Telecommunications networks can be classified in terms of their *topology,* or shape. Three common topologies are the star, bus, and ring.

Star Networks. A **star network** often consists of a host computer that's hierarchically connected to several display terminals in a point-to-point fash-

FIGURE 7-14
A star network.

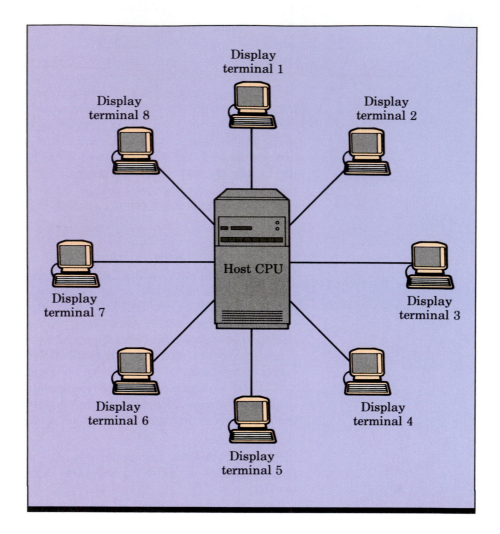

ion. This configuration is illustrated in Figure 7-14. In a common variant of this pattern, several microcomputer systems (the terminals) are connected to a larger, host computer that switches data and programs between them. The private branch exchange (PBX), discussed earlier, is another example of a star network. Star networks are especially suited to an organization with several related plants or divisions, because each plant or division may need access to common centralized files but also need to do its own local processing.

Bus Networks. A **bus network** works a lot like ordinary city buses in ground-based transportation systems. Moreover, the hardware devices are just like "bus stops" and the data like "passengers." For example, the network in Figure 7-15 contains 10 terminal stations (bus stops) at which data (passengers) are "picked up" or "let off." Cable-based local networks, discussed earlier, often utilize a bus topology. The bus line commonly consists of a high-capacity, high-speed coaxial cable, with inexpensive twisted-wire pairs dropped off each terminal station. A bus network contains no host computer.

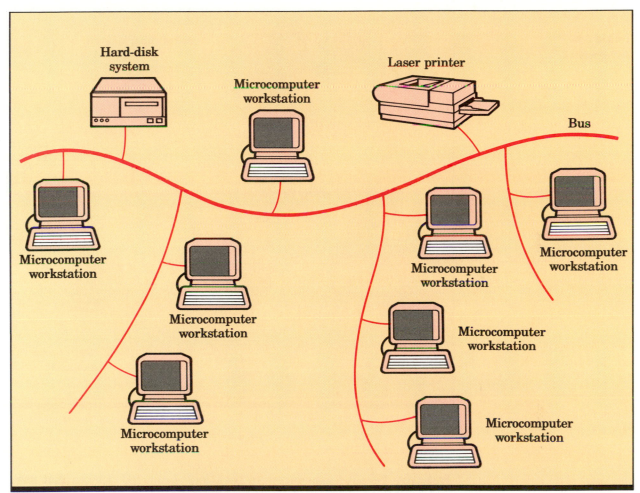

FIGURE 7-15
A bus network.

Ring Networks. A less common and more expensive alternative to both the star and bus is the **ring network,** in which a host computer is absent and a number of computers or other devices are connected by a loop. A ring network is shown in Figure 7-16. One popular form of ring network is the token-ring network pattern, which we'll discuss in the next section.

COMMUNICATIONS AMONG DEVICES

In the last few sections, we covered various types of communications media and networks. In this section, we will discuss communications standards and special communications management techniques designed to optimize the flow of communications traffic.

FIGURE 7-16
A ring network.

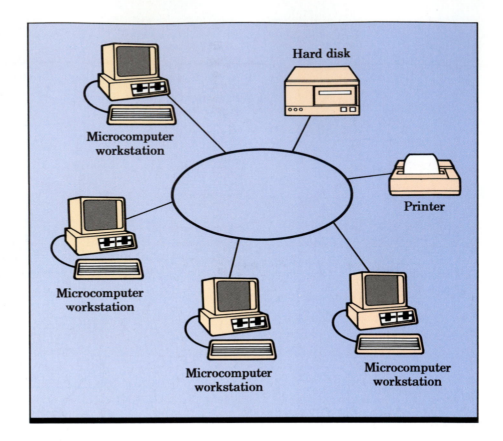

Hard disk

Microcomputer
workstation

Printer

Microcomputer
workstation

Microcomputer
workstation

Microcomputer
workstation

Protocols. Because manufacturers have long produced devices that use a variety of transmission techniques, communications standards for the industry have been a major problem. Everyone recognizes the need for standardizing transmission methods, but the form such standards should take is still widely debated. What is needed is some common agreement on matters such as communications protocols.

The term *protocol* originates from the areas of diplomacy and etiquette. For instance, at a dinner party in the elegant home of a social register family, the protocol in effect may be formal attire, impeccable table manners, and remaining at the table until beckoned to the parlor by the host or hostess. At a backwoods country barbeque, a different protocol will likely exist. In the communications field, protocols have a similar meaning.

A communications **protocol** is a collection of procedures used to establish, maintain, and terminate transmission between devices. Protocols specify matters such as how devices will physically connect into a network, how data will be packaged during transmission, how receiver devices will acknowledge sender devices (a process called *handshaking*), how errors will be handled, and so on. Just as people need an agreed-upon set of rules to communicate effectively, so do machines need a common set of rules to help them get along with one another.

For instance, a protocol called *Bisync* determines how IBM mainframes communicate with IBM 3270 display terminals and similar devices. Another protocol, known as the X.12 standard developed by the International Standards Organization (ISO), covers procedures by which companies can transmit form-based documents such as purchase orders and invoices to one another electronically—an activity called *electronic data interchange,* or *EDI.* Yet another protocol, the X.25 standard developed by ISO, defines interfacing for terminals that use packet switching on public data networks. Later in this section we will discuss two other protocols, polling and contention.

Hardware for Managing Communications Traffic

Now that we've covered some of the basic elements of telecommunications systems, let's see how these systems have been made more efficient. Several types of devices that enhance the efficiency of telecommunications networks are available. The most notable of these *communications management devices* are controllers, multiplexers, concentrators, and front-end processors.

Controllers. Controllers, which often are specialized minicomputers, supervise terminal-to-CPU communications traffic in a telecommunications environment. A large communications network may contain hundreds or even thousands of terminals, most of which are relatively low-speed display workstations. Hence, controllers relieve the host CPU of a considerable processing burden.

In large information processing systems, the peripheral devices communicate directly with the controllers, which collect the messages and communicate them to the CPU. When the CPU finishes processing the work, it sends it back to the controller, which routes the outputs to the proper peripheral devices.

Two major methods controllers use to manage terminals are polling and contention. These can be illustrated with the terminal configuration shown in Figure 7-17.

With **polling,** the controller polls the terminals in a round-robin fashion, asking each if there is a message to send. If there is, it's sent; if not, the controller queries the next terminal on its polling list. In Figure 7-17a, the terminals attached to the controller at the left may be polled in the order 1, 2, 3, 1, 2, 3, and so on. If one terminal is sending more often than the others, it can be polled more regularly. So, if terminal 3 normally accounts for 50 percent of the activity, the polling sequence might be 3, 1, 3, 2, 3, 1, 3, 2, and so forth. Polling is often used with a star network topology.

When **contention** is used, each terminal "contends" for use of the line. If a terminal can't seize the line, it gets a busy signal and must try again. The line might have enough capacity for a few terminals, but with contention there is never sufficient line capacity to service all the terminals at once. Two important forms of contention are token passing and CSMA/CD.

Token passing often is used with a ring network topology. With token passing, a small packet called a *token* is sent around a loop or ring. Each

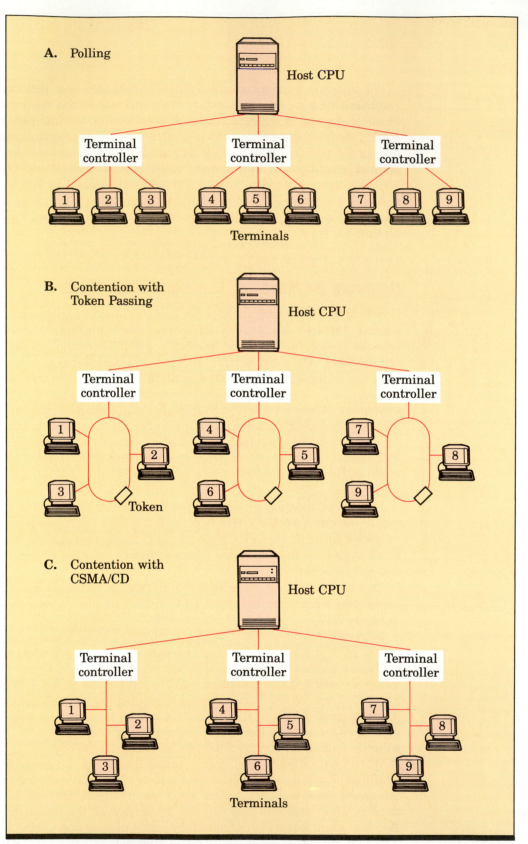

FIGURE 7-17
Terminal controllers.

packet has room for messages and addresses. As the token is passed around the ring, terminals either check to see if the token is addressed to them or seize the token so they can assign messages to it. This is illustrated in Figure 7-17b, in which each of the three controllers is using a token-passing protocol to manage the set of terminals assigned to it.

CSMA/CD is an acronym for *carrier sense multiple access with collision detection.* With CSMA/CD, which is most commonly used in bus networks, devices don't have to await either a poll or a token. On the contrary, they try to seize the controller's attention whenever they are ready. The collision detection feature ensures that the devices don't interfere with each other as they compete. CSMA/CD is illustrated in Figure 7-17c, where each controller is using a CSMA/CD protocol to manage the set of terminals assigned to it.

Multiplexers. Communications lines almost always have far greater capacity than a single terminal can use. Many terminals can work adequately at speeds of 300 bps, and voice-grade lines can transmit up to 9,600 bps. Since communications lines are expensive, it is desirable that several low-speed devices share the same line. A device called a **multiplexer** makes this possible.

Figure 7-18 illustrates the use of two multiplexers servicing several terminals and a host CPU. The first multiplexes, or combines, the data from low-speed lines into a high-speed line. The second demultiplexes the incoming character stream so that the CPU appears to get the messages from the terminals individually. The device shown in the figure, known as a *time-division multiplexer,* provides a time slice on the high-speed line for each terminal whether or not the terminal is active. A more sophisticated class of devices, called *statistical multiplexers,* allocates more time slices to busy terminals than to less active ones. Recently, with the appearance of high-speed digital lines, devices called *T1 multiplexers* have arrived on the telecommunications scene. These multiplexers have the capacity to carry as much voice and data traffic as 24 conventional (analog) phone lines.

Concentrators. A **concentrator** is a hardware device that combines control and multiplexing functions, among other things. Commonly it is a minicomputer with a memory that provides a store-and-forward capability. Thus, messages from slow devices such as asynchronous terminals can be stored at the concentrator until enough characters are collected to make forwarding to another device worthwhile.

In airline passenger-reservations systems, concentrators placed at key sites, such as Boston, New York, Los Angeles, and other transportation centers, allow several agents to share communications lines economically. Messages initiated by agents are sent to the concentrator, stored, multiplexed with messages from other agents, and transmitted at very high speeds over long-distance lines to a central processing site. Using the long-distance line in this fashion minimizes communications costs.

Front-End Processors. The **front-end processor** is the most sophisticated type of communications management device. Generally it is a programmable

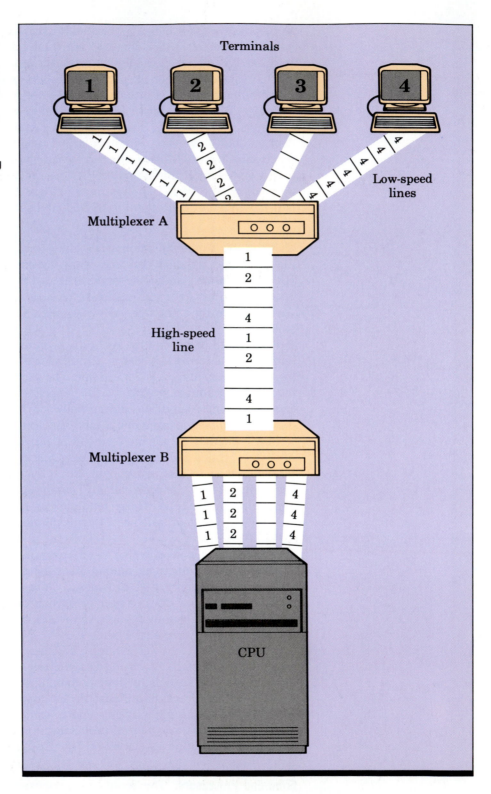

FIGURE 7-18

A system with two multiplexers. Assume that terminals 1, 2, and 4 are sending a continuous stream of characters, whereas terminal 3 is sending nothing. The messages are intertwined (multiplexed) at multiplexer A, sent over the high-speed line, and then separated (demultiplexed) at B. When the CPU transmits to the terminals, these steps are reversed.

minicomputer located at the site of the host CPU. It can perform all the communications functions of a concentrator as well as relieve the host of routine computational burdens. For example, a front-end processor can check for valid user account numbers and validate or change the format of incoming data.

SUMMARY AND KEY TERMS

Telecommunications refers to communications over a distance, such as over phone lines, via privately owned cable, or by satellite.

Messages transmitted in a telecommunications system are sent over some type of **communications medium.** Physical lines, such as **twisted-wire pairs, coaxial cable,** and **fiber optic cable,** constitute one major class of media. Messages also are commonly sent through the air, in the form of **microwave** signals. **Terrestrial microwave stations** accommodate microwave transmission when either the sender or the receiver is on the ground. **Communications satellites** reduce the cost of long-distance transmission via terrestrial microwave stations and provide better overseas communications.

The *speed* of a data-communications medium is measured in **bits per second (bps).** The slowest speeds are referred to as **narrowband transmission.** Medium-speed lines, which are the type commonly found in the public phone network, are capable of **voice-grade transmission.** The highest speeds, referred to as **wideband transmission,** are possible only with coaxial cable, fiber optic cable, and microwaves.

Communications media can be in either the simplex, half-duplex, or full-duplex mode. In **simplex transmission,** messages can be sent only in a single, prespecified direction (such as with a doorbell). In **half-duplex transmission,** messages can be sent both ways but not simultaneously (for example, as with press-to-talk phones). **Full-duplex transmission** permits transmission in two directions simultaneously (as with traffic on a busy two-way street).

Signals sent along a phone line travel in an **analog** fashion, that is, as continuous waves. Computers and their support equipment, however, are **digital** devices that handle data coded into two discrete states—0s and 1s. For two or more digital devices to communicate with each other over analog phone lines, a device called a **modem** must be placed between each piece of equipment and the phone lines. Modems perform digital-to-analog and analog-to-digital conversion. Modems can be bypassed when *digital lines* are used to interconnect devices.

To exchange data along a communications medium, two machines must "agree" on a mode of transmission and on a method of packaging data. Transmission between machines is done either in **parallel,** in which each bit of a byte is sent along a different path, or in **serial,** in which bits of a byte follow one another serially along a single path. Serially transmitted data are packaged either **asynchronously** (one byte to a package) or **synchronously** (several bytes to a package).

Common carriers are companies licensed by the government to provide communications services to the public along **wide area networks (WANs).** Carriers generally provide subscribers with access to the **switched lines** of the public telephone system. **Dedicated lines** are also available, either through common carriers or non-government-licensed vendors that sell communications media for private use.

Value-added network (VAN) vendors are firms that use the facilities of a common carrier to offer the general subscribing public additional services using those facilities. These services include information retrieval, information processing, and electronic mail.

Common carriers and VANs are most closely associated with wide area networks. Many organizations take heavy advantage of these and also build their own **local networks**—networks that link devices in a single building or at a single site. Three common types of local networks are cable-based local area networks, private branch exchanges, and hierarchical networks.

Local area networks (LANs) typically utilize transparent processors within the network, called **servers,** to manage the network and its shared facilities. A **private branch exchange (PBX)** consists of a central, private switchboard that links to devices by switched lines. A **hierarchical local network** typically consists of a powerful host CPU at the top level of the hierarchy and devices such as controllers and display terminals at lower levels. Devices on two *dissimilar* networks can communicate with each other if they are connected by a **gateway.** Devices on two *similar* networks can communicate with each other if they are connected by a **bridge.**

Telecommunications networks can be classified in terms of their topology, or shape. Three common topologies are the **star network,** the **bus network,** and the **ring network.**

A communications **protocol** is a collection of procedures used to establish, maintain, and terminate transmission between devices. Because there are so many ways to transmit data, many industry groups have pushed for certain protocols to become industry standards. These efforts notwithstanding, a number of incompatible guidelines remain in effect.

Communications management devices enhance the efficiency of telecommunications traffic flow. Common devices are controllers, multiplexers, concentrators, and front-end processors.

Controllers supervise communications traffic between the CPU and terminals. Two major methods controllers use to manage terminals are **polling,** whereby terminals are polled in an orderly (noncompeting) fashion, and **contention,** in which terminals must compete for service. Two major forms of contention are *token passing* and *carrier sense multiple access with collision detection (CSMA/CD).*

Multiplexers enable several low-speed devices to share a high-speed line. **Concentrators** perform the functions of both the controller and the multiplexer, among other things. **Front-end processors** are the most sophisticated communications management devices. They can perform the concentrator's function as well as some of the tasks the computer normally does.

REVIEW EXERCISES

Fill-in Questions

1. The telephone system, which carries most of the data sent in telecommunications systems, consists predominantly of _____ as the transmission medium.   *twisted wire prs*

2. ___*Coaxial*___ , the communications medium employed by cable television, was developed primarily to deal with a phenomenon called crosstalk that arises with lower-grade wire at high speeds.

3. In contrast to the continuous waves used to represent analog signals over phone lines, computers generate ___*digital*___ signals.

4. ___*Fiber optic cable*___ is a transmission medium that involves laser-generated light waves sent over transparent, hairlike strands.

5. Conversion from analog to digital and digital to analog is performed by a(n) ___*modem*___ .

6. ___*asynchronous*___ transmission involves sending data along a communications line in blocks of several characters at a time.

7. ___*Common carriers*___ are companies licensed by the government to provide communications services to the public.

8. ___*Asynchronous*___ transmission is a type of serial transmission in which each character is preceded by a start bit and followed by a stop bit.

9. A nonswitched line is frequently called a(n) ___*dedicated*___ line.

10. A PBX is an example of a(n) ___*star*___ network topology.

Matching Questions

Match each term with the description that best fits.

a. front-end processor   d. multiplexer
b. modem   e. controller
c. gateway   f. protocol

_d_   **1.** A device that combines several low-speed lines into a high-speed line.

_e_   **2.** A hardware device that helps the CPU manage traffic from terminals.

_b_   **3.** A device that converts digital data for transmission over the phone lines.

_a_   **4.** The most sophisticated type of communications management device.

_f_   **5.** A standard used to make communications devices more compatible.

_c_   **6.** A device that enables two dissimilar networks to communicate with each other.

Discussion Questions

1. Name some types of communications media and explain how they differ.
2. What are the differences among simplex, half-duplex, and full-duplex transmission?
3. What is packet switching?
4. Identify some alternatives for acquiring network facilities.
5. What is the difference between a local area network (LAN) and a PBX?
6. What is the difference between baseband and broadband transmission?
7. How do parallel and serial communications differ?
8. Identify the different strategies terminal controllers use to manage terminals.

Critical Thinking Questions

1. In his book *Megatrends,* author John Naisbitt states that advances in communications technology are collapsing the "information float"—the amount of time information spends in transit when being communicated from one point to another. Can you think of three business examples of collapsing information float? What is the benefit to business in each example?

2. Identify two examples of computer applications that need the type of transmission that broadband cable provides.

3. You are asked by a teacher in your former high school to give a 45-minute presentation to her students on telecommunications. She has asked you specifically to prepare a list of the half dozen or so things that every student today should know about telecommunications. What would be on your list?

C

Software

So far you've read a great deal about the hardware parts of a computer system—the CPU, storage devices, input and output equipment, and communications devices. But hardware by itself cannot process data any more than the instruments in an orchestra can play a symphony without musicians, a conductor, and a musical score. Without software a computer system would be interesting to look at, perhaps, but essentially it would represent useless hunks of metal.

As mentioned earlier, the term *software* means "computer programs." Computer programs fall into two general categories: systems programs and applications programs. *Systems programs* assist in the running of other programs. These include the operating system, language translators, and utility programs. *Applications programs*, in contrast, perform the processing tasks that directly produce the information end users need in their jobs. Among these are programs for payroll, billing, inventory control, management reports, word processing, and thousands of other tasks.

Chapter 8 discusses systems software. Chapters 9 through 11 respectively examine applications software development and the programming languages used to develop applications. Chapters 12, 13, and 14 focus on productivity software packages, such as word processing, spreadsheet, presentation graphics, and data management programs.

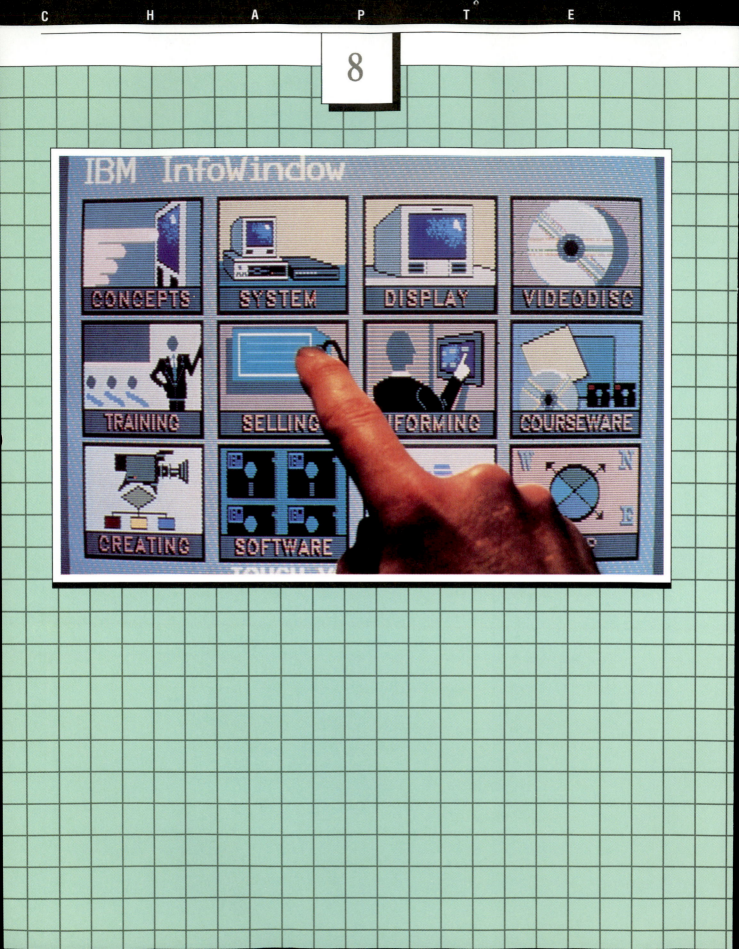

Systems Software

Objectives

After completing this chapter,
you will be able to:

1. Describe the role of
   systems software.

2. Explain the activities an
   operating system
   performs.

3. Describe several ways
   computer systems
   interleave operations to
   process data more
   efficiently.

4. Explain the role of a
   language translator and
   describe several types of
   language translators.

5. Explain the role of a utility
   program and describe
   several types of utility
   programs.

OVERVIEW

Systems software consists of programs that coordinate the various parts of the computer system to make it run rapidly and efficiently. The activities systems programs perform are quite diverse.

On most microcomputers, these programs format disks for use by your computer system, copy program or data files from one diskette to another, and enable the applications software you use to work on your display device or printer. On larger computers, systems programs perform most of the tasks their microcomputer counterparts do and many more as well. Because larger computers generally serve several people at the same time, their systems software must be sophisticated enough to be able to schedule the many jobs awaiting processing and keep track of all user activities.

In this chapter, we'll first look closely at the role of systems software. Then we'll turn to the *operating system,* the piece of systems software that controls computer system operations by assigning and scheduling resources and keeping track of user activities. Here we'll look at some of the features commonly found on operating systems that are used on both small and large computers. Finally, we will discuss *language translators* and *utility programs,* which perform other vital services for users and programmers.

THE ROLE OF SYSTEMS SOFTWARE

The basic role of **systems software** is to act as a mediator between applications programs and the computer system's hardware. Systems software goes to work on every incoming or outgoing program and block of data, putting it in a form required for processing; making available whatever hardware, software, and data resources are needed for doing the work involved; speeding up ongoing processing; or performing accounting-type tasks necessary for system control.

Most users aren't aware of what systems software is doing for them. On microcomputer systems, for example, saving a program onto disk requires that systems software look for adequate space on the disk, write the program onto "addresses" of this space, and update a directory indicating the addresses at which the program has been placed. On larger computer systems, when you log on you may not realize that systems software goes to work checking the validity of your ID number or, later, translating your BASIC program into machine language. And although it may seem to you as you sit and type at your terminal that the computer system is responding only to your commands, the system may actually be dealing with dozens of other users at almost the same time. It is systems software that makes this illusion possible.

THE OPERATING SYSTEM

Before the 1960s, human operators generally ran computers manually. For each incoming job needing processing, the operator had to reset a number of circuits on the computer by hand. In fact, every function of the computer system—input, output, processing, and storage—required substantial operator supervision and intervention.

On these early computers, jobs could be processed only in a serial fashion—one program at a time. As a result, the computers sat idle for long periods while operators took care of manual procedures between jobs.

The development of operating systems greatly improved the efficiency of computers. An **operating system** is a collection of programs that manage the computer system's activities. Operating systems have eliminated much of the manual work formerly required to process programs. Many of today's operating systems enable processing of several jobs concurrently and permit the computer to be left completely unattended by the operator while programs are running.

The primary chores of the operating system are management and control. The operating system ensures that each valid incoming program is processed in an orderly fashion and that the computer system's resources are made available to run the programs optimally.

To help you understand the role of the operating system, we can compare its activities to those of a receptionist working in the lobby of a large office. The receptionist's main duties are to screen visitors and direct them to the right people. After visitors have identified themselves satisfactorily, the receptionist finds out what they want. If, for example, a visitor wishes to chat with someone in the organization to get information for a magazine story, the receptionist might direct the visitor to a public relations person on the fifth floor. If a quick call reveals that the person is available, the visitor is routed upstairs. All visitors must sign a logbook at the reception desk before entering the premises and on their way out.

An operating system does many of the same kinds of things. For example, on a large computer system, it checks to see that people trying to gain access to the computer system are authorized users. When a user's identification number is found to be valid, he or she is signed in, or "logged on." Next, the operating system determines which of the computer system's resources will be needed to do the user's job. Then it automatically assigns these resources to the work request if and when they are available.

Generally, the user will need to tap a number of the system's resources. For example, a typical job might need the number-crunching power of the CPU, a language translator that understands the BASIC programming language, primary memory for storing intermediate results, secondary storage for storing data and programs, and a printer for output. The operating system makes all these facilities available. Finally, when the user finishes with the computer system, he or she is logged off. In effect, the operating system is the go-between, meshing the user's application program with the system's resources.

Some Popular Operating Sytems

☑ **AOS, DG**   Operating systems used on Data General minicomputers

☑ **CPF, SSP**   Operating systems available on IBM's small business systems

☑ **GCOS**   An operating system used on Honeywell Bull mainframes

☑ **Macintosh System Software**   The icon-oriented operating system used on Apple Macintosh microcomputers

☑ **MCP/AS, OS/1100**   Operating systems used on Unisys mainframes

☑ **MS-DOS**   A widely used operating system for computers that work like the IBM PC

☑ **MVS, VM**   Operating systems used on IBM mainframes

☑ **OS/2**   The operating system designed for the high end of IBM's PS/2 line of microcomputers

☑ **PC-DOS**   The operating system most widely used by the IBM PC and similar machines

☑ **UNICOS, COS**   Operating systems used by Cray supercomputers

☑ **UNIX**   A multiuser, multitasking operating system used by small computers

☑ **VAX/VMS**   An operating system used by DEC VAX minicomputers

☑ **Xenix, Venix, Ultrix, A/UX**   Four UNIX-like operating systems

Because of the central role of the operating system in managing the computer system's activities, many consider the operating system the most critical piece of software in the computer system. Without an operating system, none of the other programs can run.

The marketplace offers a wide selection of operating systems (see Figure 8-1). Like the executives who manage and control large corporations, the various operating systems differ in many important respects. For example, some operating systems are designed for only one "brand" of computer, while others are compatible with several brands. Other important differences concern ease of use, speed, number of features available, portability, and cost. Often these criteria conflict. For example, an operating system that's designed to be either easy to use or flexible generally isn't fast. In other words, the more overhead the operating system must carry, the slower it will be. And, as you might expect, a system that's packaged with an assortment of sophisticated or powerful features isn't likely to be inexpensive.

Functions of the Operating System

Now that you have a general idea of what operating systems do, we can discuss their functions in greater detail. As we examine these functions, keep in mind that not all of them apply to the operating system on *your* computer. For example, consider the differences between operating systems on sophisticated computer systems and those on relatively simple ones. The most sophisticated computers—supercomputers, mainframes, minicomputers, and top-of-the-line microcomputers—require powerful operating systems. Because these computer systems normally have several people logged on at the same time (through workstations), their operating systems must be able to accommodate the conflicting needs of the users and their jobs concurrently. In contrast, many microcomputers have operating systems that permit only one user on the computer at a time working on only one program. Therefore, features pertaining to an environment with several users and many concurrent programs simply don't apply.

Assignment of System Resources. When most computers are first activated, a major component of the operating system—a program called the **supervisor**—is also activated. On some systems, this program may be referred to as the *monitor,* the *kernel,* or something else. The supervisor will always be in primary memory when the computer is on. On many computers, other programs in the operating system are brought into primary memory from secondary storage only as they are needed. The supervisor mobilizes these other programs to perform system tasks for applications programs.

Once the supervisor activates any other program in the operating system, it relinquishes control to that program until the program has performed its role. At that point control returns to the supervisor, which may then call up other systems programs the job requires. The supervisor operates somewhat like a master of ceremonies, repeatedly introducing the next speaker on the program after the previous one has finished his or her talk.

In addition to the supervisor, a number of other operating system programs have a hand in determining which parts of the computer system will be mobilized for any given job. One of these is the **command-language translator.** This program reads instructions to the operating system that the user or programmer initiates. These instructions, which often are coded in a **command language** (sometimes referred to as a *job-control language,* or *JCL*), permit the user and programmer to specify orders for retrieving, saving, deleting, copying, or moving files; which I/O devices are to be used; which language the user or programmer is employing; any customized requests for output format; and any other special processing needs of the applications program. The command language, in effect, gives the user or programmer a channel for communicating directly with the operating system.

Operating systems can differ significantly in how command-language instructions are invoked. Take deleting a file. With operating systems such as MS-DOS and PC-DOS, which are used on many IBM microcomputers and similar machines from other manufacturers, you generally type in a command such as

ERASE FRED

to delete a file named FRED. Both MS-DOS and PC-DOS employ a *language interface,* meaning that users generally must know the syntax of a particular command language to communicate with these operating systems.

On the Apple Macintosh line of computers, icons representing operating system commands have traditionally been used in conjunction with a mouse to carry out similar operations. So, to delete FRED, you can use the mouse to point first to a file-folder-shaped icon labeled FRED and then to a wastebasket-shaped icon to activate the delete operation. Operating systems such as Macintosh System Software employ a *graphical interface,* meaning that

FIGURE 8-2
Some functions of command languages.

Some Functions of Command Languages

☑ Identifying users' names and account numbers.

☑ Retrieving, saving, deleting, moving, copying, or renaming files.

☑ Declaring any unusual requirements that exceed the standard allowances of the computer center—for example, any extraordinarily large storage, CPU time, or printed output needs.

☑ Identifying the software package, programming language, or files to be used.

☑ Identifying the organization or access methods to be used.

☑ Specifying special instructions for output—for example, the input/output device used, the number of copies of output desired, and any special printing fonts that are needed.

☑ Stating directions to operate a device in a certain way; for example, whether a display device should have 40, 80, or 132 characters per line.

☑ Assigning secret passwords to data files or programs.

users need only point to graphical icons to issue commands rather than remembering a specific syntax. Virtually any operating system that naturally uses a language interface can be complemented with a graphically oriented "shell" program, thereby overlaying it with a graphical interface. Many companies prefer to run MS-DOS, for instance, with a graphical interface.

In the absence of special command-language instructions from the user—regardless of whether these instructions are invoked through written commands or via a graphical interface—the command-language translator makes some standard assumptions about how things are to be done. These assumptions are called **defaults.** Often you can override the defaults by invoking your own commands. For instance, suppose the default on output is 24-line screen images delivered to the display and you want hard-copy output from the printer—say, 5 copies at 50 lines per page. You may be able to override the default by issuing a command such as

```
PRINTER, LINES = 50, COPIES = 5
```

In an operating system that supports written commands, you would invoke this command by typing it in as shown. In an operating system with a graphical interface, you might respectively select the PRINTER, LINES, and COPIES options from menus and have to type in only the numbers 50 and 5.

Figure 8-2 shows some functions often performed through a command language. Keep in mind that not every command language is capable of carrying out all of these functions. In general, the smaller the computer, the less powerful the associated operating system and its command language.

Figure 8-3 shows some commands you'll find helpful if you use PC-DOS or MS-DOS, both of which are predominantly single-user operating systems. Figure 8-4 shows a command screen used on a system that employs a graphical user interface. Many experts feel that in the near future, the average microcomputer user will be interacting with operating systems mostly through graphical interfaces. Figure 8-5 describes some of the commands used in UNIX, a sophisticated operating system often found on 32-bit-class

FIGURE 8-3

How various commands are implemented in PC-DOS and MS-DOS. The given commands assume a two-disk system and working from the A drive.

Command	Implementation
Formatting a disk in the A drive	FORMAT
Formatting a disk in the B drive	FORMAT B:
Copying the contents of a disk in the A drive to a disk in the B drive	DISKCOPY A: B:
Copying the contents of a file named FRED from a disk in the A drive to a disk in the B drive	COPY FRED B:
Deleting a file named FRED from a disk in the A drive	ERASE FRED
Deleting a file named FRED from a disk in the B drive	ERASE B:FRED
Invoking BASIC	BASIC
Listing the names of files stored on the disk in the A drive	DIR
Listing the names of files stored on the disk in the B drive	DIR B:

machines. Feature 8A describes the UNIX operating system more fully, and the upcoming battle it is likely to wage with OS/2, the 32-bit-class operating system that accompanies the IBM PS/2 line of computers.

Besides enabling you to do things through a command language, operating systems often make other types of assignments that are transparent to most people. For example, at any given time large computers are likely to

FIGURE 8-4

A graphically oriented command screen. Many experts feel that in the near future, the average microcomputer user will be interacting with operating systems mostly through graphical interfaces.

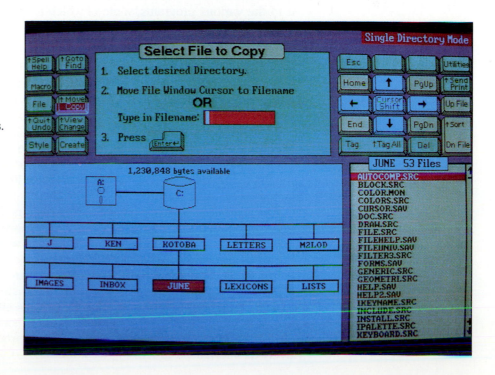

FIGURE 8-5

Some UNIX commands. UNIX, being a much more sophisticated operating system than those used with most 16-bit microcomputers, has a richer variety of commands and a deeper set of options (arguments) you can select with each command. For instance, the STTY command has about two dozen options to choose from to let you tailor the command to your particular needs.

Command	Description
AT	Execute commands in a file at a specified time of day
CAT	Display the contents of a file
CP	Copy contents of one file into another file
FIND	Search directory to find files that meet certain conditions
LS	List the contents of a directory and, also, display file information
MAIL	Send or receive electronic mail
MKDIR	Create subdirectories in the current directory
PASSWD	Change password for logging into UNIX
PR	Print a file
PWD	Display the full pathname of current directory
RM	Remove one or more files or directories
SORT	Sort lines of a file or merge two files
SPELL	Display words in file not in spelling dictionary
STTY	Set mode options for a terminal (e.g., odd or even parity, terminal speed in bps, etc.)
WC	Count lines, words, and characters in file

be processing programs from a number of users concurrently, each program having its own requirements for tape or disk devices, storage, and so on. The operating system keeps track of which facilities in the system are in use and which are free for assignment to new programs. Also, because space in main memory is at a premium, the operating system must allocate shares of it to the various programs, some of which may be very large.

Scheduling Resources and Jobs. Closely related to the process of assigning system resources to a job is that of scheduling resources and jobs. The operating system helps decide not only which resources to use (assignment) but when to use them (scheduling). This task can become extremely complicated when the system must handle a number of jobs at once.

Scheduling programs in the operating system determine the order in which jobs are processed. A job's place in line is not necessarily on a first-come, first-served basis. Some users may have higher priority than others, the devices needed to process the next job in line may not be free, or other factors may affect the order of processing.

The operating system also schedules the operation of parts of the computer system so that they work on different portions of various jobs at the same time. Because input and output devices work much more slowly than the CPU itself, millions of calculations may be performed for several programs while the contents of a single program are being printed or displayed. Using a number of techniques, the operating system juggles the various jobs to be done so as to employ system devices as efficiently as possible. Later in this section, we'll discuss some of the methods of processing a number of jobs at more or less the same time. These procedures are known collectively as *interleaved processing techniques*.

Monitoring Activities. A third general function of operating systems is monitoring, or keeping track of, activities in the computer system while processing is under way. The operating system terminates programs that contain errors or exceed either their maximum running time or storage allocations. It also sends an appropriate message to the user or operator. Similarly, if any abnormalities arise in I/O devices or elsewhere in the system, the operating system sends a message to the user's or operator's terminal.

Bookkeeping and security are two other monitoring tasks of the operating system. Records may be kept of log-on and log-off times, programs' running times, programs each user has run, and other information. In some environments, such records enable the organization to bill users. The operating system also can protect the system against unauthorized access by checking the validity of users' ID numbers and reporting attempts to breach system security. Moreover, it must protect memory such that an error in a program will not "crash" the computer system or, worse yet, corrupt vital data in other programs.

Interleaved Processing Techniques

In this section, we will examine some of the assignment and scheduling techniques that computers use to handle a large number of jobs at the same time. Sophisticated computers often take advantage of *interleaved processing techniques* such as multiprogramming, multitasking, time-sharing, virtual storage, and multiprocessing to operate more efficiently. These operating system features enable computers to process many programs at almost the same time and, consequently, increase the number of jobs the computer system can handle in any given period.

Multiprogramming. **Multiprogramming,** a term that refers to multiuser operating systems, is somewhat similar to the operation of a busy dentist's office. The dentist *concurrently* attends to several patients in different rooms within a given time period. The dentist may pull a tooth in room 1, move to room 2 to prepare a cavity for filling, move back to room 1 to treat the hole created by the pulled tooth, and so forth. As the dentist moves from patient to patient, assistants do minor tasks.

In a computer system with a multiprogrammed operating system, several applications programs may be stored in main memory at the same time. The CPU, like the dentist, works on only one program at a time. When it reaches a point in a program at which peripheral devices or other elements of the computer system must take over some of the work, the CPU interrupts processing to move on to another program, returning to the first program when that program is ready to be processed again. While the computer is waiting on data for one program to be accessed on disk, for example, it can perform calculations for another program. The systems software for the disk unit works like the dental assistants—it does background work; in this case, retrieving the data stored on disk.

Multiprogramming is feasible because computers can perform thousands of computations in the time it takes to ask for and receive a single piece of

Life after DOS

The Battle of the Operating Systems

During the 1980s, DOS was the predominant microcomputer-based operating system for most businesses. Over 14 million copies of it have been sold, making it the most widely used software package ever developed. But now that the 1990s are here, things will likely change.

OS/2 is replacing DOS as the flagship operating system for the high end of the IBM PS/2 microcomputer line. Also, more businesses are now using Apple Macintoshes, many of which are guided by the Mac's proprietary operating system. And, with an unprecedented variety of equipment in the marketplace, more and more users are looking for a standard to fit everything together. Many of these users are turning to UNIX, a hardware-independent operating system, to provide a common interface.

In 1981, Microsoft Corporation created Version 1.0 of PC-DOS specifically to work on the IBM Personal Com-

> UNIX has
> a big head start.

puter (IBM PC). It created a virtually identical operating system, called MS-DOS, a year later to run on computers similar to the IBM PC. Version 1.0 of both programs supported machines that used floppy disks. In 1983, when microcomputers with hard disks started entering the market, version 2.0 of DOS was introduced to facilitate creation of hierarchical file directories and storage of large numbers of files on a single disk.

In 1984, when a new breed of computer systems based on the Intel 80286 processor (such as the IBM PC AT) became available, the limitations of DOS became widely apparent. Versions 3.0 and 4.0 of DOS were subsequently developed to run on the new machines, but they failed to take full advantage of the new chip's capabilities. For instance, version 3.0 ran as though the 80286 were a fast 8086 chip, which is less powerful. And while version 4.0 permitted multitasking, it required all processes to fit into 640KB of RAM—the maximum amount permitted by the IBM PC and far below the amount theoretically accessible by the 80286 chip. When 80386 machines arrived in 1987, an

data from disk. Such disk I/O operations are much slower than computation, because the computer must interact with and receive communications from an external device to obtain the data it needs. It must also contend with the slower access speeds of secondary storage.

Multitasking. **Multitasking** refers to a multiprogramming capability on single-user operating systems. Thus, it refers to the ability of an operating system to enable two or more programs or program tasks from a single user to execute concurrently on one computer. This feature allows a user to do things such as edit one program while another program is executing or have two programs displayed on screen at the same time and modify them concurrently. Remember, one computer, like one dentist, can attend to only one task at a time. But the computer works so fast that the user often has the illusion that it is doing two things at once.

operating system that could support a full-fledged multitasking environment was needed. This new operating system became OS/2.

OS/2 provides a display-screen interface with a graphical, Macintoshlike look. Part of IBM's plan is to have all applications running under OS/2 look similar to users—a concept IBM includes in its *Systems Applications Architecture (SAA)*. This applications commonality will be shared both by the PS/2 line of computers and IBM mainframes. SAA is IBM's grand plan to interface many of its major product offerings.

But OS/2 is still relatively untested in the marketplace and faces stiff competition in the multivendor microcomputing world of the 1990s. Its main foe will be UNIX, a product originally developed almost two decades ago at Bell Labs as a highly portable operating system for minicomputers. Many properties make UNIX a compelling choice for the new breed of microcomputers arriving in the marketplace.

First, UNIX already has a relatively successful track record as a multiuser, multitasking operating system. Because UNIX is a multiuser system, several people can share the same processor concurrently. And because it facilitates multitasking, a user can work on several programs concurrently at a workstation.

Second, UNIX is specially built to support a wide variety of machines. Unlike other operating systems, such as MS-DOS and OS/2, UNIX is not built around a single family of processors. Computers from micros to mainframes can run UNIX, and a variety of devices from different manufacturers can easily run under UNIX while hooked into the same network.

Already a big battle between UNIX and OS/2 is looming for the 1990s. While UNIX has a big head start and is widely praised for its ability to handle the highly flexible, multivendor environment that many say will characterize the next several years, OS/2 also has some significant advantages. OS/2 will likely run faster than UNIX in environments that use Intel chips and IBM computers. Also, UNIX comes in a number of conflicting versions, which inhibits the development of standards and forestalls the reality of a definitive operating system with which all other products can easily communicate. And many people say UNIX's user interface is hard to work with. To date, UNIX has been most widely acclaimed by the programming community, which will figure less in buying decisions in the 1990s than in past decades.

One situation in which multitasking is very helpful occurs when a program has an exceptionally long processing time and the computer is needed for other work. For example, suppose you want to search through a large employee file for all people between the ages of 25 and 35 with six years of service and some experience with computers. On a relatively small computer, such a search may take several minutes, during which time you may want to use the computer for other work. With multitasking, you can use your computer to perform another task, on the same or a different program, while the search is taking place in the background. Without multitasking, you'll have to find other, offline work to do (like eating lunch) while the computer is tied up.

Because multitasking involves using the computer to interleave the processing of several tasks, it is closely associated with windowing software, which we discuss later in the chapter in the section "Utility Programs."

Time-Sharing. Time-sharing is a very popular technique for computer systems that support numerous terminals. The operating system cycles through all the active programs in the system that need processing and gives each one a small time slice on each cycle.

For example, say there are 20 programs in the system and each program is to be allocated a time slice of 1 second (the time slice usually is much smaller than this, and all slices aren't necessarily equal). The computer will work on program 1 for one second, then on program 2 for one second, and so forth. When it finishes working on program 20 for one second, it will go back to program 1 for another second, program 2 for another second, and so on. Thus, if there are an average of 20 programs on the system, each program will get a total of 3 seconds of processing during each minute of actual clock time, or 1 second in every 20-second period. As you can see, in a time-sharing system it is difficult for a single program to dominate the CPU's attention, thereby holding up the processing of shorter programs.

Both time-sharing and multiprogramming are techniques for working on many programs concurrently by allotting short uninterrupted time periods to each. They differ, however, in the way they allot time. In time-sharing, the computer spends a fixed amount of time on each program and then goes on to another. In multiprogramming, the computer works on a program until it encounters a logical stopping point, such as when more data must be read in, before going on to another. Many computers today combine time-sharing and multiprogramming techniques to expedite processing.

Virtual Storage. In the early days of computing, users who had large programs faced numerous problems loading them into main memory. Often they had to split such programs into pieces manually so that only small portions of them resided in the limited main memory space at any one time. In the early 1970s, a virtual storage feature became available on some operating systems. It permitted users the luxury of writing extremely long programs that the operating system would automatically split up and manage.

Virtual storage refers to using disk to extend main memory. This is the way it usually works. The operating system delivers programs to be processed to the virtual-storage area on disk. Here the programs generally are divided into either fixed-length "pages" or variable-length "segments." Whether the programs are subdivided into pages or segments depends on the operating system's capabilities.

A virtual storage system using *paging* breaks a program into pages. If a program is 40 kilobytes long and the system divides programs into 4 kilobyte lengths, the program is divided into 10 pages. As the computer works on the program, it stores only a few pages at a time in main memory. As it requires other pages during program execution, it selects them from virtual storage and writes over the pages in main memory that it no longer needs. All the original pages, or modified ones, remain intact in virtual storage as the computer processes the program. So, if the computer again needs a page that has been written over in main memory, it can readily fetch it. This process, illustrated in Figure 8-6, continues until the program is finished. The buffer areas shown in the figure sometimes are referred to as *spooling areas*. We'll talk more about spooling programs later in the chapter.

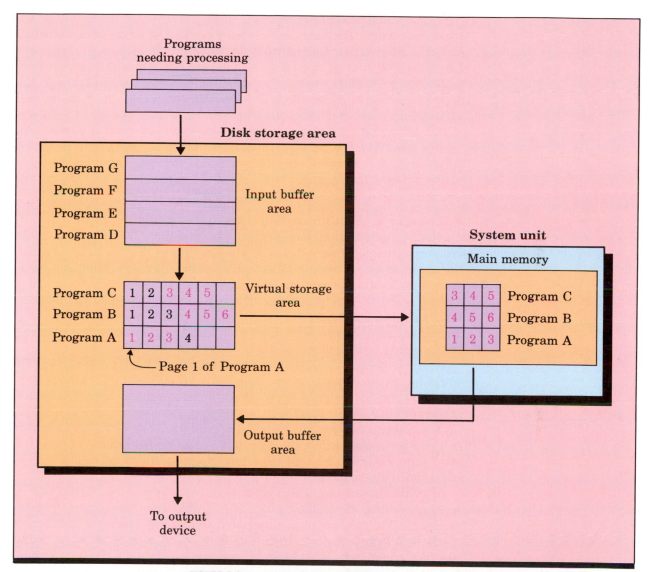

FIGURE 8-6

Virtual storage based on a paging system. In this system, programs awaiting processing are transferred from the input buffer area on disk to the virtual storage area. In the virtual storage area, programs are divided into pages of fixed length, perhaps 4,000 bytes each. When the computer is ready to process a program, the operating system transfers a certain number of pages (three in this example) into main memory. The computer then processes the program until it needs a new page, whereupon the required page is delivered to main memory, writing over the one that is no longer needed. The computer system continues in this fashion, selecting desired pages of a program from virtual storage, until the program is completed. At that point, the program output is delivered to the output buffer area of the disk to await an output device, and a new program is read into its virtual storage area.

The operating system may use a variety of rules to determine which pages to keep in main memory. One rule might require that a new page be written over the page that was used least recently. On the other hand, a page with a high overall frequency of use, even if it was the least recently used at any time, is a logical candidate for remaining in primary memory.

Segmentation works somewhat like paging except that the segments are variable in length. Each segment normally consists of a contiguous block of logically interrelated material from the program. As in paging, a segment that is needed in main memory is written over one that isn't. Many systems that use segmentation employ a combination of segmentation and paging. A program is first segmented into logically related blocks, which are further divided into pages of fixed length.

Not all operating systems on large computers use virtual storage. Although this technique permits a computer system to get by with a smaller main memory, it requires extra computer time to swap pages or segments in and out of main memory.

Multiprocessing. **Multiprocessing** refers to the use of two or more computers linked together to perform work at the same time. This, of course, often requires systems software that will realize multiple CPUs are in use and has the ability to assign work to them as efficiently as possible. While multiprogramming involves processing several programs or tasks *concurrently* on a single computer, multiprocessing involves handling multiple programs or tasks *simultaneously* (at precisely the same instant) on several computers. There are many ways to implement multiprocessing; two common ones are coprocessing and parallel processing.

With *coprocessing,* which we covered briefly in Chapter 4, a single CPU works in conjunction with specialized, "slave" processors that perform dedicated chores. For instance, many microcomputer systems today have slave processors that handle tasks such as high-speed mathematical computation, display-screen graphics, and keyboard operations. At any point in time, two or more processors within the system unit may be performing work at the same time. However, the time taken to perform an entire job will be largely constrained by the CPU.

In *parallel processing,* which is the most sophisticated and fastest type of multiprocessing, the multiple processors involved are full-fledged, general-purpose CPUs. They are tightly integrated so that they can work together on a job by sharing memory. While this may sound simple, there are many practical complications, and special software is often required (see Tomorrow box).

Multiprocessing is closely related to *fault-tolerant computing,* in which computer systems are built with important circuitry duplicated. If a critical component fails, an identical backup component takes over. While duplicate sets of processors are involved, however, only one set of processors will be in operation at any point in time.

LANGUAGE TRANSLATORS

As mentioned earlier, computers can execute programs only after the latter have been translated into machine language. There are two reasons why people don't generally write programs in this language. First, machine-

Parallel Processing

An Idea Whose Time Has Come

A general principle of work is that two or more people doing a job together can complete it faster than one of them working alone. Curiously, however, until recently few attempts have been made to apply this principle to computers. Despite the astounding evolution of computer systems over the past 50 years, most are still driven by a single central processor, or CPU. A single CPU can perform instructions only in serial, or one step at a time, whether working exclusively on one program or interleaving several.

In the race to develop ever faster computer systems for tomorrow, scientists are experimenting with ways to have two or more CPUs and memories perform tasks in parallel. For example, instead of relying on one processor to solve a lengthy calculation, a parallel-processing computer system assigns portions of the problem to several CPUs operating simultaneously. But just as it is difficult to coordinate two or more workers who are dedicated to completing a single job, so too is it difficult to integrate the parallel efforts of several processors working together at superhuman speeds. Nonetheless, many industry insiders see parallel processing as an unstoppable future reality. As it becomes harder and harder to make computers themselves faster—by, say, packing circuits closer together—parallel processing will become an increasingly important strategy for reducing the time it takes to do work.

> **Software lags far behind hardware.**

Today there are several approaches to parallel-processing computer systems observable in the marketplace. One popular approach to parallel processing is represented by the Cray-2, a supercomputer that carries a price tag of several million dollars. The Cray, like most other supercomputers, employs a common parallel design philosophy, namely hooking up a small number of expensive, state-of-the-art CPUs. The Cray-2 uses four such processors, which carry out both parallel and serial processing.

Since not everybody can afford a supercomputer, other parallel processing approaches have evolved. Another common tack is to design parallel machines with a much larger number of relatively inexpensive, off-the-shelf microprocessors. Although devices built this way are less versatile than supercomputers, together they can pack a respectable amount of power at a fraction of the cost. Some computers have been reported to use thousands of microprocessors hooked up in parallel.

A major distinction among parallel-processing architectures concerns how computers share the memory they use. "Shared memory" means that the computers linked in parallel access the same memory locations. One way this can be done is by having the computers access a single, common memory area. However, sharing memory in this way is both difficult and expensive to implement. Consequently, many parallel-processing systems allow member computers to have their own memories. Sharing data among machines having their own memories, however, requires extra processing overhead that chews up valuable machine cycles.

While a number of parallel-processing systems are now available, software lags far behind hardware. For instance, special languages are needed to decompose program tasks such that they can be sensibly allocated among several machines. In addition, complicated synchronizing techniques must be established to get the machines to share data. For example, if one processor is supposed to find a result and supply it to another processor, one doesn't want the second processor to fetch the result from memory before the first processor has put it there. When true parallel-processing software takes hold, it will necessitate an entirely new breed of programmers.

language instructions consist of complex-looking strings of 0s and 1s, for example,

$$0 1 0 1 1 0 0 0 0 1 1 1 0 0 0 0 0 0 0 0 0 0 0 1 0 0 0 0 0 0 1 0$$

Few people enjoy or are successful at writing long programs consisting of statements like this. Second, machine-language instructions must be written at the most detailed level of exposition. For example, the computer can't directly add A and B and place the result in C with a single instruction such as

$$C = A + B$$

Even a simple task like this may require three or more machine-language instructions, for example,

1. Load the value represented by A from main memory into a register.
2. Add the value represented by B from main memory into the same register.
3. Place the sum obtained into another storage area.

Such detailed statements are sometimes called *machine-level instructions,* since they cannot be subdivided further into smaller logical commands. An instruction such as C = A + B, on the other hand, is an example of a macroinstruction. *Macroinstructions* must be broken down into machine-level instructions by the computer system before they are processed. All high-level languages, such as BASIC, FORTRAN, and COBOL, use macroinstruction-type statements to spare the programmer the tedious task of explaining the work to the computer in fine detail.

A **language translator** is simply a systems program that converts an applications program written in a high-level language or an assembly language into machine language. In other words, it converts a program with macroinstructions into one with binary-based machine-level instructions. Three common types of language translators are compilers, interpreters, and assemblers.

Compilers. A **compiler** translates a high-level-language program entirely into machine language before it is executed. Every compiler-oriented language requires its own special compiler. Thus, a COBOL program needs a COBOL compiler; it cannot run on a BASIC compiler.

The program that you write in a high-level language and enter in the computer is called a **source module,** or *source program.* The machine-level program that the compiler then produces from it is called an **object module,** or *object program.*

Normally, before the object module is actually executed, it is bound together with other object modules that the CPU may need in order to process the program. For example, most computers can't compute square roots directly. To do so, they rely on small "subprograms," which are stored in secondary storage in object module form. So if your program calls for cal-

FIGURE 8-7

Compile, link-edit, Go. A compiler and a linkage editor convert a source module into a load module, which is processed by the CPU.

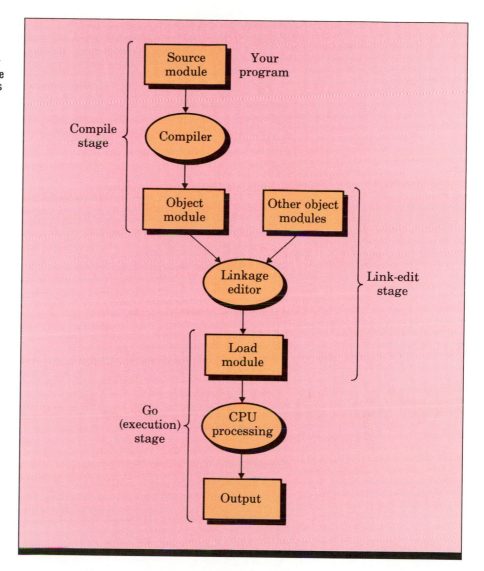

culating a square root, the operating system will bind the object module version of your program together with this square root routine to form an "executable package" for the computer. The binding process is referred to as *linkage editing,* or the *link-edit stage,* and the executable package that is formed is called a **load module.** A special systems program, called a **linkage editor,** is available on computer systems to do the binding automatically.

It is the load module that the computer actually executes, or runs. When your program is ready to run, it has reached the *Go (execution) stage.* Figure 8-7 shows the complete process from compiling to link editing to execution. Both object and load modules can be saved on disk for later use so that compilation and linkage editing need not be performed every time the program is executed.

Interpreters. An **interpreter,** unlike a compiler, does not create an object module. Interpreters read, translate, and execute source programs one line at a time. Thus, the translation into machine language is performed while the program is running.

Interpreters have advantages and disadvantages relative to compilers. Two major advantages are that interpreters are easier to use and they enable errors to be more quickly discovered in programs. Also, the interpreter itself requires relatively little storage space. Moreover, the interpreter does not generate an object module that must be stored. For these reasons, interpreters are ideal for beginning programmers and for people with limited storage space on their systems.

The major disadvantage of interpreters is that they are less efficient than compilers and, consequently, programs run more slowly on them. Since interpreters translate each program statement into machine language just prior to executing it, they can chew up a lot of time—especially when the same statements may be executed thousands of times during the course of program execution and must be reinterpreted every time they are encountered. With a compiler, in contrast, each program statement is translated only once—before the program is run. In addition, the object module of a compiled program can be saved on disk, so the source program doesn't have to be retranslated every time the program is executed.

Some programming-language packages are equipped with both an interpreter and compiler, giving the programmer the best of both worlds. This allows the programmer to work with the interpreter while rooting out program errors and, when the program is error-free, to use the compiler to save it in object-module form.

Assemblers. The third type of translator, the **assembler,** is used exclusively with assembly languages. It works like a compiler, producing a stored object module. Each computer system typically has only one assembly language available to it; thus, only one assembler is required.

UTILITY PROGRAMS

Some tasks are performed so often in the course of processing that it would be extremely inefficient if every user had to code them into programs over and over again. Sorting records, formatting disks and tapes, and copying programs from one medium to another are examples of such tasks. To eliminate the need for users and programmers to waste time writing such routines, computer systems normally have available a library of **utility programs** to perform these types of functions. Typically, utility programs reside in secondary storage and are summoned by the operating system's supervisor program when needed.

Utility programs are packaged in a variety of ways. Sometimes they are bundled into an operating system. For instance, utility programs for formatting disks, copying the contents of disks, and checking the allocation of disk space are built directly into the MS-DOS operating system. In other cases, utilities are independent programs that can be acquired from third-party vendors and made to run with a given operating system.

Five widely used types of utility programs that we will cover here are sort utilities, spooling software, windowing software, text editors, and device drivers.

Sort Utilities. *Sort utilities* are programs that sort records in a file. To appreciate how a sort utility might work, consider Figure 8-8. This program uses a *primary key,* "director," to initially sort the file. A *secondary key,* "movie title," is then used to sort movies alphabetically within each director. The example shown here activates only two sort keys. Many sorting packages will enable you to activate up to a dozen or more such keys to sort a file. Also, you can usually arrange records in either ascending or descending order on each key you name.

Sort utilities can be used in a variety of ways. For instance, you can operate one as an independent program, as Figure 8-8 illustrates. In such a case, you provide an unsorted list to the utility program as input, and a sorted list will be produced as output. Or, if you are writing a computer program and wish to sort the output, many languages permit you to imbed a "call" to the sort utility, in the form of a *sort statement,* within the computer program. Finally, many productivity software packages, such as Lotus Development Corporation's 1-2-3 and Ashton-Tate's dBASE IV, have imbedded sort utilities. These are usually invoked by highlighting onscreen the area to be sorted while pointing to a sort option on a menu.

Spooling Software. Some input and output devices are extremely slow. Tape devices and printers, for example, work at a snail's pace compared to the CPU. If the CPU had to wait for these slower devices to finish their work, the computer system would face a horrendous bottleneck. For example, suppose the computer has just completed a 5-second job that generated 100 pages of hard copy for the printer. On a printer that prints 600 lines per minute, this job would take about 10 minutes to print. If the CPU had to deal directly with the printer, primary memory would be tied up for 10 minutes waiting for the printer to complete the job. As a result, other programs would have to wait for processing while this output was being transferred from main memory to paper.

To avoid such a delay, disks on almost all large systems contain *output spooling areas* to store output destined for the printer (see Figure 8-9). As the computer processes a program, a **spooling program** rapidly transfers, or "spools," the output from main memory to the disk spooling area. The computer is then free to process another program, leaving it to the spooling program to transfer the output of the first program from disk to printer.

At any given time, the spooling area of a large computer system may contain over 100 completed jobs waiting to be delivered to output devices. As long as space remains in the output spooling area, the CPU can continue to operate without delay. Output spooling is popular on microcomputers,

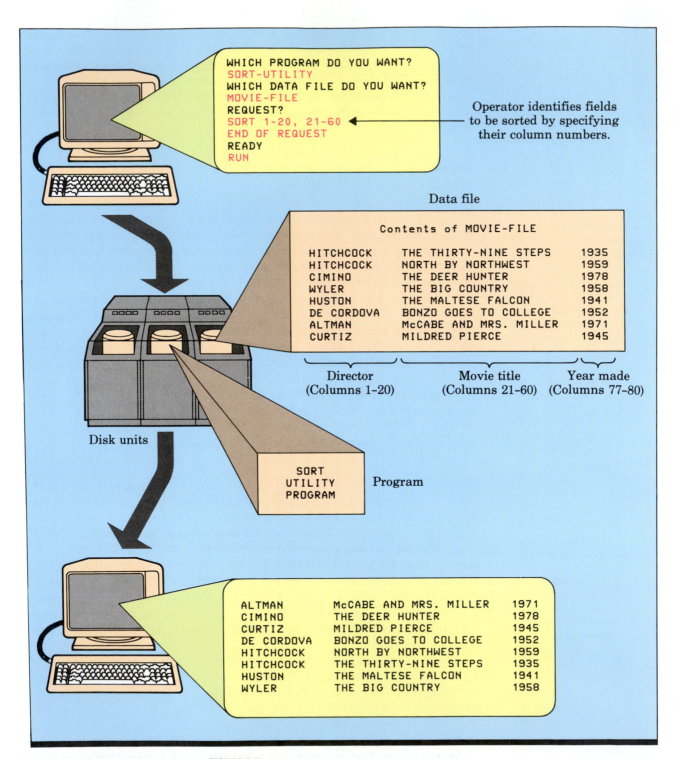

WHICH PROGRAM DO YOU WANT?
SORT-UTILITY
WHICH DATA FILE DO YOU WANT?
MOVIE-FILE
REQUEST?
SORT 1-20, 21-60
END OF REQUEST
READY
RUN

Operator identifies fields to be sorted by specifying their column numbers.

Data file

Contents of MOVIE-FILE

HITCHCOCK	THE THIRTY-NINE STEPS	1935
HITCHCOCK	NORTH BY NORTHWEST	1959
CIMINO	THE DEER HUNTER	1978
WYLER	THE BIG COUNTRY	1958
HUSTON	THE MALTESE FALCON	1941
DE CORDOVA	BONZO GOES TO COLLEGE	1952
ALTMAN	McCABE AND MRS. MILLER	1971
CURTIZ	MILDRED PIERCE	1945

Director
(Columns 1–20)

Movie title
(Columns 21–60)

Year made
(Columns 77–80)

Disk units

SORT
UTILITY
PROGRAM

Program

ALTMAN	McCABE AND MRS. MILLER	1971
CIMINO	THE DEER HUNTER	1978
CURTIZ	MILDRED PIERCE	1945
DE CORDOVA	BONZO GOES TO COLLEGE	1952
HITCHCOCK	NORTH BY NORTHWEST	1959
HITCHCOCK	THE THIRTY-NINE STEPS	1935
HUSTON	THE MALTESE FALCON	1941
WYLER	THE BIG COUNTRY	1958

FIGURE 8-8

A sort utility program in action. The terminal operator requests that a movie file be sorted alphabetically, first by director (columns 1–20) and then by movie title (columns 21–60). Note that the second sort reverses the order of the two Alfred Hitchcock movies.

FIGURE 8-9
Spooling. On large computer systems, input is spooled before it is processed and output is spooled before it is sent to the printer.

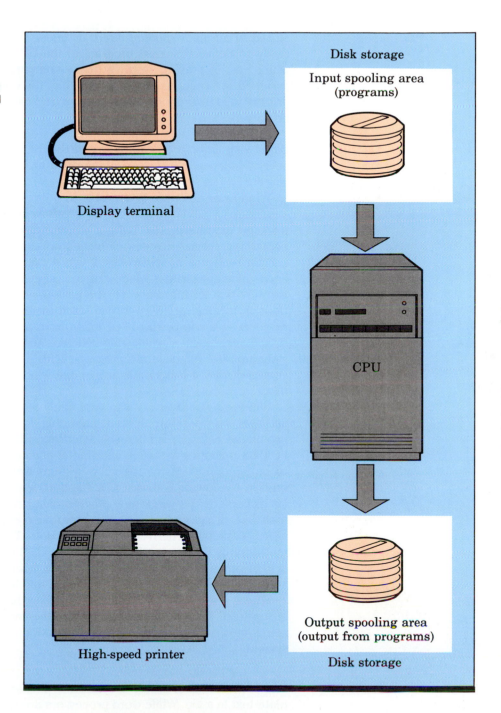

too. For example, if your printer will be tied up for 15 minutes or so typing a long document, a spooling routine will let you use your computer to edit another document while the first one is printing.

As Figure 8-9 shows, spooling is also used to hold, or stage, input on its way to the computer. As programs enter the computer system, they are stored in an *input spooling area,* or *queue.* When the operating system is ready to deliver the next program to the CPU, it checks the queue to see which one to process next. On many computer systems, priorities can be assigned to programs. If this is possible, the computer will attend to high-priority jobs before jobs that may have been waiting longer but have a lower priority.

Windowing Software. **Windowing software** refers to programs that create several independent "boxes" of information, called **windows,** on the display screen.

Windowing software is available in a number of forms. For example, the vendor may bundle it into the applications software package you buy. The package may have, say, built-in windowing routines that create windows containing special features or menus on your screen when you perform a certain sequence of keystrokes. If you depress one sequence of keys, a calendar may appear in a window; if you depress another sequence, a calculator may pop up into view. Or the package may enable you to make selections from a hierarchy of menus, each menu appearing in its own window as soon as a choice has been made from a previous menu. Ashton-Tate's dBASE uses such a windowing scheme. Also, some versions of the BASIC programming language are packaged with a windowing feature that allows you to display a program listing in one window and program results in another.

Windowing software is also commonly available as a shell program that fits over an operating system, providing it with a graphical interface. A prominent example is Microsoft Windows, which fits over the MS-DOS and PC-DOS operating systems, allowing applications run under those systems to be windowed. Many operating systems are now coming packaged with built-in windowing software as a standard feature. Probably the most familiar example is the windowing environment provided with the Apple Macintosh line of computers. Another prominent example is Presentation Manager, a product derived from Microsoft Windows, which provides a multitasking windowing interface to the OS/2 operating system (see Figure 8-10). Still another example is Open Look, a windowed version of UNIX created jointly by AT&T, Sun Microsystems, and Xerox.

Where a windowing feature accompanies the operating system, as either an optional shell or a built-in feature, the term *operating environment* is sometimes used to describe the combination of the windows and operating system.

Text Editors. A **text editor** is a software package that enables you to manipulate text in a file. While word processors are specifically targeted to manipulating text that exists in document form—say, memos, letters, and manuscripts—text editors are primarily aimed at text that exists in the form of records—say, lines of a computer program, columnar data, and so forth. With a text editor, you can often do things such as sort records in a file, delete or move fields in records, append fields to records, and so forth.

Let's look at an example. Say you are creating a bunch of records containing names and social security numbers. In each record, names are to

FIGURE 8-10

Windowing software. Windowing software, such as Presentation Manager, makes it possible for users to see independent blocks of work on the screen at the same time.

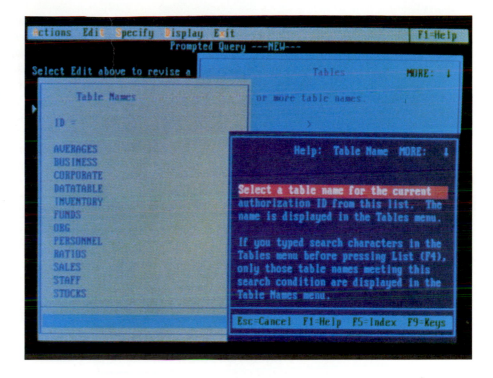

begin in column 1 and the social security numbers in column 31. But you mistakenly type in the social security numbers first and then the names. Text editors will permit you to correct this mistake quickly, with a single command that reverses the positions of the social security number and name fields in all the records.

Some text editors are *full-screen editors,* meaning that they let you move the cursor anywhere on the screen to point as you manipulate text. *Line editors,* on the other hand, constrain the cursor to a single line position on the display screen. Normally, if you want to move back to an earlier line, you must depress a special sequence of keys to tell the line editor that you want to do something out of the normal sequence of operations.

Text editors are an invaluable aid to programmers in creating and debugging programs. Many programming languages, such as BASIC, have their own built-in editors.

Device Drivers. When communicating with output hardware such as display devices and printers, applications software packages commonly rely on utility programs known as device drivers. **Device drivers** act as interfaces between applications programs and specific hardware devices.

A device driver typically works as follows. A software package you buy—say, a word processor—will often include both an installation program and a utilities disk that contains several device drivers. You install the word processor to work on a specific set of hardware devices by running the installation program. The installation program will ask you a number of questions, for instance, what type of printer and what type of monitor you are using. You answer these questions by selecting the appropriate devices from a list. As you make selections, the installation program retrieves the drivers corresponding to the selected devices and incorporates them into an "installed version" of the word processor, which it is building as the question-and-answer session is taking place. When this process is finished, the installed version of the program is ready for use on a specific hardware system.

As you later work with the installed version of the word processor, it will defer to the driver routines you have built into it to handle any hardware-specific commands. Generally, you will have to run the installation program only once—at the time you acquire the word processor. If, however, you replace one brand or model of hardware device with another, you will probably have to rerun the installation program to declare the new device.

SUMMARY AND KEY TERMS

Systems software consists of programs that coordinate the various parts of the computer system to make it run rapidly and efficiently. The basic role of systems software is to act as a mediator between applications programs and the computer system's hardware.

An **operating system** is a collection of programs that manage the computer's activities. The functions of the operating system—which include assignment of system resources, scheduling of resources and jobs, and monitoring activities—can be viewed as aspects of a single general mission: to control the computer system's operations.

Two of the most prominent programs of the operating system are the supervisor and the command-language translator. The **supervisor** controls all the other parts of the operating system. The **command-language translator** enables both users and programmers to communicate with the operating system by using a **command language.** When interfacing with the operating system, one can use the standard system **defaults,** chosen by the operating system, or request customized service through command-language instructions. On some computer systems, the operator uses a *language interface* to carry out command-language instructions. On others, which employ a *graphical interface,* the operator points on the screen to icons to carry out such instructions.

Sophisticated computers often take advantage of interleaved processing techniques, such as multiprogramming, multitasking, time-sharing, virtual storage, and multiprocessing, to operate more efficiently.

Multiprogramming is a term commonly used to describe some *multiuser* computer systems. In a computer system with multiprogramming, the computer works on several programs *concurrently*. For example, while the computer is waiting for data from one user's program to be accessed on disk, it can perform calculations for another user's program.

Multitasking refers to a multiprogramminglike capability on *single-user* operating systems. Thus, multitasking connotes the ability of two or more programs from any single user to execute *concurrently* on one computer or, more commonly, the ability of two or more tasks performed on a single program to execute concurrently.

Time-sharing is a technique in which the operating system cycles through all the active programs that need processing in the system and gives each one a small slice of time on each cycle.

Virtual storage refers to using disk to extend main memory. The operating system delivers programs to be processed to the virtual storage area, where they are subdivided into either fixed-length *pages* or variable-length *segments*.

Multiprocessing refers to the use of two or more computers, linked together, to perform work at the *same* time.

A **language translator** is a system program that converts an applications program written in a high-level language or in assembly language into machine language. There are three common types of language translators: compilers, interpreters, and assemblers.

A **compiler** translates a high-level-language program entirely into machine language before the program is executed. The program written by the user or programmer, called a **source module,** is first translated by the compiler into an **object module.** The object module version of the program is then inputted to a **linkage editor,** which combines it with supplementary object modules needed to run the program, to form a **load module.** It is the load module that the computer executes.

Interpreters read, translate, and execute source programs one line at a time. Thus, the translation into machine language occurs while the program is being run.

The third type of translator, the **assembler,** is used exclusively with assembly languages.

A **utility program** is a type of system program written to perform repetitive processing tasks. There are many types of utility programs. *Sort utilities* sort records in a file. **Spooling programs** free the CPU from time-consuming interaction with I/O devices such as printers. **Windowing software** creates several independent "boxes" (i.e., **windows**) of information on a display screen. **Text editors** enable users to manipulate text in a file. **Device drivers** act as interfaces between applications programs and specific hardware devices.

REVIEW EXERCISES

Fill-in Questions

1. _____ software consists of programs that act as a mediator between applications software and the computer system's hardware.

2. A(n) _____ is a collection of programs that manage the computer system's activities.

3. In a computer system with _____ , the computer works on several users' programs concurrently, leaving one at some logical stopping point to begin work on another.

4. _____ is a technique in which the operating system cycles through active programs in the system that need processing and gives each one a small slice of time on each cycle.

5. _____ refers to the use of two or more computers, linked together, to perform work on programs at the same time.

6. A(n) _____ is a systems program that converts an applications program written in a high-level language or in an assembly language into machine language.

7. _____ programs are systems programs written to perform repetitive processing tasks, such as formatting disks and text editing.

Matching Questions

Match each term with the description that best fits.

a. device driver
b. compiler
c. linkage editor
d. spooling software

e. interpreter
f. text editor
g. operating system

_____ 1. A language translator that reads, translates, and executes source programs a line at a time.

_____ 2. Enables a user to edit one document on a microcomputer system while printing out another.

_____ 3. A program that enables an applications software package to work on a specific hardware device.

_____ 4. Binds object modules together.

_____ 5. A piece of systems software without which a computer will do nothing.

_____ 6. A language translator that creates an object module.

_____ 7. Can do things such as append fields to records and change the order of fields in records.

Discussion Questions

1. What is systems software?

2. What is an operating system and what are its major functions?

3. Describe multiprogramming, multitasking, time-sharing, virtual storage, and multiprocessing.

4. What are the differences among a compiler, an interpreter, and an assembler?

5. Describe the differences among a source module, object module, and load module.

6. Identify several types of utility programs and explain what they do.

Critical Thinking Questions

1. UNIX has been available for about two decades, but it has only been during the last few years that it has received much attention. Why do you think this is so?

2. MS-DOS has sold millions of copies, making it the most widely used software package ever written. Now that powerful microcomputer systems are available and powerful operating systems are coming to take advantage of them, do you think a sizeable market will still exist for users who want these new computers but still want to use MS-DOS?

3. Many users of computer systems have argued that windowing environments and graphical interfaces, while potentially useful to some people, are totally undesirable for their needs. Where do you think these users are "coming from"?

Applications Software Development

Objectives

After completing this chapter, you will be able to:

1. Identify and describe the components of the program development cycle.

2. Recognize why it may be more advantageous to buy applications packages in some instances than to develop software in-house.

3. Describe a number of productivity tools and procedures computer professionals use to develop software.

OVERVIEW

If you wanted to build a house, you'd probably begin with some research and planning. You might speak to various people about home design, draw up some floor plans, estimate the cost of materials, and so on. In other words, you wouldn't start digging a hole and pouring concrete on the very first day. Producing a successful applications program also requires considerable research and planning. The process involved is called *program development*.

Years ago, the cost of hardware was the dominant concern in establishing a computer system, and developing good applications software often was a secondary concern. The cost of hardware has plunged in recent years, however, whereas the cost of labor has increased dramatically. Writing programs is a labor-intensive task. Thus, many organizations today spend most of their total computing costs on software. What's more, many large organizations have discovered that most of their software costs goes to maintaining existing programs.

In this and the next chapter, we will describe some useful practices for developing good applications programs. As you read these chapters, keep in mind that it is never enough just to write a program that works. Good programs must also be easy to understand and to maintain. A well-planned program may take slightly longer to write initially, but the subsequent savings in maintenance costs usually will make the effort well worthwhile.

THE ROLE OF APPLICATIONS SOFTWARE

Applications software consists of programs that direct computer systems to produce outputs for end users. Every computer application that interfaces with users—from video games to the tracking of a space shuttle, from printing mailing lists to compiling U.S. census returns—requires applications software.

Consider an example. It's a hot Saturday night, and you want to cool off at a local movie theater, but you don't have enough cash. You go to the automatic teller machine at your bank, slip in a plastic card, respond to the questions that appear on the screen by pressing the appropriate keys, and presto—movie money. Without an applications program, however, the convenience of automatic tellers would be impossible. It's the applications program that, among other things, tells the system what messages to put on the screen, how to respond to the keys you press, what to do if your balance is too low or if you enter the wrong ID number, and how much cash to deliver.

Creating applications software is closely related to the process of systems development, which we will discuss in detail in Chapter 17. Systems development involves the analysis, design, and implementation of complete computer systems, including hardware, systems software, applications software, data, people, and procedures. For example, if a bank without automatic teller machines considered installing them, it would probably go through the complete systems development process. Only part of that process would involve designing and creating the applications programs to make the machines do useful work.

Once the system was in place and running, however, the bank could still need new or modified applications software. It could decide, for example, to modify its automatic teller system to permit customers to make withdrawals with their credit cards as well as with their bank cards. Or a bank executive could ask to have transaction activity on the machines made available on a daily instead of weekly basis. Thus, developing software for an application normally is a continuing process.

THE PROGRAM DEVELOPMENT CYCLE

There are two ways organizations acquire applications programs: writing them internally (sometimes called in-house development) and buying them from an outside source. The method chosen generally depends on things such as the quality of software available in the marketplace, the nature and importance of the application, analyst and programmer availability, and cost. The developer of the software should follow certain steps to ensure that the software does its job.

Creating successful programs commonly involves five stages:

☐ *Analysis* Identifying and defining the problem to be solved; deciding whether or not software is appropriate; and, if it is, defining input, output, processing, and storage requirements.

☐ *Design* Planning the specific software solution to the problem.

☐ *Coding* Writing the program.

☐ *Debugging and Testing* Finding and eliminating errors in the program.

☐ *Documentation* Writing manuals for potential users of the program, maintenance programmers, and operators.

These five stages are often called the **program development cycle,** or **program life cycle.** Generally, all of these activities except documentation are carried out in the order just described. The documentation process takes place throughout the development cycle.

When a firm purchases a program from an outside source, it will not have to follow all of the stages. The vendor will take care of some of them, such as designing the program, coding, and documentation. Hopefully, most errors will be worked out of the program as well.

FIGURE 9-1

Users work closely with systems analysts in software development. The analyst's role is to assess a user's needs for computing resources and translate those needs into an orderly plan.

In a typical organization, the responsibility for successful program development is the job of systems analysts and programmers. **Systems analysts,** or simply *analysts,* specify the requirements the applications software must meet. They work with end users to assess their needs and translate those needs into a plan (see Figure 9-1). Then they determine the resources required to implement the plan. For each program, the analysts create a set of technical specifications outlining

☐ What the program must do—that is, the inputs, outputs, processing, and storage requirements
☐ The timetable for completing the program
☐ Which programming language to use
☐ How the program will be tested before being put into use
☐ What documentation is required

Some of these specifications, such as the programming language, testing methods, and documentation requirements, will follow standard organizational practices.

Next, **programmers** use these specifications to design a software solution. Later they translate that design into code—a series of statements in a programming language. **Maintenance programmers** monitor the finished program on an ongoing basis, correcting errors and altering the program as conditions change.

ANALYSIS

A problem for a systems analyst often begins as a request that a system produce specific information. The scope of the solution can range from revamping an entire system to simply providing a new piece of information on an existing printed report. **Analysis** of the problem involves two steps: (1) identifying the problem and deciding what kind of solution is called for and (2) if the solution involves software, determining the requirements the software must meet.

Identifying the Problem

The first thing a systems analyst must do in studying a potential problem is to decide if any problems do in fact exist. This may be the analyst's single most difficult task, because it involves a shrewd sense of perspective, a thorough knowledge of the end user's job, and excellent communications skills. It requires a sagacity one generally can't learn from books.

For example, suppose a sales manager complains that she is getting important information too late and the information she is getting is inadequate. The systems analyst must ascertain whether serious problems really exist. Perhaps the information the manager needs is already available, but she just doesn't know where to look for it. Also, does she really need the information she is asking for? Further, does she need it as promptly as she says she does? Getting answers to questions like these clearly requires sensitivity and tact.

In addition to determining whether these problems exist, the analyst must decide whether a computer solution is appropriate. A user has a real need for computing resources if their use will result in benefits to the organization as a whole. These benefits may be realized through reduced costs, better service, and improved information for decision making. Are the benefits of providing the sales manager with the information she needs likely to justify the associated costs of making it available?

Once the analyst has determined that one or more of these problems is serious and that the need for computer resources is legitimate, the next question concerns which approaches will best solve the problems. For the problems posed by the sales manager, some possible approaches are to:

☐ Give the manager access to an existing report or online database that will provide the information she needs

☐ Modify existing software and procedures to produce the desired information

☐ Develop new software and procedures to produce the information

☐ Acquire one or more new computer systems to serve both the manager and other users who may have similar problems with the existing system

Of course, there may be many other possibilities besides software solutions. For now, however, we will deal only with software development and defer the more general issue of systems development to Chapter 17.

Developing Software Requirements

Once the analyst has settled on a software solution, the next job is to specify the constraints the software must meet. This step involves defining the output the software is to produce, the input needed to produce this output, the processing tasks the system must perform, and the amount of storage required. Output requirements are always developed first, because you can't know what to put into a system or what to ask it to do until you know what you need to get out.

Defining Output. The analyst should define output in terms of content, format, timing, and flexibility.

☐ *Content* What type of information must the software provide, and at what level of detail? For example, a sales manager may want information on year-to-date product sales. Specifically, the manager may require sales figures on each product, subtotals taken over each region, and a grand total taken over all products and regions.

☐ *Format* How should the information be presented? Will it appear as a printed report or on a display screen? If the latter, the analyst should consult the user to see which of a number of screen formats he or she prefers. Likewise, if the output is to be a printed report, the analyst and the user must decide how to organize it.

☐ *Timing* When do users need the information? Daily? Weekly? Monthly? On demand? A sales manager might be content with sales reports on a weekly basis. Other users—for example, airline clerks, who interact directly with clients—need information constantly and also require a fast response time. Hence the analyst might recommend software that will give such users a response time of five seconds or less at least 95 percent of the time.

☐ *Flexibility* Are the solutions flexible enough so that they can be modified to meet changing conditions? For example, one bank installed a retrieval system that analysts had designed to provide information users—in this case, trust officers—had told them they needed. However, the analysts neglected to anticipate that once the system was installed, the users would begin to ask new types of questions and demand new kinds of information. Since the system wasn't flexible enough to adapt to the new requests, it was considered a failure.

Defining Input. After specifying the output, the analysts must determine what input is needed to produce it. This job involves four issues: data needed, data availability, procedures for gathering new data, and data entry.

☐ *Data Needed* What data does the application require? For example, if the application is to provide a monthly report on the sales of a particular product, the system must have data on each sale of that product and the date of sale.

☐ *Data Availability* Are the data needed currently available? For example, sales invoice records may be available that contain all the data needed to generate informative monthly reports on product sales.

☐ *Procedures for Gathering New Data* If new data are needed, how are they to be gathered? Suppose, for example, that a company is trying to decide how to market a product and wants information showing how many purchases have been for home use and how many for business use. The analyst might decide to redesign forms to provide this information.

☐ *Data Entry* How are the data to be entered into the system? For example, the analyst may have to decide whether transaction data are to be entered into the system at their source or through a centralized data-entry department. As mentioned in Chapter 6, there are compelling advantages to capturing data in machine-readable form at the time of the transaction. Also, the analyst will have to decide which precautions are necessary to ensure data enter the system error free (see Feature 9A).

Defining Processing. Processing describes the actual work the system does. The analyst must define the processing tasks involved in the application and the constraints people and equipment impose on the way those tasks are carried out.

☐ *Processing Tasks* What processing tasks must the software accomplish? Producing a sales report, for example, may require a program that can, among other things, sort a large file of sales data by date and by product, classify sales according to criteria such as product and region, and compute totals and percentages.

☐ *People Constraints* How sophisticated about computers are the people who will interact directly with the system? If they are relatively unsophisticated, the software will have to be extremely easy to learn and use.

☐ *Facility Constraints* Will the software be able to work effectively on the computer, peripheral equipment, and systems software that are available or feasible to acquire? One commonly hears stories of individuals and organizations that bought large software packages that barely fit on their current systems only to discover later that they had to substantially upgrade their facilities to get acceptable performance from the software.

Defining Storage. After determining input, output, and processing requirements, the analyst must turn to storage. Two critical issues concerning stor-

Ensuring the Validity and Accuracy of Input Data

Good Information Means Good Quality Control

Even thoroughly tested and error-free programs are not enough to guarantee correct results. If the data being fed to them are inaccurate, most programs can do relatively little to improve the situation. But even though a program might be unable to correct the data it's provided on its own, it can be supplied with utility routines that will enable it to ferret out any data that appear to be invalid, unreliable, or inconsistent. When a good quality assurance process is in effect, most of the "garbage in" should never make it to the "garbage out" stage.

A variety of control techniques can be used to flag problem data. Many of these controls operate in the realtime mode and are imbedded into the applications program

> "Garbage in" should never make it to the "garbage out" stage.

with which the end user interacts. Thus, they will immediately reject any suspect data being keyed in and, subsequently, will request the user to try again. For instance, when a program is equipped with a *field check*, a user attempting to key in data such

as a product's name (string data) into a field in which the program expects, say, product sales (numeric data) will see these data rejected. Field checks are used to inspect the individual characters of a field to ensure they are consistent with the field description in the data dictionary. Field checks are used in the batch mode, too.

Four other common controls frequently used in both the realtime and batch modes are the sign check, reasonableness check, validity check, and dependency check.

A *sign check* is commonly used in cases where an entered or computed amount must always be either positive or negative. So, for instance, if a user tried to enter a negative inventory balance, or if a program tried to create one, such a check would im-

age are access and organization methods and the amount of storage space required.

- ☐ **Access and Organization** How will users access data and, consequently, what type of organization techniques will ensure rapid access? In determining storage requirements, for instance, the analyst may decide that both sequential and direct access are required for the application at hand while an indexed-sequential organization method is best suited for providing these types of access.

- ☐ **Storage Space** What types of demands will be made on main memory and secondary storage? Every application has different storage requirements. Database processing, for instance, will likely involve relatively substantial online secondary storage requirements. An integrated software package, on the other hand, will probably demand a large amount of main memory.

mediately "raise a flag."

A *reasonableness check* ensures that certain amounts make sense. Such a check would prevent, say, the issuance of a reimbursement check for $0.00 or a weekly payroll check for $1 million.

A *validity check* prevents invalid codes or identification numbers from entering the system. So if all employee identification numbers in a company began with the letters *A, B,* or *C,* this check would reject any value beginning with a different letter.

A *dependency check* ensures that field values within a record or file are internally consistent. So, for instance, if a taxpayer declared both $100,000 in entertainment expenses and an income of $15, a dependency check would identify this situation as highly suspicious. Although

these data may be allowed to enter the system, the dependency check would almost certainly cause the taxpayer's name to be put on a list of people to be audited.

There are usually a number of other controls in effect that specifically apply to the type of processing being performed.

In realtime processing, for instance, there is usually an *echo check,* which displays or calls out each piece of data being entered for verification. Many supermarket scanners, for instance, use a voice chip to echo product descriptions and prices to both the cashier and the customer.

In batch processing, a procedure called a *sequence check* is used to ensure that all of the records being entered are in the correct order, if, indeed, they are supposed

to be. Another procedure, called *batch totaling,* makes sure that none of the records in the batch are lost as the file is passed from process to process. A batch total is the sum of all of the values in a given field on each record. It is computed whenever the file is processed, and it is compared after each round of processing with an independently computed total.

Also, where data are processed in the batch mode, a separate control program, called an *edit program,* often is used. This program enables suspect data to be culled from a transaction file before they are processed by the main applications program. Typically the edit program will produce a "clean" transaction file as well as a list of the questionable data that were extracted.

THE MAKE-OR-BUY DECISION

Once an organization has established a set of technical requirements for a software solution to a problem, it must decide whether the programs should be created in-house or acquired from a software vendor. This consideration, which often arises after the analysis stage of the program development cycle, is frequently called the *make-or-buy decision.*

Applications Packages

During the last several years, prewritten applications programs for such tasks as payroll, general-ledger accounting, financial planning, manufacturing control, and project scheduling have become increasingly available from specialized vendors for many common business functions. These programs, called **applications packages,** normally consist of an integrated set of programs, documentation (usually of fairly high quality), and possibly training. Because they often provide immediate results at a reasonable cost, applications packages are becoming ever more popular.

When contrasted with in-house-developed software, applications packages have a number of advantages and disadvantages.

Advantages. Applications packages make a great deal of sense from the viewpoint of availability, risk, expertise, and cost.

☐ *Availability* In many organizations, there are too many problems needing solution and too few programmers. End users who ask for software to be developed in-house often are relegated to a waiting list that may extend anywhere from two to four years. Once development is started—if it ever is—in-house software may take months or even years to design, code, and debug. Applications packages, in contrast, can be implemented almost immediately.

☐ *Risk* With applications packages, the buying organization knows what it's getting: a product of stated quality at a specified price. The product may also have a proven track record and an active group of users with whom to "trade notes." When software is developed in-house, it's difficult to predict what the final product will look like, when it will be finished, and what its eventual cost will be. What's more, since people tend to be overoptimistic when estimating schedules and costs, projects developed in-house are usually completed late and over budget.

☐ *Expertise* Many of the organizations that sell applications packages are experts within the niche areas they serve. Also, because software vendors typically offer analysts and programmers the greatest potential for challenge and reward in the technology field, they often draw the best talent. Systems analysts within the user organizations, in contrast, usually must be jacks of all trades to their employers. Regrettably, this results in their having to spread themselves thin.

☐ *Cost* The primary economic advantage to applications packages is relatively simple. The software's cost is distributed—that is, leveraged—over several organizations. Thus, even allowing the vendor a profit, the price per user organization can be set relatively low. Costs for in-house software, on the other hand, often are completely absorbed by a single organization. Furthermore, when an applications package has a large existing user base, new hires may already be familiar with it, saving the buyer the time and cost of training them.

Disadvantages. Although purchased software offers many compelling advantages, it is not always appropriate. If a package was originally developed for a business that works differently from the one it's being sold to and the vendor has made only superficial attempts to adapt it to the current buyer's needs, it may prove more trouble than it's worth. Also, for some applications little or no appropriate packaged software exists. In such cases, in-house

FIGURE 9-2

Advantages and disadvantages of applications packages. For applications areas in which an applications package is available, the advantages of such a package over software developed in-house may greatly outweigh the disadvantages.

Advantages and Disadvantages of Applications Packages

Advantages

☑ Lower overall cost
☑ Faster implementation
☑ Less risk
☑ Higher quality documentation
☑ Fewer analysts and programmers needed
☑ Possible availability of user groups

Disadvantages

☑ Unavailability of appropriate package
☑ Less control over applications development
☑ Possible incompatibility with existing applications

---

development is the only alternative, in which case it becomes necessary to proceed to the design stage of the program development cycle.

Figure 9-2 lists several advantages and disadvantages of using applications packages. Many industry experts feel that the advantages of applications packages far outweigh their shortcomings. They say it is only a matter of time before in-house software becomes the exception rather than the rule. Such a change will take place slowly, however. Most businesses have substantial investments in existing software and in current ways of doing work.

PROGRAM DESIGN

In the **design** stage of the program development cycle, the software requirements developed in the analysis stage are used to spell out as precisely as possible the nature of the required programming solution. The design, or plan, so formed determines all the tasks each program must do as well as how to organize or sequence them when coding the program. Only when the design is complete does the next stage—the actual coding of the program—begin.

In the early days of computing, design and coding were not clearly separated. Programmers were relatively free to solve problems their own way. They would often begin coding with a vague, disorganized notion of the requirements a program had to meet. Such an undisciplined approach created many problems.

First, a programmer might have been making substantial progress on a program only to find later that a key function had been omitted. As a result, large pieces of the program might have to be reorganized. Second, the logic behind programs written in this freewheeling way usually was obscure. What's more, each programmer had a personalized coding style. What seemed systematic to one often was incomprehensible to another. Programs written this way may have worked in the sense that they processed data correctly, but they were hard for anyone but the original programmers to understand. They were especially a nightmare for maintenance programmers, the people who had to update them whenever some aspect of the application changed. These unfortunates, faced with a jumble of confusing code, usually just patched up a program with their own bits of new code rather than starting over. The result was even more confusion. Organizations found themselves depending for critical applications on software that no one understood very well. As computer systems came to be used for increasing numbers of applications, it became clear that some order was needed to prevent financial calamity.

Structured Techniques. Beginning in the 1960s, a number of researchers began to stress program design (planning) and the merits of separating the design process from the actual program coding. Many of their proposed ideas caught on, and over the last few decades, a group of methods have evolved that have made program design more systematic and programs themselves easier to read and maintain. These methods usually are grouped together under the term *structured techniques.*

Structured methods that deal specifically with the design of programs are specifically referred to as *structured design* techniques, whereas those dealing with the coding of programs are referred to as *structured programming* techniques. Actually, **structured programming** originally referred only to the use of certain logical structures in programs themselves (we will discuss these structures in Chapter 10), but in practice it has come to apply to a whole body of both program design and coding methodologies. Today structured design and programming practices are widely reflected in programs developed in-house by firms as well as in most of the prepackaged software programs on the market.

Structured techniques represent but one solution to the problem of making programmers more productive at their jobs. Later in the chapter, we will discuss other tools organizations have used to improve the effectiveness of applications software development. Two such tools are *fourth-generation languages (4GLs)* and *reusable code modules,* both of which have their greatest impact in the program coding phase of the program development cycle. Many industry observers expect that these tools ultimately will have an even greater impact in organizations than did structured programming, but only time will tell.

Program Design Tools

Program design tools are tools that help either analysts or programmers plan and later document programs. Many such tools have been proposed. Currently four of the most important are

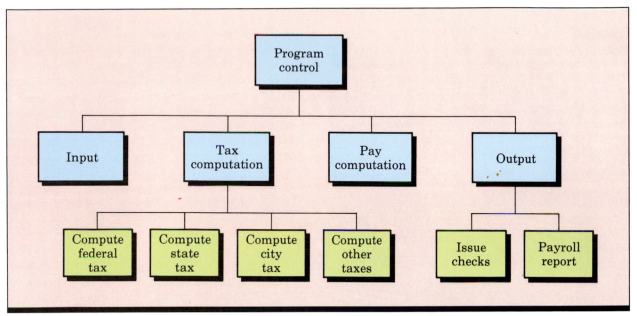

FIGURE 9-3

Structure charts. This technique subdivides a program into individual modules, each of which represents a well-defined processing task. The modules are then arranged hierarchically in a top-down fashion, as illustrated here for a payroll application. HIPO charts use a similar diagram for illustrating the hierarchy of modules in a program.

☐ Structured program flowcharts

☐ Pseudocode

☐ Structure charts

☐ HIPO (Hierarchy plus Input-Process-Output) charts

Structure charts and *HIPO charts* show how the independent parts of a program—called *modules*—relate to one another. As Figure 9-3 shows, each module represents a specific programming task, for example, calculating city tax. The modules are arranged hierarchically in what is called a top-down fashion. *Top-down* implies that the topmost modules control the ones beneath them, and as the modules are developed, the topmost ones are designed first.

Program flowcharts and *pseudocode* outline in detail the steps a program will follow. As Figure 9-4 illustrates, flowcharts show the steps and their relations to one another pictorially. Pseudocode, in contrast, outlines the program's steps in a form that closely resembles actual programming code (hence *pseudocode*).

The use of these design tools in organizations varies widely. In many organizations, systems analysts draw structure charts or HIPO charts to specify the overall design for a program, and the programmers use flowcharts or pseudocode to design the detailed, step-by-step procedures required to implement the overall design. If the programming project is large, the systems analyst may provide the programmer only with diagrams showing the highest level of detail and leave it to the programmer to do most of the fine-tuning.

FIGURE 9-4

Flowchart and pseudocode. The flowchart and pseudocode shown here count the number of temperatures over 90 degrees in a list. Flowcharts use graphical symbols and arrows to show the operations to be performed and the logical flow of the program. Pseudocode uses Englishlike statements to achieve the same objectives.

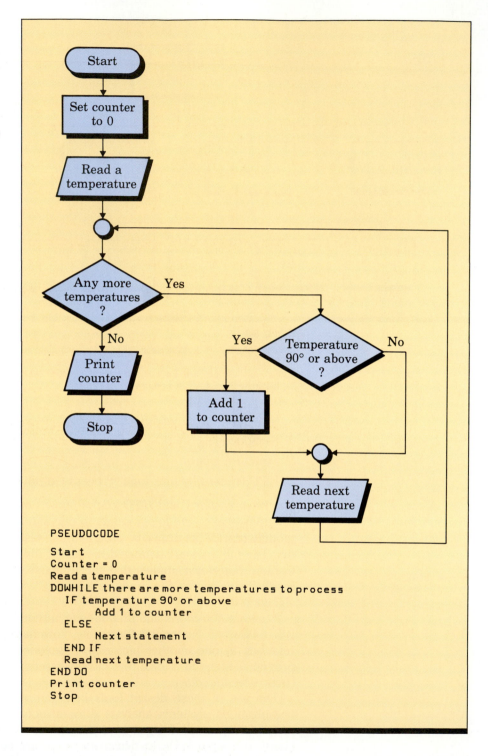

```
PSEUDOCODE

Start
Counter = 0
Read a temperature
DOWHILE there are more temperatures to process
    IF temperature 90° or above
        Add 1 to counter
    ELSE
        Next statement
    END IF
    Read next temperature
END DO
Print counter
Stop
```

Choosing a Language

An important decision that must be made during the design phase is the selection of a programming language. Many organizations code the bulk of their applications in a single prespecified language, so this decision normally is very straightforward.

The language choice is closely related to the applications environment. A business-oriented language such as COBOL, for example, is commonly used for business transaction processing applications, whereas a scientifically oriented language such as FORTRAN is more likely to be used for scientific, mathematical, and engineering applications. The use of fourth-generation languages is becoming especially popular in applications development environments in which coding speed is essential.

Because it reflects the nature of the application, the choice of programming language often also affects the selection of design tools. Some design tools are better suited to certain applications than others. An accounting problem to be coded in a structure-oriented language like COBOL is almost always better suited to structure charts and pseudocode than to flowcharts. On the other hand, scientific problems with a high degree of visual content are best planned with the aid of flowcharts.

The characteristics of some of the more popular programming languages are discussed in Chapter 11.

PROGRAM CODING

Once the program design is complete, the next step is to code the program. **Coding,** which is the job of programmers, is the actual process of writing the program in a programming language.

Programs often are keyed into the computer system with the help of a *text editor,* which we covered in Chapter 8. The text editor enables the programmer to copy blocks of code from one program to another; to replicate text strings that appear in several lines; to insert, delete, and move code; and to neatly format the program with indents and "white space." A text editor has the same utility to a programmer as a word processor does to a writer.

During the coding process, programmers often take advantage of a number of special tools and methods that help make them more productive. Several of these will be described next.

Increasing Programmer Productivity

Because programming is labor intensive, it can be a severe drain on an organization's resources when poorly managed. Among the techniques that have been used to increase programmer productivity are coding standards, fourth-generation languages, reusable code, data dictionaries, structured walkthroughs, and chief programmer teams. The purpose of these techniques is to ensure that programmers produce code rapidly while creating programs that are both as error-free as possible and easy to maintain.

Coding Standards. Many organizations enforce a set of coding standards, which are essentially a list of rules designed to inhibit personalized programming styles. These rules may cover items such as the following:

☐ *Acceptable Program Structures* Virtually all programming problems have several solutions, but some solutions are more straightforward than others. Many programming shops require programmers to use only those *program-control structures*—or conventions for grouping program statements—that follow acceptable structured programming constructs. (We will discuss these structures in Chapter 10.)

☐ *Naming Conventions* *Naming conventions* refer to uniform ways of naming variables in a program. For example, a programming shop might require that variables relating to input fields be labeled with the suffix "-IN," as in "EMPLOYEE-IN" or "ADDRESS-IN."

☐ *Comment Conventions* *Comments* within a program help explain how the program works. They are especially useful in long and logically complex programs. Most shops have conventions that dictate when and how to use comments.

Rules such as these help make programs readable and easy to maintain. If everyone in an organization writes programs using the same set of conventions, maintenance programmers always know what to expect. Unconstrained creativity is strictly discouraged in commercial programming environments.

Fourth-Generation Languages. **Fourth-generation languages (4GLs)** have evolved largely to make it easier and less time consuming to write computer programs. One type of 4GL product that is especially useful for increasing the efficiency of software development is the applications generator. An **applications generator** enables one to quickly code programs needed for a specific application without having to deal directly with a traditional "third-generation" programming language such as COBOL or BASIC. Many database management systems, for instance, are considered applications generators; they contain their own set of commands that allow users to build applications. Two widely used types of tools applications generators employ are prototyping languages and code generators.

A strategy that many computer professionals use in developing software is to create a quickly coded, "down-and-dirty" program for users to provide feedback on, successively building and refining the program into a polished product. Such a program is called a *software prototype,* and the language that facilitates creation of software prototypes is called a *prototyping language.* Prototyping languages are useful when the user is unsure of what he or she wants and when time is a limiting factor in software development. In addition, software prototypes lend some overall direction to the software

FIGURE 9-5

Software prototype development.
Prototyping is an iterative process—
after each prototype is built, the
user and analyst try it out together
and attempt to improve upon it.
Eventually, the prototype evolves
into a finished system.

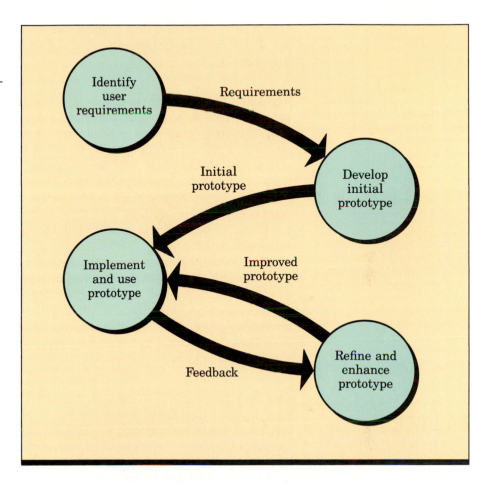

development process, and advocates claim that the finished programs often
are better as a result.

Here's how a software prototype might work. The computer professional
uses a prototyping language to create, within a couple of days, a crude prototype for a particular end user. Then the professional and the user try out
the prototype together. The user makes suggestions and, subsequently, the
prototype is both refined and expanded. Then the professional and the user
again try out the prototype (see Figure 9-5). When the prototype is improved
as far as it can be, it either becomes the finished product or is used to guide
a more ambitious applications development effort with a third-generation
programming language. Software prototypes are special cases of system prototypes, which we will cover in Chapter 17.

In cases where the prototype is to be used to guide development with a
third-generation language, a code generator is often used. A *code generator*
is a language translator that converts the code of a particular prototyping
language into the code of a particular third-generation language. So, for instance, the final version of the prototype program described earlier might
be fed into a code generator, which converts the 4GL code into COBOL. At
that point, the programming staff finishes the application in COBOL. If

COBOL is the standard development language, the organization may prefer the final version of the program be in COBOL rather than in the prototyping language.

Reusable Code. Related programs often use the same blocks of code. Take payroll programs. A company may have a dozen or more payroll programs—programs that cut checks to employees; report every check issued by the treasurer's office; report payments to the city, state, or federal government; and so on. Rather than have programmers code each of these programs from scratch, most organizations keep libraries of reusable code available. **Reusable code,** as you might guess, refers to code segments that can be used over and over again by several programs. Thus, reusable code enables programs to be "cut and pasted" quickly from pretested, error-free code segments.

Many industry experts feel that reusable code is a wave of the future in programming. They predict that someday many firms will be in the business of selling "standardized" reusable code segments rather than entire applications programs. Organizations will buy these segments and have their programmers stitch them together appropriately into complete programs. If what these experts say becomes true, programming will successfully implement the same formula that worked in the modular housing industry!

Data Dictionary Facility. A **data dictionary** is similar to an ordinary dictionary in that it contains definitions for an alphabetical list of words. The words are those encountered in the company's information processing environment. Among them would be, for example, names of fields, records, files, and programs. Thus, if we looked up the field ZIP-CODE in a data dictionary, we might find things such as:

☐ The definition of ZIP-CODE. This definition probably would include a short description of what ZIP-CODE means as well as information such as the number of characters in ZIP-CODE and whether the characters are numeric or alphabetic.

☐ The names of all the programs that use ZIP-CODE.

☐ Any alternate names that ZIP-CODE assumes in programs. For example, ZIP-CODE may be called ZCODE in one program and ZIPPER in another.

Data dictionaries can be active or passive. An *active* data dictionary is online to an application as a programmer is developing it. If, say, a programmer attempts to use a field name improperly or inconsistently, the active data dictionary will immediately warn the programmer and, possibly, prohibit the alleged infraction from being part of the finished software product. A data dictionary that is not online during application development is *passive*.

Structured Walkthroughs. Some organizations employ a technique called a structured walkthrough as a quality assurance measure for their programs.

A **structured walkthrough,** which occurs at the coding stage, is a peer evaluation of a programmer's work. The coding is evaluated by four or five other members of the staff, and a meeting is held to discuss good and bad features of the coding effort. An important topic of discussion concerns whether the program is being coded consistently and in accordance with the organization's coding standards.

Such a review process is intended to help programmers improve their coding skills and to ensure the success of important programs by subjecting them to close scrutiny. It is not intended as a formal appraisal of performance—in fact, it is recommended that the programmer's boss not participate. Walkthroughs are held early in the coding process, when errors are least costly to fix.

The term **egoless programming** is sometimes used when describing formal reviews such as structured walkthroughs. Some people consider programming an art. Thus, they are particularly sensitive to their programs' being scrutinized by others who may react negatively to the programs' more creative coding aspects. Egoless programming relates to a fundamental philosophy of review methods: One should not take constructive criticism personally.

Some organizations also conduct a walkthrough during the design stage to ensure that the analyst or programmer has properly planned the application before coding starts.

Chief Programmer Team. When a program or set of programs is expected to be very large—say, with 20,000 or more lines of code—several programmers may be assigned to the coding operation. A **chief programmer team** is simply a team of programmers coordinated by a highly experienced person called a *chief programmer*. The chief programmer assigns the program modules to the team programmers. He or she ordinarily codes the most critical modules and assigns less important ones to subordinates. The modules typically are coded in a top-down fashion, in which the higher-level modules are designed and integrated before the ones below them.

The chief programmer is also responsible for fitting all the individual modules into a workable whole by some target date. He or she normally is assisted by a *backup programmer,* who helps with the coding and integration of modules, and a *librarian,* who performs many of the clerical tasks associated with the project. Figure 9-6 shows an organization chart for a chief programmer team.

DEBUGGING PROGRAMS

Debugging is the process of ensuring that a program is free of errors, or *bugs.* Debugging is usually a lengthy process, often amounting to over 50 percent of a program's total development time.

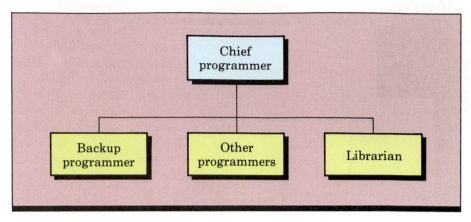

FIGURE 9-6

Organization of a chief programmer team. The chief programmer team often is compared to a surgical team. Each member has a specialized role, and there is a careful division of work.

Preliminary Debugging

The debugging process often begins after the program has been keyed. At this point, the programmer visually inspects the program, before compiling and running it, for typing errors. This is called a *desk check*. When a desk check reveals no apparent errors, the programmer submits the program to the computer for compiling and subsequent execution.

Rarely is any program error free the first time the programmer attempts to compile it. A very long program often has well over a hundred errors of one sort or another—and maybe even thousands—at the outset. The computer's systems software usually provides the programmer with a list of informative "error messages" indicating the source of many of the bugs. At this point, the programmer again checks the code to see what's wrong and then makes the necessary corrections. This desk check/compile/run/correct process may be repeated several times.

Sometimes, after the easy errors have been corrected, the programmer's desk checking may fail to weed out the remaining errors. *Diagnostic statements,* or "dummy" statements, may need to be inserted temporarily to show how the program is executing. In more drastic cases, the programmer may need to summon a special diagnostic program to find out what is being stored in computer memory when the program aborts. If all else fails, the programmer may ask someone else for help. Sometimes a few minutes of consultation can avoid several days of wasted effort. In any case, the programmer normally will have to employ many strategies to get the program in working order.

Testing

At some point in the debugging process, the program will appear to be correct. At this point, the original programmer—or, preferably, someone else—runs the program with extensive test data. Good test data will subject the program to all the conditions it might conceivably encounter when finally implemented. The test data should also check for likely sources of coding omissions; for example, will the program issue a check or a bill in the amount of $0.00? Does the program provide for leap years when dating reports? Many more program bugs often are found during the testing phase of the debugging process. Although rigorous testing significantly decreases the chance of malfunctioning when a program is implemented, there is no foolproof guarantee that the completed program will be bug free.

Purchased software also should be tested before implementation. A firm buying a package from an outside vendor must keep in mind that the programs may have been developed for a different type of company, computer, or operating system. If so, modifications may be necessary to enable the programs to work satisfactorily. In any case, few packages are completely bug free to begin with, which is another good reason for testing them thoroughly.

Proper debugging is vital, because an error that may cost a few dollars to fix at this stage in the development process may cost many thousands of dollars to correct after the program is implemented in the real world. An unusual testing challenge confronting programmers in the coming decade is featured in the Tomorrow box.

PROGRAM DOCUMENTATION

Program **documentation** includes manuals that enable users, maintenance programmers, and operators to interact successfully with a program. If you've ever had the frustration of getting something to work from poorly written instructions, you should appreciate how valuable good documentation can be.

User documentation normally consists of a user's manual. This manual should provide instructions for running the program, a description of language commands, several examples of situations the end user is likely to encounter, and a troubleshooting guide to help with difficulties. The user's manual is an extremely important piece of documentation. If it is poorly written, end users may refuse to interact with the program altogether.

Programmer documentation usually consists of any tools that will simplify maintenance of the program. These might include a program narrative, design tools such as flowcharts and structure charts, a listing of the program, and a description of inputs and outputs. There should also be a set of procedures to help programmers test the program.

Operator documentation includes manuals that assist operators in mounting tapes, printed forms, and the like that are needed to get programs up and running. Because operator documentation is machine dependent, a company purchasing a package often must rewrite this part of the vendor-supplied documentation to suit its own equipment.

Although documentation is included here as the last step in the program development cycle, you should see it as an ongoing process. For example,

T   O   M   O   R   R   O   W

January 1, 2000

A Date Maintenance Programmers Don't Look Forward To

To most people, January 1, 2000, is just another date on the calendar. And for TV sports junkies, it will be a day to get geared up for the forthcoming onslaught of college football bowl games. But to many computer professionals, especially maintenance programmers and their information processing managers, it's a day of potential infamy.

Believe it or not, there are many programs still in wide use—most notably mainframe programs that were written in the 1950s, 1960s, and 1970s—that treat the twentieth century as though it will last forever. Consequently, they contain statements such as

```
ADD 1900 TO YEAR
MOVE YEAR TO DATE
```

and permit users to input YEAR in a two-digit format.

But guess what. When we enter the twenty-first century, many programs such as these, if left in their current form, will "blow up." Consequently, a transaction taking place in the year 2000 will be treated as though it were oc-curring in 1900, when William McKinley was president. This means that many interest payments will be miscomputed, reminder-notice programs will get boggled, inventory deliveries and production schedules will go astray, and

> When we enter the twenty-first century, many programs . . . will "blow up."

files such as those comprising pension, insurance, and credit applications will reflect some interesting but erroneous transactions. Also, because some program calendars cannot accept an entry higher than the 365th day of 1999, it is feared that a lot of data will inadvertently be erased. Indeed, it will be an interesting time in history and one that will be looked on with a certain degree of gallows humor by the average onlooker, as well as with a few pangs of anxiety. It will be fun to watch, perhaps, as long as your own records don't go awry and you aren't put through monumental hassles getting them straightened out.

While it may sound like the year-2000 problem could be corrected by using some type of electronic editor to locate dates and automatically change them, it's much more complicated than that. For instance, many companies have thousands of programs that collectively involve millions of lines of code. It's difficult to track down every situation in which date computations are being made. Furthermore, the programs most in need of date maintenance are the older ones—those with which maintenance programmers are least likely to be familiar.

Many companies have set up target dates for making date checks in their scheduled program maintenance. Some plan to start scrutinizing dates around the mid-1990s, others about 1997 or 1998. When the year 2000 rolls out, however, it's likely that most eyes will be focused on the U.S. government. The feds have had computer applications up and running even before white buck shoes and pegged pants were in style, and they own 20 billion of the world's 75 billion lines of code. Also, many of their applications are much older than those in the private sector, making them more susceptible to date glitches.

as analysts develop display-screen formats in the analysis stage of development, or HIPO charts in the design stage, they should immediately put them in a form suitable for the maintenance programmer's documentation package. If they leave this task until later, they probably will forget many important details.

SUMMARY AND KEY TERMS

Applications software consists of programs that direct computer systems to produce outputs for computer users. Creating, acquiring, and maintaining good applications software are among the major information processing expenses in any organization.

In most large organizations, the development of applications software is the job of systems analysts and programmers. **Systems analysts** work with users to assess their needs, translate those needs into a list of technical requirements, and design the necessary software specifications. The design specifications then go to **programmers,** who code the programs from them. **Maintenance programmers** monitor the software on an ongoing basis, correcting errors and updating the software as applications needs change.

Creating successful programs commonly involves five stages: analysis, design, coding, debugging, and documentation. These five stages often are called the **program development cycle,** or **program life cycle.**

Analysis is the process of identifying and defining the problem to be solved; deciding whether the solution involves software; and if so, defining input, output, processing, and storage requirements.

Many organizations choose to buy their software in the form of prewritten **applications packages** rather than creating it in-house. This consideration, which often arises after the analysis stage of the program development cycle, is frequently called the *make-or-buy decision.*

In the **design** stage of the program development cycle, analysts work from the software requirements developed in the analysis stage to spell out as precisely as possible the nature of the programming solution that will enable the system to meet those requirements. A group of techniques that have made program design more systematic and programs themselves easier to read and maintain have evolved. These techniques often are grouped together under the term *structured techniques.* Techniques that deal specifically with the design and coding of programs often are referred to by the name **structured programming.**

There are many tools available for helping analysts plan structured programs, including structured program flowcharts, pseudocode, structure charts, and HIPO charts.

Once analysts have finished the program design for an application, the next stage is to code the program. **Coding,** which is the job of programmers, is the process of writing a program from a set of design specifications. Programming is labor intensive and thus can be a severe drain on an organization's resources when poorly managed. Among the techniques that have been developed for increasing programmer productivity are coding standards, fourth-generation languages, reusable code, data dictionaries, structured walkthroughs, and chief programmer teams.

Coding standards are rules that specify how programs are to be coded. Program maintenance can be a significant burden to an organization; thus, when everyone consistently follows the same set of rules, maintenance costs are reduced.

Fourth-generation languages (4GLs) have evolved primarily to make it easier and less time consuming to write computer programs. One type of 4GL product that has proven especially useful for increasing the efficiency of applications software development is the **applications generator,** which enables one to quickly code applications programs without having to deal directly with a traditional third-generation programming language such as COBOL or BASIC.

Most organizations keep libraries of reusable code available, so programmers need not code every new program from scratch. **Reusable code** refers to code segments that can be used repeatedly by several programs. Through reusable code, programs are "cut and pasted" quickly from pretested, error-free code segments.

Data dictionaries, which can be *active* or *passive,* are similar to ordinary dictionaries in that they contain definitions for an alphabetical list of words. The words are those encountered in the company's information processing environment. Data dictionaries are useful for ensuring that programs are developed quickly and consistently.

Many programming shops employ structured walkthroughs during the coding stage of program development. A **structured walkthrough** is a peer evaluation of a programmer's work. The coding is evaluated by four or five other members of the staff, and a meeting is held to discuss the program's good and bad features. The term **egoless programming** is sometimes used when describing formal reviews such as structured walkthroughs, implying that one shouldn't take constructive criticism personally.

A **chief programmer team** is a team of programmers coordinated by a highly experienced person called a *chief programmer.* The chief programmer assigns the program modules to the team programmers and coordinates the fitting of all the individual modules into a workable whole by some target date.

Debugging is the process of ensuring that a program is free of errors, or *bugs*. Debugging usually is a lengthy process, often amounting to over 50 percent of the total development time for a program.

At some point in the debugging process, the program will appear to be correct. Then the programmer—or, preferably, someone else—will run the original program with extensive *test data*. Good test data will subject the program to all the conditions it might conceivably encounter when finally implemented.

Program **documentation** includes manuals that enable end users, maintenance programmers, and operators to interact successfully with a program. Although noted as the final stage of the program development cycle, documentation is an ongoing process that must be addressed throughout the program's life.

REVIEW EXERCISES

Fill-in Questions

1. _____ define the requirements that applications software must meet to satisfy the users' needs.

2. _____ are responsible for keeping an organization's existing programs in proper working order.

3. _____ refers to the writing of computer programs.

4. A formal development process in which the work of a systems analyst or programmer is constructively reviewed by peers is called a(n) _____ .

5. A(n) _____ is a language translator that converts the code of a prototyping language into the code of a third-generation language.

6. Code segments that can be used over and over again are referred to as _____ .

7. The process of detecting or correcting errors in computer programs is called _____ .

8. A(n) _____ is a manual inspection process whereby a programmer scans a program for errors prior to submitting it to the computer for execution.

Matching Questions

Match each term with the description that best fits.

a. analysis   e. flowchart
b. design   f. pseudocode
c. chief programmer team   g. module
d. documentation   h. program design tools

_h_ 1. Flowcharts, pseudocode, structure charts, and HIPO charts.

_c_ 2. A group of programmers, often assigned to a large programming project, that is coordinated by a highly experienced programmer.

_e_ 3. A graphical design tool with boxes and arrows showing step by step how a computer program will process data.

_b_ 4. The process of planning a program, undertaken after analyzing a problem area.

_f_ 5. A technique for designing programs that uses Englishlike statements resembling actual program statements to show the step-by-step processing a program will follow.

_g_ 6. A well-defined task represented on a structure chart or HIPO chart.

_d_ 7. A written description of a program, procedure, or system.

_a_ 8. The process of studying a problem area to determine what should be done.

Discussion Questions

1. What is applications software?
2. Name the stages in the program development cycle.
3. What types of decisions must be made in defining software requirements?
4. Name some advantages and disadvantages of applications packages relative to in-house systems development.
5. Why have structured techniques evolved as a major strategy in program design?
6. Identify some ways to increase programmer productivity.
7. Why is an active data dictionary useful in program development?
8. Why is program documentation important?

Critical Thinking Questions

1. Many executives in business seem to get results by imparting their own personalized styles of management and decision making to an organization, so why shouldn't the programmer be free to create with his or her own programming style?
2. Most end users and programmers within organizations would prefer to work with a widely used applications package than a comparable soft-

ware product developed in-house. Why is this so, and what benefits and/or problems does the widely used applications package present to the organization?

3. It is a well-known fact that virtually all sizeable programs inevitably contain bugs—often many of them—when they are released for use. This being the case, what guidelines should be used when testing software?

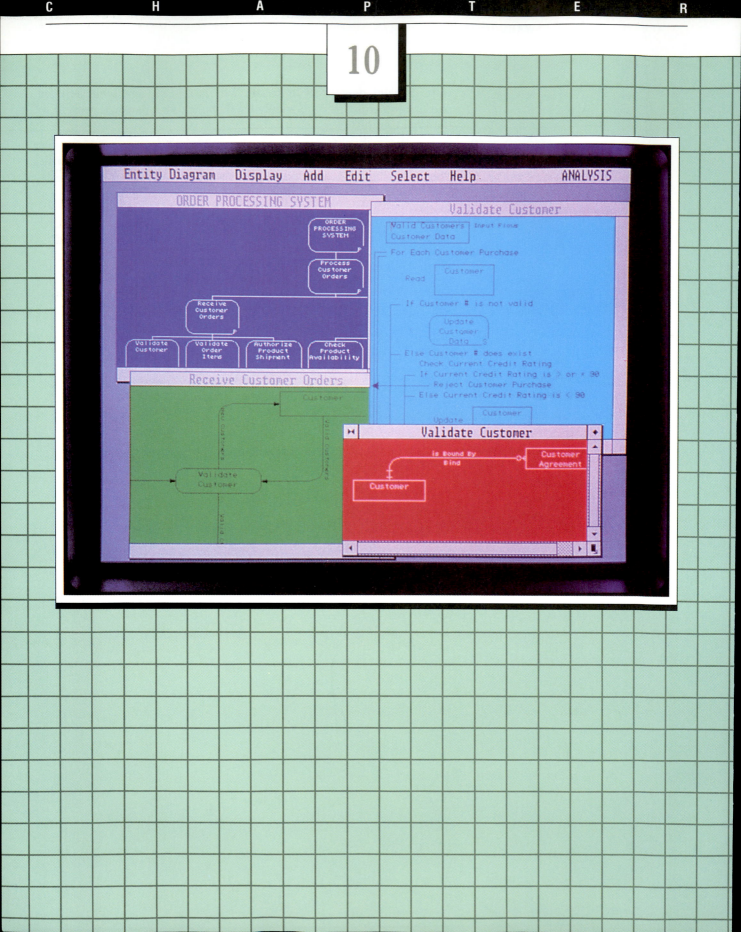

Program Design Tools

Outline

Objectives

After completing this chapter, you will be able to:

1. Describe various techniques used to make programs structured and explain why it is desirable to structure programs.
2. Identify the strengths and weaknesses of various program design tools.
3. Draw elementary flowcharts, structure charts, and HIPO charts, and create simple pseudocode and decision tables.

OVERVIEW

In Chapter 9, you learned how organizations develop applications software. In that chapter, we focused on the program development cycle, which begins with problem analysis and ends with a working program. In this chapter, we will focus on one stage of that cycle—design.

We will begin by discussing one of the earliest and most widely used program design tools: program flowcharts. Although program flowcharts are less popular than they once were for many types of commercial-level design applications, their graphical nature makes them hard to beat as a learning tool for seeing how program control structures work. Then we will describe some principles of structured programming. Next, we will discuss in detail four design tools for structured programming: structured program flowcharts, pseudocode, structure charts, and HIPO charts. Finally, we will cover decision tables and other types of design tools. Feature 10A addresses the growing importance of the user interface in software design.

WHAT ARE PROGRAM DESIGN TOOLS?

It's extremely difficult to just sit down and write a long or complex program of high quality. Before you begin coding, you need a plan for the program. **Program design tools** are essentially program planning tools. They consist of various kinds of diagrams, charts, and tables that outline either the organization of program tasks or the steps the program will follow. Once a program has been coded and implemented, program design tools serve as excellent documentation for maintenance programmers.

Many of the tools we will discuss in this chapter were developed as tools for structured programming. One of the oldest and still among the most popular design tools, however, was in use long before structured programming became widespread: the program flowchart.

Because it is hard to discuss structured programming without resorting to a design tool to help illustrate the concepts involved, we will examine program flowcharts before moving on to a discussion of structured program design and coverage of other design tools.

PROGRAM FLOWCHARTS

Program flowcharts use geometric symbols, such as those in Figure 10-1, and familiar mathematical symbols, such as those in Figure 10-2, to graphically portray the sequence of steps involved in a program. The steps in a

FIGURE 10-1
ANSI program flowchart symbols.

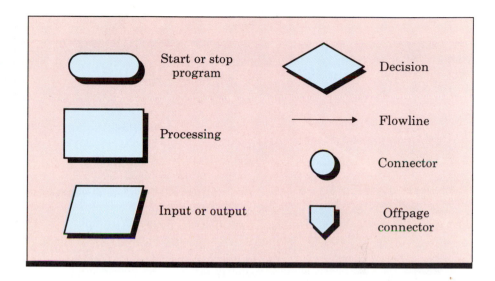

flowchart occur in the same logical sequence that their corresponding program statements follow in the program.

For many years, flowcharting symbols were nonstandardized, which made it difficult for one programmer to follow another's work. Today a number of standards exist. Among the most popular are those developed by ANSI, the American National Standards Institute (see Figure 10-1). To help you understand what these symbols mean and see how to use them, let's consider two examples.

Scanning a File for Employees with Certain Characteristics. A common activity in information processing is scanning an employee file for people with certain characteristics. Suppose, for example, a company's personnel department wants a printed list of all employees with computer experience and at least five years of company service. A flowchart that shows how to accomplish this task and also totals the number of employees who meet these criteria is shown in Figure 10-3.

This particular flowchart uses five symbols: start/stop, processing, decision, connector, and input/output. The lines with arrows that link the symbols are called **flowlines;** they indicate the flow of logic in the flowchart.

FIGURE 10-2

Mathematical symbols used in flowcharts.

Symbol	Meaning
<	Less than
≤	Less than or equal to
>	Greater than
≥	Greater than or equal to
=	Equal to
<>	Not equal to

Designing Programs for End Users

The Importance of the User/Computer Interface

One of the most important elements in the program design process goes well beyond the particular design tool chosen and the manner in which code is laid out. This element is the *user interface*—the particular way in which the entire application is presented by the computer to the end user. In many cases, the user interface can be just as important as the capabilities of the underlying product. And, odd as it may seem, well over half the code involved in writing the application may be devoted solely to the user interface.

There are many factors that contribute to the quality of the user interface, including the following.

The End User. The increasingly widespread use of computers has brought more diverse people into contact with technology than ever before. Some users are quantitatively sophisticated; others can barely add or follow instructions. Some are inquisitive and patient; others are always in a rush. Some can type; others can't and/or don't

> The user interface can be just as important as the capabilities of the underlying product.

want to. A major goal of the program design process is to identify the target audience of end users and create an interface, or even multiple interfaces, that will fit their needs.

Command Structure. Traditionally end users have worked with text-oriented interfaces that require typing in commands. During recent years, menu interfaces and graphically oriented interfaces, which require users to simply choose or point to commands or options, have been very popular. Natural-language commands, which enable users to construct commands in, say, ordinary English, also have been widely used. However, because sophisticated users complain that menus, graphics, and natural-language commands slow them down, programs often must be designed with interfaces for both novice and veteran.

Help and Memory Aids. Everyone is limited in what he or she can remember. Consequently, many programs are designed with an online help feature. When invoked, it provides assistance on matters such as command syntax and debugging. Programs also often contain a variety of features that help jog

Every flowchart begins and ends with an oval-shaped **start/stop symbol.** The first of these symbols in the program contains the word *Start* and the last the word *Stop*. The diamond-shaped **decision symbol** always indicates a question, which generally will have only two possible answers—*yes* or *no* (*true* or *false*). Decision symbols should always have one flowline entering and two flowlines (representing the two possible outcomes) exiting.

The rectangular **processing symbol** contains an action that needs to be taken—for example, "Set counter to 0" and "Add 1 to counter." The **connector symbol** provides a logical meeting point for several flowlines. The **input/output symbol** enables the logical process depicted in the flowchart to accept data or output them.

one's memory. For instance, command menus, such as those employed by Lotus 1-2-3, enable users to *recognize* commands rather than being forced to *remember* them. Also, many programs support backtracking to earlier points in the user-computer dialog so that past actions can be reconstructed.

Windowing and Graphical Interfaces. Many observers of the computer world claim that some of the best interfaces have resulted from the proliferation of microcomputers. Microcomputers have placed computing power closer to the people who know best how work should be done—the end users themselves. Perhaps the most applauded interfacing tool that has emerged from the microcomputing world is windowing (covered in Chapter 8), which was pioneered by Xerox and popularized by the Apple Macintosh. Windowing enables users to lay out work on a computer screen as they would on a conventional desktop (see photo). In fact, many users of software packages on larger computers have demanded that their software vendors provide them with windowing environments.

Undo Commands. All users make mistakes that they wish they could "have back." Undo commands make this possible. One of the most popular forms of an undo command lets users retrieve files they have just inadvertently erased from their disks.

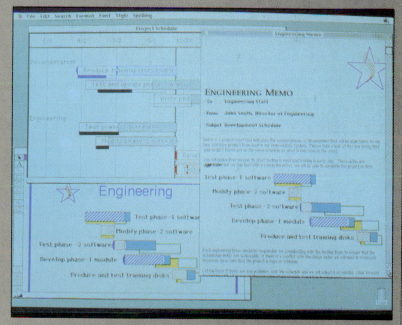

Windowing. Fitting the way users naturally do work.

The flowchart in Figure 10-3 involves a looping operation. We "read" a record, inspect it, and take an action; then read another record, inspect it, and take another action; and so on until the file is exhausted. When the computer reads a record, as indicated by the input/output symbol, it brings it into main memory and stores its contents (or field values). Here, for example, an employee's ID, name, address, phone number, department, years of service, and previous experience are being read as each record is input.

After reading and processing a record, we immediately check to see if there are any more unprocessed records left in the file. If there are no more records that need processing, we take steps to end the program. Otherwise, for the current record in memory, we check the two fields we're interested

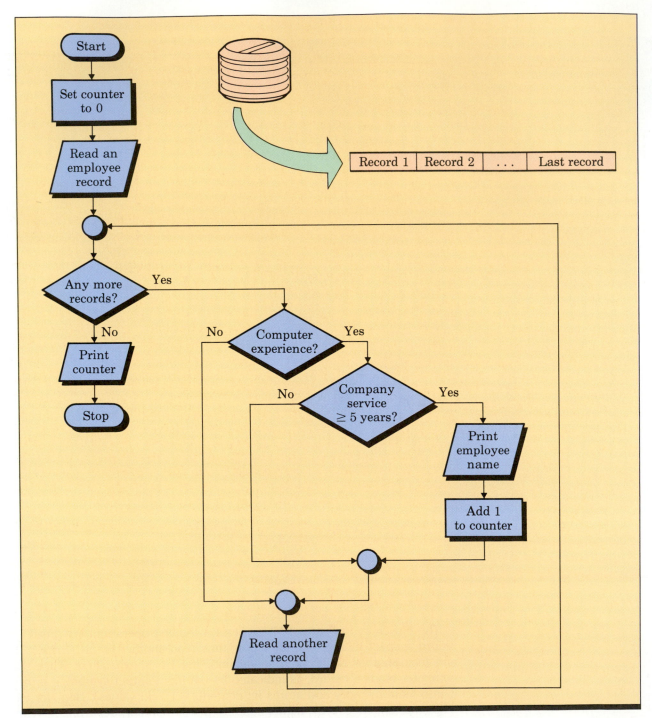

FIGURE 10-3

Scanning an employee file. The situation the flowchart represents is as follows: Print the names of all people in an employee file with computer experience and at least five years of company service. Also, count the number of such people and print out this count.

in—company service and computer experience—to see whether they meet our criteria. Only if an employee has both computer experience and at least five years of service do we print his or her name (shown by the input/output symbol). Otherwise, we bypass the print operation and immediately attempt to read the next record.

The flowchart in Figure 10-3 contains two types of branching mechanisms: a conditional branch and an unconditional branch. A program branches whenever a statement in a block of code is capable of directing the program somewhere other than the next line of code.

In a **conditional branch,** represented by the diamond-shaped decision box, the program proceeds to either of two places depending on the condition encountered in the box. For example, if we have still more records to process when we've reached the "Any more records?" box, we branch to the box indicated by the "Yes" flowline. Otherwise, we branch to the box indicated by the "No" flowline.

In an **unconditional branch,** the program proceeds to a certain step every time it comes to a particular statement. Each time we come to the statement "Read another record" at the bottom of the flowchart, for example, we make an unconditional branch back to the "Any more records?" step.

An important observation regarding the flowchart in Figure 10-3 concerns the totaling of employees who meet the selection criteria. To get this total, we *count* every employee who meets the criteria. To perform operations such as counting, we must define special areas in main memory to hold the values of the totals. We establish a name—"counter" in this example—to represent the memory area that will hold the total. At the beginning of the program, "counter" is set to zero. Whenever we find an employee who meets the selection criteria, we increase the value of "counter" by 1. After we've read the entire employee file, we output the value of "counter" just before the program ends.

With any flowchart, it's good practice to set all counts or sums (often referred to as *accumulators*) to zero at the beginning. Otherwise, when the program is coded and executed, you may get incorrect results. Setting a count or sum to a specific value at the beginning of a program or flowchart is called **initializing.**

Further Uses of Connector-Type Symbols. As we've already seen, we can use the connector symbol to provide a logical point on the flowchart for flowlines to meet. We can also use the connector symbol to prevent clutter in the flowchart or avoid the confusion resulting from the need to cross flowlines. Figure 10-4, a flowchart that computes the amounts earned by employees based on hours worked, illustrates the use of a connector symbol to prevent flowchart clutter.

We would use the **offpage connector symbol** instead of the connector symbol if we needed to continue a flowchart from one page to another. For example, we can draw the offpage connector

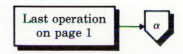

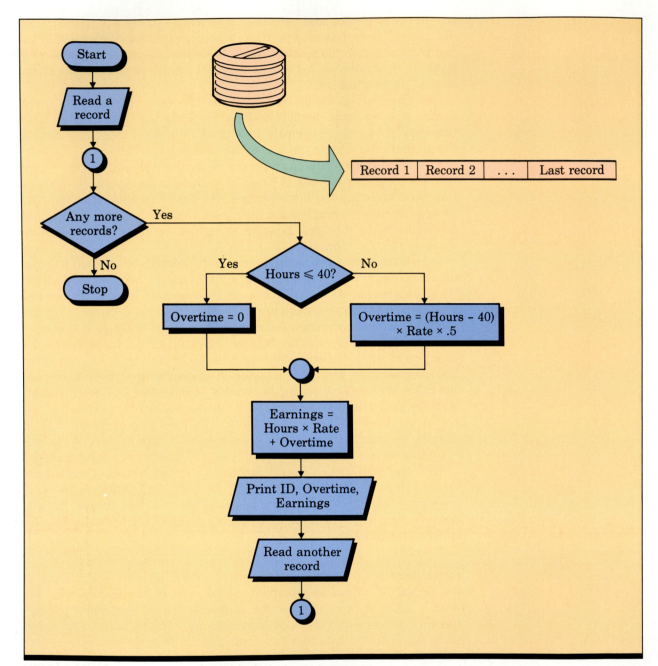

FIGURE 10-4

Computing wages. Each record processed contains an employee's ID number, the applicable hourly pay rate, and the hours worked. The amount earned by each employee is computed as Hourly rate × Hours worked for the first 40 hours worked and 1.5 × Hourly rate × Hours worked for each hour thereafter.

FIGURE 10-5

Flowcharting template. Plastic templates, used to construct various types of flowcharts, are widely available in office supply and college bookstores.

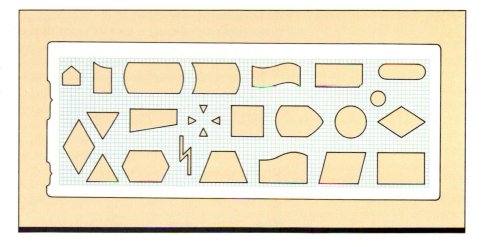

at the bottom of page 1 and, at the start of page 2, resume the flowchart with

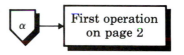

Flowchart symbols often are drawn with the aid of a plastic *flowcharting template,* such as that shown in Figure 10-5. These templates usually are available in office supply and college bookstores.

STRUCTURED PROGRAM DESIGN

Although the flowchart is a powerful tool for designing programs, it isn't always appropriate, nor does it guarantee a good program. As we mentioned in Chapter 9, most programming problems have many solutions, but some solutions are better than others. Even if a program "works" in the sense that it correctly executes the application it was written for, it is of little value if maintenance programmers can't understand and modify it.

Starting in the mid-1960s, a series of studies began to establish a body of practices for good program design. These practices often have been identi- fied with the terms *structured programming* or *structured program design.* Today there is much debate over which specific practices fall under these terms. Depending on whom you talk to, **structured programming** can refer to one or more of a variety of program design practices—using the specific control structures of sequence, selection, and looping; using pseudocode; following top-down design and development; using chief programmer teams for program development; structured walkthroughs; and so forth. Although there is no precise, universally accepted definition of structured programming, most people agree that its main thrust is to

☐ Increase programmer productivity

☐ Enhance program clarity by minimizing complexity

☐ Reduce program testing time

☐ Decrease program maintenance cost

In this section, we discuss two design practices often included under many definitions of structured programming: the use of three basic control structures and top-down design.

The Three Basic Control Structures

Advocates of structured programming have shown that any program can be constructed out of three fundamental **control structures**: sequence, selection, and looping. Figure 10-6 illustrates these structures using flowchart symbols.

A **sequence control structure** is simply a series of procedures that follow one another. A **selection** (or **if-then-else**) **control structure** involves a choice: *If* a certain condition is true, *then* follow one procedure; *else,* if false, follow another. A *loop* is an operation that repeats until a certain condition is met. As Figure 10-6 shows, a **looping** (or **iteration**) **control structure** can take one of two forms: DOWHILE or DOUNTIL.

With **DOWHILE,** a loop is executed as long as a certain condition is true ("do *while* true"). With **DOUNTIL,** a loop continues as long as a certain condition is false ("do *until* true"). You should also note another major difference between these two forms of looping. With DOUNTIL, the loop procedure will always be executed at least once, because the procedure appears before any test is made about whether to exit the loop. With DOWHILE, the procedure may not be executed at all, because the loop-exit test appears before the procedure.

The three basic control structures are the major building blocks for structured program flowcharts and pseudocode, which we discuss later in the chapter.

The Case Structure. By nesting two or more if-then-else's, you can build a fourth structure known as the **case control structure.** For example, in Figure 10-3 the two individual choices "Computer experience?" and "Company service ≥ 5 years?" could be joined into the following case structure:

Case I: No computer experience, company service < 5 years

Case II: No computer experience, company service ≥ 5 years

Case III: Computer experience, company service < 5 years

Case IV: Computer experience, company service ≥ 5 years

Many programming languages have statements that enable programmers to easily code case structures.

FIGURE 10-6
The three fundamental control structures of structured programming. Note that each structure has one entry point and one exit point.

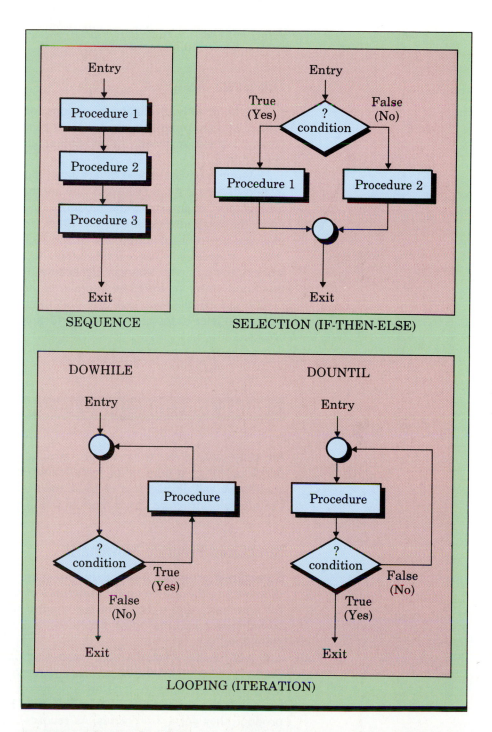

One Entry Point, One Exit Point. An extremely important characteristic of the control structures discussed so far is that each permits only one entry point into and one entry point out of the structure. This property is sometimes called the **one-entry-point/one-exit-point rule.** Observe the marked entry and exit points in Figure 10-6. The one-entry-point/one-exit-point convention encourages a modular programming approach that makes programs more readable and easier to maintain.

Top-Down Design

A long book without chapters, sections, or paragraphs would be hard to read. Likewise, programs are easier to read if they are broken down into clearly labeled segments, or **modules,** each of which performs a well-defined task.

Program modules should be arranged hierarchically, in a top-down fashion, so that their relationships to one another are readily apparent. Such an arrangement is similar to the organization charts many companies use to show the relationships among job titles. **Top-down design** indicates that modules are conceptualized first at the highest levels of the hierarchy and then at progressively lower levels. Lower-level modules should do the actual work in the program, whereas higher-level modules should perform control functions, switching from one lower-level module to another as appropriate.

The use of top-down modular constructions for designing programs is illustrated later in the chapter, in the sections on structure charts and HIPO charts.

TOOLS FOR STRUCTURED PROGRAM DESIGN

An outgrowth of the trend toward structured programming has been the development of a number of tools for structured program design. In this section we will discuss four of these tools—structured program flowcharts, pseudocode, structure charts, and the HIPO method.

Structured Program Flowcharts

Structured program flowcharts are, simply, program flowcharts that are drawn using the three control structures of structured programming. All of the flowcharts shown thus far in the chapter are structured. Figures 10-7 and 10-8 demonstrate what these structures look like when imbedded in a complete flowchart.

Figure 10-7 is a flowchart for computing payments owed to salespeople. Each record contains the name and number of units sold for each salesperson. The salespeople are paid on commission, which is a percentage of the value of sales. In addition, if they sell over 10,000 units of the company's product, they get a $100 bonus. As records are read sequentially, the payment due is computed and the salesperson's name is output with the amount due. The flowchart uses three **control structures**—SEQUENCE, SELECTION, and DOWHILE—as Figure 10-8 shows. Observe again that the flowchart is constructed entirely from fundamental control structures and that each structure has one entry and one exit point.

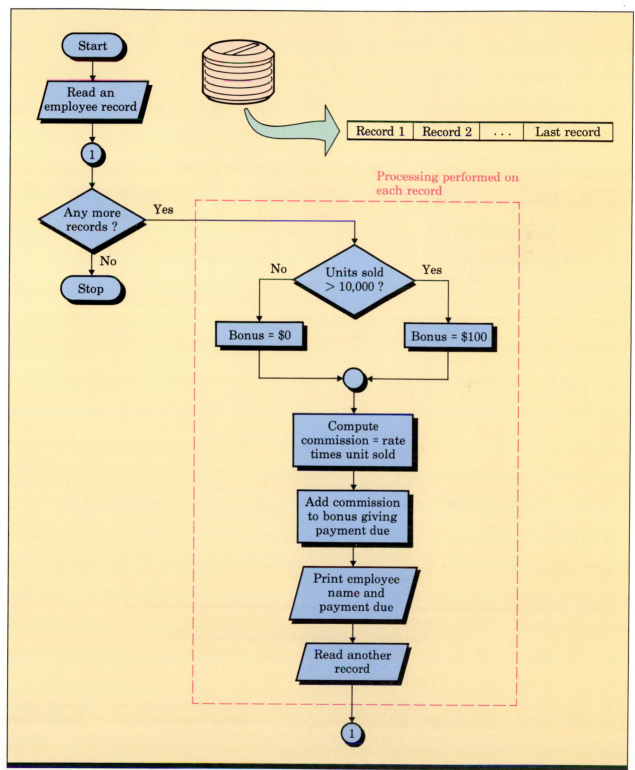

FIGURE 10-7
Computing payments due salespeople.

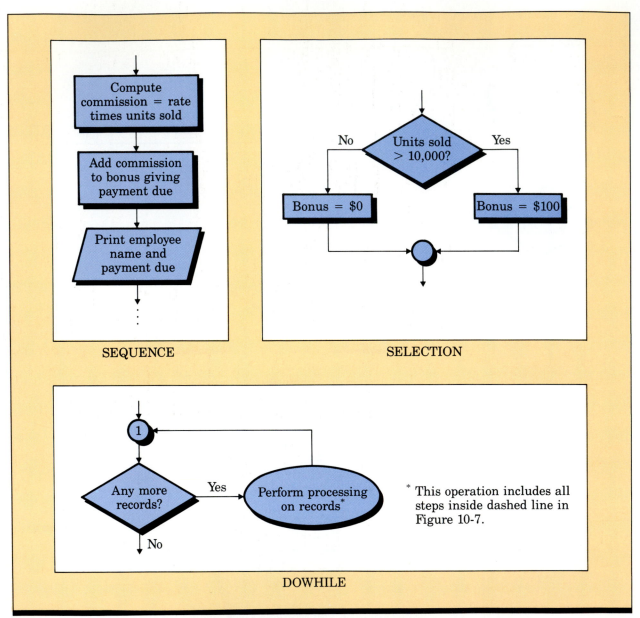

FIGURE 10-8
The three control structures as they are used in Figure 10-7.

Pseudocode

An alternative to the flowchart that has become extremely popular in recent years is **pseudocode.** This structured technique uses Englishlike statements in place of the flowchart's graphic symbols. An example of pseudocode is shown in Figure 10-9.

    Pseudocode looks more like a program than a flowchart. In fact, it's often easier to code a program from pseudocode than from a flowchart, because the former provides a codelike outline of the processing to take place. As a

FIGURE 10-9

Pseudocode for solving the employee file problem of Figure 10-3. The problem requires printing the names of all people in an employee file with computer experience and at least five years of company service. A count of the number of such people is also required as output.

```
Start
Counter = 0
Read a record
DOWHILE there are more records to process
    IF computer experience
            IF company service ≥ 5 years
                    Print employee name
                    Increment counter
            ELSE
                    Next statement
            END IF
    ELSE
            Next statement
    END IF
    Read another record
END DO
Print counter
Stop
```

result, the program designer has more control over the end product—the program itself. Also unlike a flowchart, pseudocode is relatively easy to modify and can be embedded into the program as comments. However, flowcharts, being visual, are sometimes better than pseudocode for designing logically complex problems.

There are no standard rules for writing pseudocode, but Figure 10-10 describes one set of rules that has a wide following. Note that all words relat-

FIGURE 10-10

Some rules for pseudocode. In addition to the rules shown here, governing program control structures, pseudocode often begins with the keyword *Start* and ends with the keyword *Stop*.

Sequence Control Structure

```
            BEGIN processing task
                Processing steps
            END processing task
```

The steps in the sequence structure are normally written in lowercase letters. If the steps make up a well-defined block of code, they should be preceded by the keywords BEGIN and END.

Selection Control Structure

```
            IF condition
                Processing steps
            ELSE
                Processing steps
            END IF
```

The keywords IF, ELSE, and END IF are always capitalized and tiered. The condition and processing steps normally are written in lowercase letters. The processing steps are indented from the keywords in the manner illustrated.

Loop (DOWHILE and DOUNTIL) Control Structures

```
    DOWHILE condition          DOUNTIL condition
        Processing steps            Processing steps
    END DO                     END DO
```

The keywords DOWHILE (or DOUNTIL) and END DO are always capitalized and tiered. The condition and processing steps follow the same lowercase convention and indentation rules as the selection control structure.

FIGURE 10-11

Pseudocode for solving the problem in Figure 10-7. Each employee record contains the name and number of units sold for each salesperson. As records are read sequentially, the payment is computed and the name of the salesperson is output with the amount due.

```
                              Start
                              Read a record
                              DOWHILE there are more records to process
                                IF units sold > 10000
                                       Bonus = 100
                                ELSE
                                       Bonus = 0
                                END IF
                                BEGIN payment computation
                                       Compute commission = rate times units sold
                                       Add commission to bonus giving payment due
                                END payment computation
                                Print employee name and payment due
                                Read another record
                              END DO
                              Stop
```

Loop structure | *Selection structure* | *Sequence structure*

ing to the three control structures of structured programming are capitalized and form a "sandwich" around other processing steps, which are indented. As Figure 10-11 shows, indentation is also used for readability. The keywords *Start* and *Stop* are often respectively used to begin and end pseudocode.

Action Diagrams. Pseudocode is now being widely employed in the creation of **action diagrams,** a tool used to develop applications programs rapidly while online to the CPU. Action diagrams are composed of brackets into which pseudocode statements are written (see Figure 10-12a). These statements are usually created with an *action-diagram editor*. Each control structure used in the diagram—sequence, selection, looping, or case—has its own set of brackets.

FIGURE 10-12

Action diagram elements.

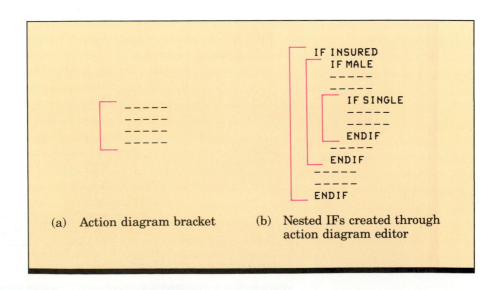

(a)   Action diagram bracket

(b)   Nested IFs created through action diagram editor

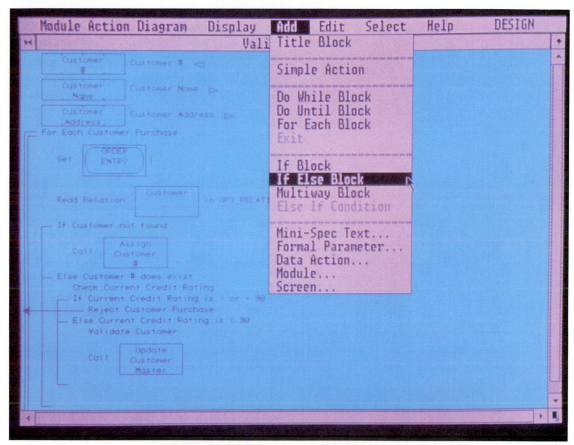

FIGURE 10-13

An action diagram. Action diagrams, which are created and modified with a special editor, are used to design and code pseudocodelike programs that are capable of being executed.

When the programmer signals that a particular control structure is to be used, the editor creates both the appropriate pseudocode keywords and brackets. For instance, as the programmer types in the IF statements in Figure 10-12b, the action-diagram editor adds the ENDIF delimiters and the associated brackets. It may even supply the ELSE clauses. The programmer can move the cursor around to edit the diagram at will, just as if he or she were creating an ordinary program.

As programmers provide various conditions or field names at certain places within the brackets, the action-diagram editor checks to see that the code is both valid and consistent with the existing code for the application. It does the latter by referring to the appropriate entries in the *active data dictionary* that exists for the application. If there is a problem, the editor will issue a warning or error message.

Once an action diagram is completed, it can be automatically translated into executable code with a *code generator.* Figure 10-13 shows an action diagram being created with KnowledgeWare's Information Engineering Workbench (IEW). Action-diagram editors are one of many computer-aided

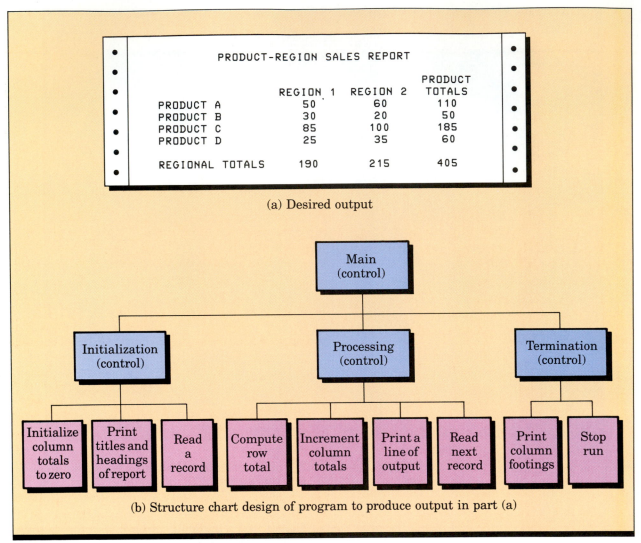

(a) Desired output

(b) Structure chart design of program to produce output in part (a)

FIGURE 10-14
Program output and the structure chart of the associated program.

software engineering (CASE) products that are helping to integrate applications software development functions (see the Tomorrow box).

Structure Charts

Structure charts, unlike flowcharts and pseudocode, depict the overall organization of a program but not the specific processing logic involved in step-by-step execution. They show how the individual segments, or modules, of a program are defined and how they relate to one another. Each module may, of course, consist of one or more fundamental control structures.

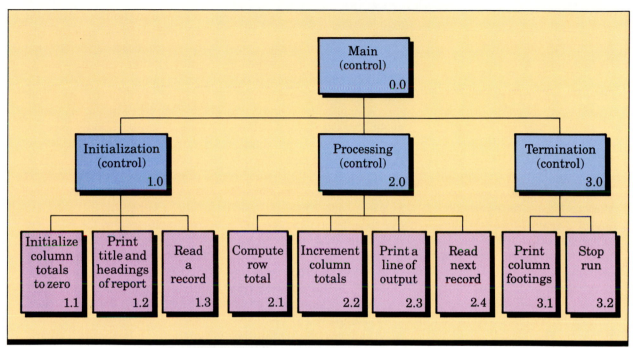

FIGURE 10-15
VTOC for the problem depicted in Figure 10-14.

A typical structure chart looks like a corporate organization chart. It consists of several rows of boxes connected by lines. Each box represents a program *module;* that is, a set of logically related operations or code. The modules in the upper rows serve control functions, directing the program to process modules under them as appropriate. The modules in the lower boxes serve specific processing functions. These modules do all the program "work." The lines connecting the boxes indicate the relationship of higher-level to lower-level modules. Figure 10-14b is a structure chart for a program that produced the sales report in Figure 10-14a.

HIPO Charts

Another useful tool for structured design is the **HIPO (Hierarchy plus Input-Process-Output) chart.** The HIPO method involves the preparation of a set of three different types of diagrams, which vary in the level of detail they address.

The most general of the diagrams is the *Visual Table of Contents (VTOC),* shown in Figure 10-15. The VTOC is identical to a structure chart, except that it contains hierarchically sequenced reference numbers in the lower right-hand corner of each module.

At the second level of detail in the HIPO method are the *overview diagrams,* which show the input, processing, and output involved in each module. Each overview diagram also has a module reference number that corresponds to a module in the VTOC diagram. Figure 10-16 shows overview diagrams for three of the modules in Figure 10-15.

CASE Tools

Automating the Program Development Process

Software development has never been an easy process. In fact, a partner at Arthur Andersen & Co. recently estimated that the average business applications program takes some 32,000 hours from start to finish—an effort worthy of a team of three dozen programmers working for almost three years. And that represents only the programs that get finished. No wonder a lot of managers are looking around for a better way to get programs developed.

In the last dozen or so years, a number of solutions have surfaced. One of the most promising is CASE (computer-aided software engineering) tools. The basic strategy CASE tools use is to automate one or more stages of the program development cycle. While CASE is in its infancy now and has a lot of bugs to be worked out, many people feel that most commercial software will be developed through a CASE-type approach at some not-too-distant future point.

Many of the CASE products now offered in the marketplace are called *software engineering workbenches*. Like a carpenter's workbench, which consists of a number of the tools of the carpentry trade—hammers, saws, chisels, drill bits, and the like—software engineering workbenches contain a number of design, programming, and maintenance tools that get software products developed faster. For instance, such a workbench might consist of an action-diagram editor, a fourth-generation language, a code generator, a feature that facilitates the development of reusable code libraries, an active data dictionary, and tools that help turn unstructured programs into structured ones. The specific tools included in the workbench vary from one vendor to another.

No company has yet developed an everything-but-the-kitchen-sink CASE package—the panacea that will cure every company's applications software development headaches. Consequently, an organization may have to shop around for several CASE products that collectively will meet its needs. This is easier said than done; many CASE tools are incompatible with one another and may not interface well with other proprietary software products the organization is using. Fortunately, CASE vendors realize this and currently are attempting to forge alliances with other vendors to establish standards that will increase CASE applicability.

Furthermore, existing CASE products are on the expensive side—a $10,000 price tag is not unusual. While that might be intimidating to the person signing the check, the unpleasant alternative is paying for more programmer time, waiting additional months for applications software to be completed, and blowing juicy market opportunities.

Currently the most successful product in the CASE marketplace is Index Technology Corporation's Excelerator (see photo), a PC-based workbench product targeted primarily to systems analysis and design and to documentation. Other big players and products in the CASE world are Computer Associates International (CA-Programmer's Workbench), Cortex Corporation (Application Factory), Nastec Corporation (Design Aid), KnowledgeWare (Information Engineering Workbench), and Cadre Technologies Inc. (Teamwork/SA). Recently a number of large firms such as McDonnell Douglas, Arthur Andersen, and Microsoft have joined the roster of CASE vendors, leveraging investments on CASE products they've used in-house by making them available to other firms.

Excelerator. The current market leader.

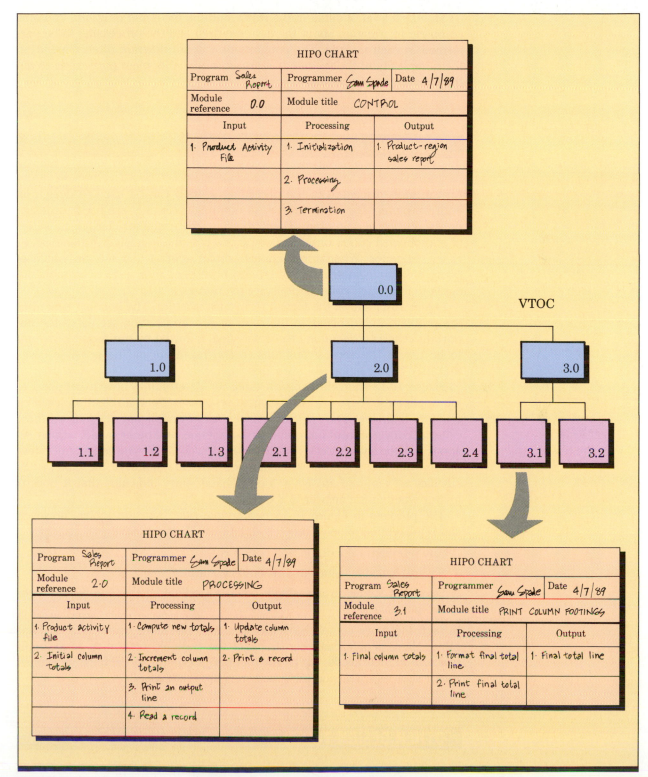

FIGURE 10-16
HIPO overview diagrams for VTOC shown in Figure 10-15.

The third level of detail in the HIPO method, the *detail diagram,* contains complete information about the data required and the processing to be performed in each module. The contents of a detail diagram often depend on the complexity of the module it represents, since its main purpose is to aid the programmer in coding.

DECISION TABLES

All the tools discussed in the preceding section can be used to design an entire program. **Decision tables,** in contrast, generally are used to design only a portion of a program. They are especially useful for clarifying a series of complicated conditions—namely, those you find in nested if-then-else, or case, structures. Whenever a choice among actions depends on which of many possible combinations of criteria have been met, a decision table ensures that no such combinations are overlooked.

Figure 10-17 shows the format for decision tables. The heading describes the problem to be solved. In the rows under the heading are listed the important criteria *(conditions)* to be satisfied, followed by the possible *actions* to be taken. The vertical columns *(rules)* represent all the possible cases that may be encountered in practice.

Figure 10-18 shows a decision table for determining how to respond to job applicants. There are two possible responses: Send a rejection letter or grant an interview. The response chosen for any applicant depends on three criteria: college education, previous experience, and other qualifications. An applicant who satisfies any two of these criteria will be granted an interview; others will get a rejection letter. In each vertical column of the table, a "Y" signifies a "yes" and an "N" a "no." A blank entry indicates that it doesn't matter whether the answer is Y or N.

The problem in Figure 10-18 is a simple one. Decision tables, however, can represent extremely complex situations. They can have

☐ Any number of condition and action rows

☐ Several Y and N values in any single column

☐ Several X values in any single column (indicating that multiple actions are possible)

In fact, the more complicated the situation, the more useful is a decision table. Many people can keep track of the possible outcomes of a simple problem in their heads, but as the number of criteria and actions multiplies, a tool such as a decision table becomes imperative.

OTHER DESIGN TOOLS

The design tools covered in this chapter are only a sampling of those commercial organizations currently use. Other widely used methods include

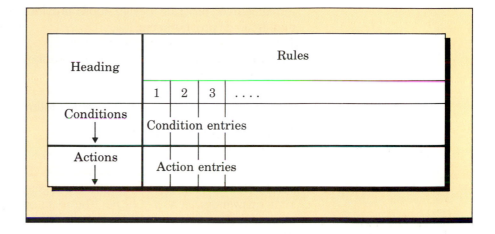

FIGURE 10-17
The format of a decision table.

Warnier-Orr diagrams, Nassi-Schneiderman charts, Meta Stepwise Refinement, Chapin charts, and a number of others. Some organizations have even created their own design tools for specialized problems. Many schools offer advanced computer courses that place these tools in their proper perspectives.

SUMMARY AND KEY TERMS

Program design tools are used for program planning. They consist of various kinds of diagrams, charts, and tables that outline either the organization of a program or the steps it will follow. Once a program is coded and

FIGURE 10-18

A simple decision table. The table specifies the following: If a job applicant does not meet at least two important criteria (conditions), send a rejection letter (the first action); otherwise, grant an interview (the second action).

Hiring Applicants		Rules					
		1	2	3	4	5	6
Conditions	College education?	N	N		Y	Y	
	Experienced?	N		N	Y		Y
	Other qualifications?		N	N		Y	Y
Actions	Rejection letter	X	X	X			
	Interview				X	X	X

implemented, program design tools provide excellent documentation for maintenance programmers.

Program flowcharts use geometric symbols and familiar mathematical symbols to depict graphically the sequence of steps involved in a program. The steps in a flowchart follow one another in the same logical sequence that their corresponding statements will follow in a program.

The lines with arrows that link the symbols in a flowchart are called **flowlines.** They indicate the flow of logic in the flowchart. Every flowchart begins and ends with a **start/stop symbol.** The diamond-shaped **decision symbol** always indicates a question and generally will have only two possible answers, such as *yes* or *no.* The rectangular **processing symbol** contains an action that needs to be taken. The **input/output symbol** indicates a read operation or the printing of a report. The **connector symbol** provides a logical intersection point for several flowlines. The **offpage connector symbol** is used instead of the connector symbol to continue a flowchart from one page to another.

A program *branches* whenever a statement in a block of code is capable of directing the program somewhere besides the next line of code. In a **conditional branch,** represented by the diamond-shaped decision box, the program proceeds to either of two places depending on the condition encountered in the box. In an **unconditional branch,** the program proceeds to a certain step every time it comes to a particular statement.

With any flowchart, it's good practice to set all counts or sums to zero at the beginning. Otherwise, when the program is coded and executed, you may get incorrect results. Setting a count or sum to a specific value at the beginning of a program or flowchart is called **initializing.**

Beginning in the mid-1960s, a series of studies began to establish a body of practices for good program design. These practices often have been identified with the terms *structured programming* or *structured program design.* Today there is much debate over exactly which practices fall under these terms.

Although there is no precise, universally accepted definition of **structured programming,** most people will agree that its main thrust is to increase programmer productivity, enhance program clarity by minimizing complexity, reduce program testing time, and decrease program maintenance cost.

Advocates of structured programming have shown that any program can be constructed out of three fundamental **control structures:** sequence, selection, and looping.

A **sequence control structure** is simply a series of procedures that follow one another. A **selection** (or **if-then-else**) **control structure** involves a choice: *If* a certain condition is true, *then* follow one procedure; *else,* if false, follow another. A **looping** (or **iteration**) **control structure** repeats until a certain condition is met. A loop can take two forms: **DOWHILE** and **DO-UNTIL.** By nesting two or more if-then-else's you can build a fourth control structure, known as a **case control structure.** All of these control structures follow the **one-entry-point/one-exit-point rule**—that is, a structure can have only one way into it and one way out of it.

Programs are easier to read if they are broken down into clearly labeled segments, or **modules,** each of which performs a well-defined task. Program modules should be organized hierarchically, in a top-down fashion, so that their relationships to one another are apparent. **Top-down design** indicates that modules are defined first at the highest levels of the hierarchy and then at progressively lower levels.

An outgrowth of the trend toward structured programming has been the development of a number of tools for structured program design. Four examples of these tools are structured program flowcharts, pseudocode, structure charts, and HIPO charts.

Structured program flowcharts are, simply, program flowcharts that are drawn by using the three control structures of structured programming. **Pseudocode** is a structured technique that uses Englishlike statements in place of the flowchart's graphic symbols. It is commonly employed in the creation of **action diagrams,** tools used to rapidly develop applications programs with an action-diagram editor and an active data dictionary. **Structure charts,** unlike flowcharts and pseudocode, depict the program's overall organization but not the specific processing logic involved in step-by-step execution. **HIPO (Hierarchy plus Input-Process-Output) charts** involve preparing a set of three different types of diagrams, which vary in the level of detail they address.

Decision tables clarify a series of complicated conditional branches. Whenever a choice among actions depends on which of many possible combinations of criteria have been met, a decision table ensures that no such combinations are overlooked.

REVIEW EXERCISES

Fill-in Questions

1. A program _____ uses geometric symbols and familiar mathematical symbols to provide a graphic display of the steps involved in a program.

2. A(n) _____ branch is an instruction used to represent a choice in a processing path.

3. A(n) _____ branch is an instruction that causes the computer to execute a specific statement other than the one that immediately follows in the normal sequence.

4. Setting a count or sum to a specific value at the beginning of a program or flowchart is called _____ .

5. In _____ design, program modules at the highest levels of the hierarchy are defined first, followed by those at progressively lower levels.

6. _____ is a program design tool that uses Englishlike statements.

7. _____ and _____ are program design tools that depict the overall organization of a program rather than the specific processing logic involved in step-by-step execution.

8. _____ are program design tools that use a tabular format and are especially useful for clarifying a series of complicated conditional branches.

Matching Questions

Match each term with the description that best fits.

a. flowlines   d. processing symbol
b. start/stop symbol   e. connector symbol
c. decision symbol   f. input/output symbol

____d____ 1. A rectangular flowcharting symbol used to represent an operation such as a computation.

____f____ 2. The flowcharting symbol used for the READ operation.

____a____ 3. The arrows that link the geometric symbols in a flowchart.

____e____ 4. A flowcharting symbol used to avoid flowchart clutter.

____b____ 5. A flowcharting symbol that begins and ends a flowchart.

____c____ 6. A diamond-shaped flowcharting symbol.

Discussion Questions

1. What is the purpose of each of the flowcharting symbols depicted in Figure 10-1?

2. Provide a flowchart that reads a list of positive values and outputs the number of those values that are greater than 25.

3. What are the objectives of structured programming?

4. Name the three fundamental control structures of structured programming, and provide an example of each.

5. What is the difference between the DOWHILE and DOUNTIL control structures?

6. Provide an example showing the similarity between the case structure and the if-then-else structure.

7. What does the one-entry-point/one-exit-point rule stipulate?

8. What is the difference between a flowchart and a structure chart?

9. Provide a pseudocode solution to the flowchart in Figure 10-4.

10. What is the purpose of a decision table?

Critical Thinking Questions

1. Computer programs have been created that distinguish people who are good credit risks from those who are not. How, would you guess, do computer programs make this distinction?

2. Feature 10A covers a number of important software design features related to the user interface. For a word processing, spreadsheet, and/or database package with which you are familiar, what do you feel are the good and bad design features as concerns the user interface?

3. The Tomorrow box discusses the use of CASE tools in software development. If you had to justify the purchase of a $10,000 CASE package to your busy boss—who, say, doesn't have even the vaguest notion of what CASE is—what would you say in that all-important first 60 seconds of your pitch?

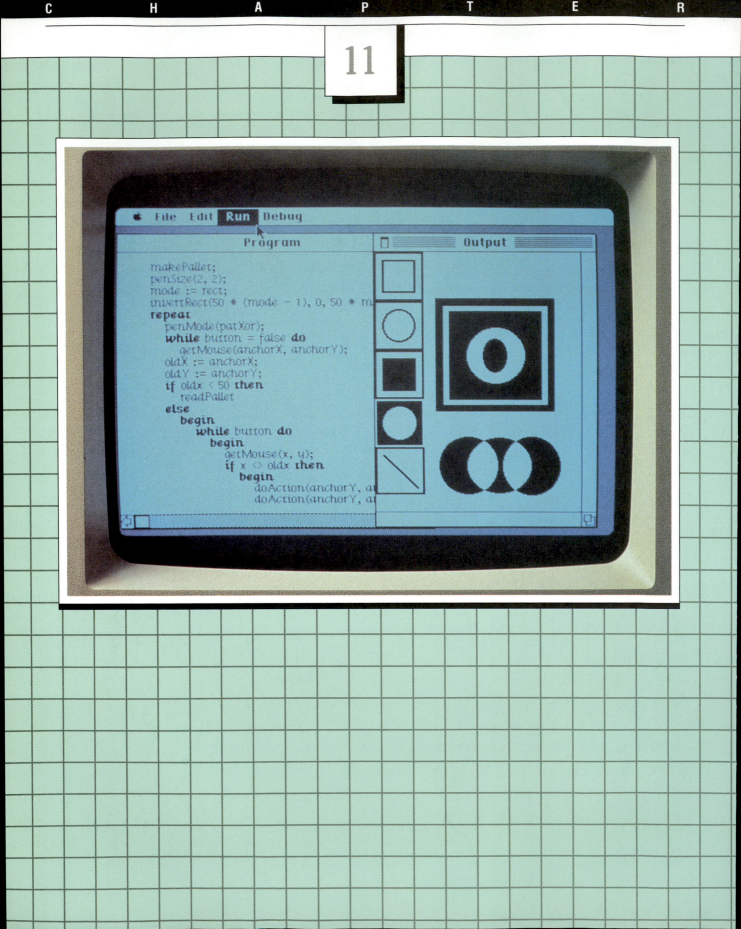

Programming Languages

Objectives

After completing this chapter, you will be able to:

1. Distinguish among low-level, high-level, and very-high-level languages.

2. Identify the uses, key features, and limitations of a number of widely used programming languages.

3. Recognize when one language is more suitable than another for a particular application.

4. Describe the role of fourth-generation languages (4GLs) and name several types of 4GLs.

OVERVIEW

Programming languages were developed so that people could get computers to do useful things. Because people vary in their ability to deal with computers and computers can do an astounding variety of complicated tasks, a large number of programming languages have come to the fore. As you will learn in this chapter, each language has been created to meet specific needs. There are languages for children and rank beginners, languages for scientists, languages to facilitate typing, languages for ongoing business applications that require regular maintenance, languages that take maximum advantage of the computer's speed, languages designed to work on extremely small computers, languages that work best on large computers, and so forth.

A **programming language** can be broadly defined as a set of rules that enable the writing of instructions for a computer. The so-called *third-generation languages*—high-level languages such as BASIC, Pascal, COBOL, and FORTRAN—account for the bulk of this chapter. These are the languages most people think of when they hear the term "programming language." Many of these languages are among the everyday tools of the professional programmer. Later in the chapter, and also in Chapters 12, 13, and 14, we'll look at several special-purpose language products that have recently evolved to make both computer and noncomputer professionals more productive. These languages have come to be known as *fourth-generation languages (4GLs)*.

A BRIEF HISTORY OF PROGRAMMING LANGUAGES

The earliest programming languages—machine and assembly languages—are called **low-level languages,** because programmers who use them must write instructions at the finest level of detail. This level is closest to that of the computer itself, namely the "base level." Each line of code corresponds to a single action of the computer system.

Machine language, which consists of strings of 0 and 1 bits, is the computer's "native tongue." Every computer has its own native machine language. Few people actually write programs in machine language anymore, but all programs written in higher-level languages eventually must be translated into machine language to be executed. We discussed the software that does the translating—assemblers, compilers, and interpreters—in Chapter 8. *Assembly languages,* which represent these detailed machine instructions in a code that is easier to understand than strings of 0s and 1s, are still frequently used by some programmers, but they are beyond the grasp of most end users. Machine language flourished during the first generation (1951–1958) and assembly languages during the second generation (1959–1964) of modern computing history.

The next languages to appear, which generally characterized the third generation of modern computing history (1965–1970) and are still very widely used today, were **high-level languages.** Included in this category are what have come to be known as the "traditional" types of programming languages, for example, BASIC, COBOL, FORTRAN, Pascal, PL/1, and APL. Well over 100 such languages are currently in use, and many of them are available in several versions. High-level languages differ from their low-level predecessors in that they require less coding detail. For example, low-level languages require programmers to assign values to specific storage locations and registers in the CPU. High-level languages, however, don't burden programmers with these tasks; the translators that convert high-level languages to machine language supply the detail. As a result, programs created in high-level languages are shorter and easier to write than those written in their low-level counterparts.

Some high-level languages, such as BASIC, are relatively easy for even users to learn. However, many users dislike programming in any high-level language whatsoever. Some feel there are too many rules to remember and the step-by-step logic involved is too complex. Others simply are too busy to do the volume of programming these languages require. Yet many of these users could benefit by writing their own programs if this task were somehow made easier. **Very-high-level languages**—many of which became widely used during the fourth generation of modern computing history (starting about 1971)—have been developed to meet this need.

We can compare a very-high-level language to a knowledgeable chauffeur. To get where we want to go, we need only give the chauffeur very general instructions, such as "Take me to City Hall," instead of detailed ones, like "From here you make a right; then three blocks later make a left. . . ." Similarly, with very-high-level languages we need only prescribe *what* the computer is to do rather than *how* it is to do it. For example, we might sum numbers with a very-high-level language by pointing on the screen to the instruction "SUM" and then pointing to the numbers to be summed. This is much easier to do than creating a mathematical looping procedure to "teach" the computer system how to sum numbers and then typing in and debugging that procedure, as would be required with a low-level or high-level language. Thus, low- and high-level languages are sometimes called **procedural languages,** because they require people to define detailed statements that represent sequential steps, or procedures, to be performed during program execution. Very-high-level languages, in contrast, are called **nonprocedural languages.**

Very-high-level languages, along with advances in interactive display technology, are bringing more people into contact with computers than ever before. These languages have some serious disadvantages, however. First, they lack flexibility; generally each is designed to do one specific kind of task. You can't, for example, process a payroll with a word processing language. Second, these languages do not adequately support many important applications. Nonetheless, for the areas in which they are available and suitable, these languages offer obvious advantages for both programmers and users. Most of the productivity software packages covered in Chapters 12 through 14 use very-high-level languages in some way.

ASSEMBLY LANGUAGES

Assembly languages are like machine languages in that each line of code corresponds to a single action of the computer system. But assembly languages replace the 0s and 1s of machine language with symbols (called *mnemonics*) that are easier to understand and remember, such as *A* for "Add" and *L* for "Load." Because they are closely related to machine languages, which take particular advantage of the structures of the computers they run on, assembly-language programs often consume less storage and run much faster than their easier-to-use high-level-language counterparts. This executional efficiency constitutes their primary advantage. Many of the word processing and spreadsheet packages available at your local computer store, for example, are written largely in assembly language rather than, say, in BASIC or Pascal.

Unfortunately, assembly-language programs take longer to write and are more difficult to maintain than programs coded in higher-level languages. Also, like programs written in machine language, they are machine dependent. An assembly-language program that works on an IBM PS/2 computer, for example, would need substantial modification to run on an Apple Macintosh IIX, which is built around a different microprocessor chip than that used by the IBM. With hardware costs decreasing and software development costs on the rise, assembly languages are gradually losing their competitive edge to higher-level languages for many applications. Nonetheless, they are still used because of their speed, efficiency, and ability to meet special-purpose needs.

Figure 11-1 shows some assembly-language commands.

FIGURE 11-1

Some examples of assembly-language commands. Note that, as opposed to most high-level languages, there are several commands for each "type" of operation. For example, L, LR, and ST are all "move" operations. The appropriate operation to use depends on whether you want to move values from one register to another, from main memory to a register, or from a register to main memory. It is not unusual for an assembly language to have *two dozen or more* different commands just to move data.

Command	Example	Description
LR	LR 7,4	Load the contents of register 4 into register 7.
L	L 8,X	Load the contents of the main-memory location defined by the variable X into register 8.
ST	ST 5,X	Store the contents of register 5 in the main-memory location defined by the variable X.
AR	AR 5,2	Add the contents of register 2 to the contents of register 5, storing the result in register 5.
A	A 5,X	Add the contents of the main-memory location defined by the variable X to the contents of register 5, storing the result in register 5.
SR	SR 5,2	Subtract the contents of register 2 from the contents of register 5, placing the result in register 5.
S	S 5,X	Subtract the contents of the main-memory location defined by the variable X from the contents of register 5, placing the result in register 5.
B	B LOOP	Branch to the statement labeled LOOP.

BASIC

In the early days of computing—before microcomputers, display devices, and sophisticated communications systems—writing and debugging programs were painfully slow processes. Users and programmers submitted their punched-card programs to the computer system operator and then waited as much as several hours or a day or two for the results. Often the program didn't work, and the user or programmer received a list of cryptic error messages. These had to be properly diagnosed, the bugs corrected, and the program resubmitted. Getting even a modest program written and debugged could take several days or weeks. Thus, it took a great deal of persistence to be successful at programming, and many people just weren't interested.

Nonetheless, computer scholars realized that the computer was potentially a tool that would benefit noncomputer professionals in many ways if only they could be encouraged to learn programming. Clearly there was a need for an easy-to-learn beginner's language that would work in a "friendly," nonfrustrating programming environment.

BASIC (Beginner's All-purpose Symbolic Instruction Code) was designed to meet this need. It was developed at Dartmouth College in conjunction with the world's first time-sharing system. With BASIC, students communicated with the computer through their own terminals, and turnaround time usually was a matter of seconds. A modest program could easily be conceived, coded, and debugged in a few hours. BASIC also proved to be extremely easy to learn, and many students found it possible to write programs after only a few hours of training.

Over the years, BASIC has evolved into one of the most popular and widely available programming languages. Because it is easy to use and the storage requirements for its language translator are small, it works well on almost all general-purpose microcomputers. The many versions of BASIC available range from "stripped-down" ones suitable for pocket computers to powerful mainframe versions that rival the processing power of COBOL.

Figure 11-2 shows a sample BASIC program.

Key Features

Almost every key feature of BASIC is related to its ease of use for beginners. Among such features are simplified naming of variables, optional formatting, conversational programming mode, and simple diagnostics.

Simplified Naming of Variables. The rules for classifying and naming variables in BASIC generally are simple. Variables are classified as either numeric (for example, UNITS = 6) or alphanumeric (for instance, GREETING\$ = "HELLO"). Variable names can begin with any letter of the alphabet. This straightforward naming convention permits beginners to move on quickly to other features of the language.

```
 10      REM PROGRAM TO COMPUTE SALES
 20      REM AUTHOR - C.S. PARKER
 30      PRINT "    DESCRIPTION          PRICE        UNITS       TOTAL VALUE"
 40      A$="\                   \     $###.##      #,###       $###,###"
 50      READ N$,P,U
 60      WHILE N$ < > "LAST RECORD"
 70        S=P*U
 80        PRINT USING A$;N$,P,U,S
 90        READ N$,P,U
100      WEND
110      DATA "SMALL WIDGETS",150,100
120      DATA "LARGE SKY HOOKS",200,50
130      DATA "BLIVETS",100,3000
140      DATA "LAST RECORD",0,0
150      END
```

(a) A BASIC program.

```
       DESCRIPTION          PRICE        UNITS       TOTAL VALUE
     SMALL WIDGETS         $150.00         100        $ 15,000
     LARGE SKY HOOKS       $200.00          50        $ 10,000
     BLIVETS               $100.00       3,000        $300,000
```

(b) Output from the program.

FIGURE 11-2

A sample BASIC program and its output. This program is designed to accept as input the name of a product, its unit selling price, and the number of units sold, and to output this information along with the total dollar value of sales.

Optional Formatting. Languages such as COBOL have a detailed set of rules for specifying the format of inputs and outputs. Although such "data declaration" rules are useful for complex programs, they are often a distraction for the beginner. The need to master them can interfere with learning how computers solve problems. With most versions of BASIC, however, one can almost completely ignore formatting data at the outset and address such advanced techniques later.

Conversational Programming Mode. Because BASIC was specifically designed to work on terminals, almost all versions readily enable users and programmers to "converse" interactively with the computer. This characteristic allows beginners to use BASIC to write programs that accept input as they are running.

Simple Diagnostics. The quality of the error messages a language generates is extremely important for a beginner. Error messages are supposed to indicate why a program has failed to work. But if a 200-line program doesn't work and the error messages are confusing or too technical, the result is often frustration. BASIC's error messages are easier to understand than those of most other languages. Also, many versions of BASIC come with an online syntax checker that identifies certain kinds of errors in each line of code as it is keyed into the computer system.

Limitations

Some experts feel that BASIC's chief strength—ease of learning and use—is also its major drawback. Because beginners can get started quickly, they sometimes start off on the wrong foot by sacrificing good programming habits for quick results. Many versions of BASIC support unstructured, trial-and-error coding, so it's easy to write confusing, poorly organized programs. Also, since so many versions of BASIC are available, a program developed on one computer may need substantial modifications to run on another. Finally, because most versions of BASIC use interpreters rather than compilers, BASIC programs often run slowly compared with programs in other languages.

PASCAL

Pascal, named after the mathematician Blaise Pascal, is a relatively new programming language. It was developed about 1970 by Professor Niklaus Wirth of Zurich, Switzerland. Figure 11-3 shows a sample Pascal program.

Key Features

Pascal was originally created to fill the need for a teaching vehicle that would encourage structured programming. Its key features are a structured orientation and memory efficiency.

Structured Orientation. Although BASIC remains a strong favorite among beginners, Pascal is far superior to most versions of BASIC (and even COBOL) in its structured programming capability. To say that Pascal is a structured language means that, generally speaking, Pascal programs are made up of smaller subprograms, each of which is itself a structured program. This modular "building-block" approach makes it easier to develop large programs. In addition, most versions of Pascal contain a rich variety of control structures with which to manipulate program modules in a systematic fashion.

Pascal also has an explicit data declaration facility to aid in program development. Because every Pascal variable must be declared at the beginning of each program or subprogram with respect to the data type it supports, many errors can be detected before a program reaches the testing stage.

Finally, Pascal supports an abundance of data types and even lets you create new ones. For example, you can declare a data type called FRIENDS, with values of ERNIE, SARAH, and MIGUEL, and another type called ENEMIES, with values DARTH, BARTH, and GARTH. Later you can manipulate these sets of names in your program by referencing the corresponding data type. If you want to, you can even create a third data type, called ACQUAINTANCES, that consists of all names declared under both FRIENDS and

```
PROGRAM SALES (INPUT, OUTPUT);
(* PROGRAM TO COMPUTE SALES *)
(* AUTHOR -- C. S. PARKER *)

VAR  UNITS, INDEX        :INTEGER;
     PRICE, TOTAL        :REAL;
     PART                :ARRAY [1..20] OF CHAR;


BEGIN
WRITELIN ('    DESCRIPTION           PRICE        UNITS       TOTAL VALUE ');
FOR INDEX :=. 1 TO 20 DO
  READ (PART[INDEX]);
  READLN (PRICE, UNITS);
WHILE NOT EOF DO
    BEGIN
    TOTAL := PRICE * UNITS;
    FOR INDEX := 1 TO 20 DO
      WRITE (PART[INDEX]);
      WRITELIN ('      $', PRICE:6:2, UNITS:11,'     $', TOTAL:9:2);
    FOR INDEX := 1 TO 20 DO
      READ (PART [INDEX]);
      READLN (PRICE, UNITS);
    END;
END.
```

(a) A Pascal program.

```
     DESCRIPTION             PRICE          UNITS        TOTAL VALUE
   SMALL WIDGETS            $150.00          100         $ 15,000
   LARGE SKY HOOKS          $200.00           50         $ 10,000
   BLIVETS                  $100.00        3,000         $300,000
```

(b) Output from the program.

FIGURE 11-3

A sample Pascal program and its output. This program solves the same sales problem as does the BASIC program in Figure 11-2.

ENEMIES. This is yet another example of Pascal's structured, building-block orientation.

Because its structured emphasis leads to good programming practices, Pascal has been enthusiastically received. Experts generally consider it an important language for anyone studying computer science or learning programming. Moreover, the College Entrance Examination Board has chosen Pascal as the required language for advanced-placement courses in computer science for high schools.

Memory Efficiency. Pascal compilers are extremely small given the language's processing power. Thus, Pascal can be easily implemented on most microcomputers. This feature also makes the language ideal for educational environments.

Limitations

Pascal's major weakness is that it has marginal input/output capabilities. Thus, it is less suitable than COBOL for business transaction processing applications. As a problem-solving language, however, Pascal can give both FORTRAN and BASIC a run for their money.

COBOL

COBOL (COmmon Business-Oriented Language), first introduced in the early 1960s, is the primary business transaction processing language in use today. Until it appeared, there was no language particularly suited to applications such as payroll, billing, payables, receivables, and general ledger— all of which typify business transaction processing. After all, the early language pioneers were engineers and mathematicians, not accountants. As more and more businesses purchased computer systems, however, the need for a transaction-processing-oriented language became apparent. Representatives from the major computer manufacturers met in Washington with users from industry and government to discuss such a product. Subsequently they formed a committee to draft a language, and the result was COBOL.

Figure 11-4 illustrates a sample COBOL program.

Key Features

Many features differentiate COBOL from other languages. Almost all of them—including machine independence, self-documentation, and input/output orientation—relate to COBOL's business transaction processing focus.

Machine Independence. Business transaction processing programs generally have to last a long time. For example, a company may expect to use many of its payroll or accounts receivable programs for 10 or even 20 years. During this time span, the organization may buy new hardware or change completely from one computer system to another. Thus, programs written for one system should be able to run on another with little modification. In other words, the language in which the programs are written should be relatively machine independent. COBOL was specifically developed to meet this important requirement.

In 1968, the American National Standards Institute (ANSI) first established a successful COBOL standard. This was revised in 1974, and again in 1985. The latter standards have been created so that, generally speaking, programs developed under earlier standards will work on them. Over the years,

```
IDENTIFICATION DIVISION.
  PROGRAM-ID. SALES.
  AUTHOR. PARKER.

ENVIRONMENT DIVISION.
CONFIGURATION SECTION.
  SOURCE-COMPUTER. VS9.
  OBJECT-COMPUTER. VS9.
INPUT-OUTPUT SECTION.
  FILE-CONTROL.
    SELECT DISKFILE ASSIGN TO DISK-A1F2-V.
    SELECT PRINTFILE ASSIGN TO SYSLST.


DATA DIVISION.
FILE SECTION.
FD  DISKFILE
    LABEL RECORDS ARE STANDARD.
01  DISKREC.
    05 PART-DESCRIPTION-IN    PIC X(20).
    05 PRICE-IN               PIC 999.
    05 UNITS-SOLD-IN          PIC 9(5).
FD  PRINTFILE
    LABEL RECORDS ARE OMITTED.
01  PRINTLINE                 PIC X(120).
WORKING-STORAGE SECTION.
01  FLAGS.
    05 WS-END-OF-FILE.        PIC X(3) VALUE 'NO'.
01  HEADING-LINE.
    05 FILLER                 PIC X(9)  VALUE SPACES.
    05 FILLER                 PIC X(11) VALUE 'DESCRIPTION'.
    05 FILLER                 PIC X(10) VALUE SPACES.
    05 FILLER                 PIC X(5)  VALUE 'PRICE'.
    05 FILLER                 PIC X(7)  VALUE SPACES.
    05 FILLER                 PIC X(5)  VALUE 'UNITS'.
    05 FILLER                 PIC X(4)  VALUE SPACES.
    05 FILLER                 PIC X(11) VALUE 'TOTAL VALUE'.
01  DETAIL-LINE.
    05 FILLER                 PIC X(5)  VALUE SPACES.
    05 PART-DESCRIPTION-OUT   PIC X(20).
    05 FILLER                 PIC X(4)  VALUE SPACES.
    05 PRICE-OUT              PIC $ZZ9.99.
    05 FILLER                 PIC X(5)  VALUE SPACES.
    05 UNITS-SOLD-OUT         PIC ZZ,ZZ9.
    05 FILLER                 PIC X(5)  VALUE SPACES.
    05 SALES-VALUE            PIC $ZZZ,ZZ9.
```

FIGURE 11-4

A sample COBOL program and its output. This program solves the same sales problem as does the BASIC program in Figure 11-2.

vendors have supplied language translators that meet these standards. Consequently, within the limits described, COBOL programs written to standard generally will work on any type of computer system with little modification.

Self-Documentation. Because business transaction processing programs must last a long time, they need ongoing maintenance. As business conditions change, the programs often must be modified. For example, a change in tax policy could require several modifications in a payroll program. Since

```
PROCEDURE DIVISION.
010-HOUSEKEEPING.
    OPEN INPUT DISKFILE
         OUTPUT PRINTFILE.
    READ DISKFILE
         AT END MOVE 'YES' TO WS-END-OF-FILE.
    PERFORM 020-HEADINGS.
    PERFORM 030-PROCESSIT
         UNTIL WS-END-OF-FILE = 'YES'.
    CLOSE DISKFILE
          PRINTFILE.
    STOP RUN.
020-HEADINGS.
    WRITE PRINTLINE FROM HEADING-LINE
         AFTER ADVANCING 1 LINE.
030-PROCESSIT.
    MULTIPLY    UNITS-SOLD-IN
         BY      PRICE-IN
         GIVING SALES-VALUE.
    MOVE PART-DESCRIPTION-IN TO PART-DESCRIPTION-OUT.
    MOVE PRICE-IN            TO PRICE-OUT.
    MOVE UNITS-SOLD-IN       TO UNITS-SOLD-OUT.
    WRITE PRINTLINE FROM DETAIL-LINE
         AFTER ADVANCING 1 LINE.
    READ DISKFILE
         AT END MOVE 'YES' TO WS-END-OF-FILE.
```

(a) A COBOL program.

```
    DESCRIPTION              PRICE           UNITS           TOTAL VALUE
  SMALL WIDGETS           $150.00            100            $ 15,000
  LARGE SKY HOOKS         $200.00             50            $ 10,000
  BLIVETS                 $100.00          3,000            $300,000
```

(b) Output from the program.

FIGURE 11-4 *continued*

programmers tend to switch jobs often, the person doing the maintenance is unlikely to be the program's original author. Thus, it's extremely important that program logic be easy for others to follow. As we saw in Chapters 9 and 10, good design techniques promote logical, easily maintainable programs. As the program in Figure 11-4 suggests, COBOL lends itself to good program design through easy-to-read program statements, an outline-style aggregation of statements into logically related blocks (such as paragraphs and divisions), and adherence to standard program control structures.

Input/Output Orientation. Business transaction processing, in contrast to scientific and engineering applications, involves manipulation of large files with many records. Thus, much of the work in business transaction processing applications relates to reading and writing records, an area in which COBOL is designed to be particularly effective. COBOL contains provisions for defining the format of input and output records explicitly and easily. For example, it is a very straightforward process to edit dollar amounts on output with dollar signs, decimal points, and commas, and also to round off these amounts.

Limitations

Because COBOL programs use long, Englishlike names and specify formats in fine detail, they tend to be lengthy. Since lengthy programs take time to develop and maintain, COBOL is partly responsible for applications backlogs in many companies. In such firms, it often takes two to four years from the time an application is first approved until it is coded. (This has led some companies to adopt easier-to-code fourth-generation languages, which we'll discuss in the last section of the chapter.) Also, COBOL's business transaction processing orientation often makes the language unsuitable for scientific or engineering applications, which are characterized by complicated formulas.

Despite its limitations, however, COBOL is very good at what it does—business transaction processing. Currently some 70 to 80 percent of transaction processing applications in large firms are coded in COBOL. With millions of dollars invested in COBOL programs and thousands of programmers versed in COBOL use, the language will likely endure for many more years (see Feature 11A). Despite the many complaints that COBOL is old-fashioned, cumbersome, and inelegant, if you're interested in making money as an applications programmer, COBOL is still clearly your best bet.

FORTRAN

FORTRAN (FORmula TRANslator), which dates back to 1954, has the distinction of being the first high-level programming language to enjoy wide use. It has shown remarkable "staying power" and today is the oldest surviving commercial high-level language. In a world where everything seems to be changing rapidly, FORTRAN has been altered remarkably little in 30 years. FORTRAN was designed by scientists and is oriented toward scientific and engineering problem solving. Figure 11-5 illustrates a sample FORTRAN program.

Business transaction processing applications involve sophisticated input/output operations and relatively simple computations. Scientific and engineering applications, in contrast, require complex computations and relatively simple input/output operations. Determining the trajectory of a rocket, for example—a classic engineering application—requires intricate, precise computations. Preparing a payroll, on the other hand—a typical business transaction processing application—involves reading numerous employee records and writing many checks and reports, but the computations performed on each record are relatively simple.

Because of its ability to perform sophisticated computations, however, FORTRAN has proven useful for certain kinds of business applications.

COBOL, Circa 1990

A Closer Look at the Top Transaction Processing Language

COBOL, developed in the 1960s, has unwittingly become the Rodney Dangerfield of programming languages: Among many computer professionals, it gets no respect. Indeed there are numerous clumsy aspects of COBOL that, because they were created years ago and are very ingrained into the language, will probably remain targets of criticism. But one can't ignore the fact that about 75 percent of mainframe transaction processing applications are still coded in COBOL. Like the air we breathe, COBOL will be around for awhile.

Perhaps, to the surprise of many, COBOL is getting more competitive as an applications development alternative. While some might point to this as a COBOL renaissance, others are quick to point out that COBOL, with its long-standing dominance in transaction processing applications, never died.

Today a great part of the effort to streamline COBOL is expended along two major fronts: making maintenance easier and creating the conversions necessary for operating COBOL effectively in microcomputing environments.

Maintenance Ease. Because there are so many COBOL applications currently "out there," a great deal of effort traditionally has been devoted to facilitating maintenance of the current stock of programs. Some estimates hold that maintaining old COBOL programs consumes up to 80 percent of the software dollar in DP shops.

> About 75 percent of mainframe applications are still coded in COBOL.

Major attempts aimed at making maintenance less painful have been the ANSI COBOL 85 standard (which makes new COBOL programs more maintainable than those written under earlier standards), structured *retrofit software* (which converts unstructured COBOL programs written under earlier standards into structured COBOL programs that meet current standards), *reusable code* libraries (which enable old COBOL code to be "cut and pasted" into new applications programs), and fourth-generation-language enhancements (such as *code generators,* which enable programmers to rapidly write programs in a streamlined code that is later translated into bug-free COBOL).

Microcomputing. With microcomputers assuming increasing importance, it stands to reason that somehow COBOL will have to come to grips with them. This translates into enabling users to develop COBOL programs at microcomputer workstations, running complete COBOL applications on microcomputers, and dealing with the distributed processing environments that are likely for the future.

The latest crop of business-oriented microcomputers is equipped with faster processing speeds, greater memory capacities, windowing environments, and hard-disk capabilities. Not only have all of these developments made full-fledged COBOL on microcomputers a reality, but programmers are actually beginning to favor COBOL microcomputing environments. At New York's Chase Manhattan Bank, microcomputer-based COBOL already is being used to create programs that track credit authorization for commercial clients—and much more cost effectively than was possible with mainframes.

The future of COBOL will lie in its ability to be integrated effectively with new technologies. If COBOL "misses the boat" in this respect, it is almost certain that another language will fill the void and take the lead.

```
C THIS PROGRAM COMPUTES SALES
C AUTHOR - C.S. PARKER

        CHARACTER PART*20
        INTEGER COUNT, RECORDS, UNITS

        READ (5, 100) RECORDS
        WRITE (6, 200)

        DO 999 COUNT = 1, RECORDS
        READ (5, 110) PART, PRICE, UNITS
        TOTAL = PRICE * UNITS
        WRITE (6, 210) PART, PRICE, UNITS, TOTAL
999     CONTINUE

100     FORMAT (I4)
110     FORMAT (A20,F6.2,I4)
200     FORMAT (5X,'DESCRIPTION',12X,'PRICE',7X,'UNITS',5X,'TOTAL VALUE')
210     FORMAT (1X, A,'        $',F6.2,I11,'        $',F9.2)

        STOP
        END
```

(a) A FORTRAN program.

```
    DESCRIPTION          PRICE          UNITS       TOTAL VALUE
SMALL WIDGETS          $150.00            100       $ 15000.00
LARGE SKY HOOKS        $200.00             50       $ 10000.00
BLIVETS                $100.00          3,000       $300000.00
```

(b) Output from the program.

FIGURE 11-5

A sample FORTRAN program and its output. This program solves the same sales problem as does the BASIC program in Figure 11-2.

These applications entail problem-solving activities rather than routine processing of business records. Some examples are sales and econometric forecasting, determining the least expensive way to manufacture a product (linear programming), and simulating complex production processes.

Key Features

A key feature of FORTRAN is its ability to express sophisticated formulas easily. Complicated algebraic expressions are written in FORTRAN in nearly the same way as they are in conventional mathematical notation. Although BASIC, which was created as a simplified version of FORTRAN, is competitive in this area, many people consider FORTRAN superior for two reasons: faster program execution and a large bank of preprogrammed routines.

Fast Program Execution. Since scientific and engineering programs are characterized by numerous computations and frequent looping, execution speed is a primary concern. FORTRAN generally uses a compiler as its language translator. Most FORTRAN compilers are so effective at "number crunching" that they are even superior in this respect to the compilers of most modern languages. The reasons for this date back to the 1950s. When FORTRAN was first developed, it had to compete with assembly languages for execution efficiency, and this quality has remained an important factor in its design ever since.

Preprogrammed Routines. Programmers who work on scientific, engineering, and mathematical applications often find that huge portions of their programs involve solving problems that others have tackled before. For example, an econometric forecast may entail computing the determinant or inverse of a matrix. Likewise, a statistical test may involve fitting a curve to a set of field observations. Fortunately, several libraries of precoded FORTRAN routines (called *subroutines*) are available for doing just these sorts of things. All the programmer needs to do is find the subroutine in one of the libraries available and incorporate it into his or her program. This can save weeks or even months of painstaking coding and testing.

Limitations

FORTRAN was developed well before structured programming began to be emphasized, so it is somewhat weak in this area compared with many of the newer languages. However, the latest ANSI standard in FORTRAN, created in 1977, provided the language with a number of structured facilities to make it competitive with some of the modern structured languages. Nonetheless, many existing commercial FORTRAN programs and subroutines were written under the 1966 ANSI standard, in an age predating the arrival of structured programming theory.

Also, the logic of FORTRAN programs is more difficult to follow than that of many other languages, and it is very easy to make a typographical error that results in a program that is syntactically correct but produces erroneous results. Nonetheless, FORTRAN will probably remain a popular scientific and engineering language for years to come. It has a large base of loyal, satisfied users, and its compilers are widely available.

OTHER PROGRAMMING LANGUAGES

PL/1

PL/1 (Programming Language 1) was introduced in the mid-1960s by IBM as a general-purpose language; that is, it was designed for both scientific and business transaction processing applications. It's an extremely powerful language, with strong capabilities for structured programming. Variants of PL/1, such as PL/C (created at Cornell) have been developed for teaching purposes.

Despite PL/1's high credentials, however, it has been used less widely than one might expect. There are several reasons for this. First, the language initially was available only on IBM machines, and other computer manufacturers were slow to adopt it on their equipment. Since IBM mainframes were less common in academic settings than in industry, few programmers learned to use PL/1 in school. Second, COBOL had had a substantial head start in business transaction processing. Not only did companies have substantial investments in working COBOL programs, but also COBOL programmers have always been more available in the marketplace. Third, BASIC and FORTRAN already were well entrenched in scientific, engineering, and business problem-solving applications. They were generally perceived as easier to use than PL/1, and their language translators were more widely available. Nonetheless, PL/1 developed a respectable following, and those that use the language swear by it.

APL

APL (A Programming Language) began in the early 1960s as a mathematical notation created by a Harvard professor to teach courses. Somewhere along the way, through the support of IBM, it evolved into a full-blown programming language.

The major objective of APL is to enable programmers to code rapidly. It is a tremendously compact language and can be used only with a special keyboard. Like BASIC, it is highly interactive.

APL has two modes of operation: calculator and program. In the *calculator mode,* APL is like a powerful desk calculator. The user types in an APL expression, and the computer system instantly supplies a response. APL uses a special set of symbols to enable users to perform complex mathematical computations in a single step. For example, the single statement

$$(+ / X) / \rho X$$

computes the average of a predefined list of numbers (called X). The $+/$ part sums the numbers of the list, the ρ (rho) part counts the size of the list, and the $/$ divides the sum by the count to produce the average. Another APL command,

$$\nabla X$$

can be used to sort the list, again in a single step. The same special symbols can be used to write complete computer programs in the *program mode.*

Supporters claim that APL programs can be written in a minute fraction of the time it takes to write comparable FORTRAN programs. After all, look at all the code you can cram into a single statement. Critics argue that APL is difficult to learn because it uses too many special symbols and employs certain programming conventions that are completely contrary to those of other languages. Most APL programs are extremely difficult for anyone but the original programmer to read. This trait is often acceptable in scientific and engineering environments, however, where programs often have short useful lives.

Ada

For many years, much of the software created for the armed services was written in machine or assembly language. In the 1970s, many branches of the services began to convert applications to high-level languages. There was no single standard for all the branches, however, and systems developed by one branch were not always compatible with those of the others. The U.S. Department of Defense soon declared a moratorium on these divergent efforts and directed the branches to cooperate in creating a single language standard. Existing languages were surveyed and, for one reason or another, rejected. The end result, in 1980, was the development of a new structured language, **Ada,** named after the Countess of Lovelace, a colleague of the nineteenth-century computer pioneer Charles Babbage.

Ada's design is based largely on Pascal. Ada, however, is a much bigger and more complex language. It includes several features that have no counterparts in Pascal, such as realtime control of tasks, exception handling, and abstract data types.

It is still too early to tell what effect Ada will have both within and beyond the Department of Defense. Its supporters predict that the language will be widely embraced by both the academic and business worlds. Critics point to PL/1 and history. "Who," they ask, "needs another programming language?"

C

C, created under the auspices of Bell Labs in the early 1970s, is a high-level language with many of the advantages of an assembly language. It's so named simply because its earlier versions were called A and B. Today, due largely to its role in packaged software development and, to a lesser degree, its association with the UNIX operating system, C is one of the hottest languages for programmers to learn.

For the past several years, the packaged applications software market has been extremely competitive. Once a software product—such as a word processor, spreadsheet, or database management system—is developed for one microcomputer system, it becomes crucial to develop versions of it for the other leading microcomputer systems as soon as possible. The earlier a software product is available in the marketplace, the harder it is for competing products to make a go of it. Thus, packaged software developers need a "mid-range" language—one that has both the portability of a high-level language like Pascal and the execution efficiency of a low-level assembly language. C, which is sometimes referred to as a "portable assembly language," conveniently fills this niche. C is also structured, which makes modifications easy to implement and test, and is far easier to learn than an assembly language.

UNIX, described in Chapter 8 as a popular operating system on smaller computers, is largely written in C; so, as UNIX's popularity continues to grow, so does C's. C and UNIX also share the same "toolkit" programming approach—that is, if a feature you like isn't available in the language, you can add it yourself.

C is used primarily by computer professionals. Code written in C looks somewhat like that in Pascal. However, C is not a language for beginners.

Logo

Logo is a programming language that also represents a philosophy of learning. It was developed in the 1970s by Seymour Paepert of MIT, who incorporated into its specification some of the learning theories of Swiss psychologist Jean Piaget. Logo has been very popular with children, many of whom find it both easy to learn and exciting.

Logo is *easy to learn* because its instructions are relatively straightforward. For example, the following program,

```
FORWARD 25 RIGHT 90
FORWARD 25 RIGHT 90
FORWARD 25 RIGHT 90
FORWARD 25 RIGHT 90
```

creates a square with 25 units on a side. The first command draws one side and points the cursorlike device on the screen 90 degrees to the right. The second command draws the second side, and so forth. As the programmer becomes more advanced, he or she can use a more sophisticated command to do the same thing, for example,

```
REPEAT 4 (FORWARD 25 RIGHT 90)
```

You can appreciate how easy Logo is to learn and use when you consider how you would draw a square in another language you are familiar with.

Logo is *exciting* because it has a lot of psychological hooks that get children involved. For example, one of Logo's strengths is graphics—and how many kids do you know who prefer writing accounting programs to drawing pictures on a screen? Also, Logo calls its triangle-shaped, cursorlike device a *turtle*. The turtle can be given commands such as FORWARD (to move), RIGHT or LEFT (to turn), PENUP (to raise the turtle's pen and allow it to move without drawing a line), and PENDOWN (to lower the pen). Inhibitions about using a computer are reduced as children imagine the cursorlike device as an animal leaving a trail on the screen and not just a boring, insensitive, run-of-the-mill cursor. Logo's *turtle graphics* have found their way into other languages as well, including Pascal.

RPG

Most business reports have a number of characteristics in common. For example, they usually contain a title page, column headings, a main body, column totals and subtotals, and page footings. **RPG** (Report Program Generator), developed by IBM in the early 1960s to produce reports quickly on small computers, capitalizes on these format similarities. Unlike the languages discussed so far in this chapter, RPG is a very-high-level, nonprocedural language. However, because it is generally considered somewhat a traditional "programmer's language," it's included in this section.

RPG works as follows. Programmers provide facts about what a report should look like. These facts often are supplied on special forms, which are subsequently machine coded. The information declared on the form includes answers to questions such as the following:

☐ *What* records in a file will be used to produce the report?

☐ *What* fields should be read from each record?

☐ *What* computations are to be done?

☐ *What* totals and subtotals should be taken?

☐ *How* will the report be formatted?

The RPG language package then determines how the job will be done and creates (generates) a computer program to produce the report. When used for the right kinds of tasks, RPG can save a considerable amount of coding and debugging time compared to a procedural language such as COBOL.

Several improvements have been made in RPG over the years. Updated versions, such as RPGIII, currently are very popular. Because RPG compilers normally are small, the language is widely used on small business systems. RPG is not standardized like many of the high-level languages, however, so different versions exist for different computer systems.

Smalltalk

Smalltalk, pioneered by Alan Kay at the University of Utah in the late 1960s, represents a significant departure from conventional programming languages. Specifically, Smalltalk is an *object-oriented programming language;* that is, it consists of objects and messages rather than the operands and operations found in traditional languages such as BASIC, COBOL, FORTRAN, and assembly languages.

What Kay first envisioned as he developed Smalltalk was a notebook-sized computer with a flat screen. The user would point to graphical icons and text options on the screen during processing. For instance, if the user wanted to retrieve a file from memory, he or she could point to a *message* icon that allowed retrieval of files. Then the computer would list all file names on the screen. At this point, the user would point to a particular file (that is, the *object* on which the message is to be invoked).

It is expected that as graphical user interfaces increase in prominence, the use of object-oriented languages such as Smalltalk will rise correspondingly. Some experts feel that at some point in the future, object-oriented languages will dominate the programming language landscape.

LISP and Prolog

LISP (for LISt Processor) and Prolog are languages prominent in the field of artificial intelligence. As you'll learn in Chapter 16, artificial intelligence is the field that studies how machines can be used to mimic human intelligence.

LISP, surprisingly, is the second oldest programming language that is still in wide use (FORTRAN is the first). It is based primarily on putting symbols such as data values, variables, and operations into meaningful lists. For instance, the three-symbol list

$$* \; A \; A$$

is used to produce A^2.

LISP, unlike BASIC and FORTRAN, is not oriented toward formula-type problem solving. Its power lies in its ability to manipulate symbols that stand for numbers. For instance, a LISP program could easily be coded to simplify an expression such as

$$N \; + \; N \; + \; N$$

to 3*N. Getting languages such as FORTRAN or BASIC to do the same thing would take a lot more effort.

Prolog, another artificial-intelligence language especially suited to symbol manipulation, was introduced about 1970. Unlike LISP, however, Prolog is a nonprocedural language. Also unlike LISP, which usually runs best on a special "LISP machine" (a computer specially configured to run LISP programs), Prolog is designed to work on an ordinary computer. Prolog advocates claim that it takes less time to get an application up and running in Prolog than it does in LISP.

Only time will tell whether Prolog will overtake LISP as the leading artificial-intelligence language. Currently LISP, which predates Prolog by more than a decade, has the edge. Prolog received a big boost in the early 1980s when the Japanese chose it to be the standard language for their push into "fifth-generation computing."

FOURTH-GENERATION LANGUAGES (4GLs)

Machine language and assembly language characterized the first and second generations of computing, respectively. During the third generation, languages such as FORTRAN, BASIC, and COBOL became dominant. Today, in the fourth generation of the computer age, a new breed of languages has

FIGURE 11-6

Types of fourth-generation languages (4GLs). 4GLs have evolved to make both end users and programmers more productive.

☑ **Report generators**   Used to generate reports quickly

☑ **Retrieval and update languages**   Used to retrieve information from files or databases and to add, delete, or modify data

☑ **Decision support system tools**   Used to create financial schedules, budgets, models of decision environments, and the like

☑ **Graphics generators**   Used to quickly prepare presentation graphics

☑ **Applications packages**   Prewritten programs for applications such as word processing, payroll, and various accounting tasks

☑ **Applications generators**   Used to quickly prepare applications programs, without having to resort to programming in a third-generation language

arrived. These languages are appropriately called **fourth-generation languages (4GLs).**

4GLs are still in a highly evolutionary stage, and many scholars disagree over exactly what a 4GL is. One property most 4GLs share, however, is an emphasis on improving the on-the-job productivity of either end users or programmers. Thus, 4GL products are commonly referred to as *productivity software.*

The 4GLs found in the market are diverse and serve a wide range of application areas. Some are targeted to users, some to programmers, and some to both. In addition, some are primarily procedural, others are chiefly nonprocedural, and still others have strong procedural and nonprocedural components.

Six types of 4GLs commonly found in commercial software products are report generators, retrieval and update languages, decision support software tools, graphics generators, applications packages, and applications generators (see Figure 11-6). Many of these language functions overlap in a single product. For instance, Lotus Development Corporation's 1-2-3 is a decision support system tool with facilities for report generation, retrieval and update, and graphics generation.

Report Generators. A *report generator* is a tool that enables you to prepare reports easily. For instance, many report generators allow you to create reports by declaring which data fields are to be represented as columns, which columns are to be sorted, and how control breaks are to be taken. Figure 14-3, in Chapter 14, shows a simple example of using a report-generation 4GL.

Retrieval and Update Languages. As more and more busy people learned to use computers to search through large files and databases, it became increasingly important to develop language products that would make this process as painless as possible. *Retrieval and update 4GLs* allow you to retrieve or update such data without having to spend weeks learning a complicated programming syntax to do so. Some of these language products require you to learn relatively simple commands, while others let you point to onscreen menu selections wherever possible. One of the best known of the retrieval and update 4GLs is **HyperTalk,** which enables you to pro-

T   O   M   O   R   R   O   W

HyperTalk

Will It Become a Major Form of Programming in the 1990s?

Ask several users what Apple's HyperCard is, and you might get a shrug accompanied by an answer like "I'm not sure, but I use it to keep addresses, phone numbers, appointments, and visit records with clients" or "You can use it to write programs." Still another familiar response is "It helps me organize slides for project presentations."

Perhaps because Hyper-Card can do so many things, just what it is and how it works can be confusing. Basically, HyperCard is a personal toolkit that enables users to create, customize, or use information involving text, graphics, video, voice, music,

and animation. It is accompanied by an easy-to-use Englishlike programming language called *HyperTalk*—an object-oriented language similar to Smalltalk. HyperTalk is not a newcomer to the programming world; it was introduced by Ted Nelson in 1965. But powerful computers such as the Macintosh, with their graphical user interfaces, weren't available back then. So it wasn't until August 1987, when Bill Atkinson (see photo) of Apple Computer introduced HyperCard to the world, that HyperTalk was actually implemented into a usable product.

The basic concept behind HyperCard, and the "clone" products to follow it, is the *card.* Data are created and placed onto cards. Each card,

which is somewhat similar in concept to the traditional 3-by-5-inch index card, may consist of one or more screenfuls of data. Also on each card may be one or more *buttons,* which, when selected by a mouse, can pull up another card to the screen, create a sound, play music, make a series of images appear on the screen (i.e., animation), and so on.

A collection of cards and their buttons is called a *stack.* In the world of HyperCard, the navigational mechanisms that enable one to use a stack is equivalent to a program in the environment of languages such as BASIC and COBOL. And when you buy a Hyper-Card stack, you need Hyper-Card to create new data for it or to run it just as you would need a BASIC language translator if you bought a BASIC program. Because HyperCard and HyperTalk are capable of

cess a variety of data (text, graphics, voice, or video) on "cards" that can be linked in numerous ways (see the Tomorrow box and Window 4). Apple's HyperCard, which uses HyperTalk, is a familiar 4GL product.

Decision Support Software Tools. *Decision support software tools* provide computing capabilities that help people make decisions. Perhaps the most familiar of such tools is the spreadsheet package, which we cover in Chapter 13. Other examples of decision support software tools are modeling packages, which allow you to create complex mathematical models, and statistical packages, which facilitate statistical analysis.

Graphics Generators. *Graphics generators,* often called *presentation graphics routines,* are tools that help you prepare graphs. If, for instance, you want

involving a number of different media, such as music and animation in addition to conventional text and graphics, the term *hypermedia* is often used to describe multimedia HyperCard or HyperTalk applications.

Today applications for HyperCard abound. An auto repair shop uses HyperCard to manage maintenance records, calculate and print bills, and post all parts used to an inventory record. Shop personnel currently are thinking of expanding this application to include an optical disk device so they can access parts catalogs more quickly. Another company has collected almost 2,000 images of artifacts and treasures from the National Gallery of Art and placed them on optical disk along with a video-guided tour and a videotaped history of the museum. There these images can be ac-

cessed by lecturers and historians via a HyperCard program. Medical and pre-med students at Brown, Cornell, and Dartmouth study pathology

through hypermedia. The list of applications is virtually endless. Window 4 presents a photoessay of some hypermedia applications.

HyperCard's inventor. Atkinson.

data to be put into the form of a pie chart, the graphics generator will ask you to both identify the data to be graphed and declare the type of graph you want. It will also ask you for your preferences as regards matters such as coloring, texturing, and legends. After you satisfactorily respond to all of the questions, the graph is automatically prepared. We cover graphics generators more fully in Chapter 13; Figure 13-12 illustrates using a menu-driven graphics generator.

Applications Packages. An *applications package* is a "canned" program designed to perform some common business application, such as payroll, accounts receivable, invoicing, or word processing. Like a graphics generator, an applications package usually asks the user a number of questions. The responses are subsequently used to assign values to parameters within the package, to customize it to the application needs of the specific user or organization. A word processor, for instance, asks each user questions about line spacing, margins, justification, and so forth. The responses to these questions facilitate customizing the word processing environment to each user.

Applications Generators. An *applications generator* is a package that enables you to quickly code applications software. These packages work in a variety of ways. For instance, some applications generators enable systems analysts and users to work together to develop menu screens for a new system. We covered such an application in Chapter 9.

Many applications generators contain *code generators,* routines that allow programs written in a proprietary prototyping language to be automatically translated into a third-generation language such as COBOL. Some applications generators also contain powerful *specifications languages,* which translate a program design—say, one depicted by a diagram—directly into executable code.

Generally speaking, applications generators require more programming knowledge than do applications packages. In an applications package, all you need to do is satisfactorily answer questions to get the application up and running. In an applications generator, you are often involved with some form of conventional programming. A familiar example of an applications generator is Ashton-Tate's dBASE.

SUMMARY AND KEY TERMS

A **programming language** can be broadly defined as a set of rules that enables instructions to be written for a computer.

The earliest programming languages—machine and assembly languages—are called **low-level languages,** because programmers who code in them must write instructions at the finest level of detail. These languages were the only ones available to programmers during the *first* and *second generations* of computer history.

The next languages to appear were the **high-level languages.** Included in this class are what have come to be known as *third-generation* programming languages—BASIC, COBOL, FORTRAN, Pascal, PL/1, APL, and many others. High-level languages differ from their low-level predecessors in that they require less coding detail and make programs easier to write.

Very-high-level languages, which characterize the *fourth generation* of computing history, are those in which users prescribe *what* the computer is to do rather than *how* it is to do it. These languages make programming much easier. Low- and high-level languages are sometimes called **procedural languages,** because they require people to write detailed statements representing specific steps to be performed during program execution. Very-high-level languages, in contrast, are called **nonprocedural languages.**

Assembly languages are like machine language in that each line of code corresponds to a single action of the computer system. But assembly languages replace the 0s and 1s of machine language with symbols that are easier to understand and remember. The big advantage of assembly language programs is executional efficiency; they're fast and consume little storage compared with their high-level counterparts. Unfortunately, assembly-language programs take longer to write and maintain than programs written in high-level languages. They are also very machine dependent.

BASIC (Beginner's All-purpose Symbolic Instruction Code) was designed to meet the need for an easy-to-learn beginner's language that would work in a "friendly," nonfrustrating programming environment. Over the years, BASIC has evolved into one of the most popular and widely available programming languages. Because it is easy to learn and use, and because the storage requirements for its language translator are small, it works well on almost all microcomputers. Nearly every advantage of BASIC is related to its ease of use for beginners. Among these advantages are simplified naming of variables, optional formatting, conversational programming mode, and simple diagnostics. A key weakness in many versions of BASIC is that their ease of use may lead to sloppy programming practices.

Pascal, named after the mathematician Blaise Pascal, is a relatively new programming language. Pascal was created primarily to fill the need for a teaching vehicle that would encourage structured programming.

COBOL (COmmon Business-Oriented Language) is the primary transaction processing language in use in organizations today. Almost all of its key features relate to its transaction processing orientation. These include machine independence, self-documentation, and input/output orientation. The primary disadvantage of COBOL is that programs written in it tend to be lengthy, making them time-consuming to develop and maintain. Also, COBOL is usually unsuitable for scientific, mathematical, or engineering applications.

FORTRAN (FORmula TRANslator), which dates back to 1954, is the oldest surviving commercial high-level language. It was designed by scientists and is oriented toward scientific, mathematical, and engineering problem solving. The key strengths of FORTRAN are fast program execution and a large bank of preprogrammed subroutines. The weaknesses include some drawbacks in the area of structured programming.

PL/1 (Programming Language 1) was introduced in the mid-1960s by IBM as a general-purpose language; that is, it was designed for both scientific and transaction processing applications. It's an extremely powerful language and has strong capabilities for structured programming.

APL (A Programming Language) was developed in the early 1960s to enable programmers to code rapidly. It is an extremely compact language and is used with a special keyboard.

Ada is a relatively new structured language initiated by the U.S. Department of Defense. It is still too early to guess how successful it will be in the business and academic worlds.

C combines the best features of a structured, high-level language and assembly languages. Currently it's one of the hottest languages for programmers to learn, largely because of its role in packaged software development and, to a lesser degree, its association with the UNIX operating system.

Logo is a programming language that also represents a philosophy of learning. It's been very popular with children, many of whom find it both easy to learn and exciting.

RPG (Report Program Generator) was developed by IBM in the early 1960s to produce reports quickly on small computers. Programmers provide facts on special coding forms about what a report should look like, and after the forms are machine coded, the RPG package determines how the job will be done and creates (generates) a computer program to produce the report.

Smalltalk, pioneered at the University of Utah in the late 1960s, represents a significant departure from conventional programming languages. For one thing, it is an *object-oriented programming language;* that is, it consists of objects and messages rather than the operands and operations found in traditional languages such as BASIC, COBOL, FORTRAN, and assembly language.

LISP (for LISt Processor) and **Prolog** are used to develop applications that incorporate some degree of artificial intelligence. LISP (the second oldest programming language that is still widely used, behind FORTRAN) is a procedural language that is often implemented on a special, dedicated computer system. Prolog, created about 1970, is a nonprocedural language designed to run on an ordinary computer.

Fourth-generation languages (4GLs) are easy-to-learn, easy-to-use languages that are targeted at improving workers' on-the-job productivity. Six types of 4GLs commonly found in commercial software products are report generators, retrieval and update languages (which include **HyperTalk** products), decision support software tools, graphics generators, applications packages, and applications generators.

REVIEW EXERCISES

Fill-in Questions

1. _____ is a language that was developed at Dartmouth College to meet the need for an easy-to-learn beginner's language that would work in a "friendly," nonfrustrating programming environment.

2. The oldest surviving commercial high-level language is _____.

3. _____ is the primary transaction processing language in use today.

4. _____, created about 1970, was developed primarily to fill the need for a teaching vehicle that would encourage structured programming.

5. _____ was introduced in the mid-1960s by IBM as a powerful, general-purpose language.

6. _____ has both the portability of a high-level language and the executional efficiency of assembly languages.

7. A programming language still widely used in the field of artificial intelligence, although it predates both BASIC and COBOL, is _____.

8. Report generators, retrieval and update languages, applications packages, and applications generators are all examples of _____ languages.

Matching Questions

Match each term with the description that best fits.

a. low-level languages
b. high-level languages
c. very-high-level languages
d. procedural languages
e. nonprocedural languages
f. assembly language
g. machine language

_____ 1. The language that works with 0s and 1s.

_____ 2. Machine and assembly languages.

_____ 3. Nonprocedural languages.

_____ 4. Languages that work by having the programmer give the computer system step-by-step instructions for solving a problem.

_____ 5. Problem-dependent, very-high-level languages.

_____ 6. A low-level language that uses symbols such as *A* for "Add" and *L* for "Load."

_____ 7. Procedural languages such as BASIC, COBOL, and FORTRAN.

Discussion Questions

1. What are the primary differences among low-level, high-level, and very-high-level languages?

2. What are the chief strengths and weaknesses of assembly languages?

3. What are the particular strengths and weaknesses of BASIC?

4. What needs are served by the following languages—BASIC, COBOL, FORTRAN, Pascal, C, APL, RPG, and Prolog?

5. Which features of COBOL make this language attractive for transaction processing applications?

6. Many people feel that PL/1 is superior to COBOL and FORTRAN, yet it's less widely used than those languages. Why?

7. What motivated the development of Ada?

8. Identify several types of fourth-generation languages and the purposes each one serves.

Critical Thinking Questions

1. If there are so many programming languages around today, why are new ones constantly being developed? Do any of these new programming languages really have a chance at wide acceptance, given the number of languages now in use?

2. A well-known software expert once commented that among the languages of today, the most likely to be around by year 2000 are COBOL and FORTRAN. Ironically, these are among the two oldest languages in wide use. What is the significance of this?

3. Given that powerful productivity software packages such as dBASE and 1-2-3 are now available to help end users, is it still useful for the average business student to learn how a traditional, third-generation programming language works?

Hypermedia

The User Interface That May
Revolutionize Programming

Hypermedia (see the To-morrow box in this chapter) is a technology that might make an orchestra conductor envious of the ordinary user. Press a button, and screenfuls of information appear on a computer monitor. Press another, and related video images emerge from a nearby TV screen. Press yet another, and related talk or music blast out of an adjacent sound system. You are in control of all of these media, each of which has a veritable mountain of interesting information in the form of text, graphics, video, or sound ready at your beck and call. The possibilities of such a technology, which only got started in earnest in 1987, are almost endless, ranging from business to entertainment. In this Window, we look at some of the environments in which hypermedia is currently being applied.

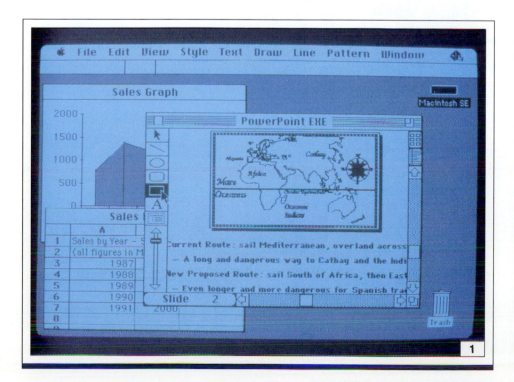

1 Hypermedia emerged in commercial product form with Apple's HyperCard, introduced to the world by its developer, Bill Atkinson, to standing-room-only crowds at the August 1987 Macworld Expo in Boston. Atkinson showed, to the oohs and aahs of the audience, how one could create related data in the form of electronic "cards," which theoretically could be interrelated in any way desired, and how one could create "buttons" on these cards that (when selected with a mouse) would do things such as dial phone numbers or activate sounds from the computer's audio unit. Apple packaged HyperCard as a standard item with every Macintosh sold, which immediately made it available to thousands of users.

STACKWARE

A group of related cards and the file that stores them are collectively called a *stack*. Today many types of stacks designed to work on the average microcomputer system are commercially available. On this two-page spread, we'll look at a few of these.

2, 3 Brøderbund Software's DTP Advisor is a stack that provides a tutorial on desktop publishing, enabling you to choose fonts and walking you through page layout basics. On any particular screen, the buttons may be either pieces of art that you can select or conventional menu/icon choices. DTP Advisor also contains a module to help you manage projects.

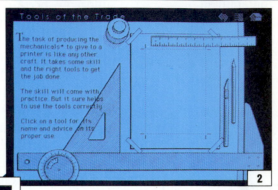

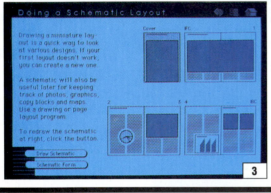

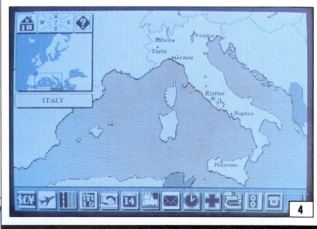

4, 5 Mediagenic's Business Class is a stack designed for people who do business overseas, travel abroad for business or pleasure, or just want to learn more about the world. It offers information on local currencies, transportation, hotels, social customs, climates, and holidays in 65 countries. It also lets you add your own information to the stack and use an automatic dialing feature. In the cards shown here, the buttons are located at the bottom of the screen.

366

6–9 Focal Point is a stackware product that integrates 18 business applications, including a monthly and daily appointment calendar, a to-do list, address cards, a telephone speed dialer, a telephone log, a deadline reminder, a billing log, and expense reports. So, for instance, you can select a client's name from an address book, whereupon Focal Point will automatically dial the number, record the call in a phone log, and present an appropriate client record on the display screen. There is also a "launch" facility to summon other applications software, such as a spreadsheet.

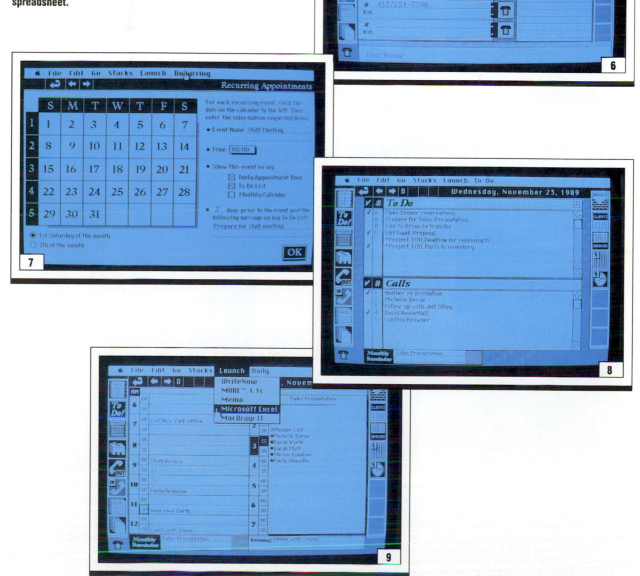

MULTIMEDIA APPLICATIONS

The full power of hypermedia is realized when you hook up a microcomputer system to other devices—say, a television set or video monitor, an optical disk system, and/or a stereo system. Here's how the overall system might work. Suppose you want to learn about the "Roaring Twenties." You first call up the appropriate stack on your computer system. The stack lets you select from a large, hierarchically structured menu of choices, each one containing different subject materials about this era. You may be able to summon scores of articles, old newspaper clippings, or photos, all of which you can lay out in windows on your monitor. You may also be able to activate buttons, embedded in the text you pull up, to choose from among several optical-disk-stored video clips, which you can watch on a nearby video screen. And to really put you in the spirit, the stack might let you access some of the old tunes of Rudy Vallee or the Goofus Five, which will be output through your computer's audio unit or a separate speaker system.

10 One of the most ambitious hypermedia undertakings to date is that of Cornell University's Medical College. Traditionally, pathology professors have had to store 35mm slides on hundreds of carousels. And because it's hard to cram all one needs to say into a single lecture period, professors often must end lectures with the all too familiar comment "We have no time to cover this stuff, but you're responsible for it anyway." Now hypermedia and high-capacity disk systems—which allow any of thousands of text-based facts, slides, and animated images to be rapidly summoned—offer an alternative, and one that may someday completely revolutionize education in many areas. Nonetheless, don't expect to say good-bye to the traditional lecture. A charismatic and inspirational instructor still has motivating powers that a computer system has not yet attained and may never master.

11

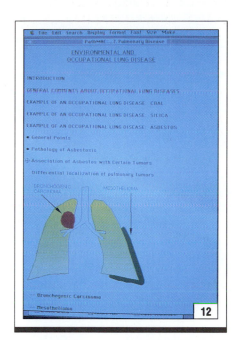

12

11 Students often begin by summoning a master menu showing the topics available on the system. The topics may be presented as modules or chapters of a book.

12 As students choose topics, they are presented with increasingly fine detail and other choices about where to go next. As they read on, they will encounter buttons that represent text or images stored on either magnetic disk or videodisk.

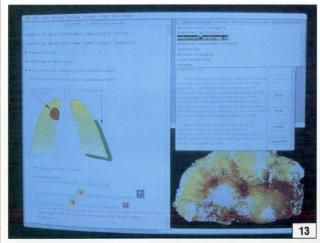

13

13 Students can lay out images in windows just as they might arrange hard-copy information on a desk. A zooming feature allows the student to size the windows as desired, to inspect detail or to just get an overview of how parts of something fit together.

14 The video monitor can be used to inspect stills or short animated segments. The success of Cornell University's hypermedia project has inspired hopes of someday extending the system to general hospital use, so that doctors have instant access to patient and treatment information.

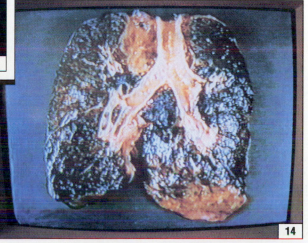

14

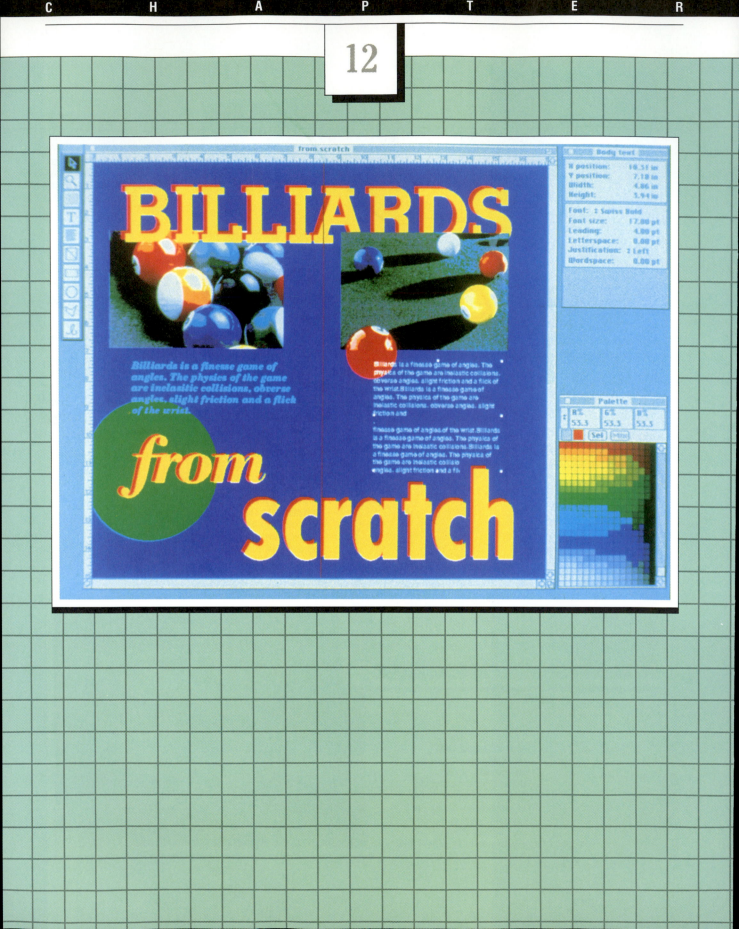

Word Processing and Desktop Publishing

Objectives

After completing this chapter, you will be able to:

1. Describe what word processing is and several ways in which it may be implemented on computer systems.

2. Identify the operations you must master to effectively use word processing software.

3. Explain the features common to many word processing packages.

4. Describe the differences between low-end and high-end desktop publishing packages and identify the components of many desktop publishing systems.

OVERVIEW

Word processing and desktop publishing are technologies that deal with the manipulation of words. *Word processing* enables a computer system to serve as a powerful typewriting tool. In using the computer in this way, one can quickly create, edit, and print documents as well as manage them in a way no ordinary typewriter can do. *Desktop publishing,* available only since high-powered microcomputers entered the marketplace, carries word processing a step further. With desktop publishing hardware and software, one can create documents that look as though they were prepared by a professional print shop.

In this chapter, we'll first cover word processors. Here we'll explore in detail some of the types of word processors currently available and many of the features that differentiate one word processor from another. Then we'll turn to desktop publishing and the hardware and software found on both low-end and high-end desktop publishing systems. We'll also examine why it's getting increasingly difficult to determine where word processing ends and desktop publishing begins.

WORD PROCESSING

When you use your computer to do the kinds of work you normally do on a typewriter, you're doing word processing. **Word processing** is the use of computer technology to create, manipulate, and print text materials such as letters, legal contracts, manuscripts, and other documents. Word processing is such a time-saver, in fact, that most people who learn to do it let their typewriters gather dust. As you will discover in this chapter, the two primary features that differentiate word processing from ordinary typewriting are computer-assisted *text editing* and *print formatting* (see Figure 12-1). But before we examine how these tasks are carried out, let's look at some of the types of word processors currently available in the marketplace.

Types of Word Processors

There are several ways you can perform word processing. First, you can do it on either a dedicated word processing system or a general-purpose computer system. Second, you can work with either a WYSIWYG (What-You-See-Is-What-You-Get) word processor or one that depends heavily on embedded formatting codes to tell you what you will subsequently see in print. Third, you can use either a general-purpose or a special-purpose word processing software package. Fourth, you can choose either a dedicated word processing package or an integrated software package. Now we will look at each of these options in turn.

FIGURE 12-1

Text editing and print formatting.
Text-editing operations allow you to
"cut and paste" text materials in
electronic memory. Print-formatting
operations let you output those
materials in a visually appealing
way.

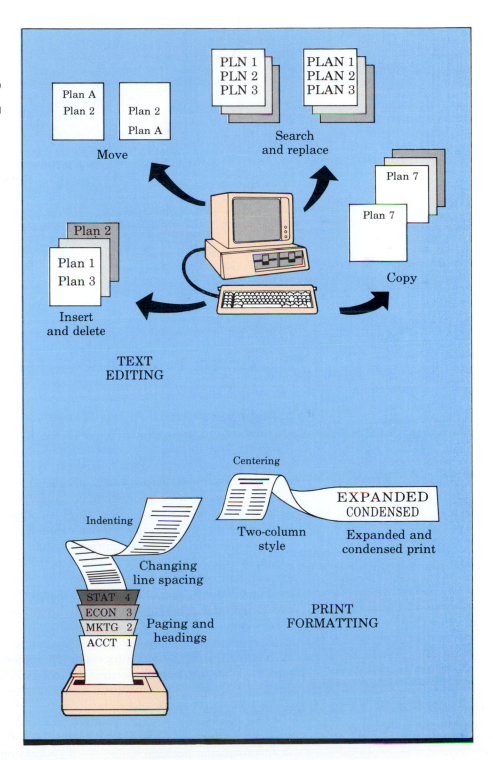

FIGURE 12-2

WordPerfect. WordPerfect Corporation's WordPerfect currently is the best-selling word processing package, claiming close to a one-third market share.

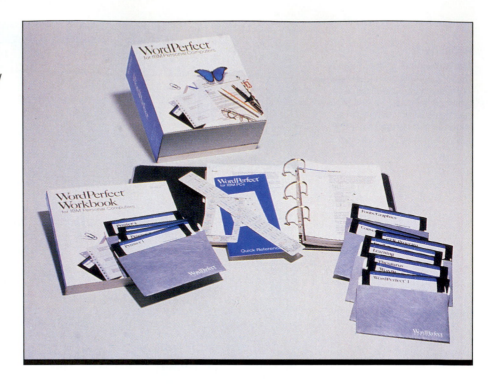

Dedicated versus General-Purpose Computer Systems. One of the best—and also one of the most expensive—ways to do word processing is to use a computer system specially dedicated to this purpose, that is, a *dedicated word processing system.* Generally these systems are microcomputers that are rigged with special keyboards and monitors and packaged with special software to make word processing as painless as possible. For people such as secretaries and authors, who need a computer system exclusively for high-volume word processing, a dedicated system often is the best way to go. Unfortunately, the special-purpose nature of these systems makes them inefficient for and sometimes incapable of doing things other than word processing. So if you need a single system for a wide variety of purposes—say, word processing, spreadsheets, data management, and writing your own BASIC or Pascal programs—a dedicated word processor generally is a poor choice. A general-purpose computer system is usually more appropriate.

General-purpose computer systems are configured to do a variety of tasks. Most people perform word processing on a general-purpose computer system. If you want to prepare a letter, for instance, you load a word processing software package onto the system; if you want to prepare a budget, you load a spreadsheet program; and so on.

Word processing software packages are widely available for virtually all sizes of computers. Figure 12-2 shows WordPerfect, today's best-selling word processing package. Other word processing packages that are widely used include Word, WordStar, XyWrite, and MultiMate. You might pay as little as $100 for a software package or several hundred dollars, depending on the size of the computer you are using and the level of sophistication you require from the software.

FIGURE 12-3

Screen-oriented word processing.
The best screen-oriented packages
approximate WYSIWYG—what you
see (on the screen) is what you get
(in print). Because fancier
documents require more complex
software and hardware, not all
screen-oriented packages approach
the ideal of WYSIWYG. Instead,
they use embedded print-formatting
codes on the display to describe
how a document will look when it is
output.

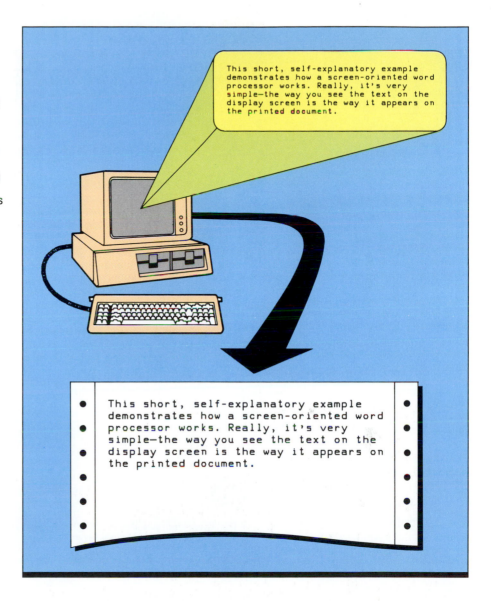

WYSIWYG versus Embedded Formatting Codes. The vast majority of word processors in use today are screen oriented. Screen-oriented word processors display on the screen exactly, or almost exactly, how a document will appear before it's printed. Each screen line corresponds to a printed-page line, so you are rarely surprised at how the document looks when it's subsequently printed. Figure 12–3 shows a document being prepared by a screen-oriented package and what it looks like when printed out.

With the ideal screen-oriented package, what you see (on the screen) is precisely what you get (in print); in other words, the image on the screen and the image on the printed page correspond exactly. This feature is commonly referred to as **WYSIWYG,** for What You See Is What You Get. WYSIWYG most often occurs in the desktop publishing world. There, users frequently employ high-resolution graphics monitors capable of showing a

Buying a Word Processing Package for Your Micro

The Choices Today Are, in a Word, Staggering

Just a few years ago, buying a word processing package and support hardware was a relatively straightforward task. Only a handful of packages were available, and the choices among printers were very limited. Today dozens of quality word processing packages are in the marketplace, and most of them come with a variety of adjunct routines—spelling checkers, thesauruses, mail merge programs, desktop publishing features, and the like—that complicate the choice. Moreover, an ever wider variety of printers and printing standards are now available.

But not to worry. The more things change, as someone once said, the more things remain the same. While the number of options available to the buyer has indeed increased, the process involved in selecting a system has changed very little.

Analyzing Needs. First, make a list of everything you want the word processor you buy to do. Most word processors in the marketplace are designed to satisfy a wide range of basic needs. Often, it is the "feel" of the word processor and the presence of certain of the more advanced features that are used to differentiate one product from another.

You can get the feel of any word processor by trying it out at a store, at school, or at a friend's house. As far as the more advanced features go, consider: Do you need a spelling checker? Must you have a thesaurus? Does the work you have planned require desktop publishing features? Keep in mind that the advanced features often require special equipment. A spelling checker and thesaurus, for example, work best with a hard disk. Many forms of desktop publishing require a laser printer.

List Products and Alternatives. Next, list the products you'd like to look at further. If you aren't familiar with many of the available products (see figure), make a preliminary visit to a computer store to get an idea. Many of the leading microcomputer publications, such as *PC Magazine* and *Infoworld,* periodically compare the leading word processors, so also visit your favorite library and do some digging. Keep in mind that specialized word processors also are available. These meet the particular needs of people such as musicians, mathema-

variety of fonts, sometimes scaled to different sizes, onscreen simultaneously. However, the resolution on the average microcomputer monitor is continually improving, and WYSIWYG will almost surely become more commonplace in everyday word processing environments.

Unfortunately, most screen-oriented word processors and monitors in use today fall far short of the WYSIWYG ideal. In fact, boldface, italic, and underline characters often do not display onscreen even though they will be output as such on the printed document. To achieve a number of such print-formatting effects, many word processors use *embedded formatting codes.* Typically the user places these codes before and after a word or phrase that is to be output in a special way. The code placed before the word or phrase alerts the printer to turn on a formatting feature; the code following the word or phrase turns off the feature. Some word processors display these codes onscreen at all times, while others reveal them only on demand.

ticians, and movie scriptwriters.

While shopping for a word processor, don't forget the printer. Most word processors will function well only on a limited number of printers. These are usually listed in the written documentation accompanying the word processor. Be aware that the printer you have in mind may be unable to handle some of the more advanced features of the package. For example, not all printers will print subscripts and superscripts even if your word processing package supports them.

Examine the Products. At this point, you will want to look more closely at as many word processors and printers as you have the time and patience to examine. Word processors can vary dramatically in the way they implement commands, and a package that has the right feel to one person might seem totally un-natural to another. So you should visit your local computer store to test out some products. Often the salesperson will have a demonstration to show you. You should also "test drive" the products yourself, ideally on the same type of printer you will be using. Perhaps something the demonstration didn't get into (or deliberately hid) is particularly important to you. Maybe the quality of the actual printed documents looks inferior to those in the promotional literature. Before the test drive, you may want to reread those comparative studies you've collected from the library to make sure that the packages you're considering don't have a "skeleton in the closet."

Product Comparison and Choice. Now is the time to separate the best packages from the also-rans and to do some hard thinking about the quality you're getting for the cost. Generally, as with anything else, the more you pay, the more quality you get. With word processing software and printers, you can get surprisingly good quality at a relatively low price. In making the final choice, you may wish to review your most pressing needs and rate each package on each need. Then you can choose the one that appears best overall.

- ☑ WordPerfect
- ☑ Microsoft Word
- ☑ WordStar
- ☑ PC-Write
- ☑ MultiMate Advantage
- ☑ XyWrite
- ☑ MacWrite
- ☑ Volkswriter
- ☑ DisplayWrite
- ☑ PFS: Professional Write

Market leaders. WordPerfect and Word alone account for about half of word processing sales.

General-Purpose versus Special-Purpose Word Processing Packages. Most word processing software products in use today are *general-purpose packages;* that is, they are designed to suit the needs of a variety of users, such as secretaries, authors, and "average" microcomputer users. However, a number of *specialized word processors* are commercially available to meet the unique demands of users in certain niche areas. For example, some word processors offer an abundance of special symbols for mathematically oriented documents. Others are designed to meet the unique needs of movie scriptwriters or musicians. However, the vast majority of software in the marketplace is aimed at people with ordinary needs.

Dedicated Word Processing Packages versus Integrated Software Packages. Most people who do word processing use a *dedicated word processing pack-*

age—that is, a package targeted exclusively to meeting various word processing needs. Most of the packages most familiar to the general public (see Feature 12A for a sample of these) fall into this category. However, some software products combine the ability to word process with the ability to perform other, dissimilar functions, such as spreadsheeting and database management. This latter category of products is most commonly referred to as *integrated software packages*. We'll discuss integrated software packages more fully in Chapter 14.

The remainder of this chapter will address dedicated, general-purpose word processing packages targeted to general-purpose computers. By far, these are the types of word processors that most people encounter in practice.

Learning to Use a Word Processor: The Basics

No matter what type of car you drive, certain operations are basic for all cars—turning the ignition on and off, moving from a stationary position, stopping, and so forth. Yet each of these operations may be implemented in different ways on different cars. The ignition may be on the steering column in one car and on the dashboard in another. Or one car may have standard transmission and another automatic.

Word processing packages are very much like cars in this respect. Almost all packages perform certain basic operations, but each implements these operations in its own way. For example, most packages contain a centering command, since most people who type have to center text (such as titles and headings) at one time or another. One package may center text when, say, the characters *O* and *C* are typed in (with the control key held down), a second when the F2 function key is depressed, and a third when the shift key and F6 function-key combination is invoked. Moreover, every word processing package must be able to save or delete documents. If you went into your local computer store and randomly picked five word processing packages off the shelf, you'd probably find five different ways to save or delete text.

Virtually all word processing packages have some method of implementing these basic operations, because such operations often account for 90 percent or more of the commands invoked during the course of word processing a document. This basic set of word processing commands may be classified as general operations, entering and editing operations, and print-formatting operations.

General Operations. To use virtually any type of productivity software package—word processor, spreadsheet, or whatever—on your computer, you need to know how to carry out a number of general operations. These operations, listed in Figure 12-4, are the functional equivalents of starting and stopping a car.

Entering and Editing Operations. Nearly every word processor contains entering and editing operations that carry out the following tasks. These tasks are associated with keying in and manipulating text on the screen.

FIGURE 12-4

General operations needed for operating any productivity software package. Depending on the package you use, the file that you work on may contain a word-processed document, a worksheet, a graph, a collection of database records, or even something else.

General Operations for Using Productivity Software

☑ **Accessing** your package from the operating system

☑ Informing the package that you either want to **create** a new file or to **retrieve** an old one from disk

☑ Commanding the package to **save** a file onto disk

☑ Commanding the package to **print** a file

☑ Commanding the package to **delete** a file that's on disk

☑ Indicating to the package that you want to **quit** working on your current file and do something on another file

☑ **Terminating** your work on the package and getting back to the operating system

---

☐ *Moving the Cursor* Moving the cursor around the screen is a task that many word processors offer well over a dozen ways to do. Usually you can move the cursor a character, a word, a line, or a screen at a time, and to the beginning or end of a document as well. You can usually move the cursor either by typing in a command or by depressing one of several function keys or cursor-movement keys. Many word processing users acquire a mouse to obtain additional cursor-movement capabilities.

☐ *Scrolling* Scrolling lets you move contiguous lines of text up and down on the screen similarly to the way the roll on a player piano unwinds. When scrolling down, for example, as lines successively disappear from the top of the screen, new ones appear from the bottom. With many word processing packages, you can use the up-arrow and down-arrow keys to scroll a document line by line. By using the PgUp and PgDn keys, you can scroll even faster—page by page instead of line by line (see Figure 12-5).

☐ *Line Return* A line return is often accomplished by hitting the "Return key"—called an Enter key—as you would on a standard typewriter. This is sometimes referred to as a *hard carriage return.* Virtually all word processors also have a *wordwrap* feature so you don't have to hit the Enter key at the end of each line. Wordwrapping automatically produces a *soft carriage return* when the cursor reaches a certain column position at the right-hand side of the page.

☐ *Inserting and Deleting* Inserting and deleting are two of the most basic editing operations. For example, suppose you typed in

```
THE HAVE WON THE CHAMPIONSHIP
```

and forgot to type in the name of the winning team. So, if the Hoboken Zephyrs won the championship, you'd have to insert the phrase HOBOKEN ZEPHYRS between THE and HAVE.

If you later decided you wanted to delete the word HOBOKEN, the word processor would enable you to do this as well. Most packages also

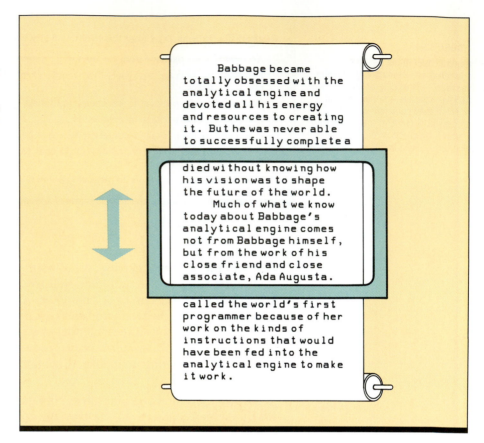

FIGURE 12-5

Scrolling. With many word processors, depressing the PgUp or PgDn key enables you to scroll the document up or down to view contiguous screen-size pages on the display. By starting at the beginning of the document and successively depressing the PgDn key, you can scroll through the entire document to proofread it. You can use the PgUp key to refer to preceding screen pages.

let you mark blocks of words and insert or delete text a block at a time in any portion of the document.

☐ *Moving and Copying* Moving and copying are operations that allow you to "cut and paste" text with a word processor. *Moving* means identifying a specific block of text and physically relocating it in a new place in the document, thus removing it from its original location. *Copying* is similar to moving except that a copy of the block remains in the original place as well. Figure 12-6 illustrates the difference between moving and copying.

☐ *Searching and Replacing* Searching and replacing are extremely useful features. They enable you to search automatically for all occurrences of a particular word or phrase and change it to something else. For example, say you've typed out a long document that repeatedly refers to a person named "Snider." If you've misspelled this name as "Schneider," you can instruct the word processor to look up all occurrences of "Schneider" and change them to "Snider."

Some people take dangerous shortcuts in searching and replacing. For example, suppose you ask the word processor to change all occurrences of "chne" to "n." This will change all "Schneider" occurrences to "Snider," but it will also change a name such as "Schneymann" to "Snymann," which you probably did not intend.

FIGURE 12-6

Moving versus copying. With moving, the highlighted line no longer appears in its original position in the document, whereas with copying it does.

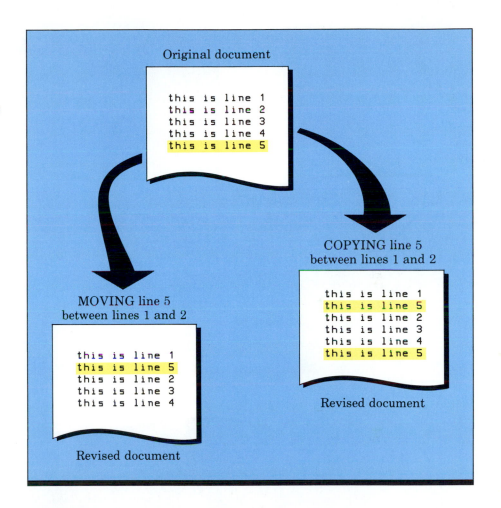

Print-Formatting Operations. Print-formatting operations tell the printer how to output the text onto paper. These operations include the following functions:

☐ *Adjusting Line Spacing* Adjusting line spacing is an important word processing operation. Suppose, for instance, you've typed a paper single-spaced, but your English 101 instructor wants all the essays you hand in double-spaced. No problem. Virtually all word processors will enable you to adjust the line spacing to double-space in a matter of a few seconds or minutes. Many packages will also permit triple-spacing, fractional blank lines between text lines, and several other line spacing options.

☐ *Indenting* Indenting, or adjusting margins, is useful when you are typing a paper with lots of quotes and want to set off these passages from the main text. Many word processors allow you to choose among several types of indenting styles.

☐ *Reformatting* Reformatting normally is necessary when you insert text, delete text, change line spacing, or readjust margins in your document. Figure 12-7 illustrates these four occasions for reformatting. After making

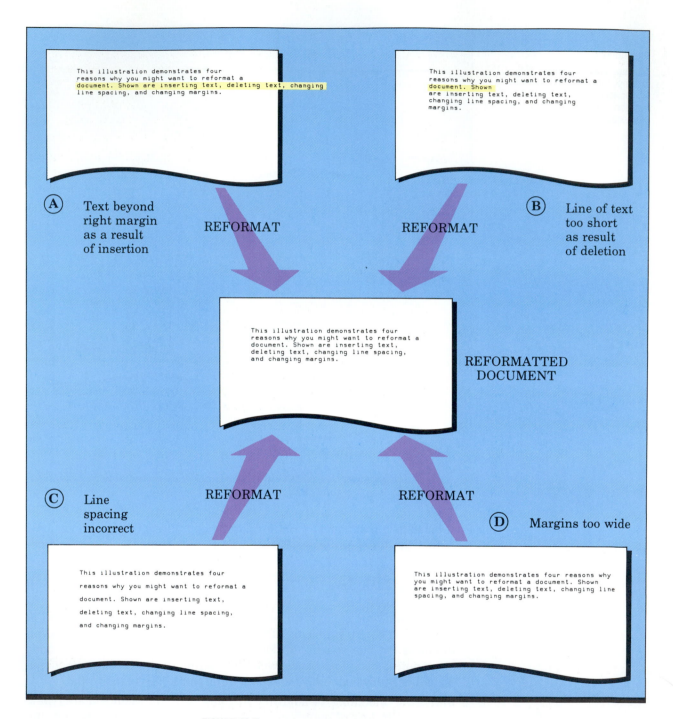

FIGURE 12-7

Four occasions to reformat a document. Shown are (a) inserting text, (b) deleting text, (c) changing line spacing, and (d) changing margins.

the insertion, deletion, choice of new line spacing, or choice of new margins, you may need to issue one or more commands to reformat the appropriate sections of the document. Some packages reformat automatically after each edit.

☐ *Centering* Centering text is a very important task for most people. Word processing packages usually require you to have the cursor on the line containing the text to be centered when invoking the centering command.

☐ *Tabbing* Tabbing is a formatting feature that typists have relied on for years. Figure 12-8 shows three useful ways to tab text. The tab at the beginning of the paragraph (Figure 12-8a) and tab-stopping of numbers into columns (Figure 12-8b) often are done merely by depressing the tab key on the keyboard. The paragraph tab (Figure 12-8c) usually is done with a special command issued through the word processing package.

☐ *Pagination* Pagination lets you choose whether or not to number pages in a document. For example, you may want page numbers placed on class reports but not on short letters. Many word processing packages will place page numbers wherever you specify.

☐ *Headers and Footers* Headers are titles printed at the top of a page; *footers* are titles printed at the bottom. Some word processors give you a lot of flexibility with respect to headers and footers. For instance, you can print both headers and footers on the same page and even alternate the title placed in a header or footer. This textbook, like many other books, alternates headers—module letter and module title are on the left-facing pages and chapter number and chapter title on the right-facing pages. Many word processors also allow page numbers to appear in a header or footer and give you several choices about where to place them.

☐ *Style Selection* Style selection features enable you to output characters in a variety of typefaces (called **fonts**) and typeface sizes (called **point sizes**) as well as boldface, italicize, underline, subscript, or superscript characters. Both the word processor and the printer on your system must support a particular styling feature in order for you to use it. Figure 12-9 shows a variety of styles used with word processors.

☐ *Multiple Columns* Multiple-column formatting lets you print text in a columnar format similar to that used in newspapers and magazines. If you are doing multiple-column formatting, it is especially useful to have a feature that eliminates orphans and widows (discussed later in the chapter).

☐ *Footnoting* A footnoting feature allows you to create, edit, and delete footnotes in a document. Typically the routine that manages the footnoting is designed to remember footnote references and automatically renumber footnotes if you insert or delete any.

Learning to Use a Word Processor: Advanced Operations

In addition to the basic operations we've just covered, the more sophisticated word processors enable you to do a number of other useful tasks. Some of these may be especially valuable if you are a professional typist or

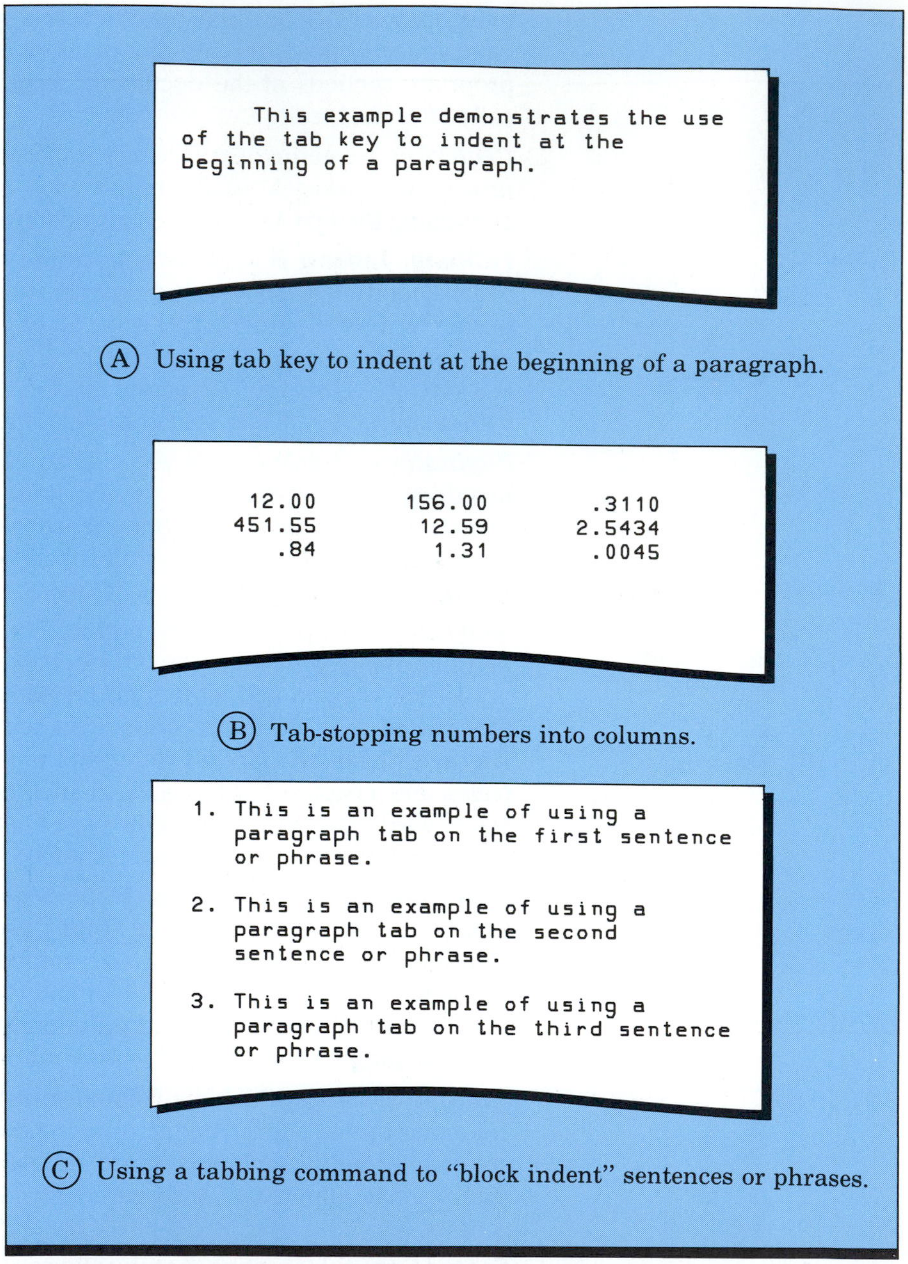

FIGURE 12-8
Three useful tab invocations in word processing. Tabbing can be done through the Tab key or function keys. Most word processing packages enable you to create your own tab stops, as well.

```
        This example demonstrates the use
of the tab key to indent at the
beginning of a paragraph.
```

(A) Using tab key to indent at the beginning of a paragraph.

```
    12.00        156.00        .3110
   451.55         12.59       2.5434
      .84          1.31        .0045
```

(B) Tab-stopping numbers into columns.

```
1.  This is an example of using a
    paragraph tab on the first sentence
    or phrase.

2.  This is an example of using a
    paragraph tab on the second
    sentence or phrase.

3.  This is an example of using a
    paragraph tab on the third sentence
    or phrase.
```

(C) Using a tabbing command to "block indent" sentences or phrases.

an author or if your business requires a lot of correspondence. Several such tasks are discussed next.

Proportional Spacing. On many printers, text is *monospaced;* that is, each character takes up the same amount of horizontal space. This textbook, on the other hand, like most others, was typeset on a system that *proportionally spaces* characters. **Proportional spacing** is a feature that allocates more horizontal space on a line to some characters than to others. For ex-

Style	Point Size	Sample
ITC New Baskerville Roman	12	Hello
ITC New Baskerville Italic	12	*Hello*
ITC New Baskerville Bold	12	**Hello**
Futura Condensed	12	Hello
Optima Medium	12	Hello
Park Avenue	12	*Hello*
Brush	12	*Hello*
Tiffany	12	ABC
Tiffany Demi	24	**ABC**
Tiffany Heavy	72	**ABC**

FIGURE 12-9

Type styles. Depending on your word processing software and hardware, there may be a large number of typefaces and point sizes available for you to print documents.

ample, a capital *M* takes up more space than does a lowercase *i*. A microspacing feature may also be available. With **microspacing,** fractions of a full blank space are inserted within each line in places where they won't likely be noticed, so that the left- and right-hand margins are flush. Proportional spacing and microspacing are shown in Figure 12-10.

Both your word processor and your printer must support proportional spacing and microspacing in order for your documents to achieve a typeset look. Many desktop publishing packages take proportional spacing and microspacing a step further by using a *kerning* feature (see Feature 12B).

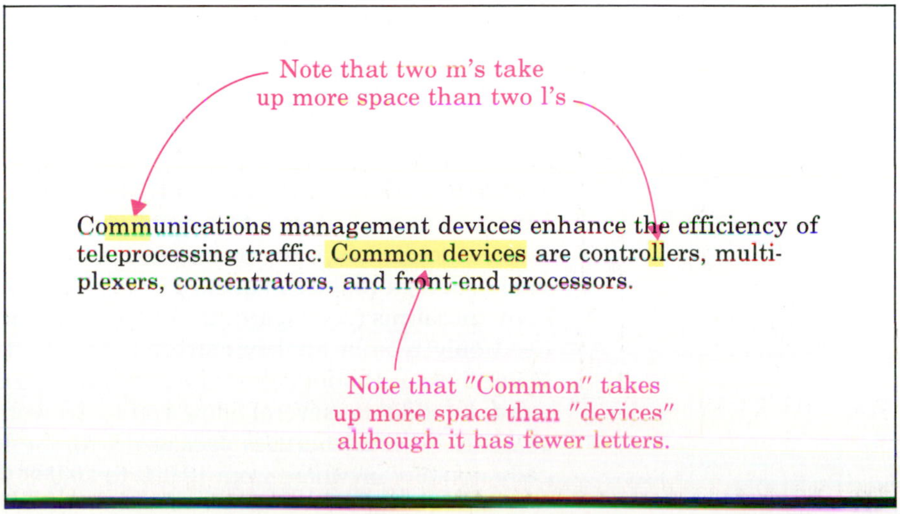

FIGURE 12-10

Proportionally spaced characters with microspacing. With proportional spacing, more horizontal space on a line is allotted to some characters than to others. Microspacing inserts fractional spaces between characters to make the line appear more attactive to the eye.

Note that two m's take up more space than two l's

Communications management devices enhance the efficiency of teleprocessing traffic. Common devices are controllers, multiplexers, concentrators, and front-end processors.

Note that "Common" takes up more space than "devices" although it has fewer letters.

FIGURE 12-11

Using a spelling checker. Many spelling checkers stop to highlight words they don't recognize when scanning a document in the batch mode. Here the checker can't find "glossery" in its dictionary and, below the dotted line, offers the operator some replacement suggestions. Many spelling checkers automatically make a replacement when the operator depresses the assigned key—the *A* key, in this example.

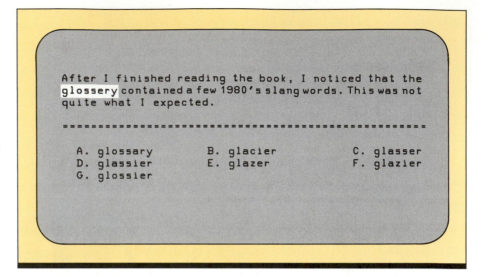

Spelling Checker. Many word processing packages include a routine that reads through a document and searches for misspelled words. This routine and its accompanying word dictionary are collectively known as a **spelling checker.** If a spelling-check feature does not come with your word processor, one may be available as a supplemental package from an independent vendor.

The capabilities of spelling checkers can vary dramatically. Some spelling checkers have dictionaries that contain around 10,000 words, while others have 100,000 or more. A particularly important feature is the ability to place additional words into a dictionary. A writer of a computer text or medical article, for example, uses very specialized terms, most of which aren't in the dictionaries of standard spelling checkers.

Many spelling checkers have both a batch and a realtime checking feature. The *batch feature,* which virtually all spelling checkers have, enables you to scan an entire document for misspelled words. The *realtime feature,* which is usually practical only if you have a hard disk, assists you as you type by beeping whenever you key in a word it doesn't recognize.

Spelling checkers often also come with a *word-count feature* and a feature that displays onscreen suggestions on how to properly spell a word it doesn't recognize (see Figure 12-11).

Thesaurus Feature. A **thesaurus feature** allows you to check words for possible synonyms. To use a thesaurus, you first flag a word you wish to replace in your document. If the thesaurus feature recognizes the word, it will provide onscreen replacement suggestions in a form resembling that of a hardcopy thesaurus (see Figure 12-12). Often, when you see a word you like, you need only type in the key corresponding to it to perform the replacement. Many thesaurus routines also automatically reformat text after replacing a word. In addition, several allow you to do word searches within other word searches. The thesauruses packaged with the leading word processors typically contain anywhere from 10,000 to 20,000 words.

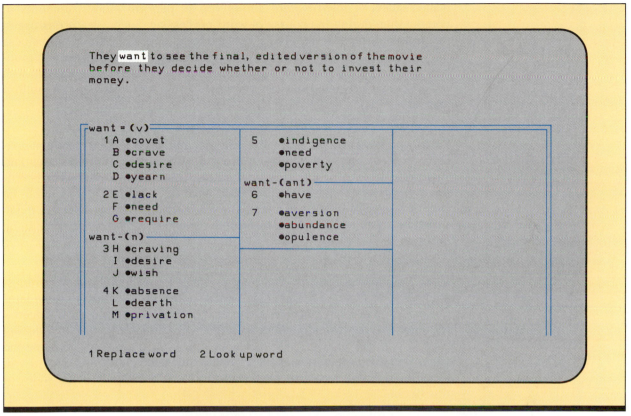

They want to see the final, edited version of the movie
before they decide whether or not to invest their
money.

```
┌want = (v)──────────────────────────────────────┐
│   1 A •covet        5    •indigence             │
│     B •crave             •need                  │
│     C •desire            •poverty               │
│     D •yearn     ┌want-(ant)─────────            │
│              │   6    •have                     │
│   2 E •lack      │                              │
│     F •need      │   7    •aversion             │
│     G •require   │        •abundance            │
│want-(n)──────────┘        •opulence             │
│   3 H •craving                                  │
│     I •desire                                   │
│     J •wish                                     │
│                                                 │
│   4 K •absence                                  │
│     L •dearth                                   │
│     M •privation                                │
└─────────────────────────────────────────────────┘

1 Replace word     2 Look up word
```

FIGURE 12-12

Using a thesaurus. In many word processors, you point to a word to be "looked up" by positioning the cursor on it and then invoke the thesaurus feature. Here the operator has pointed to *want,* and the replacement suggestions in the middle of the screen have appeared. Many thesaurus routines automatically make a replacement when you depress the key that corresponds to it. Here, words preceded by dots are themselves thesaurus entries; by choosing option 2 on the last screen line, you can perform a word search within a word search.

Mailing List/Mail Merge Programs. A **mailing list program** is used to generate mailing labels. With such a program, you can usually sort records on a specific field (such as zip codes) or extract records having special characteristics (such as all alumni from the class of 1975 living in San Francisco) prior to processing the labels. Mailing list programs are specialized versions of *file managers,* which we will discuss in Chapter 14.

A **mail merge program** is specifically designed to produce form letters. This type of program is so named because it usually prints such letters in volume by merging a file containing a list of names and addresses with a file containing a form letter.

Although many word processors themselves will let you do modest amounts of mailing list or form letter preparation, you may wish to acquire supplemental packages for these tasks if you need to process a sizable number of routine letters on a frequent basis.

Math Feature. A *math feature* allows you to perform modest amounts of computation during the course of word processing. Such a feature is useful for preparing expense reports, simple budgets, and other types of business documents that require little more than summing columns or rows of numbers. If you need to do more sophisticated forms of math, you might do well to acquire an integrated software package (with a spreadsheeting capability) instead.

Redlining. When editing the hard-copy documents of others, many people use a colored pen—often red—to cross out certain words or phrases and substitute others. This process is called **redlining.** After a document is redlined, the original author can see both what he or she originally wrote as well as the changes made by the editor. The redlining feature found in many word processors provides the electronic equivalent of the manual redlining process.

Index and Table-of-Contents Preparation. Many top-of-the-line word processors allow you to individually "tag" words or phrases so that you can later prepare an index or a table of contents. For instance, if you have tagged a few hundred words in a book for an index, you can later invoke an *indexing routine* that will arrange these words in alphabetical order and provide the pages on which the words appeared. Most indexing routines also allow you to create index subheadings similar to the ones that appear in the index of this book.

Orphan and Widow Elimination. Orphans and widows are aesthetically undesirable line breaks (see Figure 12-13). In the world of document processing, the first line of a paragraph is called an *orphan* when it is separated from the rest of the paragraph by a page or column break. The last line of a paragraph is called a *widow* when it is separated from the rest of the paragraph by being forced onto a new page or column. Many word processing packages allow you to eliminate widows and orphans by establishing a minimum number of lines that can be separated by a page or column break.

Sorting. A useful word processing feature is *sorting,* say, arranging a list of names in alphabetical order or arranging addresses by zip code for mailing purposes. As handy as this feature may seem, however, it often is either unavailable or relatively cumbersome to use in many word processors.

Embedded Typesetting Codes. Sometimes word-processed text is sent directly to a compositor for typesetting. When this is done, considerable savings can result if *typesetting codes,* such as codes for special fonts or complex printing effects, are embedded into the document before it is sent to the typesetter. Many of the more powerful word processing packages targeted for commercial environments offer this feature.

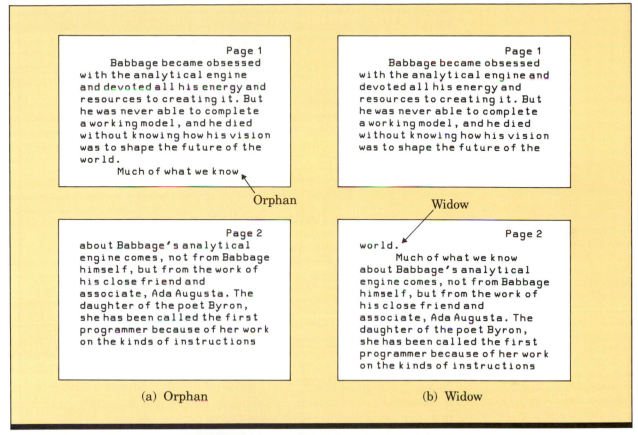

FIGURE 12-13

Orphans and widows. Orphans and widows are aesthetically undesirable line breaks that many word processors can eliminate.

Presentation Graphics. Many business documents include presentation graphics such as bar charts, pie charts, or line charts. Consequently, many word processors provide *interfacing* with spreadsheet and presentation graphics packages to enable simple graphs to be imported into a word-processed document. An alternative to using such an interface is to obtain an integrated software package that provides spreadsheeting and presentation graphics capabilities along with word processing.

Style Sheets. A feature that several word processors have begun to incorporate—and that is standard fare in desktop publishing packages—is the style sheet. A **style sheet** is a collection of font and formatting specifications that is saved as a file and later used to prepare documents in a particular way. So, for instance, if your letters to clients are to conform to a certain letterhead style, use a specific font and point size, and contain a personalized heading or footing on every page beyond the first one, you can declare all of these specifications in a style sheet that you invoke when preparing such letters. Reports, on the other hand, would likely use a different style sheet.

DESKTOP PUBLISHING

The late 1970s introduced desktop computing, an entire computer system capable of fitting on a desktop. Thanks to other big improvements on software and hardware fronts, we now have **desktop publishing**—a microcomputer-based publishing system that fits on a desktop. Desktop publishing systems let you combine on a page elements such as text (in a variety of fonts), art, and photos, thus creating attractive-looking documents that look like they came off a printer's press.

Components of a Desktop Publishing System

The desktop publishing systems currently available differ widely, and most of them are evolving rapidly. There are both low-end desktop publishing systems, which are targeted to meeting simple needs, and high-end ones.

Low-End Systems. At the low end of the desktop publishing market are inexpensive software packages that will work in concert with many ordinary impact dot-matrix printers and a 16-bit computer with at least 256 KB of main memory. These packages are adequate for users who want to prepare documents such as newsletters, restaurant menus, and announcements; that is, documents that need to be output in a style that is slightly more lively than that possible with many simple word processors.

Low-end packages often have their own built-in word processors and can accept files created from a number of leading word processing packages. Word-processed text is enhanced with various prestored fonts (available in different point sizes), prestored art images (called **clip art**), and lines and boxes that you can create to suit your needs. Composing newsletterlike pages with multicolumn formats and banners also is usually possible.

Today, the high end of the word processing market is rapidly evolving toward low-end desktop publishing applications. WordPerfect Corporation's WordPerfect (see Figure 12-14) and Microsoft's Word are just two examples of word processors that are moving in this direction.

High-End Systems. By buying at the high end of the desktop publishing market, you gain additional flexibility and the ability to produce documents that are more attractive and complex. Advantages include a wider selection of fonts and scaling features, the ability to integrate high-quality photographic images and complex art, a greater number of element-manipulation features for making up pages, the ability to handle color, and compatibility with a larger number of packages that complement various stages of the publication process. The finished page can be produced at a very high resolution, either on a laser printer or a professional typesetting system (see Figure 12-15).

Many high-end desktop publishing systems include the following:

FIGURE 12-14

The marriage of word processing and desktop publishing. Features such as graphics, multiple fonts, scaling options, imported art elements, and text wrapped around display type or art are bringing many word processing packages closer to the desktop publishing world. The two-page spread shown here has been scaled onscreen so that the operator can get a general feel for layout. For editing purposes, a document would be scaled to a larger and highly readable point size.

☐ *High-End Microcomputer System* High-quality desktop publishing requires (1) a microprocessor that packs plenty of power, (2) a respectable amount of RAM, and (3) a hard disk with plenty of storage. Manipulation of graphical fonts, photos, and clip art can be computationally intensive. A mere two-page newsletter, for instance, can require 200 KB of storage and a half-page scanned image another 500 KB. Such work requires a system unit like those based on the Intel 80286, 80386, or 80486, or the Motorola 68020, 68030, or 68040 processors. The system should have at least 1–4 MB of RAM and 20–40 MB of hard-disk storage.

☐ *Laser Printer* Most laser printers for microcomputer-based desktop publishing applications are available in the $2,000 to $10,000 range. These devices have their own built-in microprocessors, RAM, and ROM. Many such laser printers output at a resolution of either 300 dpi (dots per vertical and horizontal inch, or 90,000 dots to the inch) or 600 dpi. If you require higher resolution than this, you'll need software that will produce

Getting Familiar with Typography

A Look at Some of the Terms of the Typographer's Trade

At one time, most computer buffs cared little about the somewhat arcane terminology used in the publishing industry. Then, quite suddenly, came desktop publishing. Now, if you are going to wade through a trade book or a reference manual to understand how a particular desktop publishing package works, you'd better know your serifs from your ascenders.

Many professional graphic designers devote years to the study of typography. Fortunately for the part-time desktop publisher, such an immersion into the publishing field is hardly necessary. One can get by just by learning a few terms, most of which apply to type. Following is a miniglossary of some of the most useful terms to know:

Ascender The portion of a lowercase character that falls above the x-height (see figure).

Baseline The imaginary line formed by connecting the bottommost parts of characters on a line, ignoring descenders (see figure).

Body-copy typeface The typeface used for the main text, or "body," of a document. Body-copy typefaces are chosen to guide the eye along comfortably on a page and are usually serif.

Descender The portion of a lowercase character that falls below the baseline (see figure).

Display typeface The typeface used in banners, headings, or decorative text on a page. Display typefaces usu-ally are greater than 12 points.

Folio A page number.

Font Traditionally, a term that refers to the complete set of characters in a particular typeface and point size, for instance, 12-point Helvetica. In practice today, many people use the terms *font* and *typeface* interchangeably.

Halftoning The process of converting a continuous-tone photographic image into a series of dots.

Kerning Adjusting the spacing between certain character combinations to create a more visually consistent image. For instance, the two letters *AW* naturally appear to have more space between them than the two letters *MN*, and a kerning feature can be applied to reduce the disparity.

Phototypesetting The process of transferring a page image to film or photosensitive paper so that it can

files that professional typesetting equipment (which work at 1,200 dpi or more) can read.

☐ *Fonts* A variety of fonts for desktop publishing applications are available. Fonts are of two types: bit-mapped and outline. *Bit-mapped fonts* are described by a fixed configuration of dots. While they are the least expensive type of font, you cannot scale them to different point sizes. *Outline fonts* consist of mathematical curves that describe how characters are shaped. They are more expensive than bit-mapped fonts, but you can scale them to virtually any point size you want.

Some fonts are available in ROM chips that can be packaged into the laser printer you buy. You can acquire additional fonts in disk form and download them into the laser printer's RAM. Painting/drawing packages

be printed out by a very-high-resolution output device called a *phototypesetting machine* (such as a Linotronic 300).

Pica A unit of type measure commonly used to determine the depth of a set of lines, a paragraph, a photo, or a piece of art on a page. There are six picas to an inch.

Point The smallest unit of type measure, commonly used when referring to the size of type on a page. There are 12 points to a pica and 72 points to an inch (see figure).

Roman Nonslanted type; often contrasted with *italic* type.

Rule A line on a page; for instance, the accompanying figure is ruled in that it is enclosed in a box formed by lines.

Sans serif A typeface without serifs, such as Helvetica.

Screen A measure, usually expressed as a percentage, of grey-scale or color intensity.

For instance, a 70 percent black screen is dark grey, and a 20 percent black screen is light grey; a 90 percent yellow screen translates into a bright yellow, and a 10 percent yellow screen into a pale yellow. All of the artwork in this text is colored with screens, which consist of tightly or loosely packed dots. (You can see the dots under a magnifying glass.)

Script A typeface that looks like handwriting or calligraphy.

Serif Short lines used to fin-ish off the main strokes of a character to give it a distinctive styling (see figure).

Style A variation within a typeface. For instance, the image in photo 5 of Window 5 is done in four styles of the Times typeface—roman, bold, italic, and bold italic.

Vertical justification The ability to insert fractional lines within a page so that the top and bottom margins of all pages are even.

X-height The height of the lowercase letter *x* in a particular typeface (see figure).

enable you to create your own fonts. This is an especially useful feature if you are developing a personalized corporate logo.

☐ *Page-Makeup Software* The programs that allow you to combine a variety of text, photo, and art elements into a finished page are called **page-makeup software.** Often the software relies on a specific *page description language (PDL)* to facilitate this. Many PDLs, such as Adobe's Post-Script (which has become the de facto PDL standard for the Apple Macintosh), are compatible with professional typesetting systems. The page-makeup software you use must be compatible with the software used to develop text or illustration files. Among the most familiar high-end page-makeup packages are PageMaker and Ventura Publisher. Because page makeup is the central function in desktop publishing, page-makeup programs are often loosely referred to as "desktop publishing packages."

FIGURE 12-15

High-end desktop publishing. The gazelle in the image shown here was scanned from a copyright-free book and modified with art software, which was also used to create the logo on the wine label. The map was taken from a clip art library and cropped, again with the art software. Both the map and label were then read into a page layout program, where they were combined with text, fonts, lines, and boxes to produce the finished page image.

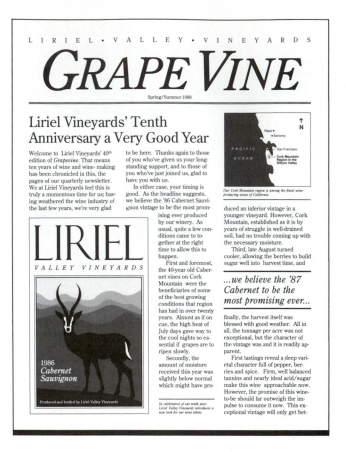

□ *Painting/Drawing Software and Hardware* Many painting/drawing software packages are available today. These packages—which include such products as Illustrator, Freehand, PaintBox, McDraw, and McPaint —allow you to create your own art images from scratch or to start with someone else's and enhance them. Most of the spectacular art images in the Windows of this text were created with painting/drawing software packages (see especially Windows 3 and 8).

Hardware such as the mouse and digitizing tablet, which work with these software packages, are covered in Chapter 6. If you want color, you'll need both software that will produce color separations and an output device that will allow color.

□ *Graphics-Oriented Monitor* Most monitors used with microcomputer systems contain a relatively small (13-inch) screen that can display about a third of a page at a time. On such screens, the resolution usually is adequate for standard text and some simple graphics. For heavy desktop publishing applications, however, it generally is preferable to have a much higher screen resolution (to fine-tune detailed graphics) and to see either a full-page or a two-page layout on the screen at one time (see Figure 12-16). Monitors designed for these purposes often have screens up to 50 percent larger than the typical microcomputer display screen. A

FIGURE 12-16

Monitors. Grey-scale monitors, which often are capable of fitting a full single page or a two-page spread onto a screen in a readable point size, are a popular choice with professional desktop publishers.

number of them use analog guns and can output up to 256 shades on a grey scale that begins at pure white and ends at pure black.

Color monitors are also available for desktop publishing applications, but they are more expensive than either monochrome or grey-scale monitors. An additional problem that color-monitor users face is that the colors on the display screen will not exactly match the colors output in hard-copy form.

☐ *Image Scanner* An image scanner (see Figure 6-30 on page 196) allows you to scan photographs, drawings, or text and digitize them directly into computer memory. Later you can edit the image with painting/drawing software and hardware. Some image scanners also use *optical character recognition (OCR)* software, which enables them to recognize certain characters rather than just digitizing them. Such a feature allows you to later edit any text you enter with the scanner.

Window 5 provides a glimpse of some of the capabilities of today's high-end desktop publishing systems, in which the finished output is produced in hard-copy form on a laser printer or professional printer's press. Tomorrow's systems will likely place a greater emphasis on dissemination of published information in screen, or soft-copy, form (see the Tomorrow box).

SUMMARY AND KEY TERMS

Word processing and desktop publishing are technologies that deal with the manipulation of words.

Word processing refers to using computer technology to create, manipulate, and print text materials such as letters, legal contracts, manuscripts, and other documents.

High-Definition Television

Its Reach Will Include Screen Publishing—and Maybe Even Altering the Balance of World Power

On the surface, it looks like just a technology that provides a better television set. But on finer inspection, it is a concept so revolutionary that it may completely restructure many computer-related industries—and even the balance of power in the world. It's known as *high-definition television (HDTV)*.

For almost half a century, the television industry has depended on analog transmission and analog TV sets. HDTV, which instead uses digital technology, promises far greater picture clarity (see photos), screens that measure from 30 to 40 inches to 3 to 5 feet, and compact-disk-quality sound. Furthermore, like conventional computers,

HDTV sets contain microprocessors and memories.

HDTV will go well beyond the role today's ordinary TV plays. Because HDTV is a digital product, it can be more closely integrated with the spate of applications now available to digital computer systems. For the publishing industry, this means the possibility of screen publishing. Many experts say that at some future point, it will be possible to pick up a remote-control, notepad-sized, flat-screen television set and read high-definition screen pages similarly to the way you read conventional book pages. Because the image is digitized, you can zoom the type up to a larger point size if your eyesight is poor. And you can access books or magazines without having to search around the house for them.

In such a futuristic world,

there will be no distinction between the online database services you see today, such as CompuServe and Nexis, and video data generated by the entire entertainment industry. You can use the flat HDTV screen to access television programs, movies, and live concerts, as well as virtually any other type of information available in digital form—books, magazines, catalogs, whatever. Screen publishing eventually will be both convenient for the consumer and the most cost-effective way to disseminate published material.

HDTV will also affect other areas of the publishing industry. Already a Japanese company has found a way to convert HDTV images onto printing plates. And when HDTV is perfected, "desktop movie production" and "desktop MTV" may become available to anyone with the proper equipment and the desire to create.

Because television is such

There are several ways to perform word processing. First, you can do it on either a dedicated word processing system or a general-purpose computer system. Second, you can work with either a **WYSIWYG** (What-You-See-Is-What-You-Get) word processor or one that depends heavily on embedded formatting codes to tell you what you will subsequently see in print. Third, you can use either a general-purpose or a special-purpose word processing software package. Fourth, you can work with a dedicated word processing package or an integrated software package.

Using a word processor—or, for that matter, any type of productivity software package—requires learning several general operations. These opera-

an integral part of everyday life, many experts predict that HDTV will become the driving force behind the semiconductor industry, a position computer systems now hold. If that happens, the balance of power in the semiconductor industry will likely shift from the United States to Japan and Europe, which are now much further ahead in HDTV research. Many experts feel that the country leading the pack in the race to market HDTV products will gain a major share of world economic power.

While the stakes in the race to deliver HDTV are high, there are still many practical problems to be worked out.

First, HDTV requires that more data be transmitted to receiver units; today's broadcasting equipment and standards are simply inadequate. Currently two possibilities for delivering this added transmission punch to the home are fiber optic cable and di-rect broadcast satellite (DBS). While fiber optic cable already connects large phone arteries between cities, many say that DBS, which will consist of small satellite dishes on the tops of homes and businesses linked directly to satellite, will be a reality before the mid-1990s.

Second, HDTV will not be cheap. In fact, you may pay as much as $3,000 for a low-end set when HDTV first becomes available and before mass ac-ceptance begins to drive the price down.

The barriers notwithstanding, with television a virtual fixture in the average home and the potential for integration with other consumer products so great, most observers say that HDTV is a technology that just can't miss. And when it comes, say some experts, expect an applications revolution the likes of what the personal computer brought in the 1980s.

See the difference. Resolution from conventional TV (left) compared with that from HDTV (right).

tions include *accessing* the package from the operating system, informing the package that you either want to *create* a new file or *retrieve* an old one, commanding the package to *save* a file, commanding the package to *print* a file, commanding the package to *delete* a file, indicating to the package that you want to *quit* working on your current file and do something on another file, and *terminating* the package and getting back to the operating system.

Learning to use a word processor at a minimal level involves mastering a number of elementary entering and editing operations as well as several print-formatting commands. Entering and editing operations include moving the cursor, scrolling, line return, inserting and deleting, moving and copying, and searching and replacing. Among the print-formatting operations one must learn are adjusting line spacing, indenting, reformatting, centering, tabbing, pagination, setting up headers and footers, **font** and **point size** selection, multiple-column formatting, and footnoting.

Sophisticated users of word processing packages often require software and hardware that provide **proportional spacing** and **microspacing** to produce typeset-quality output. In addition, advanced users often utilize a **spelling checker**, a **thesaurus feature, mailing list programs, mail merge programs,** a math feature, **redlining** capability, an index and table-of-contents preparation feature, orphan and widow elimination, sorting capabilities, embedded typesetting codes, presentation graphics, and **style sheets.**

Desktop publishing is the term used to describe microcomputer-based publishing systems that can fit on the top of a desk. A desktop publishing system may incorporate on a single page such elements as word-processed text, a variety of fonts in different point sizes, original art pieces and **clip art,** and scanned images (e.g., photographs).

Low-end desktop publishing systems—which are adequate for newsletters, restaurant menus, and announcements—are targeted to relatively simple microcomputer systems. High-end desktop publishing systems—which are capable of producing highly complex and attractive outputs—often include a powerful microcomputer system, a laser printer, a large variety of fonts and painting/drawing options, **page-makeup software,** a graphics-oriented monitor, and an image scanner.

REVIEW EXERCISES

Fill-in Questions

1. Most word processors have a(n) _____ feature that automatically produces a soft carriage return.

2. _____ is a word processing feature that allocates more horizontal space on a line to some characters than to others.

3. A(n) _____ program is used to generate mailing labels.

4. A(n) _____ word processing system is a computer system exclusively designed for word processing applications.

5. WYSIWYG is an acronym for _____ .

6. The first line of a paragraph is called a(n) _____ when it is separated from the rest of the paragraph by a page or column break.

7. PDL is an acronym for _____ .

8. Prestored art images used in a desktop publishing environment are referred to as _____ .

Matching Questions

Match each term with the description that best fits.

a. copying   **d.** inserting
b. redlining   **e.** scrolling
c. proportional spacing   **f.** moving

_e_   **1.** Moving contiguous lines of text up and down on screen similarly to the way the roll on a player piano is unwound.

_b_   **2.** A feature particularly useful when one person must edit another's written work.

_a_   **3.** An operation that involves replication.

___   **4.** An operation that entails physically relocating text so that it no longer appears in its original location.

_c_   **5.** A word processing feature that gives text a typeset-quality look.

_d_   **6.** An operation you would use on a word processor to quickly change the string MISSIPPI to MISSISSIPPI.

Discussion Questions

1. Identify several ways in which word processing can be implemented on a computer system.
2. What is the difference between monospacing and proportional spacing?
3. What is the difference between a batch and a realtime spelling checker?
4. What are orphans and widows?
5. Identify the components of a high-end desktop publishing system.
6. Why is it getting ever more difficult to distinguish word processing from desktop publishing?

Critical Thinking Questions

1. Spelling checkers are said to be of greatest utility to people who can spell reasonably well. Why do you think this is so?
2. Comment on this statement: "Now that desktop publishing is available, the professional typesetting and print shop is doomed."
3. Word processing and desktop publishing present undeniable benefits to organizations that can effectively utilize them. Can you think of any problems that these technologies pose to the average organization?
4. Some people think that high-definition TV (see the Tomorrow box) will have an impact on the world similar to that of the microcomputer. What do you think accounts for such a rave review?

Desktop Publishing

The State of the Art

What you can publish on a desktop today is, in a word, amazing. In less than a decade, the desktop publishing industry has evolved from a dream to a highly sophisticated reality—one characterized by powerful art and illustration systems, electronic darkrooms, and a spate of fonts and clip art pieces to satisfy almost every need. In this Window, we'll see why desktop publishing systems are exciting to virtually anyone who needs to process documents—from secretaries to publishers themselves.

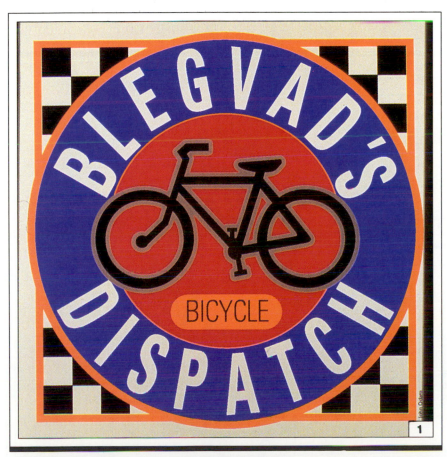

1 Illustration and painting systems enable desktop composition of attractive logos. Even if you don't have a color printer, you can proof the color image on your color monitor, save it in a disk file, and have it output—at a very high resolution—by a compositor who has a sophisticated imaging system compatible with your software.

TYPEFACES

Perhaps the most basic element of the published page is the typeface, or font. Many desktop publishing packages offer a variety of standard typefaces, and often you can buy any others you need separately. Adobe Systems Incorporated, for instance, which provided the samples shown on this page, has a library of over 350 typeface styles available for desktop publishing applications.

2–4 Three widely used typefaces are Courier, Helvetica, and Times. Courier is a monospace font that is useful when a typewritten look is desired. Helvetica is used to achieve a clean, modern feel and also is visually compatible with a wide range of other typefaces, which may need to appear on the same page. Times is useful for a wide variety of text applications.

5 Many typefaces are available in a number of styles, as shown here for Times.

Times Bold Italic — HEALTH

Times Bold — HIGH ANXIETY

Times Roman

Times Italic

BY MICHAEL BAYLAND

Nearly forty years ago W.H. Auden termed our frenetic century "the age of anxiety." And that was before Three Mile Island and AIDS. Small wonder then that when the National Institute of Mental Health recently set out to see which mental problems most plagued Americans, anxiety disorders came in first. Eight percent surveyed in three sample cities reported phobic fears, panic attacks and extreme nervousness severe enough to interfere with normal life. That means over 13 million very anxious citizens–a number some experts even call conservative.

If you're human you know anxiety: tongue-tied embarrassment at the office Christmas party, sweaty palms before you

sign the contract for your co-op, an inner thud when the phone rings in the middle of the night. Unpleasant perhaps, but useful. Anxiety is a mind/body signal wired into our brains to warn us of danger and gear us up to fight or flee. "It's the normal reaction to what we perceive as a threat to well-being," says Michael R. Liebowitz, M.D., director of the Anxiety Disorders Clinic at the New York State Psychiatric Institute. "It has real survival value."

For most people, the anxiety that appears before an event normally recedes once they gain confidence. But for others it does not. The pulse races faster, butterflies flutter more frantically, the voice quavers and the mind goes blank. For these people, who triple check the stove each time they go out, anxiety is a way of life. Dr. Liebowitz compares such anxiety to a burglar alarm that trips every time a door

It's enough to make a Chicken Little out of anyone

SPECIAL EFFECTS

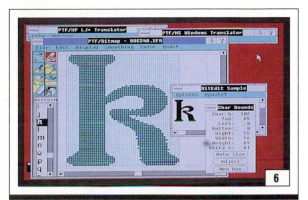

6 Packages such as Z-Soft's Publisher's Type Foundry are useful for custom creation of fonts and logos. An outline editor lets you create character or symbol shapes; a bit-map editor lets you fine-tune each character or symbol dot by dot.

7, 8 Without the availability of large libraries of clip art, which can be quickly modified and incorporated into new images, it would be impossible to get art-intensive newspapers such as *USA Today* out on time.

9 With computers, images can be retouched in ways beyond those available to the traditional photographer. Many people feel it is only a matter of time before the conventional darkroom is completely replaced by an electronic one.

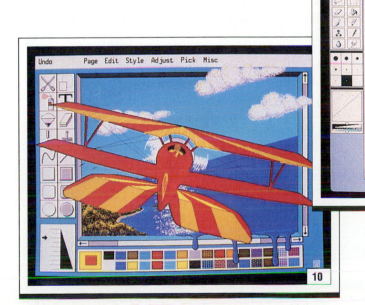

10 Often an art image is created by scanning a preliminary image into memory and then, as suggested here, coloring it to one's liking by selecting colors from a palette.

PAGE CREATION

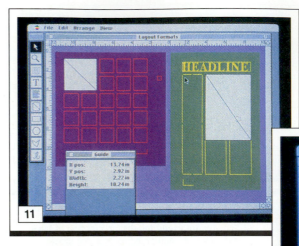

11

11 One of the first steps in creating a page is planning a general layout.

12 Once the layout is created, art and word-processed text must be read into a page-makeup program and sized appropriately. Many desktop publishing packages enable the user to dynamically change fonts and point sizes while developing the page layout onscreen.

12

13 A zooming feature, which "blows up" images, is handy when checking out details on a page.

14 When fine-tuning a page, the user may wish to summon a palette (when available) to do color touch-ups. Because desktop publishing is easier to do with a large number of elements onscreen at the same time, many users prefer 19-inch monitors for such applications.

13

14

THE FINISHED PAGE

15 This page illustrates a wide mixture of fonts and art elements. The bull and bear drawings were developed from previously scanned-in images. Using a special art tool, the designer was able to change the colors and shapes of the animals (note how the bear begins to sprout horns as it is transformed into a bull). When the center illustration was completed, it was transferred to a page-makeup program, where text, the left sidebar, and the page-number diamond were added.

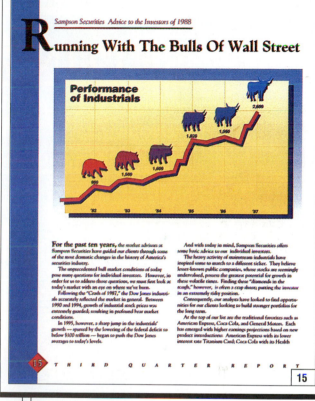

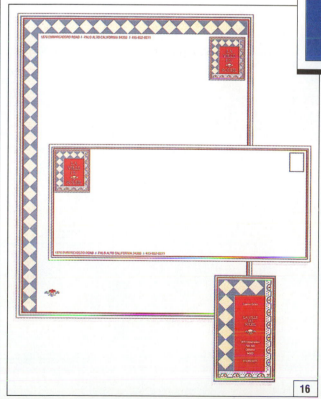

16 Desktop publishing systems are also useful for producing corporate identity packages. The basic logo design used here was first hand-sketched and then scanned into an illustration system, where it was refined. The ornaments were photocopied from copyright-free art, likewise scanned, and then scaled and replicated to fit the required dimensions.

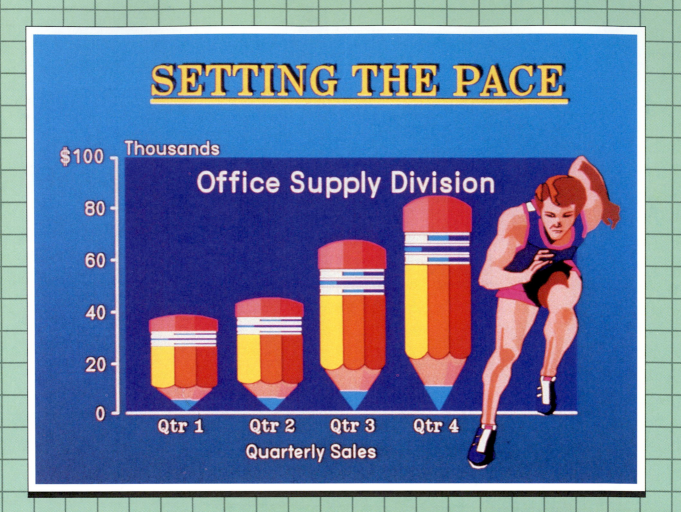

Spreadsheets and Presentation Graphics

Objectives

After completing this chapter,
you will be able to:

1. Describe what spreadsheet
   packages do and how they
   work.

2. Identify the operations you
   must master to effectively
   use spreadsheet software.

3. Explain the similarities
   and differences among
   spreadsheet packages.

4. Describe how presentation
   graphics packages work,
   some of the differences
   among them, and the
   images they let you create.

OVERVIEW

Today, one of the most important software packages any businessperson—from president to secretary—must learn is the *electronic spreadsheet.* Spreadsheet software is to the current generation of end users what the pocket calculator was to previous generations: a convenient means of performing calculations. But while most pocket calculators can compute and display only one result each time you enter new data, electronic spreadsheets can present you with hundreds or even thousands of results each time you enter a single new value or command. What spreadsheets can do and how they work are two of the primary subjects of this chapter.

From spreadsheets we move on to *presentation graphics software,* which is designed to present the results of business computations in a visually oriented, easily understood way. This class of software is among the easiest types of business software to learn and use. Today many spreadsheet packages are equipped with built-in presentation graphics features. Also, many dedicated presentation graphics packages, which enable you to produce higher-quality presentation images than those possible with spreadsheet packages, are commercially available.

SPREADSHEETS

Electronic spreadsheets first came to public notice in the late 1970s when a Harvard Business School student and a programmer friend produced a microcomputer package called *VisiCalc* ("the VISIble CALCulator"). To call it a huge success would be an understatement. VisiCalc shattered sales records for software and, according to many experts, revolutionized microcomputing. Also, it perhaps once and for all put to rest the question "Can a businessperson do anything serious with a microcomputer?" VisiCalc was easy to use and clearly made managers who mastered it more productive.

Today, although VisiCalc is gone from the scene, spreadsheet software for all sizes of computers abounds in the marketplace. Among the leading spreadsheet packages currently available for microcomputers are 1-2-3, Excel, SuperCalc, and Quattro, with 1-2-3 far and away the leader in sales (see Figure 13-1 and Feature 13A). Technically speaking, most of these products are *integrated software packages* in that they supplement spreadsheeting capabilities with one or more other functions.

FIGURE 13-1

Lotus Development Corporation's 1-2-3. 1-2-3 has long been the best-selling spreadsheet package, a position it has held for over half a decade.

How Spreadsheets Work: A Quick Overview

The principle behind electronic spreadsheets is to view the display screen as a *window* looking in on a big grid, called a **worksheet.** The worksheet is similar to the large columnar paper on which accountants frequently work.

Buying a Spreadsheet Package for Your Micro

Will 1-2-3 Remain Users' First Choice?

Since its introduction in 1983, Lotus Development Corporation's 1-2-3 has been one of the most successful microcomputer software products ever concocted. Today it still commands over a 60 percent market share among spreadsheet products, but it is facing stiffer competition than ever before. Among all microcomputer software products, the spreadsheet market may be the most competitive— and one where some of the greatest bargains abound.

With few exceptions, most spreadsheet packages do many of the same types of things. 1-2-3 has set the de facto standard; it has been so popular that competitors are afraid to stray too far from it for fear that consumers will find their products deficient. In fact, some spreadsheets look so much like 1-2-3 that they are barely legal.

Analyzing Needs. The critical parameters that often differentiate spreadsheet products in the marketplace today tend to be cost, use of graphics, speed, modeling capabilities, compatibility with other products, and the number of worksheet dimensions allowed. Also, a number of niche features, such as support for particular plotters and imaging devices, sometimes distinguish products. But when all

is said and done, most spreadsheet users' needs are relatively simple and most of the packages in the market are more than adequate to meet them.

List Products and Alternatives. The accompanying figure lists eight packages that collectively account for most spreadsheet sales. As you would when choosing a word processor, ask questions and read comparative studies if you're generally unfamiliar with the products on the market. Many microcomputer journals periodically contain articles that rate the leading spreadsheet products on important selection criteria.

If presentation graphics ranks among your needs, you will probably want to look at packages with built-in graphics routines. Standalone graphics packages also are available, but they generally are targeted to more sophisticated users. You may also have to consider acquiring a graphics board for your monitor as well as a laser printer. If you require hard-copy color output, consider a plotter.

Examine the Products. Of the various types of productivity software, spreadsheet packages probably have the fewest surprises likely to surface during a demonstration or test drive. This, of course, is because many of them work the same way. Nonetheless, it's always best

to get familiar with the features of the products you're considering. You may also want to reread the comparative studies on the packages prior to the demonstration, to make sure you don't overlook anything.

Product Comparison and Choice. Because many spreadsheet packages have the same "standard" features for manipulating cell values, it's often a certain "feel" or "bells and whistles" that distinguishes one product from another. For example, if you enjoy working with a graphically oriented (display screen) interface, such as the one pioneered by the Apple Macintosh, it may be hard to find a package that beats Microsoft Excel. The prices of most spreadsheet products fall into the $100-to-$500 range, with the high end of the market occupied by products such as 1-2-3, SuperCalc, and Excel, and the low end by "clones" that have the look and feel of 1-2-3.

☑ 1-2-3
☑ Excel
☑ Quattro
☑ SuperCalc
☑ Smart Spreadsheet
☑ Lucid 3-D
☑ Multiplan
☑ VP-Planner

Market leaders. 1-2-3 still dominates, but some say Excel is more state-of-the-art.

FIGURE 13-2

An electronic spreadsheet package at work. It's their *recalculation feature*—the ability to quickly rework thousands of tedious calculations—that makes spreadsheet packages so valuable to users.

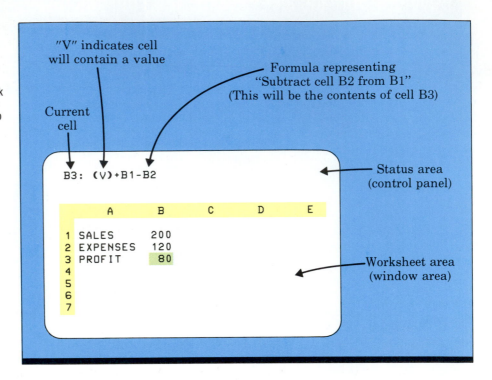

"V" indicates cell will contain a value

Formula representing "Subtract cell B2 from B1" (This will be the contents of cell B3)

Current cell

B3: (V)+B1-B2

Status area (control panel)

	A	B	C	D	E
1	SALES	200			
2	EXPENSES	120			
3	PROFIT	80			
4					
5					
6					
7					

Worksheet area (window area)

It may consist of, say, 256 rows and 64 columns. Each of the 16,384 (256 × 64) *cells* formed at the intersection of a row and column may contain a word, number, or formula. Of course, the display screen is too small to permit viewing more than a few rows and columns at any given time. However, users can press keys on the keyboard (usually the arrow keys) that will move the worksheet around, letting them view other portions of it through the window. The discussion that immediately follows concerns primarily two-dimensional spreadsheet applications. Later in the section, we'll look at the multidimensional capabilities rapidly being infused into most major spreadsheet packages.

The use of an electronic spreadsheet is illustrated in Figure 13-2. In this example, we are computing a business income statement, where expenses are 60 percent of sales and profit is the difference between sales and expenses. The *status area,* or *control panel,* is the portion of the screen where users perform tasks such as placing text or numbers into the worksheet cells. In most commercial spreadsheet packages, columns are identified by letters and rows by numbers and each cell by a letter-and-number pair. Furthermore, a *label* (L) is an entry that cannot be manipulated mathematically, while a *value* (V) is an entry that can. In the figure, we have entered the following six commands into the status area:

1. A1 (L) SALES   4. B1 (V) 200
2. A2 (L) EXPENSES   5. B2 (V) .6*B1
3. A3 (L) PROFIT   6. B3 (V) +B1-B2

As we issue each command in the status area, that command is processed and the results are automatically transferred to the worksheet in the *worksheet area* (or *window area*). In commands 1 through 4, a direct transfer occurs. In commands 5 and 6, the computer first makes the computation indicated by the formulas and then transfers the result to the corresponding worksheet cells.

Electronic spreadsheet packages are particularly useful for "what-if" types of queries. For example, suppose we wish to know what profit will result in Figure 13-2 if sales are changed to $5,000. If we simply enter the command

$$B1 \quad (V) \quad 5000$$

the spreadsheet package automatically reworks all the figures according to the prestored formulas. Thus, the computer responds

```
SALES       5000
EXPENSES    3000
PROFIT      2000
```

Electronic spreadsheets can perform in seconds recalculations that would require several hours to do manually or by writing a program in a high-level language. In fact, it's this **recalculation feature** that makes spreadsheets so popular, and it is probably the single most important thing you should know about them. In the future, it is likely that most of the leading spreadsheet packages will do far more than just make recalculations for you—they will also be able to tell you *why* something happened as a result of the recalculations (see the Tomorrow box).

A particularly attractive aspect of spreadsheet packages is that you can learn to prepare budgets and financial schedules with them after only a few hours of training.

Learning to Use a Spreadsheet: The Basics

Now that you've gotten a quick idea of how spreadsheet packages work, let's look more closely at a few important features common to most of them.

General Operations. As mentioned in Chapter 12, computer users must learn several general operations in order to use virtually any productivity software package. These operations—which in the case of spreadsheet packages include tasks such as accessing the spreadsheet from the operating system, saving worksheets, retrieving worksheets, and the like—were highlighted in Figure 12-4 (page 379). You should carefully note how each of these commands are invoked with the spreadsheet package you plan to use.

Physical Makeup. Spreadsheet products are strikingly alike in their physical makeup, particularly in screen layout, pointing mechanisms, and procedures for filling in cells.

T O M O R R O W

"Why Analysis"

The Next Major Battlefield in the Spreadsheet Wars?

One of the things people like so much about spreadsheets is their ability to perform "what-if analysis." But by the turn of the century, many people will want their spreadsheet packages to perform some type of "why analysis" as well.

What-if analysis, which involves using a recalculation feature, is really what makes today's spreadsheet a spreadsheet. Without it, you'd be just as well off with a pocket calculator. What-if analysis enables the user to look at many sets of data that bear on a decision, to ultimately improve the quality of that decision.

There are a number of ways to perform what-if anal-

ysis in practice. For instance, a teacher using a system that awards an A to students with grades above 90 and a B to students with grades between 80 and 89 can recalculate grades by asking a spreadsheet, in essence, "What if an A started at 88 and a B started at 75?" Or an executive using a spreadsheet package to look at the profitability of a new product might have the spreadsheet recalculate the worksheet by essentially asking it, "What would happen to our 'bottom line' if we raised prices by 5 percent?"

Over the years, spreadsheet vendors have tried to enhance this basic recalculation feature by differentiating their products from competitors in various ways. Today two of the major competitive

battlegrounds are multidimensionality and graphics interfaces. But tomorrow, a major hook in getting consumers into one's corner may well be "why analysis"—the ability to ask the computer why something happened and get a suitable explanation.

"Why analysis" is based on a concept known as *expert systems.* An expert system is a computer software system that is capable of providing the type of advice that normally would be attributable to a human expert. In a spreadsheet environment, the user would pose a question to the spreadsheet in a natural language—say, English or Spanish. The spreadsheet would look for key words in the sentence and reconstruct the question in a form it would understand. Then it would analyze the current worksheet or past worksheets and give the user an onscreen

□ **Screen Layout** As Figure 13-2 shows, a spreadsheet display consists of two major sections: a **worksheet area,** or **window area,** and a **status area,** or **control panel.**

Many worksheet areas permit thousands of rows and hundreds of columns. Each **cell** is identified by its column and row; for example, cell K25 is found at the intersection of column K and row 25. The arrow keys on the keyboard let you scroll the window to other parts of the worksheet to view them or to enter new data (see Figure 13-3).

The status area generally is used to display the coordinates and contents of the cell on which you are currently working, called the **current cell,** or **active cell.** Also usually displayed is a menu of useful worksheet commands—for instance, commands to *edit* the worksheet, to *copy* con-

explanation in the user's natural language.

With "why analysis," for instance, an executive disturbed by a set of escalating expense figures on a worksheet could ask:

WHY ARE ACTUAL OPERATING EXPENSES GREATER THAN PLANNED OPERATING EXPENSES?

Then the package may provide a useful graphic and explanation (see photo):

CORP TOTAL OPERATING EXPENSES WENT UP BECAUSE CORP EQUIPMENT REPAIR, CORP SALARIES AND WAGES, AND CORP EMPLOYEE BENEFITS INCREASED

This type of feature may sound extremely futuristic,

but it is already available to a certain extent on some modeling packages, such as Execucom's microcomputer-based IFPS/Plus. *Modeling packages* perform many of the same types of functions as spreadsheets, but they use a different user interface and they are better suited to peo-

ple such as financial analysts and operations research personnel—who need to build sophisticated models. But with modeling packages now offering such capabilities, one has to believe that the spreadsheet packages—which enjoy a larger market share—can't be far behind.

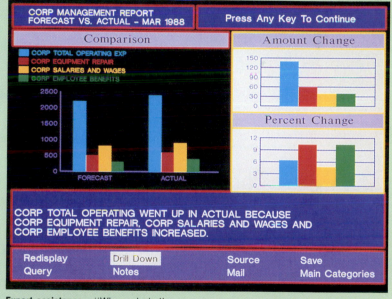

Expert assistance. "Why analysis."

tents in worksheet cells, and to *print* the worksheet. The specific commands used vary among spreadsheet packages.

☐ *Pointing Mechanisms* Most spreadsheet packages provide two pointing mechanisms: a cursor and a cell pointer, or highlight. The **cursor** is associated with the status area; it points to the place in that area where the next character typed in will appear. The **cell pointer,** or **highlight,** is associated with the worksheet area; it points to the current cell.

Both the cursor and cell pointer are labeled in Figure 13-3. Depressing any of the arrow keys, which changes the current cell, changes the display in the status area. Note in the figure that when the right-arrow key is depressed, the current cell in the status area changes from D4 to E4, and, of course, the cell pointer highlights cell E4 (instead of D4) in the

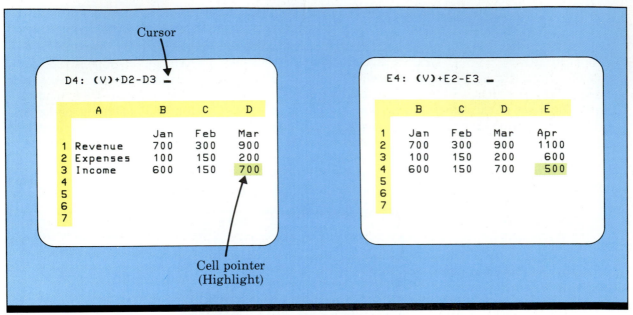

Cursor

D4: (V)+D2-D3 ▃

	A	B	C	D
		Jan	Feb	Mar
1	Revenue	700	300	900
2	Expenses	100	150	200
3	Income	600	150	700
4				
5				
6				
7				

Cell pointer
(Highlight)

E4: (V)+E2-E3 ▃

	B	C	D	E
1	Jan	Feb	Mar	Apr
2	700	300	900	1100
3	100	150	200	600
4	600	150	700	500
5				
6				
7				

FIGURE 13-3

Scrolling the worksheet to see other parts of it. In this figure, the right-arrow key has been depressed once, producing the screen at the right from the screen at the left.

worksheet area. Many people prefer using a mouse, rather than the keyboard, to move around the worksheet.

☐ *Cell-filling Procedures* In most spreadsheet products, a cell can contain either a label or a value. A **label** is an entry that cannot be manipulated mathematically; a **value** is an entry that can. Some spreadsheets automatically assume that an entry that starts with a letter is a label unless it is preceded by the $+$, $-$, or @ characters.

A value is generally one of three types: a *numeric constant* (for example, 200), a *formula* (such as $+B1-B2$, which tells the computer that the value in the current cell is computed as the value in cell B1 minus the value in cell B2), or a *function* (for example, @SUM(B1 . . B3), which tells the package that the value in the current cell is computed as a function—in this case, the sum—of the values in cells B1, B2, and B3). Feature 13B more fully describes the use of functions.

As you type in a label or value for a cell, the status area displays the keystrokes. If you make a mistake, you can send the cursor back to the point of error and type over your mistake. When you are satisfied with what you've typed in, you depress the Enter key, which will automatically transfer the appropriate status-area contents into the current worksheet cell. Then you move on to the next cell with one of the arrow keys and do the same thing.

An increasing number of spreadsheet packages are gravitating toward graphical user interfaces that sport pull-down menus and windowing envi-

A Short Guide to Spreadsheet Functions

Using Them Is as Easy as 1-2-3

Among the handiest features of a spreadsheet package are its functions. These prestored formulas allow you to quickly perform any of a wide range of tasks, from something as simple as finding the sum of a list of numbers to such complex tasks as discounting an uneven cash flow stream into an equivalent present or future value.

In many widely used spreadsheet packages, functions are invoked with the @ character. In 1-2-3, for example, the function

```
@SUM(A1..A20)
```

will sum the values in cells A1 through A20. Or, if you want to find out how much a 20-year annuity of $1,000/year that starts next year is worth today at 8 percent interest compounded annually, you can use the function

```
@PV(1000,.08,20)
```

Other spreadsheet packages provide similar forms of these two functions.

Here's a list of some commonly used functions that you'll find in most of the major spreadsheet packages. Following the name of each function is an argument list, which typically specifies a set of parameters or a range of cells. The second column describes the function.

Arithmetic and Statistical Functions

@SUM (range)	Calculates the sum of all values in a range
@MAX (range)	Finds the highest value in a range
@MIN (range)	Finds the lowest value in a range
@COUNT (range)	Counts the number of nonempty cells in a range
@AVG (range)	Calculates the average of values in a range
@STD (range)	Calculates the standard deviation of values in a range
@ABS (cell or expression)	Calculates the absolute value of the argument
@LN (cell or expression)	Calculates the natural logarithm of the argument
@LOG (cell or expression)	Calculates the base-10 logarithm of the argument
@SQRT (cell or expression)	Calculates the square root of the expression

Financial Functions

@PV (period payment, rate, number of payments)	Calculates the present value of an annuity at a specified interest rate
@FV (period payment, rate, number of payments)	Calculates the future value of an annuity at a specified interest rate
@PMT (present value, rate, number of payments)	Calculates an annuity (period payment) equivalent to a given present value at a specified interest rate
@NPV (rate, range)	Calculates the net present value of the cash flows in a range at a specified interest rate

Conditional Functions

@IF (conditional expression, value if true, value if false)	Supplies to a cell a value that depends on whether the conditional expression is true or false
@CHOOSE (pointer value, list of possible values)	Chooses one value in a list of values, based on the pointer value

Date Functions

@TODAY	Calculates today's date (in days since December 31, 1899)*
@DATE (month, day, year)	Calculates the number of days that have elapsed since the date specified in the argument and December 31, 1899*

*December 31, 1899, serves simply as a fixed reference point. In combination, the TODAY and DATE functions can be used to calculate the number of days past due on invoices or the number of days an account has existed.

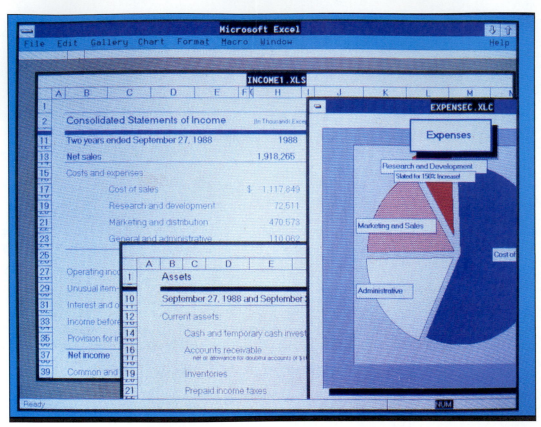

FIGURE 13-4

Graphical interface. The current trend in spreadsheet software is toward graphical interfaces, which provide windows and pull-down menus, allow presentation graphics to appear onscreen simultaneously with spreadsheet data, and provide options for scaling worksheets to different sizes.

ronments (see Figure 13-4). These features were pioneered by Microsoft's Excel for the Apple Macintosh. With the success of Excel and with better graphics now available on all of the leading microcomputers, however, such interfaces are rapidly becoming an industry standard.

Entering and Editing Operations. In addition to enabling users to type in labels and values and have results calculated and displayed immediately, spreadsheet packages have numerous features that facilitate entering and editing data. Following is a sampling of the most important of these features:

☐ *Inserting and Deleting* Virtually all spreadsheet packages allow you to insert a new column or row into a worksheet. Also, you can delete a column or row you no longer need. Generally, inserting or deleting involves moving the cell pointer to the appropriate position on the worksheet (relative to the row or column to be added or deleted) and issuing the proper command. Figure 13-5a illustrates inserting a blank row to make a worksheet more attractive.

☐ *Copying* Most spreadsheets have a command that enables you to copy the contents of one cell (or several cells) into another cell (or several others). The command usually works by prompting you for a "source range" that contains the data to be copied and a "destination range" that will receive the copied data. A valid *range* is a collection of contiguous worksheet cells—for example, F8 . . Z8, B9 . . B28, and B9 . . C10.

If you are copying cells that contain formulas, you generally will be asked to state whether you want the cell references in the formulas to be "relative," "absolute," or "mixed." For example, say you want the value of each cell in column C to equal the corresponding column A entry minus the corresponding column B entry. In other words, you want

$$C1 = A1 - B1$$
$$C2 = A2 - B2$$
$$C3 = A3 - B3$$
$$C4 = A4 - B4$$

Generally you can do this by placing the cell pointer at C1 and typing +A1−B1. Then you can copy this formula into cells C2 . . C4 in the manner described by specifying *relative replication*. Had you asked instead for *absolute replication,* the spreadsheet package would have copied the formula verbatim and all four cells would erroneously contain the expression +A1−B1. Figures 13-5b and 13-5c show relative and absolute replication respectively. Many spreadsheet packages also allow *mixed replication*—a combination of absolute and relative replication—in which a row (column) value can be kept constant while letting a column (row) value vary.

☐ *Moving* "Cutting and pasting" often is just as important in developing worksheets as it is in creating word-processed documents. Almost all spreadsheet packages enable you to move any row or column into another row or column position on the worksheet. For example, suppose you decide to move row 5 into the row 2 position, as in Figure 13-5d. When moving, the software automatically revises such that cell references point to the new worksheet locations. If your spreadsheet package lets you cut and paste larger areas, you may be able to move, say, a contiguous 20-by-40 block of cells from one part of the worksheet to another.

☐ *Editing Values* Since spreadsheets are particularly useful for preparing financial schedules, it follows that many of the worksheet cells will contain values that represent monetary amounts. Most packages provide facilities that enable you to quickly put dollar signs, commas, and decimal points into these values (for example, changing 90000 to $90,000.00). Editing figures with percent signs (%) usually is an equally straightforward process.

☐ *Selecting Column Widths* Most packages allow you to change the width of columns on the spreadsheet. With many packages, you can assign widths to each column individually or you can select only a single, "global" width that applies to all columns. Many spreadsheet packages also have a "spillover feature," which permits particularly long labels to spill over into adjacent columns, provided those cells are empty.

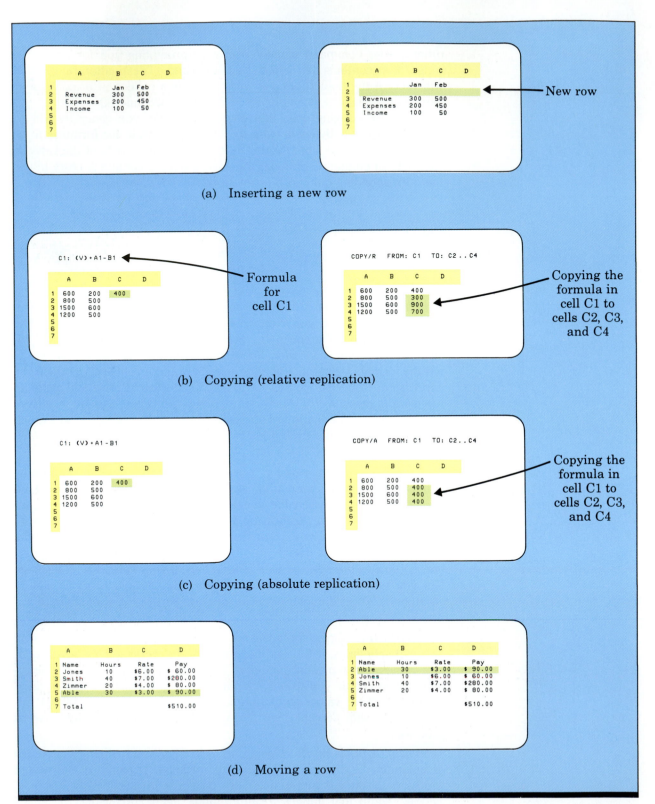

(a) Inserting a new row

(b) Copying (relative replication)

(c) Copying (absolute replication)

(d) Moving a row

FIGURE 13-5
Entering and editing operations.

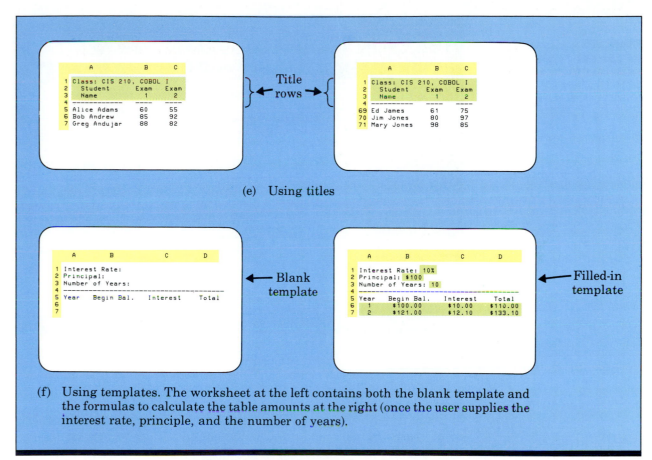

(e)   Using titles

(f)   Using templates. The worksheet at the left contains both the blank template and the formulas to calculate the table amounts at the right (once the user supplies the interest rate, principle, and the number of years).

FIGURE 13-5 *(continued)*

☐ *Establishing Titles* Most spreadsheet packages have a "titles command" that allows you to keep a portion of the worksheet locked in place on the screen when you are scrolling the rest of the worksheet. For example, if we used the titles command to establish the first three rows of Figure 13-5e as titles, we can use the down-arrow key to scroll through data in the worksheet while the titles remain on the screen.

☐ *Using Templates* A **template** is a worksheet in which rows and columns are prelabeled. Also, many cells already contain formulas. The only thing missing are the data. Thus, all of the work involved in setting up the worksheet has already been done, leaving you more time to enter and analyze data. A template is shown in Figure 13-5f.

Learning to Use a Spreadsheet: Advanced Operations

In addition to the basic operations we've just covered, many of the leading spreadsheet packages offer a rich variety of advanced features. In some cases, the spreadsheet package itself contains these features; in other cases,

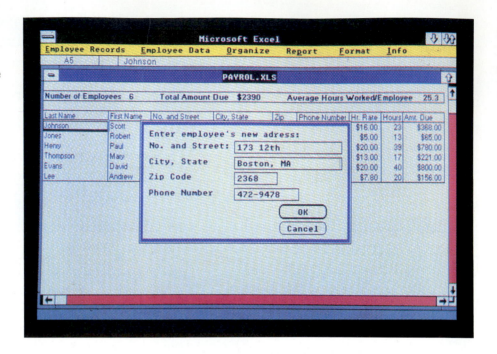

FIGURE 13-6

The spreadsheet's data management facility. With a large worksheet, it's handy to have a feature that enables you to easily create, edit, or extract records.

you have to buy the features from an "aftermarket" vendor that specializes in add-on routines.

Three features advanced spreadsheet users find useful are data management, macro facilities, and presentation graphics. Here we discuss the first two features and defer discussing presentation graphics until the next section of the chapter.

Data Management. Most spreadsheets contain a facility for managing data (see Figure 13-6). Two popular options in most spreadsheet programs' data management toolkits are sorting and searching (information retrieval).

☐ *Sorting* The ability to sort is a handy feature in almost any type of business software package. With a word processor, sorting enables you to prepare alphabetical listings of names as well as indexes, directories, and glossaries. With a spreadsheet package, you might find a sort facility handy for preparing phone and office directories, ordered listings of overdue accounts, and reports identifying fast-moving or high-selling products.

Many teachers use the spreadsheet's sort feature to keep grade books on students. Such a grade book can be maintained throughout the term in alphabetical order by student name, and at the end of the term, student records can be sorted according to final averages. Some spreadsheet packages also contain a *data distribution facility* so that a teacher can, among other things, quickly find the number of students with averages between 90–100, 80–89, 70–79, and so on.

FIGURE 13-7

Macro facility. This two-cell 1-2-3 macro, named C, lets you set a column width to 20 characters by merely depressing the Alt key and hitting the C key.

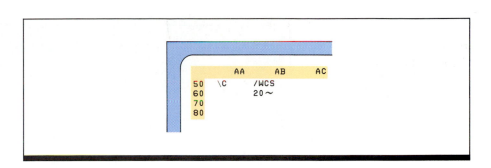

Many spreadsheet packages allow you to sort on more than one key. For example, you may wish to sort company employee records by department and by employee name within departments. In the terminology of sorting, "department" would be declared the primary key and "employee name" the secondary key. Sorting by multiple keys is illustrated in Figure 2-13d on page 53 and in Figure 8-8 on page 272.

□ *Searching*   Often each row in a worksheet represents some type of record. For example, if the worksheet stores company records, each row might contain a company name, a complete mailing address, a phone number, and so on. If the worksheet is large (some can store more than 8,000 records), it's handy to have a feature that will automatically extract records for you based on search criteria that you specify. For instance, you may wish to get a list of companies in Philadelphia, the address of Kane Publications, or a list of advertising firms with over 100 employees. A search facility will enable you to gather this information rapidly and accurately.

Macro Facility.   One of the most appreciated things about spreadsheet packages is that they let you do a lot of information processing without having to know how to program. However, if you do have the talent to write programs and the spreadsheet package you are using has a macro facility, you can really put your worksheets into high gear.

A **macro facility** enables you to write programs within your worksheet. Each *macro* is, in fact, a program. It consists of a series of keystrokes that the spreadsheet package executes every time you invoke the macro. In 1-2-3, for example, the two-cell macro shown in Figure 13-7 lets you automatically set column widths to 20 columns. When you depress the Alt key followed by the name of the macro (C), seven keystrokes (/WCS20⁓) are automatically made for you. Roughly translated, these keystrokes mean invoke the command menu (/), issue the worksheet command (W) off of this menu, select the column-width option (C), choose the set option (S), set the column width to 20 characters (20), and hit the Return key (⁓).

Macros often are written in contiguous worksheet cells, as Figure 13-7 shows. Frequently the macro is written in a remote set of cells so as not to interfere with worksheet labels and values that will later be output. If you are really skilled at writing macros, you can write long programs and even programs that loop. Like any other program, a macro must be given a name.

FIGURE 13-8

Spreadsheet utilities. Spreadsheet aftermarket products comprise a multimillion-dollar industry, sporting such widely used products as (a, left) Funk Software's Sideways, which lets you print extra-long worksheets sideways, and (b, right) Personics Corporation's SeeMORE, which lets you fit large worksheets onto a screen by displaying them in a compressed mode.

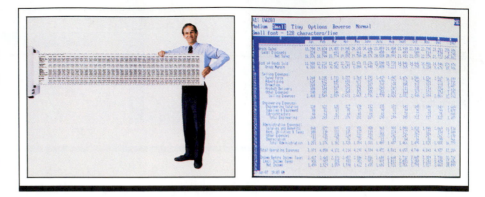

Add-on Packages

During the last decade or so, a $100 million "aftermarket" industry has sprouted up to meet the continuing demands of spreadsheet users. The companies comprising this industry make and sell *add-on packages*—spreadsheet utilities that enhance (or "add value" to) the major spreadsheet programs in the market, making them more powerful, easier to use, more flexible, and so forth. If you need your spreadsheet package to do something it isn't currently equipped to do, chances are there's an aftermarket vendor that has just the feature you need available as an add-on package.

The number of add-on products available for the leading spreadsheet packages is enormous. Funk Software's Sideways (see Figure 13-8a), a print utility that enables worksheets with too many columns to be printed lengthwise on standard letter-sized paper, is generally considered the earliest add-on package for spreadsheets. It is still one of the most popular. Personics Corporation's SeeMORE (shown in Figure 13-8b) can push more of a worksheet onto the screen by converting the characters on the display into one of four size modes—normal, medium, small, and tiny. The tiny mode can display up to 170 characters by 53 rows, depending on the graphics standard in use. There is even an add-on product (called ManuPlan) that will check a manufacturing worksheet to see if it meets production objectives and deploys resources efficiently.

Aftermarket vendors frequently sell templates that can be used with spreadsheet programs. One of the most common examples is the federal income tax forms that everyone who gets paid fills out each year (see Figure 13-9). Many tax-form templates also come equipped with built-in calculators, enabling them to be operated independently of any spreadsheet package. Income tax returns are commonly submitted today on diskettes, and it is expected that electronic filing of returns will continue to become more popular in future years.

Multidimensional Spreadsheets

Spreadsheet packages that allow developing worksheets with more than two cell dimensions are now available. These are sometimes referred to as *mul-

FIGURE 13-9

Graphically oriented templates.
The income tax form shown here is identical to the forms the government prints out. Through the spreadsheet, the form has an automatic recalculation feature. You can (a, left) display a whole form on the screen at one time or (b, right) zoom into any part of it for greater detail. When completed to your satisfaction, the filled-in forms can be sent to a laser printer or submitted in electronic form to the government.

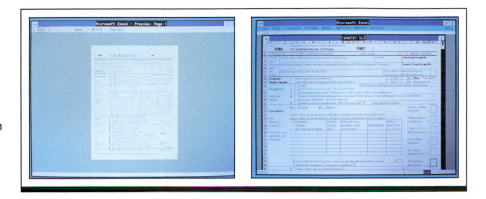

tidimensional spreadsheets. In fact, it's reasonable to assume that most of the leading spreadsheet packages that currently lack multidimensional capabilities will have them in the near future.

In a three-dimensional (3-D) package, each cell has three coordinates. For instance, the cell in column A, row 1 of the twelfth worksheet is referred to as cell 12A1. Users can specify both relationships that apply among rows and columns of a single worksheet and relationships that apply over a set of worksheets. So, for instance, one could establish that all of the cells in the thirteenth worksheet (representing a summary of the year 1989) are to be calculated by summing respective cells in worksheets 1 through 12 (representing the 12 months of 1989). The use of 3-D worksheets is illustrated in Figure 13-10.

A 3-D feature allows a set of worksheets to be read like an "electronic book," with each page (worksheet) capable of adding detail to the one that precedes it. For example, you could form a thirteenth worksheet by summing results in the other 12 worksheets or by applying a trend analysis to the cells in these worksheets. In the first case, each cell of the thirteenth worksheet will contain a sum and in the second case a forecasted value. As another example, you can store macros "under" the cells to which they apply, that is, in the cells defined by the third dimension of a conventional two-dimensional worksheet.

PRESENTATION GRAPHICS

Typically spreadsheets manipulate text, that is, words and numbers. Graphics packages, on the other hand, manipulate pictures, or graphic images. These packages make it possible to generate images relatively painlessly on either a display device, a printer, a plotter, or a film recorder.

There are two general types of graphics software: presentation graphics software and CAD software. **Presentation graphics software** enables you to draw bar charts, pie charts, and the like to present data to others in an

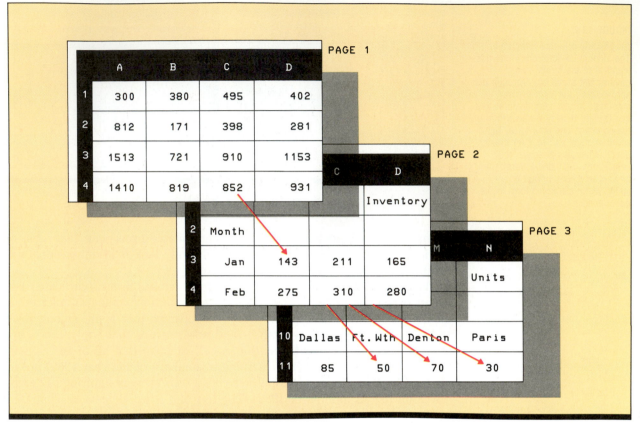

FIGURE 13-10

A multidimensional worksheet facility. With a multidimensional feature, users can prepare a hierarchy of interrelated worksheets, each of which presents a finer level of detail about a company, product, or cost.

informative and/or convincing way. Often a person can get the point suggested by the data much more quickly by looking at a presentation graphic than by reading text-based output with the same information content (see Figure 13-11). *Computer-aided design (CAD) software,* on the other hand, is used to design products such as houses, clothing, cars, planes, and microchips, as well as to create art and advertising images. Because spreadsheet software often is integrated with a presentation graphics feature, we discuss presentation graphics in this chapter and defer CAD software until Chapter 16.

Types of Packages. A variety of presentation graphics packages exist in the marketplace. Most of them fall into one of two classes: dedicated presentation graphics packages and presentation graphics packages that are bundled (integrated) with spreadsheet software.

☐ *Dedicated Packages* Dedicated packages provide the most powerful types of graphics features—for instance, a wider selection of texturing patterns (such as solid, speckled, and cross-hatched), legend fonts, graph

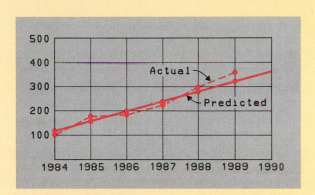

Sales ($000,000)		
Year	Actual	Predicted
1984	100	120
1985	180	160
1986	190	200
1987	230	240
1988	300	280
1989	360	320

(a) Tabular (spreadsheet) format   (b) Line chart (presentation graphics) format

FIGURE 13-11

The power of presentation graphics. Often a person looking at a presentation graphic can spot trends or make comparisons much more quickly than when looking at raw data. For managers who need to evaluate hundreds of data items daily, presentation graphics saves time and contributes to more effective decision making.

types, and device drivers. Many also come with clip art libraries and enable you to interface with painting/drawing software packages to edit the graphs you create. In short, if your presentation graphics needs are extensive, a dedicated package is more likely to contain the types of features you require.

☐ *Integrated Packages* Unfortunately, dedicated packages lack the calculation and data-modeling features available with spreadsheets, so you have to either type data directly into them or import data to them from a spreadsheet package. Integrated packages overcome this limitation by integrating both functions into a single product. Integrated packages are ideal for users who require the strong data manipulation or information processing capability that a spreadsheet package affords and whose presentation graphics needs are relatively modest.

Most presentation graphics packages are capable of producing at least simple types of bar charts, line charts, and pie charts. Dedicated packages can produce several other types of information-intensive images as well (see Figure 13-12).

Using a Package. Generally, once you invoke the graphics package, you decide on the type of graph to be created, identify the data to be used in plotting the graph, and supply your preferences on matters such as titles, coloring, and texturing. Like other productivity software, a graphics package usually lets you perform such basic operations as saving, deleting, and printing. To get the output in hard-copy form, you normally need either a dot-matrix impact printer that can work in a graphics mode, an ink-jet printer,

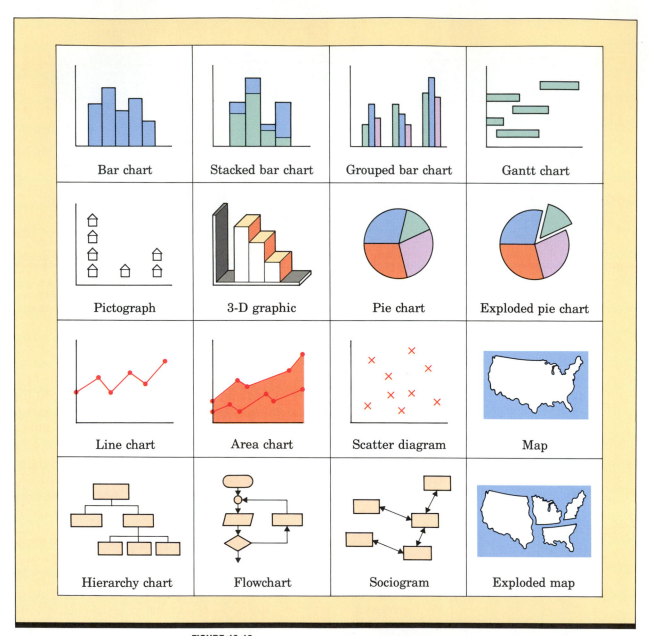

FIGURE 13-12

Types of presentation graphics. Most presentation graphics packages at least allow users to construct bar charts, line charts, and pie charts. Many packages provide a wide number of other options as well, some of which are shown here.

a laser printer, a plotter, or a film recorder. (We discussed such output devices in Chapter 6.) Integrated packages generally lack drivers for sophisticated output devices such as film recorders, but you may find the driver you need from an aftermarket vendor.

An example of a presentation graphics package in operation is shown in Figure 13-13. First you are offered a menu such as that shown in

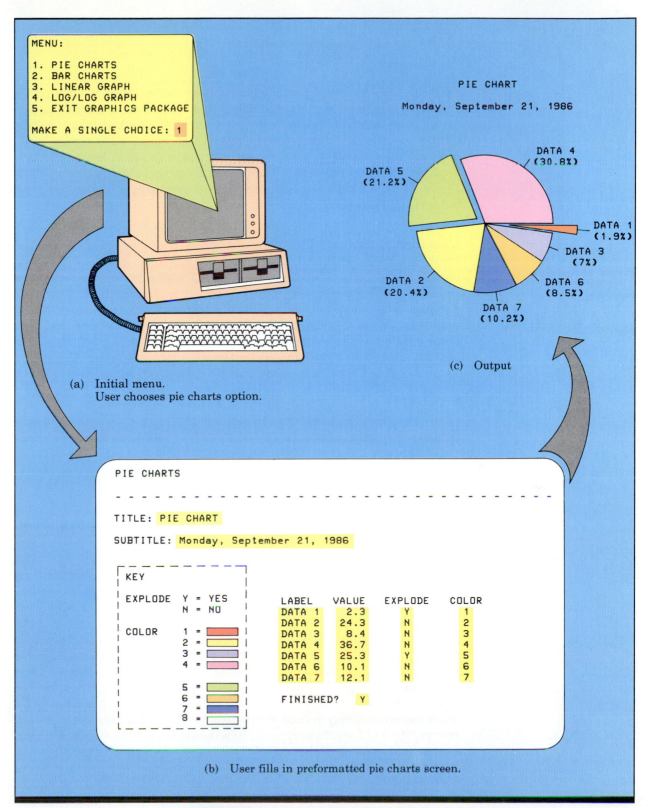

MENU:

1. PIE CHARTS
2. BAR CHARTS
3. LINEAR GRAPH
4. LOG/LOG GRAPH
5. EXIT GRAPHICS PACKAGE

MAKE A SINGLE CHOICE: 1

(a) Initial menu.
    User chooses pie charts option.

PIE CHART

Monday, September 21, 1986

DATA 4 (30.8%)
DATA 5 (21.2%)
DATA 1 (1.9%)
DATA 3 (7%)
DATA 6 (8.5%)
DATA 7 (10.2%)
DATA 2 (20.4%)

(c) Output

PIE CHARTS

- -

TITLE: PIE CHART

SUBTITLE: Monday, September 21, 1986

KEY

EXPLODE Y = YES
         N = NO

COLOR   1 =
         2 =
         3 =
         4 =

         5 =
         6 =
         7 =
         8 =

LABEL	VALUE	EXPLODE	COLOR
DATA 1	2.3	Y	1
DATA 2	24.3	N	2
DATA 3	8.4	N	3
DATA 4	36.7	N	4
DATA 5	25.3	Y	5
DATA 6	10.1	N	6
DATA 7	12.1	N	7

FINISHED?   Y

(b) User fills in preformatted pie charts screen.

FIGURE 13-13

How some presentation graphics packages work. (a) Initial menu; user chooses pie chart option. (b) User fills out the preformatted pie charts screen. (c) The completed pie chart output.

Figure 13-13a. After you select the pie chart option, a "form" appears on the screen for you to fill in (Figure 13-13b). Often the screen is entirely preformatted, and once you type an entry into a field, the package automatically tabs to the next field. When you're finished, you type a *Y* (to signify "yes") in the appropriate place. Then the graphic image shown in Figure 13-13c is produced on an output device. Note that the entries in the Value column of Figure 13-13b are automatically calculated as percentages of the total when output on the pie chart.

Show-Package Software. Presentation graphics packages often are used to create images for animated slide shows for use in important meetings and client presentations. The images are created with a presentation graphics package, the slides are produced on a film recorder, and the slide show—complete with attention-getting, movielike features such as wipes, pans, and fade-outs—is put together on show-package software. Window 6 describes more fully the creation of computer-generated slide shows and also illustrates a number of state-of-the-art presentation graphics.

SUMMARY AND KEY TERMS

Electronic spreadsheets first came to public notice in the late 1970s when a product named VisiCalc was developed. The principle behind electronic spreadsheets involves viewing the display screen as a *window* looking in on a big grid, called a **worksheet.** The worksheet is similar to the wide, columnar paper on which accountants frequently work.

Spreadsheet packages are particularly valuable because they provide a **recalculation feature;** that is, they can perform in seconds recalculations that would require several hours to do manually or by writing a program in a high-level language. Users can learn to prepare budgets and financial schedules with spreadsheet packages after only a few hours of training. In fact, this recalculation feature is what makes electronic spreadsheets so popular, and it is probably the single most important thing you should know about them.

Worksheets commonly consist of two major sections: a **status area, or control panel,** and a **worksheet area, or window area.** Most worksheet areas have columns that are labeled by letters and rows that are labeled by numbers. Every worksheet **cell** is identified by its column and row. The status area generally is used to display the coordinates and the contents of the cell currently being worked on—which is called the **current cell, or active cell**—as well as a menu of useful worksheet commands.

Most spreadsheet packages offer two pointing mechanisms: a cursor and a cell pointer, or highlight. The **cursor** is associated with the status area and points to the place where the next character typed in will appear. The **cell pointer,** or **highlight,** is associated with the worksheet area and points to the current cell.

In most spreadsheet products, a cell can contain either a label or a value. A **label** is an entry that cannot be manipulated mathematically, and a **value** is an entry that can. A value generally is one of three types: a numeric constant, a formula, or a function.

Spreadsheet packages also have numerous features that facilitate entering and editing data. Some of the *basic* entering and editing operations include inserting and deleting rows or columns, moving or copying the contents of cells from one part of the worksheet to another, editing dollar amounts and other values, selecting column widths, and establishing titles. Also, **templates** enable you to perform work on worksheets in which many cells already have labels or values, leaving you to supply only the data.

Advanced spreadsheet operations include sorting data, searching for records that meet certain criteria, using a **macro facility** to embed programs into a worksheet, and taking advantage of special "add-on" utilities sold by aftermarket vendors. In addition, many spreadsheets enable you to arrange data in more than two dimensions, to develop more sophisticated types of models.

Presentation graphics software lets you draw bar charts, pie charts, and the like to present information to others in a visual, easily understandable way. Presentation graphics packages are either dedicated or integrated. *Dedicated* packages provide the most sophisticated types of graphing capabilities, while *integrated* packages consist of modest graphics routines that support a particular spreadsheet.

Once you invoke a graphics package, you decide on the type of graph to be created, supply or identify the data to be used in plotting the graph, and indicate your preferences on matters such as titles, coloring, and cross-hatching. Like other types of productivity software, graphics packages usually let you do things such as save, delete, and print graphs.

REVIEW EXERCISES

Fill-in Questions

1. The principle behind electronic spreadsheets involves viewing the display screen as a(n) _____ looking in on a big grid, called a(n) _____ .

2. Most spreadsheet packages provide two pointing mechanisms: a(n) _____ and a(n) _____ .

3. Another name for the worksheet's status area is the _____ .

4. Three types of copying operations available in many spreadsheet packages are _____ , _____ , and _____ replication.

5. A worksheet in which all rows and columns are prelabeled, and formulas are supplied, is called a(n) _____ .

6. The spreadsheet feature that allows users to embed small programs in a worksheet is called a(n) _____ .

7. _____ packages are spreadsheet utilities commonly sold by aftermarket vendors.

8. Most presentation graphics packages fall into one of two categories: _____ packages and _____ packages.

Matching Questions

Match each term with the description that best fits.

a. +B1-B2*C2
b. @SUM
c. D4

d. JOHN SMITH
e. 200
f. F18..F28

_____ 1. A label.
_____ 2. A range.
_____ 3. A numeric constant.
_____ 4. A formula.
_____ 5. A cell.
_____ 6. A function.

Discussion Questions

1. What types of purposes are served by an electronic spreadsheet?
2. What is the difference between a label and a value in a spreadsheet?
3. What are the differences among relative, absolute, and mixed replication?
4. Of what use is a template to users of spreadsheet software?
5. What does a spreadsheet's macro facility allow you to do?
6. What types of graphical images can you construct with presentation graphics software?

Critical Thinking Questions

1. Is the average spreadsheet user actually "programming" when preparing a worksheet? Defend your response.
2. Lotus Development Corporation's 1-2-3 is one of the most widely used software packages of all time, outselling its competitors in the spreadsheet marketplace by a hefty margin. What, do you feel, accounts for 1-2-3's enormous popularity?
3. You need a plotter for your microcomputer system and want to spend no more than $500. You will use the plotter to prepare simple color

graphs of bar charts, pie charts, and line charts. Some calls to local computer stores reveal that you can get about five or six product demonstrations. What questions should you get answered during these demonstrations?

4. Spreadsheets, oddly enough, evolved from word processors. What similarities are there between these two types of software packages?

5. Comment on this statement: "Nobody should graduate from a business school today without learning how to use a spreadsheet package."

6

Presentation Graphics

A Picture Is Worth a
Thousand Words

Presentation graphics involves the use of computer graphics techniques to present information to others in a useful and interesting way. Often data are first assembled into meaningful information with a spreadsheet package. Then a graphics package—which may also contain relatively sophisticated art software—is used to put the information into a pictorial format. Frequently, output is sent to a film recorder, plotter, or sophisticated printer.

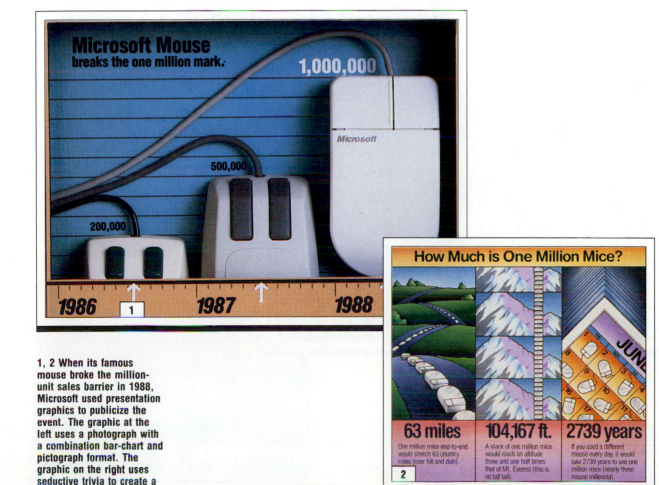

1, 2 When its famous mouse broke the million-unit sales barrier in 1988, Microsoft used presentation graphics to publicize the event. The graphic at the left uses a photograph with a combination bar-chart and pictograph format. The graphic on the right uses seductive trivia to create a memorable impression.

LINE, BAR, AND PIE CHARTS

3–5 Line charts, bar charts, and pie charts—and their countless variations—are the most basic and widely used forms of presentation graphics. Line charts and bar charts are ideal for showing trends and time comparisons, while pie charts are best for comparing individual parts to one another or to a whole.

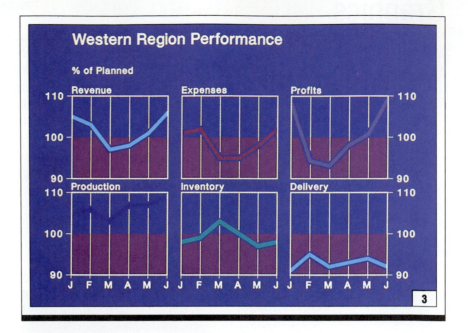

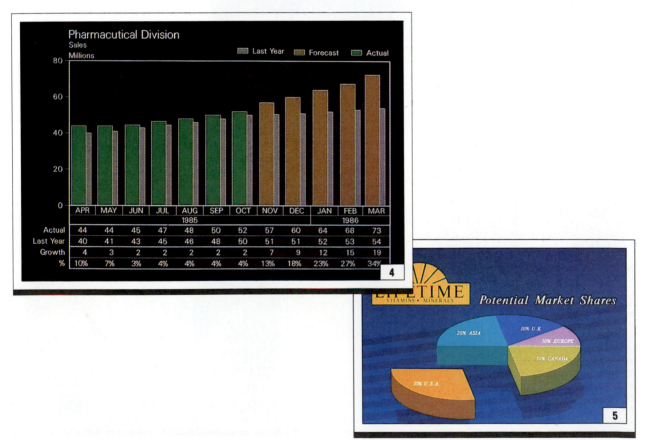

PICTOGRAPHS

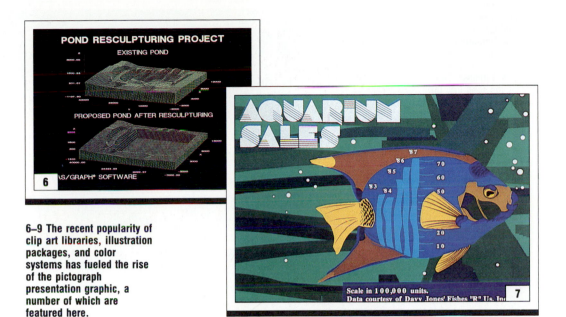

6–9 The recent popularity of clip art libraries, illustration packages, and color systems has fueled the rise of the pictograph presentation graphic, a number of which are featured here.

EMBEDDED PHOTOGRAPHS

10–13 Presentation graphics for annual reports to stockholders and for important meetings are increasingly employing embedded photographs for additional impact. The photos are read into the computer system with a scanner, digitally retouched or resized, and often, as shown here, output to a very-high-resolution film recorder.

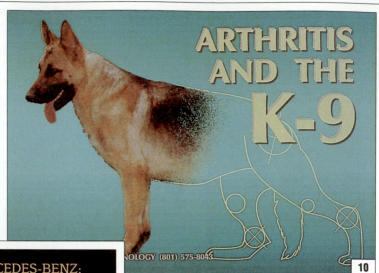

ARTHRITIS AND THE K-9

...NOLOGY (801) 575-8043

10

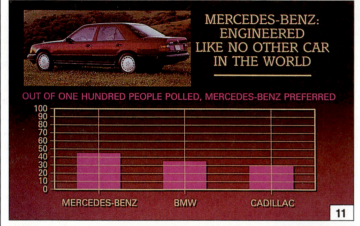

MERCEDES-BENZ: ENGINEERED LIKE NO OTHER CAR IN THE WORLD

OUT OF ONE HUNDRED PEOPLE POLLED, MERCEDES-BENZ PREFERRED

MERCEDES-BENZ   BMW   CADILLAC

11

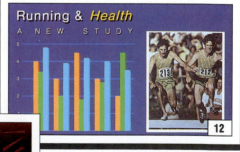

Running & *Health*
A N E W S T U D Y

12

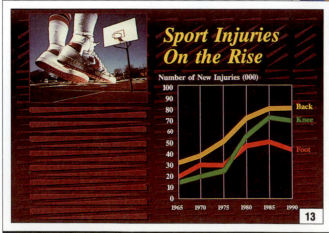

Sport Injuries On the Rise

Number of New Injuries (000)

Back
Knee
Foot

1965 1970 1975 1980 1985 1990

13

SHOW PACKAGES

One of the hottest presentation graphics concepts in recent years is the self-running or user-controlled slide show. With the proper *show-package system,* you can create or simply input a related set of "slide" images and store them in compact form on a diskette or hard disk. Then you command the system to run the entire show on a color monitor, either automatically or by pressing a key to move from one image to the next. Furthermore, some systems let you specify how long to display each image, summon an arrow and move it around the screen as a pointer, make elements on the screen change color or flash on and off, and create simple "special effects" such as fades and wipes.

14–16 General Parametrics' VideoShow has emerged as one of the front runners among show-package systems. VideoShow supports many of the leading presentation graphics packages in the market.

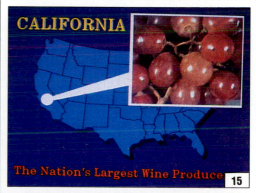

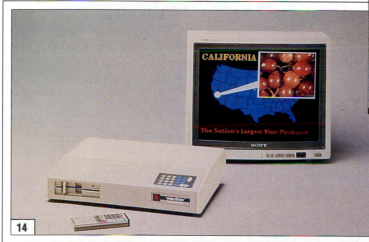

17 Effective presentations often require the use of title slides. You may be able to have the show-package system slowly fade the title image before replacing it with the next slide—an effect called a *fade*—similar to the way credits disappear off the screen in many movies and TV shows.

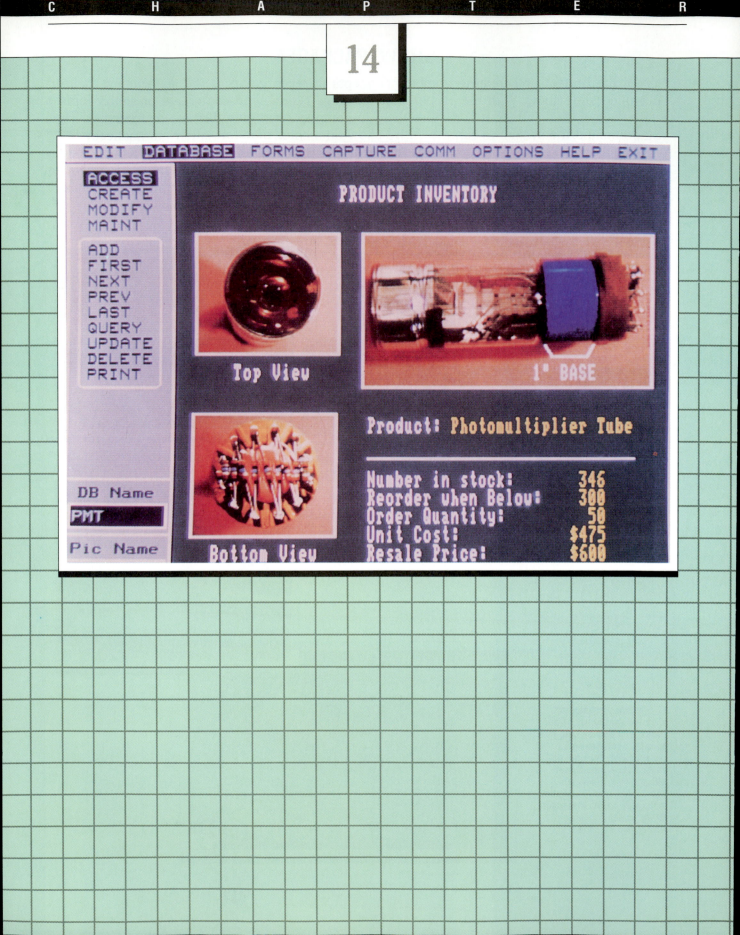

EDIT **DATABASE** FORMS CAPTURE COMM OPTIONS HELP EXIT

ACCESS
CREATE
MODIFY
MAINT

ADD
FIRST
NEXT
PREV
LAST
QUERY
UPDATE
DELETE
PRINT

DB Name

PMT

Pic Name

PRODUCT INVENTORY

Top View

1" BASE

Bottom View

Product: Photomultiplier Tube

Number in stock: 346
Reorder when Below: 300
Order Quantity: 50
Unit Cost: $475
Resale Price: $600

File Managers and Database Management Systems

Objectives

After completing this chapter, you will be able to:

1. Describe what file managers can do and how they work.
2. Explain what database management systems are and how they differ from file managers.
3. Identify the various approaches used for database management on both large and small computer systems.
4. Understand what integrated software does and where it is appropriate.

OVERVIEW

People often have a need to summon large amounts of data rapidly. An airline agent on the phone to a client may need to quickly search through mounds of data to find the lowest-cost available flight path from Tucson to Toronto two weeks hence. The registrar of a university may have to swiftly scan student records to find the grade-point averages of all students who will graduate in June. An engineer may need to test several structural-design alternatives against volumes of complicated safety and feasibility criteria before proceeding with a design strategy.

In this chapter we'll cover the type of software used specifically for such *data management* tasks. In a sense, this class of software is rapidly replacing the thick, hard-copy manuals that people have had to wade through to fetch the information their jobs require. Data management software often is categorized into two major types: *file managers* and *database management systems*. As with other popular types of software products, numerous data management software packages are available for both large and small computer systems. File managers are easier to use and understand, so we'll discuss them first. Then we'll turn to database systems. Finally, we'll look at *integrated software packages,* which usually include a data management feature with the word processing, spreadsheet, and graphics functions described in Chapters 12 and 13.

Before reading this chapter, you should review the section in Chapter 2 entitled "Organizing Data for Computer Systems" (pages 43–46) and the "Data Organization" section in Chapter 5 (pages 153–159). In this chapter, the terms *file, record,* and *field* (introduced in Chapter 2) are used throughout the discussions on data management. The Chapter 5 topics, *organization* and *access,* are what data management really is all about: organizing data on disk so you can effectively retrieve them in the manner you require.

FILE MANAGEMENT SOFTWARE

A **file manager,** or *record management system,* is a software package that enables you to organize data into files and to access the data a single file at a time. For example, you might first use the package to search for and print out the names of all recipes in a recipe file in which kumquats are an ingredient. Minutes later, you may summon the same package to scan an employee file and total the number of employees in your organization whose birthdays are in April. In the world of data management, files are sometimes referred to as *flat files,* meaning that they lack the multidimensionality imparted by the database structures we'll be describing later in the chapter.

You can use a file manager to create and store as many files as you want. But because you can point to only one file at a time, file managers can be cumbersome to use for interrelating data located in different files. So you'd

FIGURE 14-1

An onscreen form (template) representing an employee record. Such forms can be filled out while displayed on the screen.

be unable to find, say, the birthday of the employee in your employee file who gave you the candied-kumquats recipe in your recipe file without making two separate file calls and issuing two separate queries, one to each file.

The one-file-at-a-time drawback aside, file managers are both powerful and extremely useful. Besides enabling you to search for records with specific characteristics, most packages permit you to sort records, search for records, and produce both summary information and detailed reports from selected records. They also let you add, delete, and modify data.

How File Managers Work

Let's look at an illustrative example to get a feel for how file managers process data. Suppose an organization has 1,000 employees. The organization maintains a "form" on each employee like the one shown on the display screen in Figure 14-1. Such an *onscreen form,* or **template,** is commonly used for entering data into either files or databases. Each file created will have its own distinctive template.

As you place data into the records of a file, you start with an unfilled template for each record to be keyed in. Then you repeatedly fill the templates at the keyboard and save the records onto disk. At any later point, you can modify or delete records from the file and add new ones.

Setting Up a File. Before we examine some of the ways we can process the employee file, let's look more closely at the template in Figure 14-1. Notice that it contains 10 fields: NAME, SOCIAL SECURITY NUMBER, STREET, and so on.

With most file management packages, users can design their own templates. In creating a template for a recipe file, for example, a chef will likely set up a recipe-name field, an ingredients field, and a directions field. And, perhaps, even a field for calories. Generally, the file management package will contain a DESIGN FILE option that will enable you to design whatever types of templates you need for your applications. The records in a given file usually must have the same format and conform to the template chosen.

To enable you to create templates or process file data, many file management packages provide you with an "opening menu" of choices, like the one shown in Figure 14-2, as soon as you call the package from the operating system. At this point, you must choose one of the given menu options and supply the name of the file you wish to process.

So, for example, if you are setting up a template for the 1,000-record employee file previously mentioned, you select option 1, DESIGN FILE, and create a name for the file—say, EMPLOYEE-FILE. Then the package will likely summon a routine that will ask you a series of questions about how you want to design the template for this file. Here you name the fields, define the maximum length of the data in each field, and make some choices as to how the template will look on the screen. Many packages will let you set up templates that require more than one screen.

After designing the EMPLOYEE-FILE template, you go back to the opening menu and select option 2, ADD, to fill out 1,000 copies of the form—one for each employee—and place them onto disk.

File Maintenance. Once you have stored records on disk, you can add new records (opening menu option 2—ADD) or delete records representing departed employees (option 7—REMOVE). Furthermore, if a record contains outdated data, you can change these data by requesting the update mode (option 4—SEARCH/UPDATE) on the menu.

Extracting Information. Besides performing file maintenance operations, you can extract information for screen display and, if you desire, produce printed reports. For example, you might use the search/update feature on the opening menu to scan the file for the names of all employees in department 544 or the names of all employees whose salaries exceed $40,000. You can direct any of this information to the screen and, if you wish, print it.

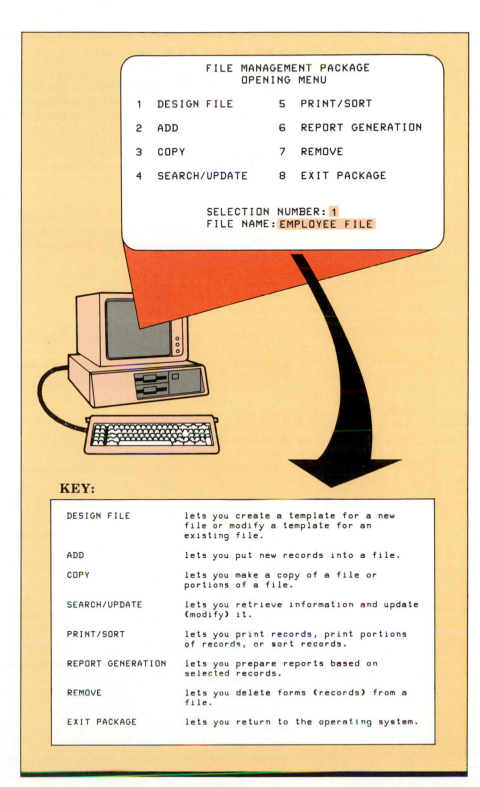

FILE MANAGEMENT PACKAGE
OPENING MENU

1 DESIGN FILE   5 PRINT/SORT

2 ADD   6 REPORT GENERATION

3 COPY   7 REMOVE

4 SEARCH/UPDATE   8 EXIT PACKAGE

SELECTION NUMBER: 1
FILE NAME: EMPLOYEE FILE

KEY:

DESIGN FILE	lets you create a template for a new file or modify a template for an existing file.
ADD	lets you put new records into a file.
COPY	lets you make a copy of a file or portions of a file.
SEARCH/UPDATE	lets you retrieve information and update (modify) it.
PRINT/SORT	lets you print records, print portions of records, or sort records.
REPORT GENERATION	lets you prepare reports based on selected records.
REMOVE	lets you delete forms (records) from a file.
EXIT PACKAGE	lets you return to the operating system.

You may also want to produce mailing labels. Thus you can extract the NAME, STREET, CITY, and ZIP fields from selected records by invoking opening menu option 5, PRINT/SORT. You can then sort these "reduced records" by zip code before sending them to the printer. (The postal service offers reduced rates for large mailings that are presorted by zip code.)

Some packages also allow you to produce very sophisticated written reports. For example, you may wish to produce a salary report on all employees in departments 212 through 214, sorted by department and totaled. Again you go back to the opening menu, select option 6, REPORT GENERATION, and identify EMPLOYEE-FILE as the file you wish to process. Then the file management package will likely present you with a report generation questionnaire, such as the one shown in Figure 14-3a, so you can describe how to prepare the report. You merely fill out the questionnaire, hitting the Enter key after placing your responses into each field. The package will then produce the report (Figure 14-3b). In some cases, such as that in Figure 14-3, the file manager will automatically format the report, supply the current date, and number pages.

DATABASE MANAGEMENT SYSTEMS

A *database management system* differs from a file manager primarily in that it enables immediate, "seamless" access to data that conceivably could span several files. As a rule, because database management systems are more technically complex than file managers, they are also more expensive and more difficult to master.

Let's look at a situation where a database management system might be useful. You're a sales manager, and an order comes in for 10,000 units of product A-211. You first need to find out if the order can be filled from stock in inventory. If it can't, you next need to know how long it will be before enough stock is available. You have an impatient client on the phone and require an immediate response.

The following scenario would be ideal for you. At the display terminal on your desk, you key in the product number, A-211. The computer system responds with a screen that shows the status of this product, including the current level of uncommitted stock, future delivery dates, and future delivery amounts. Within seconds, you are able to satisfy the client's request and place the order.

The type of task just described is especially suited to a database management system, because rapid access to more than one file's worth of data is required. Traditionally, an inventory file is used to store current stock levels, while a vendor order file is used to keep track of future shipments from vendors. The very notion of files is often transparent to the database end user, who sees only screenfuls of information and usually has no idea from where the database system is extracting the information.

FIGURE 14-3

Using a file manager to produce a report. On the display screen, the user fills in blanks on a questionnaire that covers what the report is to look like. The file manager does the rest.

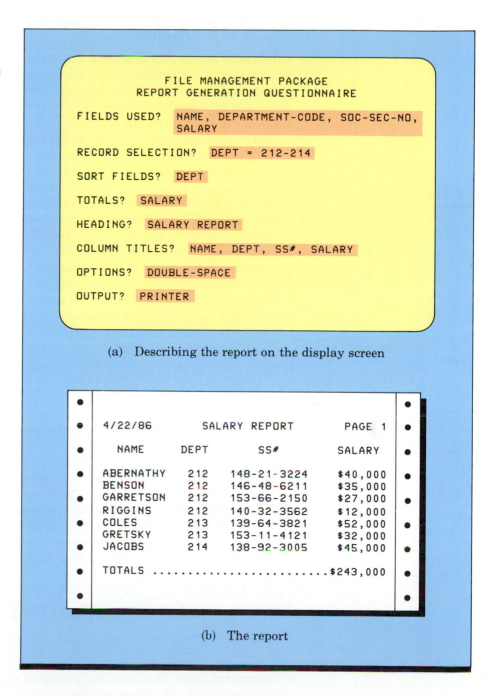

(a) Describing the report on the display screen

(b) The report

You should also observe that a file manager might be unsuitable for the job just described. With a file manager, you'd have to (1) point to the inventory file, (2) make the stock-level inquiry, (3) point to the vendor-order file, and (4) make the shipment inquiry. Because this serial, "file-conscious" process would be slower than having all the data integrated in a manner transparent to the user, both service to clients and efficiency would suffer.

The Database Approach

A **database management system (DBMS)** is a sophisticated software system for storing and providing easy access to data. The data themselves are placed on disk in a **database,** which is simply an integrated collection of data. Data in a database are set up in a standard format and in a manner that will allow several means of access. While we basically address text data in this chapter, virtually any type of data—text, graphics, voice, or video—can exist in a database (see Feature 14A).

A database may be roughly thought of as a collection of interrelated "files" of data. In a nondatabase environment, these data would likely exist as flat files. However, the notion of files in a "true" database environment differs somewhat from that in flat-file environments. You might think of a single "master file"—the database—in which all occurrences of all data items are stored only once, and a collection of *logical files,* whose fields consist not of actual data but of addresses that show where the actual data are stored in the database. So, for example, a "student file" in a college or university database environment may contain only the addresses at which student data are located in the database. Similarly, a "class file" may contain addresses at which class rosters may be found. Data such as the ID or social security numbers of students, which logically would appear in both files, need to physically appear in the database only once. Even though traditional data files do not physically exist in a true database environment, it helps to have a logical notion of them.*

End users and programmers gain access to the DBMS through either an easy-to-use *retrieval/update language* that accompanies the database package or via an *applications program* written in a programming language. Usually the retrieval/update language is an easy-to-use fourth-generation language (4GL) that is designed for noncomputer professionals, while the programming language is either COBOL or a report-generation-oriented 4GL. The DBMS serves as an interface between the person and the data. It will locate the data and convert them from the common format into the format the end user or programmer requires. A database processing scenario for a university environment is illustrated in Figure 14-4.

Advantages and Disadvantages of Database Management

A "true" DBMS offers several advantages over traditional, file-based systems. Four such advantages are:

☐ *Integrated Data* Theoretically, programs written in any language the DBMS supports can utilize any data in the database. This possibility enables information that normally would be stored in several independent files to be accessed quickly by end users.

---

*Many database systems targeted to microcomputers use *physical files,* similar to those in flat-file systems, to store data. Although such packages allow users to link data among these files in a way that's relatively transparent to the user, the fact that each file stores its own data leads to some storage redundancy and lack of integrity (see page 448).

FIGURE 14-4

A college or university database environment. Database technology makes it possible to combine and efficiently store data that traditionally have existed as separate files.

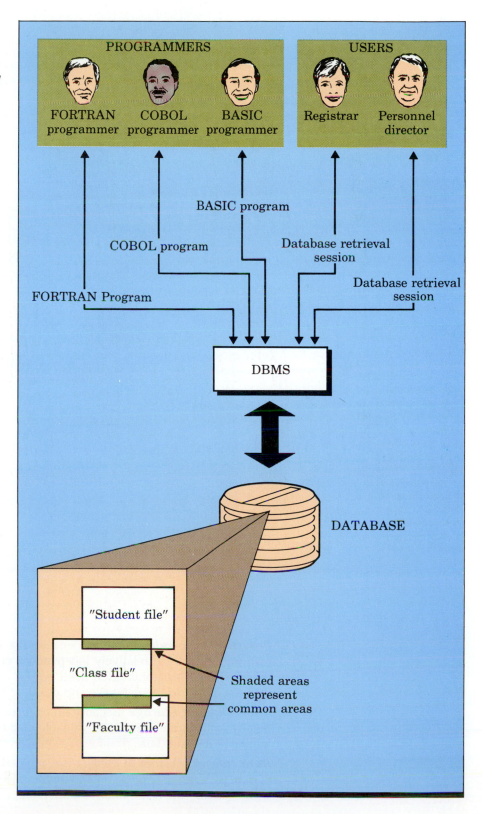

Photo Databases

A New Solution to an Old Problem

A common problem organizations face is the need to fetch picture information. A museum may have to access images of art treasures. A fine-arts professor may need to show students what Boston's Faneuil Hall or William Randolph Hearst's San Simeon looks like. A photo stock house may have to catalog its vast collection of images. A vendor in Seattle may want to show its product line to clients who can be reached at video workstations in Kansas City. And the list goes on.

Historically, such organizations and individuals kept large picture files, which they could access only manually. With the recent availability of optical disk systems and suitable retrieval software, however, they can turn to so-called "photo databases" to accomplish the same result—and both faster and better as well.

Many photo databases are not true database management systems; rather, they are flat-file products. It's uncertain precisely how they have come to be called *databases*—perhaps through the hype of overzealous vendors or through outright confusion. Nonetheless, many of the flat-file systems now in use will likely migrate to database technology at some point in the near future.

At Manhattan-based retailer Polo Ralph Lauren, staff designers now have online access to tens of thousands of photographs covering scores of topics. If, say, someone in home furnishings wants to examine art deco styles or kitchens to create a design, he or she can electronically cull images covering those particular themes from the database, and even turn them into hard-copy form. While Polo's initial motivation for acquiring the system was to trim costs, the organization has found that the database also has increased creativity.

The National Archives & Records Administration in Washington, D.C., has a different type of a problem for which it is considering the use of photo databases. In its archives are over 15 billion original records, many of which consist of priceless documents dating back to the American Revolutionary War. The value of holding these documents lies in showing them to the public and to historical researchers who chronicle important events. Unfortunately, the fragile nature of these documents makes them difficult to handle. Currently some 1.5 mil-

☐ **Program-Data Independence** Because the database data are in their own format and are relatively independent of the languages that access them, existing programs often need not be changed when new types of data are added to the database and obsolete types are culled.

☐ **Nonredundant Storage** Because all occurrences of the same data need be physically stored only once, valuable disk space can be saved by eliminating redundant data.

☐ **Data Integrity** Errors of conflict are avoided because, since each piece of data is stored only once, an update to a piece of data provides all users with access to the same information.

lion documents are being scanned and entered into a videodisk photo database as part of a pilot project. Special software now in use on the system allows developers to visually enhance the documents to obtain better clarity than the originals. Anheuser-Busch also has turned to a similar type of photo database to catalog its corporate memorabilia, as has the museum at the University of California at Berkeley.

In the areas of security and personnel, many companies now use picture databases to store photographic images of employees (see photo). Many real-estate firms also have access to online photo databases when doing searches for homes covered in multiple listing services. And some manufacturers are using picture databases to keep images of assemblies and subassemblies on file, which enables workers who need to see how a particular unit is

built to get to relevant information quickly. It is expected that some day fire departments will have street maps and maps of certain buildings on file in photo databases, thereby enabling them to get to fires faster and formulate

strategies for combatting them. And, of course, photo databases are good candidates for inclusion in a hypermedia application (see Chapter 11 Tomorrow box and Window 4). Further potential uses seem almost endless.

Employee record. Advances in optical disk technology will sharply increase use of photo databases.

These technical advantages translate into valuable practical benefits: fewer personnel, faster response to problems, better service to customers, quicker adaptability to new and changing environments, and, of course, better overall data management.

However, there are several disadvantages to database processing that an organization or individual should consider. The major shortcoming is *cost*. Significant expenses normally are incurred in the following cost areas:

☐ *Database Software* A sophisticated DBMS is expensive. An organization may have to spend between $50,000 and $300,000 to obtain one for its mainframe. Microcomputer packages typically cost somewhere in the $300–$800 range.

☐ *New Hardware* A DBMS requires a great deal of main memory and secondary storage, and accessing records can be time consuming. Thus, an individual or organization might find it necessary to upgrade to a bigger, more powerful computer system after acquiring a DBMS.

☐ *Specialized Training of Personnel* Both database systems and databases themselves can be very complex. Large organizations need highly specialized personnel to develop and support them, and naturally such people are costly. Microcomputer-based systems are easier to learn and use, but still are considerably more difficult to master than file managers, spreadsheets, and word processors.

☐ *Conversion Effort* In organizations, moving from a traditional file-oriented system to a database management system often entails a large-scale, expensive conversion. Data must be reorganized and programs rewritten. Fortunately, this is a one-time expense.

Cost, however, is not the only problem. Database processing can increase a system's vulnerability to failure. Because the data are highly integrated in the database, a problem with a key element might render the whole system inactive. Despite the disadvantages, however, DBMSs have become immensely popular with both organizations and individuals.

How a DBMS Works: The Basics

Now that you have a notion of what DBMSs are, let's see how they work. How a DBMS works depends largely on what type of DBMS it is, so we'll start our discussion there.

Types of Database Management Systems. A relatively wide variety of database management systems are available for both large and small computers. Each DBMS organizes database data according to some predefined model, called its *data structure*. A **data structure** specifies relationships among data. As you may remember from Chapter 5, you should organize data according to the way you want to access it. So, given how you think you might access data, some data structures, and therefore DBMSs, will be more advantageous than others. Three major types of data structures in database processing are hierarchical (tree) structures, network structures, and relational structures.

Hierarchical and *network* structures have been around the longest and are still quite useful for many types of applications, particularly those geared to traditional, companywide transaction processing tasks. These two data structures offer a large base of tested programs and experience, and the security systems accompanying the products that conform to them have been well tested through years of use.

Because hierarchical and network data structures are relatively complicated for the typical end user, on the other hand, the database products based on them require professional help to set up and use. Generally this type of work is done by a knowledgeable professional called a **database administrator (DBA).** In large organizations, several people may carry out

FIGURE 14-5
Widely used commercial database products and their underlying data structures.

Commercial Database Product	Vendor	Underlying Data Structure
FOCUS	Information Builders Int'l.	Hierarchical
IMS, DL/1	IBM	"
Ramis II	D & B Computer Services	"
ADABAS	Software AG of North America	Network
DMS 1100	Unisys	"
IDMS	Cullinet	"
IDS II	Honeywell Bull	"
Image	Hewlett-Packard	"
Total	Cincom	"
dBASE IV	Ashton-Tate	Relational
Guru, KnowledgeMan/2	Micro Data Base Systems	"
Ingres	RTI	"
Oracle	Oracle	"
rBASE, System V	Microrim	"
SQL/DS, DB2	IBM	"
Supra	Cincom	"

the DBA function. In contrast, virtually all DBMSs targeted to microcomputers follow the *relational* data model, which is much easier for noncomputer professionals to work with.

In hierarchical and network systems, if data are to be accessed in a certain way, the DBA must formally establish a "navigational path" to allow that type of access. End users aren't free to create new paths on the fly. On the other hand, in relational systems, there are no preexisting paths to worry about. As you will see shortly, the data exist in tables and users are free to browse through the data and combine (i.e., *relate*) them as they see fit.

Because of their simplicity and flexibility, relational models are ideal for applications such as *decision support systems* (see Chapter 16), in which users require flexibility in accessing data authorized to them. Having preexisting paths into the database generally is faster, however, so hierarchical and network databases are useful in environments where people will access the database in predictable ways, such as traditional transaction processing applications.

Figure 14-5 lists some widely used commercial database products and the data structures they use.

Setting Up the Database. The process of setting up, or organizing, the database may involve many steps. Data must be stored as efficiently as possible, indexes and paths may have to be established for rapid access, tight security may have to be established, and so forth. In a large organization, the database administrator performs these tasks. But on most microcomputer systems, such details must be tended to by ordinary users.

One task performed by anyone setting up a database is data definition. **Data definition** is the process of describing data to the DBMS prior to entering them. For example, suppose you've informed your microcomputer's

relational database package that you want to create a table called
EMPLOYEE-SALARY. The package may ask you to describe each data field
of the records that will go into the table. You might respond as follows:

Field Name	Field Type	Width	Decimals
SOC-SEC-NUM	C	9	–
EMPLOYEE-NAME	C	30	–
EMPLOYEE-SALARY	N	8	2

Roughly translated, you've just stated that each record you subsequently
create will have three fields. SOC-SEC-NUM is the first field and will consist
of character (C) data having a maximum length of 9 characters. EMPLOYEE-
NAME, the second column, will use 30 characters. EMPLOYEE-SALARY, the
third column, will consist of numeric (N) data that are at most eight characters long and have two decimal places. Each table *row* will consist of an
employee record—namely, a particular employee's social security number,
name, and salary. The DBMS will use the entries just described to set up a
data dictionary for the application. Character data, incidentally, are those
data on which you can't perform arithmetic operations, while numeric data
are those on which you can.

Processing Data. The process of using the database in some hands-on fashion is called **data manipulation.** Two common ways to manipulate data in
a DBMS are with a retrieval/update language and with a programming language.

End users such as managers, airline clerks, and university registrars typically use the DBMS's retrieval/update language to manipulate data. The **re-
trieval/update language** generally consists of easy-to-use 4GL commands.
The 4GL enables noncomputer professionals to interact with the database
without having to learn a traditional programming language (and possibly
one with a very complicated syntax).

A programmer often uses some sort of *programming language* to write
an application-specific program. In the case of microcomputer packages, the
programmer usually has only one choice: the proprietary 4GL or "database
language" supplied with the DBMS. With DBMS packages targeted to larger
computers, programmers usually have several familiar high-level languages
to work with, including COBOL, PL/1, and BASIC. Typically the DBMS vendor
will extend the power of each of these interfacing languages with a set of
database-specific commands. There will likely be a report-oriented 4GL
available also, for the programmer to prepare "quickie" reports when time
or cost considerations are paramount.

Database Management on Microcomputers

Microcomputer-based DBMSs are predominantly relational. As mentioned
earlier, they are also simple to learn and use relative to DBMSs on large
computer systems. Many of them come with only a single proprietary lan-

FIGURE 14-6

Two database relations. In relational database systems, data exist in tables such as these. Data from two or more files can be combined, or *related*. Through the use of simple database commands, these data can later be extracted and output by the user.

Employee		
Name	**Office Location**	**Department**
Doney	Phoenix	Accounting
Black	Denver	Sales
James	Cleveland	Sales
Giles	San Diego	Accounting
Smith	Miami	Accounting
Fink	San Diego	Sales
. . .	. . .	. . .

Office	
Location	**Manager**
San Diego	Hurt
Cleveland	Holmes
Miami	Jonas
Phoenix	Alexis
. . .	. . .

guage that has commands for data definition, retrieval/update, reporting, and programming functions. For example, in dBASE, a popular microcomputer-oriented DBMS, the CREATE command is used to set up the database, the BROWSE command to look through the database, and the DOWHILE command to set up loops for programs. Although there is no standard relational database language, a number of vendors have chosen to model the retrieval/update features in their languages after IBM's SQL (Structured Query Language).

Setting Up the Database. Data in relational databases must be put into *tables,* such as those in Figure 14-6. Each table has a name—in this example, EMPLOYEE and OFFICE. These tables are similar in concept to *files.* Moreover, their rows are like *records* and their columns are like *fields.* Many of the tables have one or more columns in common with other tables. It is through these columns that the data in the tables are *related.* In our example, the EMPLOYEE and OFFICE tables are related through the "city" column in each (called OFFICE-LOCATION in the first and LOCATION in the second). Defining data in a relational database often is performed in the manner described on pages 451–452.

Processing Data. If, say, we wanted to retrieve the names of all employees in the San Diego office in Figure 14-6, we could use a retrieval command such as

```
SELECT NAME
   FROM EMPLOYEE
WHERE OFFICE-LOCATION = 'SAN DIEGO'
```

The system would access the EMPLOYEE table to select the names of all employees who work in San Diego. This retrieval operation, as you can see, would involve only one table.

The power of relational database systems, however, lies in their ability to link data in more than one table. Suppose, for example, that we wanted to know which employees worked under an office manager named Jonas. We would enter a command such as

```
SELECT NAME
   FROM EMPLOYEE
WHERE OFFICE IS IN
   (SELECT LOCATION FROM OFFICE
   WHERE MANAGER = 'JONAS')
```

The system would find Jonas in the OFFICE table, determine that he or she managed the office in Miami, and then use the EMPLOYEE table to find all employees who work in Miami. In other words, the system would relate these tables to retrieve the needed information.

When applied on a large scale to databases with many tables and numerous interrelations, this principle gives users considerable freedom in the information retrieval process. Commands similar to those just shown make it possible to modify, insert, or delete entries or tables in the database system—that is, *update* data—as well as *retrieve* information. In addition, when several such retrieval/update commands are put together and saved, they form a program. Other commands packaged into microcomputer-based DBMSs allow users to loop, compare, and perform arithmetic on data fields.

The subject of selecting a microcomputer-based database system or file management system is covered in Feature 14B.

Database Management on Large Computers

On large computer systems, DBMSs are necessarily more complex than their microcomputer counterparts. First, they must deal with the problem of several users trying to access the database, perhaps simultaneously. Second, because database technology began evolving at a time when many organizations had thousands of dollars already invested in programs written in popular high-level languages, DBMS vendors had to design their products to interface with these languages.

Setting Up the Database. Large DBMS packages usually have a special language dedicated to the data definition function. This language has generically come to be known as the **data definition language (DDL).** Besides simply defining data, a major function of the DDL in these large packages is security—protecting the database from unauthorized use.

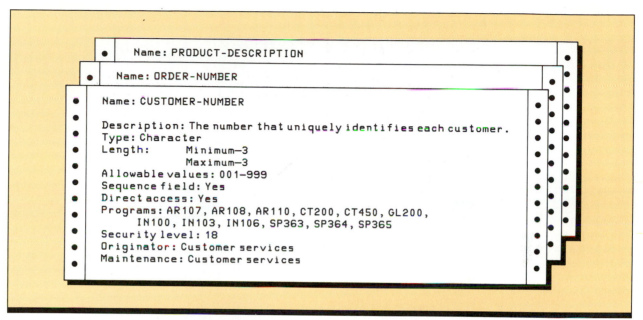

```
    •  ┌─  Name: PRODUCT-DESCRIPTION
    •  │  Name: ORDER-NUMBER
    •  │  Name: CUSTOMER-NUMBER
       │
       │  Description: The number that uniquely identifies each customer.
       │  Type: Character
       │  Length:        Minimum—3
       │                 Maximum—3
       │  Allowable values: 001—999
       │  Sequence field: Yes
       │  Direct access: Yes
       │  Programs: AR107, AR108, AR110, CT200, CT450, GL200,
       │       IN100, IN103, IN106, SP363, SP364, SP365
       │  Security level: 18
       │  Originator: Customer services
       │  Maintenance: Customer services
```

FIGURE 14-7

Data dictionary facility. Among the many things the data dictionary manages are characteristics for each data field, as shown here. The data dictionary can also be used to keep track of program and system descriptions.

Because a large database management system in a firm is used by several people, the accompanying database is particularly vulnerable to security problems. For example, unscrupulous employees may attempt to alter payroll data, access privileged salary or financial account data, or even steal or erase data. To avoid these possibilities, the DBA may assign passwords when setting up the database, to determine which users access which data. This practice gives users only restricted views of the full database. For example, users working on a mailing list application that accesses an employee database will be locked out of access to data such as employee salaries. Also, the DBA can allow some users to modify certain data and give other users of those data only retrieval privileges. For example, in an airline's passenger reservation database, a regular clerk or agent may not be allowed to rebook a special-rate passenger on an alternate flight, but a high-level supervisor, who knows the password, may be able to do so.

Many database management systems, especially those on larger computers, come with a sophisticated data dictionary facility, a feature that considerably extends the scope of the data definition function. The **data dictionary** contains definitions and properties for an alphabetical list of words. Among these words are names of fields, files, and programs located in the database environment. Included under each field entry in the dictionary, for instance, is information such as the number of characters in the field; whether the field is character, numeric, or some other type; the level of security or access attached to the field (employee salaries, for example, would likely allow very limited access); and any alternate names by which the field is known in programs (see Figure 14-7). Included under each pro-

Buying Data Management Software for Your Micro

Decide Whether You Need a File Manager or a Full-fledged DBMS

Data management software consists of programs that enable you to store large banks of records. The software allows you to locate specific records, cull records with specific characteristics, sort records, prepare reports, and create mailing labels.

More so than either word processing or spreadsheeting, data management is a "workhorse" application, requiring lots of number-crunching power to make computationally intensive activities such as sorting and searching proceed quickly, and a great deal of secondary storage capacity to accommodate large files or databases. A general rule of thumb in selecting a system is that the more records you need to store and process, the more powerful the hard-

ware and software you select must be.

Analyzing Needs. The first thing you should do is make a list of the types of files or databases you will be processing, the number of records that will be involved, and the type of processing you intend to do. If you will do relatively simple work, a file manager may adequately meet your needs. If you will require processing of interrelated files, however, you will want a database manager.

Choosing the right data management package may be one of the most critical software decisions you will ever make. Unlike word-processed documents and worksheets, which usually serve to meet a temporary or ad hoc need, the records you develop with your data management system may be with you for years. Therefore, you should choose a system with the

long term in mind, anticipating your needs at least five years into the future.

Three additional things you might add to your checklist of data management needs are ease of learning and use, speed, and backup and recovery.

With respect to ease of learning and use, data management packages can vary considerably. Generally speaking, file managers are much easier to work with and much less expensive than DBMSs. Also, some database systems are targeted to advanced users with a bent for programming and really are inappropriate for the average end user. Therefore, you may have to trade off sophistication for ease of use.

Speed is an important consideration, because sorting and searching can consume a lot of time. Because data management packages differ in how they organize and access data, some are much faster than others for these common types of data man-

gram or data-file entry is information such as identities of authorized users and, in the case of distributed databases, the site at which the program or data resource can be found (see the Tomorrow box).

The dictionary facility ensures that a programmer uses field names correctly when developing new programs for the database environment, that end users access only data specifically authorized for their use, and that updates made to any item in the database environment are proper and are reflected throughout the system.

Processing Data. DBMSs targeted to larger computer systems often contain separate language packages to handle retrieval/update and programming

agement work.

Backup and recovery of records are vital in data management. Try to visualize the consequences of an entire database on your hard disk somehow being accidentally erased. Then consider the types of backup equipment and procedures you would need to implement to make recovery as painless as possible.

Listing Products and Alternatives. Next, list the software package candidates (see figure). If you aren't familiar with the available packages, visit a computer store or look at comparative product reviews in the microcomputer journals at your local library. The leading journals typically publish such reviews periodically.

Because processing speed and secondary storage capacity are usually critical in data management, you will likely need a reasonably powerful microcomputer system and a hard disk. If performing hard-disk backup is time consum-

ing with floppy disks, you may also want to consider a streaming tape device. All of these extra hardware elements can add considerable cost to your computer system.

Examining the Products. If you can test product candidates at your local computer store, you'll be able to see firsthand which works best for some of the types of work you have in mind. Assessing speed will be difficult unless you can find adequate test data. If this is not possible, you should look carefully at reviews that make such tests. Also, you should assess ease of use and the quality of the vendor documentation. If the documentation on a product you like is poor or too advanced, check your local bookstore for a well-written trade book on the product.

Product Comparison and Choice. This is where you cull the best products from the rest of the lot and scrutinize them closely on the basis of performance and cost. If

you are purchasing data management software to run a company, reliability and support will become additional factors to weigh into your final decision. Thus, you may choose a mature product with a proven track record or base your buying decision on the type of support that will be available when something goes wrong.

File Managers
- ☑ PFS: Professional File
- ☑ Reflex: The Analyst
- ☑ Q & A
- ☑ Filing Assistant

Database Managers
- ☑ dBASE
- ☑ Paradox
- ☑ Oracle
- ☑ RBase
- ☑ Team-up
- ☑ KnowledgeMan
- ☑ Foxbase
- ☑ Clipper

Market leaders. Ashton-Tate's dBASE claims over half the packages sold.

---

tasks. Also, both sets of tasks pose their own array of problems that the typical microcomputer DBMS owner doesn't encounter.

For example, on large computer systems (or microcomputer systems linked by a network), users often need to access the same data at more or less the same time. This can cause several problems. For example:

☐ Only one seat is available on a flight. Two agents seize it at the same moment and sell it to different customers.

☐ A program is tallying a series of customer balances in a database. When it is halfway finished, another program controlled by someone else transfers $5,000 from account 001 (which the first program already has tallied)

T   O   M   O   R   R   O   W

Distributed Databases

Today's Rarity, Tomorrow's Standard

For many years, both database vendors and corporate DBAs have discussed the need for distributed databases. While some corporations, such as New York–based Chemical Bank, have gone to great expense to build such systems on their own, to date very few companies have distributed databases. With many of the major database vendors in the process of releasing products in this area, however, the situation may well change—and rather soon.

The concept of a distributed database is relatively simple. Instead of a single database existing on a large, centralized mainframe—currently the most widespread practice—the database is divided among several smaller

> Users should work under the illusion that all the data are stored on their own machines.

computers that are hooked up in a network. These computers are likely to be state-of-the-art PCs, each with, say, 60 to 100 megabytes of local secondary storage.

In a distributed DBMS, data are divided among the member databases so as to optimize system performance measures such as communications cost, response time, and storage capacity. Moreover, data can be left at the sites at which they are most needed and best managed. A user calling into the database generally will have no idea where the data are coming from; they could be stored in a machine in the same building, in a different state, or even in a different country.

When the user makes a request to a distributed DBMS, it is up to the DBMS to determine how to best get the data; how it will do this should be transparent to the user. Theoretically, users should be able to work under

---

to account 999 (which it hasn't). Thus, the first program will "double count" the $5,000 and obtain erroneous results.

To prevent such **concurrent access** problems, most database systems allow users to place a temporary "lock" on certain blocks of data to ensure that no other modifications to these data will be made during their processing.

Another problem unique to DBMSs on large computer systems relates to the need of these DBMSs to tie into programs coded in popular high-level programming languages. An interfacing feature known as a **data manipulation language (DML),** however, solves this problem. The DML is simply a set of commands that enable the language the programmer normally works with to function in a database environment. For example, if the programmer writes programs in COBOL, a COBOL DML must be used. The DML may consist of 30 or so commands, which the programmer uses to interact with data in the database (Figure 14-8 provides a sample of these commands).

Thus, a COBOL program in a database environment consists of a mixture of standard COBOL statements and COBOL DML statements, such as the

the illusion that all the data are stored on their own machines.

The integrated, distributed database environment of tomorrow is a far cry from the traditional, nonintegrated distributed database environment of today. In traditional database environments, users generally must know where the information they need is located. For instance, if the user is in New York and the information is on a local mainframe, the user must know how to call up the mainframe and how to download the data. And if the information is in Chicago, the user probably will have to know this in order to phone Chicago to get the information. This can pose a serious problem if the user is unfamiliar with the Chicago DBMS and must depend on some "stranger" in Chicago to make the retrieval. The resulting loss of control and the delays can be considerable.

With traditional distributed systems, if the user must frequently call up several DBMSs, he or she will probably get bogged down learning the syntax and idiosyncracies of each system. Each of these systems may have been built at different times and use different interfaces. In a truly distributed DBMS, there is a common, seamless interface among member systems. Thus, the user need learn only one command structure to get information from any workstation hooked into the network, resulting in minimum delays for customers.

Still another benefit of the distributed system is the economies realized through using several small machines in place of a single large one. For instance, in a centralized system, a new mainframe may be needed to manage the larger bank of data as the DBMS grows. Upgrading a mainframe can cost several hundred thousands or even millions of dollars. With a distributed system, on the other hand, an organization will likely need to add just one or a few more small stations, at a cost of only a few thousand dollars, to accommodate the extra capacity. Thus, the organization can easily deal with growth by adding to the system in small increments rather than in giant blocks.

following small block of code, which deletes an employee's record from a database:

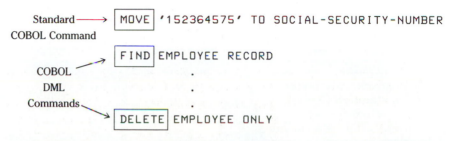

The program containing this mixture of statements is then fed to the DBMS's COBOL precompiler, as shown in Figure 14-9. The **precompiler** translates this program into a standard COBOL program, which then can be executed with the regular COBOL compiler available on the system.

High-level languages that are supported by their own DMLs are called **host languages.** Several host languages may be available on any particular

DML Command	Purpose
CREATE	Creates a record
STORE	Stores data in the database
FETCH	Retrieves data from the database
INSERT	Inserts a record
MODIFY	Changes data in a record
FIND	Locates a record
DELETE	Deletes a record

FIGURE 14-8

Some typical DML commands. Where available, such commands extend the language with which the programmer normally works, tailoring it to a database environment.

system. Languages that a DBMS commonly employs as hosts are COBOL, FORTRAN, PL/1, and BASIC.

INTEGRATED SOFTWARE PACKAGES

This and the previous chapters have described various types of productivity software—specifically word processors, spreadsheets, presentation graphics packages, file managers, and database management systems. An **integrated software package** is one that bundles two or more of these software functions, and perhaps others, into a single "megapackage." Symphony and Jazz—which bundle a spreadsheet, file manager, presentation graphics routine, word processor, and communications software—are examples of integrated software products. So is Framework, which combines a spreadsheet,

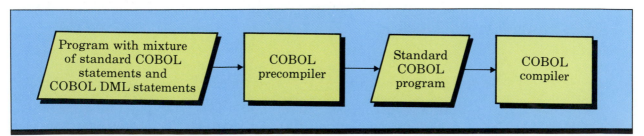

FIGURE 14-9

Use of a COBOL precompiler. The COBOL precompiler translates a COBOL program written with DML commands into a regular COBOL program, which can be run on a standard COBOL language translator.

Pros and Cons of Integrated Software

Advantages

☑ You need to learn only a single command structure

☑ A bundled package costs less than purchasing all of the components separately

☑ Integrating data among the package components is straightforward

Disadvantages

☑ You may be paying for a number of functions you don't really need

☑ Packages dedicated to single applications often are stronger in those applications than are integrated packages

☑ Integrated packages can be complex and require a lot of memory

FIGURE 14-10

Advantages and disadvantages of integrated software packages.

database management system, presentation graphics routine, word processor, and communications software.

Integrated software packages give you the convenience of having to learn only a single command or menu structure rather than suffer through the software-approach differences of three or four vendors. In addition, a bundled package normally costs less than a system of individually purchased software components. Perhaps most important, you can integrate data generated from the various package components—for example, insert a graph into a word-processed document—because all the software components are compatible with one another.

On the negative side, integrated packages typically have one or two strong components and several weak ones. Thus, an author, who likely requires a top-of-the-line word processor, often is better off getting a dedicated word processing package and leaving alone integrated packages that also cater to spreadsheet or database users. A second disadvantage of these packages is that some of the features may be of little use to the user. For example, a user without phone access certainly wouldn't get his or her money's worth out of a communications-software feature.

Figure 14-10 summarizes some of the advantages and disadvantages of integrated software packages.

SUMMARY AND KEY TERMS

A **file manager,** or *record management system,* is a software package that enables one to organize data into files and process the data a single file at a time.

Many file managers employ an *onscreen form,* or **template,** to help users create a file's records. Later, records can be updated or deleted from the file and new ones added.

A **database management system (DBMS)** differs from a file manager primarily in that it enables immediate, "seamless" access to data that might span several files. As a rule, because database management systems are more technically complex than file managers, they are also more expensive and more difficult to master.

The data in a DBMS are placed on disk in a database. A **database** is an integrated collection of data. End users and programmers gain access to the DBMS through an easy-to-use *retrieval/update language* that accompanies the DBMS or via an *applications program* written in a programming language (e.g., COBOL or a report-oriented 4GL).

The major advantages of a DBMS include integrated data, program/data independence, nonredundant storage, and data integrity. These technical advantages translate into fewer personnel, better service to customers, faster response to problems, and more rapid adaptation to new and changing environments. The major disadvantage of a DBMS is cost. Significant expenses include the costs of purchasing database software, upgrading hardware, acquiring specialized personnel, and converting to a database system.

A wide variety of database management systems are available for both large and small computers. Each DBMS organizes database data according to some predefined model, called a **data structure,** which specifies relationships among data.

Three types of data structures important in database processing are *hierarchical (tree)* structures, *network* structures, and *relational* structures. Hierarchical and network databases are relatively complex for end users to set up and use on their own and generally are installed with the help of a professional known as a **database administrator (DBA).** Virtually all DBMSs targeted to microcomputers follow the relational database model, which is much easier for noncomputer professionals to understand and use.

One task performed by anyone setting up a database is **data definition,** the process of describing data to the DBMS prior to entering them.

The process of using the database in some hands-on fashion is called **data manipulation.** Two common ways to manipulate data in a DBMS are with a **retrieval/update language** and with a *programming language.*

Many microcomputer-oriented DBMSs come with only a single proprietary language that has commands for data definition, retrieval/update, reporting, and programming functions. Large computer systems that use sophisticated DBMSs usually have a special language dedicated to each of these tasks. For example, a **data definition language (DDL)** handles data definition chores, placing key data for applications development and security purposes into a **data dictionary.** A **data manipulation language (DML)** extends the language the programmer normally works with into a database environment. Languages supported by their own DMLs are called **host languages.** A program called a **precompiler** translates DML commands into host-language commands, which in turn can be executed on the regular compilers available at the computer site.

On large computer systems, DBMS packages must also deal with the problem of several users trying to access the database at the same time. To prevent such **concurrent access** problems, most database systems allow users to place a temporary "lock" on certain blocks of data to ensure that no other modifications to these data will be made during their processing.

An **integrated software package** bundles one or more individual productivity software functions—such as word processing, spreadsheets, presentation graphics, file management or database management, and the like—into a single "megapackage."

REVIEW EXERCISES

Fill-in Questions

1. The two major types of data management packages are _DBMS_ and _filemgo_.

2. The onscreen form used to create records in a data management environment is often called a(n) _template_.

3. An integrated collection of data is called a(n) _database_.

4. The three most common types of database data structures are the _network_, _hierarchial_, and _relational_ structures.

5. On large, companywide database management systems, a knowledgeable professional known as a _DBA_ often is called upon to set up the database and assist users.

6. The problem of _concurrent_ access often arises when two or more people try to seize and modify data at the same time.

7. SQL is an acronym for _structured query language_

8. A software package that combines a database management system with a word processor and a spreadsheet is called a(n) _integrated software pkg_

Matching Questions   *Match each term with the description that best fits.*

a. precompiler   d. retrieval/update language
b. data definition language (DDL)   e. host language
c. data manipulation   f. data definition

  _B_   **1.** A language used to describe database data.

     2. A language supported by a DML (data manipulation language).

  _a_   **3.** A translator used to translate DML commands into commands that can be input to a regular language translator.

  _d_   **4.** A database software product that permits programmers and nonprogrammers to easily retrieve, add, delete, or modify database data with simple, Englishlike commands.

  _f_   **5.** Organizing data in the database so that programmers and users have good access to them, data are stored as efficiently as possible, and the database's security is maintained.

  _c_   **6.** A task that can be performed through either a retrieval/update language or a programming language.

Discussion Questions

1. What is a file manager?
2. What is a database management system, and how does it differ from a file manager?
3. Identify the advantages and disadvantages of database management systems.
4. What is the difference between data description and data manipulation?
5. How do database management systems solve the problem of concurrent access?
6. What is an integrated software package?

Critical Thinking Questions

1. An owner of a small personnel agency is about to purchase a well-known database package to manage a growing client list on a microcomputer system. One of her employees is a computer whiz and has suggested writing the database package himself, to make it better fit the agency's needs. What should the owner do in this situation—say yes, say no, or gather more information?

2. Comment on this statement: "The most successful integrated software product of the future will be virtually all-inclusive, combining an operating system; language translators to handle COBOL, FORTRAN, BASIC, Pascal, and many other such languages; database management

routines; spreadsheet and presentation graphics routines; communications functions; and a variety of other functions."

3. Many people feel that, to the average business, the choice of a database management system is much more important than the choice of a word processor or a spreadsheet package. What do you think?

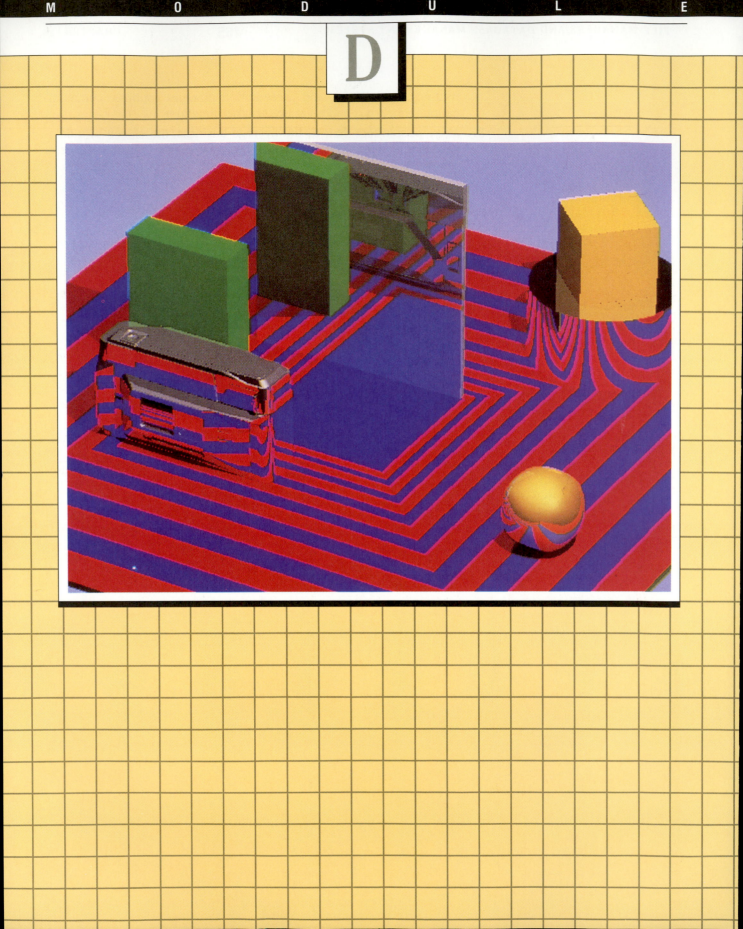

Computer Systems

This module integrates many of the concepts from earlier chapters, which introduced various parts of computer systems. A computer system consists of the computer itself and the support equipment, programs, data, procedures, and people in its environment. In other words, all the components that contribute to making the computer a useful tool can be considered part of a computer system.

Chapters 15 and 16 discuss various types of computer systems. Chapter 15 focuses on personal computer systems—their principal hardware parts, the software available for them, and how to acquire a system for business or home use. Chapter 16 addresses the applications of small and large computer systems in businesses and other organizations, including transaction processing, information reporting systems and decision support systems, office automation, and manufacturing and design. This chapter also covers artificial intelligence, an area that is expected to have a far-reaching impact on any type of system that would benefit from some type of humanlike guidance. Chapter 17 discusses how organizations build computer systems.

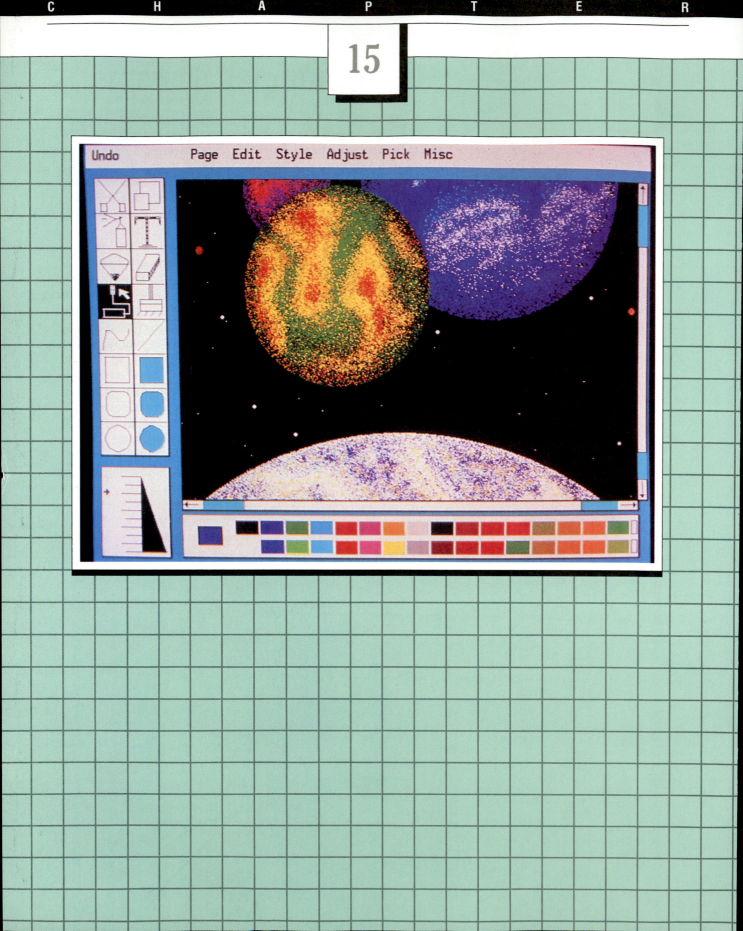

Microcomputer Systems

Outline

Objectives

After completing this chapter, you will be able to:

1. Distinguish among the various types of microcomputer systems currently on the market.

2. Identify the major hardware and software components of most microcomputer systems.

3. Explain how to go about selecting a microcomputer system and how to maintain it.

OVERVIEW

Often affordably priced between a few hundred and a few thousand dollars, microcomputer systems have been available since the mid-1970s. The earliest systems were targeted to electronics hobbyists, but rapid improvements on both software and hardware fronts shortly made them practical for business and home use. Today microcomputer-based processing is the fastest-growing area in the computer field. Some industry observers predict that in the next few years as many as 100 million systems will be in operation.

We'll begin this chapter by covering the types of hardware and software commonly found with microcomputer systems. Where appropriate, we'll look at product differences that are particularly important to know about when buying (or leasing) systems. Then we'll cover various topics of interest to virtually any microcomputer user, such as where to go to learn more about microcomputer systems and how to maintain a microcomputer system once it's on your desk.

TYPES OF MICROCOMPUTER SYSTEMS

Microcomputer systems, as we mentioned earlier, are computer systems driven by microprocessors. A **microprocessor** is a computer—having both a control unit and an ALU—that is engraved on a silicon chip no larger than a fingernail. The CPU and other microprocessor chips, memory chips, and various types of circuitry are packaged into a unit called the *system unit.* The system unit often is informally called "the computer," but, technically speaking, it is the CPU chip that most experts refer to as the computer. Besides microcomputer systems, microprocessors are found in scores of consumer products, for instance, electronic scales, watches, washers and dryers, and video arcade games.

Personal computer systems technically are microcomputer systems used by individuals to meet various *personal* needs both at work and at home. The terms *personal computer system* and *microcomputer system* often are used synonymously in practice.

Microprocessors can be classified in many ways, for example, by the number of bits they can manipulate per operation. The microprocessors that power electronic gadgets such as watches and toys typically manipulate a small number of bits at one time, often 2, 4, or 8. The microprocessors that serve as the CPUs in microcomputer systems, on the other hand, typically handle 16 or 32 bits at once.

Classifying Microcomputer Systems

Most general-purpose microcomputer system units currently available for business and home use can be classified as being either portable (including laptop) or desktop (also see Figure 15-1).

FIGURE 15-1
Three microcomputer systems. (a, left) Laptop. (b, middle) Portable. (c, right) Desktop.

Portable and Laptop Units. **Portable computers** are designed for users who would like to use a microcomputer at several sites. These computers are characterized by being lightweight (4 to 18 pounds) and compact (able to fit into a briefcase). Technically speaking, the most lightweight portable computers—which can be used on one's lap, if desired—are called **laptop computers.** Typical users of portable units include field engineers, sales representatives, executives who travel a lot, and people who need to give computer-assisted management presentations in places where it would be inconvenient to lug in a larger unit (see Window 7).

Although many portables are just as powerful as their larger desktop cousins (discussed next), they tend to be more expensive, have small and hard-to-read screens, and have a dense arrangement of keys. These disadvantages notwithstanding, portability is "in" these days, and laptop computers currently are one of the fastest growing segments of the microcomputer industry.

Desktop Units. **Desktop computers** are those found most often in schools, homes, and businesses. These are the computer systems that have become household names—IBM PC; IBM PS/2; Apple II, IIe, IIc, and the Macintosh line; Tandy 1000, 2000, 3000, and 4000; Compaq Deskpro 286 and 386; the NeXT Computer System; Commodore Amiga; and so forth.

Desktop units fall into one of two categories: single-user systems and multiuser systems. *Single-user systems,* as their name implies, can be operated by only one user at a time, while *multiuser systems* can accommodate several users concurrently. Multiuser systems are sometimes called *supermicrocomputers,* or *supermicros.* Despite their multiuser potential, supermicros often are employed as single-user systems.

HARDWARE

Many desktop microcomputer systems contain at least five pieces of hardware: the system unit itself, a secondary storage device, a video display unit, a keyboard, and a printer. In some microcomputer systems, all or most of

FIGURE 15-2

A microprocessor chip in its carrier package. The carrier package is plugged into the system unit's system board, which also contains a limited amount of memory.

these devices are housed in a single hardware unit; with others, you can select each device separately. We'll now look at each of these devices in detail. Then we'll discuss how they and other hardware devices are fitted together into a "typical" system.

The System Unit

The **system unit** often consists of at least a CPU chip, memory (RAM and ROM) chips, internal boards on which these and other chips are mounted, ports that provide connections for external devices, a power supply, and internal circuitry to hook everything together. We discussed many of these hardware devices in some detail in Chapter 4. Here we'll expand on that discussion.

Microprocessor Chips. Every microcomputer system unit contains a specific microprocessor chip as its CPU. This chip is put into a carrier package, as shown in Figure 15-2, and the carrier package is mounted onto a special board that fits inside the system unit.

Most microcomputer systems made today use CPU chips that are manufactured by either Intel or Motorola. The Intel line of chips—such as the 8086, 8088, 80286, 80386, and 80486—is used on the microcomputer systems made by IBM and companies that make "IBM-look-alike" microcomputer systems. The Motorola line of chips—including the 68000, 68020, 68030, and 68040—is used on the Apple Macintosh line of computers and the NeXT Computer System. Figure 15-3 lists the names of some popular system units and the CPUs that run them.

The type of CPU chip in a computer's system unit also greatly affects what one can do with the computer system. Software is written to work on a specific chip, and an applications program that works on one chip generally does not function on another unless modified. So if the CPU chip that supports your computer is rare, you will have difficulty finding applications programs that will run on it.

Working alongside the CPU chip in many system units are *specialized processor chips,* such as numeric coprocessors and graphic processors. The role of these chips is to perform specialized tasks for the CPU, thereby enhancing overall system performance.

RAM. The primary memory of microcomputer systems, like any microprocessor, consists of circuits etched onto silicon chips. This kind of primary memory is commonly called **random access memory (RAM).** Most desktop microcomputer systems in use today have between 256 kilobytes and 4 megabytes of RAM. Many computer systems allow memory expansion (within limits) directly on the system board or through an add-in board when RAM is insufficient.

Most RAM is *volatile,* meaning that the contents of memory are lost when the computer is shut off. *Nonvolatile* RAM, called *CMOS RAM,* is also available, but it is more expensive. (CMOS RAM is mounted onto boards contain-

Vendor	Product	Type	CPU
Apple Computer, Inc.	Macintosh 512KB Enhanced, Macintosh Plus, Macintosh SE	Desktop	Motorola 68000
	Macintosh II	Desktop	Motorola 68020
	Macintosh IIX, Macintosh IICX, Macintosh SE/30	Desktop	Motorola 68030
Compaq Computer Corp.	Deskpro Model 2	Desktop	Intel 8086
	Deskpro 286 Model 1, Deskpro 286 Model 20	Desktop	Intel 80286
	Deskpro 386 Model 40, Deskpro 386 Model 70	Desktop	Intel 80386
	Compaq Portable	Portable	Intel 8088
	Compaq Portable II, Compaq Portable III	Portable	Intel 80286
Data General Corp.	DG/One Model 2T	Portable	Intel 8088-2
Hewlett-Packard Co.	Vectra PC	Desktop	Intel 80286
IBM Corp.	PC, PC/XT	Desktop	Intel 8088
	PC AT	Desktop	Intel 80286
	PS/2 Model 25, PS/2 Model 30	Desktop	Intel 8086
	PS/2 Model 50, PS/2 Model 60	Desktop	Intel 80286
	PS/2 Model 70, PS/2 Model 80	Desktop	Intel 80386
NeXT Inc.	The NeXT Computer System	Desktop	Motorola 68030
PC's Limited	Turbo	Desktop	Intel 8088-2
	286-12	Desktop	Intel 80286
	386-16	Desktop	Intel 80386
Tandy Corp./Radio Shack	Tandy 1000SX	Desktop	Intel 8088
	Tandy 3000HL	Desktop	Intel 80286
	Tandy 4000	Desktop	Intel 80386
Toshiba America, Inc.	T1100 Plus	Portable	Intel 8086
	T5100	Portable	Intel 80386
Zenith Data Systems	Z-159	Desktop	Intel 8088-2
	Z-286	Desktop	Intel 80286
	Z-386	Desktop	Intel 80386

FIGURE 15-3

Some widely used system units and their CPUs. Virtually all of the leading microcomputer systems use a CPU chip made by either Intel or Motorola.

ing small batteries, which allow the chips to retain data and programs for several months or more. The batteries are automatically recharged every time the system unit is turned on.)

ROM. ROM stands for **read-only memory.** It consists of nonerasable random access hardware modules that contain programs. These modules are plugged into one or more boards inside the system unit. You can neither write over these ROM programs (that's why they're called *read-only*) nor destroy their contents when you shut off the computer's power (that is, they're nonvolatile).

Often key pieces of systems software are stored in ROM. For instance, on the IBM PC, PC AT, PS/2, and similar computers, the routine used to bring applications programs in and out of the central processor—called the *Basic Input/Output System (BIOS)*—is stored in ROM.

Internal and External Interfaces. Many system units contain a limited number of *internal* "slots" into which the user can mount **add-in boards.** Where this can be done, it offers a great deal of flexibility in personalizing a system. For example, if you needed more main memory, you would acquire a *memory expansion board.* This board contains the appropriate number of additional memory chips and the circuitry needed to get your computer system to access them. For instance, to run the OS/2 operating system (which requires a bare minimum of 1 MB of RAM) on the IBM PS/2 Models 50 and 60 (which are based on the Intel 80286 processor), you would use a memory expansion board. If, on the other hand, you wanted to put an Intel 80386 processor into an IBM PC AT (which contains a slower, 80286 processor), you would opt for an *upgrade board.*

Many types of add-in boards currently are available in the marketplace. Most of these boards provide either a basic function that is unavailable with the system unit or a "value-added" capability that enhances an existing function. With new machines and new capabilities being announced regularly, the number of boards is increasing rapidly. Figure 15-4 lists several types of boards and the functions they perform.

In addition to internal interfaces, many microcomputer systems provide communications with detached devices through *external* I/O ports. **Ports** are sockets into which specific types of "standard" peripherals can be plugged. As mentioned in Chapter 7, ports are of two types—*parallel* and *serial.* Parallel ports are faster and use more expensive cables. Devices such as modems almost always connect to serial ports, while printers connect to either serial or parallel ports, depending on the type of computer and printer. Also, many microcomputer systems contain a special port for a keyboard, display device, and a mouse. These ports are generally located at the back of the system unit.

There is a practical limit to the number of peripheral devices a simple CPU can handle. Generally, each new device interfaced through an add-in board or port adds to the burden the CPU must manage, thereby possibly downgrading system performance.

Bus. The CPU connects to RAM, ROM, internal interfaces, and external interfaces through circuitry called an *I/O* (for *input/output*) **bus.** Thus, the I/O bus hooks up the CPU to every online hardware device in the system, enabling data to be exchanged and processed. On newer computers such as the IBM PS/2 line (Model 50 and higher) and the Macintosh IIX, this bus enables additional CPUs, on add-in boards, to compete for system resources and gain full control of the microcomputer system.

FIGURE 15-4

Add-in boards for microcomputer systems. Add-in boards can provide a microcomputer system with either brand new capabilities or enhancements to existing features.

Board Type	Purpose
☑ Cache card	Provides the microcomputer system with logic to do disk caching
☑ Concurrent-processor board	Contains a CPU that can be run concurrently with the CPU on the system board
☑ Coprocessor board	Uses specialized processor chips that speed up over-all processing in the microcomputer system
☑ Disk controller card	Enables a certain type of disk unit to interface with the microcomputer system
☑ Display adapter board	Enables a certain type of display device to interface with the microcomputer system
☑ Emulator board	Allows the microcomputer system to function as a communications terminal to a large computer system
☑ Fax board	Provides facsimile capabilities for the microcomputer system
☑ Graphics adapter board	Enables the computer system to conform to a particular graphics standard
☑ Memory expansion board	Allows additional RAM to be put into the microcomputer system
☑ Modem board	Provides modem circuitry on a board
☑ Multifunction board	Provides several independent functions on a single board
☑ Upgrade board*	Contains a CPU that can be used in lieu of the CPU on the system board

*Also known as an accelerator board or a turbo board.

This powerful feature—known as *Micro Channel Architecture (MCA)* on computers on the high end of the PS/2 line and *Nubus* on the Mac II series of computers—enables you to, say, give an IBM PS/2 Model 60 the functionality of a Mac II simply by inserting an add-in board. Alternatively, you conceivably can configure several 80386 processor boards into your IBM PS/2 Model 80 and assign them to different applications that are to be run concurrently. Thus, one CPU can be working on a spreadsheet application while another is performing a background database search. Having each CPU dedicated to a specific application and the host CPU coordinating each will make the work go much faster than it would if the host had to do everything.

On both the Mac II series of computers and the high end of the PS/2 line, the I/O bus has a 32-bit-wide path. Recently an *EISA* (Enhanced Industry Standard Architecture) standard has become available so that IBM PC AT users, whose systems have older, 16-bit buses, can upgrade to the MCA world. Boards conforming to EISA enable PC AT users to use their computers in an environment that permits concurrent processors and greater amounts of RAM. EISA has also been widely adopted by vendors producing IBM-look-alike computer systems. The Tomorrow box in this chapter addresses the mounting issue of upgrading the large bank of still useful microcomputer systems that have been technologically leapfrogged by newer devices.

T   O   M   O   R   R   O   W

Mainframe Power on a Desktop

Personal Computing with the '486 in the Coming Decade

When the IBM PC made its debut in 1981, it gave the public the power of yesterday's mini on a single microprocessor chip—the Intel 8088. As the 1990s begin, the wallop of today's low-end mainframe is here—on a desktop—in the form of the Intel 80486, or '486, chip. As hardware and software products that take full advantage of this chip's power enter the market, we can expect to see an amazing variety of desktop applications emerge in the world of IBM and IBM-compatible microcomputing. (The Apple Macintosh world, with the Motorola 68040 processor, will undergo a similar transformation.)

> Don't discard that '286 or '386 processor yet.

The Intel 80486 squeezes the power of 1 million transistors into an area smaller than a fingernail. Its predecessor, the 80386 chip, was able to achieve circuit widths 1/50th the diameter of a human hair, but the 80486 chip is able to fit four times that number of circuits into the same area.

The bottom line: microcomputers that can perform at mainframe speeds. The 80386 chip provided clock speeds of 16, 20, and 25 MHz (megahertz), but early 80486 chips will yield speeds in the 33-to-50-MHz range.

Already there are many types of applications for the new chip. For the desktop user, computation- and storage-intensive applications such as sophisticated modeling, computer-aided design and manufacturing (CAD/CAM), high-end publishing, large-database information retrieval, and image processing are now a greater reality than ever before. While all of these applications can be done to some extent on less powerful processors, sophisticated users may easily find themselves running out of the

Secondary Storage

As with larger computers, the primary memory of microcomputers can hold only the data and programs the computer is currently processing. If you want to keep data and programs for repeated use, you must have a secondary storage unit. Both disk devices and other storage hardware are available for use with microcomputers.

Diskettes. For desktop systems, **diskette** remains by far the most popular storage medium. Although diskettes are available in several sizes (diameters), the 5¼-inch and 3½-inch ones are the most popular. Diskettes have various other properties; for example, they may be double-sided, double-density, soft-sectored, and the like. We discussed these and other properties in detail in Chapter 5. The diskettes you use must be compatible with the diskette drives on your microcomputer system.

number-crunching power and storage a processor such as the 80486 can provide.

The '486 chip is also now being widely integrated into larger computers. For instance, a number of computer systems today employ several '486 microprocessors working in parallel. Some of these systems are in the same league as the top-of-the-line mainframes and supercomputers currently available—and at only a small fraction of the price. But don't count out the conventional computer systems prematurely. Parallel processors require special software, and the resulting expense can make the price tag on a piece of hardware seem almost inconsequential.

Many owners of 80286- and 80386-based machines feel their systems are being in-stantly eclipsed by the '486 processor, but functional obsolescence is unlikely to happen for some time. Most experts strongly advise "Don't discard that '286 or '386 computer yet!" Several reasons support this viewpoint.

First, many of yesterday's systems are totally adequate for tomorrow's needs. For instance, there are still many users around who need little more than a simple spreadsheet or word processing package. Many of them can get along just fine even if they have only a simple 8088-based system, such as an IBM PC. And, realistically speaking, even yesterday's '286 processor, along with a 40 MB hard disk, will continue to serve most personal types of uses well into the future—even the maintenance of rel-atively large personal data-bases.

Second, many of the applications that work on '286 and '386 processors still don't take full advantage of those processors' power; that is, even though the hardware is available, the software for them lags far behind. As more applications that run on UNIX and OS/2, which address more RAM than MS-DOS, become available, owners of these older machines will benefit.

Finally, the current crop of '486 machines are expensive. Unless an application comes along that both requires '486-class power and packs a type of functionality that users feel they can't live without, it will likely be a few more years before a steady migration to these machines occurs.

Hard Disks. In Chapter 5, we discussed **hard disks** and hard-disk drives for microcomputer systems. In Winchester devices, the disks, access arms, and read/write heads are sealed in the same container. Hard-disk systems are much faster than diskette systems and can store much more, but they are comparatively expensive. Although many microcomputer users don't need and/or can't afford hard disks, these devices are today considered the standard for business applications.

Other Devices. Four other widely used types of secondary storage devices are hard cards, disk cartridges, cartridge tapes, and optical disks (see Figure 15-5). We discussed all of these devices in some detail in Chapter 5.

The Keyboard

For most people, a personal computer system would be useless without a **keyboard,** which often is the main vehicle for input. Potential buyers should carefully evaluate keyboards considering several factors.

FIGURE 15-5

Optical disk. The 256 MB optical disk on NeXT Inc.'s NeXT Computer System is removable and allows both writing and erasing. It can store the equivalent of 300 to 400 complete books and includes sophisticated searching and indexing capabilities.

First, not all keyboards have the same key arrangement as that on a standard typewriter nor do they have the same number of keys. For example, the QWERTY keyboard uses the conventional typewriter format, while the newer and more conveniently designed Dvorak keyboard uses another arrangement (see Figure 15-6). A typical keyboard may contain anywhere from 80 to 110 keys.

Second, the keyboards on most microcomputer systems have several special keys that involve specific software routines. A Delete key, for example, deletes characters from the screen, and a PgUp key flips through page-length units of a file one at a time. Also, there are several function keys. Each software package defines these keys in certain ways, and, in many instances, you can program them with your own instructions. The number of special keys, as well as their capabilities and placement, varies widely among manufacturers.

Third, keyboards differ with respect to touch. Some are sculpted to match the contours of the fingertips, for instance, while others have either flat (calculator-style) keys or a flat membrane panel with touch-sensitive keys. Also, manufacturers space keys differently, so keys that feel just right to one person may seem too far apart to another. Key spacing can be a real problem

FIGURE 15-6

QWERTY and Dvorak keyboards. Although most people are trained on QWERTY keyboards, proponents of the Dvorak keyboard claim that device significantly increases typing speed. Dvorak keyboards place the five vowels under the fingertips of the left hand and the five most-used consonants under the fingertips of the right.

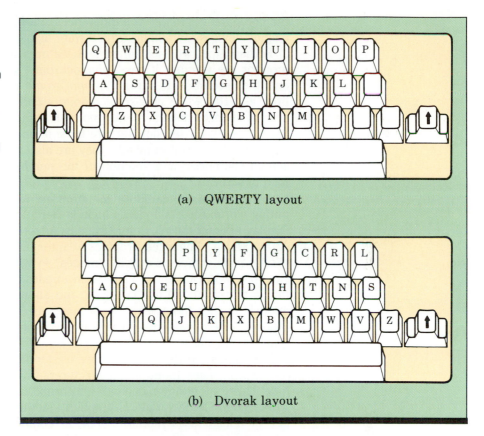

(a) QWERTY layout

(b) Dvorak layout

for word processing users who need a portable computer, because the keyboards on these units are designed to be as compact as possible. Still another difference regarding touch is that some keyboards make a faint clicking sound each time you depress a key, while others are completely silent.

Finally, many keyboards are detached hardware units that you can place wherever convenient. Others are built into the display or system unit. While the trend today is clearly toward detachable keyboards, this design feature is not always feasible.

As we discussed in Chapter 6, you may want other input devices to supplement keyboard operations. One of the most popular of these is the **mouse,** a cursor-movement device that's a standard item on computers such as those in the Apple Macintosh line. Many other computer systems support the mouse as an optional device. The mouse is especially useful in making selections from graphical user interfaces.

The Monitor

Almost every microcomputer system has a video display unit, or **monitor.** It allows you to see your input as you enter it and the computer's output as the computer responds. The differences among monitors and other types of display devices are numerous and were highlighted in Chapter 6.

Perhaps the two most important features to consider when selecting a monitor are whether it has a monochrome, grey-scale, or a color display and the resolution it permits. *Monochrome monitors* are available for as little as $100, while *grey-scale monitors* and *full-color monitors* may cost several hundred dollars. *Analog monitors,* which work under a principle similar to that of a television set, are far superior for color or grey scales than *digital monitors*. Unfortunately, they are also more expensive. Resolution, or screen sharpness, is a function of the number of pixels packed into each inch of screen.

A number of standards for monitors are in effect. In the IBM microcomputing world, these standards include Hercules monochrome, Monochrome Display Adapter (MDA), Color Graphics Adapter (CGA), Multi-Color Graphics Array (MCGA), Enhanced Graphics Adapter (EGA), and Video Graphics Array (VGA). Such standards specify "modes" in which the monitor can run. For example, VGA can run in 17 different modes. One mode divides the screen into a matrix of 320 by 200 pixels and allows 256 colors to be displayed; another divides the screen into a matrix of 720 by 400 pixels and permits monochrome display only. The Apple Macintosh world has a similar set of graphics standards.

In response to the large number of standards and modes now available for display, many monitor manufacturers have developed *multiscan monitors.* These monitors can handle both analog and digital signals and can work under a wide variety of graphics standards. Also available are a number of nonstandard monitors that, in combination with special graphics adapter boards, will produce super-high-resolution images for an IBM PS/2, Macintosh IIX, or other 32-bit computer.

The Printer

If you will use your computer system for any purpose other than playing computer games, you'll probably need some form of printed output. For example, you may want a copy of a computer program you just debugged or perhaps a paper you just wrote.

As with monitors, the differences among **printers** (discussed in Chapter 6) are numerous. The two most popular types of microcomputer-oriented printers are impact dot-matrix printers and (nonimpact) laser printers. Both types of printers produce characters formed by tiny dots.

Impact dot-matrix printers are the most inexpensive type of microcomputer printer. Characters are printed serially—that is, one after another—by pins in the printhead that strike the paper. Many dot-matrix printers sold today use a single row of nine pins. Several high-end printers that use two rows of 12 pins are also available. The more pins in the printhead, the higher the print quality. On IBM microcomputers and similar devices, impact dot-matrix printers connect to the system unit through a parallel port. On the Apple Macintosh line of computers, printers often connect through a serial port.

Laser printers produce one page of output at a time, just as a copying machine does. In fact, many laser printers use the same "engine" (usually made by Canon or Ricoh) and the same principle (putting electrically charged toner onto paper) as copying machines do. Laser printers are superior to impact dot-matrix printers with respect to print quality, speed, and graphics; however, they are also more expensive.

Other Hardware

In addition to the devices discussed so far, many other hardware units are commonly found on microcomputer systems. Two popular ones are modems and power managers.

Modems, which we discussed in some detail in Chapter 7, are used to convert the binary pulses a computer system generates into analog pulses that are compatible with phone lines. Modems often connect to the computer's serial port.

Many microcomputer system owners also invest in a unit called a **power manager** (see Figure 15-7). Power managers enable you to turn on all your computer hardware devices—for example, the system unit, monitor, and printer—and even a nearby lamp or two with the flick of a single switch. They also usually perform *surge suppression,* which prevents random electrical power spikes from causing damage. The power going into most homes and offices is uneven, and power spikes can "zap" your RAM at unexpected times. This may result in loss of memory when your system is on. Some power managers can also handle "brownouts" (the reverse of a power spike) and even "blackouts" (complete loss of power).

Of course, still other hardware devices can be interfaced to microcomputer systems, but it probably would take a book the size of this text to adequately describe them all. With today's microcomputers packing the power of yesterday's mainframe, many of the types of input and output devices available for larger computers—particularly laser printers, hard disks, and film recorders—are now available for microcomputers. There is also now a greater variety of hardware available for microcomputer systems than for larger computer systems, which is largely due to the growing number of microcomputer users and product developers interested in microcomputers.

APPLICATIONS SOFTWARE

The types of tasks that some microcomputer systems can handle are extensive. Historically, as microcomputer-based applications needs grew, software firms and individual entrepreneurs quickly stepped in to satisfy the demand. In this section, we discuss some important microcomputer system applications and the software that accommodates them.

FIGURE 15-7

Power manager. The CPU and its support devices feed into the power manager, which is plugged into a standard wall outlet. This permits you to turn all your equipment on or off with the flick of a single switch.

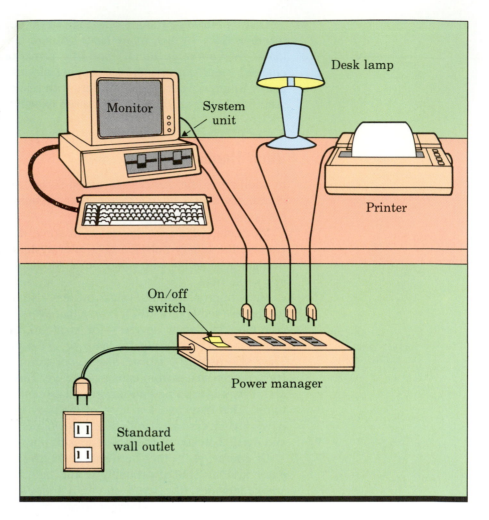

Productivity Software

Productivity software, some examples of which we discussed in detail in Chapters 12, 13, and 14, are fourth-generation language (4GL) products designed to make workers more productive. Some important types of productivity software packages available for microcomputers are listed and described in Figure 15-8.

When two or more of these productivity functions (and perhaps others) are combined into a single product, the resulting software is commonly referred to as an **integrated software package.** For example, Microsoft Works is an integrated software package that combines spreadsheets, file management, and presentation graphics into a single product. Other examples are Lotus Development Corporation's Symphony and Ashton-Tate's Framework.

Many productivity software products package the program disks, an easy-to-follow tutorial disk, and a reference manual into an attractive, shrink-wrapped box. When buying such a package, make sure you get the version intended for both your system unit and your operating system.

FIGURE 15-8
Types of productivity software.
Productivity software packages are designed to make both end users and computer professionals more productive at their jobs.

Package Type	Description
☑ Word processor	Turns the computer system into a powerful typewriting tool
☑ Spreadsheet	Turns the computer system into a sophisticated electronic calculator and analysis tool
☑ Presentation graphics	Turns the computer into a tool that can be used to prepare overheads, slides, and presentation materials for meetings
☑ File manager and database manager	Turns the computer system into an electronic research assistant, capable of searching through mounds of data to prepare reports or answer queries for information
☑ Communications software	Enables managers to call up remote computers for such things as financial information, marketing information, and news
☑ Desktop publishing	Turns the computer system into a tool that can be used to produce documents that look like they were produced at a professional print shop
☑ Desk accessory	Provides the electronic equivalent of tools commonly found on an office desktop—calendars, address files, and calculators, for instance
☑ CASE (computer-assisted software engineering)	Automates and integrates many of the tasks performed by computer professionals, thus enabling them to develop systems and software faster and more effectively
☑ Expert system	Enables workers to tap into expert knowledge to support them in their work

Educational Software

Education by computer can take many forms and benefit people of all ages. For instance, you can learn arithmetic, spelling, music, foreign languages, chemistry, and even programming languages by interacting, at your own pace, with instructional programs available from a number of software firms. These programs vary widely in difficulty. An elementary one might require you to compute the daily profit earned at a front-yard lemonade stand, while a complex one might necessitate creating three-dimensional surfaces with multivariate calculus.

A number of software products are also available to support microcomputer-based courses in various disciplines. Some of these courses are addressed in Feature 15A.

Home Software

Although we're still a long way from seeing a computer in every home, it seems inevitable that the home computer will someday be as prevalent as the home telephone. In fact, the phone and computer may even be bundled together into one product.

The Electronic University

Using Your PC and TV to Get an Education—and Maybe Even a Degree

The electronic university, once considered in the realm of science fiction, has arrived and is thriving. Today more than half a million students get a formal education outside the classroom with the assistance of electronic media.

Electronic education is not a new idea. In 1957, CBS implemented the concept by airing a program called "Sunrise Semester" to New York television audiences. The program offered a course in comparative literature and was shown weekdays at 6:30 a.m. While it did attract a modest following, *Sunrise Semester* subsequently was dropped.

Few people wanted to get up at that hour to get educated.

But electronic education was far from dead. Technological innovations such as the PC, satellite dish, videocassette recorder (VCR), and electronic mailbox have all

> **Electronic education is a product in growing demand.**

contributed to making electronic education a viable reality, and maybe even a trend. For instance, New York Institute of Technology's American Open University offers self-paced courses, for degree credit, that one can link up to via a PC and a modem. Stu-

dents communicate with professors through electronic mailboxes, calling up professors' mailboxes to get tests or assignments and depositing all work back in the mailboxes when finished. As hypermedia develops as a technology, such approaches to electronic education will improve dramatically.

The conventional TV set and the VCR also play an important role in electronic education. At Rensselaer Polytechnic Institute in Troy, New York, lectures are beamed live by satellite to employees at selected IBM, General Electric, and General Motors facilities. Students taking a specific course usually assemble in a group in a conference room at their company site, where they listen to each lecture on a television monitor. Videotapes of the lectures are also made at the company site for students who are ab-

---

The most popular use of computers in the home is electronic games. Home computer systems intended for extensive game playing generally can be equipped with a game controller to load prepackaged cartridges; a joystick, which looks like the stick shift in an automobile (and can move spaceships, computer characters like Mario and Luigi, and the like in different directions on the monitor screen); and an audio output unit, which makes sounds to accompany onscreen action. Most of these games use a standard TV set as the display device.

Computers are, of course, also used in the home for productivity and educational purposes. For example, computer systems are now inexpensive enough to be considered for purchase as a powerful home typewriter or a sophisticated household calculator. Also, you can acquire communications software to make banking or securities transactions or interface with a large information-retrieval network. With respect to education, parents often bring computers into their homes so that their children can learn a pro-

sent or want to view the lectures again. Columbia University and Virginia Polytechnic Institute have similar programs available to companies.

A management school set up by the Western Behavioral Sciences Institute in La Jolla, California, uses a different approach to electronic education. Students participate with instructors in live teleconferences and debates, which are set up similarly to the "Nightline" TV show. Participants at different sites see and hear one another as they sit in specially equipped rooms.

Still another way electronic universities are implemented is through lavishly produced videotape shows packaged together into courses. One such course, a series of French programs filmed in France, was created by the Public Broadcasting System (PBS) for around $5 million. A number of leading universities also have formed consortiums to produce such courses. A college or university needing a telecourse buys materials from the networks or consortiums and makes them available to students who are electronically enrolled at their institutions. Students watch the courses at home and are asked to complete tests either via PC or by sitting in at proctored exam sessions. While these extravagant productions are feasible for introductory courses, which have large enrollments, live satellite often is more attractive for higher-level courses.

By far, the greatest beneficiary of an electronic university is the student who works full-time and, due to business trips or a variable work schedule, finds it hard to commit to specific times. Also, at places such as the University of Alaska, which traditionally has had to fly professors to campuses in out-of-the-way places like Sitka or Barrow, the electronic university concept is a true blessing.

Proponents of electronic education point out that studies have shown that their students perform as well as or even better than "traditional" students. Also, they argue, many students who get an electronically disseminated education would get no education at all if all education were forced through a conventional classroom. Detractors feel that education suffers when the student learns in solitude. Regardless, electronic education is a product in growing demand and with potentially low costs, and it is likely that millions of people will someday turn to it as an alternative or supplement to regular classroom instruction.

gramming language, learn how to use a word processor, or pick up a variety of other computer-based skills.

You can also use your microcomputer to manage your home environment automatically. Computers can help regulate temperature, manage fuel consumption, open and close drapes, control kitchen appliances, turn lights on and off, supervise security, and even monitor the watering of your garden.

SYSTEMS SOFTWARE

The most important piece of software on any microcomputer system is the **operating system.** A variety of operating systems are available for microcomputers. Among the best known of these are OS/2, MS-DOS, PC-DOS, UNIX, and Macintosh System Software.

Operating systems are developed to conform to the physical limitations of specific CPU chips. Often they are written in the assembly language available with the chip. Chips differ in such respects as the number of registers they offer, the amount of RAM they can address, and the types of ROM they use for support. As a result, their assembly languages, which address specific memory modules and storage locations, are not interchangeable. Since prepackaged application programs are written to interface with particular operating systems, an applications program that works with one operating system usually does not work with another. Thus, choosing the right operating system is critical.

PC-DOS and MS-DOS, which are single-user operating systems designed for 16-bit Intel microprocessor chips, are the major operating systems used on 16-bit IBM microcomputer systems and similar machines. OS/2 and UNIX, two multiuser operating systems, are expected to make a similar impact as microcomputer-based applications truly evolve beyond the 16-bit word size. On the Apple Macintosh line of computers, the most widely used operating systems are UNIX and the Mac's proprietary operating system, Macintosh System Software.

Other microcomputer-based systems software includes language translators and utility programs, such as editors, windowing programs, print spoolers, modem software, and terminal emulators. We covered these types of software in some detail in Chapters 7 and 8.

SELECTING AND MAINTAINING A SYSTEM

Now that you know about the typical hardware and software found in microcomputer systems, let's turn to how you decide what type of system to buy, how to shop for such a system, where you can pick up knowledge that will make your system more useful, and how to care for your system.

Choosing a System

Selecting a microcomputer-based system for home or business use must begin with the all-important question "What do I want the system to do?" Once you've decided the types of applications for the system, you must decide what applications software to buy, given your budget constraints. Finally, you need to select the hardware and systems software that will best meet the requirements imposed by your earlier choices.

Often people can justify the purchase or lease of a microcomputer system on the basis of one or two applications. For example, many managers do so much "what-if" financial planning that a spreadsheet capability alone is enough to justify the entire computer system cost. And, of course, many writers find word processing capability so indispensable to their livelihoods that they care little what else the computer system can do. On the other hand, if you're uncertain about what you want a system to do for you, you'd better think twice about buying one. Computer systems that are heavily configured to serve certain applications (say, word processing) are often poor at others (such as computer graphics), so you can easily make some expensive mistakes if you're uncertain.

Shopping for a System

Where should you shop for hardware and software? One possibility is your local computer store. Many stores, such as Computerland and Micro Age, carry a number of vendors' products in their showrooms (see Feature 15B for a list of prominent manufacturers of microcomputer-based products). Generally the salespeople at these stores are relatively knowledgeable about computers and will help you try out the equipment before you buy or lease. As with a stereo system, you can buy a whole computer system at once or the individual components separately. You'll find that many complete systems include the offerings of more than one vendor, because few companies manufacture a full line of products for personal computers.

When contemplating computer stores as a possibility for buying a system, an important consideration is service and support. Some stores sell only hardware and software. Others may provide you with a service contract that covers timely replacement of malfunctioning equipment. Still others sell complete support, which may extend to matters such as helping you set up your business on a computer system, providing you with customized training, and lending you backup equipment in emergency situations. As a general rule, the more service and support you get with your system, the more you must pay.

Another possible source of computer products is mail-order firms. These companies regularly publish price lists in microcomputer journals and will ship products to you on request. Because these companies don't have to pay for a showroom, their prices usually are lower than those of computer stores. Also, some of them have access to an enormous stock of goods and can get almost any item to you quickly via a private shipper such as UPS or Federal Express. A disadvantage of mail-order shopping, however, is that you need to know exactly what you want, since most mail-order firms don't maintain showrooms. Also, buying something by mail generally is riskier than buying it locally, even when you know what you want. Nonetheless, the mail-order business has been thriving for several years, and a number of firms have established solid reputations for service.

Learning More about Microcomputers

A wealth of resources is available to those who want to learn more about personal computer systems and their uses. Classes, computer clubs, computer shows, magazines, newspapers, newsletters, books, and electronic media are all sources of information about microcomputers.

Classes. A good way to learn any subject is to take an appropriate class. Many colleges and universities offer microcomputer-oriented courses for

The Microcomputer Industry

A Look at Who the Big Players Are

Only a dozen or so years ago, many of the companies that produce today's most familiar microcomputer products did not even exist. But what a difference a decade can make! Several of these firms now rake in more than $1 billion a year in revenue. Almost overnight, the microcomputer industry has laid claim to being both the fastest-growing and the largest segment of the computer industry. Below we will look at some of the big players in each major market segment of this industry.

System Units. IBM, Apple, and Compaq are the three big names in desktop microcomputers. But many other companies—such as Tandy, Hewlett-Packard, and PC's Limited—have become highly successful largely by producing IBM "look-alikes." This strategy has been necessary because most of the available microcomputer software is

> IBM, Apple, and Compaq are the three big names in desktop microcomputers.

IBM compatible. In the laptop field, some of the biggest names are Zenith, Toshiba, GRiD, and Tandy.

Software. Among the largest independent software producers are Lotus Development Corporation (1-2-3, Symphony, and Jazz), Microsoft Corporation (DOS and OS/2 operating system software, BASIC language translators, Word, Excel, and Works), Ashton-Tate (dBASE and Framework), Computer Associates International (SuperCalc), Borland International (SideKick, Quattro, and Turbo Pascal), and WordPerfect Corporation (WordPerfect). At one time, many of these companies were single-product firms. Today, the software leaders are aggressively diversifying, internally developing new products and acquiring smaller companies with successful, related product lines.

Monitors and Printers. With the exception of a few U.S. companies, such as IBM,

both undergraduate and continuing-education students. Probably the fastest way to find out about such courses is to phone a local college and ask to speak to the registrar or someone in a computer-related academic department.

Clubs. Computer clubs are another effective vehicle for getting an informal education in computers. They are also a good place to get an unbiased and knowledgeable viewpoint about a particular product or vendor. Generally clubs are organized by region, product line, or common interests. Apple computer enthusiasts join clubs such as Apple-Holics (Alaska), Apple Pie (Illinois), or Apple Core (California). Clubs such as The Boston Computer Society, on the other hand, serve the needs of a more diverse group of microcomputer buffs. Many clubs also function as buying groups, obtaining software or hardware at reduced rates. Computer clubs range in size from two or three members to several thousand.

Qume, Wyse, and Hewlett-Packard, these two segments are dominated by the Japanese. Some of the major players are Epson, Toshiba, Amdek, Brother, Fujitsu, Canon, NEC, and C. Itoh.

Computer and Memory Chips. The chip markets are ruled by Intel, Motorola, and the Japanese. Intel and Motorola make chips for most of the leading system units.

Modems. Ten years ago, who would have thought that someday you'd watch a major college bowl game and see an award such as "Hayes Microcomputer Player of the Game"? Hayes is today's dominant name in microcomputer modems. Many other manufacturers are in the business of producing Hayes-compatible modems.

Add-in Boards. Hercules was one of the first big names in add-in boards. Like the Hayes modem, Hercules' monochrome display board, which facilitates monochrome graphics, has become somewhat of a de facto standard in the industry. Today, because of the large number of products and specifications around, there is a very wide variety of board products in the marketplace (see Figure 15-4). Other major manufacturers of boards are Quadram, AST, STB, and Tallgrass.

Disk Systems. A number of floppy disk, magnetic hard disk, and optical disk drive manufacturers are currently in the market. Some of the more familiar names in the magnetic disk drive marketplace are Control Data, IBM, Seagate, and Tandon. In the optical disk drive marketplace, Canon and IBM are big names. Companies such as Iomega and Plus Development have done well making hard cards and disk cartridges.

Diskettes. This is one of the most fiercely competitive segments. After all, there are few significant ways to differentiate diskettes. If the diskette "works" (that is, the quality is sufficiently high—which is usually the case with a familiar brand name), price is the only remaining consideration. Most diskettes are sold by companies that don't make them; they buy diskettes from other firms and put their labels on them. If you want a familiar name on the label, you may pay $1 or more per diskette. Generic diskettes (which may be made by the same manufacturer as the more expensive variety) may cost as little as 25 cents apiece when purchased in quantities of 100.

Shows. Computer shows give you a firsthand look at leading-edge hardware and software products. Such shows typically feature a number of vendor exhibits as well as seminars on various aspects of computing. The annual West Coast Computer Faire, held in the San Francisco area, is one event specifically oriented toward smaller computers.

Periodicals. Periodicals are another good source of information about microcomputers. Magazines such as *Byte, Popular Computing, PC,* and *Macworld* (see Figure 15-9) focus on microcomputers. Computer magazines vary tremendously in reading level. You can probably find and browse through all of these publications and more at your local bookstore or computer store.

Books. One of the best ways to learn about any aspect of personal computing is to read a book on the subject. A host of soft- and hardcover books

FIGURE 15-9

A variety of microcomputer periodicals. Dozens of periodicals, many published monthly, cater to both general and specialized microcomputer needs.

are available, ranging from simple to highly sophisticated. Included are "how-to" books on subjects such as operating popular microcomputer systems or productivity software packages, programming in microcomputer-based languages, and the technical fundamentals of microcomputers. You can find such books in your local library, computer stores, and bookstores.

Electronic Media. One easy way to learn a subject in our electronic age is to pick up a training disk or view a videotape or television show devoted to the subject. Today many microcomputer-oriented software packages, for instance, are sold with training disks that provide screen-oriented tutorials showing which keys to press and the results. Also, a large selection of videotapes are available for standard videocassette units, so you can see how something works simply by watching your television. Television shows such as "The Computer Chronicles," which may feature a program on optical disks one week and on bus architectures the next, are especially targeted to microcomputer users.

Caring for a System

Microcomputer systems consist of sensitive electronic devices, so they must be treated with appropriate respect. In Chapter 5, we observed some of the safeguards to be taken when handling disks. Let's now turn to some of the other precautions.

Dust, Heat, and Static. Each of those tiny processor and memory chips in your hardware units are packed tightly with hundreds or even thousands of circuits. Dust particles circulating in the air can easily settle on a chip and cause a short circuit. Many people buy dust covers that fit snugly over each of their hardware devices to prevent foreign particles in the air from causing hardware failure.

System units that support add-in boards require cooling fans. These boards generate heat, and too much heat inside the system unit can cause all sorts of problems. When inserting boards, you should place them as far apart as possible to avoid heat buildup. Also, most boards draw power off the system's main power unit (as do many internal hard disks), so you have to be particularly careful about overtaxing the power unit.

Static electricity is especially dangerous because it can damage chips, destroy programs and data in memory, or disable your keyboard. To ensure that those nasty little electrical discharges from your fingertips don't wreak havoc, you might consider buying an antistatic mat to place under your workstation chair or an antistatic spray for your keyboard. Static electricity is more likely in dry areas and in the winter, when there's less humidity in the air.

Other Concerns. CRT-type monitors work by having a phosphorescent surface "lit up" by an electronic gun (see Feature 6A in Chapter 6). If you keep your monitor at a high brightness level and abandon it for an hour or two, the phosphorescent surface could be "torched" rather than merely lit up. This means that ghostlike character images will be permanently etched on the screen, making it harder to read. Most monitors made today automatically shut off if not used for several minutes to prevent this from happening.

Disk drives and printers are particularly prone to failure, because they are electromechanical devices. You should clean the heads on your disk drives periodically and, at the same time, check to see that they haven't slipped out of alignment. Misregistered heads usually can be adjusted easily. And, of course, never insert a warped disk into a drive.

If you have an impact dot-matrix printer, the most vulnerable mechanism in the unit is the print head. Such a print head, like a typewriter key, will wear down over time. Nonetheless, you can take precautions to prevent rapid wear, such as making sure the head is cleaned periodically, not using the printer excessively for graphics (which wears down the head more rapidly), and ensuring that the head is not adjusted for carbon copies (which makes the head strike harder) if you want only single copies.

Naturally, as with other electronic devices, you shouldn't switch hardware units on and off excessively.

SUMMARY AND KEY TERMS

Microcomputer systems are computer systems driven by microprocessors. **Microprocessors** serve as the central processors in microcomputer systems, as well as in products such as electronic scales, digital watches, children's learning toys, microwave ovens, washers and dryers, and video games. **Personal computer systems** are, technically, microcomputer systems individuals use to meet various personal needs at work or at home. The terms *personal computer system* and *microcomputer system* often are used synonymously.

Microcomputer system units currently available for business and home use often are classified into two categories: portable and desktop. **Portable computers** are designed for users who frequently need to transport a computer around from site to site. The portable computers that are most lightweight and comfortable enough to be used on one's lap are called **laptop computers. Desktop computers** are those most often found in schools, homes, and businesses. Examples are the IBM PC, PC AT, and PS/2; Apple II line and the Macintosh line; Tandy 1000, 2000, 3000, and 4000; Compaq Deskpro 286 and 386; NeXT Computer System; and Commodore Amiga. Desktop units fall into one of two categories: *single-user* or *multiuser systems.*

Many microcomputer systems contain at least five major pieces of hardware: the system unit itself, a secondary storage device, a video display unit, a keyboard, and a printer.

The **system unit** often consists of at least a CPU chip, memory chips, internal boards on which these and other chips are mounted, ports that provide connections for external devices, a power supply, and internal circuitry to hook everything together.

The CPUs on most microprocessor systems are made by either Intel or Motorola. Generally, the more bits the chip can manipulate at one time, the faster it is and the greater the amount of main memory it can accommodate. The primary memory chips on microcomputer systems are commonly referred to as **RAM,** for **random access memory.** Memory chips that contain nonerasable programs are referred to as **ROM,** for **read-only memory.**

Many system units contain a limited number of *internal* "slots" into which **add-in boards** can be mounted. Also, many system units have *external* I/O **ports** that enable peripherals to be plugged into them.

The CPU connects to RAM, ROM, and internal/external interfaces through circuitry called an I/O **bus.** Some widely used bus architectures are *Micro Channel Architecture* (MCA), used on the high end of the IBM PS/2 line of computers; *NuBus,* used on the high end of the Apple Macintosh line of computers; and *EISA,* used to help 16-bit IBM PC AT computers and compatibles "graduate" into the newer, 32-bit world.

As with larger computers, the primary memory of microcomputers can hold only the data and programs the computer is currently processing. If you want to keep data and programs for repeated use, you must have secondary storage. Two popular secondary storage media are **diskette** and **hard disk.**

For most people, a microcomputer system would be useless without a **keyboard,** which often is the main vehicle for input. Potential buyers should carefully evaluate keyboards before deciding on one. Many other input devices are available to supplement keyboard operations, most notably the **mouse.**

Almost every microcomputer system has a video display unit, or **monitor.** Most of the monitors in the marketplace are either *monochrome, grey-scale,* or *color,* and either *digital* or *analog. Multiscan* monitors, which can deliver both analog and digital signals and work under a variety of graphics standards, are also available.

If you are using your computer system for any purpose other than playing games, you'll probably need some form of printed output. Two popular **printers** used in microcomputer systems are **impact dot-matrix printers** and **laser printers.**

Two other hardware units commonly found on microcomputer systems are **modems** and **power managers.**

There is a practical limit to the number of peripheral devices a single CPU can handle. Generally each new device interfaced through an add-in board or port adds to the burden the CPU must manage, thereby possibly downgrading system performance.

Applications software for personal computers includes **productivity software** (both single-function packages and **integrated software packages**), educational software, and home software. Systems software includes the computer's **operating system,** language translators, and utility programs.

Selecting a microcomputer-based system for home or business use must begin with the all-important question "What do I want the system to do?" Once you've decided what types of applications the system must service, you must decide what applications software to buy given your budget constraints. Finally, you must select the hardware and systems software that will best meet the requirements imposed by your earlier choices.

There are numerous options available when seeking a microcomputer system, including computer stores and mail-order firms.

A wealth of resources for learning more about microcomputer systems and their uses exist. Classes, computer clubs, computer shows, magazines, training disks and videocassettes, and books are all good sources of information about computers.

Microcomputer systems consist of sensitive electronic devices, so they must be treated with respect. You should be particularly careful to protect the system from dust, heat buildup, and static discharge. Disk drives and printers are particularly prone to failure, because they are electromechanical devices.

REVIEW EXERCISES

Fill-in Questions

1. RAM is an acronym for _____ .
2. ROM is an acronym for _____ .
3. A CPU on a silicon chip is called a(n) _____ .
4. Memory whose contents are not destroyed when the power is shut off is _____ .
5. As with larger computers, _____ on smaller computers allocate the hardware of a specific computer system to the demands of applications programs.
6. A device that enables microcomputer users to communicate with remote computers over ordinary phone lines is called a(n) _____ .
7. A feature on a power manager called _____ prevents random electrical power spikes from damaging a microcomputer system.
8. An add-in board capable of providing several independent functions is called a(n) _____ board.

Matching Questions

Match each term with the description that best fits.

a. multiscan   e. port
b. VGA   f. board
c. RAM   g. NuBus
d. ROM   h. mouse

_____ 1. Nonerasable hardware modules.

_____ 2. Often found at the back of the system unit.

_____ 3. With microcomputing systems, synonymous with primary memory.

_____ 4. A graphics standard.

_____ 5. A term used to describe monitors that can work under a variety of graphics standards.

_____ 6. A cursor-movement device.

_____ 7. Refers to an architecture used to connect the CPU to input and output devices on some Apple Macintosh computers.

_____ 8. A device into which processor and memory chips plug directly.

Discussion Questions

1. Identify the major types of microcomputing systems, and explain how they differ.
2. What are the major pieces of hardware in a microcomputer system?
3. Distinguish among a microprocessor, a microcomputer system, and personal computer system.
4. What is Micro Channel Architecture?
5. Identify and describe several types of add-in boards used with microcomputer systems.
6. Name several applications for a microcomputer system.
7. Name some places where you can acquire a microcomputer system.
8. Identify some concerns in caring for a microcomputer system.

Critical Thinking Questions

1. Almost every year or every other year a new, major microprocessor chip is introduced, and it leads to a new "family" of faster, more capable computer systems. What problems does this pose to a typical corporation?
2. Why, do you think, are so many companies in the business of producing IBM-compatible microcomputers?
3. Multiuser desktop computers are often completely owned and operated by a single user. What, do you think, accounts for this?

A Computer for the Road

Laptop Use Starts to Take Off

As recently as the early 1980s, portable computers were considered just an interesting novelty. They were about the size and weight of sewing machines, and their displays were notoriously hard to read. Moreover, a hard disk that could run on batteries was still a dream. Then, within the span of a few years, technology improved dramatically. Today laptops in the four-pound class that have the power of many cutting-edge desktop computers are available. Also, the battery-powered hard disk is now a reality, and backlighting has vastly improved the readability of displays. Laptops currently are the fastest-growing segment of the microcomputer industry, and sales revenues may be as high as $5 billion by 1992—five times the level of 1988 sales. In this Window, we explore some of the uses to which laptops have been put.

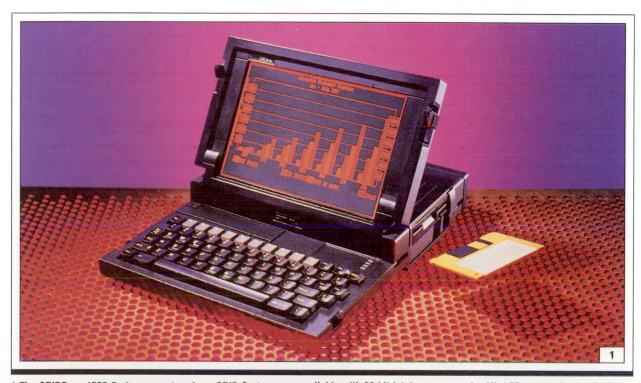

1 The GRiDCase 1500 Series computers from GRiD Systems are available with 32-bit Intel processors, backlit LCD or gas plasma displays, and 20MB or 40MB hard disks, as well as support for VGA graphics, mainframe terminal emulation, and local area networking.

EDUCATION

2, 3 Laptops are becoming more popular than ever in educational environments. At a growing number of colleges, students now take exams on laptops rather than in blue books.

BUSINESS TRIPS

4, 5 Because they are so compact and lightweight, laptops can easily be stuffed into a briefcase and carried along on business trips. And because they can be operated on batteries when a wall socket isn't handy, you can even use them on a plane or train, or in a car or bus.

CLIENT PRESENTATIONS

6–8 One of the most popular uses of laptops is in sales. Laptops provide field salespeople with the computer models they need to analyze a client's financial situation—during a sales call, when the client is in a receptive mood—and with the tools they need to obtain key selling information. Giants such as Kodak, Hewlett-Packard, Chrysler, and Ciba-Geigy are among the many firms that have placed thousands of laptops in their salespeople's hands.

FIELD WORK

9, 10 For people who need access to computing power in the "boonies"—say, out in an oil field or in the woods—laptops are an ideal solution. Laptops are frequently used as computational or data-collection devices, as shown here.

C H A P T E R

16

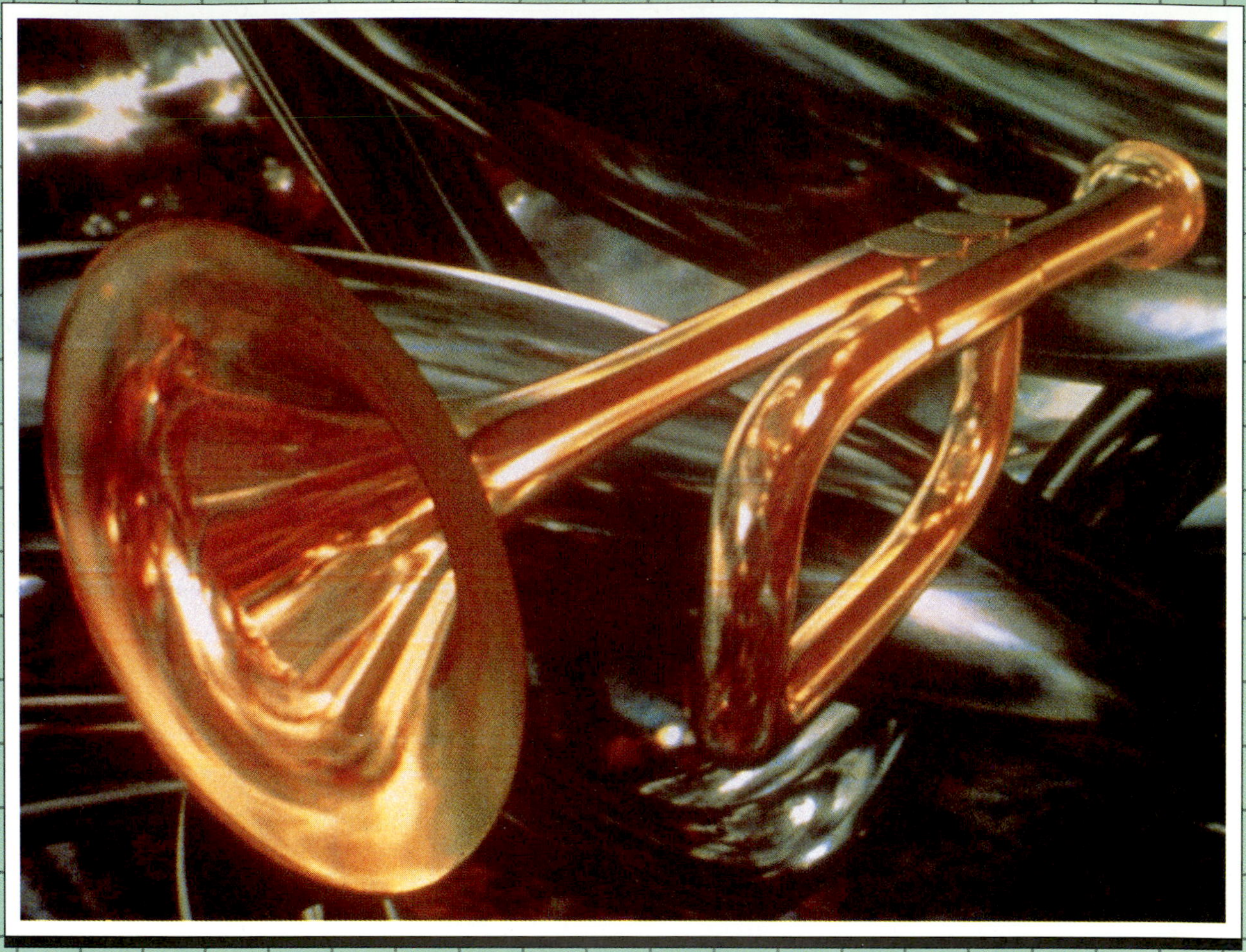

Business Systems

Objectives

After completing this chapter, you will be able to:

1. Describe several types of computer systems commonly found in business and other environments.

2. Explain how a number of elements discussed in previous chapters fit together into a complete computer system.

3. Appreciate, through Window 8, how designers work with computers to create interesting images.

4. Explain the role of artificial intelligence in improving the quality of applications software.

OVERVIEW

Now that we've covered various types of hardware and software, let's focus on how these combine into complete computer systems in businesses and other organizations. Undoubtedly you've already encountered many types of computer systems. When you go to the supermarket, you generally see electronic cash registers and various hand-held or laser scanning devices that obviously are parts of some supermarket system. Or, when registering for classes, perhaps you've observed someone at a display terminal checking to see whether a certain class you want to take is still open or whether you've paid all your bills—apparently a procedure of a registration system. Also, almost all organizations have accounting systems to help handle their business transactions, and many maintain manufacturing systems that assist in running their factories.

There are perhaps hundreds of types of computer systems in existence today. Many systems in businesses, nonprofit organizations, and government fall into one or more of four categories:

☐ *Transaction Processing Systems* Systems in this category perform record keeping and other accounting tasks that organizations handle regularly.

☐ *Management Information Systems* These systems provide managers with predefined types of information on a periodic basis or with capabilities to meet customized information needs.

☐ *Office Systems* These systems cut down on the time-consuming paperwork normally generated in an office and make office workers more productive.

☐ *Design and Manufacturing Systems* This category includes computers that are used to design and make products as well as guide robots in factories.

In the following pages, we'll look more closely at each of these basic types of systems. We'll also explore the area of *artificial intelligence,* which can lend each of these systems powers that we would normally attribute to humans.

TRANSACTION PROCESSING SYSTEMS

Virtually every company must support a number of routine operations, most of which involve some form of tedious recordkeeping. These operations, such as payroll and accounts receivable, were some of the earliest commercial applications of computers in organizations and are still among the most important. Because these systems heavily involve processing of business transactions—such as paying employees, recording customer purchases and

| DATE: | | | | | | | | $\dfrac{90\text{-}1200}{0414}$ |

SMITH COMPANY

PAY

CHECK NUMBER

TO THE
ORDER OF

VALLEY BANK

Employee number	Employee name		Dept.	Pay period	Pay period ended	Check no.	Check date
Earnings and statutory deductions							
Hours	Rate	Regular pay	Overtime pay	Other pay	Gross pay	Fed. w/tax	F.I.C.A. tax	State tax
Voluntary deductions							
Medical ins.	Life ins.	Credit union	Union dues	Charity	Savings bonds	All others	Net pay
Social Security and W-2 information							
Social security no.	Exempt	Y.T.D. gross	Y.T.D. fed. w/tax	Y.T.D. F.I.C.A.	Y.T.D. state tax	Not negotiable

FIGURE 16-1
A paycheck and earnings statement.

payments, and recording vendor receipts and payments—they are called **transaction processing systems.** As you'll see in the following pages—and from taking a beginning accounting course—most transaction processing operations are highly interrelated.

Payroll. *Payroll systems* compute deductions, subtract them from gross earnings, and write paychecks to employees for the remainder (see Figure 16-1). These systems also contain programs that prepare reports for managerial and taxing agencies of the federal, state, and local governments. Moreover, many have links to bank systems where direct deposits are made for firms' employees.

Order Entry. Many organizations handle some type of order processing on a daily basis. Customers either call in orders by phone, send in written orders by ordinary mail or by computer, or place orders in person. The systems that record and help manage such transactions are called *order-entry systems*.

For instance, mail-order-catalog firms such as Eddie Bauer, L. L. Bean, and Lands' End process orders daily from customers who want outdoor equipment or clothing. Retailers such as Sears and B. Dalton, who maintain shopping premises, also require order-entry systems, because the goods they offer for sale are not always in stock. Even the airlines' passenger reservations systems have order-entry components, since air and hotel reservations often are made in advance.

In many cases, the order-entry system must also interface with an inventory control system, because products' stock levels are reduced by customer orders and increased by supplier receipts.

Inventory Control. The units of product that a company has in stock to sell at a given moment are called its *inventory*. An *inventory control system* keeps track of the number of units of each product in inventory and ensures that reasonable quantities of products are maintained.

The term *inventory* may not necessarily refer to tangible merchandise on a shelf. For example, in airline passenger reservation systems, inventory refers to the seats available for sale on flights. In a college's course registration system, inventory refers to the slots for each class that are still open for enrollment. Auto showroom dealers usually consider inventory as any uncommitted cars scheduled for manufacturing, sometimes in other parts of the world.

Let's see how an inventory control system might work, using the case of a mail-order firm that sells outdoor equipment. You call a toll-free number to place an order. A clerk takes your order and types it into a terminal that ties into an inventory control system. The system then checks to see if the goods you want are in stock. If they are, the goods are made available for shipment and the number of units ordered is automatically subtracted from inventory balances. If not, the goods may be placed on back order. As soon as the goods are shipped, the accounts receivable system is notified of your order so it can bill you.

Besides automatically monitoring stock levels, almost all inventory control systems generate an assortment of reports for management. Among these documents are inventory stock status reports (shown in Figure 16-2) and summaries listing fast-moving and slow-moving items, back orders, and the like.

Accounts Receivable. The term *accounts receivable* refers to the amounts owed by customers who have made purchases on credit. Because about 90 percent of the business transacted in the United States is done on a credit

```
SMITH COMPANY        ***INVENTORY STOCK STATUS***        9/29/89      PAGE 1

ITEM            ITEM          BEG   QTY   QTY    ON    ON    AVAIL   UNIT
             DESCRIPTION      QTY   REC   SOLD  HAND  ORDER          PRICE

1002   RESISTOR-TYPE B         0    600   200   400   100    500     .15
1003   RESISTOR-TYPE D         0      0     0     0   100    100    2.20
1006   RESISTOR-TYPE E         0      0     0     0    50     50    6.85
1008   SEALING TAPE-1 INCH   200    100    50   250     0    250    3.00
1010   SEALING TAPE-1.5 INCH 100      0    30    70     0     70    3.71
1012   LIGHT FIXTURE-TYPE 6    0      0     0     0     0      0    4.31
1014   LIGHT FIXTURE-TYPE 7    0      0     0     0     0      0    4.03
1015   HEX SCREW             300    250    50   500   200    700     .65
1016   BIT NUT                0    600   100   500     0    500     .21
1018   WRENCH                 0     30    30     0   100    100    8.55
1020   SOCKET SET           250     40    80   210     0    210   30.35
```

FIGURE 16-2

Inventory stock status report. Inventory systems often are tied into transaction processing systems. As delivery or sale transactions are processed, the number of units of stock involved is added or subtracted from electronically kept inventory records. These records are used to produce reports such as this one, either periodically or on demand.

basis, the *accounts receivable system* is a critical computer application in most companies. The system keeps track of customers' purchases, payments, and account balances. It also calculates and prints customer statements and provides information to management. Other output includes sales analyses, which describe changing patterns of products and sales, as well as detailed or summary reports on current and past-due accounts.

When interest rates are high, the accounts receivable system's billing procedures can be especially critical because the sooner a bill is mailed, the sooner it will be paid and the sooner the receipts can begin earning interest for the company. Also, studies have shown that delays in billing increase the likelihood of nonpayment.

Accounts Payable. The term *accounts payable* refers to the money a company owes to other companies for the goods and services it has received. In contrast to receivables, which reflect a portion of the money coming in, payables reflect part of the money being spent.

An *accounts payable system* keeps track of bills and often generates checks to pay them. It records who gets paid and when, handles cash disbursements, and advises managers whether they should accept discounts offered by vendors in return for early payment. The last function is important because the interest the firm could earn by delaying payment may outweigh the value of discounts for early payment.

General Ledger. A *general ledger (G/L) system* keeps track of all financial summaries, including those originating from payroll, accounts receivable, accounts payable, and other sources. It also ensures that the company's

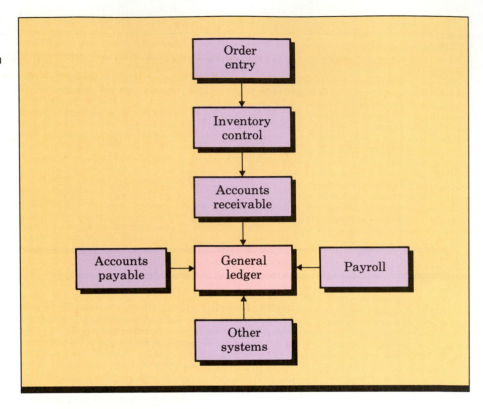

FIGURE 16-3
The relationship among transaction processing systems.

books balance properly. A typical G/L system may also produce accounting reports such as income statements, balance sheets, and general ledger balances.

Once a company decides to computerize one or more of the routine activities just discussed, it must decide whether to develop the appropriate software itself or buy it from a vendor. Payroll packages are the most popular software to buy from vendors, because payroll operations are similar in many companies and the cost of keeping up with federal, state, and city tax legislation is often too high for a company to bear by itself. Inventory control packages are the least popular, because inventory practices differ widely among companies.

Figure 16-3 illustrates the relationships among the various systems described in this section.

MANAGEMENT INFORMATION SYSTEMS

In the early days of commercial computing, businesses purchased computers almost exclusively to perform routine transaction processing tasks. Used in this way, the computer could cut clerical expenses considerably. As time passed, however, it became apparent that the computer could do much more than replace clerks. It could also provide information to assist management in its decision-making role.

A system that generates information for use by decision makers often is called a **management information system (MIS).** With an MIS, management can incorporate much more information into decisions and spend less time gathering it. As a result, managers have more time to do the things they do best—think creatively and interact with people.

Two major types of information systems are information reporting systems and decision support systems. Before we discuss these, however, let's look at the types of managers found in organizations and their special information needs.

Managers and Information Needs

The major function of a management information system is to provide managers at many levels with the kind of information they regularly need.

Top-level managers, for example, spend much of their time plotting the company's long-term future. This process is called *strategic planning.* To establish goals and objectives for achieving them, top-level managers often need information about critical events and trends in data—for key areas within the company, for the company as a whole, and for the national or international economy. Decisions made by top-level managers involve matters in which vision, perspective, judgment, and intuition are prominent components. A great deal of the information relevant to these managers involves events that occur outside their firms.

The information needs of *middle-level management* differ somewhat. In order to carry out the strategic plans devised by their superiors, these managers need plans of their own. Such plans often are called *tactical plans.* A tactical plan determines how a strategic objective will be accomplished. Middle-level managers especially need information systems to keep them apprised of what's happening in their departments. In the manufacturing area, for instance, middle-level managers need information that describes any problems in the performance of production, such as missed deadlines or cost overruns. Data summarizing inputs, costs, targets, and outputs is especially useful for meeting these information needs.

Lower-level management has still another set of priorities and information needs. Supervisors must coordinate and control workers' activities so that tactical goals are met. This is commonly called *operational planning and control.* Lower-level managers need information on current operations that will help them effectively manage workers and materials, for instance, information on current inventories and stock due from suppliers, on finished orders scheduled for shipment during the current week, on purchases of raw materials that must be made immediately, or on workers who will be available the following week.

Many of the transaction processing tasks mentioned earlier generate data most directly relevant to lower-level management. When these data are summarized and consolidated, they become the information that many middle-level managers need to perform their jobs. Until the recent boom in

FIGURE 16-4

The three levels of management and the tasks performed at each level. Each level of management involves a different mix of planning and control activities.

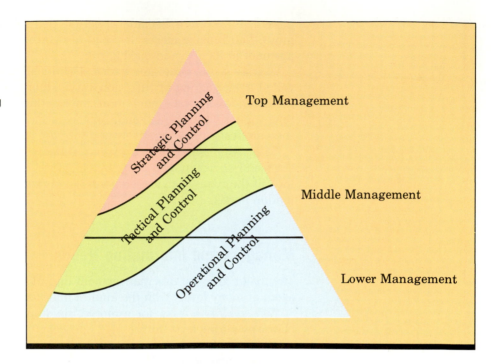

easy-to-use microcomputing software and financial databases covering domestic and international news, few top-level managers wanted to interact with computers in any way. Today, however, although high-level planning involves a lot of information that is difficult to formally integrate into a computer system, top-level managers are realizing that computers are increasingly becoming useful tools for performing many of the tasks they need to do.

The pyramid in Figure 16-4 illustrates the roles of the three levels of management.

Information Reporting Systems

Information reporting systems were the first type of MIS. They provide management with preselected types of information, generally in the form of computer-generated reports. The types of information managers receive are preplanned just like the information you see on your monthly checking account statements. The individual *values* on your statements, such as check numbers and amounts, may change from month to month, but the *types* of information you receive remain the same. Also, all people mailed checking account statements receive exactly the same type of information.

A typical report from an information reporting system might be an inventory control report that is distributed every morning to an inventory control manager, like that illustrated in Figure 16-2. Many information reporting systems provide managers with information that is a by-product of the data generated through transaction processing, as this example illustrates. The types of reports information reporting systems produce are shown in Figure 16-5.

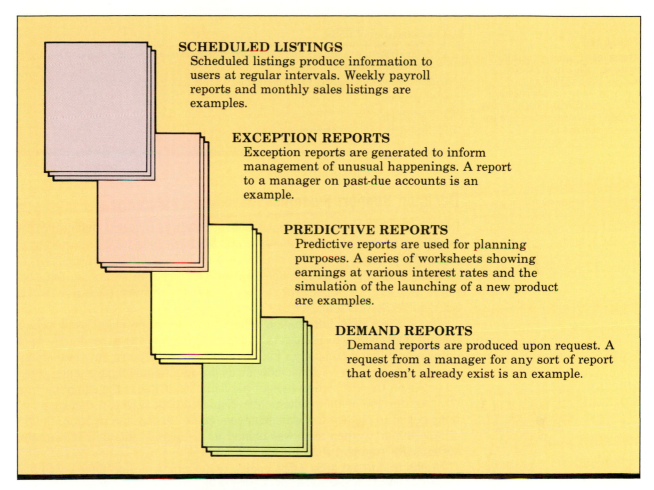

SCHEDULED LISTINGS
Scheduled listings produce information to users at regular intervals. Weekly payroll reports and monthly sales listings are examples.

EXCEPTION REPORTS
Exception reports are generated to inform management of unusual happenings. A report to a manager on past-due accounts is an example.

PREDICTIVE REPORTS
Predictive reports are used for planning purposes. A series of worksheets showing earnings at various interest rates and the simulation of the launching of a new product are examples.

DEMAND REPORTS
Demand reports are produced upon request. A request from a manager for any sort of report that doesn't already exist is an example.

FIGURE 16-5
Reports produced by an information reporting system.

When information reporting systems first became popular in the 1960s, they were plagued by some serious problems. Many company executives, perhaps misled by the hype of computer experts (as well as by their own computer illiteracy), expected far more from the systems than the systems could actually provide. For example, many firms ambitiously undertook the design of some "total system" that would link up every level of the organization and, more or less, do everything a computer system could possibly do for everybody. When executives and users discovered that no information system could systematically provide information about all aspects of a business or anticipate all of its needs, many became disillusioned.

Despite the failings of some overambitious efforts, however, many information reporting systems survived. They have provided undeniable benefits to the organizations that developed them, and many of them still play vital roles in those organizations.

FIGURE 16-6

Properties of decision support systems. Since most decision support systems have a top-management focus, it is important that they be flexible enough to meet changing requirements and also be easy to learn and to use.

Characteristics of DSSs
☑ Support for the "unstructured" decision environments commonly encountered by high-level managers
☑ Flexibility in allowing users to specify their own output requirements
☑ Ease of use
☑ Fast response
☑ High degree of user involvement

Decision Support Systems

During the 1970s, many companies began to call for systems that could field questions as they occurred to managers. Such systems were expected to be particularly useful to top-level managers, whose requirements for information are somewhat unpredictable and unstructured. In response, the computer industry developed the **decision support system (DSS).** What exactly a DSS does is a matter that's still evolving.

The earliest MISs, information reporting systems, provided fixed, preformatted information to managers. A typical product was a hard-copy computer report that a company's information systems department circulated at regular intervals to various individuals or functional departments. Every manager on the circulation list got the same report with the same information. As developments in interactive display technology and database systems began to change the way managers could receive information, the decision support system term was coined to distinguish this new information systems environment from the traditional one.

Unlike traditional MISs, DSSs enable managers to design their own information systems. They equip managers with tools for modeling customized decision support environments, manipulating data, and collecting information. Thus, the primary distinction between an information reporting system and a DSS is that the former provides certain fixed types of information while the latter gives managers the tools they need to develop their own information. And while traditional MISs rely on hard-copy reports, most DSSs employ some interactive technology, such as microcomputer systems or display terminals. Figure 16-6 lists these and some of the other properties that distinguish DSSs from information reporting systems.

Let's put DSSs into perspective with an example. To assist with making product pricing decisions, a sales manager uses a DSS that has been set up on a mainframe to retrieve sales data. At a display terminal, the manager first requests the price of an item. Then he or she decides to ask for the average price of several other items, and then for the inventory turnover of yet a different item. The manager can pose his or her own questions as the need evolves and receive answers at once. At the end of the interactive session, the manager uses the DSS to prepare a summary of significant findings and some bar charts for a meeting.

Executive support systems (ESSs), which are DSSs customized to the special needs of individual executives, are covered in Feature 16A.

OFFICE SYSTEMS

In recent years, computer technology has been applied to the task of increasing productivity in the office. The term **office automation (OA)** has been coined to describe this trend. Office automation can be achieved through a wide variety of technologies and processing techniques, several of which we discuss in this section.

Word Processing and Desktop Publishing

By far the most widespread of the OA technologies is word processing. As stated in Chapter 12, **word processing** refers to technologies that enable computer systems to automate a variety of typing and document preparation tasks. Today most word processing is accomplished with general-purpose word processing packages used on general-purpose computer systems. Since we already have discussed word processing extensively, we will not go into the details here.

Desktop publishing, which involves the use of desktop microcomputer systems to produce documents that rival those of professional print shops, was also covered extensively in Chapter 12 and in Window 5. Today word processing and desktop publishing are increasingly overlapping, and many people use the term *document processing* to describe what they feel is evolving from the merger of these two fields.

Electronic Mail

Electronic mail, or *E-mail,* makes it possible to do things such as sending letters, manuscripts, legal documents, and the like from one terminal or computer system to another. Following are some examples of electronic mail usage:

☐ A secretary in New York places a document containing both text and pictures into a **facsimile (fax) machine,** such as the one pictured in Figure 16-7. The fax machine digitizes the page image and transmits it over ordinary phone lines to Los Angeles. In Los Angeles, another fax machine receives the electronic page image and reproduces it in hard-copy form. All of this takes place in less than a minute. Microcomputer systems can be equipped with *fax boards* that enable them to send output to fax machines.

☐ Two people communicate over a **voice mail** system, in which the sender's spoken messages are digitized by voice tone and stored in memory on an answering device at the receiver's location. When the receiver presses a "listen" key, the digitized message is reconverted to voice mode.

☐ A manager within a company types a memo and electronically routes it to the **electronic mailboxes** of selected company employees (see Figure 16-8). The electronic mailboxes are located in the company mainframe's

FIGURE 16-7

Facsimile machine. With a facsimile (fax) machine, hard-copy document images can be sent from one location to another—perhaps thousands of miles away—within seconds.

Executive Support Systems

Computers Arrive at the Top Floor

Traditionally executives and computers have mixed about as well as oil and water. Granted, those working at the top have signed checks for billions of dollars of computer equipment over the years. But personally they have been averse to using them.

A litany of both excuses and valid reasons for this reluctance has been heard throughout the course of modern time. Computers are too unfriendly. Why should I waste time learning to use a computer when we have a staff of middle managers who are paid to do the job? Computers are for technocrats, not executives. What if I can't figure out how to use the system and suffer ego loss and humiliation in front of subor-

dinates? There is no earthly reason for me to have to touch a computer system when the hard-copy reports I get daily do the job. And on it has gone—until recently.

Now executives in many industries are realizing that it will soon be impossible to exist without their own personal desktop systems. Why the sudden change of heart? Well, computers are now offering both rapid access to corporate and environmental data and information-gathering capabilities that executives find absolutely seductive. Not only are the systems targeted to them easy to use; they no longer have to wait for an assistant to get back from the computer center with armfuls of output to get answers. With the right type of system, all it takes is a few keystrokes or mouse clicks to get what they want and in the exact form

they require. Yes, the *executive support system (ESS)* has indeed arrived.

Consider, for example, the executives at Kraft's Grocery Product Group. Until recently, each afternoon the president and vice-president received piles of hard-copy reports covering the previous day's sales. With over 500 products and 33,000 grocery stores to review on performance, their top priority might well have been to avoid drowning in a sea of paperwork. Today these same executives have their own desktop computer workstations from which they can access critical information, in any manner they choose, almost as soon as they get to work in the morning.

As some executives see it, the business world is so competitive and fast paced these days that they no longer can afford to be ignorant about how to use a computer. Among their favorite applications are using database man-

secondary storage, and most of the employees have terminals or microcomputer workstations that can access the mainframe.

☐ A typist word processes a manuscript on a microcomputer system and electronically transmits it over the phone lines to a hard disk on an author's system. The author is not home, but communications software on her computer system enables the phone to be answered and the manuscript to be accepted.

As with many other evolving concepts in the world of computers, electronic mail is a term that's not defined without controversy. For example, some people consider electronic mail as referring exclusively to commercial

agement systems to access corporate and financial data pertinent to their industries, using electronic mail systems to streamline contact with subordinates, and using customized spreadsheet programs that enable them to quickly tumble their favorite ratios or to display important trends in a graphical format.

Executive support systems weren't born overnight. The rapid growth of personal computers, which has dragged a number of "ordinary" people into the computer arena, has helped create a solid market for easy-to-learn, easy-to-use software products. Also, because many executives can't type, many of them require graphical or menu interfaces that let them merely point at their choices. Until only recently, few off-the-shelf products were available that did this. Also, gradual advances in communications technology have made it possible for executives to access by computer one of their most im-

portant information sources —events happening outside the company. In many companies, executive support systems are customized to each executive's needs. And there are individualized training sessions to boot.

Industry analysts feel that

executive support systems are about to take off. By the early 1990s, ESSs could grow into a $100 million industry— a fivefold increase from 1986. Some analysts predict that more than a quarter of all executives will be using ESSs by the mid-1990s.

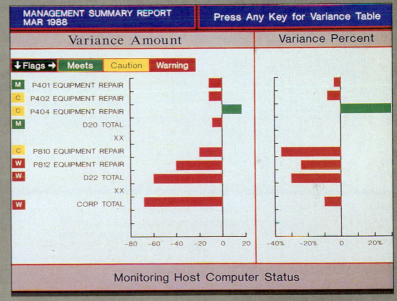

ESSs. Executives like graphs and color-coded buttons that give fast, preliminary assessments.

services that offer an electronic-document delivery alternative that competes with the post office system.

Desk Accessories

Desk accessories, or *desktop organizers,* are software packages that provide the electronic equivalent of features commonly found on an office desktop. Desk accessory software varies among vendors, but many offer features such as a calendar, clock, calculator, and rolodex-type file (see Figure 16-9). Often the feature is activated through a window that appears when a specific sequence of keys is depressed. Following is a list of several desk accessory features:

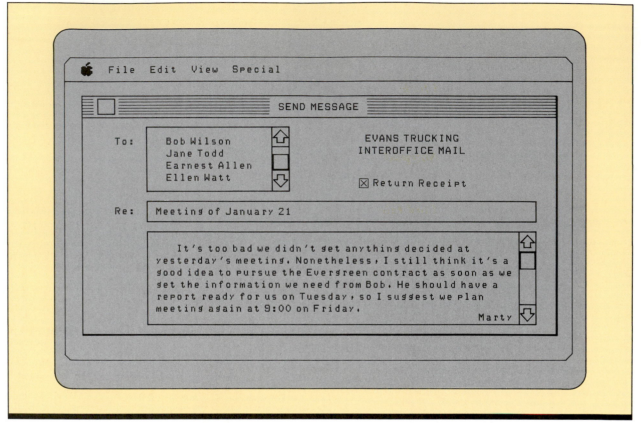

FIGURE 16-8

Electronic mailboxes. Using an electronic mailbox system, an employee can send messages or work to others without leaving his or her desk.

☐ *Calculator* Most calculator utilities come with screen graphics that provide an image of the calculator in the display-screen window. Some can also export the calculations back to your applications program.

☐ *Calendar* Calendar programs usually have two levels. At one level, they simulate the wall calendars you have at home. Each graphical image sent

FIGURE 16-9

Desk accessories. (a, left) A pop-up calculator. (b, right) An electronic calendar.

to the window is a grid of the days in a particular month. When you hit specific sequences of keys, you can move forward or backward to other months. At the other level, the graphical image sent to the screen is an appointment-book page for a particular day that enables you to view, add, or delete entries.

☐ *Clock* Besides giving you the time, some packages have an online alarm-clock feature that causes the audio unit in your computer to beep or chime. Some clocks will even interrupt your application with a prepro-grammed message.

☐ *Notepad* Many desk accessory programs offer full-screen notepads for writing notes, letters, and other text. In some cases, you may be able to export notepad text back to your applications program.

☐ *Card File* A card-file feature allows you to store and recall the electronic equivalent of a rolodex card file on your microcomputer system. Many programs offer a communications interface so that you can look up the number of an online information service or database and dial it automat-ically.

Desk accessory software is becoming increasingly popular with micro-computer users. Borland International's SideKick is probably the most familiar example of such microcomputer-based packages. Also, desk acces-sory routines are now commonly found in *HyperTalk* products on micro-computers. For instance, HyperTalk card files (called *stacks*) often are used to store a mix of client records—addresses, phone numbers, memos, orders, and invoices—in an easy-to-use cardlike form. On larger computers, desk accessories are commonly bundled into so-called *integrated office systems,* such as IBM's PROFS or Data General's CIO.

Decision Support Tools

Since many office decisions are made by white-collar workers, it's under-standable that many offices maintain decision support systems. Among the *decision support tools* useful in such a setting are spreadsheets, presentation graphics, plotters and laser printers, color monitors, and relational database systems. All of these software and hardware tools have contributed to streamlining life at the office and were discussed earlier in the book. These tools have automated decision processes that were once carried out exclu-sively with the assistance of "ancient" devices such as pencils, pads of pa-per, file folders, and filing cabinets.

Teleconferencing

Teleconferencing enables a group of people to meet electronically, thereby conserving the time and expense of physically getting together in one spot. Three types of teleconferencing technologies are audio teleconferencing, video teleconferencing, and computer teleconferencing.

Of these three technologies, *audio teleconferencing* has been around the longest. It allows a conference to take place among several people on a

FIGURE 16-10

A video teleconference. In video teleconferencing, participants at different sites can both see and hear one another.

phone system. Such meetings are commonly known as "conference phone calls."

Video teleconferencing systems permit participants to see as well as hear one another on video screens (see Figure 16-10). Although such video systems are gaining popularity, they have the disadvantage of requiring expensive, specially equipped rooms. Also, they are relatively ineffective in situations where physical confrontation among participants is important. Eventually, however, person-to-person video teleconferencing through "picture phones" may become a widespread reality.

Computer teleconferencing allows a conference to take place through electronic mailboxes, even when all the participants aren't using the computer system at the same time. For instance, computer conferencing might be made available to a group of executives who are investigating the feasibility of a big merger during a hectic two-week period. Participants can broadcast messages to all other participants at any time or can retrieve all or any part of the proceedings of the entire "conference." In fields such as newspaper publishing and automobile design, computer teleconferencing is allowing workers to regularly communicate with one another from their own workstations during the course of everyday work. This computer-age phenomenon, called *workgroup computing,* is described in the Tomorrow box in this chapter.

Telecommuting

One of the most interesting ways in which computer technology has automated the office is **telecommuting,** that is, enabling people to work at home on a terminal or microcomputer workstation linked up to an organization at another location. Many word processing operators and computer programmers, for example, telecommute either entirely or in part to their jobs, perhaps because they prefer to do so or because they are more productive at home.

FIGURE 16-11

Telecommuting. Telluride, nestled in the Uncompahgre National Forest of southwest Colorado, used to be one of America's best-kept secrets. Today it is becoming a favorite spot for telecommuters, who communicate with their offices in cities such as Chicago and Washington via fax machines and satellite dishes.

Telecommuting can save workers both the time and expense involved in traveling to work. It can also save businesses the expense of maintaining office and parking space. On the negative side, telecommuting limits the interpersonal contact that often makes working in an office lively and productive. Also, telecommuting requires a major cultural adjustment for organizations accustomed to on-site supervision of employees.

Telecommuting is beginning to catch on as a life-style trend for executives and independent consultants as they look for new ways to combine business and pleasure in their lives. For instance, many executives will spend days at home or on a boat, telecommuting by microcomputer workstation or by fax machine with the office. In fact, the town of Telluride, Colorado—an isolated, picturesque mining town that is now a popular ski resort—recently organized a task force on economic diversification to find ways to attract certain types of telecommuters (see Figure 16-11). One of their most prominent telecommuters to date is John Naisbitt, author of *Megatrends,* who keeps in touch with his Washington, D.C., office by phone and facsimile machine.

T   O   M   O   R   R   O   W

Workgroup Computing

A Trend That Will Change How Working People Interact

When personal computers first started appearing in offices, they gave people a good excuse to be alone. Armed with a copy of Lotus 1-2-3 or dBASE, an employee could spend hours at his or her personal workstation, keyed into a private environment and oblivious to the goings-on around the office. Now that office networks are starting to be implemented, however, some of that may change.

Workgroup computing is a recently coined term used to describe people linked up on a common network to communicate with one another about a common job or problem (see photo). Some of the other names used to describe this phenomenon are *groupware* and *shareware,* both of which relate to the specific software used in the group application. While people indeed are starting to work on computers together, many of these efforts are still in the pioneering stage and much of the now-needed shareware is yet to come. Four applications recently developed for workgroup computing involve computer conferencing, publishing, claims processing, and CASE tools.

With an E-mail network, workers can engage in a technique called *computer teleconferencing* (see page 516), in which a worker can broadcast a message to everyone in a group or to certain individuals. Some groups that have used computer teleconferencing claim it enables much faster decision making, gets more people involved in the decision-making process, and avoids tying up time in routine staff meetings that would accomplish the same thing. In addition, higher-level managers can use their terminals to peek in on the conference, eliminating the need for formal reports. Although many such conferences are carried out locally, it's also possible to have "virtual workgroups" of people scattered about geographically. In this type of arrangement, when an urgent problem comes up at one location, an organization can distribute a description to the mailboxes of experts at other sites, who may be able to suggest some solutions.

In the publishing world, where deadlines can be tight and people need to get answers quickly from colleagues in order to proceed, workgroup computing is really finding a home. When a writer

DESIGN AND MANUFACTURING SYSTEMS: CAD/CAM

So far, we've looked at computers at work crunching out operational documents such as paychecks and bills, supplying information to managers when and where they need it, and streamlining various functions around the office. Now let's look into the design labs and out on the factory floor to see how computers are used there. Computers are widely used in organizational settings to improve productivity both at the design stage—through computer-aided design (CAD)—and at the manufacturing stage—through computer-aided manufacturing (CAM).

or editor is part of a group, single-user workstations that are not part of a network can lead to chaos. After all, if, say, the writer and two editors are working on the wording of an article at the same time, it becomes difficult to coordinate the changes into a product that everyone agrees to. When implemented in a group environment, publishing software needs a locking feature so that concurrent access to, say, an article or chapter is not possible while someone is making key changes to it. Virtually all of the desktop publishing packages available today are single-user systems, but multi-user packages are expected to emerge in the next year or two.

In the field of insurance, it's common for several types of photos and documents to be generated as a claim is being processed. For instance, an adjuster may take a picture of a damaged car and prepare an adjustment form. An estimate and a claim form will also need to be prepared. Gradually, a file on each claim will be developed, and people within the claims department of the insurance company will need to see the file, sign off on certain documents, and add other documents. With such products as the Wang Integrated Image System (see Figure 6-4 in Chapter 6), this type of workgroup processing application is now possible on computer.

In the world of software development, programmers often are assigned pieces of the same program to work on concurrently or sequentially. With the rise of automated program development tools—commonly referred to as CASE (computer-aided software engineering) products—it soon will be possible for programmers to more easily share and synchronize work online.

Groupware will be an evolutionary, trial-and-error phenomenon as it takes hold. Many experts believe that as pioneering vendors get groupware products out to users and obtain feedback, they will come to more fully understand how people can use computers to work together in groups.

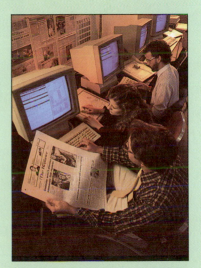

Shareware. A new breed of software and way of working.

Computer-Aided Design (CAD)

Using **computer-aided design (CAD),** product designers can dramatically reduce the time they spend at the drawing board. For example, using light pens and specialized graphics workstations (see Figure 16-12), engineers can sketch ideas directly into the computer system and then instruct it to analyze the proposed design in terms of how well it meets a number of design criteria. Using the subsequent computer output, designers can modify the drawings until they achieve the desired results.

Before the arrival of CAD, designers had to manually produce preliminary sketches and, then, advanced designs incorporating refinements on the sketches. Then, after models were built and tested, designers had to prepare production drawings, which were used to build the equipment needed to

FIGURE 16-12

Computer-aided design. High-resolution technical workstations enable design engineers to create any of a variety of products, from cars and aircraft to rug patterns and running shoes.

manufacture the new product, whether a truck or a toaster. Today computer-aided assistance with all of these tasks is fairly common. CAD is especially helpful in designing products such as automobiles, aircraft, ships, buildings, electrical circuits (including computer chips), and even running shoes.

Besides playing an important role in the design of durable goods, CAD is very useful in fields such as art, advertising, and movie production. Window 8 provides several examples of how CAD is implemented in various work environments.

Computer-Aided Manufacturing (CAM)

Computer applications are not limited to the design phases of product development; in fact, computers were used on the factory floor well before engineers used them interactively for design. Every day more and more aspects of the production process on the factory floor are becoming computerized.

Computer-aided manufacturing (CAM) includes the use of computers to help manage manufacturing operations and control machinery used in those processes. One example is a system that observes production in an oil refinery, performs calculations, and opens and shuts appropriate valves when necessary. Another system, commonly used in the steel industry, works from preprogrammed specifications to automatically shape and assemble steel parts. CAM is also widely used to build cars and ships, monitor power plants, manufacture food and chemicals, and perform a number of other functions.

FIGURE 16-13

An industrial robot. Robots take on jobs that are too physically demanding, monotonous, dangerous, or expensive for humans to perform. The robot shown here is folding cartons.

One type of CAM that seems to have caught the attention of people everywhere is **robotics,** the study of the design, building, and use of robots. Robots are machines that, with the help of a computer, can mimic a number of human motor activities to perform jobs that are too monotonous or dangerous for their flesh-and-blood counterparts (see Figure 16-13). Some robots can even "see" by means of embedded cameras and "feel" with sensors that permit them to assess the hardness, temperature, and other qualities of objects. Robots can represent substantial savings to a corporation, since they don't go on strike, don't need vacations, and don't get sick.

The auto industry uses robots to weld and paint cars. Electronics firms employ robots to assemble calculators. Robots help mine coal and even build other machines. In fact, a well-known sushi chef in Japan is not a human but a robot. So too are a few internationally famous "painters." In Japan, there is even a robot that can read standard sheet music (via optical recognition of notes) and play the music with real-life instruments!

Despite global fascination with robot technology, robotics has been slow to catch on in the United States and Europe, where unions fear workers will lose their jobs to machines. On the other hand, in Japan, where many companies virtually guarantee workers employment until age 60, robots have been quickly embraced. Japan is now the world's leading robot producer, representing more than half of the worldwide market.

ARTIFICIAL INTELLIGENCE

A computer is a device that, when given some instructions, can perform work at extremely fast speeds, drawing on a large memory. Also, it can be programmed with a set of rules or guidelines that enable it to draw certain types of conclusions based on the input it receives. A good deal of human mental activity involves these same processes. For this reason, the ability of computer systems to perform in ways that would be considered intelligent if observed in humans is commonly referred to as **artificial intelligence (AI).** Consequently, the computer systems that embody principles of artificial intelligence are frequently called *artificial intelligence systems.*

The Evolution of AI

The field of AI evolved from attempts to write programs that would enable computers to rival skilled humans at games such as chess and checkers, to prove difficult mathematical theorems, and so forth. Early attempts to use computers to do humanlike thinking primarily exploited the awesome speed of computers. For example, the first chess programs instructed computer systems to make decisions by looking several plays ahead and calculating the effects of all possible moves and countermoves. Unfortunately, planning even 10 moves ahead is a burdensome chore, even for a computer. Also, it is not the way skilled chess players think. Most chess masters rely on intuitive rules of thumb called *heuristics.* For example, one highly successful heuristic for playing chess is to control the center of the board. As programmers began supplying computers with the logic for using such heuristics, the quality of chess-playing programs improved dramatically. And as programmers began to incorporate the same type of "built-in intelligence" into other types of applications, the field of AI started to attract serious notice. In fact, many industry experts now see AI as the key to the fifth generation of computing.

Today the four main areas of AI are expert systems, natural languages, vision systems, and robotics.

Expert Systems

Expert systems are an outgrowth of the heuristics-based chess-playing programs of the 1950s and 1960s, when the "expert knowledge" of chess masters was built into programs. Today expert systems are successfully used in many fields.

In medicine, for instance, an expert system might be used to incorporate the thinking patterns of some of the world's leading physicians. For example, a system might be given a configuration of symptoms exhibited by a patient. If these symptoms might lead to the diagnosis of a disease the program knows something about, the program may ask the attending physician for information about specific details. Ultimately, through questioning and checking the patient's condition against a large database of successfully di-

FIGURE 16-14
Benefits of expert systems.

Benefits of Expert Systems
☑ Capture the knowledge of company experts who someday will retire, resign, or pass away
☑ Place expert knowledge into machine-readable form, where it can be summoned at any time
☑ Train new hires to solve problems the way experienced professionals do
☑ Are not vulnerable to problems such as fatigue, emotion, and overwork, all of which plague human experts

agnosed cases, the program might draw conclusions that the attending physician may never reach otherwise—and much more quickly as well.

Expert systems have enormous applications potential in business, where they can be used to capture the knowledge of expert business professionals into an active form and subsequently employed to improve decision making within the firm or to train individuals (see Figure 16-14). Today the application of expert systems to the solution of business problems is just beginning to occur on a widespread basis.

Figure 16-15 shows a number of present and proposed applications for expert systems in business.

FIGURE 16-15

Business examples of expert systems. Within the coming decade, say many industry analysts, expert system routines will become standard items in scores of software products.

Business Area	Application
☑ Tax accounting	Assisting tax accountants by providing advice on the best tax treatment for an individual or corporation
☑ Repair	Assisting machine repairpeople by providing expert diagnosis of malfunctions
☑ Insurance sales	Helping an insurance agent tailor an insurance package to a client, given the client's insurance, investment, financial planning, and tax needs
☑ Portfolio planning	Determining the best securities portfolio for a client, given the client's growth and equity objectives
☑ Manufacturing	Finding the best way to design, produce, stock, and ship a product
☑ System design	Determining the optimal hardware and software configuration to meet a set of user requirements
☑ Multinational planning	Providing expert advice on whether a given business strategy will work in different countries, each with its own laws and customs
☑ Government tax auditing	Using a complex set of criteria and a knowledge base of past audit cases to decide which individuals and companies to audit, so as to maximize overall return
☑ Credit authorization	Deciding whether to grant credit to individuals and companies based on both their past histories and other similar credit cases
☑ Training	Putting new hires into computer-simulated situations in which their performance is aided by or compared with experts

Natural Languages

One of the greatest challenges that scientists in the field of AI currently face is providing computer systems with the ability to communicate in *natural languages*—English, Spanish, French, Japanese, and so forth. Unfortunately, this challenge has not been easy to meet. People have personalized ways of communicating, and the meanings of words vary with the contexts in which they are used. Also, the heuristics people employ to understand what others are saying are highly complex and still poorly understood by language researchers.

Nonetheless, researchers have made some big strides toward getting computers to listen to and respond in natural languages. Some of the important applications in the voice input and voice output areas, both of which heavily depend on natural-language processing, were covered in Chapter 6.

Vision Systems

Vision systems are systems that enable computer-controlled devices to "see." A vision system might work as follows. Parts produced in a manufacturing process are sent along an assembly line for inspection. A vision system located at a station along the line takes a digital photograph of each part as it passes by the station. The photo is decomposed into vital data that are compared to other data—showing how the part would look if it were produced correctly—in the vision system's electronic memory. An expert system within the vision system uses heuristics to judge whether the part has been correctly made or is flawed. If the part is flawed, the system determines the nature of the flaw and the necessary corrective action.

Robotics

We've already seen that *robotics* plays an integral role in computer-aided manufacturing (CAM) systems. Although many robots may seem "dumb," they are often aided by a number of other artificial intelligence techniques to enable them to identify objects and states in their environments and act accordingly. There are now robots designed for warehouses, for instance, that are equipped with vision systems. These "eyes" allow them to gauge distances and speeds while they navigate among stationary stores of goods and moving fork-lift trucks. And scientists are busy at work producing ant-sized robots that will be able to fit inside the human body and perform delicate tasks such as unclogging arteries. The ultimate AI product, of course, will be a robot that's virtually indistinguishable from a human being. Such a robot could be scaled to virtually any dimension and given superhuman powers. AI, of course, is still far from realizing this goal.

SUMMARY AND KEY TERMS

Many computer applications in business, industry, and government fall into one or more of four categories: transaction processing systems, management information systems, office systems, and design and manufacturing systems.

Transaction processing systems generally perform tasks that involve the tedious recordkeeping organizations handle regularly. Among these tasks are payroll, order entry, inventory control, accounts receivable, accounts payable, and general ledger.

Management information systems (MISs), which fall into two classes—information reporting systems and decision support systems—give decision makers access to needed information. An **information reporting system** provides management with preselected types of information, generally in the form of computer-generated reports. A **decision support system (DSS),** on the other hand, provides managers with tools for modeling customized decision support environments, manipulating data, and collecting information, thereby enabling them to design their own information systems.

In recent years, computer technology has been applied to increasing productivity in the office. The term **office automation (OA)** has been coined to describe this trend. Automating the office can be done through a wide variety of technologies and processing techniques, including **word processing** and **desktop publishing; electronic mail** systems such as **facsimile (fax) machines, voice mail** systems, and **electronic mailboxes; desk accessories;** decision support tools; **teleconferencing;** and **telecommuting.**

Computers are widely used in industry to improve productivity both at the design stage—through **computer-aided design (CAD)**—and at the manufacturing stage—via **computer-aided manufacturing (CAM).** One type of CAM that has caught a great deal of attention is **robotics**—the study of the design, building, and use of robots.

The ability of some computer systems to perform in ways that would be considered intelligent if observed in humans is referred to as **artificial intelligence (AI).** The four main applications of AI techniques are expert systems, natural languages, vision systems, and robotics.

Expert systems are an outgrowth of the heuristics-based chess-playing programs of the 1950s and 1960s, when the "expert knowledge" of chess masters was built into programs. Today expert systems are successfully used in many fields.

One of the greatest challenges scientists in the field of AI currently face is the development of computer systems with the ability to communicate in *natural languages* such as English, Spanish, French, and Japanese. Although this challenge has been difficult to meet, researchers have made some big strides toward getting computers to listen to and respond in natural languages.

Vision systems enable computer-controlled devices to "see." Vision systems are commonly used in manufacturing environments to inspect products for flaws.

Today *robotics* plays an integral role in both computer-aided manufacturing (CAM) systems and other systems. Although many robots may seem "dumb," they are often aided by a number of other artificial intelligence techniques that enable them to identify objects and states in their environments and act accordingly.

REVIEW EXERCISES

Fill-in Questions

1. The term _____ refers to computer systems that perform humanlike tasks.

2. The term _____ refers to money owed to a company by customers who have made purchases on credit.

3. A(n) _____ system keeps track of all financial summaries and produces accounting reports such as balance sheets, income statements, and the like.

4. CAD is an acronym for _____ .

5. A(n) _____ system makes it possible to send letters, memos, and so on from one computer terminal to another.

6. _____ is an OA technology that allows a group of people to meet electronically, thereby saving the time and expense of physically getting together in one spot.

7. The study of the design, building, and use of robots comprises the field of _____ .

Matching Questions

Match each term with the description that best fits.

a. transaction processing system   d. DSS
b. CAM   e. CAD
c. expert system   f. word processing

_____ 1. A system possessing artificial intelligence.

_____ 2. Pertains to the recordkeeping tasks that organizations handle on a day-to-day basis.

_____ 3. The use of computers to assist in the preparation of letters, memos, documents, and the like.

_____ 4. Refers to the use of computers in design.

_____ 5. Pertains to the use of interactive computer systems for decision support.

_____ 6. Refers to the use of computers in manufacturing.

Discussion Questions

1. Name several functions performed by transaction processing systems.

2. What is the difference between an information reporting system and a decision support system?

3. Identify some of the computing technologies that comprise OA.

4. What is the difference between computer-aided design and computer-aided manufacturing? Provide some examples of each.

5. What is meant by artificial intelligence?

6. What types of benefits do expert systems provide?

Critical Thinking Questions

1. There is a great deal of confusion with regard to computer terminology. For instance, many people refer to almost every computer system as a "management information system." Also, the term "artificial intelligence" is widely applied to systems that save people a great deal of work—even when such systems do not use techniques that mimic human intelligence. Why, do you think, is there such confusion?

2. Whereas robots can perform many jobs adequately, there are a number of other jobs for which robots may never be used. What are three such jobs?

3. Several studies have claimed that despite the billions of dollars being spent on office automation during the past several years, there has been no appreciable gain in white-collar-worker productivity. How do you account for this?

4. Until very recently, executives have been willing to sign checks for computers but have been unwilling to use computers directly in their own work. Why, would you guess, has this been the case?

5. What two devices in Chapter 6 does a fax machine most resemble? Identify any similarities.

The World of CAD

A Brief Pictorial Introduction to Computer-Aided Design

8

As you've seen in some of the other Windows, computer systems are capable of producing spectacular images. But how are these images created? It would take an entire book to adequately describe this process, but this Window will give you some insights into several of the methods computer designers commonly use when confronted with a design challenge. In the first four pages, we'll study a few of the favorite techniques of designers. Then we'll explore in depth three applications of computer graphics. Here you'll see how the so-called "optical illusion" is created, how marketers conceptualize a package design, and how a magazine cover design is produced.

1 Shown here is an attractive graphic in which the image file itself was "mapped" onto a file element—the right-facing magazine page. Sophisticated computer graphic techniques allow flat, two-dimensional images to be rescaled and mapped onto curved, three-dimensional surfaces, as illustrated in the photo.

BASIC TECHNIQUES

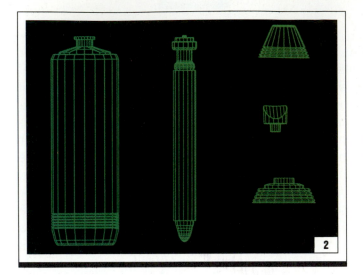

2, 3 Three-dimensional computer graphics models often are first created as wireframe diagrams onto which a surface is later applied.

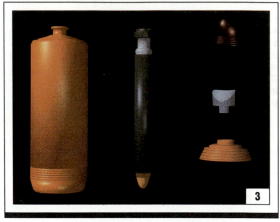

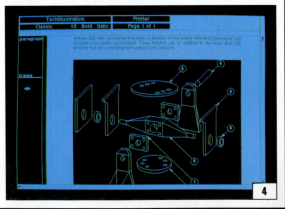

4 Images of product subassemblies often are developed from images in a component parts database, as this photo shows. The subassembly can be exploded, as illustrated here, and, with the assistance of a desktop publishing package, used to create a specifications manual.

5 A three-dimensional image can be rotated to permit viewing from any angle. At any point in the viewing, the image can be enlarged on the screen through a process called *zooming.* The image shown here was produced on a display having a 1,024-by-1,024-pixel resolution and allowing 256 colors or grey shades to be displayed simultaneously.

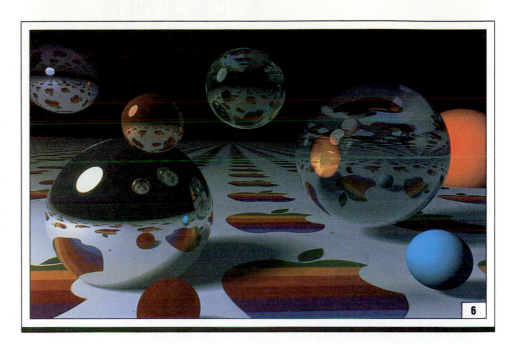

6 Reflections were created in this image by mapping the Apple logos on the image floor onto the contour of the spheres, whose shapes are mathematically known. The shadow effects were created by defining the coordinates of the light source and spheres in space, and then determining mathematically where shadows would fall. Shadows are touched up to look realistic by airbrushing them around the edges.

7 A common technique graphics designers use is distortion. When an image is mapped onto a surface and the surface is distorted, the image is distorted as well.

8 You can replicate virtually any computer image just as you would copy text with a word processor. And, as shown here, you can then treat each replicated image in its own special way. The sidebar at the right of the image illustrates the use of blending software to provide color gradation.

SPECIAL EFFECTS

9–13 Once an image has been either scanned-in or created on the computer, it can be treated with a number of special effects, as shown in the panel of photographs on this page. Here color properties such as hue, intensity, and saturation are varied to produce a number of moods.

CREATING THE OPTICAL ILLUSION

14

15

16

14–16 Optical illusions often are created by *composite imaging,* that is, forming an image from two or more other images. Here a sleepy cove, a ship, and a picturesque cloud formation are read separately into digital storage with a color image scanner. These serve as the basic ingredients for the composite image.

17 The composite image is formed by overlaying the images and cutting away the unneeded parts.

17

18

18 The finished image is produced by exporting the composite art into a desktop publishing package, where it is combined with text and display fonts.

CREATING A PACKAGE DESIGN

19 One of the first steps in package design is creating a suitable logo. Because the computer is being used to manipulate the logo image, the designer can try out dozens of color and style variations in less than an hour. In this image, the sliding bars at the bottom of the screen enable the designer to choose colors from a palette and to vary their percentages.

20 A finished label.

21 A label mapped onto a cylindrical surface—a juice can.

23 A completely simulated supermarket display, or *plan-o-gram,* enables the designer to view on screen how a product might appear when part of a larger display or when placed alongside a competitor's products.

22 By replicating the can six times, a six pack is created. Here, the six pack is illuminated with an artificial light source to simulate how it may actually appear when presented to the consumer for purchase consideration. The cans are created in three dimensions, enabling them to be rotated and inspected at various angles.

CREATING A MAGAZINE COVER

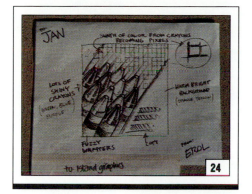

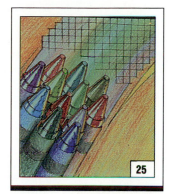

24 Most designs begin with preliminary sketches. Here the designer and publisher, located at different sites, use a fax machine to rapidly refine the hand-drawn sketch that will form the cover subject.

25 The final drawing is xeroxed (fax paper is too slippery), hand colored with art pencils, and read into the computer system with a color image scanner.

26 Illustration software on the computer system is used to make refinements to the crayon shapes and to perfect the colors.

27 The illustration software is used to add other elements to the drawing, one at a time.

28 The designer uses a zooming feature on the computer system to closely inspect each detail.

29 Once the drawing is finished, it is combined with a title logo, other art elements, and text to produce the finished magazine cover.

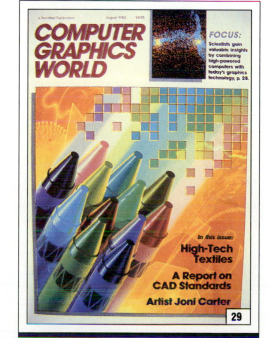

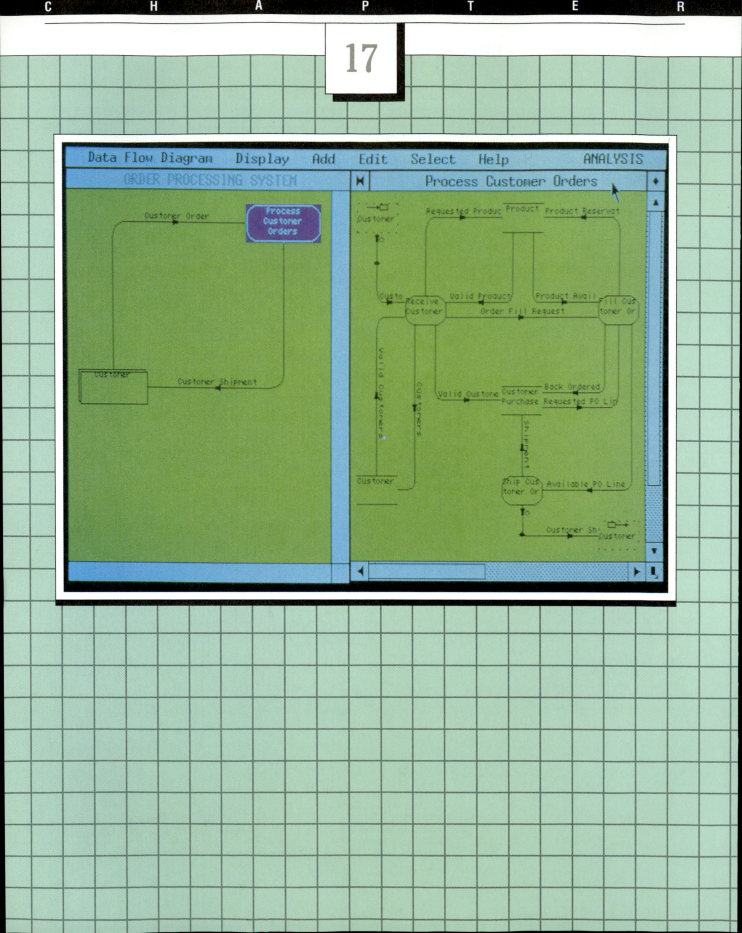

Systems Development

Objectives

After completing this chapter, you will be able to:

1. Explain what a system is.
2. Describe the traditional and nontraditional approaches used to develop systems.
3. Describe the role of the systems analyst in systems development.
4. Identify and describe the components of the systems development life cycle (SDLC).

OVERVIEW

As you saw in Chapter 16, all organizations have various sorts of systems, for example, transaction processing systems, management information systems, office systems, and CAD/CAM systems. Such systems require considerable planning and follow-up effort. The process that includes planning and implementing any type of system, whether computerized or not, is called *systems development.*

Unfortunately, since no two organizations are exactly alike and ways of doing things differ among organizations, there is no sure-fire formula for successful systems development. A procedure that works well in one situation may fail in another. These facts notwithstanding, there is a set of general principles that, if understood, will enhance the likelihood of the system's success. Those principles are the subject of this chapter.

Systems development often is subdivided into five steps, or phases: preliminary investigation, systems analysis, system design, system acquisition, and system implementation. Collectively these phases often are called the *systems development life cycle (SDLC).*

In this chapter, we'll closely examine three approaches to systems development. First, and throughout most of this chapter, we'll look at the *traditional approach* to systems development, in which phases of the life cycle are performed sequentially. Then we'll cover a process called *prototyping,* in which a temporary system model called a "prototype" is created and refined. Finally, we'll look at situations in which *end users* take primary responsibility for systems development.

ON SYSTEMS

A **system** is a collection of elements and procedures that interact to accomplish a goal. A football game, for example, is played according to a system. It consists of a collection of elements (two teams, a playing field, referees) and procedures (the rules of the game) that interact to determine which team is the winner. A transit system is a collection of people, machines, work rules, fares, and schedules that get people from one place to another. Similarly, a computer system is a collection of people, hardware, software, data, and procedures that interact to perform information processing tasks.

The function of many systems, whether manual or computerized, is to keep an organization well managed and running smoothly. Systems are created and altered in response to changing needs within an organization and shifting conditions in its surrounding environment. When problems arise in an existing system or a new system is needed, systems development comes into play. **Systems development** is a process that consists of analyzing an applications environment, designing a new system or making modifications to an old one, acquiring needed hardware and software, and getting the new or modified system to work.

Systems development may be required for any of a number of reasons. New laws may call for the collection of data never before assembled. The government may require new data on personnel, for example. The introduction of new technology, especially new computer technology, may prompt wholesale revision of a system. For instance, an organization may wish to convert certain operations in a transaction processing system from the batch mode to the realtime mode, as many colleges have done with their course registration systems over the last decade or so. Or, a company may decide to convert certain applications into a database or network environment. These and other kinds of pressure often can bring about major changes in the systems by which work is done in an organization.

As you read this chapter, you should consider certain facts about the nature of systems development:

☐ It is impossible to foresee every conceivable condition a system will encounter in the future. Because business, economic, and technological conditions are always changing, and users themselves are never sure of their needs, some modifications are usually necessary in any system at some point. For instance, as voice technology improved, some colleges further modified their registration systems in the late 1980s to enable students to register for classes over touch-tone phone, directly with the computer and without human assistance.

☐ Even if perfection were attainable, normally it is economically infeasible to try to solve every conceivable problem. A system that attempts to do everything might be so complicated that it would be impossible to administer efficiently, if at all.

☐ Often systems must be chosen with respect to hardware and software resources already in place. So, for instance, a systems designer who feels managers should have desktop microcomputers might nonetheless acknowledge that option as unwise if those same managers already have mainframe terminals that perform adequately.

☐ Often there is considerable uncertainty as to which system will work best in a given situation. Systems development is not an exact science like mathematics, in which a solution can be proven correct. As with most decisions in life, you're never sure that the alternatives you choose are the best ones.

RESPONSIBILITY FOR SYSTEMS DEVELOPMENT

In the typical business organization, a number of people share responsibility for the development of systems. The *chief information officer (CIO)* holds primary responsibility for systems development. Often this position is at the level of vice-president. One of the CIO's duties is to oversee the formulation of a five-year plan that maps out which systems are to be studied and possibly revamped during that period. Because information processing affects not only the accounting functions in most firms but also most other departments, including marketing, manufacturing, and personnel, a *steering committee* composed of top-level executives normally approves the plan. This committee also sets broad guidelines for performing computer-related activities. However, it does not become highly involved with technical details or the administration of particular projects, which are the responsibility of the *information systems department.*

The Information Systems Department

The **information systems department** varies widely in structure from one company to another. In one form the department is divided into three parts, as shown in Figure 17-1. The *data processing* area has primary responsibility for the development of large transaction processing systems, that is, those systems costing over $100,000 or so and affecting the entire organization. The *information center* normally is involved with smaller projects, say, those that help individual end users or end-user departments select microcomputer resources for their own, local use. The *office automation (OA)* area is in charge of ensuring that the organization takes full advantage of technologies such as word processing, desktop publishing, electronic mail, and the like. Increasingly, organizations are seeking the help of *systems integrators* (see the Tomorrow box) as either an alternative to developing systems inhouse or in cases where in-house resources do not exist.

Data Processing Area. The **data processing area** predates other areas within the information systems department and is still considered by many to be the most important. After all, if their computers stopped processing transactions, most large organizations would have to shut down.

Within the data processing area, the *systems analysis and design group* analyzes, designs, and implements new software and hardware systems. As we discussed in detail in Chapter 9, the *programming group* codes computer programs from program design specifications created by the systems analyst. The *operations group* manages day-to-day processing once a system has become operational.

The person most involved with systems development is the **systems analyst.** Generally speaking, the systems analyst's job is to both plan and implement large systems that will use the computers the organization has or will acquire. When such a system is needed, the systems analyst interacts with current and potential end users to produce a solution. The analyst generally is involved in all stages of the development process, from the preliminary investigation to implementation.

We can easily understand the varied activities of the systems analyst by dividing the process of systems development into five steps, or phases:

☐ Phase 1: Preliminary investigation

☐ Phase 2: Systems analysis

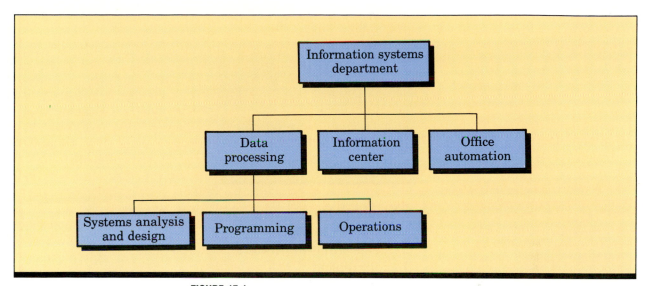

FIGURE 17-1

A possible organizational structure for an information systems department.

☐ Phase 3: System design

☐ Phase 4: System acquisition

☐ Phase 5: System implementation

Collectively these phases often are referred to as the **systems development life cycle (SDLC),** because they describe a system from the time it is first studied until the time it is put into use. When a new business pressure necessitates a change in a system, the steps of the cycle begin anew.

The role of the systems analyst in the five phases is shown in Figure 17-2. In the next several sections of this chapter, we will first consider the earliest

FIGURE 17-2

The role of the systems analyst in the five phases of systems development.

Role of the Systems Analyst

☑ **Preliminary investigation** During this phase the analyst studies the problem briefly and suggests a few possible solutions so that management can decide whether the project should be pursued further.

☑ **Systems analysis** If management decides after the preliminary investigation that further systems development is warranted, the analyst must study the existing applications area in depth and make specific recommendations for change.

☑ **System design** During this phase the analyst develops a model of the new system and prepares a detailed list of benefits and costs. Both the model and the list are incorporated into a report to management.

☑ **System acquisition** Upon management approval of the design model, the analyst must decide what software and hardware to obtain.

☑ **System implementation** After the components of the system have been acquired, the analyst supervises the lengthy process of adapting old programs and files to the new system, prepares specifications for programmers, and so forth.

T   O   M   O   R   R   O   W

Systems Integrators

Will They Provide a Major Solution to Systems Development in the 1990s?

A *systems integrator* is a firm that provides systems development assistance for other organizations. Systems integration is really not a new concept; the government has for years used these firms to do much of its systems development work. But recently a new twist has emerged—one that may signal a significant future trend.

That twist concerns the private sector. Traditionally most private-sector firms have chosen to do the bulk of their systems development in-house, with little help from the outside. A number of recent changes in technology and business, however, are making that alternative increasingly undesirable.

> The number of companies in the systems integration area has increased dramatically.

First, the number of companies in the systems integration area has increased dramatically in the last several years. As computer-related costs for most Fortune 500 companies began to spiral in the 1980s, many of those firms decided to use their large MIS staffs and bases of expertise to enter niche areas in the computer industry. Thus, familiar names such as Sears, Boeing, Celanese, Weyerhauser, John Deere, and JC Penney—none of them traditionally known for their computer expertise—are now in the systems-building business, creating both software and systems in the applications areas they know best. And, scores of entrepreneurs within these firms have left to found their own firms.

Second, until only recently, there was very little high-quality packaged software for sale. If an organization wanted a system, it had to build one from scratch. Today, however, there is a growing base of useful programs and systems that can, so to speak, be bought off the shelf, eliminating the need for time-consuming systems development and the inherent risks.

and most conventional approach to systems development, sometimes called the **traditional SDLC approach.** In this approach, which is common with the transaction processing systems built by the data processing area, each phase of the life cycle is completed before the next phase begins. Later in the chapter, we'll consider alternative development approaches.

Information Center. The **information center (IC)**—sometimes also called the microcomputer support center or corporate computer store—is one of the latest additions to many information systems departments. It was conceived to help the individual end users in the organization make intelligent choices about the microcomputer hardware and software they need to better perform their jobs, as well as to promote an orderly acquisition of microcomputing resources within the organization as a whole. Many ICs are staffed primarily with *information center consultants* (systems analysts having special skills in the microcomputing area) and with *trainers.*

Perhaps the biggest fear with any systems-building effort is that the cost and the development time of the new software will spiral out of control. This concern can be eliminated to some degree if one can get an experienced software/systems house involved and get them to make promises on paper.

Third, the diversity of systems in an organization today makes it difficult to find people who are jacks of all trades. At one time, virtually the only computer system any organization had was a mainframe-based transaction processing system, which probably came from a single vendor. Now it has scores of personal computers with their customized decision support systems, CAD systems, expert systems, desktop publishing systems, electronic mail systems, complex communications networks, end-user interfaces, and so on. The number of vendors represented can easily number in the hundreds. Moreover, many technologies and applications interweave, adding to the degree of complication involved. It is not unusual for the demands of a new project to be completely beyond the capabilities of the in-house staff.

And these reasons represent only the most compelling ones for considering a systems integrator. Two more reasons are that systems integrators represent an outside point of view and, because integrators pay more than average, they usually land some of the best talent. To management, which gets tired of hearing about the backlog of computer-related work requests, the integrator provides a quickie solution to a new project that threatens to disrupt the current flow of work and add to the regular payroll.

Just how far systems integration will come as a systems development solution for private-sector firms in the 1990s will depend on a number of things. Often companies are afraid to give up some control, especially when they don't fully understand the complexity of the projects involved. Also, systems integration is still relatively new to most companies, on both the buying and selling ends. Thus, it's difficult to predict how rapid the acceptance will be and how users will react to the failures that are likely to occur as they feel their way through integration.

ICs often are set up similarly to a typical microcomputer store. A user walks in and talks to a consultant about specific microcomputing needs. Perhaps the user is a sales manager who needs a small decision support system to keep track of a field sales force. The manager and consultant sit down at one or two machines and experiment with some appropriate, off-the-shelf software. (This experimentation process is called *prototyping,* and we will cover it later in the chapter.) Eventually, they put together a small system. Training may also be offered to users through self-paced videocassettes or classes.

Office Automation (OA) Area. In many organizations, the **office automation (OA) area** is both the newest and the smallest group within the information systems department. The OA area is responsible for developing a cost-efficient, integrated approach to using office technologies such as electronic document processing and electronic mail. Typical duties, which resemble those of the IC, are establishing a long-range plan, arranging product demonstrations, and helping end users and end-user departments select systems.

PHASE I: THE PRELIMINARY INVESTIGATION

The first thing the systems analyst does when confronted with a new systems assignment is conduct a **preliminary investigation,** or *feasibility study*. The purpose of this investigation is to define the problem at hand and suggest some possible courses of action. Accordingly, the investigation should examine the nature of the problem, the scope of the project created by the problem, possible solutions, and the approximate costs and benefits of the alternatives.

The Nature of the Problem. Determining the true nature of a problem is one of the key steps in the preliminary investigation. The analyst must take care to distinguish *symptoms* from *problems* at the outset.

For example, suppose an analyst is talking to a warehouse manager who complains that inventories are too high. This may be so, but this fact in itself is not enough to warrant corrective action. It's a symptom, not a problem. There is a problem, however, if these high inventories are forcing the company to build a new, expensive warehouse or if they are unnecessarily drawing on funds that could be used for profit opportunities. Yet even if there is a definable problem, the company may be unable to do anything about it; that is, the problem may not be solvable. For example, the high inventories may be due to a shipping or receiving strike somewhere else.

The analyst must also determine the relative magnitude of a problem. Everyone in an organization has problems he or she wants solved, but solutions for some problems are more important than for others.

The Scope of the Project. In the preliminary investigation, the analyst also has to determine the scope of the project created by the problem. Scope is a function of the nature of the problem and of what management is *willing to spend*. An organization may be ready to spend $100,000 or only $1,000. Scope is also a function of what management is *willing to change*. Understandably, people in organizations often hesitate to switch from one procedure to another. If a new system demands too many adaptations, it will probably fail.

Because most systems in a typical organization are interrelated, the analyst must draw some clear boundaries around the systems or subsystems to be studied. Although one almost always finds scores of problems that require attention in any system, one learns to accept some things as given and to find the best solution possible given the constraints of the situation. Completely new systems aren't always the answer. Sometimes a patchwork solution or minor alteration of an old system is all that is necessary. Developing a new system from scratch is commonly called *top-down* systems development, while developing new systems relative to systems currently in place is called *bottom-up* systems development.

Possible Solutions. Once the nature and scope of the problem have been defined, a number of solutions may become apparent. The important question at this point is: Does the problem have a simple, inexpensive solution that requires no further study, or is a new system or substantial alteration called for?

One common mistake is to assume that all problems can be satisfactorily solved by computers. Actually, the computer often only makes matters worse. An application that is infrequent and that involves only a few hours of work is almost always better done the old-fashioned way: manually. Also, for some problems there may be no absolutely satisfactory solutions. For example, no company can completely avoid customers who don't pay their bills, no matter how comprehensive its billing system is. It is more useful to think of minimizing some problems than of eliminating them entirely.

Costs and Benefits. During the preliminary investigation, the analyst should also provide a rough estimate of the costs and benefits of each recommended solution. How much should the company expect to spend on hardware and software? How much time and money would be saved by installing a computer system?

Report to Management. At the end of the preliminary investigation, the analyst writes a report to management briefly describing the problems and offering some recommendations. If the problems have a simple solution that requires no further study, the analyst should state this clearly. If the recommendations involve extensive changes that require further study and expense, the analyst should outline the reasons for the proposed changes and summarize their costs and benefits. Once management has a ballpark estimate of the benefits and financial commitment involved, it can decide whether to abandon the project, implement an inexpensive or temporary solution immediately, or press forward to the next phases of systems development.

PHASE II: SYSTEMS ANALYSIS

Let's assume that based on the report evolving out of the preliminary investigation, management has decided to pursue systems development further. At this point, the **systems analysis** phase begins. During this phase, the main objectives are fact collection, analysis, and a report to management.

FIGURE 17-3

An organization chart. An organization chart provides an overview of company operations and shows the relationships among employees and the work they perform.

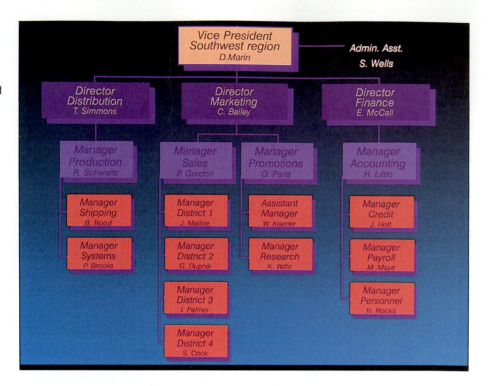

Fact Collection

The goal of fact collection is to gather information about the type of work being performed in the application under study and to ascertain what resources end users need. Later in this phase, the collected facts should enable the analyst to come up with some possible solutions. Deciding which facts to collect depends largely on the problem being studied. Four sources of information on the applications area and end-user needs are written documents, questionnaires, interviews, and observation.

Written Documents. Written documents such as special forms, manuals, diagrams, letters, and other materials can provide helpful information about how the current system functions. For example, an organization chart such as the one in Figure 17-3, which covers the company functions being studied, is an especially useful document. At the outset of a project, it will be difficult to determine which documents will be most helpful. Naturally, one can't gather everything in sight without drowning in a sea of paperwork. Therefore, the analyst should concentrate on collecting documents that tell the most about how the system works, as well as those that bear on the key problems.

Questionnaires. Questionnaires sent to system users are helpful for many reasons. They enable the analyst to obtain information from a large number of people rapidly and inexpensively. Also, they permit anonymous responses. If system users are geographically dispersed, questionnaires may be the only feasible means of getting information from them. However, questionnaires have a number of limitations. If too few users respond, results may be biased. Also, it is quite easy to create questions that are misleading, are confusing, and produce biased answers in unpredictable ways.

Interviews. Interviews and questionnaires generally serve the same purpose: to gather information from system users. Questionnaires are helpful for amassing a great deal of information rapidly, while interviews allow flexibility in following up interesting lines of questioning that the analyst could not have anticipated in a questionnaire. Also, interviews can be closely tailored to respondents. Like writing questions, interviewing is a skill.

Observation. Observation requires the analyst to go to the workplace to watch the flow of work directly. Sometimes, by listening to what people say to one another and watching what they do, the analyst can detect interesting discrepancies between what they said during the interviews and what they do in fact. Observation can also answer questions such as: Does the system actually work the way the people involved think it does? Is anything happening that I didn't expect?

Analysis

After the analyst has gathered information about the application and the current system, he or she must analyze it to reach some conclusions. These conclusions will serve as the basis for the report to management at the end of the systems analysis phase. Three useful tools for performing analysis are diagrams, checklists, and synthesis.

Diagrams. Diagrams of both the existing system and any proposed ones sometimes can be particularly helpful. Two commonly used diagram tools are data flow diagrams and system flowcharts.

Figure 17-4 shows a **data flow diagram** for the order-entry operation of a mail-order firm. Data flow diagrams provide a visual representation of data movement in an organization. They do not refer to any specific hardware devices; hence, they are commonly called *logical design* tools. Logical design tools portray how a system conceptually works rather than how it is implemented in particular hardware and/or software. Premature commitments to certain types of hardware may limit how the analyst thinks about the system and make some promising possibilities easily overlooked.

With **system flowcharts,** on the other hand, the analyst selects specific kinds of hardware devices and software. Because they show how the system is to be implemented, system flowcharts are referred to as *physical design* tools.

Figure 17-5 illustrates how a system flowchart could be created for a portion of the system depicted in Figure 17-4. Note that the symbol for online storage in Figure 17-5 indicates the need for a disk unit and the symbol for a document indicates the need for a printer. System flowcharts are not the same as *program flowcharts* (discussed in Chapter 10), which outline the steps that a program follows in processing data.

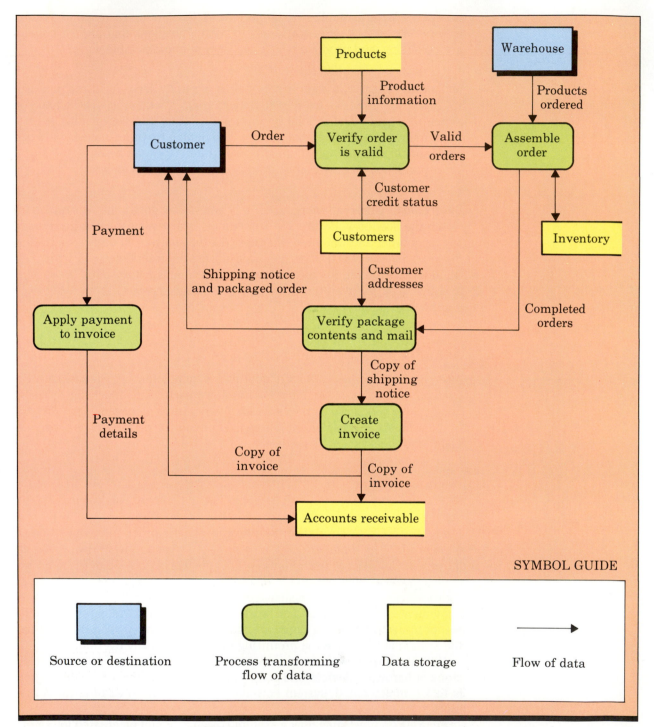

FIGURE 17-4

A data flow diagram for a mail-order firm. An order triggers the processes of verification and assembly of the goods ordered, and payment is recorded by accounts receivable.

FIGURE 17-5

A system flowchart. This flowchart depicts a portion of the system shown in Figure 17-4.

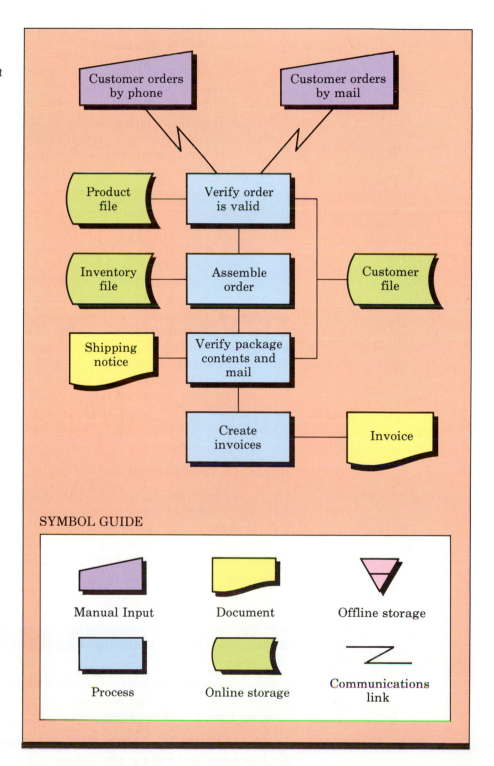

Checklists. Checklists also can prove particularly helpful in analysis. Separate checklists can be developed for

- ☐ *System Goals* For example, an accounts receivable system should get bills out quickly, identify good and bad credit risks for management, and rapidly inform customers about late payments.
- ☐ *The Kinds of Information Needed to Meet These Goals* For example, what information does management need to identify good and bad credit risks? How will this information be collected and disseminated? What timing is required to get information to managers when they need it?
- ☐ *Strengths and Weaknesses of the Current System* For example, how does the present system measure up against these goals and information needs?

There are several other types of checklists the analyst might employ depending on the requirements of the problem. Common sense eventually will dictate which type of checklist is most appropriate for the situation at hand.

Synthesis. At some point, the moment of truth will arrive: The analyst will need to provide some recommendations and be able to back them up. This is clearly the most unstructured part of the analysis and therefore the most difficult. The analyst must be able to *synthesize,* or combine, a number of seemingly unrelated facts into a coherent whole to reach a decision. Because almost every system differs in some respect, the analyst can't depend on a textbook or formula approach for help here. The ability to synthesize is also characterized by a high degree of common sense.

Report to Management

After collecting and analyzing the data, the analyst must report findings to management. This report covers many of the same subjects as the report at the end of the preliminary investigation, but it is much more thorough. The length and detail of the report should be sufficient to convince management whether it should or should not proceed to the next stage of development—system design.

PHASE III: SYSTEM DESIGN

If the analysis phase indicates that a new system is needed, the system design phase of the development process begins. The **system design** phase normally consists of four steps:

1. Review the goals and scope of the project.
2. Develop a model of the new system.
3. Perform a detailed analysis of benefits and costs.
4. Prepare a system design report.

Review of the Goals and Scope of the Project

The design of the new system must conform to the goals and scope approved by management in the analysis phase. Thus, it is always wise for the analyst to review these matters carefully before proceeding with the design. They define both the direction and the limits of the development of the project.

Development of a Model of the New System

Once the analyst understands the nature of the design problem, it is usually helpful to draw a number of diagrams of the new system. Both the data flow diagrams and the system flowcharts discussed earlier can show, respectively, how data will logically flow through the new system and how the various physical components of the system will fit together.

When designing a system, the analyst must take into account output requirements; input requirements; data access, organization, and storage; processing; system controls; and personnel and procedure specifications. Figure 17-6 covers some of the issues that must be addressed in the design specification.

Analysis of Benefits and Costs

Most organizations are acutely sensitive to costs, including computer system costs. Costs include both the initial investment in hardware and software and ongoing costs such as personnel and maintenance. Some benefits can be computed easily by calculating the amount of labor saved, the reduction in paperwork, and so on. These are called *tangible benefits,* because they are easy to quantify in dollars.

Other benefits, such as better service to customers or improved information for decision makers, are more difficult to convert into dollar amounts. These are called *intangible benefits.* Clearly the existence of intangible benefits makes it more difficult for management to reach firm decisions. On projects with a large number of such benefits, management must ask questions such as "Are the new services that we can offer to customers worth the $100,000 it will cost us?" In comparing alternative ways to spend the firm's money, management must also take into account taxes and the timing of benefits and costs.

System Design Report

Once the design has been completed and benefits and costs assessed, the analyst prepares a system design report for management. This report should provide all the facts to be weighed before the system receives final approval. The analyst might preface such a report with a three- to five-page cover letter summarizing the primary recommendations, the reasoning used to draw conclusions, and other important information. The report itself con-

FIGURE 17-6

Issues to cover during the system design specification. System design ultimately addresses all major elements of a computer system—hardware, software, data, people, and procedures.

System Design Issues

Output Considerations

☑ What types of information do users need?

☑ How often is this information needed? Annually? Monthly? Daily? On demand?

☑ What output devices and media are necessary to provide the required information?

☑ How should output be formatted or arranged so that it can easily be understood by users?

Input Considerations

☑ What data need to be gathered?

☑ How often do data need to be gathered?

☑ What input devices and media are required for data collection?

Storage Considerations

☑ How will data be accessed and therefore organized?

☑ What storage capacity is required?

☑ How fast must data be accessed?

☑ What storage devices are appropriate?

Processing Considerations

☑ What type of functionality is required in the software?

☑ What type of processing power is required? A mainframe? A minicomputer? A microcomputer?

☑ What special processing environments must be considered? A communications network? A database processing environment?

System Controls

☑ What measures must be taken to ensure that data are secure from unauthorized use, theft, and natural disasters?

☑ What measures must be taken to ensure the accuracy and integrity of data going in and information going out?

☑ What measures must be taken to ensure the privacy of individuals represented by the data?

Personnel and Procedures

☑ What personnel are needed to run the system?

☑ What procedures should be followed on the job?

---

tains all the details on the system design as well as the associated costs and benefits.

PHASE IV: SYSTEM ACQUISITION

Once a system has been designed and the required types of software and hardware have been specified, the analyst must decide from which vendors to buy the necessary components. This decision lies at the heart of the **system acquisition** phase.

FIGURE 17-7

A point-scoring approach for evaluating vendors' bids.

Criterion	Weight (Maximum Score)	Vendor 1 Score	Vendor 2 Score
Hardware	60	60	40
Software	80	70	70
Cost	70	50	65
Ease of use	80	70	50
Modularity	50	30	30
Vendor support	50	50	50
Documentation	30	30	20
		360	325

Vendor 1 has
highest total score

RFPs and RFQs

Many organizations formulate their buying or leasing needs by preparing a document called a **request for proposal (RFP).** This document contains a list of technical specifications for equipment and software determined during the system design phase. An RFP may range from a few pages to hundreds, depending on the magnitude and complexity of the acquisition. The RFP is sent to all vendors who might satisfy the organization's needs. In the proposal they send back to the initiating organization, vendors recommend a hardware and/or software solution to solve the problem at hand and specify a price.

In some cases, an organization knows exactly which hardware and software resources it needs from vendors and is interested only in a quote on a specific list of items. In this case, it sends vendors a document called a **request for quotation (RFQ),** which names those items and asks only for a quote. Thus, an RFP gives a vendor some leeway in making system suggestions, while an RFQ does not.

Evaluating Bids

Once vendors have submitted their bids or quotes in response to the RFP or RFQ, the acquiring organization must decide which bid or quote to accept. Two useful tools for making this choice are a vendor rating system and a benchmark test.

Vendor Rating System. One system for rating vendors is illustrated in Figure 17-7. In many **vendor rating systems,** such as the one in the figure, important criteria for selecting computer system resources are identified and each is given a weight. In Figure 17-7, for example, the "60" for hardware and "30" for documentation may be loosely interpreted to mean that hardware is twice as important as documentation to this organization. Each vendor that submits an acceptable bid is rated on each criterion, with the associated weight representing the maximum possible score. Then the buyer totals the scores and chooses, if possible, the vendor with the highest total. Although such a rating tool does not guarantee that the best vendor will always have the highest point total, it has the advantage of being simple to apply and objective. If several people are involved in the selection decision, individual biases will tend to be "averaged out."

Benchmark Test. After tentatively selecting a vendor, some organizations make their choice conditional on the successful completion of a "test drive," or **benchmark test.** Such a test normally consists of running a pilot version of the new system on the hardware and software of the vendor under consideration. To do this, the acquiring organization usually visits the vendor's benchmark testing center and attempts to determine how well the hardware/software configuration will work if installed. However, benchmark tests are expensive and far from foolproof. It's very possible that the pilot system will perform admirably at the benchmark site but the real system, when eventually installed at the site of the acquiring organization, will not.

PHASE V: SYSTEM IMPLEMENTATION

Once arrangements for delivery of computer resources have been made with one or more vendors, the **system implementation** phase begins. This phase includes all the remaining tasks necessary to make the system operational and successful.

To ensure that the system will be working by a certain date, the analyst must prepare a timetable. One tool for helping with this task is project management software, illustrated in Figure 17-8, which shows how certain implementation activities are related and when they must start and finish.

Implementation consists of many activities, including converting programs and data files from the old system to the new one, debugging converted and new applications programs, documentation, training, appraising the new system's performance, and ongoing maintenance. If the system has been designed well, it should be flexible enough to accommodate changes over a reasonable period of time with minimal disruption. However, if at some point a major change becomes necessary, another system will be needed to replace the current one. At this point, the systems development life cycle—from the preliminary investigation to implementation—will begin all over again.

FIGURE 17-8

Project management. Claris Corporation's MacProject II lets one organize, plan, and present projects as well as link subprojects.

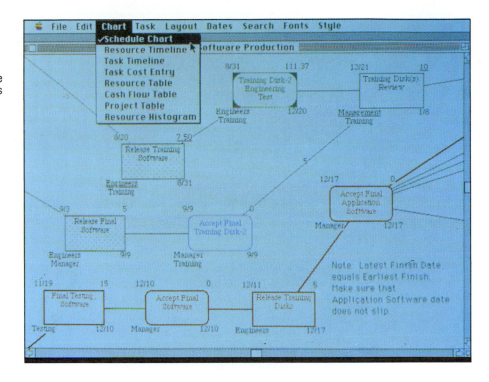

PROTOTYPING

In developing systems, it's often inappropriate to follow the five phases of systems development in perfect sequence. Some hardware and software may have to be acquired early on—perhaps as part of the system design phase— to direct the remainder of the development effort. There are several reasons for this.

First, systems often take too long to analyze, design, and implement. By the time a system is finally put into operation, important new needs that were not part of the original plan may surface. Second, the system being developed often is the wrong one. Managers almost always have difficulty expressing their informational needs, and it is not until they begin to use a system that they discover what it is they really need.

So to avoid the potentially expensive disaster that could result from completing every phase of systems development before users ever lay their hands on anything, many analysts have advocated prototyping as part of systems development. In **prototyping,** the focus is on developing a small model, or *prototype,* of the overall system. Users work with the prototype and suggest modifications. The prototype is then modified, resulting in an improved prototype. As soon as the prototype is refined to the point where higher management feels confident that a larger version of the system will succeed, either the prototype can be gradually expanded or the organization can go "full steam ahead" with the remaining steps of systems development. Information centers commonly use prototyping approaches to assist users in building decision support systems (DSSs).

END-USER DEVELOPMENT

End-user development is a relatively new form of systems development—one that has evolved from the microcomputing revolution. It is defined as a systems development effort in which the end user is primarily responsible for the development of the system. This is in contrast to traditional types of development, in which a qualified computer professional, such as a systems analyst, takes charge of the systems development process.

As you might guess, end-user development is feasible only in cases where the system being acquired is relatively inexpensive. A good example is the situation in which an end user purchases a microcomputer system and develops applications on his or her own. In developing the system, the end user might follow a prototyping approach or a method similar to traditional development.

One of the most serious problems facing organizations today is deciding how far to let end users go in creating their own systems. Although the information center may exert some control over how these systems are initially developed, it does not eliminate the threat that "homemade" data will later wend its way into critical decision-making processes that should be part of a larger, more formal system. If the user's microcomputing needs are seen as potentially disruptive to the organization in this regard, the analyst should recommend that the user's problem be handled as part of a professionally undertaken systems development effort. Some of the problems involved with managing end-user development are discussed in Feature 17A.

SUMMARY AND KEY TERMS

A **system** is a collection of elements and procedures that interact to accomplish a goal. The function of many systems, whether manual or computerized, is to keep an organization well managed and running smoothly.

Systems development is a process that consists of analyzing a system, designing a new system or making modifications to the old one, acquiring the needed hardware and software, and getting the new or modified system to work. Systems development may be required for any number of reasons, such as changes in government regulations, shifting business conditions, new computer technology, and so forth.

Managing End-User Development

Uncontrolled Growth in PC Usage Becomes a Major Management Problem

A decade or so ago, when the first microcomputers started trickling in to corporations, few people correctly assessed how rapidly they would proliferate within the office ranks. Today PCs account for over half the total annual computing tab in many organizations. Also, because of the way these systems are usually acquired and developed, they have posed a serious problem within the ranks of computer management.

In many organizations, PCs are acquired through departmental budgets. If, say, someone in the sales department feels that a microcomputer is needed, the cost of such a system may be estimated and then hidden within a line item of an upcoming budget request. Or if there is money left unallocated in the current budget, the system may be purchased right away, with little or no development. In very few cases, report several researchers, are such purchases ever formally justified. While one or two microcomputers acquired informally would not pose a serious problem, the reality in many corporations is that this haphazard buying behavior characterizes hundreds of purchases.

Consequently, many organizations have little feel for how much they are spending in total on microcomputers. While a number of companies have charged their informa-

> Many organizations have little feel for what they are spending in total on microcomputers.

tion centers (ICs) with coordinating microcomputer purchases, it is often the end user or end-user department that has the final say on which system is ultimately purchased. The strategy many ICs take to force end users to conform to a common buying pattern is to withhold any type of assistance or ongoing systems support unless the purchase is made from a list of acceptable hardware and software products.

But even if the end user buys from the IC-designated product list, there are still a lot of problems to work out. A big one is getting users to be independent enough to recognize and solve their own problems once they get their feet wet setting up an application and using the new system. Just a few years ago, many ICs were able to give most of their users full sup-

port and were easily able to dispatch consultants to end-user areas to help troubleshoot problems or set up new applications. But today, most ICs are so overloaded with requests that end users are being advised that they will have to be on their own most of the time.

In response, many end-user departments have hired their own microcomputer consultants, or *business systems analysts.* For many firms, this arrangement is more satisfactory than the previous one. Business systems analysts often are intimately familiar with both microcomputers and the end-user areas in which they serve.

In most organizations, the end user has been forced to acquire a certain degree of computer literacy. This has required not only getting a minimal amount of knowledge about how computers work but getting some knowledge about proper systems management—such as maintaining adequate backup and security, documenting important results and establishing audit trails (in case results must be reconstructed from inputs), upgrading systems, and setting up controls to guarantee the accuracy and integrity of data. At many companies, such knowledge is disseminated through in-house courses coordinated by the IC. At other companies, users often are left to pick up this knowledge the hard way—through experience.

The chief information officer, or someone with a similar title, holds primary responsibility for the overall direction of systems development. The technical details are the responsibility of the **information systems department,** which consists of the **data processing area, information center (IC),** and **office automation (OA) area.** The **systems analyst** is the person who is most closely involved with the development of systems from beginning to end.

Systems development often is divided into five phases: preliminary investigation, systems analysis, system design, system acquisition, and system implementation. Collectively these phases are often referred to as the **systems development life cycle (SDLC),** because they describe a system from the time it is first studied until the time it is put into use. When a new business pressure necessitates a change in a system, the steps of the cycle begin anew.

In the **traditional SDLC approach** to systems development, the first thing the systems analyst does when confronted with a new systems assignment is to conduct a **preliminary investigation,** or *feasibility study.* This investigation addresses the nature of the problem under study, the potential scope of the systems development effort, the possible solutions, and the costs and benefits of the solutions. At the end of the preliminary investigation, the analyst writes a report to management containing a brief description of the problem and some recommendations.

If, based on the report evolving out of the preliminary investigation, management decides to pursue systems development further, the **systems analysis** phase begins. During this phase, the main objectives are to study the application in depth (to find out what work is being done), to assess users' needs, and to prepare a list of specific requirements the new system must meet. These objectives are accomplished through fact collection, analysis, and a report to management.

The goal of fact collection is to gather evidence about what types of work are being done and what types of information users need. Four useful sources are written documents, questionnaires, interviews, and observation.

Once gathered, facts must be analyzed. A number of tools are useful for this task, including **data flow diagrams, system flowcharts,** and checklists. The object of the analysis is to synthesize facts to reach concrete conclusions about specific requirements that any new system must meet.

After collecting and analyzing the data, the systems analyst must report findings to management. This report covers many of the same subjects as the report at the end of the preliminary investigation, but it is much more thorough.

The **system design** phase of systems development consists of four steps: (1) reviewing the goals and scope of the project, (2) developing a model of the new system, (3) performing a detailed analysis of benefits and costs, and (4) preparing a system design report.

Once a system has been designed and the required types of software and hardware specified, the analyst must decide from which vendors to buy the necessary components. This decision lies at the heart of the **system acquisition** phase.

Many organizations formulate their buying or leasing needs by preparing a document called a **request for proposal (RFP).** This document lists the technical specifications for equipment and software determined during the system design phase. In some cases, an organization knows exactly which hardware and software resources it needs from vendors and is interested only in a quote on a specific list of items. In this case, it sends vendors a document called a **request for quotation (RFQ),** which names those items and asks for a quote.

Once vendors have responded to the RFP or RFQ, the organization must make selections among the vendor alternatives. Two useful tools for making such a choice are a vendor rating system and a benchmark test. In most **vendor rating systems,** important criteria for selecting computer system resources are identified and weighted. Information systems personnel then rate each vendor on each criterion. A **benchmark test** normally consists of running a pilot version of the new system on the hardware and software of the vendors under consideration.

Once arrangements have been made with one or more vendors for delivery of computer resources, the **system implementation** phase begins. This phase includes all the remaining tasks necessary to make the system operational and successful, including programming and file conversion, debugging, documentation, training, performance appraisal, and maintenance.

Prototyping is an approach to systems development in which the five phases of the systems development life cycle are not conducted serially; rather, the focus is on developing a small model, or *prototype,* of the overall system. Users work with the prototype and suggest modifications. As soon as the prototype is refined to the point where higher management feels confident that a larger version of the system will succeed, either the prototype can be gradually expanded or the organization can proceed with the remaining steps of systems development.

End-user development is a systems development approach in which the end user is primarily responsible for building the system. This is in contrast to traditional types of systems development, in which a qualified computer professional, such as a systems analyst, takes charge of the systems development process. End-user development is feasible only in cases where the system being acquired is relatively inexpensive.

REVIEW EXERCISES

Fill-in Questions

1. The _____ holds primary responsibility for systems development in an organization.

2. A(n) _____ committee composed of executives in key departments and other members of top management normally approves a plan for systems development.

3. At the end of the preliminary investigation, the systems analyst writes a report to _____ with a brief description of the problem and some recommendations.

4. _____ refers to systems development in which users are primarily responsible for the development effort.

5. Developing a model of a new system is part of the _____ phase of the systems development life cycle (SDLC).

6. Benefits that are easy to quantify in dollars are called _____ benefits.

7. In many _____ systems, the buying organization identifies important criteria for selecting computer system resources and gives each a weight. Subsequently, each vendor submitting a bid is rated on each criterion, with the associated weight representing the maximum possible score.

8. A(n) _____ consists of running a pilot version of a new system on the hardware and/or software of a vendor being considered for resource acquisition.

Matching Questions

Match each term with the description that best fits.

a. design
b. implementation
c. preliminary investigation
d. analysis
e. acquisition

_____ 1. The final phase of the SDLC.
_____ 2. The phase of the SDLC that involves studying the current system in depth.
_____ 3. The phase of the SDLC that involves RFP or RFQ preparation, vendor rating systems, and benchmark tests.
_____ 4. The first phase of the SDLC.
_____ 5. The phase of the SDLC that follows systems analysis.

Discussion Questions

1. What is systems development?

2. Describe and compare the traditional SDLC, prototyping, and end-user development approaches to systems development.

3. What are the main duties of the systems analyst?

4. Identify the five phases of the systems development life cycle.

5. What is the purpose of the preliminary investigation?

6. Why are reports sent to management at the end of both the preliminary investigation and systems analysis phases of development?

7. Why must output requirements be addressed before all other considerations when developing a model of a new system?

8. What types of items should be incorporated in the reports sent to management by the systems analyst?

9. What is the purpose of the RFP and RFQ?

10. What is the difference between top-down and bottom-up systems development?

Critical Thinking Questions

1. What are several reasons why an organization using a vendor rating system may choose to buy from a vendor other than the most highly rated one?

2. What types of problems are likely to surface when end users rather than trained computer professionals develop computer systems within an organization?

3. Can the prototyping approach to development be useful in situations in which computer systems are not involved? If you think so, provide an example.

4. Many observers of the computing scene have pointed out that some of the biggest problems in getting a system to work properly are people-related. Provide several examples that show how people problems can make a system fail.

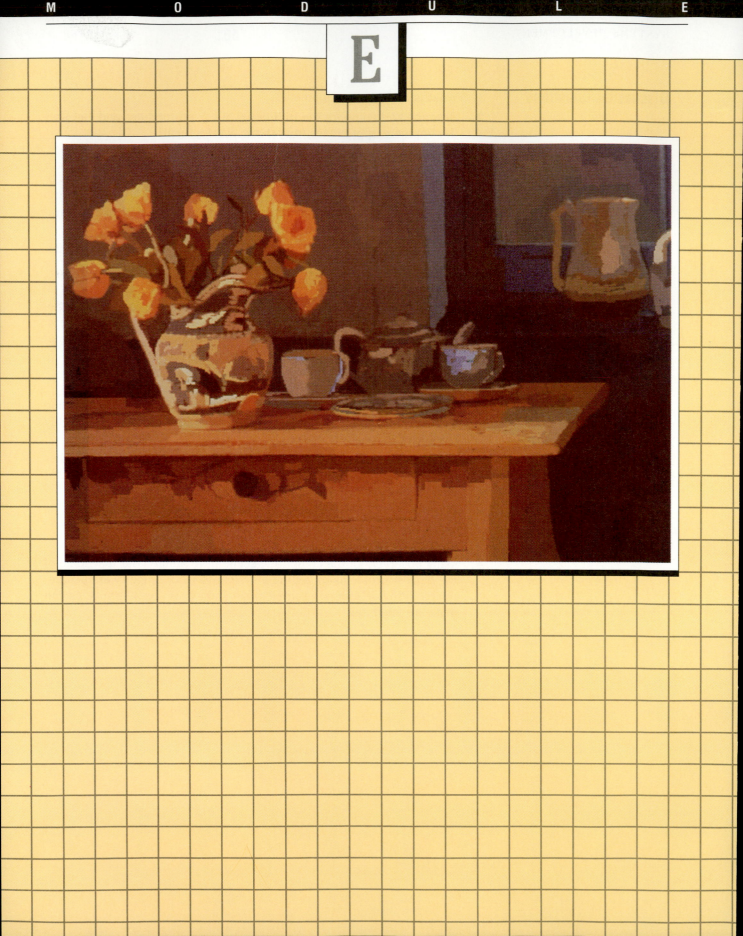

Computers in Society

No study of computers is complete without a look at the impact these machines have had on the very fabric of our society. In the workplace, computers have created many jobs and careers but also have made others obsolete. Likewise, in society as a whole, they have created both opportunities and problems. Many people praise them as a major source of progress. Others wonder if we are indeed any better off today than we were before ENIAC.

Chapter 18 covers the important subject of computer-related jobs and careers. Chapter 19 discusses many of the opportunities and problems created by the proliferation of computers.

18

Career
Opportunities

Objectives

After completing this chapter, you will be able to:

1. Identify the various types of employment available to those seeking a job in the computer field.

2. Understand the alternatives available to those seeking a career as a computer professional.

3. Describe the differences among computer curricula offered by colleges and universities.

4. Describe the resources available to computer professionals as they continue learning about computers.

OVERVIEW

If you're interested in obtaining computer-related employment, welcome to a relatively "hot" job market. The demand for computer professionals in government and industry has been booming over the past 10 to 15 years, and this general trend is expected to continue well into the 1990s. Both the increasing dependence of organizations on computing and communications technologies and the rapid proliferation of technology products in the marketplace have created more opportunities for computer-related careers than ever before.

The explosive demand for computer professionals has been accompanied by an unusually acute shortage of qualified people, a trend that is also expected to persist for some time. A major cause of this shortage is the dwindling supply of teachers in the field. Because graduates of computer fields can earn almost as much as their professors as soon as they graduate, many would-be instructors are lured away by high-paying jobs in government and industry. Without teachers, colleges and universities are hard-pressed to expand their academic programs to meet the growing demand. Also, schools find computer curricula particularly expensive to maintain. They must pay top salaries for good teachers and continually acquire costly hardware and software. When academic budgets are being cut, as is often the case today, this need is difficult to fulfill.

Thus, a degree in a computer field (if you get into a program) will probably land you several job offers and a good starting salary if your grades are high enough. But beware. Being a computer professional is not for everyone. If you have neither an aptitude nor an interest in computers—a field that involves grasping a relatively large number of technical concepts—you'd better try your hand at something else. As in other fields, high salaries generally are earned only by people with talent and dedication, and often only after many years of hard work.

One of the many myths that has propagated in the computer field is that virtually anyone can become a millionaire or be president of his or her own company before age 30, as did many of the founders of the microcomputer revolution of the 1970s and 1980s (see Feature 18A). Actually, nothing could be further from the truth. Nonetheless, with the right ingredients for success—talent, hard work, patience, and a game plan—who knows? As hinted earlier, the opportunities are plentiful.

We'll begin this chapter by looking at some of the jobs and careers possible in the computer field. Next, we'll cover the various educational paths to follow to prepare for entry-level jobs. Finally, we'll discuss finding a job and ways to maintain professional skills and develop new ones.

JOBS AND CAREERS

There are so many jobs that classify one as a "computer professional" that it's impossible to adequately cover them all in a single chapter. Here we'll consider only those that involve, either directly or indirectly, supplying end users with computer-generated information. These jobs require substantial training in a specific computer field. Included are equipment operators, programmers, systems analysts, and computer managers, as well as a number of specialized jobs such as database administrator, EDP auditor, telecommunications specialist, and knowledge engineer. Excluded are computer salespeople, personnel engaged in manufacturing computer hardware, and service engineers.

In this section, we'll first look at some specific jobs that qualify one as a computer professional. Then we'll consider ways to combine jobs into various career paths.

Computer Jobs

Figure 18-1 shows how computer jobs are organized in a typical organization.

Computer Operations Personnel. Computer operations personnel include data-entry operators, computer equipment operators, system librarians, and managers who supervise the day-to-day running of computing centers. All these people perform a service for others working with large computer systems. Their responsibility lies primarily in making the operating environment for companywide information processing as efficient as possible.

Data-entry operators transcribe data files, programs, and other documents into machine-readable form. At one time, this process involved keypunching onto cards. With the decline in punched-card usage, data entry on key-to-tape and key-to-disk devices became the norm. At some point in the future, voice input technology will completely revolutionize the data-entry function and make typing skills superfluous. A high-school diploma and good typing skills are today the major requirements for entry-level data-entry jobs. Increasingly, with advances in source data automation equipment, many data-entry chores that were once performed by centralized data-entry departments are being shifted to the end-user level.

Computer operators are responsible for setting up equipment for various jobs, mounting and dismounting tapes and disks, and monitoring computer operations. If a program is in an "endless loop," a terminal breaks down, a user is performing an unauthorized activity, or the computer "crashes," the operator is the one who initiates a solution to the problem. Since many commercial computers run nearly 24 hours a day, an operator's responsibilities extend over a single 8-hour shift. Entry-level personnel in this area should have at least an associate's degree from a community college or a certificate from a technical institute. Some companies train operators on the job, while others require experience with a particular system.

Birth of a Start-up

The Autodesk Story

Probably everyone who begins a career in computers has some thoughts about eventually starting his or her own company, or at least getting in on the "ground floor" of a company that's poised to take off. There is no master blueprint for success for small computer firms that eventually wind up big. All of them have a different story to tell.

Autodesk, Inc., the producers of the wildly successful AutoCAD software package (see photo), are no exception. Incredibly, Autodesk did not start out as a CAD (computer-aided design) company. The firm originally was founded by John Walker and Dan Drake, two programmers who had been running a small computer hardware company. In late 1981, they invited several of their talented programmer friends to a meeting at Walker's house, at which they discussed their intention to begin a company. Their goal was simple: They would use a shotgun approach that entailed developing several PC software products concurrently. They would then test market them and focus subsequent efforts on those that looked promising.

Although the initial venture was rather ill defined, Walker and Drake got most of the meeting attendees hooked. So, armed with just under $60,000 and a lot of hope, they soon incorporated. For-

tunately, they were at a point in history when microcomputer use was just about to take off worldwide, so one thing they definitely had on their side was being in the right place at the right time.

One of the projects on which the group decided was AutoCAD. Since no computer design packages had yet been developed for microcomputers, and such packages for larger computer systems often cost $100,000 or more, this project seemed viable. Ironically, the project was panned by the venture capitalists they approached, who felt their target market was too narrow and the product would not succeed unless it was bundled with hardware, to form a complete computer system.

Virtually the only background in CAD applications the company had was one

System librarians are responsible for managing data files and programs stored offline on tapes, disks, microfilm, and all other types of storage media. These media may contain backup copies of important programs and data files, items that are stored offline because they are not needed on a day-to-day basis, and archival data kept for legal purposes. The librarian catalogs all the library items, purges materials no longer needed, and prevents unauthorized access to restricted material. A high-school education and some knowledge of information processing concepts generally are enough to qualify for an entry-level position as a system librarian.

Computer operations managers oversee the entire operation of the computer system. Their duties include scheduling jobs to be run, hiring and assigning operations personnel, supervising machine maintenance, and monitoring operations to ensure that the system runs efficiently. This is not an entry-level position. Computer operations managers often must have at least three to five years of experience in the operations field.

programmer's previous experience in writing a small CAD program. But undaunted by lack of experience and money, the group worked as a team to expand the application. And in the typical seat-of-the-pants style that characterizes many start-up firms, they finished the product just a few hours before piling into a car to get to the November 1982 COMDEX show, where they had purchased a demonstration booth to show their innovation to the world.

The remainder of the story sounds like a rewrite of *A Star is Born*. The product drew huge, excited crowds at the show. The firm's founders and many others who had tiny shares went on to become millionaires. Because there were no venture capitalists involved, there was no one to skim off the lion's share of the profits. Today Autodesk's revenues are above the $100 million mark, and the firm has almost 500 employees. It is the leading producer of microcomputer-based CAD software in the world, with an enviable 40 percent market share. Besides having been used on scores of conventional applications, AutoCAD has also been employed to help design an America's Cup yacht, arrange lighting on a Michael Jackson tour, and raise a sunken ship from the clutches of Australia's Great Barrier Reef.

AutoCAD. A shotgun approach that worked.

Programmers. Programmers generally fall into one of two categories: systems programmers and applications programmers.

Systems programmers write and maintain systems software. Since this class of programs is very technical, systems programmers must have a good technical knowledge of computers. Often they have had rigorous training in subjects such as assembly languages, compiler design, operating systems, and computer system architecture. An entry-level job usually requires a college degree in a technically oriented field such as computer science.

Applications programmers write and maintain the programs that serve end users. Because there's still a shortage of people in this area in many parts of the country, entry-level requirements vary widely. Many applications programmers have computer-related degrees from four-year or community colleges. Others are certified by technical institutes. In some cases, companies hungry for applications programmers have hired people with degrees in other areas virtually "off the street," trained them, and pressed

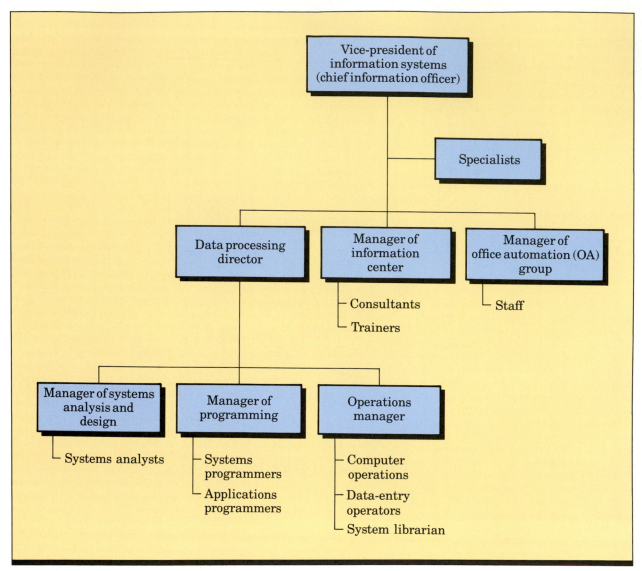

FIGURE 18-1
An organization chart showing common computer jobs and their relation to one another.

them into service. In general, however, a person seeking an entry-level job as an applications programmer should have a college degree in a computer-related field or in an applied field such as business or science (with a significant number of computer courses supplementing the training in the chosen applied field). A knowledge of accounting and COBOL is also useful.

Some people make programming a career, advancing from trainee to senior-level or chief programmer. In some cases, advancement involves specializing in a certain area, such as banking or database applications. Many organizations allow employees to move from programming to positions in systems analysis. This is not always the best career path, however. Program-

FIGURE 18-2

The role of the systems analyst.
The systems analyst translates the business requirements of end users and management into a technical system specification that is passed on to programmers and other computer professionals. Like any other person who serves in a translator capacity, the systems analyst must be familiar with the languages and customs of two different "worlds."

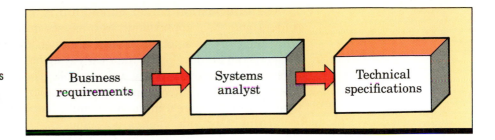

mers must spend a lot of time working alone on technical problems, and many have chosen this profession because they enjoy solitude and independence. Systems analysts, in contrast, spend most of their time dealing with other people and must have excellent communications skills.

Systems Analysts. **Systems analysts** plan and implement computer systems. They form the critical interface between management and end users and, later, between end users and programmers. Management dictates the priority of the problems to be solved. Handed a problem, the analyst must work with users to find the best solutions. The analyst then translates these solutions into a system design and sets the technical specifications for applications programs to be written by programmers (see Figure 18-2). The general duties of the analyst are covered in detail in Chapters 9 and 17.

Good systems analysts must literally be jacks of all trades. They must have a high level of technical knowledge about computers, computer systems, and the computer industry in order to design state-of-the-art systems. They also must be personable and possess excellent communications skills, because they have to interact with many different kinds of people, including managers, end users, and programmers. They must be as comfortable speaking "computerese" with experts as they are speaking English with people who have no technical knowledge. Systems analysts should also have some background in business, since most information processing systems are business oriented. They certainly should be familiar with business terms such as *accounts receivable, pro forma cash flow, direct costs, gross margin,* and *inventory turnover.* Some knowledge of accounting is a particularly helpful asset.

Many systems analysts have college degrees in computer-related fields. Some positions, such as the programmer/analyst slot in small companies (which combines the programmer and systems analyst functions), are entry level. Most companies require systems analysts to have a few years of computer-related experience.

Information Center Personnel. The *information center*—the in-house "computer store" established to help end users meet informal computing needs, thereby making them more productive in their jobs—is staffed primarily by consultants and trainers. Most of the applications the information center services are microcomputer related.

The **information center consultant** is an analyst skilled in microcomputers and their applications who assists current and potential end users with their microcomputing needs. Although the users themselves often are responsible for developing their own systems, the consultant makes suggestions and helps them in any way possible. The educational requirements for the information center consultant are similar to those for the systems analyst. A special interest in microcomputer applications is a must.

Trainers provide classes on some aspects of microcomputing. For instance, a class on using Lotus 1-2-3 may be given to a particular department within the company, or a course on microcomputing fundamentals may be offered on a sign-up basis to any interested company employee. Trainers often have a college degree in a computer-related field, but many do not. Important qualifications other than a specific type of college degree are knowledge of microcomputers and an ability to teach.

Office Automation (OA) Personnel. Many firms have an *OA group,* consisting of about two to eight people, charged with strategy and implementation of OA technologies such as document processing and electronic mail. These people often perform many of the same systems analyst and trainer roles as data processing and information center personnel—advising end users and end-user departments on technologies, building systems with these technologies, and bringing users "up to speed." Educational requirements are similar to those for personnel holding comparable positions within the data processing department and the information center.

Specialists. The vast majority of computer-related positions within organizations—especially at the entry level—fall into one of the categories we just covered. As the computer industry has expanded and grown more sophisticated over the last two decades, however, a number of *specialist* positions have evolved. For instance, many firms now employ *PC managers,* also called *business system analysts.* These people are hired directly by a particular functional department within the organization—say, the marketing department or the personnel department—to help that department with its particular microcomputing applications. Also, many firms have *telecommunications specialists,* who help them with communications-related needs. Several specialist positions are listed and described in Figure 18-3.

Management. At the highest level of computer management are positions such as data processing director, information center director, OA director, and vice-president of information systems. The exact titles of these jobs vary from company to company.

The **data processing director** oversees all data processing personnel, including programmers, systems analysts, and operations personnel. He or she is given a budget and a long-range plan by the vice-president of information systems. In turn, the director sets up budgets and plans for the areas under his or her control. Generally, this position requires several years of computer-related experience in a variety of jobs. Most of the data processing director's responsibilities relate to the upkeep and development of trans-

FIGURE 18-3

Specialists. Listed are a number of specialist positions that exist in the computer field.

Position	Function
☑ Database administrator	Responsible for setting up and managing large, critical databases within the organization
☑ EDP auditor	Responsible for certifying that both the information and the information processing systems within the organization meet a certain set of standards
☑ PC manager (business system analyst)	Responsible for PC-related applications within a particular functional work group (for example, the marketing department)
☑ Telecommunications specialist	Responsible for major telecommunications applications within the organization
☑ Knowledge engineer	Responsible for setting up and maintaining the base of expert knowledge used in expert system applications
☑ Security specialist	Responsible for seeing that the organization's hardware, software, and data are protected from computer crime, natural disasters, major human errors, and the like
☑ Project manager	A systems analyst responsible for managing a major systems development project
☑ Consultant	A person hired by the firm for purposes such as giving advice and training

action processing systems. The data processing director is usually the second most important person in the information systems department, behind the chief information officer (CIO).

The **information center director** and the **OA director** are in charge of all activities relating to the information center and the OA group, respectively. Some of the most important decisions these people make concern staffing, training, and providing ongoing support for end users. These positions generally require several years of business experience and a strong background in microcomputing and end-user applications.

The **vice-president of information systems,** sometimes generically referred to as the **chief information officer (CIO),** oversees routine transaction processing and information reporting activities as well as planning in the newer computer-related areas, such as telecommunications, database processing, office automation, and the information center. He or she also works with key company executives to establish the overall direction of computer activities for the company. In recent years, a major role of the CIO has been determining how to use information processing resources strategically, to achieve competitive advantage for the firm. The CIO job usually requires a master's degree in business or computers and extensive computer-related and managerial work experience. A recent survey indicated that the average work experience for a vice-president of information systems is almost 15 years.

Figure 18-4 shows some recent average salaries reported for computer-related jobs. Keep in mind that averages can be misleading because some industries and companies pay better than others. In general, you will find

FIGURE 18-4
Recent salaries for computer-related jobs.

Job Title	Annual Salary
Chief information officer	$67,643
Director of data processing	$54,189
Manager of information center	$42,203
Senior systems programmer	$57,846
Senior systems analyst	$41,518
Senior applications programmer	$36,397
Senior systems analyst/programmer	$38,974
Junior systems programmer	$47,462
Junior systems analyst	$25,599
Junior applications programmer	$22,947
Junior systems analyst/programmer	$23,620
Manager of computer operations	$37,072
Computer operator	$21,346
System librarian	$20,887
Data-entry operator	$16,838
Word processing operator	$17,930
Database administrator	$36,579
Telecommunications specialist	$33,998
Consultant	$48,810

Source: *Datamation,* October 1, 1988, pp. 58–59, 62–63.

some of the best-paying and most challenging jobs at the leading-edge software houses.

Although money is often a compelling reason to prefer one job over another, you should weigh a number of other factors. Among the most important of these are advancement opportunity (both inside and outside the firm), challenge, job location, work environment, and job security.

Career Options

There are many ways to build computer-based careers. Three such possibilities are establishing a career path, specializing in a niche area, and molding a career around a particular lifestyle. Deciding on a particular career strategy is the focus of the Tomorrow box.

Career Path. The traditional way to build a career is to select a *career path,* or track, within a particular organization. You begin with an entry-level job and then move up the organizational ladder into positions of ever-increasing responsibility. For example, suppose you join a company with an organization chart like the one shown in Figure 18-1. You might start as a programmer trainee; later, become a full-fledged applications programmer; and finally, after many years' experience, become a manager. A managerial position requires a broad exposure to a number of computer-related functions as well as an ability to plan and direct other people. If you supplement your work experience with additional education or an advanced degree, you might continue up the ladder to a high executive position.

Specialty Niche. A second career possibility is to specialize in a highly marketable *niche area* of information processing, especially one in which the demand for your services is likely to remain strong. There are several ways to do this.

Some people specialize by focusing on a certain *industry*. For example, you might choose to become an expert in the analysis and design of computer systems for banks or insurance companies. Or perhaps the airline industry fascinates you. In any case, if you have detailed knowledge of the kinds of computer-related problems a specific industry faces and know how to solve those problems, you will have an advantage when seeking jobs in that industry.

Another way to specialize is to choose a specific *technology* or *product* area. Some such areas where you commonly find specialists are database processing, telecommunications, desktop publishing, expert systems, and business applications for the Apple Macintosh line of computers. A database expert, for instance, will be in demand by any company that relies heavily on database systems. The growing prominence of Apple Macintosh computers in business environments is creating a demand in business for Macintosh specialists.

Still another option is to specialize in some computer-related *function*. For instance, people interested in teaching may have promising careers as trainers awaiting. People who can write clearly and concisely are a great asset to any organization as documentation writers for software and hardware systems.

Lifestyle. A third possibility is to mold a career around a certain *lifestyle*. For example, some people, for various reasons, prefer to work only part time or during unusual hours. Programming is ideally suited for these people, because it allows a great deal of independence. Programmers are pretty much on their own once they understand the technical specifications of a project. Some programmers, in fact, telecommute—they do their jobs at home on a terminal or microcomputer. This not only saves them gas and commuting time but also can spare them from unproductive office politics. And if they get their jobs done on schedule, no one cares if they take the kids to the playground in the afternoon or work from 1 a.m. to 5 a.m. Other prime candidates for working at home are data-entry clerks and documentation writers. Of course, working at home is not for everyone. Some people need the social stimulus of an office to work well.

T   O   M   O   R   R   O   W

Looking at a Career as a Business

Consider Formulating a Strategic Plan for Your Future

Virtually all major companies use some type of strategic plan to plot their course for the future. A strategic plan, which often encompasses a relatively long period—perhaps 10 or more years—starts with a vision of the future, an assessment of the company, and an evaluation of the company's competitive environment.

Thus, a company might begin the strategic planning process by considering what it wants to become (that is, its mission), its inherent strengths and weaknesses, the nature of its consumers, the strengths and weaknesses of competitors, and so on. From this profile it develops a *strategy*—a course of action

for accomplishing its mission—and then a specific list of long- and short-term objectives and policies. Thus the strategic planning process provides a comprehensive "game plan" that answers all of the pertinent what, when, where, and how questions regarding carrying out the mission. From time to time, unanticipated conditions will warrant altering parts of the plan.

Just as many businesses have profited from a strategic plan, so can you, whether you plan to work for yourself or for someone else. Like a business, you must formulate goals, objectives, and a game plan for achieving them. And just as a business starts the strategic planning process by formulating a mission and looking at itself, its consumers, and its competitors, so

must you. Here's a sample of some of the issues you may encounter during the strategic planning process.

Mission. What are you really after in life? Among your needs for money, respect, challenge, love, a family, adventure, stability, which are most important? What type of career would be ideal for meeting your needs?

Personal Strengths and Weaknesses. Are you resourceful? Do you get along well with people? What types of work are you best and worst at? What types of work do you like and dislike? Are you strong enough, either financially or emotionally, to accept risks? Do you really have the motivation and drive to make things happen in your life? Do you have any "hang-ups" that might hold you back? (No matter how much it may hurt, it pays to assess yourself honestly.)

Your Environment. What types of companies or indi-

FORMAL EDUCATION FOR ENTRY-LEVEL JOBS

Going to school is one of the best ways to train for an entry-level position in computers. Although you can learn a great deal on your own or through on-the-job training, a degree or certificate often is a requirement for obtaining a job. It convinces potential employers that you've had formal training in certain areas and that you've met the standards of a particular institution. In other words, it legitimizes your claim that you know something and are willing to work hard. Although it is often a year or longer before new employees begin to produce a return for a company, most firms prefer their new employees to arrive on their first day as fully equipped to do useful work as possible. Some companies offer training programs for new employ-

viduals could benefit from the skills and services you have to offer? Whom are you competing against, and how do you stand relative to specific competitors? What trends are taking place in the world that will affect your future?

Strategies. Considering what you want and all the forces that will affect its achievement, what do you need to do? For instance, if you want to become an executive in a large firm, getting an MBA degree will be one viable strategy toward that goal. On the other hand, if you want to own your own business and you are risk averse, learning how to better deal with risk and possible failure may become a major strategy.

Objectives. What timetable must you establish to achieve your goals? What must you do this year, this month, or *right now* (after you finish reading this box) to be certain that you will meet the timetable you set?

Policies. What good habits must you form to help you accomplish your goals? What bad habits must you break?

While all of this looks good in theory, it is also true that many strategic plans are never met. Both companies and individuals often start the planning process with the best of intentions and then put the plan aside and forget all about it. Strategic planning is just like going on a diet. To succeed, you must work almost daily at assessing your progress and refining your plan. You must also be enough of a doer to carry out what you set down on paper.

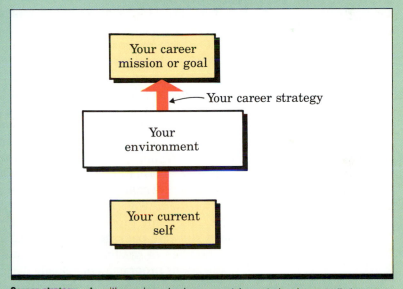

Career strategy. As with running a business, you take control or be controlled.

ees to familiarize them with the company, the particular industry in which it competes, or the details of a specific project.

Many types of schools beyond high school offer some type of education in computers. These include four-year colleges and universities, two-year community colleges, and technical institutes. Course offerings vary widely among such schools. Also, some schools emphasize computer theory, while others focus on the more practical aspects of computing.

Computer Curricula

If you're interested in pursuing formal academic study in computers, there are many curricula available to you. Here we cover the most common of these. The specific names given to such programs vary widely among schools.

Computer Information Systems. The **computer information systems (CIS) curriculum** often is coordinated by a college or department of business. The primary emphasis is on directly providing services for end users, and many of the computer courses have a "business applications" flavor. These courses often include an introduction to computers, microcomputer fundamentals, COBOL programming, a second programming language such as BASIC or FORTRAN, systems development, database processing, and management information systems. Most schools also offer training in a variety of optional subjects, such as decision support systems, telecommunications, office automation, expert systems, and EDP auditing.

Because the degree program is coordinated by the business school, students must also take several business courses. These courses can be particularly helpful to anyone aspiring to be a systems analyst or manager. Most graduates of these programs assume entry-level work as applications programmers or programmer/analysts.

Two associations of computer professionals—the Data Processing Management Association (DPMA) and the Association for Computing Machinery (ACM)—have proposed model curricula for the CIS area. These curricula propose such things as specific core and elective CIS courses as well as required business courses. Many schools adhere to one or the other model, while some have developed curricula independent of these models.

Computer Science. The **computer science curriculum** often is coordinated by a college or department of computer science, mathematics, or engineering. The training provided is much more technical than that offered in a computer information systems program, because the primary emphasis is on software design. Graduates of these programs often find jobs as systems programmers, with responsibility for designing compilers, operating systems, and utility programs. They are also sought for the design of sophisticated software packages such as database management systems. A surprising number of graduates of these programs, however, take positions as applications programmers. Usually these students have prepared themselves by cross-registering for business-oriented courses such as COBOL, database processing, and systems development. Some have even taken an accounting course or two, since accounting generally is considered the language of business. Of course, cross-registration works both ways: Computer information systems majors often enroll in computer science courses, such as assembly-language programming and operating systems, which enable them to sharpen their technical skills.

Computer Engineering. Some schools also support a **computer engineering curriculum.** This degree program is intended primarily to prepare students to design computer hardware systems. Graduates of such programs usually are sought by hardware manufacturers.

Computer Operations. In addition to their other computer offerings, community colleges and technical institutes typically provide practical training in **computer operations.** Students enrolled in these courses often plan to become computer or data-entry operators. These courses involve a great deal of hands-on, practical training, enabling students to quickly move on to entry-level positions in government and industry.

Many schools periodically have their curricula reviewed by representatives from national and local companies. This ensures both that curricula remain up to date and that graduates are being trained with marketable skills. Although there is no consensus about which specific type of academic training is best for entry-level programmer or analyst jobs in business, many companies prefer graduates with a strong technical and/or business background, a desire to learn the ins and outs of a particular organization, and an ability to identify with user needs.

MAINTAINING SKILLS AND DEVELOPING NEW ONES

One of the things people find exciting about the computer field is its rapid rate of change. Someone with "computer fever" trying out new equipment or software is like an excitable five-year-old opening birthday presents. But rapid change also has a less pleasant side to it—the need for constant retraining. When a computer system you've known and loved for the past several years is unplugged and wheeled away for a newer one, you will have to retrain. If the new system involves many recent technologies that you are unfamiliar with, the retraining may take a long time.

Retraining is a fact of life in the computer field. If you want to keep yourself current and marketable, you must have some knowledge of the latest technologies. There are a variety of ways to effectively "retool" yourself or develop new skills. Among them are attending classes, seminars, and exhibitions; reading; using training disks and tapes; and participating in professional associations.

Attending Classes. Many universities, community colleges, and computer institutes offer courses on a nondegree or continuing-education basis. These courses are particularly visible in large cities, where there's a large market for such services. Many of the courses are taught at night to accommodate people who work during the day. Some companies also hold regular classes and even have schools for training employees in the latest computer technologies.

A more ambitious possibility is to enroll in a graduate school. Many universities have master's and doctoral degree programs in areas such as computer information systems, computer science, and computer engineering.

Attending Seminars. Many individuals and companies offer nationwide seminars on a variety of computer topics (see Figure 18-5). An expert on telecommunications, for example, may travel the lecture circuit with an inten-

FIGURE 18-5

Seminars. A selection of seminar announcements on a variety of topics. Seminar topics vary enormously. There are some targeted to computer professionals and others aimed at ordinary people wanting to learn more about a specific topic.

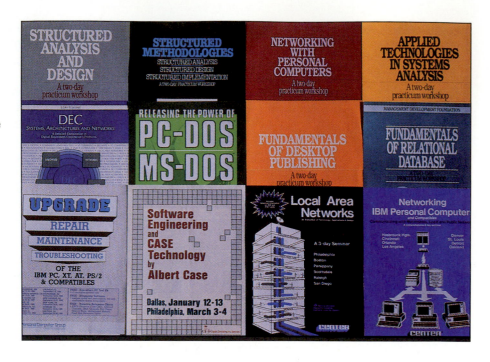

sive, three-day seminar on the subject, charging, say, $650 per person. The speaker may present the seminar on January 11, 12, and 13 in Phoenix; on January 15, 16, and 17 in Los Angeles; then on to San Francisco; and so on. Some seminars, especially those conducted by hardware and software vendors, are offered free. Many computer trade publications maintain lists of seminars and details about them.

Attending Exhibitions. Vendors of computer products frequently participate in joint trade shows to demonstrate new hardware and software to the public. Three of the largest trade shows are the annual U.S. National Computer Conference (NCC); the international, several-times-a-year Computer Dealer Expo (COMDEX) shows; and San Francisco's annual West Coast Computer Faire. Such shows commonly attract hundreds of vendors and thousands of visitors. Today, however, there is a definite trend toward smaller, specialized shows.

Reading. Reading is one of the most inexpensive ways to learn about new technologies. Fortunately computer literature abounds, and several sources carry up-to-date information.

The most current information is found in the so-called computer newspapers. *Computerworld,* which many professionals regard as the *Wall Street Journal* of the computer establishment, contains news items and special features of general interest to a wide audience of professionals (see Figure 18-6). Several other newspapers are targeted to smaller audiences. Among

FIGURE 18-6

Computerworld. Published weekly, *Computerworld* is one of the most successful computer publications aimed at a wide audience.

Data Communications
Targeted to communications specialists

Personal Publishing
Targeted to users of desktop publishing systems

Computer Graphics World
Targeted to computer graphics professionals

Modern Office Technology
Targeted to OA personnel

CIO
Targeted to chief information officers

Byte
Targeted to technically oriented users of small computer systems

FIGURE 18-7

Computer journals. Many computer journals, such as those shown here, are targeted to a specific, "niche" audience.

these are *PC Week* and *Macintosh Today,* which specialize in developments of particular interest to the IBM and Macintosh microcomputing worlds, respectively.

A second source of written information is the computer journals (see Figure 18-7), many of which are published monthly. Each journal generally is targeted to a specific audience—small-computer users, the banking industry, and so on—and prints articles of potential interest to its readership.

A third source is books. If there's a specific topic you want to learn about in some depth, there usually are several books available to meet this need. Some of these are written at very technical levels; others are aimed at readers who are relatively unsophisticated about computers. One way to learn more about computers is to go to your local library or bookstore and browse through the shelves devoted to computer books to find ones that seem interesting and readable.

A fourth source of materials is the topical reports issued periodically by research companies such as Auerbach and Datapro (see Figure 18-8). These reports, many of which contain fewer than 30 pages, are assembled into

FIGURE 18-8

Datapro reports. Computer managers and professionals often consult publications such as those published by Datapro to find the most up-to-date, objective information about specific products and technologies.

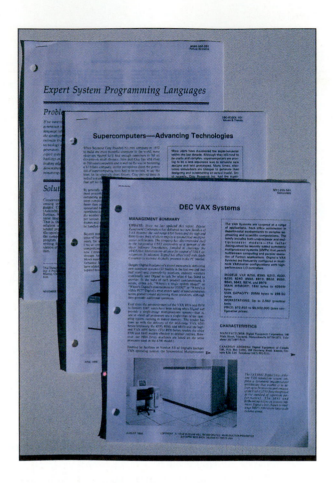

looseleaf binders. Each binder contains current information on related topics that is hard to find in other sources. Some of the information may also be available in textbooks, but these topical reports are far more current. Also, these reports often contain useful comparisons of specific computer products.

A fifth source is the marketing brochures of the computer product vendor. Although such literature often is biased toward the vendor's products, some of it is extremely well presented and informative. Also, much of this information is available free of charge.

Using Training Disks and Tapes. With the boom in microcomputing products have come a spate of tutorial disks and videocassette tapes for learning about almost any aspect of computing. For instance, many of the leading word processing, database management system, and spreadsheet packages are available with learning or demonstration diskettes. When you insert one of these into a disk drive on your microcomputer system, the diskette "holds you by the hand," perhaps by providing sequences of display screens show-

FIGURE 18-9
Organizations joined by computing professionals.

Computer Organizations

American Federation of Information Processing Societies   (AFIPS)

AFIPS is a consortium of several professional organizations, among which are the American Institute of Certified Public Accountants (AICPA), the American Statistical Association (ASA), and the Institute of Electrical and Electronics Engineers (IEEE). AFIPS represents the interests of its constituent organizations.

Association for Computing Machinery   (ACM)

The ACM is the largest professional association devoted specifically to the advancement of knowledge about computers and computer-related areas. Many of its members are from computer science faculty at colleges and universities. ACM has many special-interest groups (SIGs) in which its members may participate, such as SIGGRAPH (computer graphics), SIGSMALL (small computers), and so on.

Association for Systems Management   (ASM)

The ASM is an international organization dedicated to the advancement of systems professionals in business and government. It publishes the *Journal of Systems Management,* a monthly journal that is widely read by information systems professionals.

Data Processing Management Association   (DPMA)

The DPMA is an organization dedicated to the advancement of knowledge in the areas of data processing and information systems. It publishes *Data Management,* a monthly journal that is widely read by computer professionals.

Society for Information Management   (SIM)

SIM is composed of information systems managers, systems analysts, and information systems educators. SIM cosponsors an annual International Conference on Information Systems, which provides a forum for new research ideas in the information systems area.

EDP Auditors Foundation

The EDP Auditors Foundation is an organization composed of professionals specializing in auditing computer systems. It regularly publishes a journal called *The EDP Auditor.*

ing what the package will do when you press certain keys or by showing an animated presentation. Videocassettes generally are even easier to use and are geared to educate through one of the ways in which people most like to digest information—by watching television. Besides vendors of computer products, many third-party firms sell training disks and tapes, usually of the most popular software packages.

Joining Professional Associations. Computer people often join professional associations to keep up to date. Members of these associations stay current through meetings, workshops, conferences, and informal contact with other people having similar interests. Many associations have local chapters in major cities. Organizations such as the ACM (Association for Computing Machinery) and DPMA (Data Processing Management Association) also have student chapters. Furthermore, joining a professional association often is a good way to learn about job openings. Figure 18-9 lists some major associations.

SUMMARY AND KEY TERMS

The demand for computer professionals in government and industry has been booming over the past decade, and this trend is expected to continue into the 1990s. Computer professionals include operations personnel, programmers, systems analysts, trainers, specialists, and managers.

Computer operations personnel include data-entry operators, computer operators, system librarians, and computer operations managers. **Data-entry operators** transcribe data files, programs, and other documents into machine-readable form. **Computer operators** set up equipment for various jobs, mount and dismount tapes and disks, and monitor computer operations. **System librarians** manage data files and programs stored offline on tapes, disks, microfilm, and all other types of storage media. **Computer operations managers** oversee the entire operation of the computer system. Their duties include scheduling jobs to be run, hiring and assigning operations personnel, supervising machine maintenance, and monitoring operations to ensure that the system runs efficiently.

Programmers generally fall into one of two categories: systems programmers and applications programmers. **Systems programmers** write and maintain systems software. **Applications programmers** write and maintain the programs that serve end-users' needs.

Systems analysts plan and implement computer systems. They form the critical interface between management and users and, subsequently, between users and programmers.

The information center is staffed primarily by consultants and trainers. The **information center consultant** is an analyst skilled in microcomputers and their applications who assists current and potential users with their personal needs. **Trainers** provide classes, often on some aspect of microcomputing.

Many firms have an OA group, consisting of about two to eight people, charged with strategy and implementation with respect to OA technologies such as document processing and electronic mail. These people often perform many of the same analyst and trainer roles as people working in the data processing department or information center.

As the computer industry has expanded and become more sophisticated over the last two decades, a number of *specialist* positions also have evolved. For instance, many firms now employ specialists such as PC managers (also called *business system analysts*), database administrators (DBAs) and telecommunications specialists.

At the highest level of computer management are positions such as data processing director, information center director, OA director, and vice-president of information systems. The **data processing director** oversees all personnel involved with transaction processing, including programmers, systems analysts, and operations personnel. The **information center director** and the **OA director** are in charge of all activities relating to the information center and the OA group, respectively. The **vice-president of information systems,** sometimes referred to as the **chief information officer (CIO),** oversees routine transaction processing and information reporting activities as well as planning in the newer computer-related areas such as telecommunications, database processing, office automation, and the information center.

There are many ways to build computer-based careers. One possibility is to begin with an entry-level job and then move up the organizational ladder into positions of greater and greater responsibility. A second option is to specialize in a highly marketable "niche" area of computer processing where the demand for your services is likely to remain strong. For example, many people specialize by concentrating on a specific industry, technology, or function. A third possibility is to mold a career around a certain lifestyle.

Going to school is one of the best ways to train for an entry-level position in computers. Many types of schools offer some kind of education in computers. These include four-year colleges and universities, two-year community colleges, and technical institutes.

If you're interested in pursuing studies in computers many curricula are available to you. The **computer information systems (CIS) curriculum** often is coordinated by a college or department of business. The primary emphasis is on directly providing services for end users, and many of the computer courses have a "business applications" flavor. The **computer science curriculum** frequently is coordinated by a college or department of computer science or engineering. The training provided is geared toward software design. Some schools also support a **computer engineering curriculum.** This degree program is aimed primarily at preparing students to design computer hardware systems. In addition to their other computer offerings, community colleges and technical institutes typically provide practical training in **computer operations.** Students enrolled in these courses often plan to become computer or data-entry operators.

Retraining is a fact of life in the computer field. There are a variety of ways to maintain your skills and develop new ones. Among them are attending classes, seminars, and exhibitions; reading; using training disks and tapes; and participating in professional associations.

REVIEW EXERCISES

Fill-in Questions

1. _____ transcribe data files, programs, and other documents into machine-readable form.

2. _____ are responsible for setting up equipment for various jobs, mounting and dismounting tapes and disks, and monitoring computer operations.

3. _____ are responsible for managing data files and programs stored offline on tapes, disks, microfilm, and all other types of storage media.

4. _____ oversee the entire operation of the computer system, including scheduling jobs to be run, hiring and assigning operations personnel, supervising machine maintenance, and monitoring operations to ensure that the system runs efficiently.

5. _____ write and maintain systems software.

6. _____ write and maintain the programs that serve end users.

7. _____ plan and implement computer systems. They form the critical interface between management and users and, subsequently, between users and programmers.

8. The _____ oversees all personnel involved in transaction processing, including programmers, systems analysts, and operations personnel.

Matching Questions

Match each term with the description that best fits.

a. computer information systems curriculum
b. computer science curriculum
c. computer engineering curriculum
d. computer operations curriculum

_____ **1.** The degree program tailored primarily to training students to design computer hardware systems.

_____ **2.** The degree program, often coordinated by a college or department of business, that trains students as applications programmers and systems analysts.

_____ **3.** The degree program, sometimes coordinated by a college of engineering or department of mathematics, that primarily trains students in the design of systems software.

_____ **4.** The degree program that trains students as data-entry operators, computer equipment operators, and the like.

Discussion Questions

1. Why is there such a big difference between the demand for computer professionals and the supply of qualified ones?

2. Discuss the types of work involved in performing each of the following jobs: data-entry operator, computer operator, system librarian, computer operations manager, systems programmer, applications programmer, systems analyst, information center consultant, data processing director, vice-president of information systems.

3. Describe some ways to build computer-based careers.

4. Are all academic computer curricula the same? Discuss.

5. Identify several ways you can effectively maintain your computer skills and develop new ones.

Critical Thinking Questions

1. Many people think that programmers make poor systems analysts. What do you think accounts for this viewpoint?

2. Many industry experts say that for the most part, large, centralized data-entry departments will no longer be needed in the 21st century. How do you account for this?

3. What, do you think, are the most important skills (of any type) that someone seeking a career in computers should possess? Confine your list to five skills or fewer.

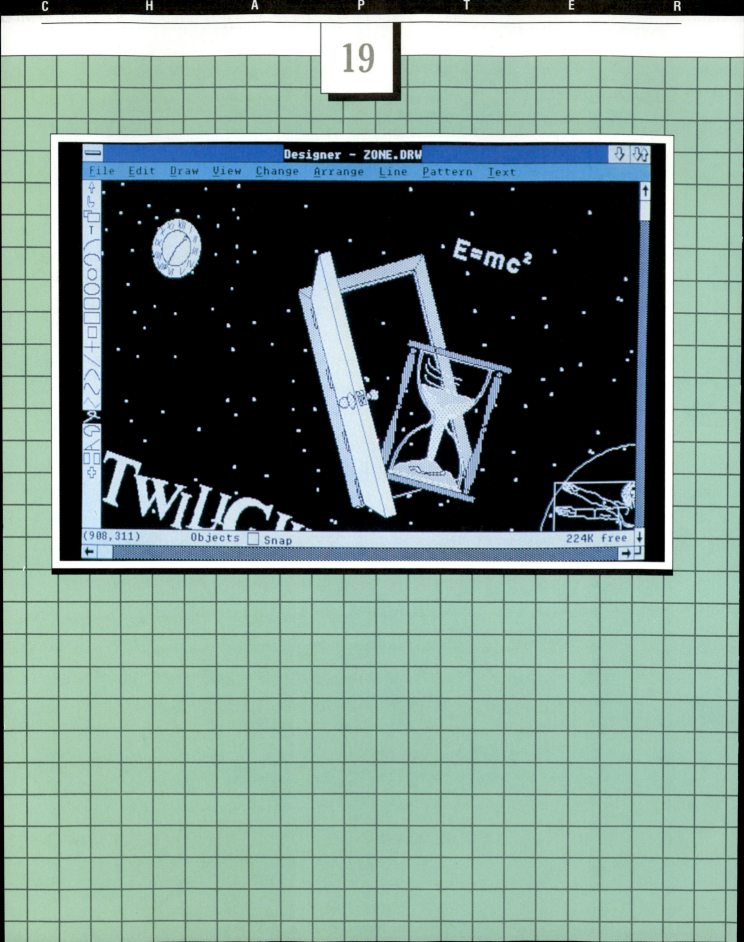

Computers in Our Lives: The Costs and the Benefits

Objectives

After completing this chapter, you will be able to:

1. Describe some of the health-related concerns people have regarding computers.

2. Explain what is meant by computer crime, and describe several types of computer crime.

3. Appreciate that computer technology can be abused to encroach on people's privacy, and describe some of the legislation enacted to prevent such abuses.

4. Describe several applications in which computers affect the day-to-day life of the average person.

OVERVIEW

Since the early 1950s, when the era of commercial computing began, computers have rapidly woven their way into the very fabric of modern society. In the process, they've created both opportunities and problems. Consequently, they've been both cursed and applauded—and for good reason.

So far in this book, we've focused on the opportunities. We've examined the impact computers have had in organizations and on the people who work there. Through the text and Windows, we've seen how these machines have been put to work on routine transaction processing tasks, used to provide managers with better information for decision making, and employed to design and manufacture better products. In this chapter, we'll examine some of the impact that computer technology has had or will likely have on our personal lives—our lives outside the workplace (see also the Tomorrow box).

But before we look at these social benefits, let's examine some of the problems computers have created. Although the "computer revolution" has brought undeniable benefits to society, it has also produced some troubling side effects. Like any fast-paced revolution, it has been disruptive in many ways. Some jobs have been created, others lost, and still others threatened. In addition, an increasing variety of health-related concerns regarding people's working with computer-related technologies have surfaced. Computers have also immensely increased access to information, creating new possibilities for crime—even at the international level—and threatening personal privacy. Clearly some controls to limit the dangers these awesome machines pose will always be needed. In this chapter, we highlight three important problem areas: computers and health in the workplace, computer crime and ethics, and computers and privacy. Feature 19A addresses some of the legal problems created by the existence of computers.

COMPUTERS, WORK, AND HEALTH

Computers have been said to pose a threat to both our mental and physical well-being. Although the body of scientific evidence supporting this claim is far from conclusive, and will likely be that way for many more years, we should all be aware of the major concerns raised about the possible effects of computers on our health.

Stress-related Concerns

Emotional problems such as financial worries, feelings of incompetence, and disorientation often produce emotional *stress*. These problems, in turn, may have been triggered by layoff or reassignment, fear of falling behind, or job burnout.

Layoff or Reassignment. One of the first criticisms leveled at the entry of computers into the workplace was that their very presence resulted in job-related stress. When computers came in, many people were laid off and had to find new jobs. Clerical workers especially worried about job security. Many feared the full potential of computers in the office, never knowing when machines might replace them. These fears are still widespread today.

But even a number of people who were not laid off found that their jobs had changed significantly and that they had no choice but to retrain. Airline agents, for example, had to learn how to manipulate a database language and to work with display terminals. Many secretaries were pressured into picking up word processing (and perhaps electronic spreadsheets, electronic data management, and electronic mail) to keep in tune with state-of-the-art office work. Many of these workers never made the transition successfully, and many who did found that the use of computers had depersonalized certain aspects of their jobs.

Fear of Falling Behind. The microcomputing boom has placed computing power of awesome dimensions at everyone's fingertips. Some researchers perceive a widespread fear that failure to learn how to use these machines will make one "fall behind." An example is parents who fear that their children will suffer in school without the latest educationally oriented microcomputer system installed in their home. Another example is the numerous non-computer-oriented executives, managers, and even educators who see themselves being upstaged by their computer-knowledgeable colleagues. The surge of interest in microcomputers has even made many programmers who work in mainframe environments feel they are somehow falling behind.

Burnout. Burnout is caused not by fear of computers (*cyberphobia*) but by overuse of them (*cyberphelia*). Perhaps the classic example of burnout-by-computer is the pale, workaholic programmer who seems to live in another world. The infusion of microcomputers into home and office has raised new concerns about what will happen to children who withdraw into their computer systems, to terminal-bound executives who have inadvertently been swept into the tide of the computer revolution, or to couples or families whose intimacy may be threatened by computer overuse in their homes.

To date, little research has been done on computer burnout. What makes this area so controversial is the compelling flip-side argument that most victims of computer burnout would burn out on something else if computers didn't exist.

Ergonomics-related Concerns

Ergonomics is the field that addresses such issues as making products and work areas comfortable and safe to use. With respect to technology, ergonomics covers the effects on workers of things such as display devices and computer workspaces. Let's consider some of the major fronts of ergonomic research.

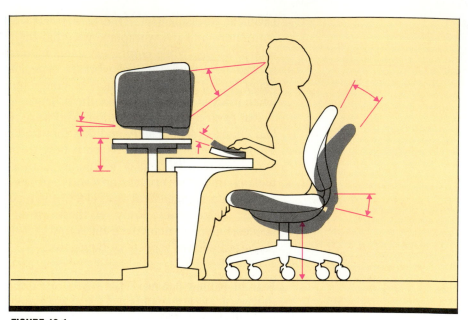

FIGURE 19-1

Ergonomics. Features such as detachable keyboards, tilt capabilities on both keyboard and display, and adjustable furniture have all contributed to making life more pleasant for display device users.

Dangers Posed by Display Devices. For nearly a decade, large numbers of data-entry operators have reported a variety of physical and mental problems stemming from their interaction with display devices. The complaints have centered on visual, muscular, and emotional disorders resulting from long hours of continuous display device use. These include blurred eyesight, eyestrain, acute fatigue, headaches, and backaches. In response to these problems, several states have passed laws that curb display device abuse. Consequently, vendors of these devices have redesigned their products with features such as tiltable screens and detachable keyboards to make them more comfortable to use.

Workspace Design. Display devices are not the only things that can torture people at workstations. For example, the furniture may be nonadjustable, forcing the terminal user into awkward postures that are guaranteed to produce body kinks. Or the lighting may be so bright that it causes a headache-producing glare on the display screen. There may even be disconcerting noise levels present due to poorly designed office equipment or acoustics. Ergonomics researchers are constantly studying such problems, and the results of their efforts are becoming apparent in the consumer products now being offered to the ergonomics-conscious buyer. Figure 19-1 illustrates some principles of good workspace design.

Pregnant Operators. Recently concerns have emerged regarding the effects of radiation levels in display devices on the unborn fetuses of pregnant operators. A recent study of 1,500 pregnant female display-device operators in California found that women who used display devices more than 20 hours a week had almost twice as many miscarriages as women who did other kinds of office work. However, the researchers were unable to conclude whether the miscarriages resulted from the equipment or from workspace- and stress-related factors such as sitting in a cramped position, extreme deadline pressure, and lack of job autonomy. Many researchers in this area tend to think that the latter group of factors rather than display device use accounted for the miscarriages.

Software Ergonomics. The branch of ergonomics that deals with hardware-related issues, such as display-device flicker and radiation levels, is sometimes referred to as *hardware ergonomics,* and as you might expect, the branch dealing with software-related issues is called *software ergonomics.* A program's ease of learning and use, for example, affects both the productivity and the well-being of the operator. Thus, one feature increasingly being incorporated into programs of all types—even operating systems—are menu and graphical user interfaces. Menu interfaces allow users to point to familiar commands and options rather than having to fully memorize them; graphical interfaces eliminate some of the burden of keyboard data entry.

Other Areas of Concern

Besides stress- and ergonomics-related concerns, there are many other health-related worries regarding computers. One is whether we are coming to rely on them too much. Dr. Joseph Weizenbaum of MIT, a luminary in the field of artificial intelligence, has voiced another concern: Will future generations rely on computers so much that they lose sight of the fundamental thought processes that computers are intended to model? Many teachers complain that some children who own pocket calculators can't even do arithmetic by hand.

There is no question, of course, that computers have altered the structure of work and play just as mechanized farm machinery has changed the nature of agriculture and airplanes, and automobiles the nature of travel. Many people have accepted these disruptions as the price of "progress." Yet almost everyone wonders somewhat about the type of world we are creating for ourselves.

COMPUTER CRIME AND ETHICS

Computer crime is loosely defined as the use of computers to commit unauthorized acts. The law is spotty on computer crime. The federal government, through the Computer Fraud and Abuse Act of 1986, has made it a felony to knowingly and fraudulently access programs or data of value in federal-level computers. Most states also have laws that address some as-

Computers and the Law

Legal Issues Raised by Computers

Given that the effect of computers has been so far-reaching, it was perhaps only inevitable that many legal issues would surface that somehow involved computers. Many of the cases that wind up in court involve electronic-age matters that the people who years ago wrote the laws never anticipated, and that juries and judges do not fully understand themselves. While new areas in which the computer is a major factor in a legal hassle are always cropping up, many of the problems seen so far can be categorized into one or more of the following five areas.

Ergonomics-related. Ergonomics refers to the development of products and workspaces that are comfort-

> Can a company copyright a user interface for a software package?

able and safe for an operator to use. But how safe are some of these products, most of which we have not been familiar with on a long-term basis? And are many of these products being abused by

employers and configured into uncomfortable and even dangerous work environments? A number of these concerns have developed into legal battles in the courts.

Computer Crime. Ever since Alexander Graham Bell invented the telephone, technology has been used to help commit crimes. Computer systems, because they are used to make financial transactions and to store sensitive data, have been a favorite target of criminals. As the detailed treatment of computer crime in this chapter suggests, a computer crime can be committed in a wide variety of ways. Unfortunately, while some companies have successfully prosecuted computer criminals, the majority of computer crimes never make it to court.

pect of computer crime. But such laws notwithstanding, computer crime is hard to pin down.

One reason is that it is often difficult to decide when an unauthorized act is really a crime. No one would doubt that a bank employee who uses a computer system to embezzle funds from customers' accounts is committing a crime. But what about an employee who "steals time" on the company mainframe to balance a personal checkbook for a home or business? Or someone who uses the same computer to word process a personal letter to a friend? Aren't those acts also unauthorized? Where do you draw the line?

Another problem in pinning down computer crime is that judges and juries often are bewildered by the technical issues involved in such cases. Also, companies that discover computer criminals among their employees frequently are reluctant to press charges because they fear adverse publicity.

Types of Computer Crime

Computer crime has many forms. Some cases involve the use of a computer for theft of financial assets, such as money or equipment. Others concern

Privacy. Because computers can store massive quantities of data, some very sensitive, what type of data about an individual can be disseminated and to whom is a matter of legal concern. Public-interest groups are continually fighting the government with regard to creating new databases that would violate the right to privacy that is guaranteed to every citizen. Regrettably, there are relatively few privacy laws that pertain to the private sector.

Fault. Judges and juries frequently hear cases in which the primary issue is who is at fault. When a computer is involved, however, the conflict can indeed be more difficult to resolve. For instance, if a bank and a client allegedly make an electronic transaction over a computer network, and the transaction is lost or altered in transit, who is responsible if there are damages? Also, recently in Texas, a patient died from an overdose of radiation because there was a bug in the software that was supposed to monitor his treatment. Should the blame be assigned to the programmer, the company that developed the system, and/or the hospital?

Ownership and Copyright. One of the interesting issues that has recently surfaced in the courts is: Can a company copyright a user interface for a software package? For instance, lawyers for Lotus Development Corporation have claimed that certain "clone" vendors have come too close to copying their menu, command, and worksheet interfaces. In many such cases, however, the courts have disagreed, arguing that user interfaces represent ideas and that no one can own an "idea." (Ideas, as legally defined, are not protected under copyright law.) There have also been a few cases in court in which companies that collect and package public-record data for sale in hard-copy form have sued other companies that have used these data to create their own electronic databanks, which are also sold. Were the original, packaged data ever owned? Are hard-copy data the same as electronic data, which may have been enhanced with a new, value-added component? The courts are still feeling their way around such murky, electronic-age legal issues.

the copying of information processing resources such as programs or data to the owner's detriment. Still other cases involve manipulation of data such as grades for personal advantage. By far, the majority of computer crimes are committed by insiders.

The cost of computer crime to individuals and organizations is estimated at billions of dollars annually. No one knows for sure what the exact figure is, because so many incidents are either undetected or unreported.

As in many fields, a specialized jargon has evolved in the area of computer-related crime. Following is a sampling of some of the specific forms computer crime can take.

Data Diddling. *Data diddling* is one of the most common ways to perform a computer crime. It involves altering key production data on the computer system in some unauthorized way. Data diddlers often are found changing grades in university files, falsifying input records on bank transactions, and the like.

The Trojan Horse. The *Trojan horse* is a procedure for adding concealed instructions to a computer program so that it will still work but will also perform unauthorized duties. For example, a bank worker can subtly alter a program that contains thousands of lines of code by adding a small "patch" that instructs the program not to withdraw money from a certain account.

Salami Shaving. *Salami shaving* involves altering programs so that many small dollar amounts—say, a few cents' worth of interest payments—are shaved from a large number of selected transactions or accounts and deposited in another account. The victims of a salami-shaving scheme generally are unaware that their funds have been tapped, because the amount taken from each individual is trivial. The recipient of the salami shaving, however, benefits from the aggregation of these small amounts, often substantially.

Superzapping. *Superzapping* is a technique made possible by a special program available on most computer systems—a program that bypasses all system controls when the computer "crashes" and cannot be restarted with normal recovery procedures. This program, in effect, is a "master key" that can provide access to any part of the system. The superzap program is a highly privileged "disaster aid" that very few computer system professionals are authorized to use. In the wrong hands, it can be used to perform almost any unauthorized task.

Trapdoors. *Trapdoors* are diagnostic tools, used in the development of systems programs, that enable programmers to gain access to various parts of the computer system. Before the programs are marketed, these tools are supposed to be removed. Occasionally, however, some blocks of diagnostic code are overlooked. Thus, a person using the associated systems program may get unauthorized views of other parts of the computer system.

Logic Bombs and Computer Viruses. *Logic bombs* are programs or short code segments designed to be executed at random or at specific times to perform unauthorized acts. In one documented case, a programmer inserted into a system a logic bomb that would destroy the company's entire personnel file if his name was removed from it. Sometimes the term **computer virus** is used to describe a logic bomb in which a piece of unauthorized code is transmitted from program to program during a copy operation and destroys data or crashes the computer system as soon as it is unwittingly executed (see Feature 19B).

Scavenging. As its name implies, *scavenging* involves searching through trash cans, offices, and the like for information that will permit unauthorized access to a computer system. Students, for example, will sometimes look through discarded listings at the mainframe computer site for an identification number that will open to them the resources of others' accounts. Many organizations use document shredders to deter scavengers.

Computer Viruses

The Most Talked-about Computer Disease of Our Time

If your computer system catches a virus, it will probably be you who wants the Excedrin.

A computer virus is a small block of code that is purposely hidden inside a larger program and designed to replicate itself on a disk or in memory. When a virus-bearing program is processed with other programs, the virus attaches a copy of itself onto the other programs, thereby "infecting" them. The virus also contains a mechanism that makes it pull a prank or outright crime at a specific time or moment—say, on April Fool's Day or when an infected program performs a certain operation. Often people who concoct virus-bearing programs have something malicious in mind, such as destroying data or bringing a computer system to a complete halt.

To date, the most famous virus implanted in a computer system is the one in November 1988 that disabled thousands of computers that were hooked into Arpanet, a nationwide network connecting scores of colleges, universities, and research labs. After a computer system in the network read a program containing the viral code, the virus went to work filling up the

> What will happen when the "heavyweights" get into the act?

system's main memory with garbage, effectively choking out legitimate applications and grinding the system to a halt. The virus eventually was traced to a graduate student, who claimed he had not intended it to do any harm (the virus did not, in fact, destroy data). Intentions aside, millions of dollars of damage was done and the case is now under grand jury investigation.

The famous virus of '88 caused a number of issues to surface. First was the realization that viruses are capable of doing inestimable amounts of damage. Today the world is increasingly depending on communications systems—the type of system in which viruses have the greatest reach and thus potential for doing damage. Second was the realization that, to date, viruses have been the tools of amateur hackers. What will happen when the "heavyweights"—those involved with organized crime, international terrorism, and corporate espionage—get into the act? The notions of leading corporations having viruses clog their systems or of nuclear power stations being fed erroneous data are not farfetched nightmares. Third was the realization that some type of legislation to control computer system tampering is long overdue. Congress is now considering a bill that will make it a federal crime to insert a virus into certain computers.

To date, a number of "vaccine programs" for combatting computer viruses have surfaced. Many of them are designed to scrutinize code for suspicious patterns. For instance, some vaccines are designed to test programs for contamination by setting the system clock to suspicious dates to see if anything unusual happens. Although this type of vaccine isn't foolproof, it does effectively test for viruses that are set to detonate when the system clock reaches a certain value.

Data Leakage. Some pieces of data generated by organizations are highly confidential and not intended for outsiders' eyes. Generally these organizations carefully control any computer output that leaves their premises. In *data leakage,* however, confidential data are coded in sophisticated ways so that they can be removed undetected. For example, sensitive data can be transformed through a coding process into useless nonsense. Then, after they leave the premises unnoticed, they are decoded into the original output and used for unauthorized purposes.

Wiretapping. There are many documented cases of people who have wiretapped computer systems to obtain information illegally. Some transmission facilities, such as satellites, are highly susceptible to *wiretapping* (as evidenced by those "illegal" rooftop dishes that intercept cable TV). Others, such as fiber optic cable, are extremely difficult to penetrate.

Software Piracy. Software piracy, the unauthorized copying or use of a computer program, is often a crime. A person who makes an unauthorized copy of a program can be guilty of breaking copyright laws. It is definitely a crime to copy a program and then attempt to sell it for profit. The law is generally more lenient if one just uses an unauthorized copy that was made by someone else, but this use may constitute a crime as well. Whether a law is being broken or not, the software pirate is likely cheating someone out of deserved royalties.

Hacking. Hacking is a computer term referring to the activities of people who "get their kicks" out of using computers or terminals to crack the security of some computer system. Many people engage in hacking purely for the challenge of cracking codes; others do it to steal computer time or to peek at confidential information. Intentions aside, hacking often is considered a breaking-and-entering crime just like forced entry into someone's car or home.

Preventing Computer Crime

There are many ways organizations can combat computer crime.

Hire Trustworthy People. Employers should carefully investigate the background of anyone being considered for sensitive computer work. Some people falsify resumés to get jobs. Others may have criminal records. Despite the publicity given to groups such as hackers, studies have consistently shown that most computer crimes are committed by insiders.

Beware of Malcontents. The type of employee who is most likely to commit a computer crime is one who has recently been terminated or passed over for a promotion, or one who has some reason to "get even" with the organization. In cases where an employee has been terminated and potential for computer crime exists, records should be updated immediately to indicate that the person involved is no longer an employee.

Separate Employee Functions. An employee with many related responsibilities can more easily commit a crime than one with a single responsibility. For example, the person who authorizes adding new vendors to a file should not be the same one who authorizes payments to those vendors.

Restrict System Use. People who use a computer system should have access only to the things they need to do their jobs. A computer operator, for example, should be told only how to execute a program and not what the program does. People who need only to retrieve information should not be given updating privileges too.

Limit Access to Programs and Data. On many systems, users can restrict access to programs and data with *passwords*. For example, a user might specify that anyone wanting access to a program named AR-148 must first enter the password FRED. Users can change passwords frequently and also protect particularly sensitive files with several passwords. Today many organizations use measures such as *access cards* and sophisticated *biometric security devices* (see Feature 19C) in place of or in combination with passwords.

Use Site Licensing. Software vendors often protect their products from unauthorized copying with site licenses. A **site license** allows organizations buying a software product to make copies of it and to distribute the copies among employees for internal use.

Disguise Programs or Data Through Encryption. Some users and vendors encrypt data or programs to protect them. **Encryption** is the process of disguising data and programs by using some coding method. The encrypting procedure must provide for both coding and decoding. As with passwords, the encryption method should be changed regularly if it is protecting particularly sensitive materials.

Devise Staff Controls. Overtime work should be carefully scrutinized, because computer crimes often occur at times when the criminal is unlikely to be interrupted. Sensitive documents that are no longer needed should be shredded. Access to the computer room or program/data library should be strictly limited to authorized personnel. **Callback devices,** which hang up on and call back people phoning in from remote locations, should be used in communications systems to deter hacking and virus implantation.

Monitor Important System Transactions. The systems software should include a program for maintaining a log of every person gaining or attempting to

Biometric Security Systems

The High-Tech Alternative to the Lock and Key

At one well-known scientific laboratory, people wanting access to certain secured areas must place the palms of their hands against a plastic panel, where they are electronically scanned to verify the people's identities. In a number of homes across the world, if someone wants to get in the front door without someone on the other side opening it, he or she must speak to a voice recognition system that matches the voice against a stored voiceprint. At a Texas firm, employees who want to retrieve valuables from the vault must peer into a mechanism that studies the patterns of blood vessels in their eyes to determine who they are.

Such identification systems are *biometric security devices.* When a person attempts to get access to an area guarded by such a device, it reads a physical trait that is recognized as unique in individuals, digitizes the trait into an electronic pattern, and compares it against the known patterns stored in its memory. If it finds a match, it permits the person access; if not, it may give off a silent alarm. Fine as it might have been for centuries as a security device, the venerable metal key has always suffered the disadvantages of being able to be lost or duplicated. Not so with biometric security devices.

Biometric security devices commonly fall into one of two categories. *Physiological devices* work by recognizing

some physical characteristic, such as a fingerprint (see photo), handprint, or blood vessels in the retina of the eye. *Behavioral devices,* on the other hand, attempt to recognize a learned characteristic, such as the pattern of one's voice, one's signature, or one's typing habits. For instance, the typing-habit systems—based on a principle called "keystroke dynamics"—may test 100 or more different keystroke patterns during a typical user logon session. Among the variables used in the authentication process are key pressure, typing rhythms, and letter patterns.

The effectiveness of a security device largely depends on the particular type of technology in use. Early biometric systems, introduced a little over a decade ago, often rejected people whom they should have cleared. How-

gain access to the system. The log should contain information on the terminal used, the data files and programs used, and the time at which the work began and ended. Such a log allows management to isolate unauthorized system use.

Conduct Regular Audits. Unfortunately, many crimes are discovered by accident. Key elements of the system should be subjected to regular **audits**—inspections that certify that the system is working as expected—to ensure that no foul play is taking place.

Educate Employees. One of the best ways to prevent computer crime is to educate employees about security matters. People should be told about various types of computer crime and the conditions that foster them, informed

ever, accuracy has improved dramatically in recent years. Many systems now accept the wrong person less than 1 percent of the time and reject the right person less than 5 percent. The right person has a greater chance of being rejected on a voice system, say, if he or she has a cold, is eating food or chewing gum, or is speaking right after a strenuous jog up several flights of stairs.

To date, the largest consumer of biometric devices has been the government, especially defense-related facilities. However, a number of companies in the private sector—including giants such as Hertz, Chemical Bank, General Electric, and Merrill Lynch—have also joined the fold.

A plan now on the drawing boards is to use biometric devices to ensure that truckers with bad driving records in one state cannot be licensed in another state. And a number of financial institutions are talking seriously about storing biometric patterns on consumer-issued smart cards (see the Tomorrow box in Chapter 2), which many insiders expect to be common-place by the turn of the century. Who knows—when you sign a bank deposit slip in the year 2005, a device may be monitoring both your signature and the time it takes you to write it, comparing them with patterns stored on your card.

Fingerprint recognition. No match, no entry.

of the seriousness of computer crime, and instructed on what to do when they suspect a computer crime is taking place or is about to occur. Because most people are relatively unaware of how others can use computers illegally, a computer crime can be committed in front of several witnesses without their knowing that a crime is taking place.

Ethical Issues

Ethics refers to standards of moral conduct. For example, telling the truth is a matter of ethics. An unethical act isn't always illegal, but sometimes it is. For example, purposely lying to a friend is unethical but normally is lawful, but perjuring oneself as a courtroom witness is a crime. Whether or not criminal behavior is involved, ethics play a significant role in shaping the law and in determining how well we get along with other people.

Computer ethics refers to standards of moral conduct demonstrated in computer-related matters. Today one of the most important concerns in the computer ethics area is the use of someone else's property in an unauthorized way. Let's look at two examples.

☐ People tend to casually use computer resources in ways that, although not criminal, are ethically questionable. For instance, some people regularly use a software package they don't own for personal purposes, claiming they are doing so just to "get the feel of it." Although most vendors encourage limited experimentation with their products, they frown on someone who hasn't bought the package but owns and uses it regularly.

☐ A student may casually eavesdrop, on a university mainframe system, on data not intended for his or her use. This may entail neither a prosecutable crime nor a major security threat, but that makes the act no less ethically reprehensible.

Many scholars feel that educating people about ethical matters is being pushed aside today in the rush to achieve measurable results. The question of who is responsible for providing education about ethics is a major concern.

COMPUTERS AND PRIVACY

Almost all of us have some aspects of our lives that we prefer to keep private. These may include a sorry incident from the past, sensitive medical or financial facts, or certain tastes or opinions. Yet we can appreciate that sometimes selected people or organizations have a legitimate need for some of this information. A doctor needs accurate medical histories of patients. Financial information must be disclosed to credit card companies and college scholarship committees. A company or the government may need to probe into the lives of people applying for unusually sensitive jobs.

However, no matter how legitimate the need, once personal information has been made available to others there is always the danger that it will be misused. Some of the stored facts may be wrong. Facts may get to the wrong people. Facts may be taken out of context and used to draw distorted conclusions. Facts may be collected and disseminated without one's knowledge or consent. People who are victimized may be denied access to incorrect or sensitive data. With respect to information processing, **privacy** refers to how and by whom information about individuals is used.

The problem of how to protect privacy and ensure that personal information is not misused was with us long before electronic computers existed. But modern computer systems, with their ability to store and manipulate unprecedented quantities of data and to make those data available to many locations, have added a new dimension to the privacy issue. The greater the ability to collect, store, use, and disseminate information, the greater the potential for abuse of that information.

Legislation

Since the early 1970s, the federal government has sought to protect citizens' rights by passing legislation to limit the abuse of computer data banks. Some important laws enacted for this purpose are the Fair Credit Reporting Act, the Freedom of Information Act, the Education Privacy Act, and the Privacy Act.

The *Fair Credit Reporting Act (1970)* is designed to prevent private organizations from unfairly denying credit to individuals. It stipulates that people must have the right to inspect their credit records. If a reasonable objection about the integrity of the data is raised, the credit reporting agency is required by law to investigate the matter.

The *Freedom of Information Act (1970)* gives individuals the right to inspect data concerning them that are stored by the federal government. The law also makes certain data about the operation of federal agencies available for public scrutiny.

The *Education Privacy Act (1974)* protects an individual's right to privacy in both private and public schools that receive any federal funding. It stipulates that an individual has the right to keep matters such as course grades and evaluations of behavior private. Also, individuals must have the opportunity to inspect and challenge their own records.

The *Privacy Act (1974)* primarily protects the public against abuses by the federal government. It stipulates that collection of data by federal agencies must have a legitimate purpose. It also states that individuals must be allowed to learn what information is being stored about them and how it's being used, and have the opportunity to correct or remove erroneous or trivial data.

Most privacy legislation, as you can see, relates to the conduct of the federal government and the organizations to which it supplies aid. Some state governments have enacted similar legislation to protect individuals from abuses by state agencies. The federal government currently is developing private-sector privacy guidelines similar to those of federal and state agencies.

COMPUTERS IN OUR LIVES: TODAY AND TOMORROW

The number of uses to which computers have been put is so large and heterogeneous that it almost defies classification. As you've seen, computers are valuable, on-the-job tools whether you are a company executive, a manager, an engineer, a marketing research analyst, an accountant, a financial analyst, a lawyer, a doctor, a dentist, a real estate broker, an architect, or even a farmer or rancher. And although it may be hard to believe, the impact of the computer on those occupations and others is just beginning.

Outside the workplace, computers have also asserted their presence into our lives. Let's see how.

FIGURE 19-2

Microprocessor-driven bread baker. Auto Bakery is but one of scores of consumer products that employ microcomputer and memory chips to automatically perform processes that would otherwise be handled manually.

Computers for Home and Personal Use

When inexpensive microcomputer systems first became widely available in the late 1970s, many people predicted that soon there would be a computer system in every home. After all, computers are useful tools, and look what happened in the case of other great inventions, such as the car, phone, and television. We are still far from a society in which every home has a desktop personal computer system. However, those brainy little microcomputer and memory chips that are used to make desktop computers are finding their way into scores of other products purchased for personal use. Following are several examples.

Electrical Gadgets. Today almost everybody uses a variety of electrical gadgets—television sets, stereo systems, videocassette recorders (VCRs), washing machines, cameras, phones, kitchen appliances, and so on. Increasingly these products are coming packaged with built-in microprocessors and solid-state memories that provide a variety of special functions. The electronic components in your VCR, for instance, enable you to "program" the VCR to record programs while you are away. Built-in components on your stereo system provide features such as "quartz tuning" and let you save your favorite radio stations in memory for easy access through push buttons. Electronic processors and memories in kitchen appliances can accept instructions, store them, and perform them according to a designated timetable (see Figure 19-2).

Computerized Cars. The car is one product that has been enhanced in a variety of ways through built-in microprocessors and memories. Some of the earliest microprocessors were employed as control mechanisms, for instance, as regulators in electronic ignition systems. Lately they have been employed in a variety of more "exotic" applications, and it is not unusual for a car to have over two dozen electronic chips of one form or another. In fact, creative use of microcomputing gadgets within cars is becoming a major selling point of cars themselves (see the Tomorrow box in Chapter 1).

Computerized Homes. Today homes all over the world are being built with computer-controlled devices that greet and identify visitors, monitor and water your lawn while you're away, and automatically regulate the temperature in your home. Although the potential for this type of microcomputer application seems far-reaching, it is limited by the reality that many people want their homes to reflect an ambience in which computers play no part.

Personal Robot Servants. Although most robots today are utilized to perform dangerous work in factories, personal robot servants are also being built and marketed for the home. A few "robot stores" have even sprouted up to sell robot kits or fully assembled robots to the public. Home robots are still very much in their infancy, but some now can perform acts once thought impossible, such as greeting specific people by name and busing snacks to people around the house.

Home Banking and Shopping. Electronic funds transfer (EFT) systems have long existed. The earliest systems enabled funds to be wired between banks. Later came the automatic teller machine. Most recent to the scene are home-computer-based communications packages and services that enable you to make transactions at banks, brokerage houses, travel agencies, and/or retail stores. Today the promise of home banking and shopping remains unfulfilled, although some industry observers see both of these applications as future giants.

Cottage Industries. We are living in an age where information—the very thing that computers are best at producing—has become a highly salable commodity. As business-related computing products continue to drop in price, it is likely that many more of them will be used to create or enhance home-based businesses, or *cottage industries.* To some extent, this phenomenon has been observed with the availability of powerful desktop microcomputer systems. The feasibility of home-based businesses has also been fueled by technologies such as desktop publishing, "personal copiers," inexpensive facsimile machines, modems, laptop computers, and satellite dishes.

Computers in Education

Some of the earliest electronic computers were installed in academic institutions in the 1940s and 1950s, where they were either studied as a curiosity in their own right or used to perform calculations rapidly. Thus, one of the earliest applications of computers in education involved the training of engineers, who had to know how to build computers.

As computers found their way into businesses, data processing and information systems courses evolved in business schools. Some academic visionaries, such as John Kemeny at Dartmouth College in the 1960s, realized early on that computers would be useful for performing work in an ever wider variety of disciplines. And so BASIC was developed and rapidly became part of every student's life at Dartmouth.

Today computers and education are combined in a wide variety of ways (see Figure 19-3). Let's look at a few of these.

Learning about Computers. Learning about computers involves taking courses that teach you about things such as general computer principles or hands-on use of a specific software package. As with many other disciplines, the very act of learning about computers can be done from several perspectives. Chapter 18 touched on a few of these, for example, *computer science* (a technically oriented perspective), *computer information systems* (a business perspective), and *computer operations* (a hands-on, operational perspective). In a large university, it's common to see 50 or more courses collectively devoted to covering these multiple emphases. Many large businesses and independent training firms also provide computer courses.

FIGURE 19-3
Education. Computers are widely used today to teach courses of all types, at all levels of the educational system.

Computer-Enhanced Instruction. Computers are also now widely used to assist in the process of teaching.

With *computer-assisted instruction (CAI),* the student and computer take part in an interactive dialog. For example, a high-school algebra student using a CAI package may be given a problem on the screen to solve. If the answer given is correct, the package poses another problem, perhaps one that's more advanced. If the answer is wrong, the package may go into a "remedial mode" in which it either gives hints, shows how to solve the problem, or provides another problem on the same level. Each student progresses at his or her own pace. At the end of the session, the student is graded. A "progress report" may also be provided.

A closely related technology is *computer-managed instruction (CMI).* In a CMI system, the computer merely supervises students, perhaps directing them to read certain books or see certain library films on their own. On completing one assignment, students return to their computer workstations for testing and, perhaps, further assignments. Thus, with CMI, students aren't limited to materials that can be stored and disseminated by a computer system. CMI can be implemented as a supplemental technique in a course or, on a larger scale, by a so-called "electronic university" (see Feature 15A).

New technologies such as *videodisk* and *hypermedia* are also just beginning to be used to assist in the educational process (see pages 368–369 of Window 4 for an example). Of course, no computer-enhanced instructional tool has ever been recognized as a solution that will meet every teaching need. In many situations the computer may never seriously challenge the purely human, personal approach to education.

Problem Solving. One of the first applications of computers in education was solving difficult problems. Today, students in a wide variety of disciplines use computers to perform such tasks as producing cash flow statements, developing business strategies through what-if scenarios, simulating product designs, planning facilities, testing decision alternatives, computing mathematical curves, and producing course papers. The list is almost endless. Also, virtually every professor involved in research uses computers in one form or another to discover new scientific facts or to just become more efficient at getting work done.

FIGURE 19-4

Computer football. Computer football games have become much more sophisticated in recent years. Not only has the graphics resolution improved, but also many games come packaged with screen shots of screaming fans and angry coaches, and with audio programs that simulate fan excitement.

Computers in Entertainment and Leisure Activities

There are so many entertainment and leisure activities that support computer use that these applications are virtually impossible to enumerate. So let's consider a few selected applications of general interest—sports, movies and television, music, and art.

Sports. Among the earliest applications of computers in sports were highly simplified computerized baseball games. You selected opposing lineups and then issued a RUN command at your terminal. Subsequently the computer would use random numbers to simulate a ballgame and, within seconds, print out a box score. Not very interesting, perhaps, but better things were to come. Today there are some very sophisticated products that enable you to "participate" in sports such as baseball, football, auto racing, and flying without ever leaving the comfort of your living room (see Figure 19-4).

In the world of televised sports broadcasting, the computer has been nothing less than impressive. Take those flashy graphics, for instance. There are attractive screens of scores and statistics, possibly a digitized freeze-frame of tennis or racing-car action you saw live just seconds ago, and fully animated, cartoonish sequences of fantasy flights over a basketball court or football field. The fast-paced world of computer graphics and animation has made all of this possible.

And, of course, there are all those impressive player statistics. After all, what else but a computer could quickly determine for you that José Canseco batted .314 against right-handers and .289 against left-handers prior to tonight's game? Professional ballclubs now have behind-the-scenes computer people to prepare statistics for the announcers in the broadcast booth. Also, in sports such as baseball, football, tennis, hockey, and basketball, and in

FIGURE 19-5

Computer-generated movies. *Tin Toy,* by Pixar's John Lasseter and William Reeves, became the first so-called ''computer-generated movie'' ever to receive an Oscar at the Academy Awards.

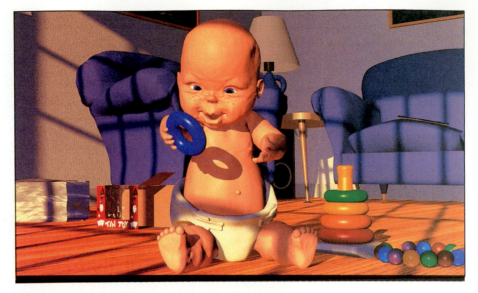

© 1988 Pixar

Olympic competitions, coaches and managers are trusting computers to analyze player performances and game plans. Even some ballplayers—such as the 1988 World Series MVP, pitcher Orel Hersheiser of the Dodgers—have their own laptop computers and personal databases to help them develop playing strategies.

Combine all of these applications with electronic scoreboards, computer-controlled ticketing, and all the other computerized activities performed by any profit-making enterprise and you have one very impressive array of computing power in the sports industry today.

Movies. Computers and movies first met when computers became the subjects of movies. Robots were among the earliest computer technologies to be worthy objects of moviemaking. Then, with the 1950s, UNIVAC I, and the ominous presence of the Cold War and atomic weapons, movies began to portray the computer as an infallible, Big-Brother-type of device that insensitive powermongers would use to rule the world. A major emphasis in movies today, of course, is the notion that computer systems are indeed fallible and that a human software oversight can cause some global disaster.

In the last several years computers have figured prominently in the actual creation of movies. For example, movies such as *Who Framed Roger Rabbit?* would have been impossible without computers to keep track of and integrate the numerous special effects involved. Many scenes in that film used computers to combine live images, drawings, and dynamic electronic models. Also, the colorized versions of old classics such as *The Maltese Falcon* and *Yankee Doodle Dandy* would not have been possible without computers, nor would the restored versions of many old color films whose original prints have faded. In the 1989 Academy Awards, the computer virtually won an Oscar in its own right when the computer-generated movie *Tin Toy* was the top-vote getter in the animated short film category (see Figure 19-5).

FIGURE 19-6

Music synthesizer. With a synthesizer, sounds can be created and stored, and then either played directly from memory or distorted in new and interesting ways.

Some people feel that the day is not too far distant when the majority of images you see in movies or on television will be computer-generated, and indistinguishable from real-life images to most viewers. Since computers are more than ever being used to "enhance" images, it's getting ever more difficult to separate fantasy and reality.

Music. While creating music may be an art, the notion of sound is a matter of physics. Musicians frequently use computers called *electronic synthesizers* to store sounds, recall them from memory to have them played, and distort them in new and unusual ways (see Figure 19-6). The use of computer technology in creating music is a widespread reality today, and artists ranging from Stevie Wonder (popular music) to Herbie Hancock (jazz) to Pierre Boulez (classical music) have accepted technology as an important force in the creation of their works. Musicians use the computer like writers use a word processor, but, instead of words, they store, edit, and cut-and-paste sounds. Today many musical pieces are so rich with electronically produced sounds that it's difficult for a nonexpert to tell what came directly from an instrument and what was electronically enhanced.

The computer plays many other important roles in the music industry today. For example, DJs and their staffs use computer-controlled equipment to edit and organize music for their radio shows. Also, written musical scores are prepared with desktop publishing systems that use specialized fonts, document preparation software, and laser printers (see Figure 19-7).

FIGURE 19-7

Sheet music. Desktop publishing systems with musical fonts are widely used to place notes and lyrics on paper.

Art. At one time virtually the only way you could create an artistic image was to paint, draw, weave, sculpt, and the like completely by your own hand. Then the Gutenberg press arrived, and images could be mass produced. Although that event probably created panic among people contemplating a calligraphy career, the would-be Renoirs and Van Goghs had little to worry about.

The industrial revolution gave further rise to the so-called industrial arts, and machines such as the Jacquard loom (see Chapter 3), which could weave under program control, appeared. When photography arrived in the mid-1800s, it threatened the painters of the day, but it later evolved into an art form of its own, with a different set of standards.

Now that the computer has arrived, there are new perceived threats to artists on all levels—but there are also great opportunities. With a computer, images of virtually any shape can be created, colored in any of millions of colors, enlarged, rotated, blended, combined with other images, illuminated by one or more shadow-casting light sources, and so forth. Also, colors, positions, and shapes of objects can be changed at electronically fast speeds to create new images. For example, a computer was used to generate the image in Figure 19-8 as well as the stunning images in Windows 3 and 8. A computer enables the artist to see a variety of images and store the

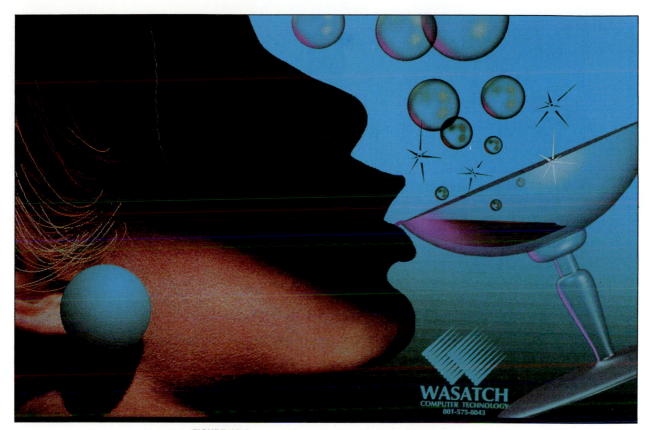

FIGURE 19-8

Computer art. Computer art is rapidly becoming an acknowledged art form, with many shows and exhibitions held worldwide each year.

most promising of them, all in a span of time that would be impossible with only canvas and brush.

Nonetheless, painters are still far from being replaced. Like photography, computer art is becoming an art form in its own right.

Computers in Science and Medicine

Science and medicine account for a wide variety of computer applications. In this section, we'll look specifically at how computers are used for weather forecasting, space exploration, environmental simulations, patient diagnosis, life-support systems, and the treatment of handicapped people.

Science. One of the earliest applications of computer power in a scientific field was weather forecasting. To predict the weather accurately, data on current weather conditions must be input to the computer, which then analyzes mounds of data on past conditions. Because predicting weather is a round-the-clock chore that requires supercomputer-sized computational

FIGURE 19-9

Simulation. The use of computers in simulating a ship's wheelhouse makes it possible to train students to captain seagoing vessels without always going to the expense and time of actually bringing a ship out into the water.

and storage capacity, it is done at a national level at places such as the National Center for Atmospheric Research (NCAR) in Boulder, Colorado. Of course, the computer now plays a big part in presenting TV viewers with interesting weather graphics.

Another ongoing application of computers in science is the exploration of space. So many computations need to be done to send people and spacecraft into the universe that space travel with any degree of safety would be impossible without computers. Computers are also used to enhance and study photographs taken in space.

Simulation involves building a mathematical model of a real-life object or situation and thoroughly testing it with "dummy data" before the object is built or the situation encountered. Computer-aided design (CAD), for example, often involves simulation. A car, say, may be modeled on a computer screen. Then, before the car is actually built, the computer simulates real-life events such as accidents and stresses. Similarly, many airplane pilots and sailors today are trained in special "cockpits" or "control rooms" that simulate other craft in the immediate vicinity, departures and arrivals at airports or harbors, and the like (see Figure 19-9 and Window 9). Simulation is also useful to both government and business for predicting economic changes in society, the environmental impact of new policies, and consumer reaction to the effects of price changes.

FIGURE 19-10

Computers and the handicapped. There are now hundreds of specialized computer applications to help the handicapped. In this photo, computers are being used to help special education students.

Medicine. It is indeed comforting to know that computers are hard at work ensuring that you remain healthy and live longer.

Computer-assisted diagnosis refers to a number of hardware or software technologies that assist physicians in diagnosing patients' conditions. One example is inputting data about a patient's condition to a software program that compares the condition to previously diagnosed ones in a large patient database. The program then outputs relevant statistics to help the attending physicians diagnose the ailment. Many of these programs are considered expert systems in that they employ artificial intelligence techniques that enable them to actually draw some conclusions for the physician.

Computer tomography, sometimes referred to as CAT or PET scanning, is another computer-assisted diagnosis technique. It employs X-ray hardware and computer technology to provide physicians with three-dimensional pictures of the organs in a person's body. Thus, the physicians have more information on which to base a diagnosis than they would from a traditional two-dimensional X-ray.

Computerized life-support systems provide nursing support, although they usually bear no human resemblance. These systems monitor bedridden patients, freeing their flesh-and-blood counterparts from the need for uninterrupted observation. A system might continuously monitor signs such as heart rate, temperature, and blood pressure and sound a silent alarm if something goes wrong.

Today computers are being used in many ways to help the handicapped. Computer-aided instruction (CAI), for example, has been used successfully to help slow learners (see Figure 19-10). Portable computers have been used to artificially simulate the human voice, enabling cerebral palsy victims to "speak." Also, vision systems, which contain sensors to determine distances of objects and computer systems to determine objects' identities or properties, are evolving to enable blind people to "see."

T   O   M   O   R   R   O   W

Technology Breakthrough Areas

Where Tomorrow's Great Innovations Are Likely to Be Found

No one has a crystal ball to predict the future. Technology predictions are especially risky because one must look into the future through eyes that heavily focus on the world as it is today.

In the 1940s, for instance, the director of the Harvard Computational Laboratory predicted that the computer industry would never amount to much, since no more than a half-dozen machines (such as the one used at Harvard at the time) could handle the world's demand. As things turned out, some half-century later millions of microcomputers that sell for several hundred dollars or less are widely available—and these tiny machines can run circles around that gargantuan Harvard computer. The telephone, too, was at one time seen as a device that would receive limited use because many observers doubted there would ever be enough telephone operators to handle any sort of widespread demand.

Despite these caveats, a number of breakthrough areas seem imminent in the near future. On the hardware front, we can expect to see breakthroughs with respect to speed, memory capacity, size, and cost. Speed will be enhanced by fitting circuitry ever closer together, by devising new ways to process data, and by discovering better materials with which to build computers. Memory capacity is improving because new methods for storing more data in less space on media are continually being found. And because computer and memory hardware are becoming more dense, both their cost and their size are shrinking.

On the software front, there has been a strong trend toward making programs completely independent of their data. In addition, someday most programs will likely contain several artificial intelligence (AI) components, enabling computer systems to perform at human or even superhuman levels in many areas. Embedded AI routines will be to tomorrow's software industry what embedded microprocessors have been to today's hardware sector. Parallel processing is also seen as a major breakthrough area, with respect to both software and hardware.

The accompanying figure lists a number of these and other leading-edge breakthrough areas.

Technology Breakthrough Areas

☑ Expert systems widely embedded into software products

☑ Microprocessor and storage chips embedded into an ever increasing number of hardware products

☑ Very-high-level language products and graphics interfaces that make it even easier for people to do more sophisticated types of things with computers and communications technology

☑ Parallel processing architectures replacing conventional, serial architectures, thereby creating computer systems that are orders of magnitude faster

☑ Impressive improvements in speech recognition—possibly to 10,000–20,000 words by the beginning of the twenty-first century

☑ Optical recognition products that make it even easier to input anything on paper and manipulate it within the computer system

☑ The marriage of computers and high-definition television

☑ Video disk emerging as a major mass-consumer product

☑ High-resolution, flat-panel displays displacing conventional CRTs

☑ An all-digital phone system

☑ Fiber-optic cable emerging as a major communications medium

☑ Compact disks that can store a few gigabytes of data

SUMMARY AND KEY TERMS

Since the early 1950s, when the era of commercial computing began, computers have rapidly woven their way into the very fabric of modern society. In the process, they have created both opportunities and problems.

One of the first criticisms leveled at the entry of computers into the workplace was that their very presence resulted in stress. Stress-related concerns triggered by the so-called computer revolution include fear of layoff or reassignment, fear of falling behind, and job burnout. In addition to these problems, a number of concerns related to **ergonomics**-related issues, such as display device usage and workspace design, have surfaced. Moreover, many people worry about our society's apparent overreliance on computers.

Computer crime is loosely defined as the use of computers to commit unauthorized acts. Some states have laws that address computer crime directly; others do not. In practice, however, computer crime is hard to pin down even in states that have such laws. It often is hard to decide when an unauthorized act is really a crime, judges and juries often are bewildered by the technical issues involved, and companies frequently are reluctant to press charges.

Computer crime has many forms. Types of computer crime include data diddling, the Trojan horse technique, salami-shaving methods, unauthorized use of superzap and trapdoor programs, logic bombs, **computer viruses,** scavenging, data leakage, wiretapping, **software piracy,** and **hacking.**

There are many ways organizations can combat computer crimes: hiring trustworthy people, taking precautions with malcontents, separating employee functions, restricting system use, limiting access to programs and data, **site licensing,** devising staff controls, **encrypting** particularly sensitive programs and data, using **callback devices,** monitoring important system transactions, conducting regular **audits,** and educating employees.

Computer ethics refers to standards of moral conduct displayed in computer-related matters. Today one of the most important concerns in the computer ethics area is using someone else's property in an unauthorized way.

Most people want some control over the kinds of facts that are collected about them, how those facts are collected and their accuracy, who uses them, and how they are used. Modern computer systems, with their ability to store and manipulate unprecedented quantities of data and make those data available to many locations, have added a new dimension to the personal **privacy** issue.

Today the number of uses to which computers have been put is so large and heterogeneous that it almost defies classification. The bulk of this text has examined the uses of computers in the ordinary business workplace. Outside this workplace, computers of some sort are found in the home, in educational institutions, in entertainment and leisure activities, and in science and medicine.

REVIEW EXERCISES

Fill-in Questions

1. Fear of computers is known as _____ .
2. _____ is the field that covers the effects of factors such as equipment and computer workspaces on employees' productivity and health.
3. _____ refers to standards of moral conduct shown in computer-related matters.
4. The unauthorized copying or use of computer programs is known as software _____ .
5. The _____ Act is designed to prevent private organizations from unfairly denying credit to individuals.
6. The _____ Act protects an individual's right to privacy in both private and public schools that receive federal funding.

Matching Questions

Match each term with the description that best fits.

a. computer virus   d. hacking
b. data diddling   e. trapdoor
c. salami shaving   f. superzap

_____ 1. The deduction of small amounts from a large number of randomly selected accounts.
_____ 2. Refers to a program that can bypass all system controls.
_____ 3. Transmitted through a copy operation.
_____ 4. A diagnostic tool that allows viewing of computer storage.
_____ 5. The altering of an organization's production data.
_____ 6. Using a terminal or microcomputer system to illegally break into a large computer system.

Discussion Questions

1. Identify some specific problems caused by the rapid spread of computer use in society.
2. Describe some ways that computers may affect our health or well-being.
3. Why is computer crime so difficult to pin down?

4. Name some of the forms computer crime can take.

5. How does a computer virus work?

6. Provide some examples demonstrating unethical behavior regarding the use of computers.

7. Name some rights of individuals that computer privacy laws have tried to protect.

8. Identify some ways in which computers affect us in our daily lives.

Critical Thinking Questions

1. A clerk in a steel company uses a company-owned desktop computer, on company time, to keep track of baseball statistics. Is a crime being committed?

2. A defense lawyer gets a computer researcher to electronically enhance photographs taken at the scene of an accident to prove her client wasn't completely at fault. The enhanced photographs appear to show that there was some prior damage to the plaintiff's car, which, if true, would contradict statements made by the plaintiff. What problem might the lawyer have in presenting the case?

3. By whom and how should ethics be taught?

4. Computer systems are used today to assist in finding missing children. When provided a photo of the child, the computer system can output what the child might look like, say, 1, 2, 5, 10, or even 20 or more years into the future. How, would you guess, can computer systems do this?

Computer Models

How Computers Are Used to Model Reality

Computers are frequently used to set up models of real-world phenomena. These models, in turn, are used to predict events before they happen, to train people, to create stunning visual effects, and to perform a variety of other useful tasks. In this Window, we look at a few applications in which computer modeling is widely used.

1 This image was created using thousands of tiny polygons—called *fractals*—that are mathematically fitted together to mimic reality. The image shown here consumes only 1,500 bytes of storage, which is several hundred times less space than that required for conventional picture images (which are stored pixel by pixel). Because fractals are mathematically described, they can be blown up to larger sizes without significant loss in resolution.

FACILITY PLANNING

Computer-aided design (CAD) techniques are today used to help architects construct real-life electronic models of buildings and other facilities. Consequently, several design alternatives can be rapidly conceived and tested, and then submitted to the client for approval. Not only is the client usually excited by getting to see the "final product," but much of the risk associated with the structure's turning out other than expected is eliminated.

2–5 Solid (three-dimensional) CAD modeling offers a unique opportunity for architects to conceptualize a project well before the first shovel breaks ground. Here, "walkthrough animation" allows both the architect and client to start at the building entrance, tour every nook and cranny of a proposed facility, and exit through the rear door. Lighting algorithms can be used to beam in light from indoor or outdoor sources, simulating real-life illumination.

6

7

6, 7 When a computer-stored image of an existing site in Lynchburg, Virginia (photo 6), is combined with a scaled, computer-stored, solid model of a proposed building, the result (photo 7) is a realistic portrayal of what the future may hold.

8

10

9

8–10 An unimproved lot in North Carolina (8) is provided, through the magic of a CAD package, roadways and scanned-in magnolia trees (9). Then, the outdoors scene is "mapped" onto a window of an office building (10), giving the future owner of the building the look and feel of the architect's proposal.

COMPUTER SIMULATION

11

11–18   Computers are frequently used to simulate aircraft operation before aircraft are built and put into use and, also, to train pilots. The Evans & Sutherland imaging systems used to produce these highly complex scenes generate frames in realtime at a rate of about 50 frames per second. Realtime simulation means that the frames are not prestored in the computer but are created—on the fly, so to speak— each time the simulation program is run.

The Evans & Sutherland systems are programmed to simulate a variety of real-life situations. During training, for instance, pilots are exposed to hazards such as fog or lightning storms (photo 15) and mountains or cliffs (photo 16), as well as to a variety of landing and takeoff situations (photos 17 and 18). The system is also programmed to create unusual special effects, such as rotor wash on the ocean surface (photo 13).

12

13

14

Number Systems

A

In Chapter 4, you learned that fixed-length codes such as EBCDIC and ASCII are often used to represent numbers, letters of the alphabet, and special characters. Although these codes are handy for storing data and transporting them around a computer system, they are not designed to do arithmetic operations. For this type of use, data must be stored in a "true" binary form that can be manipulated quickly by the computer.

This appendix covers several fundamentals of numbering systems. The two primary systems discussed are the decimal numbering system (used by people) and the binary numbering system (used by computers). Also discussed are the octal and hexadecimal numbering systems, both of which are shorthand ways of representing long strings of binary numbers so they are more understandable to people.

A *number system* is a way of representing numbers. The system we most commonly use is called the *decimal,* or base 10, system (the word *decimal* comes from the Latin word for *ten*). It is called *base 10* because it uses 10 symbols—the digits 0, 1, 2, 3, 4, 5, 6, 7, 8, 9—to represent all possible numbers. Numbers greater than nine are represented by a combination of these symbols.

Because we are so familiar with the decimal system, it never occurs to most of us that we could represent numbers in any other way. In fact, however, there is nothing that says a number system has to have 10 possible symbols. Many other numbers would do as a base.

We saw in Chapter 4 that the *binary,* or base 2, system is used extensively by computers to represent numbers and other characters. Computer systems can perform computations and transmit data thousands of times faster in binary form than they can using decimal representations. Thus, it's important for anyone studying computers to know how the binary system works. Anyone contemplating a professional career in computers should also understand the *octal* (base 8) and *hexadecimal* (base 16) systems. But before we examine many of the number systems used in the computing world—and learn how to convert numbers from one system into another—let's look more closely at the decimal numbering system. Insight into how the decimal system works will help us understand more about the other numbering systems.

THE DECIMAL NUMBERING SYSTEM

All numbering systems, including the decimal system with which we work in our everyday lives, represent numbers as a combination of ordered symbols. As stated earlier, the **decimal*** (or base 10) system has 10 acceptable

---

*Terms used in this appendix can be found in the Glossary at the end of the book.

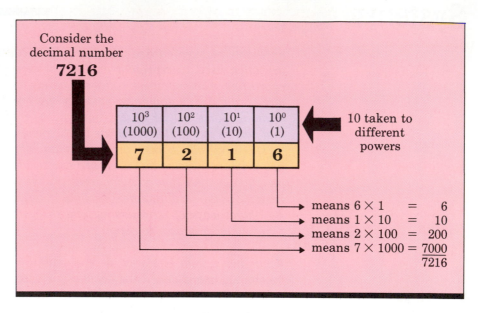

Consider the decimal number

7216

10^3 (1000)	10^2 (100)	10^1 (10)	10^0 (1)
7	**2**	**1**	**6**

10 taken to different powers

means 6×1 = 6
means 1×10 = 10
means 2×100 = 200
means 7×1000 = 7000
                       7216

symbols—the digits 0, 1, 2, . . . , 9. The positioning of the symbols in a decimal number is significant. For example, 891 is a different number than 918 (with the same symbols occupying different positions).

The position of each symbol in any decimal number represents the number 10 (the base number) raised to a power, or exponent, that is based on that position. Going from right to left, the first position represents 10^0, or 1; the second position represents 10^1, or 10; the third position represents 10^2, or 100; and so forth. Thus, as Figure A-1 shows, a decimal number like 7,216 is understood as $7 \times 10^3 + 2 \times 10^2 + 1 \times 10^1 + 6 \times 10^0$.

THE BINARY NUMBERING SYSTEM

The **binary,** or base 2, system works in a manner similar to the decimal system. One major difference is that the binary system has only two symbols—0 and 1—instead of ten. A second major difference is that the position of each digit in a binary number represents the number 2 (the base number) raised to an exponent based on that position. Thus, the binary number 11100 represents

$$1 \times 2^4 + 1 \times 2^3 + 1 \times 2^2 + 0 \times 2^1 + 0 \times 2^0$$

which, translated into the decimal system, is 28. Another example of a binary-to-decimal conversion is provided in Figure A-2.

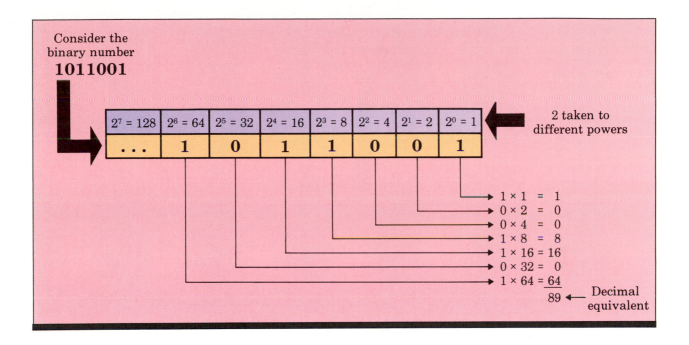

FIGURE A-2

Binary-to-decimal conversion. To convert any binary number to its decimal counterpart, take the rightmost digit and multiply it by 2^0 (or 1), the next to rightmost digit and multiply it by 2^1 (or 2), and so on, as illustrated here. Then add up all the products so formed.

Converting in the reverse direction—from decimal to binary—is also rather easy. A popular approach for doing this is the *remainder method*. This procedure employs successive divisions by the base number of the system to which we are converting. Use of the remainder method to convert a decimal to a binary number is illustrated in Figure A-3.

To avoid confusion when different number bases are being used, it is common to use the base as a subscript. So, referring to Figures A-2 and A-3 for example, we could write

$$89_{10} = 1011001_2$$

In addition, when we are using number systems other than the decimal system, it is customary to pronounce each symbol individually. For example, 101_2 is pronounced "one-zero-one" rather than "one hundred one." This convention is also used with other nondecimal systems.

The binary system described here is sometimes referred to as *true-binary representation*. True-binary representation does not use a fixed number of bits, as do EBCDIC and ASCII, nor is it used to represent letters or special characters.

Decimal-to-binary conversion using the remainder method. In this approach, we start by using the decimal number to be converted (89) as the initial dividend. Each successive dividend is the quotient of the previous division. We keep dividing until we've reached a zero quotient, whereupon the converted number is formed by the remainders taken in reverse order.

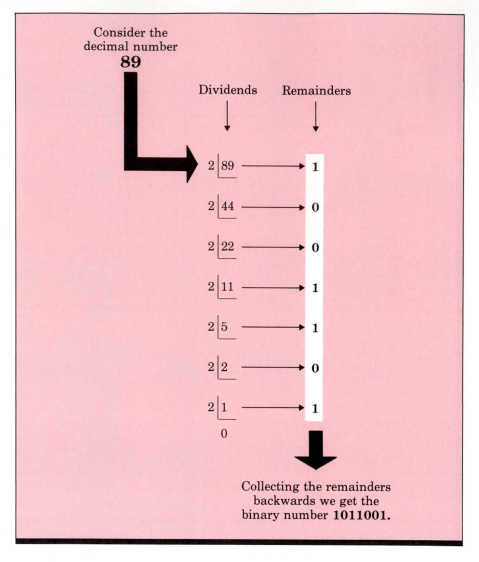

Consider the decimal number **89**

Dividends   Remainders

2	89	→	1
2	44	→	0
2	22	→	0
2	11	→	1
2	5	→	1
2	2	→	0
2	1	→	1
	0		

Collecting the remainders backwards we get the binary number **1011001.**

THE OCTAL NUMBERING SYSTEM

Because large binary numbers—for example, 11010100010011101_2—can be easily misread by programmers, binary digits are often grouped into units of three or four that, in turn, are represented by other symbols. The octal system uses a grouping of three. Some computer manufacturers use the octal system extensively with their hardware and software documentation, so it is a handy system to know.

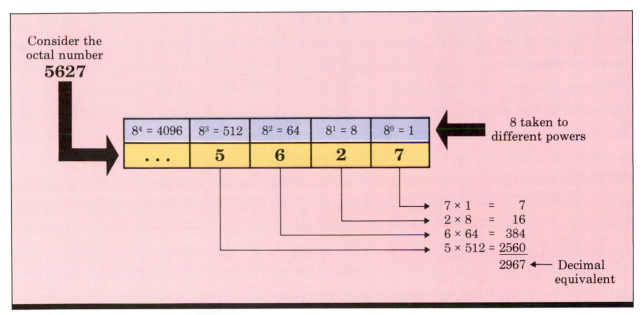

FIGURE A-4

Octal-to-decimal conversion. To convert any octal number to its decimal counterpart, take the rightmost digit and multiply it by 8^0 (or 1), the next to rightmost digit and multiply it by 8^1 (or 8), and so on, as illustrated here. Then add up all the products so formed.

As you may already have guessed, the **octal** (or base 8) system uses eight symbols—0, 1, 2, 3, 4, 5, 6, 7. The position of each digit in an octal number represents the number 8 (the base number) raised to an exponent based on that position. Thus, a number in base 8 looks like a decimal number, but it has a different meaning than the same pattern of digits in base 10. The base 8 number 725, for example, means

$$7 \times 8^2 + 2 \times 8^1 + 5 \times 8^0$$

which, translated into base 10, is 469. A second example illustrating conversion from octal to decimal is provided in Figure A-4. The procedure employed in this conversion process closely parallels the one used to change binary numbers to decimal numbers.

We can find the octal counterpart of a decimal number by employing the remainder method we used with binary numbers. Instead of successively dividing by 2, however, we divide by 8. Figure A-5 illustrates this process.

To convert from base 8 to base 2, we separately convert each octal digit to three binary digits. The table in Figure A-6 will help with this process. So, for example, to convert 7136_8 to base 2, we get

$$\begin{array}{cccc} 7 & 1 & 3 & 6 \\ 111 & 001 & 011 & 110 \end{array}$$

FIGURE A-5

Decimal-to-octal conversion using the remainder method. To convert 469_{10} to an octal number, we start our successive divisions by 8 using 469 as the initial dividend. Each successive dividend is the quotient of the previous division. As in Figure A-3, we divide until we've reached a zero quotient and form the converted number by taking the remainders in reverse order.

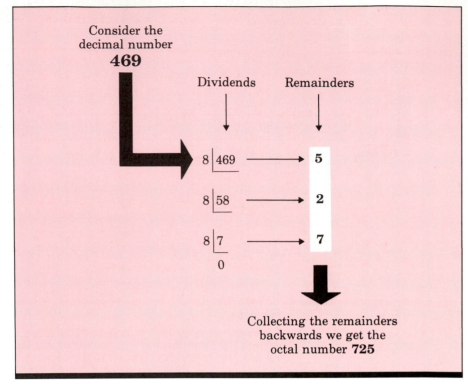

Consider the decimal number **469**

Dividends   Remainders

8 | 469 ⟶ **5**

8 | 58 ⟶ **2**

8 | 7 ⟶ **7**

    0

Collecting the remainders backwards we get the octal number **725**

or 111001011110_2. To convert the other way, from base 2 to base 8, we go through the reverse process. If the number of digits in the binary number is not divisible by 3, we add leading zeros to the binary number to force an even division. Thus, for example, to convert 1101100011_2 to base 8, we get

$$001 \quad 101 \quad 100 \quad 011$$
$$1 \qquad 5 \qquad 4 \qquad 3$$

or 1543_8. Note that two leading zeros were added to make this conversion.

FIGURE A-6

Octal characters and their binary counterparts.

Octal Character	Binary Equivalent
0	000
1	001
2	010
3	011
4	100
5	101
6	110
7	111

Often diagnostic messages are output to programmers in hexadecimal (or *hex*) notation. Hex is a shorthand method for representing the 8-bit bytes that are stored in the computer system.

Hexadecimal means base 16, implying that there are 16 different symbols in this numbering system. Since we have only 10 possible digits to work with, letters are used instead of numbers for the extra 6 symbols. The 16 hexadecimal symbols and their decimal and binary counterparts are shown in Figure A-7.

Hexadecimal, like octal, is not itself a code the computer uses to perform computations or to communicate with other machines. It does, however, have a special relationship to the 8-bit bytes of EBCDIC and ASCII-8 that makes it ideal for displaying messages quickly. As you can see in Figure A-7, each hex character has a 4-binary-bit counterpart, so any combination of 8 bits can be represented by exactly two hexadecimal characters. Thus, the letter *A* (represented in EBCDIC by 11000001) has a hex representation of C1.

Let's look at an example to see how to convert from hex to decimal. Suppose you receive the following message on your display screen:

PROGRAM LOADED AT LOCATION 4F6A

This message tells you the location in primary memory of the first byte in your program. To determine the decimal equivalent of a hexadecimal num-

FIGURE A-7

Hexadecimal characters and their decimal and binary equivalents.

Hexadecimal Character	Decimal Equivalent	Binary Equivalent
0	0	0000
1	1	0001
2	2	0010
3	3	0011
4	4	0100
5	5	0101
6	6	0110
7	7	0111
8	8	1000
9	9	1001
A	10	1010
B	11	1011
C	12	1100
D	13	1101
E	14	1110
F	15	1111

ber such as 4F6A, you can use a procedure similar to the binary-to-decimal conversion shown in Figure A-2 (refer to Figure A-8).

To convert the other way—from decimal to hex—we again can use the remainder method, this time dividing by 16. A decimal-to-hex conversion using the remainder method is illustrated in Figure A-9.

To convert from base 16 to base 2, we convert each hex digit separately to four binary digits (using the table in Figure A-7). Thus, for example, to convert F6A9 to base 2, we get

$$\begin{array}{cccc} \text{F} & 6 & \text{A} & 9 \\ 1111 & 0110 & 1010 & 1001 \end{array}$$

or 1111011010101001_2. To convert from base 2 to base 16, we go through the reverse process. If the number of digits in the binary number is not divisible by 4, we add leading zeros to the binary number to force an even division. So, for example, to convert 1101101010011_2 to base 16, we get

$$\begin{array}{cccc} 0001 & 1011 & 0101 & 0011 \\ 1 & \text{B} & 5 & 3 \end{array}$$

or $1B53_{16}$. Note that three leading zeros were added to make this conversion.

A table summarizing all of the conversions covered in this appendix is provided in Figure A-10.

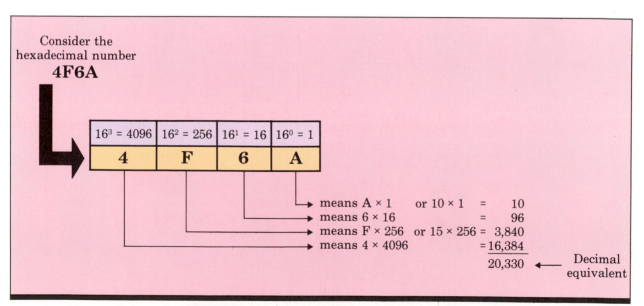

FIGURE A-8

Hexadecimal-to-decimal conversion. To convert any hexadecimal number to its decimal counterpart, take the rightmost digit and multiply it by 16^0 (or 1), the next to rightmost digit and multiply it by 16^1 (or 16), and so on, as illustrated here. Then add up all the products so formed.

FIGURE A-9

Decimal-to-hexadecimal conversion using the remainder method. To convert 20330_{10} to a hexadecimal number, we start our successive divisions by 16 using 20330 as the initial dividend. Each successive dividend is the quotient of the previous division. As in Figure A-3, we divide until we've reached a zero quotient and form the converted number by taking the remainders in reverse order.

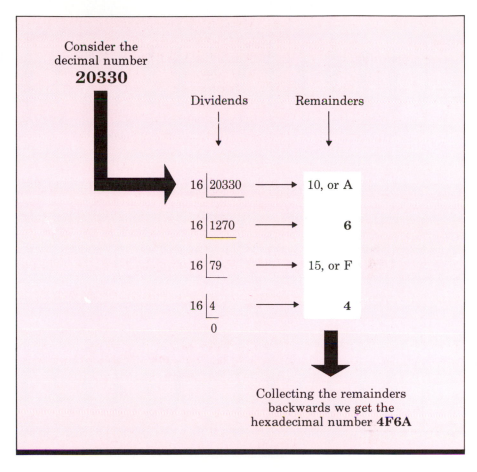

Consider the decimal number
20330

Dividends   Remainders

16 ⎹ 20330 ⟶ 10, or A

16 ⎹ 1270 ⟶ **6**

16 ⎹ 79 ⟶ 15, or F

16 ⎹ 4 ⟶ **4**

0

Collecting the remainders backwards we get the hexadecimal number **4F6A**

SUMMARY AND KEY TERMS

A *number system* is a way of representing numbers.

The number system we most commonly use is called the **decimal,** or base 10, system. It is called base 10 because it uses 10 symbols—the digits 0, 1, 2, 3, 4, 5, 6, 7, 8, 9—to represent all possible numbers. The position of each symbol in any decimal number represents the number 10 (the base number) raised to a power, or exponent, which is based on that position.

The **binary,** or base 2, system works in a manner similar to the decimal system. One major difference is that the binary system has only two symbols—0 and 1—instead of ten. A second major difference is that the position of each digit in a binary number represents the number 2 (the base number) raised to an exponent based on that position.

From Base	To Base			
	2	8	10	16
2		Starting at rightmost digit, convert each group of three binary digits to an octal digit.	Starting at rightmost digit, multiply binary digits by 2^0, 2^1, 2^2, etc., respectively. Then add products.	Starting at rightmost digit, convert each group of four binary digits to a hex digit.
8	Convert each octal digit to three binary digits.		Starting at rightmost digit, multiply octal digits by 8^0, 8^1, 8^2, etc., respectively. Then add products.	Convert to base 2; then to base 16.
10	Divide repeatedly by 2; then collect remainders in reverse order.	Divide repeatedly by 8; then collect remainders in reverse order.		Divide repeatedly by 16; then collect remainders in reverse order.
16	Convert each hex digit to four binary digits.	Convert to base 2; then to base 8.	Starting at rightmost digit, multiply hex digits by 16^0, 16^1, 16^2, etc., respectively. Then add products.	

Because large binary numbers can be easily misread by programmers, binary digits often are grouped into units of three or four that, in turn, are represented by other symbols. The **octal,** or base 8, numbering system corresponds to a grouping of three binary digits. The octal system has eight symbols—0, 1, 2, 3, 4, 5, 6, 7. The position of each digit in an octal number represents the number 8 raised to an exponent based on that position.

The **hexadecimal,** or base 16, system is used to represent a grouping of four binary digits. There are 16 different symbols in this system. Since we have only ten possible digits to work with, the letters A–F are used instead of numbers for the extra six symbols. The position of each digit in a hexadecimal number represents the number 16 raised to an exponent based on that position.

It is a relatively straightforward process to convert any value in one numbering system into a value in another system.

Instructions: Provide an answer to each of the following questions.

1. Convert the following binary numbers to decimal numbers.
   a. 1011_2 _____
   b. 101110_2 _____
   c. 1010011_2 _____

2. Convert the following octal numbers to decimal numbers:
   a. 17_8 _____
   b. 275_8 _____
   c. 3106_8 _____

3. Convert the following decimal numbers to binary numbers:
   a. 51_{10} _____
   b. 260_{10} _____
   c. 500_{10} _____

4. Convert the following decimal numbers to octal numbers:
   a. 92_{10} _____
   b. 153_{10} _____
   c. 6133_{10} _____

5. Convert the following binary numbers to hexadecimal numbers:
   a. 101_2 _____
   b. 11010_2 _____
   c. 111101000010_2 _____

6. Convert the following binary numbers to octal numbers:
   a. 11_2 _____
   b. 1010_2 _____
   c. 10011101000001_2 _____

7. Convert the following hexadecimal numbers to binary numbers:
   a. $F2_{16}$ _____
   b. $1A8_{16}$ _____
   c. $39EB_{16}$ _____

8. Convert the following hexadecimal numbers to decimal numbers:
   a. $B6_{16}$ _____
   b. $5E9_{16}$ _____
   c. $CAFF_{16}$ _____

9. Convert 72_8 to hexadecimal.

10. Drawing on techniques you've learned in this appendix, how would you convert the base 6 (yes, six) number 451_6 to a decimal number?

1. a. 11
   b. 46
   c. 83

2. a. 15
   b. 189
   c. 1606

3. a. 110011
   b. 100000100
   c. 111110100

4. a. 134
   b. 231
   c. 13765

5. a. 5
   b. 1A
   c. F42

6. a. 3
   b. 12
   c. 23501

7. a. 11110010
   b. 000110101000
   c. 0011100111101011

8. a. 182
   b. 1513
   c. 51967

9. 3A

10. $(4 \times 6^2) + (5 \times 6^1) + (1 \times 6^0) = 175$

A Beginner's Guide to BASIC

BASIC (Beginner's All-purpose Symbolic Instruction Code) is one of many programming languages widely in use today. A programming language is a set of rules used to create a computer program. The computer program is what you enter into the computer system to produce results.

A BASIC computer program is very similar to a recipe. It consists of a list of instructions the computer must carry out in a specified sequence to produce the desired result. Each of the instructions in a BASIC program must be written in strict accordance with the rules of the BASIC language. These rules are referred to as syntax. If you make a seemingly trivial syntax error in writing the program, such as misspelling a word or omitting a comma, the computer system will reject your program or give unexpected, incorrect results.

The purpose of this Appendix is to teach you how to write useful, simple BASIC programs. BASIC is one of the easiest to learn of all the major programming languages. You should be able to create programs for business use, game playing, and performing difficult, repetitive computations after reading this Appendix and practicing on a computer.

Many versions of the BASIC language are available today. This Appendix has been written to conform as closely as possible to the most common BASIC usage, the guidelines for minimal BASIC proposed by the American National Standards Institute (ANSI). Thus, the programs that follow will work on most machines. In this Appendix, program outputs are distinguished from programs and their inputs by a color background.

The need to practice BASIC on a computer can't be emphasized enough. Programming, like driving a car or playing a sport, is a skill that is mastered mostly by practice. Since it is easy for a beginner in any endeavor to make mistakes at the beginning, practicing can initially be very frustrating (can you remember your first day with a musical instrument?). However, if you really want to learn BASIC, and if you start by writing simple programs rather than complicated ones, you will find BASIC relatively easy. So, be patient—and start playing with your computer as soon as possible.

Here's what's on the following pages.

Section 1
A BASIC Primer

A SIMPLE EXAMPLE

Let's get into BASIC immediately by looking at a relatively simple problem and developing a BASIC program to solve it. The example given in Figure B1-1 will show you both some of the rules of BASIC and the manner in which computers carry out instructions in a logical, step-by-step fashion.

The problem is to write a BASIC program that adds the numbers 8 and 16. We want the computer to print the answer like this:

THE ANSWER IS 24

There are many ways to solve this problem, including the one shown in Figure B1-1.

The six numbered instructions in the figure make up a *BASIC program*. In most cases, you will be typing in instructions such as these at a keyboard hooked up to a computer. When you have finished typing the instructions, you then normally type the word RUN to command the system to execute (that is, to carry out) your program. You should study this program carefully before proceeding further. Sometimes the purpose of an instruction will be obvious. The following comments should clarify the other instructions.

Before we go into detail about precisely how the program works, you should observe the following important points about the program in Figure B1-1:

1. Each of the six numbered instructions is a *BASIC program statement.* The computer completes the operation described in each statement. It then automatically moves on to another statement.

   Each BASIC program statement begins with a key word that tells the computer what type of operation is involved: for example, REM, READ, LET, PRINT, DATA, and END. These key words may be thought of as the vocabulary of the

FIGURE B1-1
A simple BASIC program.

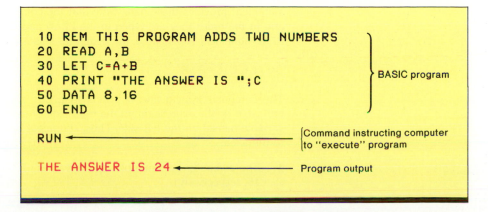

```
10  REM THIS PROGRAM ADDS TWO NUMBERS  ⎫
20  READ A,B                           ⎪
30  LET C=A+B                          ⎬  BASIC program
40  PRINT "THE ANSWER IS ";C           ⎪
50  DATA 8,16                          ⎪
60  END                                ⎭

RUN ◀────────────────────  Command instructing computer
                           to "execute" program

THE ANSWER IS 24 ◀────────  Program output
```

computer system when you are writing BASIC programs. You must always stay strictly within this vocabulary. If, for example, you substitute DATUM or DATTA for DATA in line 50, the computer system will not know what you want to do.

2. Each program statement is identified by a *line number;* for example, 10, 20, 30, and so on. Line numbers are normally written in increments of 10 rather than 1, which allows you easily to insert new statements in the program later. All line numbers must be integers (whole numbers), and all lines must have different line numbers.

   The computer will always execute statements in the sequence specified by the line numbers unless instructed to do otherwise. Ways to do this are discussed later in this section. Because the line numbers specify the order of program statements, you can type in the lines in any order, such as 30, 60, 10, 50, 20, and 40. Before the computer system runs your program, it will automatically put all the statements in proper order (by line number).

3. In this program three *variables* (A, B, and C) are used. When the computer system begins to execute the program, it will set up separate storage locations for A, B, and C. A storage location can be thought of as a "bucket" that can hold only one item (for example, a number) at a time.

   The storage locations represent the memory of the computer with respect to the program being run. For example, when we ask the computer in line 40 to print the value of C, the computer consults its memory to find the value.

   It is possible, as we will see in later programs, to change the values of variables such as A, B, and C several times during the execution of a program. It is because their values are allowed to change that they are known as variables. When A, B, and C are given new values, their old values are lost.

Now let's see, statement by statement, how the program works.

```
10 REM THIS PROGRAM ADDS TWO NUMBERS
```

The REM (remark) statement is actually ignored by the computer. However, even though the computer doesn't use it, the REM statement is very helpful. It allows you to place informative comments (such as the program title or description) in the body of the program.

```
20 READ A,B and 50 DATA 8,16
```

The READ and DATA statements are always used together in BASIC. The READ statement instructs the computer to assign data to the specified variables. The DATA statement provides these data. Note that the computer assigns values one at a time and in the order they are typed in the READ and DATA statements. Thus, when the READ statement is executed, the computer sets A equal to 8 and B equal to 16.

```
30 LET C=A+B
```

The computer system always reacts to a LET statement by computing the value indicated by the expression on the right side of the "=" sign and assigning it to the variable named on the left side. Thus, statement 30 will cause the following actions to be taken:

1. The computer system looks up the values of A and B in memory (finding 8 and 16, respectively).

2. The values of A and B are added (producing 24).

3. The value of the right side of the expression (24) is assigned to C.

```
40 PRINT "THE ANSWER IS ";C
```

The PRINT statement is used when we want the computer system to output something, for example, the results of a computation. The PRINT statement above consists of three elements:

1. A phrase appearing inside quotes (THE ANSWER IS). The computer system will print this phrase exactly as it appears. These *literal* phrases are handy in PRINT statements to label output.

2. A formatting character (;). The semicolon instructs the computer system to leave only one space between the literal phrase and the value of C.

3. A variable (C). The computer system will look up the value of C in memory and print its value.

If you are using a display device, PRINT instructs the computer to display the information on the screen. On IBM microcomputer systems and many other machines, you must use the command LPRINT in your program if you wish to direct output to your printer instead.

```
60 END
```

On many computer systems, the END statement physically must be the last statement in the program. It instructs the computer system that the program is finished.

At this point, you can start to see how BASIC works. Now is a good time to test your knowledge of some of the fundamental concepts just introduced by practicing on your computer system. You might try some of the following suggestions:

1. Type and run the BASIC program in Figure B1-1. Did you get the same result as in this Appendix?

2. Try altering the PRINT statement so that it produces nicer output. For example, to get the computer system to output

```
THE SUM OF 8 AND 16 IS 24
```

your PRINT statement should look like

```
PRINT "THE SUM OF ";A;" AND ";B;" IS ";C
```

3. Try making the expression in statement 30 more complicated to see what the effects are. For example, A and B could be multiplied by specifying A * B instead of A + B in statement 30. Note that in BASIC an asterisk is used to tell the computer to multiply. Multiplication is explained in more detail later.

4. Tinker with the DATA statement by changing the data values (try some negative numbers or numbers with decimal points). Also, experiment to see if it matters where the DATA statement appears. Try placing it as the first, second, or third statement of your program.

Running BASIC programs is a relatively simple task and is described in some detail later in this section. All you need to concentrate on at this point are the RUN and LIST commands, as well as the instructions relating to correcting or changing lines. The RUN command executes your program and produces output. The LIST command will display the lines of your program in proper order on your display device. So get started now! If you can write simple programs today, the complicated ones you encounter later will seem much easier.

A TOUGHER EXAMPLE

The program we just looked at was rather simple. The values of the variables didn't change, and the computer wasn't asked to execute a statement out of numerical order. In most programs, however, the values of the variables do change, and the computer is asked to *branch* to a statement other than the one that immediately follows.

Let's now consider a program that reflects these two added complications. We will write a program to compute and output the squares of 8, 16, and 12.

Before *coding* (that is, writing out) this problem in BASIC, let's consider what tasks are involved in solving this problem. In addition, let's think about the order in which these tasks must be presented to the computer. The tasks themselves, together with the order in which they are performed, are referred to as an *algorithm*. Designing an algorithm is not that different from building a house. You don't start putting the roof together before you've fully designed the whole structure and decided when the roof will be made relative to other sections.

At first glance, it seems that the following algorithm is attractive for solving our problem:

1. Read a number.
2. Square the number.
3. Print out the result of step 2.
4. Return to step 1.

The fundamental structure involved here is called a *loop*. Thus, the computer system is to read 8, square it (producing 64), output the result (64), loop back to step 1, read 16, square it, and so on. There is one major problem with the four-step solution just described: Once the computer system fully processes the last number (12) and goes back to step 1, there are no more numbers to read. Thus, we need to instruct the loop when to stop. This problem is frequently solved by putting a *trailer* (or *sentinel*) *value* (such as -1) at the end of the data list and directing the computer to leave the loop immediately after this value is read. Thus, we could refine our algorithm as follows:

1. Read a number.
1.5 If the number $= -1$, go to step 5; otherwise process step 2.
2. Square the number.
3. Print out the result of step 2.
4. Return to step 1.
5. End the program.

Although this procedure is complete and produces correct results, many professional programmers include an extra "Read" step to make the procedure *structured*. Many programming languages (such as Pascal and COBOL) make it difficult to code satisfactory programs unless this extra step is taken. As you will learn later on, structured programs result in program logic that is easy to follow.

B-6

FIGURE B1-2

A program for computing and outputting the squares of several numbers.

```
 10 REM    TITLE:  PROGRAM B1-2
 20 REM    DESCRIPTION:  THIS PROGRAM READS
 30 REM    NUMBERS, SQUARES THEM, AND OUTPUTS
 40 REM    THE RESULTS.
 50 REM        AUTHOR - C.S. PARKER
 60 REM         DATE - 7/25/89
 70 REM ************VARIABLES**************
 80 REM      A = THE NUMBER TO BE SQUARED
 90 REM      B = THE SQUARE OF THE NUMBER
100 REM ********************************
110 READ A
120 IF A =-1 THEN 180
130 LET B=A^2
140 PRINT "THE SQUARE OF ";A;" IS ";B
150 READ A
160 GOTO 120
170 DATA 8,16,12,-1
180 END
RUN
THE SQUARE OF 8 IS 64
THE SQUARE OF 16 IS 256
THE SQUARE OF 12 IS 144
```

Inserting the extra Read step (step 3.5) and modifying step 4 so that it points back to step 1.5, we get

1. Read a number.
1.5 If the number = −1, go to step 5; otherwise process step 2.
2. Square the number.
3. Print out the result of step 2.
3.5 Read another number.
4. Return to step 1.5.
5. End the program.

Once the algorithm is completely designed, coding it in BASIC becomes relatively straightforward, as you will see by observing the program in Figure B1-2. The program has been liberally enhanced with REM statements; remember, these are ignored by the computer. It will take the computer 18 steps to execute this program fully, as shown in Figure B1-3. Later, in Section 3 of this Appendix, you will see that the IF and GOTO statements can be replaced by the WHILE and WEND statements, respectively, to form a functionally identical type of looping pattern.

WRITING ACCEPTABLE BASIC EXPRESSIONS

Now that we've covered some broad fundamentals concerning how BASIC works, let's consider more closely rules for writing BASIC instructions. This subsection addresses allowable characters, formation of variables and constants, and writing of mathematical expressions.

Step	Statement Executed	Value of A in Storage	Value of B in Storage	Action Taken
1	110	8		8 taken from data list and assigned to A
2	120	8		$8 \neq -1$; therefore, proceed to next statement
3	130	8	64	B computed
4	140	8	64	Computer system prints THE SQUARE OF 8 IS 64
5	150	16	64	16 taken from data list and assigned to A
6	160	16	64	Computer directed to line 120
7	120	16	64	$16 \neq -1$; therefore, proceed to next statement
8	130	16	256	B computed
9	140	16	256	Computer system prints THE SQUARE OF 16 IS 256
10	150	12	256	12 taken from data list and assigned to A
11	160	12	256	Computer directed to line 120
12	120	12	256	$12 \neq -1$; therefore, proceed to next statement
13	130	12	144	B computed
14	140	12	144	Computer system prints THE SQUARE OF 12 IS 144
15	150	-1	144	-1 taken from data list and assigned to A
16	160	-1	144	Computer directed to line 120
17	120	-1	144	$-1 = -1$; therefore, proceed to line 180
18	180	-1	144	The program ends

FIGURE B1-3
Steps the computer system must take to fully execute the problem in Figure B1-2.

BASIC Character Set

When you are typing in a program you must use only those characters that are understood by the version of BASIC available to your computer system. Such characters are known as the BASIC *character set*. They fall into three groups:

☐ Alphabetic: ABCDEFGHIJKLMNOPQRSTUVWXYZ

☐ Numeric: 0123456789

☐ Special: . , + & ! < > / @ ( ) - * = (and so on)

Variables

Variables are of two fundamental types: numeric and string. *Numeric variables* can be assigned only numbers, whereas *string variables* can be assigned any combination of alphabetic, numeric, and special characters. Let's look at numeric variables first.

Numeric Variables. The following program contains six numeric variables:

```
10 LET A=6.5
20 LET B=8.04
30 READ C1,C2,C3
```

```
40 LET D=A+B-(C1+C2+C3)
50 PRINT D
60 DATA 3,2,0.04
70 END
RUN
9.5
```

Each variable (A, B, C1, C2, C3, and D) is allocated a storage location by the computer at execution time. Each location may store a number while your program is executing.

BASIC varies in the way numeric variable names may be created by the programmer. The most universal convention is to allow the name to be composed of either

1. A single alphabetic character (for example, A, B, and D)

2. A single alphabetic character followed by a single digit (for example, C1, C2, and C3)

Thus, for example, the following numeric variable names are allowable under this convention:

```
C8, F1, X, I, I8, T
```

while the following are not:

☐ C12   Too many characters

☐ 8C   First character not alphabetic

☐ F&   Second character must be numeric

If your computer system was purchased within the past few years, it probably allows longer numeric variable names in BASIC—up to 40 characters long in many systems. This allows variable names to be chosen as better reminders of what the variables stand for. The first character must still be alphabetic; other characters can be letters or digits.

In this Appendix, we will stick with the older convention, since it will work on any computer system using BASIC.

String Variables. A *string* is a collection of related characters; for example,

```
JOHN Q. DOE
1600 PENNSYLVANIA AVENUE
THX-1138
```

Strings may be assigned to variable names and manipulated by computer systems. For example, the following program contains only string variables:

```
10 LET A$="AT THIS EXAMPLE"
20 LET B$="LOOK CAREFULLY "
30 PRINT B$;A$
40 END
RUN
LOOK CAREFULLY AT THIS EXAMPLE
```

There are two string variables in this short program: A$ and B$. The computer allocates storage space to string variables in essentially the same way it allocates storage to numeric variables. In other words, the storage location set up for A$ contains the string

AT THIS EXAMPLE

and the location set up for B$ contains the string

LOOK CAREFULLYb   (b represents a blank space)

Since A$ and B$ are variables, they can contain different strings throughout the course of the program, but only one string at any given time. An important difference between numeric and string variables is that we can perform conventional arithmetic with numeric variables but generally not with string ones.

BASIC varies in the way string variable names may be created by the programmer. The original and most universal rule is to use a single alphabetic character followed by a dollar sign ($). Thus, with this convention the following string variable names are allowable:

A$, B$, C$, T$, Z$

but the following are not:

☐ F1   Dollar sign is not second character

☐ P2$ Too many characters

☐ T   Dollar sign missing

☐ $ Leading alphabetic character missing

Again, many newer systems allow longer names.

Some computer systems require that the string assigned to a string variable be enclosed in quotes; for example,

```
10 READ A$
20 PRINT A$
30 DATA "EVERY GOOD BOY DOES FINE"
40 END
RUN
EVERY GOOD BOY DOES FINE
```

Constants

Like their variable counterparts, *constants* may be either numeric or string. Unlike variables, however, the value of a constant doesn't change (although constants can be assigned to variables, which can change).

Numeric Constants. A *numeric constant* is simply a number, for example, 81, −54, .001. When creating arithmetic expressions in BASIC, it is often useful to assign numbers to or to use numbers in combination with numeric variables. Some examples are

```
☐ 10 LET A=5.0          5.0 is a numeric constant
☐ 10 LET B=A+2          2 is a numeric constant
☐ 10 LET C=.01*A+B      .01 is a numeric constant
```

While the numeric constant chosen can be an integer number or a number with a decimal point, the use of commas or dollar signs is not allowed as part of the constant itself. The following are invalid representations of numeric constants in a BASIC program:

```
☐ 10 LET A=2,000        Comma invalid; LET A=2000 valid
☐ 100 DATA $6,$3.52     $ invalid; DATA 6,3.52 valid
```

In many cases we would like to precede a number by a $ sign. This can be done very simply, as the following short example suggests:

```
10 LET A=5.21
20 PRINT "$";A
30 END
RUN
$ 5.21
```

String Constants. A *string constant* is simply any collection of allowable BASIC characters enclosed in quotes; for example,

```
"HELLO 12?"
"GOODBYE MY LOVELY"
"145-86-7777"
```

String constants can be assigned to string variables, such as

```
10 LET A$="EVERY GOOD BOY DOES FINE"
```

or be declared independently of any variables, as in the following PRINT statement:

```
10 PRINT "THE VALUE OF INVENTORY IS $";X
```

A string constant is often referred to as a literal. On many computer systems, string constants appearing in DATA statements need not be enclosed in quotes.

Mathematical Expressions

BASIC allows the programmer to create complex mathematical expressions involving numeric variables and numeric constants. The following operations are permitted:

Operation	BASIC Symbol Used
Addition	+
Subtraction	−
Multiplication	*
Division	/
Exponentiation	^ or sometimes **

For example, suppose A = 1, B = 3, and C = 2. The following statements would produce the results indicated:

☐ 1 0   L E T   D = A + B - C   D is assigned a value of 2. The previous value of D is lost.

☐ 1 0   I F   B = A + C   T H E N   7 0   A+C is computed as 3. Since that is the value of B, the computer branches to statement 70.

☐ 1 0   L E T   C = B / 2   The right-hand side equals 1.5, which is assigned to C. The previous value of C is lost.

☐ 1 0   P R I N T   A * B   A and B are multiplied, and the product, 3, is printed.

Now consider a more complicated expression, such as:

$$1 0 \quad L E T \quad C = C - A + B / (C + 4)^{\wedge} 2$$

The question arises here as to which operation the computer will perform first. BASIC and many other languages recognize the following order of operations (commonly known as the *hierarchy of operations*):

1. All operations within parentheses are performed first, starting with the innermost set of parentheses.

2. Exponentiation is performed next.

3. Multiplication and division are performed next, and the computer executes these from left to right in the expression.

4. Addition and subtraction are performed last, also left to right.

Thus, the expression just given would be evaluated as follows under this set of rules:

Step	Operation Performed
1	(C + 4) evaluated; result is 6
2	6^2 evaluated; result is 36
3	B/36 evaluated; result is .083333
4	C − A evaluated; result is 1
5	1 is added to .083333; result is 1.083333
6	C is assigned the value 1.083333; the previous value of C is lost

To be fully sure that you understand the hierarchy of operations, you should study the following examples. Assume in the examples that W = 1, X = 2, Y = 3, Z = 4.

Example 1   1 0   L E T   A = Y / W * Z
A would be assigned a value of 12, since division and multiplication, being on the same level of hierarchy, are performed left to right.

Example 2 `10 LET B=(X+Y)*(W+1)^2`

B would be assigned a value of 20. Parenthetical expressions are evaluated first, then exponentiation, and finally multiplication.

Example 3 `LET C=((Z-W)*X)^2/2`

C would be assigned a value of 18. The computation in the innermost parentheses is performed first, yielding $Z-W=3$. Then contents of the outermost parentheses are evaluated, yielding $3*2=6$. After all of the parenthetical expressions are evaluated, the 6 is squared. Finally, the result of all the previous operations, 36, is halved to produce 18.

MORE ON ELEMENTARY BASIC STATEMENTS

So far, we've informally shown the use of the REM, READ, DATA, IF, LET, PRINT, GOTO, and END statements. Let's consider further the permissible usage of these statements.

READ and DATA Statements

As mentioned earlier, the READ and DATA statements are always used together. When a READ is executed, the computer will assign values appearing in the DATA statements to the respective variables named in the READ. The format of each of these statements is shown below:

> Line # READ list of variables (separated by commas)
> Line # DATA list of data items (separated by commas)

The DATA statements actually are never executed by the computer. Between the time the RUN command is issued and the program is executed, the computer system extracts all of the values from the DATA statements and prepares a "data list." It is this list that is referenced each time a READ is encountered. The DATA statement itself is ignored during program execution.

It is useful to think of a "pointer" attached to the data list. The pointer initially points to the first value in the data list. When this value is assigned, it then points to the second item, and so on. For example, consider the READ and DATA statements for the program in Figure B1-2. The pointer initially points to the 8. When statement 110 is executed, the 8 is assigned to A and the pointer moves to the 16; when the next READ (statement 150) is executed, 16 is assigned to A (the previous value, 8, being erased) and the pointer moves to the 12; and so on. When the -1 is finally assigned to A, the data list is exhausted.

There can be several DATA statements in a BASIC program, a fact that is observable in the solved review problems at the end of the section. In most implementations of BASIC, DATA statements can be placed anywhere before the END statement. It is critical to keep in mind that data are executed in the order they appear in the DATA statements, and if there are several DATA statements, the earliest of these will be used first.

IF Statement

The simplest form of the IF statement follows this format:

Line # IF relational-expression $\begin{Bmatrix} \text{THEN} \\ \text{GOTO} \end{Bmatrix}$ line number

A *relational expression* is one that contains one of the relational operators in the following table:

Operator	Meaning
<	Less than
<=	Less than or equal to
>	Greater than
>=	Greater than or equal to
=	Equal to
<>	Not equal to

For example, the following are allowable IF statements:

□ 10 IF A>B THEN 170
(A>B is the relational expression.)

□ 10 IF A-B<=C-D THEN 180
(A−B<=C−D is the relational expression.)

□ 10 IF A<>C*(D-E)^F THEN 220
(A<>C*(D−E)^F is the relational expression.)

The computer executes an IF statement as follows:

1. The expression on each side of the relational operator is computed, resulting in a single value on each side.

2. If the statement is true (for example, A>B, where A=3 and B=1), the computer branches to the statement number appearing after the THEN (or GOTO); otherwise the computer goes to the statement that appears immediately after the IF. The IF statement is an example of a *conditional branch*.

An IF statement can contain a relational expression involving string variables; for example,

          10 IF S$="LAST RECORD" THEN 220

Thus, if the string LAST RECORD were stored in S$, this statement would be true.

Later, in Section 3, we'll cover the IF/THEN/ELSE statement, a much more powerful form of the IF statement.

LET Statement

The LET statement typically uses the following format:

Line # LET variable-name = expression

An important requirement of this format is that only a single variable name is allowed to appear on the left-hand side of the = sign. Thus,

```
10 LET A=6*B-C^(N-1)
10 LET D=0
```

are allowable, whereas

```
LET A+B=C
```

is not. A single variable must appear on the left-hand side because once the right-hand side expression is computed down to a single value, a storage location (as represented by a single variable) must be declared to store this value. Remember, A, B, C, and so on are acceptable names for storage locations, whereas A+B is not.

The = sign of the LET statement is more properly referred to as an *assignment* (or *replacement*) *symbol* than an "is equal to." To understand the basis of this nomenclature, consider the perfectly acceptable BASIC statement

```
10 LET I=I+1
```

This statement makes absolutely no sense if we interpret the = sign as meaning "is equal to." However, if we interpret this statement as instructing the computer to determine the value of I+1 and to assign the number obtained back to I, it does make sense. Thus, if the value 6 were initially stored in I, this statement would add 6 to 1 and assign the result, 7, back to I (erasing the 6 that was there previously).

In most versions of BASIC, the appearance of the word LET is optional in a LET statement. Thus,

```
10 I=I+1
```

is perfectly acceptable.

PRINT Statement

The PRINT statement, being the main vehicle for obtaining BASIC output, is so pivotal that a separate section in this Appendix is devoted exclusively to its use (see Section 4). So far we have seen that one acceptable form of the PRINT statement is

$$\text{Line \# PRINT} \begin{Bmatrix} \text{literal,} \\ \text{variable, or} \\ \text{expression} \end{Bmatrix} ; \begin{Bmatrix} \text{literal,} \\ \text{variable, or} \\ \text{expression} \end{Bmatrix} ;...$$

Thus, the following statements are allowable:

☐ `50 PRINT "A=";A`
    If 6 is stored in A, the output is
    `A=6`
☐ `50 PRINT A;B;C*Z;M$`
    If 6 is stored in A, 72 in B, 16 in C, 2 in Z, and " ARE THE ANSWERS" in M$, the output is
    `6 72 32 ARE THE ANSWERS`

Problem Decomposition

Learning the Art of Breaking a Problem into Component Parts

One of the sad facts of life is that people often give up when trying to solve a complex problem. In many cases the problem is very solvable, but people just stare at it, become intimidated, and quit before even getting started.

An approach that many have used successfully when confronting a tough problem is to *decompose* it into easier-to-solve subproblems. For example, think about writing a textbook such as this one or even a novel. You don't start by writing the first page of Chapter 1, then the second page, and so on. You start by making a broad outline of what each chapter will cover. Then you need to expand each chapter outline to a more detailed list of topics. Once this "skeleton" is erected, you may then want to start writing some of the chapters you find most fascinating—making each of the chapters a project in itself, with its own set of goals and deadlines. And so forth. Most authors think decomposing a book project into manageable pieces is not only the most logical way, but also the *only* way to proceed.

Writing a computer program often involves a similar process of decomposition. It helps, for example, to decompose the program into the *output, input,* and *processing* required—and to take each of these details in turn. For example, say you're required to write a program such as the one in Problem 7, which computes the amount due from students. The *outputs* you must produce are the name of each student and the amount of his or her bill. The *inputs* you're given (i.e., the things that *vary* for each student considered) are the names of the students, credit hours, and scholarship amounts. You're also given a tuition fee formula and an activity fee schedule, but since those *don't vary* on input, they can be built into the *processing* logic of the program.

You can decompose the processing logic further, as follows:

□ `50 PRINT A$;B$`

If "HIGH " is stored in A$ and "SCHOOL" in B$, the output is

```
HIGH SCHOOL
```

Other versions of the PRINT statement are covered in Section 4.

GOTO Statement

The simple format of the GOTO statement is

Line # GOTO line-number

This makes it one of the easiest BASIC statements to use. For example,

```
200 GOTO 810
```

will direct the computer to statement 810. The GOTO statement is an example of an *unconditional branch.*

1. Determine *activity fee* from the credit hours taken and activity fee schedule. (This can be done by building the activity fee schedule into one or more IF statements.)

2. Determine *tuition* by multiplying credit hours by $100. (This can be done by a LET statement.)

3. Determine *billing amount* by adding the values found in steps 1 and 2 and subtracting the scholarship amount. (This can be done by a LET statement.)

Thus the solution algorithm is something like the following:

1. Read the record of a student.

2. Go through the series of processing steps.

3. Print results.

4. Loop back to next record.

Of course, you'll also need to build a mechanism into the algorithm to get it to stop when it finishes the last record.

Before you design an algorithm, it's always best to do a few computations by hand to make sure you fully understand the problem and the mental processes you are going through to solve it. Later, when you code the algorithm and get output, it's also important to check the output against hand computations to make sure the program is producing correct results.

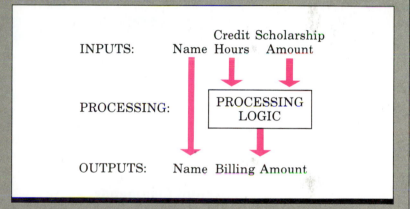

If you thought about it awhile, the decomposed problem might look like this.

Perhaps because of its simplicity, the GOTO statement is frequently overused, leading to programs that are difficult or impossible for a human to follow or "debug" easily. You should never GOTO another GOTO statement. In any case, GOTO should be used as little as possible.

REM Statement

The REM (remark) statement is a very important tool in BASIC, even though it is completely ignored by the computer when the program is executed. Its purpose is to allow you to put useful comments, or blank lines, in the program listing. The format of the REM statement is

Line # REM any remark

REMs can appear anywhere in a program. In some implementations, they must appear before the END statement.

END Statement

Generally the END statement is physically the last statement in the program; that is, it is the statement with the highest line number. When the computer encounters this statement, it terminates execution of your program. The format of the END statement is

Line # END

Some versions of BASIC do not require an END statement; however, its use is highly recommended, because it leaves no doubt in anyone's mind as to where the program ends. The END statement is frequently used in combination with the STOP statement. The STOP statement is discussed in Section 3.

DEVELOPING AND RUNNING BASIC PROGRAMS ON YOUR COMPUTER SYSTEM

Now that we've covered how to write simple BASIC programs, it's time to consider how to develop and run them on your computer system. Systems vary tremendously with regard to the specific forms of the system commands used. Fortunately, most of them have the same types of commands. These systems often differ only in the specific ways in which the commands must be typed.

System Commands

There are two major types of commands that you will use to write and run BASIC programs on your computer: *BASIC statement commands* (which are the BASIC program statements in the lines of your program) and *BASIC system commands* (which are outside of your program). We have already covered several statement commands (READ, PRINT, GOTO, and so on). These commands instruct the computer system what to do while it is executing your program.

System commands, on the other hand, are often used to tell the computer to do something before or after it executes the program. Two examples are RUN and LIST. Some examples of common system actions, and how they are implemented on several microcomputer systems, are given in Figure B1-4. The form of these commands on larger computer systems is similar. You should check the system commands for your particular computer.

Interacting with Your System

Let's say you want to "try out" your computer system by typing in the squares program of Figure B1-2. You would type in all 18 lines, pressing the Enter (or Return) key after each line, as usual. Many versions of BASIC will check each statement for correct form *(or syntax)* when you press Enter. Thus, suppose you fumble at the keyboard while typing in the eleventh line of your program, producing

```
110 READD A
```

Action Desired	IBM PS/2, IBM PC, and Compatibles (Disk BASIC)	Apple II (Applesoft BASIC)	Apple Macintosh (MS-BASIC)
Turn on System	Power switch is usually on right side of system unit	Power switch is at left rear of system unit	Power switch is at left rear of system unit
Log into System	Respond to date and time prompts	No response	Insert appropriate disk
Starting BASIC			
User response	Type BASICA (for IBM) or GWBASIC (for compatibles) to A> prompt	System comes up in BASIC, so begin typing program	Insert MS-BASIC disk
Computer response	OK		Display disk directory
User response	Begin typing program		Double click MS-BASIC icon
Computer response			Command box appears
User response			Begin typing program
System Commands*			
List program	LIST	LIST	LIST
Run program	RUN	RUN	RUN
Delete a line	DELETE line #	Type line #, then hit Enter key	Type line #, then hit Enter key
Save program	SAVE "filename"	SAVE filename	SAVE filename
Retrieve program	LOAD "filename"	LOAD filename	LOAD OPEN filename
Delete a program	KILL "filename.BAS"	DELETE filename	DELETE filename
Clear memory†	NEW	NEW	NEW
Obtain list of files	FILES	CATALOG	Files automatically appear
Log Off System			
User response	No response	No response	Select QUIT from File menu
Computer response	No response	No response	Displays directory
User response	Turn power off	Turn power off	Select CLOSE Then, from File menu, select EJECT to leave BASIC Turn power off

*Disk-based system assumed throughout. Commands on some computer systems can be typed or selected from a menu.
†Memory should be cleared (erased) before a program is retrieved or keyed in. Not clearing memory can result in the new program's being inadvertently merged with the program currently in memory.

FIGURE B1-4

System commands on three microcomputer systems.

Your keyboard probably has a backspace key that will let you fix the error if you have not hit the Enter key. If you have already hit the Enter key to send the faulty line to the computer system, the following error message might be sent to the output device:

INVALID COMMAND

At this point you may have to retype the entire line, including the line number.* The computer system will then replace the old line 110 with the corrected version.

When you have finished typing your program, you will probably be anxious for the computer to execute it immediately. Most systems require the user to type in the command

```
RUN
```

After you issue this command, one of the following will happen:

1. The program will run successfully, producing the correct answers.

2. The program will run, but produce incorrect answers. This might happen if, for example, you typed in line 130 of the squares program as

```
130 LET B=A^3
```

The program would then produce cubes of numbers instead of squares! Thus, it is important that you look at your output carefully before you decide that your program works.

3. The program stops unexpectedly in the middle of a run. This would happen in the squares program if line 170 were typed in as follows:

```
170 DATA 8,16,"HELLO",12,-1
```

The program would compute the squares of 8 and 16 successfully, but would stop (or abort) when it tried to assign the string "HELLO" to the numeric variable A. When BASIC runs into this situation while running the program, it is likely to display a message such as

```
ATTEMPT TO READ INVALID DATA ON LINE 150
```

and halt. At this point you must correct the error, or *bug,* in the program and try again. Learning how to correct, or *debug,* faulty programs is one of the most important skills you must develop to program well. As unusual as it may seem, even a good programmer can easily spend 50 percent of the time it takes to develop a program in getting rid of bugs in it. This subject will be addressed in more detail later on.

SOLVED REVIEW PROBLEMS

Example 1

Company X has anywhere from five to twenty students employed on a part-time basis during the summer. This past week five students were on the payroll. The students each worked different hours at different rates of pay, as shown in the following table:

---

*Most keyboards sold today have an Insert key, a Delete key, and a set of four arrow keys to enable you to rapidly edit your programs. On many computer systems, you can correct an error by first displaying the line containing the error, then moving to the point of the error with one of the arrow keys, then using the Insert or Delete key to make the correction, and finally entering the change by pressing the Enter key.

Student Name	Hours Worked	Rate of Pay
John Smith	20	$5.40
Nancy Jones	15	5.60
Bo Weeks	25	5.00
Millicent Smythe	40	4.80
Joe Johnson	20	5.10

The company would like you to write a BASIC program to compute and print the total pay due each student.

Solution

The program must successively read a number of *records.* Consequently, a looping structure similar to the one in the program of Figure B1-2 will be required. Each record will contain a name, hours worked, and a rate of pay—that is, a row of data from the preceding table. The number of records varies from week to week, so it will be convenient to employ a trailer record to enable the program to terminate. These considerations lead to the program in Figure B1-5, which you should study carefully.

FIGURE B1-5

A program for computing the pay due employees.

```
10 REM THIS PROGRAM COMPUTES EMPLOYEE PAY
20 REM    AUTHOR: C.S. PARKER
30 REM ************VARIABLES*************
40 REM    S$ = EMPLOYEE NAME
50 REM    H  = HOURS WORKED
60 REM    P  = HOURLY PAY RATE
70 REM    D  = PAY DUE
80 REM *********************************
90 READ S$,H,P
100 IF S$ = "LAST RECORD" THEN 230
110 D=H*P
120 PRINT S$;" HAS EARNED   $";D
130 READ S$,H,P
140 GOTO 100
150 REM *********DATA STATEMENTS*********
160 DATA "JOHN SMITH",20,5.40
170 DATA "NANCY JONES",15,5.60
180 DATA "BO WEEKS",25,5.00
190 DATA "MILLICENT SMYTHE",40,4.80
200 DATA "JOE JOHNSON",20,5.10
210 DATA "LAST RECORD",0,0
220 REM *********************************
230 END
RUN
JOHN SMITH HAS EARNED  $ 108
NANCY JONES HAS EARNED  $ 84
BO WEEKS HAS EARNED  $ 125
MILLICENT SMYTHE HAS EARNED  $ 192
JOE JOHNSON HAS EARNED  $ 102
```

Before we leave this example, let's consider some of the problems we might have run into if there were errors in the program. Also, we'll explore how we might correct such errors.

First, suppose we had typed in line 110 as follows:

```
110 D=H*R
```

When the computer encounters this statement, it has a value for S$, H, and P. However, it doesn't have a clue as to what R is, since we never assigned a value to it. In most versions of BASIC, when the computer is requested to use the value of a variable it hasn't yet encountered during execution, it assumes the value is zero. Naturally this can lead to some very surprising results in your programs. In the current problem, your program would show that everyone has earned $0.

You should quickly be able to find an error like the one just described by making a few simple deductions. For example, since all the values of D are printing as 0 and D is computed by H*R, either H or R (or both of these variables) is equal to zero.

As a second example, suppose we had mistakenly typed in line 190 as follows:

```
190 DATA 40,"MILLICENT SMYTHE",4.80
```

The computer would execute our program successfully until it had printed out

```
BO WEEKS HAS EARNED $125
```

Then we might receive a message such as the following:

```
ATTEMPT TO READ INVALID DATA ON LINE 130
```

These two lines of output give us a clue to the error. The computer successfully completed the processing of Bo Weeks's record but subsequently "bombed" on line 130. Thus, something must be amiss with the data in the next record. Now we would notice that the number 40 and "MILLICENT SMYTHE" are switched around, and BASIC cannot assign a string constant to a numeric variable.

Debugging programs is a skill that involves a lot of practice. You must learn to make deductions from the information given by the computer system (i.e., partial output, incorrect output, and error messages) to determine the source of the error.

Another technique that's recommended for particularly hard-to-find errors is the so-called dummy (diagnostic) PRINT statement. Suppose again that for line 110 you had typed

```
110 D=H*R
```

You have deduced that either H, R, or both of these variables are zero, but you still can't put your finger on the error. However, you could now type the statement

```
115 PRINT "H ="; H;" R =";R
```

The computer system would then respond with the following outputs after you typed RUN:

```
H = 20   R = 0
JOHN SMITH HAS EARNED   $ 0
H - 15   R = 0
NANCY JONES HAS EARNED   $ 0
```

and so on. Now the source of the error is obvious: R is zero for every record in the program.

Once the dummy PRINT statement has served its purpose of uncovering the error and the error has been corrected, statement 115 should be deleted so that it won't interfere with the normal output of the program. The form for doing this may be

```
DELETE 115
```

on your system, or you may be able to type simply

```
115
```

and press Enter (replacing the old statement 115 with a blank statement).

Example 2
ABC Company has a file that keeps the following information on employees:

- [ ] Name
- [ ] Sex (M or F)
- [ ] Age
- [ ] Department

The file has approximately 1,000 employees, although the exact number is usually unknown. Write a BASIC program that will print out the names of all females over age 40 who work in the accounting department.

Solution
This program involves a series of three IF statements that pose the three conditions we wish to check in each record: in other words, female?, over 40?, and accounting? If a record passes all three checks, we print the associated name; otherwise we read the next record.

Since the data file is not given, we'll make up five "program test records" (including a trailer record) to illustrate how the program works. The program is shown in Figure B1-6.

```
 10 REM THIS PROGRAM SELECTS FROM A FILE ALL
 20 REM FEMALE EMPLOYEES OVER 40 WHO WORK IN
 30 REM THE ACCOUNTING DEPARTMENT
 40 REM    AUTHOR - C.S. PARKER
 50 REM ***********VARIABLES***************
 60 REM    N$ = EMPLOYEE NAME
 70 REM    S$ = SEX
 80 REM    A  = AGE
 90 REM    D$ = DEPARTMENT
100 REM ********************************
110 READ N$,S$,A,D$
120 IF N$="LAST RECORD" THEN 260
130 IF S$="M" THEN 170
140 IF A<=40 THEN 170
150 IF D$<>"ACCOUNTING" THEN 170
160 PRINT N$
170 READ N$,S$,A,D$
180 GOTO 120
190 REM **********DATA STATEMENTS***********
200 DATA "JANE CRIBBS","F",25,"ACCOUNTING"
210 DATA "PHIL JONES","M",45,"ACCOUNTING"
220 DATA "ANNE WELLES","F",42,"ACCOUNTING"
230 DATA "MARY SMITH","F",41,"FINANCE"
240 DATA "LAST RECORD","X",99,"NONE"
250 REM ********************************
260 END
RUN
ANNE WELLES
```

EXERCISES

Instructions: Provide an answer to each of the following questions.

1. Categorize the following variables as numeric, string, or invalid:
   a. A   b. 6F   c. D1   d. B$ e. $R   f. I

2. Write a valid LET statement for each of the following formulas:

   a. $C = \sqrt{A^2 + B^2}$ c. $R = \dfrac{S + T}{U - V} - Y$

   b. $A = \left(\dfrac{B + C}{D}\right)E$ d. $A = \dfrac{3(B - 1)}{T + 2}$

3. Given $A = 2$, $B = 5$, and $C = 6$, determine the value of X in the following BASIC expressions:
   a. X=(A+B)*C   c. X=(A+C/A+1)^2/2
   b. X=C/A*B   d. X=((3*A)*B)/C-4

B-24

4. Identify the syntax errors, if any, in the following BASIC statements:

a. `10  GOTO  10  IF  X = Y`

b. `10  LET  X + Y = Z`

c. `98  IF  X - Y < = C - D  THEN  200`

d. `20  LET  F$ = F + 5.23`

5. In the expression

$$X = (Y + Z) \wedge 2 - 2 * B$$

which operation does the computer do

a. first?

c. third?

b. second?

d. last?

PROGRAMMING PROBLEMS

Instructions: Write a BASIC program to do each of the following tasks.

1. Find the sum of each of the following pairs of numbers.

> 6 and 8
>
> 13 and 25
>
> 14 and 33
>
> 19 and 41

Use trailer values at the end of your data list so that your program can sense when there are no more data.

2. Following are three sets of data. Each set of data has four variables: A, B, C, and D:

	Variables			
Set	A	B	C	D
1	8	15	10	4
2	6	5	3	2
3	4	0	5	2

Plug the values in each set of data into the following formula, and print out the results:

$$X = A - B * C + A / D$$

3. Salespeople at XYZ Company are paid a base salary of $10,000. This salary may be augmented by commissions, which are equal to 10 percent of gross sales, and by a bonus of $500. The bonus is awarded only to salespeople with over $80,000 in gross sales. Compute and output the amounts earned by each of these salespeople:

Salesperson	Gross Sales
Carlos Ortiz	$90,000
Jill Johnson	$70,000
Don Williams	$20,000
Dee Jones	$95,000
Al Ennis	$40,000

Your output should include the name of each salesperson and his or her earnings. Use trailer values at the end of your data list so that your program can sense when there are no more data.

4. Solve Problem 3 assuming that the commission is computed as follows:

If Gross Sales Are in the Range	The Commission Rate Is
$ 1–$30,000	6%
$30,001–$60,000	8%
$60,001–$80,000	10%
$80,001 and above	12%

Assume also that the bonus is still in effect.

5. Grades in a course are awarded as follows: 90 and above = A, 80–89 = B, 70–79 = C, 60–69 = D, below 60 = F. Write a BASIC program that reads the following data and assigns letter grades:

Social Security Number	Score
182-66-1919	63
321-76-4344	81
821-66-0045	90
376-38-3202	54
802-11-1481	79
346-49-8911	75

Your output should include the social security number of each student and that student's letter grade. Use trailer values at the end of your data list so that your program can sense when there are no more items to be read.

6. A company running a copying service charges the following rates:

The first 500 copies are billed at 5 cents per copy
The next 500 copies are billed at 4 cents per copy
Any additional copies are billed at 3 cents per copy

Compute and output the amount each of the following customers is to be billed:

Customer	Copies
XYZ Amalgamated	1200
ABC Industries	200
TR Systems Limited	800

Your output should include the name of each customer as well as the billing amount. Use trailer values at the end of your data list so that your program can sense when there are no more data.

7. Students at a university are billed as follows:

$$\text{Tuition} = \$100 \text{ per credit hour}$$
$$\text{Activity fee} = \begin{array}{l} \$30 \text{ for 6 hours or less} \\ \$60 \text{ for 7–12 hours} \\ \$75 \text{ for more than 12 hours} \end{array}$$

The total amount a student will be billed each semester is computed by the following formula:

$$\text{Tuition fee} + \text{Activity fee} - \text{Scholarship}$$

Compute the amounts due from the following students:

Student Name	Credit Hours This Semester	Scholarship Amount
Ed Begay	15	$700
Bill Mendoza	8	0
John Williams	3	0
Nancy Jones	12	500
Dennis Hall	6	0

Your output should include the name of each student as well as the billing amount. Use trailer values at the end of your data list so that your program can sense when there are no more data. [*Hint:* See box on page B-16.]

Section 2
Program Design Techniques

INTRODUCTION

As mentioned earlier, the design of computer programs requires considerable care. Programs used to help run businesses are usually in operation for several years, and they need to be constantly modified to meet changing business conditions. Thus, a program that is designed in a hasty fashion will often cause numerous maintenance problems over the years for programmers who have to keep it up to date. Simply stated, poorly designed programs are almost always expensive headaches. A few extra dollars spent on initial design may save hundreds of dollars later.

Many techniques have been employed over the years to design computer programs. Two of the most widely used are flowcharts and pseudocode.

FLOWCHARTS AND PSEUDOCODE

Program flowcharts, dating back to the 1940s, are among the oldest tools used to design programs. A program flowchart is a diagram that shows the flow of logic behind a computer program. For example, the flowchart in Figure B2-1 outlines the logic of the program shown in Figure B1-2. Shown alongside the program and flowchart is the corresponding pseudocode. Pseudocode is an alternate means of depicting the logic behind a computer program.

Flowcharts. As you can see from the example, a program flowchart consists of geometric symbols and arrows. Each symbol contains an operation the computer must perform, while the arrows show the flow of the program logic (in other words, which operation is to be performed next).

As you have probably already noticed, not all of the symbols have the same shape. The shape of the symbol used depends on the type of operation being performed. The symbols used in this Appendix, along with their program statement types, are shown in Figure B2-2.

You should note in Figure B2-1 that not every BASIC program statement will necessarily correspond to a flowchart symbol; conversely, not every flowchart symbol corresponds to a BASIC program statement. For example, there is no BASIC program statement counterpart to the flowcharting "START" symbol. The BASIC program shown actually begins with a REM statement. Also, there is no flowchart symbol for the DATA statement. The flowchart is intended to represent only the flow of program logic. This can be done without specifying actual values for the variables. Finally, note that the GOTO statement of BASIC has no associated geometric symbol. It is represented by an arrow leading to the appropriate instruction.

B-28

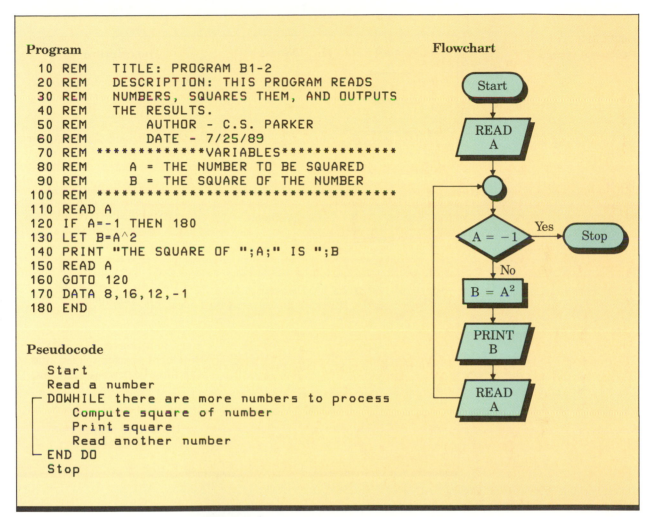

Program

```
 10 REM    TITLE: PROGRAM B1-2
 20 REM    DESCRIPTION: THIS PROGRAM READS
 30 REM    NUMBERS, SQUARES THEM, AND OUTPUTS
 40 REM    THE RESULTS.
 50 REM       AUTHOR - C.S. PARKER
 60 REM        DATE - 7/25/89
 70 REM *************VARIABLES**************
 80 REM     A = THE NUMBER TO BE SQUARED
 90 REM     B = THE SQUARE OF THE NUMBER
100 REM ********************************
110 READ A
120 IF A=-1 THEN 180
130 LET B=A^2
140 PRINT "THE SQUARE OF ";A;" IS ";B
150 READ A
160 GOTO 120
170 DATA 8,16,12,-1
180 END
```

Flowchart

Pseudocode

```
 Start
 Read a number
┌DOWHILE there are more numbers to process
│   Compute square of number
│   Print square
│   Read another number
└END DO
 Stop
```

FIGURE B2-1

Program, flowchart, and pseudocode for computing and printing the squares of several numbers (previously presented in Figure B1-2).

You should also note in Figure B2-1 that the flowchart need not contain every detail that will be specified in the program but only those that are important for understanding the logical flow. Thus, the flowchart indicates the output as PRINT B, whereas statement 140 of the corresponding program specifies in more detail:

```
140 PRINT "THE SQUARE OF ";A;" IS ";B
```

Pseudocode. Whereas program flowcharts use graphical symbols to depict program logic, *pseudocode* uses Englishlike statements. Pseudocode is widely considered to be a better tool than flowcharts for designing structured programs. While it is possible to create unstructured flowcharts, it is virtually impossible to create unstructured pseudocode.

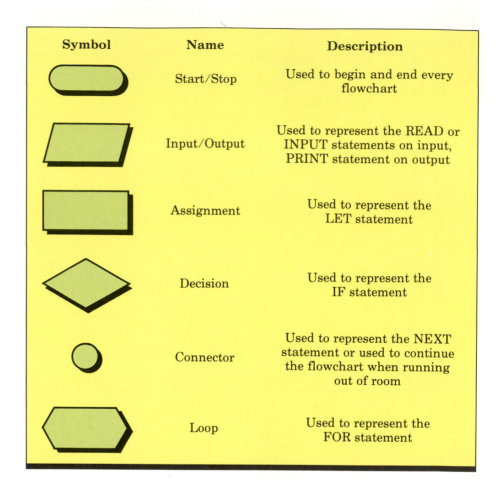

Symbol	Name	Description
	Start/Stop	Used to begin and end every flowchart
	Input/Output	Used to represent the READ or INPUT statements on input, PRINT statement on output
	Assignment	Used to represent the LET statement
	Decision	Used to represent the IF statement
	Connector	Used to represent the NEXT statement or used to continue the flowchart when running out of room
	Loop	Used to represent the FOR statement

All of the programs, flowcharts, and pseudocode represented in this text reflect a *structured* programming style. This style, which is comprehensively discussed in Chapter 10 of the text, involves the strict use of three program structures: *sequence, selection,* and *looping* (shown in Figure B2-3). Virtually every programming problem that you encounter can be satisfactorily solved by using some combination of these—and only these—three structures. Note that the flowchart and pseudocode in Figure B2-1 involve a looping structure (DOWHILE) and, within the loop, a sequence of three statements. In a DOWHILE structure, the procedure in a loop is performed *while* a condition is true, whereas in a DOUNTIL structure, the procedure in a loop is performed *until* a condition is true. Many versions of BASIC do not support the DOUNTIL looping structure, in which the procedure within a loop is always performed *at least once* and the test of the condition is performed at the bottom of the loop. In DOWHILE, in contrast, the loop procedure may not be performed at all (if the condition is initially false) and the test of the condition is performed at the top of the loop.

Just as there are many conventions used to construct flowcharts, so, too, are there many ways to develop pseudocode. The convention used in this text is to capitalize certain keywords, such as those shown in Figure B2-3, and to begin and end the pseudocode with the keywords "Start" and "Stop," respectively. Also, while

• SEQUENCE •

Flowchart

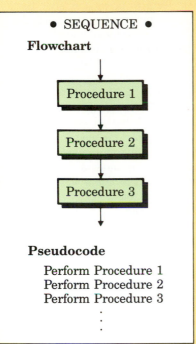

Pseudocode

Perform Procedure 1
Perform Procedure 2
Perform Procedure 3
.
.
.

• SELECTION •

Flowchart

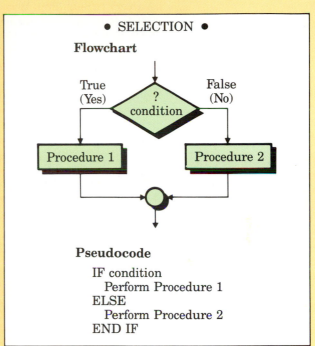

Pseudocode

IF condition
    Perform Procedure 1
ELSE
    Perform Procedure 2
END IF

• LOOPING •

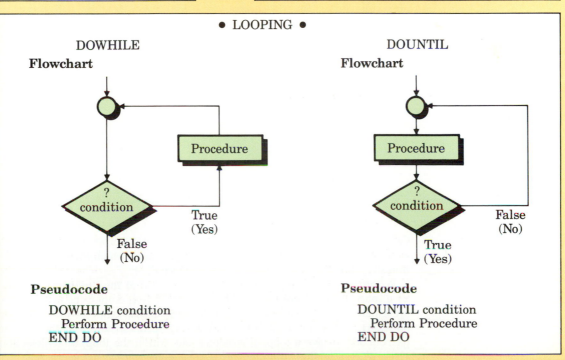

DOWHILE

Flowchart

DOUNTIL

Flowchart

Pseudocode

DOWHILE condition
    Perform Procedure
END DO

Pseudocode

DOUNTIL condition
    Perform Procedure
END DO

FIGURE B2-3

Flowchart and pseudocode forms of the three fundamental control structures—sequence, selection, and looping.

it is not mandatory, the convention chosen in this Appendix is to depict pseudocode at a very general level. Most professionals seem to prefer this style because if the pseudocode were too detailed, one might be better off just coding the program. While flowcharts can also be constructed at a general level (see Chapter 10 for examples), we've selected a detailed level here to give you better insight as to how each corresponding BASIC program works.

Both flowcharts and pseudocode are useful as design tools for developing programs and, later, as program *documentation* aids. As a design tool, the flowchart or pseudocode lets the programmer "think through" the logical design of programs prior to writing them. This can be particularly helpful for the same reason a builder of a house consults a floor plan before constructing any individual room. Once a program is written, the flowchart or pseudocode becomes a documentation aid: it generally is easier for others to understand how a program works by studying the flowchart or pseudocode rather than the program itself. Also, because of their simplicity, flowcharts or pseudocode can often be understood by nonprogrammers.

SOME FURTHER EXAMPLES

Now that we've covered some of the fundamentals of flowcharting and pseudocode, we'll look at two further examples.

First, let's consider a simple problem involving the selection structure. Team A and Team B, crosstown rivals, played each other in baseball a total of five times over the course of a season. The results were as follows:

Game	Team A Score	Team B Score
1	8	5
2	6	7
3	2	0
4	0	1
5	5	4

Create a flowchart, pseudocode, and, finally, a BASIC program that will output, for each game, the team winning the game. The solution, which involves a simple selection structure within a loop, is shown in Figure B2-4.

As our second example, let's take another look at the problem solved in Figure B1-6 (page B-24). There we were required to find all employees in a company who are female, over 40, and work in the accounting department. The associated program, flowchart, and pseudocode are shown in Figure B2-5. Note that the flowchart and pseudocode involve a looping structure and, within the loop, three selection structures. When selection structures are *nested,* as they are in the figure, note that every IF keyword is paired with an ELSE keyword and that there is an END IF terminating each structure.

Several other examples of flowcharts and pseudocode will be presented in later sections of this Appendix.

Program

```
 10 REM TITLE: PROGRAM B2-4
 20 REM A PROGRAM TO PICK WINNERS
 30 REM *************VARIABLES****************
 40 REM    I = THE NUMBER OF THE GAME
 50 REM    A = THE TEAM "A" SCORE
 60 REM    B = THE TEAM "B" SCORE
 70 REM *********************************
 80 READ I,A,B
 90 IF I=0 THEN 230
100 REM ASSUME NO GAMES END IN A TIE SCORE
110 IF A>B THEN 140
120 PRINT "TEAM B IS THE WINNER OF GAME ";I
130 GOTO 150
140 PRINT "TEAM A IS THE WINNER OF GAME ";I
150 READ I,A,B
160 GOTO 90
170 DATA 1,8,5
180 DATA 2,6,7
190 DATA 3,2,0
200 DATA 4,0,1
210 DATA 5,5,4
220 DATA 0,0,0
230 END
RUN
TEAM A IS THE WINNER OF GAME 1
TEAM B IS THE WINNER OF GAME 2
TEAM A IS THE WINNER OF GAME 3
TEAM B IS THE WINNER OF GAME 4
TEAM A IS THE WINNER OF GAME 5
```

Flowchart

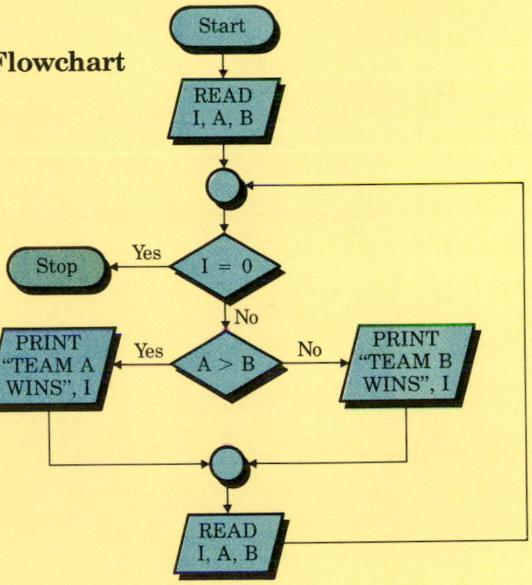

Pseudocode

```
Start
Read game number and score
DOWHILE there are more scores to process
    IF A's score > B's score
        Print "TEAM A WINS"
    ELSE
        Print "TEAM B WINS"
    END IF
    Read game number and score
END DO
Stop
```

FIGURE B2-4

Program, flowchart, and pseudocode for solving a simple baseball problem.

Program

```
10 REM THIS PROGRAM SELECTS FROM A FILE ALL
20 REM FEMALE EMPLOYEES OVER 40 WHO WORK IN
30 REM THE ACCOUNTING DEPARTMENT
40 REM    AUTHOR - C.S. PARKER
50 REM ************VARIABLES***************
60 REM    N$ = EMPLOYEE NAME
70 REM    S$ = SEX
80 REM    A  = AGE
90 REM    D$ = DEPARTMENT
100 REM *******************************
110 READ N$,S$,A,D$
120 IF N$="LAST RECORD" THEN 260
130 IF S$="M" THEN 170
140 IF A<=40 THEN 170
150 IF D$<>"ACCOUNTING" THEN 170
160 PRINT N$
170 READ N$,S$,A,D$
180 GOTO 120
190 REM *********DATA STATEMENTS**********
200 DATA "JANE CRIBBS","F",25,"ACCOUNTING"
210 DATA "PHIL JONES","M",45,"ACCOUNTING"
220 DATA "ANNE WELLES","F",42,"ACCOUNTING"
230 DATA "MARY SMITH","F",41,"FINANCE"
240 DATA "LAST RECORD","X",99,"NONE"
250 REM *******************************
260 END
```

Flowchart

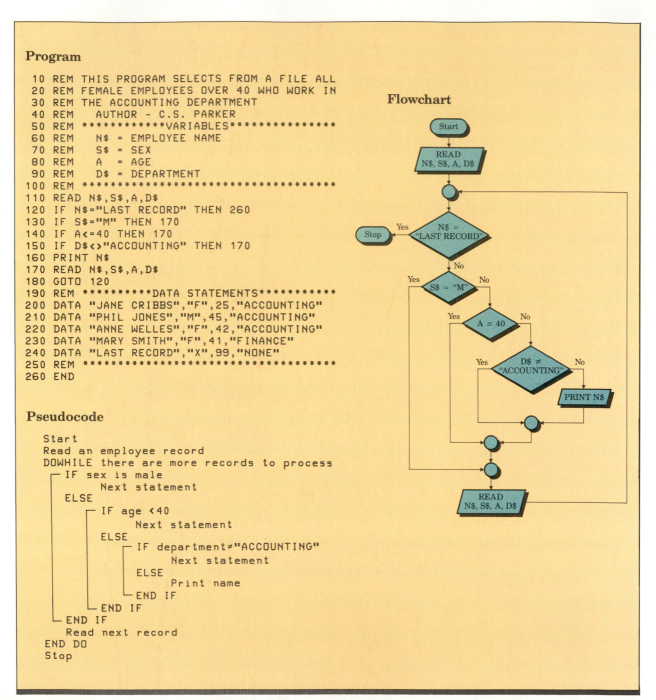

Pseudocode

```
Start
Read an employee record
DOWHILE there are more records to process
  ┌IF sex is male
  │     Next statement
  │ ELSE
  │   ┌IF age <40
  │   │    Next statement
  │   │ ELSE
  │   │  ┌IF department≠"ACCOUNTING"
  │   │  │    Next statement
  │   │  │ ELSE
  │   │  │    Print name
  │   │  └END IF
  │   └END IF
  └END IF
   Read next record
END DO
Stop
```

FIGURE B2-5

Program, flowchart, and pseudocode for solving an employee selection problem (previously presented in Figure B1-6).

Instructions: Write a flowchart and pseudocode to do each of the following tasks.

1. Three numbers (no two of which are equal) are to be read by the computer system and assigned to variables A, B, and C, respectively. Determine the largest, smallest, and middle number. (For example, if A is 3, B is 1, and C is 6, then 6 is the largest, 1 is the smallest, and 3 is the middle number.)

2. The following tax table is used to calculate the tax in a certain state:

1989 Tax Rate Schedules Table X (Single Taxpayers)	
If the Bottom Line Amount on Your Tax Return Is	**Compute Your Tax as Follows:**
$0–1,000	2% of the amount
$1,001–10,000	4% of the amount less $100
$10,001–50,000	6% of the amount less $300
Over $50,000	7% of the amount

Use this table to design a procedure to compute taxes due for a list of taxpayers.

3. A state charges the following annual fees for fishing licenses:

	Resident	Nonresident
All species	$10.00	$22.00
All species except trout	$ 7.00	$15.00

Use this table to design a procedure to compute the fee to be charged for each person buying a license. Following are some sample data to test the correctness of your procedure.

Individual	Residency Status	License Wanted
Merlon Biggs	Resident	All species
Alexis Adams	Resident	All species except trout
Arlen Bixby	Nonresident	All species
Al Allen	Nonresident	All species except trout

*For additional practice, try providing flowchart and pseudocode solutions to the problems described in Programming Problems 3-7 in Section 1 (pages B-25 through B-27). If you want to test your knowledge quickly, try Problems 4 and 7 first.

Section 3
Expanding on the
Basics of BASIC

COUNTING AND SUMMING

Now that we've covered a few fundamentals of how BASIC works, let's tackle a slightly more complicated problem. The example in Figure B3-1, a program to compute and print the average of a group of positive numbers, introduces two of the most fundamental operations in computing: counting and summing. You should observe the "mechanics" of both of these operations very carefully, since they occur in almost every large-scale programming problem.

Three important observations should be made about the program in Figure B3-1:

1. Statements 100 (LET I = O) and 110 (LET S = 0) establish *explicitly* the beginning values of I and S. Establishing beginning values for variables is called *initialization*. Most versions of BASIC will *implicitly* initialize all variables to zero before the program is executed; thus, statements 100 and 110 are usually unnecessary. It is good practice, however, to explicitly initialize certain variables to zero whether it is necessary or not on your computer system. There are two reasons for this practice:

   a. Many programming languages will not automatically initialize variables to zero. This can lead to surprising results if you didn't explicitly initialize, since numbers from someone else's program may be lurking in the storage locations assigned to your variables. Thus, your variables will assume these arbitrary values.

   b. When you initialize explicitly, the intent of your program becomes more evident. In other words, initialization is good documentation.

   Only the variables I and S require initialization to zero in this program. These are the variables that the computer needs to "look up" the values for on the right-hand side of the assignment symbol (=) in lines 140 and 150, respectively. The variables X and A don't have to be initialized, since they never appear on the right-hand side of an assignment symbol before the computer has explicitly assigned them a value.

2. Statement 140 (LET I = I + 1) *counts* the number of numbers in the list. I is initially assigned a value of zero. Each time a positive number is read into storage for X (so that the "X = −1 test" is failed in line 130 of the program), 1 is added to the current value of I. Since only one number can be assigned to I at any time, the previous value of I is destroyed and lost forever.

3. Statement 150 (LET S = S + X) *sums* the numbers in the list. As with I, S is initially zero. Each time statement 150 is executed, the current value of X is added to the current value of S. Thus, S can be seen as a "running total," as indicated in the following table:

When the Value of X Is	Statement 150 Does the Following
7	Adds 7 to the initial sum, 0, producing S = 7
23	Adds 23 to 7, producing S = 30
33	Adds 33 to 30, producing S = 63
15	Adds 15 to 63, producing S = 78
42	Adds 42 to 78, producing S = 120
−1	Statement 150 is not executed when X = −1

You should note that both the counting (I = I + 1) and summing (S = S + X) statements appear after the check for the last record (statement 130, IF X = −1 THEN 180). This is crucial. If these statements appear before the last-record check, the values of I and S will both be in error.

THE INPUT STATEMENT

The INPUT statement is one of the most useful statements in the BASIC language. It permits the program user to operate in a *conversational (interactive) mode* with the computer system. In other words, during the course of executing a program, the computer system asks the user for a response, the user answers, and then, based on the response given, the computer system asks the user for a response to another question, and so forth. The format of the INPUT statement is as follows:

Line # INPUT list of variables (separated by commas)

Figure B3-2 shows the program in Figure B3-1 rewritten with the INPUT statement. You should carefully note the following:

1. The READ statement in Figure B3-1 has been changed to an INPUT statement in Figure B3-2. With the READ statement, all data to be assigned to X are placed in an associated DATA statement; remember, READ and DATA statements are always used together. When we use INPUT X, no corresponding DATA statement is employed. Instead we supply data to the computer system as the program is running.

2. Data are supplied to the computer system as follows. Whenever an INPUT statement is encountered, a "?" is output by the system, and processing temporarily halts. At this point, we must enter as many data values as there are variables appearing after the word INPUT in the program. These values must be separated by commas. After we depress the Enter key, the system will assign the values to their corresponding variables and resume processing. If the same or another INPUT statement is encountered, the system will again respond with a question mark and await more input from the user.

3. In line 120, just before the INPUT statement, is a PRINT statement that provides instructions for the user of the program. When writing programs that include

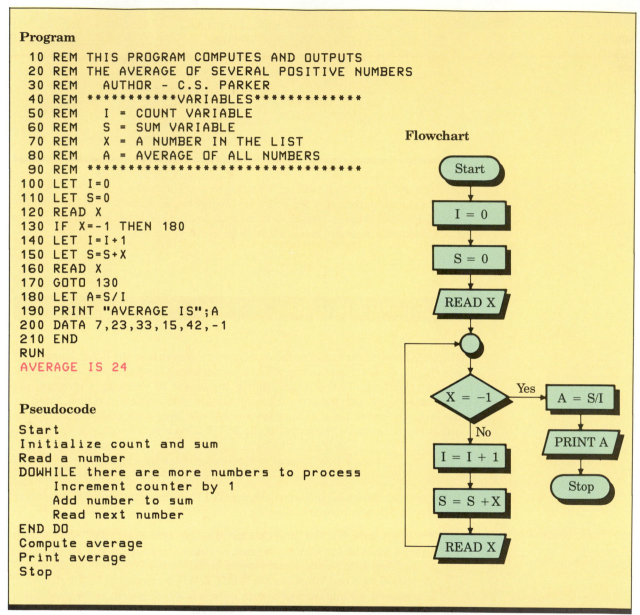

Program

```
10  REM THIS PROGRAM COMPUTES AND OUTPUTS
20  REM THE AVERAGE OF SEVERAL POSITIVE NUMBERS
30  REM    AUTHOR - C.S. PARKER
40  REM ***********VARIABLES*************
50  REM    I = COUNT VARIABLE
60  REM    S = SUM VARIABLE
70  REM    X = A NUMBER IN THE LIST
80  REM    A = AVERAGE OF ALL NUMBERS
90  REM *******************************
100 LET I=0
110 LET S=0
120 READ X
130 IF X=-1 THEN 180
140 LET I=I+1
150 LET S=S+X
160 READ X
170 GOTO 130
180 LET A=S/I
190 PRINT "AVERAGE IS";A
200 DATA 7,23,33,15,42,-1
210 END
RUN
AVERAGE IS 24
```

Flowchart

Pseudocode

```
Start
Initialize count and sum
Read a number
DOWHILE there are more numbers to process
    Increment counter by 1
    Add number to sum
    Read next number
END DO
Compute average
Print average
Stop
```

FIGURE B3-1
Computing the average of several numbers.

INPUT statements, it is always a good idea to include such a *prompting* PRINT statement before each INPUT so that the user will know both how to enter data into the computer and how to stop the program.

The major advantage of the INPUT statement over READ is that the user and computer system are involved in a dynamic dialog. In many cases, the user may not know the inputs in advance, since they depend on actions taken by the computer.

```
 10 REM THIS PROGRAM COMPUTES AND OUTPUTS
 20 REM THE AVERAGE OF SEVERAL POSITIVE NUMBERS
 30 REM    AUTHOR - C.S. PARKER
 40 REM ************VARIABLES**********
 50 REM    I = COUNT VARIABLE
 60 REM    S = SUM VARIABLE
 70 REM    X = A NUMBER IN THE LIST
 80 REM    A = AVERAGE OF ALL NUMBERS
 90 REM ******************************
100 LET I=0
110 LET S=0
120 PRINT "ENTER A POSITIVE NUMBER (OR -1 TO STOP)"
130 INPUT X
140 IF X=-1 THEN 200
150 LET I=I+1
160 LET S=S+X
170 PRINT "ENTER A POSITIVE NUMBER (OR -1 TO STOP)"
180 INPUT X
190 GOTO 140
200 LET A=S/I
210 PRINT "AVERAGE IS";A
220 END
RUN
ENTER A POSITIVE NUMBER (OR -1 TO STOP)
? 7
ENTER A POSITIVE NUMBER (OR -1 TO STOP)
? 23
ENTER A POSITIVE NUMBER (OR -1 TO STOP)
? 33
ENTER A POSITIVE NUMBER (OR -1 TO STOP)
? 15
ENTER A POSITIVE NUMBER (OR -1 TO STOP)
? 42
ENTER A POSITIVE NUMBER (OR -1 TO STOP)
? -1
AVERAGE IS 24
```

THE STOP STATEMENT

Execution of a STOP statement in a program causes the program to halt execution,
often by immediate transfer to the END statement. Figure B3-3 illustrates the use of
the STOP statement, which has the following format:

> Line # STOP

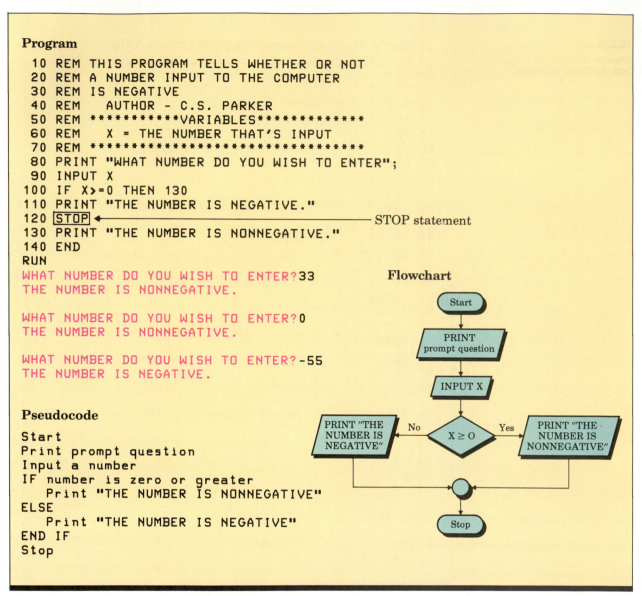

Program

```
 10 REM THIS PROGRAM TELLS WHETHER OR NOT
 20 REM A NUMBER INPUT TO THE COMPUTER
 30 REM IS NEGATIVE
 40 REM    AUTHOR - C.S. PARKER
 50 REM ***********VARIABLES*************
 60 REM    X = THE NUMBER THAT'S INPUT
 70 REM ****************************
 80 PRINT "WHAT NUMBER DO YOU WISH TO ENTER";
 90 INPUT X
100 IF X>=0 THEN 130
110 PRINT "THE NUMBER IS NEGATIVE."
120 STOP ←————————————————————————— STOP statement
130 PRINT "THE NUMBER IS NONNEGATIVE."
140 END
RUN
WHAT NUMBER DO YOU WISH TO ENTER?33
THE NUMBER IS NONNEGATIVE.

WHAT NUMBER DO YOU WISH TO ENTER?0
THE NUMBER IS NONNEGATIVE.

WHAT NUMBER DO YOU WISH TO ENTER?-55
THE NUMBER IS NEGATIVE.
```

Flowchart

Pseudocode

```
Start
Print prompt question
Input a number
IF number is zero or greater
    Print "THE NUMBER IS NONNEGATIVE"
ELSE
    Print "THE NUMBER IS NEGATIVE"
END IF
Stop
```

FIGURE B3-3
A program illustrating use of the STOP statement.

THE FOR AND NEXT STATEMENTS

The FOR and NEXT statements, which allow the programmer to loop (repeat a program section) automatically, are among the most important statements in BASIC. For example, consider the short program given in Figure B3-4.

The FOR and NEXT statements form a "sandwich," or loop. All statements inside the loop are executed the number of times determined in the FOR statement. (Note

FIGURE B3-4

Simple usage of FOR and NEXT statements.

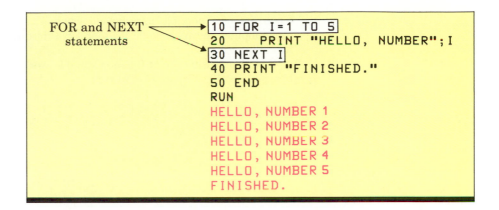

```
                          ┌─────────────────┐
FOR and NEXT ───────────► 10 FOR I=1 TO 5
statements                20    PRINT "HELLO, NUMBER";I
                          ┌─────────┐
                          30 NEXT I
                          40 PRINT "FINISHED."
                          50 END
                          RUN
                          HELLO, NUMBER 1
                          HELLO, NUMBER 2
                          HELLO, NUMBER 3
                          HELLO, NUMBER 4
                          HELLO, NUMBER 5
                          FINISHED.
```

that these statements are indented, making the program easier to read.) In Figure B3-4, I is first set equal to 1. Then everything inside the loop (that is, statement 20) is executed; I is then set equal to 2 and statement 20 is executed again; and so forth. After I is set equal to 5 and the loop is executed for the fifth time, control passes to the statement that immediately follows the NEXT statement (in other words, statement 40).

FOR and NEXT statements are always used together. They physically establish the beginning and end of the loop. Like READ and DATA, one statement makes absolutely no sense unless the other is present. The format of these statements is:

$$\text{Line \# FOR loop variable} = \begin{Bmatrix} \text{Beginning} \\ \text{value} \end{Bmatrix} \text{TO} \begin{Bmatrix} \text{Ending} \\ \text{value} \end{Bmatrix} \text{STEP increment}$$

$$\vdots$$

$$\text{Line \# NEXT loop variable}$$

The use of the loop variable, beginning value, ending value, and increment will now be explained.

The variable I in the program of Figure B3-4 is an example of a *loop variable*. Note carefully that the chosen loop variable (which can be any acceptable BASIC numeric variable) must be included in both the FOR statement and its associated NEXT statement, as indicated in the figure.

In Figure B3-4, it was implicitly assumed that the loop variable was to be incremented by 1 each time the loop was executed. The increment could also have been explicitly declared in a STEP clause:

```
10 FOR I=1 TO 5 STEP 1
```

The results produced would be the same. If, on the other hand, we rewrote line 10 as

```
10 FOR I=1 TO 5 STEP 3
```

and ran the program, the computer system would respond

```
HELLO, NUMBER 1
HELLO, NUMBER 4
FINISHED.
```

Since the next possible incremented value, 7, exceeds the terminal value of 5, the computer doesn't execute the loop for a third time but passes control to statement 40.

It is also possible to let the loop variable work "backwards." For example, if we changed line 10 of Figure B3-4 to read

```
10 FOR I=5 TO 1 STEP -1
```

we would obtain

```
HELLO, NUMBER 5
HELLO, NUMBER 4
HELLO, NUMBER 3
HELLO, NUMBER 2
HELLO, NUMBER 1
FINISHED.
```

BASIC also allows programmers to use variables in FOR and NEXT statements. For example, the following sequence is also acceptable:

```
30 FOR Z=J TO K STEP L
        .
        .
        .
70 NEXT Z
```

If $J = 2$, $K = 10$, and $L = 3$, the loop will be performed 3 times, with Z taking on values of 2, 5, and 8 as the loop is executed.

Let's now consider a more comprehensive example to further explore the concept of looping. Consider again the "averages" problem solved in Figure B3-1 (page B-38). How can we solve this problem using FOR/NEXT loops? The flowchart and program solution appear in Figure B3-5.

You should note the following features in comparing the programs, flowcharts, and pseudocode in Figures B3-1 and B3-5:

1. The logic of the program in Figure B3-5 is less complicated than that of Figure B3-1, even though the programs are the same length. A major reason for the gained simplicity is that the automatic initialization, incrementing, and testing done in the loop allow us to eliminate:

```
100 LET I=0
130 IF X=-1 THEN 180
140 LET I=I+1
```

Note also that -1 is eliminated in the DATA statement.

2. There are major differences in the flowcharts. Note especially the flowchart symbols used for FOR and NEXT, as well as the dotted line indicating automatic control back to the FOR statement.

3. FOR/NEXT logic can be simulated in pseudocode through a DOWHILE looping structure. Note that this requires a separate Set instruction before the loop to initialize the counter and a separate Add instruction at the end of the loop to increment the counter.

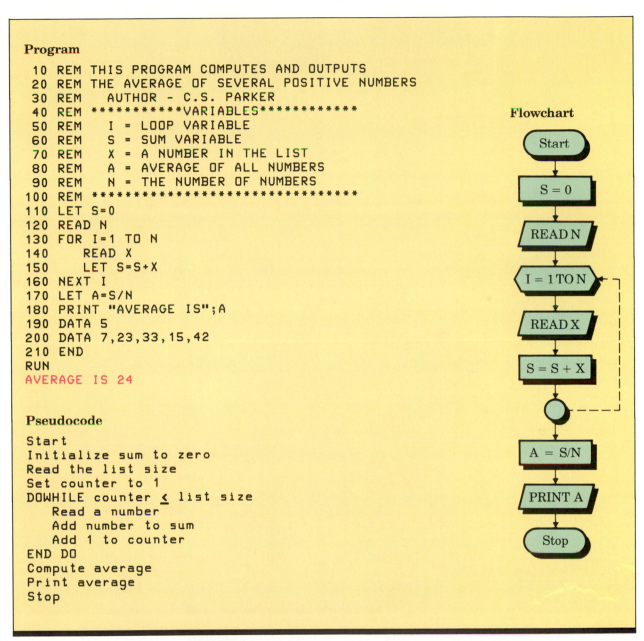

Program

```
 10 REM THIS PROGRAM COMPUTES AND OUTPUTS
 20 REM THE AVERAGE OF SEVERAL POSITIVE NUMBERS
 30 REM    AUTHOR - C.S. PARKER
 40 REM **********VARIABLES************
 50 REM    I = LOOP VARIABLE
 60 REM    S = SUM VARIABLE
 70 REM    X = A NUMBER IN THE LIST
 80 REM    A = AVERAGE OF ALL NUMBERS
 90 REM    N = THE NUMBER OF NUMBERS
100 REM ******************************
110 LET S=0
120 READ N
130 FOR I=1 TO N
140    READ X
150    LET S=S+X
160 NEXT I
170 LET A=S/N
180 PRINT "AVERAGE IS";A
190 DATA 5
200 DATA 7,23,33,15,42
210 END
RUN
AVERAGE IS 24
```

Flowchart

Start
S = 0
READ N
I = 1 TO N
READ X
S = S + X
A = S/N
PRINT A
Stop

Pseudocode

```
Start
Initialize sum to zero
Read the list size
Set counter to 1
DOWHILE counter ≤ list size
    Read a number
    Add number to sum
    Add 1 to counter
END DO
Compute average
Print average
Stop
```

FIGURE B3-5
Solution to the problem in Figure B3-1 using loops.

You may be wondering at this point why a programming structure like the one shown in Figure B3-1 would ever be used, considering how complicated it is. The major advantage of this structure is that it doesn't require the programmer to know in advance the number of data items processed. In many data processing applications, the number of records processed is unknown. In these situations, it is useful to append a trailer record at the end of the data file and use an IF statement to

A Box on Bugs

Like Their Insect Counterparts, Program Bugs Exist in Many Forms

Unless you are incredibly intelligent, careful, or lucky, chances are that any computer program that you write will not run correctly at first. Inevitably there will be one or more errors, or bugs. Here we'll look at the types of bugs you can expect—and some ways to root them out of your programs.

Types of Bugs. While there are many varieties of bugs, virtually all of them can be classified into three categories: syntax errors, runtime errors, and logical errors.

Syntax errors usually cause the most headaches for beginning programmers. These errors involve violations of the grammatical rules of the programming language. For example, the syntax of BASIC's LET statement is

```
10 LET variable-
      name=expression
```

This syntax implies that statements such as

```
10 LETT A=B
or 10 LET A+B=A
```

will result in syntax errors. In the first statement, LET is misspelled; in the second, a single variable does not appear to the left of the = sign. Although these types of errors can be annoying, BASIC generally provides informative error messages to enable you to pinpoint and correct them.

Even though your program is gramatically correct, however, there is no guarantee it will produce correct results. It may contain a *run-time error;* that is, an error that causes abnormal behavior during program execution. For example, suppose you have a statement such as

```
10 LET A=B/C
```

in your program. Gramatically speaking, this statement is correct. But if C has a value of zero at the time this statement is executed, it will cause your program to terminate. As with syntax errors, runtime errors also generally produce some type of error message, making them relatively easy to pinpoint.

One of the most time-consuming and difficult errors to diagnose is the *logical error*. This is where you have incorrect results, but your program appears to be working properly. Thus, either you've incorrectly translated the problem statement or an algorithm, or perhaps there is an error somewhere in the input data. One reason this type of error is so difficult to locate is that you get no error message—just wrong results. A second reason is that there may be many unanticipated conditions that can trigger this type of error. Thus, except for tiny programs, you can never really be 100 percent sure that your program is entirely correct.

detect it. Thus, both of these structures—the FOR/NEXT loop and I = I + 1/IF—are frequently used in programs.

Let us now consider branching within a FOR/NEXT loop. For example, suppose we wanted to read a list of 10 numbers, summing only the positive ones. This problem is solved in the short program that appears in Figure B3-6, using the variable-naming convention (lines 40 to 100) of Figure B3-5.

Note that if the number is negative ($X < 0$), we wish to bypass the summation operation ($S = X + X$) and read in the next number. However, instead of going directly to the FOR statement, we pass control to the NEXT statement (which will

Correcting Bugs. Debugging programs can often be a long process, taking longer than writing the program itself. Over the years, a number of helpful strategies have evolved to discover and correct bugs. Three of these are diagnostic printing, tracing, and the use of rigorous test data.

Diagnostic printing often involves using PRINT statements to provide you with the current value of certain variables. The use of temporary (or "dummy") PRINT statements was discussed earlier (page B-22). Once the error you are searching for is found, these PRINT statements are removed from your program. Another type of diagnostic printing strategy is *echo printing*. With echo printing, you output the values of variables as soon as they are supplied to a READ or INPUT statement. For example,

```
100 INPUT N$,P
110 PRINT "NAME: ";N$
120 PRINT "PAY :";P
```

The purpose of echo printing is to provide you the opportunity to verify that data are being entered into the computer system correctly. Unlike dummy PRINT statements, echo PRINT statements are generally a permanent part of programs.

Tracing is a technique that allows you to determine the path the computer takes through a program. When tracing is used, the computer prints out the line number of each statement it executes. Thus, you are able to determine the point in the program where the computer has halted processing. On the IBM Personal Computer, the tracing feature is activated by the TRON command and deactivated by the TROFF command. Both of these commands can be used either as BASIC program commands or as BASIC system commands. When the TRON command is activated and the program is run, the line numbers (on the IBM) are printed successively in square brackets, to prevent them from being confused with other program output.

Using rigorous *test data* is one of the most effective ways to root out logical errors in your program. Test data should be chosen so that they subject your program to as many possible situations the program will encounter when it is put into practice. You should test the program with both valid and invalid data, as well as with both ordinary and unusual data. Make sure as well that the test data cover every possible condition that you specify in your IF statements, so you can determine whether the program is branching correctly. Also, select some test data that fall on the boundaries of the problems allegedly solvable by your computer program. For example, choose data that set variables to largest- or smallest-allowable values, that cause examination of the first or last item on a list, or that fall on the borderlines of conditions specified in your IF statements. Choosing suitable test data can take time, but it is generally the only way to get a good idea if your program really works.

automatically bring us back up to the top of the loop). This raises a key point. If statement 40 were instead

```
40 IF X<0 THEN 20
```

the value of I would be erroneously reset to 1 when the THEN clause was invoked. Note that only through execution of the NEXT statement is the loop variable named in the FOR automatically incremented. If control is passed to a FOR by any statement other than its corresponding NEXT, the loop variable will be set (or reset) to its initial value.

```
10 S=0
20 FOR I=1 TO 10
30     READ X
40       IF X<0 THEN 60
50       S=S+X
60 NEXT I
70 PRINT "THE SUM IS";S
80 DATA 5,-1,3,6,-14,20,4,2,40,10
90 END
RUN
THE SUM IS 90
```

```
10 FOR I=1 TO 3
20     FOR J=1 TO 2
30         PRINT I;J
40     NEXT J
50 NEXT I
60 END
RUN
 1      1
 1      2
 2      1
 2      2
 3      1
 3      2
 ↑      ↑
 Ⓘ      Ⓙ
```

Finally, loops within loops, or *nested loops,* are allowed. Observe the short program in the left margin. The program executes the PRINT statement a total of $3 * 2 = 6$ times. The outer loop variable (I) varies the slowest; the inner loop variable (J) varies the fastest.

In writing nested-loop programs, it is always important to enclose the inner loop entirely within the outer loop. Thus, a program segment such as the one following,

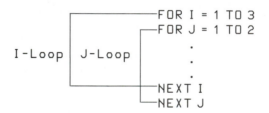

would not work because the loops cross rather than nest.

ELIMINATING GOTOS: THE IF/THEN/ELSE AND WHILE/WEND STATEMENTS

Many recent versions of BASIC enable you to use commands such as IF/THEN/ELSE and WHILE to make program coding more straightforward. IF/THEN/ELSE is a method for coding a *selection* structure, whereas WHILE is a way of coding a *looping* (DO-WHILE) structure. Both of these structures are described in Section 2 and are discussed extensively in Chapter 10 of this text. Where IF/THEN/ELSE and WHILE are available, they can make developing a program easier and eliminate many of those GOTO statements (and GOTO clauses) that can make programming logic particularly hard for people to follow.

IF/THEN/ELSE

As explained on page B-14, the simplest form of the IF statement involves testing a relational expression and branching to a line number if the value of the expression is true. This was the earliest form of the IF statement and is available in virtually all versions of BASIC. The more recent (and increasingly popular) IF/THEN/ELSE statement, as suggested by the following format, allows us to do much more than the simple IF:

$$\text{Line \# IF relational-expression THEN } \begin{Bmatrix} \text{line-number} \\ \text{other statement(s)} \end{Bmatrix}$$
$$\left[\text{ELSE } \begin{Bmatrix} \text{line-number} \\ \text{other statement(s)} \end{Bmatrix} \right]$$

The square brackets around the ELSE clause mean that this clause is optional. Later we'll look at an instance where we may not want to use an ELSE.

Let's immediately consider an example so you can see how the full form of the IF/THEN/ELSE statement works. Suppose a list of salespeople is to be processed. If a salesperson sells $5,000 or more worth of merchandise in a day, a $50 bonus is to be awarded. A salesperson not achieving that level gets no bonus.

Two short program segments representing this processing task, one using a simple IF and the other using an IF/THEN/ELSE, are provided in Figures B3-7a and B3-7b, respectively. As you can see, to accomplish the same task (determining whether or not a salesperson gets a bonus), it takes four statements with a simple IF versus a single statement with an IF/THEN/ELSE. Moreover, the IF/THEN/ELSE construct is much easier to follow, since it does not involve GOing TO line numbers. Incidentally, many computer systems require you to depress the line feed key when you *continue* a statement from one line to the next (as we've done here in line 100 of Figure B3-7b). If your computer does not have a line feed key, depress the Control (Ctrl) key while hitting the J key to get a line feed.

In some programs that you write, you may want to execute two or more statements if the value of a relational expression is true or, possibly, two or more statements if the value is false. For example, suppose a salesperson selling $5,000 or more worth of merchandise is given both a bonus of $50 and a watch (W$ = "YES"). We

FIGURE B3-7

Comparison of a simple IF statement and an IF/THEN/ELSE statement.

```
100  IF S>=5000 THEN 130
110  B=0
120  GOTO 140
130  B=50
140  . . .
```
(a)   Coding a task with a simple IF statement

```
100  IF S>=5000 THEN B=50
                  ELSE B=0
110  . . .
```
(b)   Coding the equivalent task with an IF/THEN/ELSE statement

Note: In the program segments above, S=sales and B=bonus.

might then code the statement in Figure B3-7b to inform us of this information as follows:

```
100 IF S>=5000 THEN B=50:W$="YES"
               ELSE B=0:W$="NO"
```

On many computer systems, the colon character (:) is used, as shown above, to separate statements appearing on the same line.

Finally, we mentioned earlier that the ELSE clause is optional. So, for example, if we want to increment a counter (C) by 1 every time a record is read representing a person in the accounting department (D$ = "ACCOUNTING"), we could use a statement such as

```
200 IF D$="ACCOUNTING" THEN C=C+1
```

As you can see, this form of IF/THEN/ELSE looks a lot like a simple IF statement. The only difference is that a line number need not follow the THEN clause.

WHILE/WEND

Whereas IF/THEN/ELSE can be used to avoid sloppy branching within a selection structure, many versions of BASIC have a WHILE statement to eliminate the same type of confusion in a looping (DOWHILE) structure. The WHILE statement is similar to the FOR statement in that it uses a companion statement (WEND) to mark the end of the loop. And, also similar to FOR and NEXT, all of the statements appearing between the WHILE and WEND are executed under terms specified by the first statement of the loop: the WHILE statement. The formats of the WHILE and WEND statements are as follows:

```
Line # WHILE relational-expression
       .
       .
       .
Line # WEND
```

To see how WHILE and WEND work, let's consider a simple example. Suppose we want to read numbers successively from a list of nonnegative numbers. Each time

FIGURE B3-8

Using the WHILE and WEND statements.

```
100 READ X                          100 READ X
110 IF X<0 THEN 150                 110 WHILE X>=0
120     PRINT X                     120     PRINT X
130     READ X                      130     READ X
140 GOTO 110                        140 WEND
150 . . .                           150 . . .
```

(a) Looping *without* WHILE and WEND   (b) Looping *with* WHILE and WEND

B-48

we read a number, we print it. A negative value (-1) is used as the trailer value on the list to signify its end. Two short program segments representing this processing task are given in Figure B3-8. Figure B3-8a shows how we might code the task if no WHILE statement is available, whereas Figure B3-8b shows how to proceed with the WHILE. Note that using the WHILE eliminates the confusing line-number transfers in lines 110 and 140 of Figure B3-8a. After the loop in Figure B3-8b is executed, processing resumes with statement 150.

SOLVED REVIEW PROBLEM

An auto rental company rents three types of cars at the following rates:

Car Type	Fixed Cost per Day	Cost per Mile
Compact	$10	$0.15
Intermediate	$20	$0.18
Large	$30	$0.22

Thus, for example, a person renting a compact car for 3 days and driving 100 miles would be charged $10 * 3 + .15 * 100 = 45.

Write an interactive BASIC program that will accept

☐ Customer name ☐ Number of days car held
☐ Car type ☐ Miles traveled

as input. It should output the charge for each customer. Also, have the computer add up the total charges attributable to each type of car. Use the sample data in the following table to test your program.

Customer Name	Car Type	Days Held	Miles Traveled
Jones	Large	6	500
Smith	Compact	17	3,000
Baker	Intermediate	8	250
Williams	Intermediate	4	1,000
Winston	Large	3	500

The solution to this problem is provided in Figure B3-9 (pages B-50 and B-51). You should note that the program will terminate if the user types in "GOODBYE" when asked to supply a customer name.

```
10 REM THIS PROGRAM COMPUTES THE CHARGES DUE ON
20 REM RENTED AUTOMOBILES
30 REM      AUTHOR - C.S. PARKER
40 REM **************VARIABLES*****************
50 REM     T   = CAR TYPE (1=COMPACT)
60 REM                    (2=INTERMEDIATE)
70 REM                    (3=LARGE)
80 REM     N$ = CUSTOMER NAME
90 REM     D  = DAYS CAR HELD
100 REM    M  = MILES TRAVELED
110 REM    C  = CHARGE FOR CUSTOMER
120 REM    C1,C2,C3 = TOTAL BILLINGS ON CAR
130 REM         TYPES 1,2 & 3, RESPECTIVELY
140 REM ***********************************
150 LET C1=0
160 LET C2=0
170 LET C3=0
180 PRINT "ENTER CUSTOMER NAME"
190 PRINT "     NOTE: ENTER GOODBYE TO STOP PROGRAM"
200 INPUT N$
210 IF N$="GOODBYE" THEN 470
220 PRINT "ENTER DAYS CAR HELD, MILES TRAVELED, AND CAR TYPE"
230 PRINT "     NOTE: 1=COMPACT  2=INTERMEDIATE  3=LARGE"
240 INPUT D,M,T
250 IF T=1 THEN 310
260 IF T=2 THEN 350
270 IF T=3 THEN 390
280 PRINT "CAR TYPE";T;"DOES NOT EXIST"
290 GOTO 220
300 REM COMPACT CAR CALCULATIONS
310      C=.15*M+10*D
320      C1=C1+C
330      GOTO 410
340 REM INTERMEDIATE CAR CALCULATIONS
350      C=.18*M+20*D
360      C2=C2+C
370      GOTO 410
380 REM LARGE CAR CALCULATIONS
390      C=.22*M+30*D
400      C3=C3+C
410 PRINT N$;"     $";C
420 PRINT
430 PRINT "ENTER CUSTOMER NAME"
440 PRINT "     NOTE: ENTER GOODBYE TO STOP PROGRAM"
450 INPUT N$
460 GOTO 210
470 PRINT "TOTAL CHARGES ON CAR TYPE 1 ARE   $";C1
480 PRINT "TOTAL CHARGES ON CAR TYPE 2 ARE   $";C2
490 PRINT "TOTAL CHARGES ON CAR TYPE 3 ARE   $";C3
500 END
```

FIGURE B3-9   An interactive program to determine auto rental charges

```
ENTER CUSTOMER NAME
     NOTE: ENTER GOODBYE TO STOP PROGRAM
?JONES
ENTER DAYS CAR HELD, MILES TRAVELED, AND CAR TYPE
     NOTE: 1=COMPACT  2=INTERMEDIATE  3=LARGE
?6,500,3
JONES     $ 290

ENTER CUSTOMER NAME
     NOTE: ENTER GOODBYE TO STOP PROGRAM
?SMITH
ENTER DAYS CAR HELD, MILES TRAVELED, AND CAR TYPE
     NOTE: 1=COMPACT  2=INTERMEDIATE  3=LARGE
?17,3000,1
SMITH     $ 620

ENTER CUSTOMER NAME
     NOTE: ENTER GOODBYE TO STOP PROGRAM
?BAKER
ENTER DAYS CAR HELD, MILES TRAVELED, AND CAR TYPE
     NOTE: 1=COMPACT  2=INTERMEDIATE  3=LARGE
?8,250,6
CAR TYPE 6 DOES NOT EXIST
ENTER DAYS CAR HELD, MILES TRAVELED, AND CAR TYPE
     NOTE: 1=COMPACT  2=INTERMEDIATE  3=LARGE
?8,250,2
BAKER     $ 205

ENTER CUSTOMER NAME
     NOTE: ENTER GOODBYE TO STOP PROGRAM
?WILLIAMS
ENTER DAYS CAR HELD, MILES TRAVELED, AND CAR TYPE
     NOTE: 1=COMPACT  2=INTERMEDIATE  3=LARGE
?4,1000,2
WILLIAMS     $ 260

ENTER CUSTOMER NAME
     NOTE: ENTER GOODBYE TO STOP PROGRAM
?WINSTON
ENTER DAYS CAR HELD, MILES TRAVELED, AND CAR TYPE
     NOTE: 1=COMPACT  2=INTERMEDIATE  3=LARGE
?3,500,3
WINSTON     $ 200

ENTER CUSTOMER NAME
     NOTE: ENTER GOODBYE TO STOP PROGRAM
?GOODBYE
TOTAL CHARGES ON CAR TYPE 1 ARE   $ 620
TOTAL CHARGES ON CAR TYPE 2 ARE   $ 465
TOTAL CHARGES ON CAR TYPE 3 ARE   $ 490
```

Instructions: Provide an answer to each of the following questions.

1. Identify the syntax errors, if any, in the following BASIC statements:

   a. `10 FOR I=6 TO 1 STEP 2`
   b. `10 INPUT N$,A,A1`
   c. `10 INPUT T=1, T=2, T=3`
   d. `15 IF N$="PHONY" THEN 25`
   e. `10 FOR I=-5 TO 5`
   f. `10 FOR K=3 TO A STEP 2`

2. Consider the following FOR/NEXT loop:

   ```
   10 FOR I=A TO B STEP C
         .
         .
         .
   20 NEXT I
   ```

   How many times will this loop execute if

   a. A=1, B=7, and C=1?   c. A=5, B=17, and C=3?
   b. A=1, B=7, and C=2?   d. A=5, B=1, and C=−1?

3. Consider the following program:

   ```
   10 FOR I=1 TO 5
   20 FOR J=3 TO 7
   30 A=I*J
   40 NEXT J
   50 NEXT I
   ```

   a. What is the first value assigned to A?
   b. What is the value of A at the end of the program?
   c. What is the value of A the 8th time statement 30 is executed?
   d. What is the value of A the 12th time statement 30 is executed?
   e. How many times will line 30 be executed?

PROGRAMMING PROBLEMS

Instructions: Write a BASIC program to do each of the following tasks.

1. Read a list of positive numbers, sum all of the numbers greater than 10 in the list, and output that sum.

2. Sum all even numbers from 1 to 100 and output the square root of that sum. [*Hint:* The square root of any number X is $X^{1/2}$.]

3. Read a list of positive numbers, find the average of all numbers between 10 and 20 (inclusive) in the list, and output the average.

4. Write a program that will read in the 10 values

$$-6, 8, 65, 4, 8, -21, 2, 46, -12, 42$$

and identify the highest and lowest number. [*Hint:* Declare the first number in the list as both the highest and lowest value in the list. Then let each of the remaining nine numbers "get a shot" at competing for highest or lowest value. As each number is read, check it against the current high value and low value.]

5. The following data show the weather in a city on 10 successive days: Sunny, Cloudy, Rainy, Sunny, Sunny, Cloudy, Sunny, Sunny, Rainy, Cloudy.

   Write a program to read these 10 weather observations and then count and output the number of sunny days.

6. Use FOR/NEXT loops to compute the following sums (S):

$$S = 1 + 2 + 3 + 4 + \cdots + 10$$
$$S = 3 + 6 + 9 + 12 + \cdots + 30$$
$$S = 1 + 1/2 + 1/3 + 1/4 + \cdots + 1/1000$$

7. Write a program to convert several temperatures from Fahrenheit (F) to centigrade (C). Use the INPUT statement to supply each Fahrenheit temperature to the computer system for conversion. The following formula can be used to make the conversion:

```
C=(5/9)*(F-32)
```

Use a trailer value, such as 9999 degrees, to stop your program.

8. The cost of sending a telegram is $2.80 for the first 20 (or fewer) words and 10 cents for each additional word. Write a program that will find the cost of a telegram after you have entered the number of words as input at a keyboard.

9. The population growth rate in a city has been projected at 5 percent per year for the next 10 years. The current population in the city is 31,840 residents. Write a program to find the population 10 years from now.

10. Solve Problem 3 in Section 1 (page B-25) using (a) the IF/THEN/ELSE statement in place of the simple IF statement where appropriate and (b) the WHILE/WEND statements for the looping control structure.

Section 4
Formatted Printing

SPACING OUTPUT

Producing neatly formatted output is one of the prized skills of computer programming. A sloppy-looking report, even though it contains accurate information, often is not read. Readers of reports generally are favorably inclined toward well-presented output.

So far we have learned two formatting vehicles to use with the PRINT statement:

1. The semicolon. This generally leaves a space or two between printed items.*
    When it is the last character in the PRINT statement, it forces the next output
    from the computer system to begin on the same line.

2. The "blank" PRINT statement. This is used to produce blank output lines.

There are three other techniques discussed in this section that will aid in formatting output:

1. The comma (,).

2. The TAB function.

3. The PRINT USING statement.

COMMA PRINT CONTROL

The comma works in a manner somewhat similar to the semicolon, except that

1. It produces more space between the output data items.

2. The items are printed at fixed tab stops.

The fixed tab stops define so-called *print zones*. If you are on an output device that provides 72 characters per line, the zones might be fixed as follows:

Zone 1	Zone 2	Zone 3	Zone 4	Zone 5
X———————X———————X———————X———————X———————X				
Columns	Columns	Columns	Columns	Columns
1-15	16-30	31-45	46-60	61-72

*The exception is that no spaces are provided between two strings separated by a semicolon (unless, of course, spaces appear within the string).

Use of comma in PRINT for spacing. This simple program reads in names of people, along with associated pay rates and gross pay. This information is then output into print zones.

```
10  REM THIS PROGRAM LISTS PAY RATES AND
20  REM GROSS PAY OF EMPLOYEES
30  REM    AUTHOR - C.S. PARKER
40  REM ***********VARIABLES**********
50  REM    N$ = EMPLOYEE NAME
60  REM    P  = PAY RATE
70  REM    A  = GROSS PAY
80  REM    I  = LOOP VARIABLE
90  REM ****************************
100 PRINT "NAME","PAY RATE","GROSS PAY"
110 PRINT
120 FOR I=1 TO 3
130    READ N$,P,A
140    PRINT N$,P,A        ← Print statement
150 NEXT I                   with zone spacing
160 DATA "JOHN DOE",6.30,200.15
170 DATA "MARY SMITH",7.20,316.40
180 DATA "ANN JONES",5.00,80.00
190 END
RUN
NAME                PAY RATE        GROSS PAY

JOHN DOE            6.3             200.15
MARY SMITH          7.2             316.4
ANN JONES           5               80
```

        Zone 1   Zone 2   Zone 3

In any case, you should check your output device to find out where the zones begin and end. With the zones given on page B-54, the use of commas in a PRINT statement would have the effect shown in Figure B4-1. Positive numbers printed in a zone are preceded by a blank space, negative numbers by a minus sign.

If we want to total gross pay in this program and print it neatly on output, we can add the following statements to this program:

```
115  S=0
145  S=S+A
155  PRINT
156  PRINT,,S
```

When the program is run, the output produced will look like this:

```
NAME                PAY RATE        GROSS PAY

JOHN DOE            6.3             200.15
MARY SMITH          7.2             316.4
ANN JONES           5               80

                                    596.55
```

Not Very BASIC Anymore

A Look at Some High-End Versions of the BASIC Language

When BASIC was first developed by John Kemeny and Thomas Kurtz of Dartmouth College some 25 years ago, it was a simple language, with very few frills. Its creators envisioned a language that didn't get in the way of problem solving, one that would open the world of computing to ever larger numbers of people. Although Kemeny and Kurtz succeeded in their aim, and BASIC is still among the easiest of programming languages to learn, a lot has changed in 25 years.

A general rule of software development is that no matter how good a product is, there is always a wide audience of users looking for new and improved features. For instance, the earliest versions of BASIC had no PRINT USING statement. Business users of BASIC quickly made it quite clear that some type of easy-to-use formatted-printing feature was necessary if BASIC were to be more acceptable for business applications. Later, as bit-mapped and color display screens became widely available, commands such as LINE, DRAW, CIRCLE, and COLOR were added in most versions of BASIC to accommodate users who wanted powerful graphics features. Over the years, even music commands have found their way into BASIC, enabling beginners to compose simple tunes and advanced users to create sophisticated works by coordinating prestored sounds and synthesizers.

A number of enhanced forms of BASIC now exist. Two of the most widely used of these are True Basic Inc.'s True BASIC and Microsoft Corporation's QuickBASIC. Among the most widely hailed features of these new forms of BASIC are their windowing capabilities, structured programming enhancements, and powerful help features.

With respect to windowing, both True BASIC and Quick-BASIC allow you to create separate windows on the screen and to place in them such things as program listings, program output, and command menus (see photos). So, for instance, you can examine a program listing in one window while the results are being output in another window. Or, you could summon a command-menu window to help painlessly sort or draw a graph of the output you just produced.

The structured capability of True BASIC and Quick-BASIC permits you to compose a "true" DOUNTIL structure and, also, a CASE structure. For instance, True BASIC's DOUNTIL structure has the form:

```
DO
  Procedure
LOOPUNTIL Condition
```

Many stripped-down versions of BASIC do not have a real DOUNTIL structure, which always performs the procedure in a loop *at least once* and tests to see whether a condition is true *after* the procedure is performed.

The case structure, which is a form of the selection structure, enables you to compose easy-to-follow logic in situations where any one of several actions may be appropriate, depending on the value of a variable. For instance, if different actions are to be taken when the variable X is equal to 1, 2, 3, or some other value, this logic could be coded as follows with True BASIC's case structure:

```
SELECT CASE X
CASE 1 , 2
    Perform task A
CASE 3
    Perform task B
CASE ELSE
    Perform task C
END SELECT
```

Many versions of BASIC do not have a built-in case capability, and it must be simulated with other types of logic (for an example, see the menu-selection program in Figure B5-5).

The latest version of QuickBASIC has such an outstanding help feature that you hardly need a reference manual. For instance, you can place the cursor on any command or key word, and, by pressing a key, have a wealth of pertinent syntax and use information sent to your display screen.

Both True BASIC and QuickBASIC come equipped with both a compiler and an interpreter. The compiler enables BASIC code to execute in the fastest manner possible. Thus, when a program is fully debugged, a compiler is the language translator of choice. An interpreter is slower than a compiler, but since it provides easier-to-follow error messages, it is often used when BASIC programs are being developed.

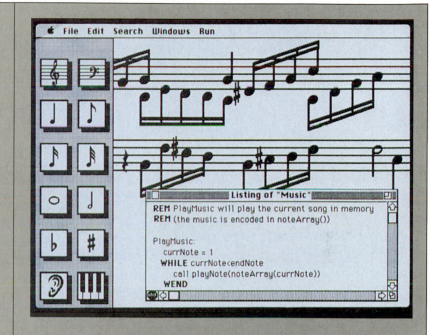

BASIC in the 1990s. QuickBASIC (top) and True BASIC (bottom) both have a windowing feature that can provide window images of listings, output, and command menus.

There are two other interesting features to note about the use of the comma for spacing in a PRINT statement:

1. If the number of items to be output in a PRINT statement is too large to fit on one line of the output device used, a "wraparound" effect will occur; for example:

```
10 FOR I=1 TO 12
20 PRINT I,
30 NEXT I
40 END
RUN
 1              2              3              4              5
 6              7              8              9             10
11             12
```

Only five data items are printed per line because only five print zones are available on the output device used. If we tried running this program on a different output device, say, one with six zones, we would get six numbers per line.

2. If a particular data item is too large to occupy a single print zone, it will "overflow" into subsequent zones; for example:

```
10 PRINT "TODAY IS MAY 16, 1990","HELLO"
20 END
RUN
TODAY IS MAY 16, 1990    HELLO
↑                        ↑
└ Begins in zone 1       └Begins in zone 3
                          (because the
                          first literal overflowed
                          into zone 2)
```

THE TAB FUNCTION

The TAB function of BASIC permits us to "tab" over to any column to start printing. Thus, with the TAB function we don't have to begin printing at a zone boundary.

The following self-explanatory example will clarify how the TAB function is used in BASIC:

```
10 PRINT TAB(10);"HELLO"
20 PRINT TAB(15);"HELLO AGAIN"
30 PRINT TAB(20);"HELLO FOR A THIRD TIME"
40 END
RUN
         HELLO
         ↑    HELLO AGAIN
         |    ↑    HELLO FOR A THIRD TIME
         |    |    ↑
         |    |    Starts in column 20
         |    |
         |    Starts in column 15
         |
         Starts in column 10
```

Note that there must be no space between the word TAB in a statement and the opening parenthesis.

It is possible to use several TAB functions on one line. You can also specify tabbing for a single, long output line that spans two PRINT statements. For example:

```
10 PRINT "PART NUMBER";TAB(20);"NAME";TAB(30);
20 PRINT "AMOUNT IN STOCK";TAB(50);"UNIT PRICE"
30 END
   RUN
PART NUMBER            NAME           AMOUNT IN STOCK       UNIT PRICE
↑                      ↑              ↑                     ↑
Column 1               Column 20      Column 30             Column 50
```

Remember, the semicolon at the end of a PRINT statement (see line 10) will keep the output device on the same line.

In many versions of BASIC, you can use variable names as tab stops; for example:

```
10 F=25
20 PRINT TAB(F);"GOODBYE"
30 END
RUN
                                        GOODBYE
                                        ↑
                                        Column 25
```

THE PRINT USING STATEMENT

The PRINT USING statement is the most powerful instruction in BASIC for formatted printing. The syntax of this statement varies considerably from system to system; however, the one presented here and in the examples to follow is used widely:

> Line # PRINT USING output-image variable;
> list of variables (separated by commas)

A program employing the PRINT USING statement appears in Figure B4-2. This program reads in names (N\$), pay rates (P), and hours worked (H). It then computes and sums the amounts earned (A = P*H). You should examine this example carefully before reading further.

The program uses two PRINT USING statements. Each PRINT USING statement refers to a variable that specifies how to format, or *image,* the output when the PRINT USING is executed. The program in Figure B4-2 contains two such *output-image variables:* A\$ and B\$. The PRINT USING statement in line 210 references A\$, containing the output images of variables N\$, H, and A. Similarly, statement 230 references B\$, containing the image of variable S. For both A\$ and B\$, the associated output image appears between quotation marks.

PRINT USING output images are formatted according to the following rules.

```
 10 REM THIS PROGRAM COMPUTES EMPLOYEE PAY
 20 REM    AUTHOR - C.S. PARKER
 30 REM ************VARIABLES***************
 40 REM    N$ = EMPLOYEE NAME
 50 REM    H  = HOURS WORKED
 60 REM    P  = PAY RATE
 70 REM    A  = AMOUNT EARNED BY EMPLOYEE
 80 REM    S  = SUM OF ALL AMOUNTS EARNED
 90 REM    I  = LOOP VARIABLE
100 REM    A$,B$ = OUTPUT-IMAGE VARIABLES FOR
110 REM                PRINT USING STATEMENTS
120 REM ********************************************
130 S=0
140 A$="\              \        ###        $##,###.##"
150 B$="SUM OF AMOUNTS                     $##,###.##"
160 PRINT "NAME                   HOURS      AMT EARNED"
170 FOR I=1 TO 3
180    READ N$,P,H
190    A=P*H
200    S=S+A
210    PRINT USING A$;N$,H,A
220 NEXT I
230 PRINT USING B$;S
240 DATA "JONES",6.5,160
250 DATA "SMITH",12.16,200
260 DATA "BAKER",5,100
270 END
RUN
NAME                   HOURS      AMT EARNED
JONES                    160      $ 1,040.00
SMITH                    200      $ 2,432.00
BAKER                    100      $   500.00
SUM OF AMOUNTS                    $ 3,972.00
```

Numeric Variables. All numeric variable values are placed in the areas occupied by the pound (number) signs (#) of their associated output images, in the order in which the variable names appear in the PRINT USING. If the variable value contains a decimal point, you can specify where it must appear and the number of digits to the left and right of it. For example, an image such as

#####.##

specifies that 1245.06 be printed as

ʁ1245.06

In many versions of BASIC, commas can also be automatically placed into numeric values. For example, an image such as

##,###.##

specifies that 1245.06 be printed as

1,245.06

If a number to be output with the last image is smaller than 1,000, the comma is replaced by a ƀ. Thus, 154.68 is output as

ƀƀ154.68

You should note that the # is a special symbol when used to specify an output image.

String Variables. The symbol pair \ \ is used to specify the maximum number of characters printed out for a string variable. The backslashes plus each space left between them represent the length of output. For example, a declaration such as

\ƀƀƀ\

will accommodate the full contents of any output strings of five characters or fewer.

Constants. Generally any characters other than # (for numeric variables) and the backslashes (for string variables) will be printed as they appear. Thus, the dollar sign in lines 140 and 150 and the phrase SUM OF AMOUNTS in line 150 appear on the output exactly as they do in the output image.

As you can see by inspecting this program, a major advantage of PRINT USING is that it allows neat decimal-point alignment in columns. This is a "must" for reports used in business. The use of comma spacing or the TAB function does not provide this luxury, since variable values start printing in the zone boundary or tab stop indicated, leaving the decimal point to fall where it may. This can be seen in Figure B4-1; note that the gross pay for Ann Jones is not neatly lined up under the gross pay of the other individuals.

The values of string variables automatically begin at the far left (left-justified) within the \ \ symbol pair. The values of numeric variables are aligned with respect to the decimal point. The following example should make this clear:

```
10 N$="BETSY JONES"
20 A=10
30 B=3.06
40 A$="\              \    ###     ###.##"
50 PRINT USING A$;N$,A,B
60 END
RUN
BETSY JONES          10    3.06
```

| First # field (15 characters) | Second # field (3 characters) | Third # field (3 characters to left of decimal point, 2 characters to right) |

If the values of any of the variables are too large to fit within the specified \ \ or # sign fields, either truncation, rounding, or output suppression (that is, spaces or nonnumeric symbols) may occur. Referring to the last example, if

```
N$="SHERIDAN P. WHITESIDE"
A=10.6
B=8321.46
```

the following output might be produced:

SHERIDAN P. WHIⱤⱤⱤⱤ11ⱤⱤⱤ******

| Truncation | Rounding | Output suppression |

SOLVED REVIEW PROBLEMS

Example 1

Compute the square root ($I^{1/2}$), cube root ($I^{1/3}$), and fourth root ($I^{1/4}$) of all integers I in the range 1–10. The output should be neatly labeled and formatted.

Solution

The program and associated output are shown in Figure B4-3. You should note the use of the comma in lines 160 and 200, which keeps the output device printing on the same line. The blank PRINT statement in line 220 is extremely important; it negates the effect of the comma on line 200 when the fourth roots are printed and sends the output device to the next output line.

Example 2

Straight-line depreciation expenses are computed by the formula:

$$\text{Annual depreciation charge} = \frac{\text{Original cost} - \text{Salvage value}}{\text{Useful life}}$$

Provide a depreciation schedule for a car that originally cost $7,328 and will be worth approximately $600 at the end of its 10-year useful life. The depreciation schedule should show (for each year) the depreciation charge, total depreciation so far, and the (undepreciated) balance.

Solution

The program and associated output are shown in Figure B4-4.

The annual depreciation charge is computed in line 210. Since the charge for each year is the same, it is computed before the FOR/NEXT loop beginning in line 250. This loop is used to compute the total accumulated depreciation, compute the undepreciated balance, and produce most of the output lines for the report. The PRINT USING statement in line 280 aligns the output neatly in formatted columns.

Example 3

The TAB function is extremely helpful for printing various types of geometrical designs. The program in Figure B4-5 uses the TAB function to print a triangle.

B-62

```
 10 REM THIS PROGRAM COMPUTES THE SQUARE ROOT,
 20 REM CUBE ROOT, AND FOURTH ROOT OF ALL
 30 REM INTEGERS IN THE RANGE 1-10
 40 REM   AUTHOR - C.S. PARKER
 50 REM ******************VARIABLES*******************
 60 REM   I = LOOP VARIABLE TO GENERATE 1-10
 70 REM   N = LOOP VARIABLE TO GENERATE EXPONENTS
 80 REM   X = THE COMPUTED ROOT
 90 REM ***********************************************
100 PRINT TAB(20);"COMPUTATIONS TABLE"
110 PRINT
120 PRINT "INTEGER","SQUARE ROOT","CUBE ROOT","FOURTH ROOT"
130 PRINT
140 FOR I=1 TO 10
150    REM PRINT OUT ROW NUMBER
160    PRINT I,
170    FOR N=2 TO 4
180       REM COMPUTE AND PRINT OUT THE REST OF THE ROW
190       X=I^(1/N)
200       PRINT X,
210    NEXT N
220    PRINT
230 NEXT I
240 END
RUN
```

COMPUTATIONS TABLE

INTEGER	SQUARE ROOT	CUBE ROOT	FOURTH ROOT
1	1	1	1
2	1.414213	1.259921	1.189207
3	1.732051	1.44225	1.316074
4	2	1.587401	1.414214
5	2.236068	1.709976	1.495349
6	2.44949	1.817121	1.565085
7	2.645751	1.912931	1.626577
8	2.828427	2	1.681793
9	3	2.080084	1.732051
10	3.162278	2.154435	1.778279

FIGURE B4-3
A program for computing roots.

The triangle in the figure consists of 11 lines of output. The top line of 21 asterisks and the bottom line of 1 asterisk are each produced by a single statement—statements 100 and 160, respectively. The middle nine lines of output consist of two asterisks each and are produced in the FOR/NEXT loop, using the variables S1 and S2. As each pass is made in the loop, S1 (which is initialized to 1) increases by one unit and S2 (which is initialized to 21) decreases by one unit, producing the collapsing sides of the triangle.

```
10  REM THIS PROGRAM COMPUTES STRAIGHT-LINE
20  REM DEPRECIATION CHARGES FOR AN AUTOMOBILE
30  REM    AUTHOR - C.S. PARKER
40  REM ********************VARIABLES********************
50  REM    C  = ORIGINAL COST OF AUTO
60  REM    N  = USEFUL LIFE
70  REM    S  = SALVAGE VALUE AT END OF USEFUL LIFE
80  REM    D  = ANNUAL DEPRECIATION CHARGE
90  REM    A  = ACCUMULATED DEPRECIATION
100 REM    U  = UNDEPRECIATED BALANCE
110 REM    I  = LOOP VARIABLE
120 REM    A$ = OUTPUT-IMAGE VARIABLE
130 REM ********************************************************
140 A$=" ##      $#,###.##         $#,###.##         $#,###.##"
150 PRINT TAB(12);"AUTO DEPRECIATION SCHEDULE"
160 PRINT
170 PRINT "YEAR   DEPR CHARGE      ACCUM DEP      UNDEP BALANCE"
180 PRINT
190 READ C,S,N
200 REM DEPRECIATION CALCULATION
210 D=(C-S)/N
220 A=0
230 U=C
240 REM PERFORM OTHER CALCULATIONS AND OUTPUT RESULTS
250 FOR I=1 TO N
260    A=A+D
270    U=U-D
280    PRINT USING A$;I,D,A,U
290 NEXT I
300 DATA 7328,600,10
310 END
RUN
```

AUTO DEPRECIATION SCHEDULE

YEAR	DEPR CHARGE	ACCUM DEP	UNDEP BALANCE
1	$ 672.80	$ 672.80	$6,655.20
2	$ 672.80	$1,345.60	$5,982.40
3	$ 672.80	$2,018.40	$5,309.60
4	$ 672.80	$2,691.20	$4,636.80
5	$ 672.80	$3,364.00	$3,964.00
6	$ 672.80	$4,036.80	$3,291.20
7	$ 672.80	$4,709.60	$2,618.40
8	$ 672.80	$5,382.40	$1,945.60
9	$ 672.80	$6,055.20	$1,272.80
10	$ 672.80	$6,728.00	$ 600.00

FIGURE B4-4
A depreciation problem.

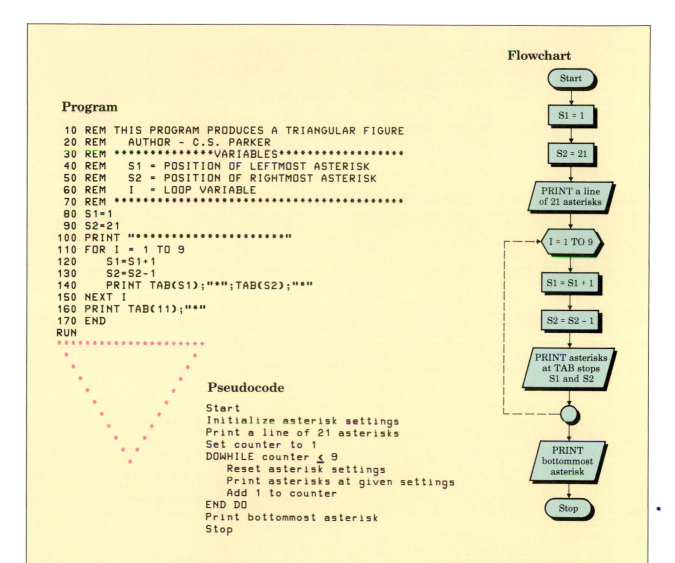

Program

```
 10 REM THIS PROGRAM PRODUCES A TRIANGULAR FIGURE
 20 REM    AUTHOR - C.S. PARKER
 30 REM *************VARIABLES******************
 40 REM    S1 = POSITION OF LEFTMOST ASTERISK
 50 REM    S2 = POSITION OF RIGHTMOST ASTERISK
 60 REM    I  = LOOP VARIABLE
 70 REM ***************************************
 80 S1=1
 90 S2=21
100 PRINT "*********************"
110 FOR I = 1 TO 9
120    S1=S1+1
130    S2=S2-1
140    PRINT TAB(S1);"*";TAB(S2);"*"
150 NEXT I
160 PRINT TAB(11);"*"
170 END
RUN
```

Pseudocode

```
Start
Initialize asterisk settings
Print a line of 21 asterisks
Set counter to 1
DOWHILE counter ≤ 9
    Reset asterisk settings
    Print asterisks at given settings
    Add 1 to counter
END DO
Print bottommost asterisk
Stop
```

Flowchart

Start

S1 = 1

S2 = 21

PRINT a line of 21 asterisks

I = 1 TO 9

S1 = S1 + 1

S2 = S2 – 1

PRINT asterisks at TAB stops S1 and S2

PRINT bottommost asterisk

Stop

FIGURE B4-5
A program, flowchart, and pseudocode for producing a triangle.

```
 10 REM THIS PROGRAM COMPUTES SUBTOTALS BY BRANCH
 20 REM    AUTHOR - C.S. PARKER
 30 REM    ***************VARIABLES*****************
 40 REM    T  = BRANCH SUBTOTAL
 50 REM    G  = GRAND TOTAL
 60 REM    N$ = SALESPERSON NAME
 70 REM    S  = SALESPERSON SALES
 80 REM    B$ = BRANCH
 90 REM    H$ = HOLDING VARIABLE FOR BRANCH
100 REM    *****************************************
110 T=0
120 G=0
130 PRINT TAB(10);"XYZ SALES REPORT"
140 PRINT
150 PRINT "NAME","SALES"
160 PRINT
170 READ N$,B$,S
180 H$=B$
190 IF N$="LAST RECORD" THEN 310
200    IF B$=H$ THEN 260
210       PRINT
220       PRINT "   SUBTOTAL - BRANCH ";H$,T
230       PRINT
240       T=0
250       H$=B$
260    G=G+S
270    T=T+S
280    PRINT N$,S
290    READ N$,B$,S
300    GOTO 190
310 PRINT
320 PRINT "   SUBTOTAL - BRANCH ";H$,T
330 PRINT
340 PRINT "   GRAND TOTAL",G
350 DATA "M. VINCENT","A",1020,"T. LOUX","A",1090
360 DATA "J. JEFFERSON","A",1400,"A.T. JONES","A",1700
370 DATA "C. SMITH","B",1100,"L. MARTINEZ","B",1400
380 DATA "M. SCHURER","C",1550,"G. SEAVER","C",1090
390 DATA "LAST RECORD","Z",0
400 END
```

```
            XYZ SALES REPORT

NAME            SALES

M. VINCENT      1020
T. LOUX         1090
J. JEFFERSON    1400
A.T. JONES      1700

    SUBTOTAL - BRANCH A     5210

C. SMITH        1100
L. MARTINEZ     1400

    SUBTOTAL - BRANCH B     2500

M. SCHURER      1550
G. SEAVER       1090

    SUBTOTAL - BRANCH C     2640

    GRAND TOTAL             10350
```

FIGURE B4-6
A control-break program and output (inset).

Example 4

The following table lists salespeople at XYZ Company, their branch affiliations, and their sales booked last week:

Name	Branch	Sales
M. Vincent	A	$1,020
T. Loux	A	$1,090
J. Jefferson	A	$1,400
A. T. Jones	A	$1,700
C. Smith	B	$1,100
L. Martinez	B	$1,400
M. Schurer	C	$1,550
G. Seaver	C	$1,090

Write a program that outputs salespeople (and their sales) by branch, subtotals sales by branch, and calculates a grand total over all branches.

Solution

The program and associated output are shown in Figure B4-6. The subtotals that "foot" each branch are examples of *control breaks*. In the program, variable B$ (branch) is referred to as the *control-break variable*. B$ "breaks" two times—when branch changes from A to B and later from B to C. At each break a subtotal is printed. Before the program ends, it prints out the final subtotal and the grand total. The program uses a "holding variable" (H$) to hold the value of B$ from the most-recently-processed record and uses a check (in line 200) to signal when a new record represents a change in branch. For this program to work, the data must be presorted by branch.

EXERCISES

Instructions: Provide an answer to each of the following questions.

1. Consider this program:

```
10 FOR I=1 TO 3
20 PRINT "HELLO NUMBER";I
30 FOR J=1 TO 4
40 PRINT X=I*J,
50 NEXT J
60 PRINT
70 NEXT I
```

a. How many lines will be printed by this program?
b. How many times will line 20 be executed?
c. What will be the fourth line printed by this program?
d. How many times will line 40 be executed?
e. What will be the value of X at the end of the program?

B-67

2. How would your answers to Exercise 1 change if the following changes were made to the program?

```
 5 LET X=0
35 LET X=X+I*J
40 PRINT X,
```

3. Consider the following program:

```
10 READ A,B,C,D,E
20 PRINT...
30 DATA (data values)
```

Write a PRINT statement for line 20 that will do the following:
a. Place the values of A, B, and C in print zones 1, 2, and 3, respectively.
b. Place the value of A in all five print zones.
c. Place the values of C, D, and E in print zones 3, 4, and 5, respectively.
d. Place the values of A, B, and C in print zones 1, 3, and 5, respectively.

4. Assume X has a value of 2590.86. Show how this value would be output when assigned to the output-image fields below. (Use b̸ to represent a blank space.)

a. `####`   c. `$#,###`
b. `##,###.##`   d. `#.##`

5. Assume N$ has a value of JONES. Show how this value would be output when assigned to the output-image fields below. (Use b̸ to represent a blank space.)

a. `\b̸b̸b̸b̸b̸b̸\`   c. `\b̸\`
b. `\b̸b̸b̸\`   d. `#####`

PROGRAMMING PROBLEMS

Instructions: Write a BASIC program to do each of the following tasks.

1. Students in a class are required to take three exams. The class performed as follows on the exams last semester:

Student Name	Scores		
	Exam 1	Exam 2	Exam 3
Jo Smith	70	80	90
Ed Lynn	40	65	59
Richard Johnson	86	93	72
Linda Harris	95	75	86
Wendy Williams	77	83	78
David Rudolph	55	83	78

Compute the average on each of the 3 exams, the average of each of the 6 students, and the overall average of the 18 scores. Print the table with these computed averages shown in their appropriate row and column positions. Use trailer values at the end of your data list so that your program can sense when there are no more records to be read.

2. Solve Problem 1 by printing letter grades in place of the average score of each of the six students. Use the following formula to assign grades to numbers: 90 and above = A, 80–89 = B, 70–79 = C, 60–69 = D, below 60 = F.

3. Redo the following table so that all of the decimal points line up and each column of data is centered below its column title:

```
NAME                GROSS PAY
----                ----------
ZELDA SMITH   $  1000
ZEB TSOSIE    $  83.25
ZENON JONES   $  .50
```

4. If P dollars are invested in an account today at a compounded interest rate of R percent per period, the amount in the account at the end of N periods is given by

$$S = P(1 + R/100)^N$$

For example, $100 will be worth $129.15 on 12/31/94 if it was invested on 12/31/89 at an interest rate of 5.25 percent compounded annually; that is,

$$\begin{aligned} S &= 100\,(1 + 5.25/100)^5 \\ &= 100\,(1.0525)^5 = 129.15 \end{aligned}$$

Produce a table showing the value of $1 at the end of 1, 2, 3, . . ., 10 years at interest rates of 10 percent, 10.5 percent, 11 percent, 11.5 percent, and 12 percent. The years should appear as rows of the table and the interest rates as columns. Make sure that your decimal points are lined up so that your output looks neat and professional.

5. Figure B4-5 shows how to use the TAB function to produce a triangle. Use the TAB function to produce a square with 10 asterisks on each side.

6. The program given in Figure B4-5 shows how to produce a hollow triangle. Revise this program so that the triangle is completely filled with asterisks.

Section 5
Advanced Topics

SUBSCRIPTING

Subscripting is one of the most useful tools in BASIC, enabling the programmer to build and store lists of numbers or strings. Such lists are commonly called *arrays.* A subscript is simply a number that refers to a position in the list or array. For example, suppose we wanted to place the data in the "averages" program of Figure B3-1 (page B-38) in a list. If we decided to call the list X, it might look as follows:

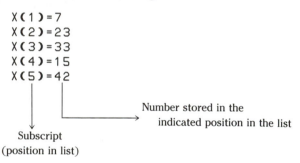

$$X(1)=7$$
$$X(2)=23$$
$$X(3)=33$$
$$X(4)=15$$
$$X(5)=42$$

Number stored in the indicated position in the list

Subscript
(position in list)

You should make certain you fully grasp the difference between a position in the list and the number stored in that position before reading further. If, for example, you were asked if $X(3) < X(4)$, how would you respond? (*Note:* 33 is not less than 15, so the answer is no.)

A Simple Subscripting Problem

Let's again find the average of a set of numbers, expanding the problem to 12 values. Also, let's assume that we wish to output the difference of each of the numbers in the list from the average. A program for solving this problem is shown in Figure B5-1. As usual, study the problem carefully before reading the commentary that follows. The first thing you may have notice is the DIM (dimension) statement in line 12. This statement instructs the computer to reserve 12* storage positions for array X. This is necessary because each number in the array is assigned to a different variable—that is, $X(1)$, $X(2)$, . . ., $X(12)$—and, as is the usual practice, each variable corresponds to a single storage location. Thus, a total of 17 storage positions will be allocated to the variables in this program, as follows:

$$X(1), \ X(2), \ X(3), \ . \ . \ ., \ X(12), \quad S, \ N, \ I, \ A, \ D$$

Specified by the DIM
statement

Nonsubscripted
variables
in program

*Many versions of BASIC will also reserve a 13th storage location, for $X(0)$. Many skilled programmers, however, choose to ignore this storage position, since other programming languages often prohibit a zero subscript.

B-70

```
10 REM THIS PROGRAM COMPUTES THE DIFFERENCES BETWEEN
20 REM NUMBERS IN A LIST FROM THE AVERAGE OF THE LIST
30 REM    AUTHOR - C.S. PARKER
40 REM ****************VARIABLES*************************
50 REM    I  = THE LOOP VARIABLE
60 REM    X  = THE ARRAY OF NUMBERS
70 REM    N  = THE NUMBER OF NUMBERS IN THE LIST
80 REM    S  = THE SUM OF THE NUMBERS IN THE LIST
90 REM    A  = THE AVERAGE OF THE NUMBERS
100 REM   D  = THE DEVIATION OF A NUMBER FROM THE AVERAGE
110 REM *****************************************************
120 REM DIM X(12)
130 LET S=0
140 READ N
150 REM READ AND SUM NUMBERS
160 FOR I=1 TO N
170    READ X(I)
180    LET S=S+X(I)
190 NEXT I
200 LET A=S/N
210 PRINT "NUMBER","AVERAGE","DIFFERENCE"
220 PRINT
230 REM RECALL VALUES, COMPUTE DEVIATIONS, AND OUTPUT RESULTS
240 FOR I=1 TO N
250    LET D=X(I)-A
260    PRINT X(I),A,D
270 NEXT I
280 DATA 12
290 DATA 5,10,11,13,4,6,8,14,2,15,1,7
300 END
RUN
NUMBER          AVERAGE          DIFFERENCE

5               8                -3
10              8                 2
11              8                 3
13              8                 5
4               8                -4
6               8                -2
8               8                 0
14              8                 6
2               8                -6
15              8                 7
1               8                -7
7               8                -1
```

FIGURE B5-1

A program for computing differences of numbers in a list from the average of the list.

Some Hints for Writing Successful Programs

In most programming languages, including BASIC, there are many ways to solve a problem. Moreover, there are good ways and bad ways. Below are some coding tips that may help you write better BASIC programs:

1. If the code you are writing looks overly complicated, stop and think of a better way to solve the problem. Beginning programmers sometimes try to do too much at one time. Often, it's advantageous to retrench and find a way to decompose the solution into easier subproblems. Most programs can be written in a very simple, straightforward manner.

2. If you can't solve an entire problem, consider solving only part of it. Oddly enough, if you've successfully solved part of the problem and you're determined to solve all of it, the solution to the remainder might later hit you when you're brushing your teeth or walking your dog.

Choose meaningful variable names.

3. Choose meaningful variable names. If you are going to represent "gross pay" by a variable, for example, use names such as G or GROSSPAY. Don't choose such names as X or VAR1.

4. Initialize all program variables used as accumulators. For example, if you have counts and sums that start at zero, and you've coded statements such as

I = I + 1 and S = S + X

to represent them, initialize I and S to zero first. Although BASIC is forgiving and will automatically set I and S to zero before it executes these statements, other languages you may learn ordinarily will not do this and may produce unpredictable results in your program.

5. Prove the correctness of every result you get from the computer. Many beginners are satisfied that their programs work as soon as they get any sort of reasonable looking output. The logic used to write the program unfortunately might be totally incorrect.

Prove every result.

6. Use comments in a program (i.e., REM statements) where appropriate. Using *too few* comments will often leave people who read your program bewildered at what it does. Unfortunately using *too many* comments will also produce the same result.

Many versions of BASIC will allow you to omit the DIM statement if the length of the array stored is 10 positions or fewer. In other words, the computer will react as if you had specified

```
120 DIM X(10)
```

in your program, even though this statement is absent. This is called *implicit* dimensioning. Most skilled programmers, however, prefer *explicit* dimensioning, where all

7. Avoid recomputing constants in a loop. For example, the code

```
100 FOR I=1 TO 10
110     A=3*B
120     READ X
130     S=S+X
140 NEXT I
150 S=S+A
```

should be rewritten as

```
100 FOR I=1 TO 10
110     READ X
120     S=S+X
130 NEXT I
140 S=S+3*B
```

Avoid tricky code.

8. Write clearly and avoid tricky code. For example, many versions of BASIC allow the two operators AND and OR. An all-inclusive IF statement that is coded in the form

```
100 IF X=3
        AND Y=2
        OR B=5
            THEN 210
```

is not as clear as the equivalent block of code:

```
100 IF X=3 AND Y=2
        THEN 210
110 IF B=5
        THEN 210
```

Some programmers insist on cramming as much code as possible into as few lines as possible, making programs very hard to read or debug.

9. Avoid unnecessary GOTO statements. For example, if the version of BASIC you are using supports the WHILE, IF/THEN/ELSE, or CASE statements, use them to avoid GOTOs.

10. Order IF statements that will appear together by putting the most frequently occurring conditions first. For example, if you put statements in the order

```
100 IF T=1 THEN 200
110 IF T=2 THEN 210
120 IF T=3 THEN 220
```

and most of the records you are examining are type 3, the computer will be going through many needless comparisons. The program would execute faster if statement 120 came first.

Use subroutines where possible.

11. Use subroutines where possible. Many languages, such as COBOL and Pascal, emphasize breaking a program up into independent modules and using subroutines or subroutinelike statements to access them. If you plan a computer career, it would be well worth your time to consider this approach to coding programs.

12. If your program is computationally intensive, it is useful to know that computers perform addition faster than multiplication. Thus a statement that computes an expression such as

```
100 A=B+B+B
```

will operate faster than one that does the same computation as

```
100 A=3*B
```

arrays are declared in one or more DIM statements. The reasons for this are similar to the ones for explicitly initializing count and sum variables to zero: The intent is made clear, the opportunity for mistakes is minimized, and the practice is a good one to adopt if you program in other languages (BASIC is among a minority of languages permitting implicit dimensioning).

Since the array in our program has 12 positions, X must be dimensioned explicitly. If the DIM statement is absent, the computer will not automatically reserve space for X(11) and X(12). Thus, the program will "bomb" when the computer attempts to manipulate one of these variables. It is, however, acceptable to reserve more storage positions in a DIM statement than you will actually use.

The DIM statement, like a DATA statement, is not executed by the computer. Although there are several acceptable places to position it, it is good practice to put it at the beginning of the program to avoid potential problems.

If several arrays need to be dimensioned, it is possible to use one DIM statement or several. For example, both

```
10 DIM A(250),X(15),Y(20),Z(200),T(6)
```

and the combination

```
10 DIM A(250),X(15)
20 DIM Y(20),Z(200),T(6)
```

are acceptable to dimension the five arrays shown.

Another interesting feature of the program in Figure B5-1 concerns statements 170 and 180, which are contained in the first loop. Each time I is incremented, a single number is taken from statement 290 and assigned to the Ith variable in the X array. Thus, when I = 1, X(1) is assigned 5; when I = 2, X(2) is assigned 10; and so on. When the computer exits the first loop and makes the computation in line 200, storage looks as follows:*

X(1) 5	X(2) 10	X(3) 11	X(4) 13
X(5) 4	X(6) 6	X(7) 8	X(8) 14
X(9) 2	X(10) 15	X(11) 1	X(12) 7
S 96	I 12	N 12	A 8
D 0			

When the second loop is encountered (line 240), the computer has all the information it needs in storage to compute the 12 differences ($D = X(I) - A$). Thus, all that needs to be done in this loop is to successively recall from storage X(1), X(2), . . ., X(12), subtract A from these values, and compute the difference, D.

You should note that it would be extremely inconvenient to solve a problem like the one in Figure B5-1 without the use of subscripts. This is so because we need to consider the values in the array twice—once to compute the average and again to compute the differences.

The general format of the DIM statement is as follows:

Line # DIM list of dimensioned arrays (separated by commas)

---

*In some versions of BASIC, I would be set to 13 even though the loop was executed only 12 times. This is because the first time NEXT is encountered, I is set to 2; the twelfth and last time NEXT is encountered, I is set to 13. Some computer systems will "roll back" this value to 12 upon leaving the loop.

B-74

FIGURE B5-2

A program that manipulates a string list.

```
 10 REM THIS PROGRAM ILLUSTRATES HOW TO HANDLE
 20 REM STRING DATA IN AN ARRAY
 30 REM   AUTHOR - C.S. PARKER
 40 REM ***************VARIABLES******************
 50 REM   I = LOOP VARIABLE
 60 REM   A$ = AN ARRAY STORING THE NAME OF FRUITS
 70 REM *****************************************
 80 DIM A$(5)
 90 REM READ LIST OF FRUITS
100 FOR I=1 TO 5
110 READ A$(I)
120 NEXT I
130 REM PRINT OUT LIST IN REVERSE ORDER
140 FOR I=5 TO 1 STEP -1
150 PRINT A$(I)
160 NEXT I
170 DATA "APPLES","ORANGES","BANANAS"
180 DATA "PEACHES","CHERRIES"
190 END
RUN
CHERRIES
PEACHES
BANANAS
ORANGES
APPLES
```

String Lists

The examples provided in the previous subsections illustrated lists of *numbers*. BASIC also allows the programmer to form lists of *strings*. For example, suppose we wish to create a list of fruits (say, APPLES, ORANGES, BANANAS, PEACHES, and CHERRIES) and then output the list in reverse order. The program in Figure B5-2 does just this. Note that subscripted string variables are named in the same way as unsubscripted *(scalar)* ones—a single letter followed by the dollar sign.

Double Subscripting

Data to be processed by the computer system are sometimes better represented in two-dimensional (table) form than in one-dimensional (list) form. For example, consider the following data, which show the vote distribution on a certain issue in different schools of a university:

	Voted Yes	Voted No	Didn't Vote
Business	205	152	38
Liberal arts	670	381	115
Engineering	306	251	47
Forestry	112	33	14

```
10 REM THIS PROGRAM READS AN ARRAY OF NUMBERS, TOTALS IT,
20 REM AND OUTPUTS EACH ARRAY VALUE AS A FRACTION OF THE TOTAL
30 REM     AUTHOR - C.S. PARKER
40 REM ************************VARIABLES************************
50 REM    V       = THE ARRAY OF NUMBERS
60 REM    I,J,M,N = LOOP VARIABLES
70 REM    S       = THE SUM OF ALL THE NUMBERS IN THE ARRAY
80 REM    P       = THE FRACTION OBTAINED
90 REM ********************************************************
100 DIM V(4,3)
110 S=0
120 REM READ NUMBERS INTO ARRAY AND ALSO TOTAL THE NUMBERS
130 FOR I=1 TO 4
140    FOR J=1 TO 3
150       READ V(I,J)
160       S=S+V(I,J)
170    NEXT J
180 NEXT I
190 REM COMPUTE FRACTIONS AND OUTPUT RESULTS
200 FOR M=1 TO 4
210    FOR N=1 TO 3
220       P=V(M,N)/S
230       PRINT P,
240    NEXT N
250    PRINT
260 NEXT M
270 DATA 205,152,38
280 DATA 670,381,115
290 DATA 306,251,47
300 DATA 112,33,14
310 END
RUN
  .088210        .065405        .016351
  .288296        .163941        .049484
  .131670        .108003        .020224
  .048193        .014200        .006024
```

FIGURE B5-3

A program that reads a table, totals all the numbers in the table, and prints the fraction that each number is with regard to the sum.

These data, which include four rows and three columns of numbers, exist naturally in the form of a table. It would be most convenient if we could give the table a name (V, for example) and store any number in the table with reference to its row and column position. For example, 115, which is in row 2 and column 3, would be referenced by the subscripted variable V(2, 3).

Fortunately, BASIC permits us to represent two-dimensional tables in the simple manner just described. Thus, we could store the table numbers in the following 12 variables:

$$
\begin{array}{lll}
V(1, 1) = 205 & V(1, 2) = 152 & V(1, 3) = 38 \\
V(2, 1) = 670 & V(2, 2) = 381 & V(2, 3) = 115 \\
V(3, 1) = 306 & V(3, 2) = 251 & V(3, 3) = 47 \\
V(4, 1) = 112 & V(4, 2) = 33 & V(4, 3) = 14
\end{array}
$$

It is relatively easy to create such a table in BASIC and to later access each number and process it as needed. To see how this might be done, refer to the program in Figure B5-3 which totals all of the numbers in the table and subsequently divides each number in the table by this total.

You should observe that in this program, as is the usual practice with subscripts, a DIM statement is immediately employed to declare the size of the table. Then nested loops are established in statements 130–180 to generate automatically the row ($I = 1, 2, 3, 4$) and column ($J = 1, 2, 3$) subscripts. Thus, the first time these nested loops are executed,

$$I = 1, J = 1, V(1, 1) \text{ is assigned 205, and } S = 0 + 205 = 205$$

The second time,

$$I = 1, J = 2, V(1, 2) \text{ is assigned 152, and } S = 205 + 152 = 357$$

and so forth.

In the nested loops in statements 200–260, we simply recall $V(1, 1)$, $V(1, 2)$, . . ., $V(4, 3)$ successively from storage and, as we do so, divide each by the table sum and print out the fraction obtained. Note that the variables (M, N) used to represent the subscripts in the second set of nested loops are different than those (I, J) used in the first set. Although we could have used I and J again, the example illustrates that any choice of a subscript variable will do as long as the proper numbers are substituted by the computer to represent the row and column involved.

Two final points on the program in Figure B5-3 deserve your close attention. First, note that the PRINT statement in line 230 contains a comma. This keeps output belonging in the same row printing on the same line. Second, note the blank PRINT statement on line 250. This statement forces the output device onto a new line, where a new row of numbers is printed.

FUNCTIONS AND SUBROUTINES

Functions

A *function* is a precoded formula that is referenced in a computer program. BASIC permits two types of functions: *library (built-in) functions* and *user-defined functions*. Two widely used library functions are INT and RND, which respectively truncate and generate random numbers. Since these functions are built into the BASIC language, the computer system knows exactly what type of action to take when it runs into one of them. Many other library functions are probably available with the version of BASIC used by your computer system. Following is a partial list of some of the more common ones:

Function	Purpose
ABS(X)	Returns the absolute value of X
SQR(X)	Calculates the square root of X (X must be $>=0$)
RND	Returns a random number between .000000 and .999999
SIN(X)	Computes the sine of X (X must be in radians)
COS(X)	Computes the cosine of X (X must be in radians)
TAN(X)	Computes the tangent of X (X must be in radians)
LOG(X)	Calculates the natural logarithm of X (X must be positive)
EXP(X)	Calculates the term e^x, where e is approximately 2.718
INT(X)	Returns the greatest integer $<=X$

You can also define your own functions. This can be useful when there is a formula you need to use repeatedly that is not a library function. User-defined functions are specified with the DEF statement. For example, suppose we wanted to compute the commission due a salesperson as

☐ 15 percent of gross sales of "brand-name" items

☐ 10 percent of gross sales of "nonbrand" items

Thus, if S1 represents gross sales of brand-name items and S2 is gross sales of nonbrand items, the commission, C, may be calculated as

$$C = .15 * S1 + .10 * S2$$

A program that computes this commission for three salespeople is given in Figure B5-4. You should inspect this program carefully before proceeding further.

Note in the program that the formula for computing the commissions is defined in line 90. The formula must be defined (with a DEF statement) before it can be used (as in statement 120).

The format of the DEF statement is

Line # DEF FNx (y) = z

where x is a single alphabetic letter chosen by the programmer, y is a list of arguments (which may be as large as five variables, depending on the computer system used), and z is a valid BASIC expression. It is also permissible to use several DEF statements in a single program. Note that the word DEF must be followed by a space and then FN. You must remember, however, to define the functions early in your program, *before* you reference them.

You should also note that the formula, or function, in the figure also contains two *dummy arguments*, S1 and S2. The only significance of dummy arguments is that they demonstrate how the function will be computed. After reading in the salesperson information in line 110, the computer system prints out in line 120 the salesperson's name and total commission due. Before the computer calculates and prints the commission, it "refers" to line 90 and substitutes A for S1 and B for S2.

A and B are called *real arguments*. Real arguments are always substituted for corresponding dummy arguments, according to their respective positioning within the parentheses, whenever the function is used in the programs.

```
 10 REM THIS PROGRAM COMPUTES SALES COMMISSIONS
 20 REM    AUTHOR - C.S. PARKER
 30 REM ****************VARIABLES**************
 40 REM    S1,S2 = DUMMY ARGUMENTS
 50 REM    A,B   = REAL ARGUMENTS
 60 REM    N$    = SALESPERSON NAME
 70 REM    I     = LOOP VARIABLE
 80 REM ***************************************
 90 DEF FNC(S1,S2)=.15*S1+.10*S2   ◄── The function is defined here
100 FOR I=1 TO 3
120     READ N$,A,B
120     PRINT N$,FNC(A,B)   ◄── The function is executed here
130 NEXT I
140 DATA "JOE SMITH",700.00,1000.00
150 DATA "ZELDA GREY",600.00,1200.00
160 DATA "SUE JOHNSON",1000.00,500.00
170 END
RUN
JOE SMITH         205
ZELDA GREY        210
SUE JOHNSON       200
```

The program could have also been written by using the same variable names as both dummy and real arguments. All that you would need to change are lines 110 and 120:

```
110 READ N$,S1,S2
120 PRINT N$,FNC(S1,S2)
```

This ability to define a function is one of the most useful and most powerful features of BASIC. It is also the capability most overlooked, even by many skilled programmers.

Subroutines

BASIC *subroutines* are partial programs, or subprograms, that are contained within a BASIC program (called the *main program*). They are particularly effective when a series of statements in a program is to be performed numerous times or, perhaps, at many different places in the overall program.

Subroutines introduce two new statements, GOSUB and RETURN, which have the following formats:

```
Line # GOSUB line number
            .
            .
            .
Line # RETURN
```

```
10 REM THIS PROGRAM DEMONSTRATES THE USE OF
20 REM SUBROUTINES AND MENUS
30 REM    AUTHOR - C.S. PARKER
40 REM ***************VARIABLES******************
50 REM   C$,A$ = ARRAYS TO HOLD EXPENSE CATEGORIES
60 REM                AND AMOUNTS
60 REM        N = NUMBER OF RECORDS
70 REM        X = MENU-SELECTION VARIABLE
80 REM    H,H$ = HOLDING VARIABLES FOR LARGEST
90 REM               EXPENSE AND CATEGORY
100 REM       T = TOTAL EXPENSES
110 REM ******************************************
120 DIM C$(100),A(100)
130 REM DATA ENTRY
140 READ N
150    FOR I=1 TO N
160       READ C$(I),A(I)
170    NEXT I
180 REM MENU AND SELECTION
190    PRINT
200    PRINT
210    PRINT "PROGRAM OPTIONS"
220    PRINT
230    PRINT "    1 - THE LARGEST CATEGORY"
240    PRINT "    2 - TOTAL COST"
250    PRINT "    3 - ALL CATEGORIES EXCEEDING $1000"
260    PRINT "    4 - END PROGRAM"
270    PRINT
280    PRINT "WHICH OPTION DO YOU WISH TO TAKE (TYPE IN NUMBER)";
290    INPUT X
300 REM CASE STRUCTURE FOR SUBROUTINE TRANSFER
310    ON X GOTO 320,340,360,380
320    GOSUB 400
330    GOTO 310
340      GOSUB 540
350      GOTO 310
360        GOSUB 650
370        GOTO 310
380            STOP
```

PROGRAM OPTIONS

   1 - THE LARGEST CATEGORY
   2 - TOTAL COST
   3 - ALL CATEGORIES EXCEEDING $1000
   4 - END PROGRAM

WHICH OPTION DO YOU WISH TO TAKE (TYPE IN NUMBER)?

CATEGORIES EXCEEDING $1000

CATEGORY	EXPENSE
SALARIES	8500
RENT	2000
ADVERTISING	1100
DEPRECIATION	1200

NEXT MENU SELECTION (TYPE IN NUMBER)?

FIGURE B5-5

A menu-selection program using subroutines. The program's output is in the inset at the right.

The GOSUB statement causes immediate branching to the first statement in the subroutine. The RETURN statement causes branching back to the main program, to the statement that immediately follows the invoking GOSUB (that is, the GOSUB that caused the branching). An example of a program that uses subroutines and the output of this program are given in Figure B5-5.

The program processes accounting expenses for the past month. Users of the program have several options—for example, finding the category with the greatest expense, computing total expenses (over all categories), or listing all categories with an expense exceeding $1,000. These options are presented to the user in the form of a *menu*. Once the user selects a choice on the menu, either a 1, 2, 3, or 4 is typed in, corresponding to the options in lines 230–260. Given the choice, the computer then branches to the appropriate subroutine to be processed (or ends the program). If, for example, the user selects option 2 (total cost), the computer branches to line

```
390 REM ************LARGEST COST SUBROUTINE**************
400    H=A(1)
410    H$=C$(1)
420    FOR I=2 TO N
430    IF A(I)<=H THEN 460
440       H=A(I)
450       H$=C$(I)
460    NEXT I
470    PRINT
480    PRINT "LARGEST EXPENSE:";H$;"  (AMOUNT =";H;")"
490    PRINT
500    PRINT "NEXT MENU SELECTION (TYPE IN NUMBER)";
510    INPUT X
520    RETURN
530 REM ************TOTAL COST SUBROUTINE***************
540    T=0
550    FOR I=1 TO N
560       T=T+A(I)
570    NEXT I
580    PRINT
590    PRINT "TOTAL COST IS...$";T
600    PRINT
610    PRINT "NEXT MENU SELECTION (TYPE IN NUMBER)";
620    INPUT X
630    RETURN
640 REM ***********$1000-OR-MORE SUBROUTINE**************
650    PRINT
660    PRINT " CATEGORIES EXCEEDING $1000"
670    PRINT
680    PRINT "CATEGORY", "EXPENSE"
690    FOR I=1 TO N
700       IF A(I)<1000 THEN 720
710          PRINT C$(I),A(I)
720    NEXT I
730    PRINT
740    PRINT "NEXT MENU SELECTION (TYPE IN NUMBER)";
750    INPUT X
760    RETURN
770 REM ************DATA STATEMENTS*****************
780 DATA 8
790 DATA "SALARIES",8500,"RENT",2000,"ADVERTISING",1100
800 DATA "UTILITIES",590,"SUPPLIES",200,"DEPRECIATION",1200
810 DATA "INSURANCE",300,"TAXES",150
820 END
```

540 and proceeds from that point until line 630 (RETURN) is encountered. It then goes back to the main part of the program and continues with the statement following the invoking GOSUB (in other words, statement 350).

The program in Figure B5-5 also demonstrates the use of the ON GOTO statement (line 310). The format of this statement is

> Line # ON case-variable GOTO line-number, line-number, . . .

A *case variable* (X in our program) is one that has values such as 1, 2, 3, and so forth that correspond to special situations, or "cases," that must be processed. If X is equal to 1, the computer branches to the first line number after the GOTO; if X is equal to 2, it branches to the second line number; and so on. The *case structure* made possible by BASIC's ON GOTO is ideal for menu-selection programs and is a special form of the selection structure discussed earlier.

Subroutines are useful because the programmer can assign complicated tasks or calculations to several subroutines and avoid cluttering up the main part of the program. Each independent task should be done in a separate subroutine, making the main program logic much easier to follow. Such a modular programming style allows new programmers hired by a company to understand more quickly how existing programs work. It also makes debugging easier, since each subroutine can be tested independently with dummy variables.

SOLVED REVIEW PROBLEM

A company that produces three products currently has eight salespeople. The sales of each product by each salesperson are given in the following table:

Salesperson	Units Sold		
	Product 1	Product 2	Product 3
William Ing	100	50	65
Ed Wilson	500	0	0
Ann Johnson	200	25	600
Edna Farber	150	30	500
Norris Ames	600	80	150
Elma Jace	100	410	800
Vilmos Zisk	300	30	60
Ellen Venn	400	0	0

The latest unit prices on products 1, 2, and 3 are $1, 1.25, and .85, respectively.

Use the preceding data to produce the following table. Use subscripted variables to represent the totals associated with the three products and eight salespeople.

```
    NAME        PRODUCT1    PRODUCT2    PRODUCT3     TOTAL

WILLIAM ING     100.00       62.50       55.25      217.75
ED WILSON       500.00        0.00        0.00      500.00
ANN JOHNSON     200.00       31.25      510.00      741.25
EDNA FARBER     150.00       37.50      425.00      612.50
NORRIS AMES     600.00      100.00      127.50      827.50
ELMA JACE       100.00      512.50      680.00    1,292.50
VILMOS ZISK     300.00       37.50       51.00      388.50
ELLEN VENN      400.00        0.00        0.00      400.00

TOTALS        2,350.00      781.25    1,848.75    4,980.00
```

A program solution to this problem is given in Figure B5-6, which appears at the right.

```
 10 REM THIS PROGRAM CALCULATES PRODUCT SALES ATTRIBUTABLE
 20 REM TO VARIOUS SALESPEOPLE IN A COMPANY
 30 REM     AUTHOR - C.S. PARKER
 40 REM ********************VARIABLES********************
 50 REM    N$    = THE SALESPERSON NAME
 60 REM    M     = THE NUMBER OF SALESPEOPLE
 70 REM    P     = THE ARRAY OF PRODUCT PRICES
 80 REM    Q     = THE UNITS OF A PRODUCT SOLD BY A SALESPERSON
 90 REM    S     = THE ARRAY SAVING PRODUCT SALES
100 REM                   IN EACH ROW BEFORE THEY ARE OUTPUT
110 REM    T     = THE ROW TOTALS
120 REM    C     = THE ARRAY SAVING THE COLUMN TOTALS
130 REM    G     = THE GRAND TOTAL OF ALL SALES
140         I,J  = LOOP VARIABLES
150 REM    A$,B$ = OUTPUT-IMAGE VARIABLES FOR PRINT USING
160 REM ****************************************************
170 DIM C(3),P(3),S(3)
180 PRINT "   NAME        PRODUCT1   PRODUCT2   PRODUCT3    TOTAL"
190 PRINT
200 READ M
210 REM INITIALIZATIONS
220 FOR I=1 TO 3
230    C(I)=0
240    READ P(I)
250 NEXT I
260 G=0
270 A$="\            \   #,###.##   #,###.##   #,###.##   #,###.##"
280 B$="TOTALS          #,###.##   #,###.##   #,###.##   #,###.##"
290 REM MAIN COMPUTATIONS
300 FOR I=1 TO M
310    T=0
320    READ N$
330    FOR J=1 TO 3
340       READ Q
350       S(J)=Q*P(J)
360       C(J)=C(J)+S(J)
370       T=T+S(J)
380       G=G+S(J)
390    NEXT J
400    PRINT USING A$;N$,S(1),S(2),S(3),T
410 NEXT I
420 PRINT
430 PRINT USING B$;C(1),C(2),C(3),G
440 DATA 8
450 DATA 1,1.25,.85
460 DATA "WILLIAM ING",100,50,65
470 DATA "ED WILSON",500,0,0
480 DATA "ANN JOHNSON",200,25,600
490 DATA "EDNA FARBER",150,30,500
500 DATA "NORRIS AMES",600,80,150
510 DATA "ELMA JACE",100,410,800
520 DATA "VILMOS ZISK",300,30,60
530 DATA "ELLEN VENN",400,0,0
540 END
```

FIGURE B5-6   A program for cross-classifying sales data.

The outer loop (lines 300–410) is used to read each salesperson's record. The inner loop (lines 330–390), which executes three times for every iteration of the outer loop, is used to multiply sales of each of the three products by its price, accumulate the row totals, and accumulate the column footings.

EXERCISES

Instructions: Provide an answer to each of the following questions.

1. Consider the following program:

```
10  DIM A(5)
20  FOR I=1 TO 5
30  READ A(I)
40  LET A(I)=A(I)+1
50  NEXT I
60  DATA 35,18,-6,42,27
```

What is the final value of

   a. A(1)?   b. A(2)?   c. A(3)?   d. A(4)?   e. A(5)?

2. Consider the following program:

```
10 DIM A(6)
20 A(1)=0
30 FOR I=2 TO 6
40 READ A(I)
50 LET A(I)=A(I-1)
60 NEXT I
70 DATA 35,18,-6,42,27
```

What is the final value of

   a. A(1)?   b. A(2)?   c. A(3)?   d. A(4)?   e. A(5)?

3. Consider the following program:

```
10 DIM A(4,4)
20 FOR I=1 TO 4
30 FOR J=1 TO 4
40 READ A(I,J)
50 NEXT J
60 NEXT I
70 DATA 12,2,0,3,1,4,2,7,6,10,9,0,11,3,8,7
```

What is the final value of

a. A(1,3)?   b. A(2,2)?   c. A(3,4)?   d. A(4,3)?

PROGRAMMING PROBLEMS

Instructions: Write a BASIC program to do each of the following tasks.

1. The following is a list of salaries of the six employees in a certain company:

Name	Salary
T. Jones	$43,000
F. Smith	$31,000
K. Johnston	$22,000
P. Miner	$18,000
C. Altman	$27,000
A. Barth	$19,000

Calculate and output the average salary for the company as well as the names of all people whose salaries exceed the average.

2. Read the 10 numbers in the following list, and then output the list in reverse order (that is, 12, 43, 6, etc.):

31, 15, 85, 36, 22, 81, 70, 6, 43, 12

3. The following list contains names and sexes of people at XYZ company: Janice Jones (female), Bill Smith (male), Debra Parks (female), Elaine Johnson (female), William Anderson (male), Art James (male), Bill Finley (male), and Ellen Ott (female).

Read the list into the computer in the order given. Then prepare and output two separate lists—one composed of all of the males and the other of all of the females.

4. Write a program that reads the following matrix,

$$\begin{bmatrix} 8 & 7 & 3 \\ 2 & 4 & 1 \\ 6 & 5 & 8 \end{bmatrix}$$

adds the number 5 to each element (number) of the matrix, and prints the result.

5. ABC Company has the following accounts receivable data:

Customer Name	Previous Balance	Payments	New Purchases
Clara Bronson	$700	$500	$300
Lon Brooks	100	100	0
Louise Chaplin	0	0	100
Jack Davies	50	0	0
Emil Murray	600	600	200
Tom Swanson	300	100	50
Lucy Allen	500	500	80

Write a subroutine that computes the new balance for each customer. Assume that unpaid portions of previous balances are assessed a 2 percent finance charge each month. The main part of your program should perform all the input/output functions necessary to support and supplement the subroutine.

BASIC STATEMENT COMMANDS

Statement	Description	Example
DEF	Sets up a user-defined function (B-78)	`90 DEF FNC(S1,S2)=.15*S1+.10*S2`
DIM	Dimensions an array (B-74)	`120 DIM X(12)`
END	The last statement in a program (B-5, B-18)	`250 END`

FOR/NEXT	The beginning and ending statements in a loop (B-41)	`160 FOR I=1 TO N`
		
		`190 NEXT I`

GOSUB/RETURN	Branch to a subroutine; Return to main program from subroutine (B-79)	`120 GOSUB 150`
		
		`190 RETURN`

GOTO	An unconditional branch (B-16)	`140 GOTO 100`
IF	A conditional branch (B-14)	`110 IF A=-1 THEN 160`
IF/THEN/ELSE	A conditional branch (B-47)	`110 IF S>5000 THEN B=500` `             ELSE B=0`
INPUT	Enables data to be entered interactively (B-37)	`80 INPUT X`
LET	An assignment (replacement) statement (B-4, B-14)	`30 LET C=A+B`
ON GOTO	Branches to a specific case (B-81)	`100 ON M GOTO 300,400,500`
PRINT	Displays or prints program output (B-5, B-15)	`160 PRINT N$`

PRINT USING	Enables neatly formatted output (B-59)	`100 A$=" ###.##"`
		
		`200 PRINT USING A$;X`

READ/DATA	Assigns values to variables from a list of data (B-4, B-13)	`20 READ A,B`
		
		`50 DATA 8,16`

REM	A program remark (B-4, B-17)	`100 REM DEPRECIATION CALCULATION`
STOP	Stops a program (B-39)	`80 STOP`

WHILE/WEND	The beginning and ending statements in a loop (B-48)	`150 WHILE X>0`
		
		`200 WEND`

Note: Numbers in parentheses in the second column are the pages on which the statement is described.

Glossary

The terms shown in boldface are presented in the text as key terms. The boldfaced number in parentheses at the end of the definition of each term indicates the page (or pages) on which the term is boldfaced in the text. The terms shown in boldface italic are other commonly used and important words often encountered in information processing environments. The boldface italic number in parentheses after the definition of each term indicates the page on which the term is first mentioned.

ABC. See Atanasoff-Berry Computer. **(66)**

Access mechanism. A mechanical device in the disk pack or disk unit that positions the read/write heads on the proper tracks. **(129)**

Accumulator. A register that stores the result of an arithmetic or logical operation. **(98)**

Action diagram. A programming tool that helps programmers code structured programs. **(324)**

Active cell. In spreadsheet software, the worksheet cell at which the highlight is currently positioned. Also called the *current cell.* **(412)**

Ada. A structured programming language developed by the Department of Defense and named after Ada Augusta Byron, the world's first programmer. **(353)**

Add-in board. A board that may be inserted into the computer's system unit to perform one or more functions. **(112, 474)**

Address. An identifiable location in storage where data are kept. Primary memory and direct-access secondary storage devices such as disk are addressable. *(97, 134)*

Address register. A register containing the memory location of an instruction to be executed. **(98)**

AI. See Artificial intelligence. **(522)**

Altair 8800. The first microcomputer system to achieve some degree of commercial success. **(78)**

ALU. See Arithmetic/logic unit. **(96)**

American National Standards Institute (ANSI). An organization that acts as a national clearinghouse for standards in the United States. *(73)*

Analog computer. A computer that measures continuous phenomena, such as speed and height, and converts them into numbers. **(94)**

Analog transmission. The transmission of data as continuous wave patterns. **(226)**

Analysis. In program and systems development, the process of studying a problem area to determine what should be done. **(285)**

Analytical engine. A device conceived by Charles Babbage in the 1800s to perform computations. This machine is considered the forerunner of today's modern electronic computer. **(63)**

ANSI. See American National Standards Institute. *(73)*

APL. See A Programming Language. **(352)**

Applications generator. A fourth-generation-language product that can be used to quickly create applications software. **(296)**

Applications package. A fourth-generation-language product that, when the user sets a few parameters, becomes a finished applications program ready to meet specific end-user needs. **(290)**

Applications programmer. A programmer who codes programs that do the useful work—such as payroll, inventory control, and accounting tasks—for end users of a computer system. Contrasts with systems programmer. **(569)**

Applications software. Programs that do the useful work—such as payroll, inventory control, and accounting tasks—for end users of a computer system. Contrast with systems software. **(50, 282)**

A Programming Language (APL). A highly compact programming language popular for problem-solving applications. **(352)**

Arithmetic/logic unit (ALU). The part of the computer that contains the circuitry to perform addition, subtraction, multiplication, division, and comparison operations. **(96)**

Artificial intelligence (AI). The ability of a machine to perform actions that are characteristic of human intelligence, such as reasoning and learning. **(522)**

ASCII. An acronym for American Standard Code for Information Interchange. ASCII is a 7-bit code widely used to represent data for processing and communications. **(102)**

Assembler. A computer program that takes assembly-language instructions and converts them to machine language. **(270)**

Assembly language. A low-level programming language that uses mnemonic codes in place of the 0s and 1s of machine language. **(71, 340)**

Asynchronous transmission. The transmission of data over a line one character at a time. Each character is preceded by a "start bit" and followed by a "stop bit." Contrasts with synchronous transmission. **(228)**

Atanasoff-Berry Computer (ABC). The world's first electronic digital computer, built in the early 1940s by Dr. John V. Atanasoff and his assistant, Clifford Berry. **(66)**

Audit. An inspection used to determine if a system or procedure is working as it should or if a claimed amount is correct. **(600)**

Auxiliary equipment. Equipment that works in a "standalone" mode, independently of direct CPU interaction. Some examples are bursters, decollators, key-to-disk units, and key-to-tape units. **(41)**

Bar code. A machine-readable code consisting of sets of bars of varying widths. The codes are prominently displayed on the packaging of many retail goods and are commonly read with wand readers. *(190)*

BASIC. See Beginner's All-Purpose Symbolic Instruction Code. **(341)**

Batch processing. Processing transactions or other data in groups, at periodic intervals. Contrasts with real-time processing. **(54)**

Beginner's All-Purpose Symbolic Instruction Code (BASIC). An easy-to-learn, high-level programming language developed at Dartmouth College in the 1960s. **(341)**

Benchmark test. A test used to measure computer system performance under typical use conditions prior to purchase. The test is analogous to the rigorous "test drive" you take with a car before you buy it. **(554)**

Binary. A number system with two possible states. The binary system is fundamental to computers because electronic devices often function in two possible states—for example "on" or "off," "current present" or "current not present," "clockwise" or "counterclockwise," and so forth. **(99, A-2)**

Bit. A binary digit, such as 0 or 1. The 0- or 1-states are used by computer systems to take advantage of the binary nature of electronics. Bits often are assembled into bytes and words when manipulated or stored. **(99)**

Bit mapping. A term, used with certain display devices and dot-matrix printers, that implies that each of the dots in the output image may be individually operator controlled. **(168)**

Bits per second (bps). A measure of the speed of a communications device. **(224)**

Blocking. The combining of two or more records (into a "block") to conserve storage space and increase processing efficiency. **(148)**

Board. A hardware device into which processor chips and memory chips are fitted, along with related circuitry. **(112)**

Bps. See Bits per second. **(224)**

Bridge. An interface that enables two similar networks to communicate. Contrast with gateway. **(237)**

Buffer. A temporary storage area used to balance the speed differences between two devices. For example, buffers are used within the computer unit to store physical records so that the logical records that comprise them may be processed faster. Buffers are also used in many terminals and data communications devices to store characters in large blocks before they are sent to another device. **(148)**

Bug. An error in a program or system. *(299)*

Burster. A device used to separate perforated, fan-fold paper into single sheets. *(187)*

Bus. A set of wires that acts as a data highway between the CPU and other devices. **(474)**

Bus network. A telecommunications network consisting of a line and several devices that are tapped into the line. The network is so named because data are picked up and dropped off at devices similarly to the way passengers are picked up and dropped off at bus stops. **(238)**

Byte. A configuration of seven or eight bits used to represent a single character of information. **(104)**

C. A programming language that has the portability of a high-level language and the executional efficiency of an assembly language. **(353)**

Cache disk. A disk management scheme whereby more data than are necessary are read from disk during each time-consuming disk fetch and stored in internal memory, to minimize the number of fetches. **(144)**

CAD. See Computer-aided design. **(519)**

CAD/CAM. An acronym for *computer-aided design/computer-aided manufacturing.* CAD/CAM is a general term applied to the use of computer technology to automate design and manufacturing operations in industry. *(520)*

CAI. See Computer-assisted instruction. *(606)*

Callback device. A device on the receiving end of a communications network that ascertains the authenticity of the sender by calling the sender back. **(599)**

CAM. See Computer-aided manufacturing. **(520)**

Cartridge disk. Magnetic disk in which a single disk platter is contained in a sealed plastic case, which in turn is mounted onto a disk unit when data are to be read from or written to the disk inside. **(142)**

Cartridge tape. Magnetic tape in which the supply and take-up reels are contained in a small plastic case, which in turn is mounted onto a tape unit when data are to be read from or written to the tape inside. **(145)**

Case control structure. A control structure that can be formed by nesting two or more selection control structures. **(318)**

Cathode-ray tube (CRT). A display device that contains a long-necked display-tube mechanism similar to that used in television sets. **(171)**

Cell. In spreadsheet software, an area of the worksheet that holds a single label or value. **(412)**

Cell pointer. In spreadsheet software, a cursorlike mechanism used to point to cells on the display screen. **(413)**

Central processing unit (CPU). The piece of hardware, also known as the *computer,* that interprets and executes program instructions and communicates with input, output, and storage devices. **(5)**

Chief information officer (CIO). See Vice-president of information systems. **(573)**

Chief programmer team. A team of programmers, generally assigned to a large programming project, that is coordinated by a highly experienced person called the *chief programmer.* **(299)**

CIO. See Chief information officer. **(573)**

Clip art. Prepackaged artwork designed to be imported into text documents, say, by desktop publishing software. **(390)**

Coaxial cable. A transmission line developed for transmitting data at high speeds. **(222)**

COBOL. See Common Business-Oriented Language. **(345)**

Coding. The writing of instructions, in a programming language, that will cause the computer system to perform a specific set of operations. **(295)**

COM. See Computer output microfilm. **(196)**

Command language. A programming language used to communicate with the operating system. **(257)**

Command-language translator. Systems software that translates instructions written in a command language into machine-language instructions. **(257)**

Common Business-Oriented Language (COBOL). A high-level programming language developed for transaction processing applications. **(345)**

Common carrier. A government-regulated private organization that provides communications services to the public. **(231)**

Communications medium. The intervening substance, such as a telephone wire or cable, that connects two physically distant hardware devices. **(221)**

Communications satellite. An earth-orbiting device that relays communications signals over long distances. **(223)**

Compiler. A computer program that translates a source program written by a user or programmer in a high-level programming language into machine language. The translation takes place before the translated program is executed. Contrasts with interpreter. **(268)**

Computer. See Central processing unit. **(5, 36)**

Computer-aided design (CAD). A general term applied to the use of computer technology to automate design functions in industry. **(519)**

Computer-aided manufacturing (CAM). A general term applied to the use of computer technology to automate manufacturing functions in industry. **(520)**

Computer-assisted instruction (CAI). The use of computers to supplement personalized teaching instruction by providing the student with sequences of instruction under program control. The progression through the instructional materials in such a system enables students to learn at their own rate. ***(606)***

Computer crime. The use of computers to commit unauthorized acts. **(593)**

Computer engineering. The field of knowledge that includes the design of computer hardware systems. Computer engineering is offered as a degree program in several colleges and universities. **(578)**

Computer ethics. A term that refers to ethical behavior with regard to computer-related issues. **(602)**

Computer information systems (CIS) curriculum. A course of study, normally offered by business schools, that prepares students for entry-level jobs as applications programmers or systems analysts. **(578)**

Computer operations. (1) The functions related to the physical operation of the computer system. (2) A curriculum offered in many schools that is oriented toward training students to enter the computer operations field. Computer operations curricula often train students to become computer or data-entry operators. **(578)**

Computer operations manager. The person who oversees the computer operations area in an organization. The computer operations manager is responsible for tasks such as hiring operations personnel and scheduling work the system is to perform. **(568)**

Computer operator. A person skilled in the operation of the computer and its support devices. The operator is responsible for tasks such as mounting and dismounting tapes and disks and removing printouts from the line or page printer. **(567)**

Computer output microfilm (COM). A term referring to equipment and media that reduce computer output to microscopic form and put it on photosensitive film. **(196)**

Computer science curriculum. A course of study that includes all technical aspects of the design and use of computers. Computer science is offered as a degree program in many institutions of higher learning. **(578)**

Computer system. When applied to buying a "computer system," the term generally refers to the equipment and programs being sold. When applied to a computer-based operation in an organization, it is commonly defined as all the equipment, programs, data, procedures, and personnel supporting that operation. **(5)**

Computer virus. A small block of unauthorized code, transmitted from program to program by a copy operation, that performs destructive acts when executed. **(596)**

Concentrator. A communications device that combines the features of controllers and multiplexers. Concentrators also have a store-and-forward capability that enables them to store messages from several low-speed devices before forwarding them at high speeds to another device. **(243)**

Concurrent access. A term that refers to two or more users attempting to interactively access the same data at more or less the same time. **(458)**

Conditional branch. An instruction that may cause the computer to execute an instruction other than the one that immediately follows in the program sequence. **(315)**

Connector symbol. A flowcharting symbol used to represent a junction to connect broken paths in a line of flow. **(312)**

Contention. A condition in a communications system in which two or more devices compete for use of a line. **(241)**

Control-break reporting. A term that refers to "breaks" in the normal flow of information in a computer report that periodically occur for subtotals and totals. *(54)*

Controller. A device that supervises communications traffic in a telecommunications environment, reducing the computer's processing burden. **(241)**

Control panel. In spreadsheet software, the portion of the screen display that is used for issuing commands and observing what is being typed into the computer system. **(412)**

Control structure. A pattern for controlling the flow of logic in a computer program. The three basic control structures are sequence, selection (if-then-else), and looping (iteration). **(318)**

Control unit. The part of the CPU that coordinates the execution of program instructions. **(97)**

Coprocessor. A dedicated processor chip that is summoned by the CPU to perform specialized types of processing. *(112)*

CPU. See Central processing unit. **(5)**

Crosshair cursor. A digitizing device that is often moved over hard-copy images of maps and drawings to enter those images into the computer system. **(194)**

CRT. See Cathode-ray tube. **(171)**

Current cell. See Active cell. **(412)**

Cursor. A highlighting symbol that appears on a video screen to indicate the position where the next character (or group of characters) typed in will appear. **(173, 413)**

Daisywheel printer. A low-speed printer with a solid-font printing mechanism consisting of a spoked wheel of embossed characters. Daisywheel printers are capable of producing letter-quality output. *(177)*

Data. A collection of unorganized facts. **(6)**

Data access. Fetching data from a device either sequentially or directly. **(153)**

Database. An integrated collection of data stored on a direct-access storage device. **(45, 446)**

Database administrator (DBA). The person or group of people in charge of designing, implementing, and managing the ongoing operation of a database. **(450)**

Database management system (DBMS). A software package designed to integrate data and provide easy access to them. **(446)**

Data definition. The process of describing the characteristics of data that are to be handled by a database management system. **(451)**

Data definition language (DDL). A language used by a database administrator to create, store, and manage data in a database environment. **(454)**

Data dictionary. A facility that informs users and programmers about characteristics of data or programs in a database or a computer system. **(298, 455)**

Data-entry operator. A member of a computer operations staff responsible for keying data into the computer system. **(567)**

Data flow diagram. A graphically oriented systems development tool that enables a systems analyst to logically represent the flow of data through a system. **(547)**

Data manipulation. The process of using language commands to add, delete, modify, or retrieve data in a file or database. **(452)**

Data manipulation language (DML). A language used by programmers to supplement some high-level language supported in a database environment. **(458)**

Data organization. The process of establishing a data file so that it may subsequently be accessed in some desired way. Three common methods of organizing data are sequential organization, indexed-sequential organization, and direct organization. **(153)**

Data preparation device. An auxiliary device used to prepare data in machine-readable form. Two examples are key-to-tape units and key-to-disk units. **(41)**

Data processing area. The group of computer professionals within the information systems department who are charged with building transaction processing systems. **(540)**

Data processing director. The person in charge of developing and/or implementing the overall plan for transaction processing in an organization and for overseeing the activities of programmers, systems analysts, and operations personnel. **(572)**

Data processing system. See Transaction processing system. ***(503)***

Data structure. The relationships among data items. **(450)**

DBA. See Database administrator. **(450)**

DBMS. See Database management system. **(446)**

DDL. See Data definition language. **(454)**

Debugging. The process of detecting and correcting errors in computer programs or in the computer system itself. **(299)**

Decimal. A number system with 10 symbols—0, 1, 2, 3, 4, 5, 6, 7, 8, and 9. **(A-1)**

Decision support system (DSS). A system that provides tools and cababilities to managers to enable them to satisfy their own information needs. **(510)**

Decision symbol. A diamond-shaped flowcharting symbol used to represent a choice in a processing path. **(312)**

Decision table. A table that shows all the circumstances to be considered in a problem as well as the outcomes from any given set of circumstances. **(330)**

Decollator. A device that automatically removes carbon interleaves from continuous, fan-fold paper. ***(187)***

Dedicated line. A line used to provide an always available point-to-point connection between two or more devices. **(232)**

Default. The assumption a computer program makes when no specific choice is indicated by the user or programmer. **(258)**

Design. The process of planning a program or system. Design is normally undertaken after a problem has been thoroughly analyzed and a set of specifications for the solution established. **(291)**

Desk accessory. A software package that provides the electronic counterpart of tools commonly found on a desktop—a clock, calendar, notepad, and rolodex file, for instance. Also called a *desktop organizer.* **(513)**

Desk check. A manual checking process whereby a programmer or user scans a program listing for possible errors before submitting a machine-readable version of the program to the computer for execution. ***(300)***

Desktop computer. A microcomputer system that can fit on a desktop. Some familiar examples are the IBM PS/2 and Apple Macintosh II. **(471)**

Desktop publishing. A microcomputer-based publishing system that can fit on a desktop. **(390, 511)**

Detachable-reel tape. Magnetic tape that is wound onto a single reel, which in turn is mounted onto a tape unit with an empty take-up reel when data are to be read from or written to the tape. **(145)**

Device driver. A utility program that enables an applications program to function with a specific hardware device. **(275)**

Diagnostic. A message sent to the user by the computer system pinpointing errors in syntax or logic. Diagnostics often are referred to as *error messages.* ***(300)***

Difference engine. A mechanical machine devised by Charles Babbage in the 1800s to perform computations automatically and print their results. **(63)**

Digital computer. A computer that counts discrete phenomena, such as people and dollars. Virtually all computers used in businesses and in the home for personal computing are digital computers. **(94)**

Digital transmission. The transmission of data as discrete impulses. **(226)**

Digitizer. An input device that converts a measurement into a digital value. **(194)**

Digitizing tablet. A digitizer that consists of a flat board and device that traces over the board, storing the traced pattern in computer memory. **(195)**

Direct access. Reading or writing data in storage such that the access time involved is relatively independent of the location of the data. **(125)**

Direct organization. A method of organizing data on a device so they can be accessed directly (randomly). **(158)**

Disk access time. The time taken to locate and read (or position and write) data on a disk device. **(134)**

Disk cylinder. All tracks on a disk pack that are accessible with a single movement of the access mechanism. **(131)**

Disk drive. A mechanism within the disk storage unit on which disk packs, diskettes, or disk cartridges are placed to be accessed. *(16)*

Diskette. A small, removable disk made of a tough, flexible plastic and coated with a magnetizable substance. **(128, 476)**

Disk pack. A group of tiered hard disks that are mounted on a shaft and treated as a unit. A disk pack must be placed on a disk unit in order to be accessed. **(129)**

Disk unit. A direct-access secondary storage device that uses magnetic or optical disk as the principal I/O medium. **(129)**

Display device. A peripheral device that contains a viewing screen. **(167)**

Display terminal. A communications workstation that consists of a display device and a keyboard. **(167)**

DML. See Data manipulation language. **(458)**

Documentation. A detailed written description of a program, procedure, or system. **(301)**

Dot-matrix character. A character composed from a rectangular matrix of dots. *(181)*

DOUNTIL control structure. A looping control structure in which the looping continues as long as a certain condition is false (i.e., "do until true"). **(318)**

DOWHILE control structure. A looping control structure in which the looping continues as long as a certain condition is true (i.e., "do while true"). **(318)**

Drum plotter. An output device that draws on paper that is rolled along a cylindrically shaped drum. *(197)*

DSS. See Decision support system. **(510)**

EBCDIC. An acronym for Extended Binary-Coded Decimal Interchange Code. EBCDIC uses an 8-bit byte and can be used to represent up to 256 characters. **(102)**

E-cycle. The part of the machine cycle in which data are located, an instruction is executed, and the results are stored. **(98)**

EDSAC. An acronym for Electronic Delay Storage Automatic Calculator. EDSAC was the world's first stored-program computer and was completed in England in 1949. **(67)**

EDVAC. An acronym for Electronic Discrete Variable Automatic Calculator. Completed in 1950, EDVAC was the first stored-program computer built in the United States. **(67)**

EEPROM. See Electrically erasable programmable read-only memory. *(109)*

EFT. See Electronic funds transfer. *(605)*

Egoless programming. A term coined to emphasize that programmers whose work is being criticized in a structured walkthrough should not let their egos stand in the way of obtaining constructive feedback. **(299)**

Electrically erasable programmable read-only memory (EEPROM). An EEPROM module capable of having its contents altered when plugged into a peripheral device. *(109)*

Electromechanical machine. A device that has both electrical and mechanical features. **(64)**

Electronic funds transfer (EFT). Pertains to systems that transfer funds "by computer" from one account to another, without the use of written checks. *(605)*

Electronic machine. A device that contains electronic components. **(66)**

Electronic mail. A facility that enables users to send letters, memos, documents, and the like from one computer terminal to another. **(511)**

Electronic mailbox. A storage area used to hold a recipient's electronic mail. **(511)**

Electronic spreadsheet. A productivity software package that enables operators to create tables and financial schedules quickly by entering labels and values into cells on a display-screen grid. **(408)**

Encryption. A method of disguising data or programs so they are unrecognizable to unauthorized users. **(599)**

End user. A person who needs computer-produced results in his or her job. **(11)**

End-user development. Systems development activities carried out by the end user. **(556)**

ENIAC. An acronym for Electronic Numerical Integrator and Calculator. Unveiled in 1946, ENIAC was the world's first large-scale, general-purpose computer. **(66)**

EPROM. See Erasable programmable read-only memory. **(109)**

Erasable programmable read-only memory (EPROM). A software-in-hardware module that can be programmed and reprogrammed under certain limited conditions, yet cannot be casually erased by users or programmers. **(109)**

Ergonomics. The field that studies the effects of things such as computer hardware, software, and workspaces on employees' comfort and health. **(591)**

Expert system. A program or computer system that can reach conclusions for a problem that requires specialized knowledge similarly to the way in which a human expert might work on the problem. **(522)**

External disk. A disk unit that is not housed within the computer's system unit. Contrasts with internal disk. *(140)*

External storage. See Secondary storage. **(10)**

Facsimile (fax) machine. A device that can transmit or receive hard-copy images of text, pictures, maps, diagrams, and the like over the phone lines. **(511)**

Fiber optic cable. A cable composed of thousands of hair-thin, transparent fibers along which data are passed from lasers as light waves. **(222)**

Field. A collection of related characters. **(43)**

File. A collection of related records. **(43)**

File directory. A directory on an input/output medium that provides data such as filename, length, and starting address for each file on the medium. **(137)**

File manager. A productivity software package used to manage records and files. **(440)**

Film recorder. A cameralike device that captures computer output onto film. **(198)**

Firmware. Software instructions that are written onto a hardware module. **(109)**

First generation. Usually refers to the first era of commercial computers (1951–1958), characterized by vacuum tubes as the main logic element. **(68)**

Flatbed plotter. An output device that draws on paper that is mounted on a flat drawing table. *(197)*

Flat-panel display. A slim-profile display device. **(171)**

Floppy disk. See Diskette. *(128)*

Flowchart. See Structured program flowchart and System flowchart. *(310, 547)*

Flowline. A flowcharting symbol used to represent the connecting path among other flowchart symbols. **(311)**

Font. A typeface. **(392)**

FORmula TRANslator (FORTRAN). A high-level programming language used for mathematical, scientific, and engineering applications. **(348)**

FORTRAN. See FORmula TRANslator. **(348)**

Fourth generation. Usually refers to the fourth era of commercial computing (1971–present), characterized by microminiaturization and the rise of microcomputing. **(77)**

Fourth-generation language (4GL). An easy-to-learn, easy-to-use language that enables users or programmers to code applications much more quickly than they could with third-generation languages such as BASIC, FORTRAN, and COBOL. **(296, 357)**

Front-end processor. A computer that is positioned in a network to screen messages sent to the main computer and also relieves the main computer of certain computational chores. **(243)**

Full-duplex transmission. A type of transmission in which messages may be sent in two directions simultaneously along a communications path. **(226)**

Function key. A special keyboard key that executes a preprogrammed routine when depressed. *(173)*

Gateway. An interface that enables two dissimilar networks to communicate. Contrast with bridge. **(237)**

GB. See Gigabyte. **(104)**

General-purpose computer. A computer capable of being programmed to solve a wide range of problems. *(7)*

Gigabyte (GB). Approximately 1 billion bytes. **(104)**

Hacking. A term that, when used with computers, often relates to using a microcomputer system or terminal to break into the security of a large computer system. **(598)**

Half-duplex transmission. Any type of transmission in which messages may be sent in two directions—but only one way at a time—along a communications path. **(224)**

Hard card. A hard disk that has been configured onto an add-in board. **(142)**

Hard copy. A permanent form of usable output, for example, output on paper or film. Contrasts with soft copy. **(167)**

Hard disk. A rigid platter coated with a magnetizable substance. **(128, 477)**

Hardware. Physical equipment in a computing environment, such as the computer and its support devices. **(11)**

Hashing. A key-to-disk mathematical transformation in which the key field on each record determines where the record is stored. *(158)*

Heuristic. An intuitively appealing "rule of thumb" that is often used as part of a trial-and-error process to find a workable solution to a problem. *(522)*

Hexadecimal. Pertaining to the number system with 16 symbols: 0, 1, 2, 3, 4, 5, 6, 7, 8, 9, A, B, C, D, E, and F. **(A-7)**

Hierarchical local network. A star-shaped local network in which a large CPU (and, possibly, communications controllers) are at the top of the hierarchy and communications terminals or small CPUs are at the bottom. **(237)**

Hierarchy plus Input-Process-Output (HIPO) charts. A set of diagrams and procedures used to describe program functions from a general to a detailed level. **(327)**

High-level language. See High-level programming language. **(339)**

High-level programming language. The class of programming languages used by most professional programmers to solve a wide range of problems. Some examples are BASIC, COBOL, FORTRAN, and Pascal. **(72).**

Highlight. See Cell pointer. **(413)**

HIPO charts. See Hierarchy plus Input-Process-Output charts. **(327)**

Host computer. In telecommunications, a computer that is used to control a communications network. *(219)*

Host language. A programming language available for use on a specific computer system or subsystem. **(459)**

HyperTalk. A fourth-generation language that enables text, graphics, voice, and video data to be stored in a cardlike format and manipulated. **(357)**

IC. See Integrated circuit. **(74)**

Icon. A graphical image on a display screen that invokes a particular program action when selected by the operator. **(174)**

I-cycle. The part of the machine cycle in which the control unit fetches an instruction from main memory and prepares it for subsequent processing. **(98)**

If-then-else (selection) control structure. See Selection control structure. **(318)**

Image scanner. A device that can "read" into digital memory a hard-copy image such as a text page, photograph, map, or drawing. **(195)**

Impact dot-matrix mechanism. A print head that forms dot-matrix characters through impact printing. **(177)**

Impact dot-matrix printer. A printer whose print head is an impact dot-matrix mechanism. **(480)**

Impact printing. The formation of characters by causing a metal hammer to strike a ribbon into paper or paper into a ribbon. Contrasts with nonimpact printing. **(177)**

Indexed-sequential organization. A method of organizing data on a direct-access medium such that it can be accessed directly (through an index) or sequentially. **(155)**

Information. Data that have been processed into a meaningful form. **(6)**

Information center. A facility in an organization that caters to end-user needs. **(542)**

Information center consultant. A systems analyst, assigned to an information center, who helps end users develop their own systems. **(572)**

Information center director. The person in charge of an information center. **(573)**

Information processing. Pertains to computer operations that transform data into meaningful information. **(7)**

Information reporting system. An information system whose principal outputs are preformatted, hard-copy reports. **(508)**

Information retrieval. Online inquiry, through a display terminal or microcomputer workstation, to computer files or databases. **(54)**

Information systems department. The area in an organization that consists of computer professionals—managers, analysts, programmers, operations personnel, trainers, specialists, and the like. **(540)**

Initialize. To preset a variable to a specified value before using it in computations. **(315)**

Input. Anything supplied to a process or involved with the beginning of a process. For example, data must be input to a computer system; or data must be keyed into the system on an input device. Contrasts with output. **(5)**

Input device. A machine used to supply data to the computer. Contrasts with output device. **(5, 37, 166)**

Input/output (I/O) media. Objects used to store data or information before or after processing. Examples include magnetic disk, magnetic tape, and paper. **(5, 40)**

Input/output symbol. A parallelogram-shaped flowcharting symbol used to represent an input or output operation. **(312)**

Instruction register. The register that holds the part of the instruction indicating what the computer is to do next. **(98)**

Integrated circuit (IC). A series of complex circuits that are etched onto a small silicon chip. **(74)**

Integrated software package. A software package that bundles two or more major software functions into a single package. **(460, 482)**

Interblock gap. The distance on magnetic tape or disk between the end of one physical record and the start of another. **(148)**

Internal disk. A disk unit that is housed inside the computer's system unit. Contrasts with external disk. *(140)*

Internal memory. See Primary memory. **(7, 97)**

Internal storage. See Primary memory. **(7, 97)**

Interpreter. A computer program that translates a source program written by a user or programmer in a high-level language into machine language. The translation takes place on a line-by-line basis as each statement is executed. Contrasts with compiler. **(270)**

Interrecord gap. See Interblock gap. **(148)**

I/O media. See Input/output media. **(5, 40)**

Issuance. The use of computers to produce transaction processing documents such as paychecks, bills, and customer reminder notices. **(51)**

Iteration control structure. See Looping control structure. **(318)**

Joystick. An input device, resembling a car's stick shift, that often is used for computer games and computer-aided design (CAD) work. **(194)**

KB. See Kilobyte. **(104)**

Keyboard. An input device composed of several typewriterlike keys, arranged in a configuration similar to that of a typewriter. Computer keyboards also have a number of special keys that initiate preprogrammed routines when activated. **(173, 477)**

Key field. A field used to identify a record. **(147)**

Key-to-disk unit. An auxiliary device that uses a keyboard unit to place data directly on magnetic disk. *(41)*

Key-to-tape unit. An auxiliary device that uses a keyboard unit to place data directly on magnetic tape. *(41)*

Kilobyte (KB). Approximately 1,000 (1,024, to be exact) bytes. Primary memory on smaller computer systems often is measured in kilobytes. **(104)**

Label. In spreadsheet software, a cell entry that cannot be manipulated mathematically. **(414)**

LAN. See Local area network. **(235)**

Language translator. A system program that converts an applications program into machine language. **(268)**

Laptop computer. A portable computer light enough to be operated while resting on one's lap. **(471)**

Large-scale integration (LSI). The process of placing a large number of integrated circuits (usually over 100) on a single silicon chip. *(80)*

Laser printer. A nonimpact printer that works on a principle similar to that for a photocopier. **(481)**

Light pen. An electrical device, resembling an ordinary pen, used to enter input by pointing to a display screen. **(174)**

Line printer. A high-speed printer that produces output a line at a time. **(186)**

Linkage editor. A system program that binds together related object-module program segments so they may be run as a unit. **(269)**

LISP. A language widely used for artificial intelligence applications. **(356)**

Load module. A complete machine-language program that is ready to be executed by the computer. Also called a *load program.* **(269)**

Local area network (LAN). A cable-based local network, without a host computer, that usually consists of microcomputer workstations and shared peripherals. **(235)**

Local network. A privately run communications network of several machines located within a mile or so of one another. **(233)**

Logical record. A data record from the point of view of an end user or programmer. **(148)**

Logic element. The electronic component used to facilitate circuit functions within the computer. *(67)*

Logo. A programming language often used to teach children how to program. **(354)**

Looping (iteration) control structure. The control structure used to represent a looping operation. Also see DOUNTIL control structure and DOWHILE control structure. **(318)**

Low-level language. A highly detailed, machine-dependent programming language. Included in the class of low-level languages are machine and assembly languages. **(338)**

LSI. See Large-scale integration. *(80)*

Machine cycle. The series of operations involved in the execution of a single machine-language instruction. **(98)**

Machine language. A binary-based programming language that the computer can execute directly. **(71, 106)**

Machine-readable. Any form in which data are encoded so that they can be read by a machine. **(5)**

Macro facility. A spreadsheet facility that enables programs to be embedded in a worksheet. **(421)**

Magnetic bubble storage. Storage that uses magnetic bubbles to indicate the 0- and 1-bit states. **(152)**

Magnetic core. A tiny, ring-shaped piece of magnetizable material capable of storing a single binary digit. Magnetic cores were popular as internal memories in second- and third-generation computers. **(72)**

Magnetic disk. A secondary storage medium consisting of platters made of rigid metal (hard disk) or flexible plastic (diskette). **(128)**

Magnetic ink character recognition (MICR). A technology, confined almost exclusively to the banking industry, that involves the processing of checks inscribed with special characters set in a special magnetic ink. **(191)**

Magnetic tape. A plastic tape with a magnetic surface for storing data as a series of magnetic spots. **(144)**

Mailing list program. A program used to generate mailing labels. **(387)**

Mail merge program. A program specifically designed to produce form letters. **(387)**

Mainframe. A large, transaction-processing-oriented computer capable of supporting powerful peripheral devices. **(14)**

Main memory. See Primary memory. **(7)**

Maintenance programmer. A programmer involved with keeping an organization's existing programs in proper working order. **(284)**

Management information system (MIS). A system designed to provide information to managers to enable them to make decisions. **(507)**

Mark I. Completed in 1944 by Harold Aiken of Harvard University, the Mark I was the first large-scale electro-mechanical computer. **(65)**

Mass storage unit. A storage device capable of storing billions of bytes of data online. **(150)**

Master file. A file containing relatively permanent data, such as customer names and addresses. **(46)**

MB. See Megabyte. **(104)**

Mechanical calculating machine. A computer that works by means of gears and levers rather than by means of electric power. **(62)**

Megabyte (MB). Approximately 1 million bytes. **(104)**

Menu. A set of options, provided at a display device, from which the operator makes a selection. *(18)*

MICR. See Magnetic ink character recognition. **(191)**

Microcomputer. See Microcomputer system. **(12, 470)**

Microcomputer system. The smallest and least expensive type of computer system. Also called a *personal computer system.* **(16, 470)**

Microfiche. A sheet of film, often 4 by 6 inches, on which computer output images are stored. *(196)*

Microminiaturization. A term that implies a very small size. **(80)**

Microprocessor. A CPU on a silicon chip. **(472)**

Microsecond. One millionth of a second. **(99)**

Microspacing. A technique used by some printers to insert fractional spaces between characters to give text a typeset look. **(385)**

Microwave. An electromagnetic wave in the high-frequency range. **(222)**

Millisecond. One thousandth of a second. **(99)**

Minicomputer. An intermediate-size and medium-priced type of computer. **(13)**

MIS. See Management information system. **(507)**

Modem. A contraction of the words MOdulation and DEModulation. A communications device that enables computers and their support devices to communicate over ordinary telephone lines. **(226, 481)**

Module. A related group of entities that may be treated effectively as a unit. **(320)**

Monitor. (1) A video display. (2) The supervisor program of an operating system. **(167, 257, 479)**

Monochrome. A term used to refer to a display device that operates in a single foreground color. *(170)*

Mouse. A device used to rapidly move a cursor around a display screen. **(174, 479)**

Multiplexer. A communications device that interleaves the messages of several low-speed devices and sends them along a single, high-speed transmission path. **(243)**

Multiprocessing. The *simultaneous* execution of two or more program sequences by multiple computers operating under common control. **(266)**

Multiprogramming. The execution of two or more programs, possibly being run by different users, *concurrently* on the same computer. **(261)**

Multitasking. The ability of a single-user operating system to enable two or more programs or program tasks to execute concurrently. **(262)**

Nanosecond. One billionth of a second. **(99)**

Narrowband transmission. Low-speed transmission, characterized by telegraph transmission. **(224)**

Network. A system of machines that communicate with one another. *(231)*

Nonimpact printing. The formation of characters on a surface by means of heat, lasers, photography, or ink jets. Contrasts with impact printing. **(181)**

Nonprocedural language. A very-high-level, problem-dependent programming language that informs the computer system *what* work is to be done rather than *how* to do the work. Contrast with procedural language. **(339)**

Nonvolatile storage. Storage that retains its contents when the power is shut off. Contrast with volatile storage. **(125)**

Object module. The machine-language program that is the output from a language translator. Also called an *object program.* **(268)**

OCR. See Optical character recognition. **(189)**

Octal. Pertaining to the number system with eight symbols—0, 1, 2, 3, 4, 5, 6, and 7. **(A-5)**

Office automation (OA). The use of computer-based, office-oriented technologies such as word processing, desktop publishing, electronic mail, video teleconferencing, and the like. **(511)**

Office automation (OA) area. The group of computer professionals within the information systems department that is charged with managing office-related computer activities within the organization. **(543)**

Office automation (OA) director. The person in charge of the office automation (OA) area. **(573)**

Offline. Anything not in or prepared for communication with the CPU. Contrasts with online. **(41)**

Offpage connector symbol. A flowchart symbol used to connect other flowchart symbols logically from page to page. **(315)**

One-entry-point/one-exit-point rule. A rule stating that each program control structure will have only one entry point into it and one exit point out of it. **(319)**

Online. Anything ready for or in communication with the CPU. Contrast with offline. **(41)**

Operating system. A collection of systems software that enables the computer system to manage the resources under its control. **(74, 255, 485)**

Optical character recognition (OCR). The use of light reflectivity to identify marks, characters, or codes and the subsequent conversion of such symbols into a form suitable for computer processing. **(189)**

Optical disk. A disk read by laser beams rather than by magnetic means. **(151)**

Original equipment manufacturer (OEM). A company that buys hardware from manufacturers and integrates it into its own systems. *(83)*

Output. Anything resulting from a process or involved with the end result of a process. For example, processed data are output as information; or information may be printed using an output device. Contrast with input device. **(5)**

Output device. A machine used to output computer-processed data, or information. **(5, 37, 166)**

Page-makeup software. Programs used to compose page layouts in a desktop publishing system. **(393)**

Page printer. A high-speed printer that delivers output one page at a time. **(187)**

Parallel transmission. Data transmission in which each bit in a byte has its own path and all of the bits in a byte are transmitted simultaneously. Contrasts with serial transmission. **(228)**

Parity bit. An extra bit added to the byte representation of a character to ensure that there is always either an odd or an even number of 1-bits transmitted with every character. **(106)**

Pascal. A structured high-level programming language that is often used to teach programming. **(343)**

Pascaline. A mechanical calculating machine developed by Blaise Pascal in the 1600s. **(62)**

PBX. See Private branch exchange. **(237)**

Peripheral equipment. The input devices, output devices, and secondary storage devices in a computer system. **(40)**

Personal computer. See Personal computer system. **(12, 470)**

Personal computer system. See Microcomputer system. **(16, 470)**

Physical record. A block of logical records. **(148)**

Picosecond. A trillionth of a second. **(99)**

Pixel. On a display screen, a single dot used to compose dot-matrix characters and other images. **(168)**

Plotter. An output device used for drawing graphs and diagrams. **(197)**

PL/1. See Programming Language/1. **(351)**

Point-of-sale (POS) system. A computer system, commonly found in department stores and supermarket environments, that uses electronic cash register terminals to manage and record sales transactions and, possibly, to perform other data-handling functions. **(190)**

Point size. A measurement used in the scaling of typefaces. **(383)**

Polling. In data communications, a line control method in which a computer or controller asks one terminal after another if it has any data to send. **(241)**

Port. An outlet on the computer's system unit through which a peripheral device may communicate. **(113, 474)**

Portable computer. A microcomputer system that is compact enough to be easily carried about. **(471)**

POS system. See Point-of-sale system. **(190)**

Power manager. A device that controls the power going to several other devices in a computer system. **(481)**

Precompiler. A computer program that translates an extended set of commands available with a programming language into standard commands of the language. **(459)**

Preliminary investigation. In systems development, a brief study of a problem area to assess whether or not a full-scale systems project should be undertaken. Also called a *feasibility study.* **(544)**

Presentation graphics package. A productivity software package used to prepare line charts, bar charts, pie charts and other information-intensive images. **(423)**

Primary key. A key in a record that is often used to physically arrange or to access a record. Generally, each record has a different value for its primary key. For example, many records kept on individuals use social security number as a primary key. *(271)*

Primary memory. Also known as *main memory* and *internal storage,* a section of the CPU that temporarily holds data and program instructions awaiting processing, intermediate results, and output produced from processing. **(7, 97)**

Printer. A device that places computer output onto paper. **(177, 481)**

Privacy. In a computer processing context, refers to how information about individuals is used and by whom. **(602)**

Private branch exchange (PBX). A switching station that an organization acquires for its own use. **(237)**

Procedural language. A high-level programming language designed to solve a large class of problems. Procedural languages work by having the programmer code a set of procedures that tell the computer, step by step, how to solve a problem. Contrasts with nonprocedural language. **(339)**

Processing. See Information processing. **(5)**

Processing symbol. A rectangular flowcharting symbol used to indicate a processing operation such as a computation. **(312)**

Productivity software. Fourth-generation-language-based software—such as word processors, spreadsheets, presentation-graphics packages, file managers, and database management systems—designed to make workers more productive at their jobs. **(482)**

Program. A set of instructions that causes the computer system to perform specific actions. **(6)**

Program design tool. A tool, such as a flowchart, pseudocode, or structure chart, that helps the systems analyst or programmer decide how a program is to work. **(310)**

Program development cycle. A process consisting of all the steps an organization must go through to bring a computer program into operation. The steps of the program development cycle include analysis, design, coding, debugging and testing, and documentation. Also called the *program life cycle.* **(283)**

Program flowchart. A visual design tool showing step by step how a computer program will process data. Contrasts with system flowchart. **(310)**

Program life cycle. See Program development cycle. **(283)**

Programmable read-only memory (PROM). A software-in-hardware module that can be programmed under certain restricted conditions and cannot be altered or erased once programmed. **(109)**

Programmer. A person whose job is to write, maintain, and test computer programs. **(11, 284)**

Programming language. A language used to write computer programs. **(7, 338)**

Programming Language/1 (PL/1). A structured, general-purpose, high-level programming language that can be used for scientific, engineering, and business applications. **(351)**

Prolog. A language widely used for artificial intelligence applications. **(356)**

PROM. See Programmable read-only memory. **(109)**

Proportional spacing. A printing feature that allocates more horizontal space on a line to some characters than to others. **(384)**

Protocol. A set of conventions used by machines to establish communication with one another in a telecommunications environment. **(240)**

Prototyping. A systems development alternative whereby a small model, or prototype, of the system is built before a full-scale systems development effort is undertaken. **(555)**

Pseudocode. A technique for structured program design that uses Englishlike statements to outline the logic of a program. Pseudocode statements closely resemble actual programming code. **(322)**

Queue. A group of items awaiting computer processing. *(274)*

RAM. See Random access memory. **(108, 472)**

RAM disk. A disk management system in which a portion of RAM is set up to function as disk memory. **(143)**

Random access. See Direct access. **(125)**

Random access memory (RAM). Any memory capable of being accessed directly. In the world of microcomputers, the acronym RAM generally applies only to primary memory. **(108, 472)**

Read-only memory (ROM). A software-in-hardware module that can be read but not written on. **(109, 473)**

Read/write head. A magnetic station on a disk access mechanism or tape unit that reads or writes data. **(124)**

Realtime processing. Updating data immediately in a master file as transactions take place. Contrasts with batch processing. **(55)**

Recalculation feature. The ability of spreadsheet software to quickly and automatically recalculate the contents of several cells based on new operator inputs. **(411)**

Record. A collection of related fields. **(43)**

Redlining. A word processing facility that provides the electronic equivalent of the editor's red pen. **(388)**

Reduced instruction set computing (RISC). A term referring to a computer system that gets by with a fewer number of instructions than conventional computer systems, thereby reducing system overhead and, in many cases, decreasing the time needed to process programs. **(95)**

Register. A high-speed staging area within the computer that temporarily stores data during processing. **(97)**

Relational data structure. A data structure in which data are represented in tables, which may be interrelated by the user. *(451)*

Report Program Generator (RPG). A report-generation language popular with small businesses. **(355)**

Request for proposal (RFP). A document containing a general description of a system that an organization wishes to acquire. The RFP is submitted to vendors, who subsequently recommend specific systems based on the resources they are able to supply. **(553)**

Request for quotation (RFQ). A document containing a list of specific hardware, software, and services that an organization wishes to acquire. The RFQ is submitted to vendors, who subsequently prepare bids based on the resources they are able to supply. **(553)**

Resolution. A term referring to the sharpness of the images on an output medium. *(168)*

Response time. The time it takes the computer system to respond to a specific input. *(286)*

Retrieval/update language. A fourth-generation language specifically tailored to information retrieval and updating operations. **(452)**

Reusable code. Program segments that can be reused several times in constructing applications programs. **(298)**

RFP. See Request for proposal. **(553)**

RFQ. See Request for quotation. **(553)**

Ring network. A telecommunications network in which machines are connected serially in a closed loop. **(239)**

RISC. See Reduced instruction set computing. **(95)**

Robotics. The field devoted to the study of robot technology. **(521)**

ROM. See Read-only memory. **(109, 473)**

RPG. See Report Program Generator. **(355)**

Secondary key. A key field, subordinate to the primary key, used to search through or arrange a file or database. Unlike with a primary key, two records can have the same value for a secondary key. *(271)*

Secondary storage. Storage, provided by technologies such as disk and tape, that supplements primary memory. Also called *external storage.* **(10)**

Secondary storage device. A machine, such as a tape unit, disk unit, or mass storage device, capable of providing storage to supplement primary memory. **(37)**

Second generation. Usually refers to the second era of commercial computers (1959–1964), characterized by transistor circuitry. **(71)**

Sector. A pie-shaped area on a disk. Many disks are addressed through sectors. **(135)**

Selection. The process of going through a set of data and picking out only those data elements that meet certain criteria. **(51)**

Selection (if-then-else) control structure. The control structure used to represent a decision operation. **(318)**

Semiconductor memory. A memory whose components are etched onto small silicon chips. **(80)**

Sequence control structure. The control structure used to represent operations that take place sequentially. **(318)**

Sequential access. Fetching records in storage ascendingly or descendingly by the key field on which they are physically ordered. **(125)**

Sequential organization. Arranging data on a physical medium either ascendingly or descendingly by some key field. **(154)**

Serial transmission. Data transmission in which every bit in a byte must travel down the same path in succession. Contrasts with parallel transmission. **(228)**

Server. A shared device, such as a laser printer or high-capacity hard disk, on a local area network (LAN). **(235)**

Simplex transmission. Any type of transmission in which a message can be sent along a path in only a single prespecified direction. **(224)**

Simulation. A technique whereby a model of a real-life object or situation is built and tested prior to constructing the object or encountering the situation. *(612)*

Site license. A right acquired by an organization that enables employees to freely use or copy software for specific, authorized purposes. **(599)**

Smalltalk. An object-oriented programming language. **(355)**

Soft copy. A nonpermanent form of usable output, for example, display output. Contrasts with hard copy. **(167)**

Software. Computer programs. **(11)**

Software piracy. The unauthorized copying or use of computer programs. **(598)**

Solid-font mechanism. The printing element on a printer, such as a daisywheel printer, that produces solid characters. Contrasts with dot-matrix mechanism. **(177)**

Sorting. The process of arranging data in a specified order. **(54)**

Source-data automation. Making data available in machine-readable form at the time they are collected. **(188)**

Source module. The original form in which a program is entered into an input device by a user or programmer, prior to being translated into machine language. Also called a *source program.* **(268)**

Spelling checker. A program often used adjunctively with a word processor to check for misspelled words. **(386)**

Spooling program. A program that temporarily stores input or output in secondary storage to expedite processing. **(271)**

Star network. A network consisting of a host device connected directly to several other devices. **(237)**

Start/stop symbol. A flowcharting symbol used to begin and terminate a flowchart. **(312)**

Status area. See Control panel. **(412)**

Storage. Pertains to memory areas that hold programs and data in machine-readable form. **(5)**

Storage register. A register that temporarily stores data that have been retrieved from primary memory prior to processing. **(98)**

Streaming tape. A cartridge tape used exclusively for backup purposes. *(145)*

Structure chart. A program design tool that shows the hierarchical relationship among program modules. A structure chart closely resembles the common organization chart. **(326)**

Structured program flowchart. A flowchart embodying many of the principles of structured programming. **(320)**

Structured programming. An approach to program design that uses a restricted set of program control structures, the principles of top-down design, and numerous other design methodologies. **(292, 317)**

Structured walkthrough. A formal program development practice in which the work of a systems analyst or programmer is constructively reviewed by peers. **(299)**

Style sheet. A collection of font and formatting specifications that can be saved as a file and later used to format documents in a particular way. **(389)**

Summarizing. The process of reducing a mass of data to a manageable form. **(51)**

Supercomputer. The fastest type of computer. Typically, supercomputers are found in engineering or scientific research environments. **(14)**

Supervisor. The central program in an operating system. The supervisor has the ability to invoke other operating system programs to perform various system tasks. **(257)**

Support equipment. All the machines that make it possible to get data and programs into the CPU, get processed information out, and store data and programs for ready access to the CPU. **(5, 36)**

Surge suppression. The act of protecting a microcomputer system from random electrical power spikes. *(481)*

Switched line. A communications line that feeds into a switching center, enabling it to reach virtually any destination in the network by means of a telephone number. **(232)**

Synchronous transmission. The transmission of data over a line a block of characters at a time. Contrasts with asynchronous transmission. **(228)**

System. A collection of elements and procedures that interact to accomplish a goal. **(538)**

System acquisition. The phase of the systems development life cycle in which equipment, software, or services are acquired from vendors. **(552)**

System board. A board that contains the computer and its primary memory. Sometimes called a *motherboard.* **(112)**

System design. The phase of the systems development life cycle in which the parts of a new system and the relationship among them are formally established. **(550)**

System flowchart. A systems development tool that shows the physical parts of a system and how they relate to one another. Contrasts with program flowchart. **(547)**

System implementation. The phase of systems development that encompasses activities related to making the computer system operational and successful once delivered by the vendor. **(554)**

System librarian. The person in the computer operations area responsible for managing data files and programs stored offline on tapes, disks, microfilm, and other types of storage media. **(568)**

System unit. The hardware unit that houses the computer and its primary memory, as well as a number of other devices, such as add-in boards and related circuitry. **(36, 108, 470)**

Systems analysis. The phase of the systems development life cycle in which a problem area is thoroughly examined to determine what should be done. **(545)**

Systems analyst. A person who studies systems in an organization in order to determine what actions need to be taken and how these actions may best be achieved with computer resources. **(284, 540, 571)**

Systems development. The process of studying a problem or opportunity area, designing a system solution for it, acquiring the resources necessary to support the solution, and implementing the solution. **(538)**

Systems development life cycle (SDLC). The process consisting of the five phases of system development: preliminary investigation, systems analysis, system design, system acquisition, and system implementation. **(541)**

Systems programmer. A programmer who codes systems software. Contrasts with applications programmer. **(569)**

Systems software. Computer programs, such as the operating system, language translators, and utility programs, that do background tasks for users and programmers. Contrasts with applications software. **(50, 254)**

Tape unit. A secondary storage device on which magnetic tapes are mounted. **(146)**

Telecommunications. A term that refers to transmitting data over a distance—over the phone lines, via privately owned cable, or by satellite, for instance. **(216)**

Telecommuting. The substitution of working at home, and being connected through electronic devices to others at remote locations, for the commute to work. **(516)**

Teleconferencing. Using computer and communications technology to carry out a meeting in which the participants need not all be present at the same site. **(515)**

Teleprinter terminal. A low-speed printer containing a keyboard. **(188)**

Template. A prelabeled onscreen form that requires only that the operator fill in a limited number of input values. **(419, 441)**

Terabyte. Approximately 1 trillion bytes. **(104)**

Terminal. Technically speaking, any device that is not a host device. *(219)*

Terrestrial microwave station. A ground station that receives microwave signals, amplifies them, and passes them on. **(222)**

Text editor. A utility program that enables an operator to manipulate text in a file. **(274)**

Thesaurus feature. A routine, often accompanying a word processor, that enables electronic lookup of word synonyms. **(386)**

Third generation. Usually refers to the third era of commercial computers (1965–1970), characterized by integrated circuit technology. **(73)**

Time-sharing. Interactive processing in which the computer is shared by several users at more or less the same time. The computer system interleaves the processing of the programs so that it appears to each user that he or she has exclusive use of the computer. **(264)**

Top-down design. A structured design philosophy whereby a program or system is subdivided into well-defined modules, organized in a hierarchy, which are developed from the top of the hierarchy down to the lowest level. **(320)**

Touch-screen device. A display device that can be activated by touching a finger to the screen. **(175)**

Track. A path on an input/output medium on which data are recorded. **(128)**

Trackball. A cursor-movement device that consists of a sphere resting on rollers, with only the top of the sphere exposed outside its case. **(194)**

Traditional SDLC approach. An approach to systems development whereby the five phases of the systems development life cycle are carried out serially. **(542)**

Trainer. A person who provides education to end users about a particular program, system, or technology. **(572)**

Transaction file. A file of occurrences, such as customer payments and purchases, that have taken place over a period of time. **(46)**

Transaction processing system. A system that processes an organization's business transactions. Operations falling into the transaction processing category include payroll, order entry, accounts receivable, accounts payable, inventory, and general ledger. **(503)**

Transistor. A circuit device that dominated second-generation computers. **(71)**

Twisted-wire pairs. A communications medium consisting of pairs of wires twisted together and bound into a cable. The public-access telephone system consists mainly of twisted-wire cabling. **(221)**

Unconditional branch. An instruction that causes the computer to execute a specific statement other than the one that immediately follows in the normal sequence. **(315)**

UNIVAC I. The first commercial electronic digital computer. **(68)**

Universal product code (UPC). The bar code that is prominently displayed on the packaging of almost all supermarket goods, identifying the product and manufacturer. A variety of optical scanning devices may be used to read the codes. **(190)**

UPC. See Universal product code. **(190)**

Updating. The process of bringing something up to date by making corrections, adding new data, and so forth. **(54)**

Upward compatible. A computer system that can do everything that a smaller model in the line or the previous model can do, plus some additional tasks. *(73)*

Utility program. A program used to perform some frequently encountered operation in a computer system. **(270)**

Vacuum tube. The circuit device that dominated first-generation computers. **(68)**

Value. In spreadsheet programs, a cell entry that can be manipulated mathematically. Contrasts with label. **(414)**

Value-added network (VAN). A term that most commonly refers to a service offered over the public-access phone network by a firm other than the phone company, thereby adding value to the network. **(233)**

VAN. See Value-added network. **(233)**

Vendor rating system. An objective point-scoring procedure for evaluating competing vendors of computer products or services. **(553)**

Very-high-level language. A problem-specific language that is generally much easier to learn and use than conventional high-level languages such as BASIC, FORTRAN, COBOL, and Pascal. **(339)**

Very-large-scale-integration (VLSI). The process of placing a very large number of integrated circuits (usually over 1,000) on a single silicon chip. *(80)*

Vice-president of information systems. The person in an organization who oversees routine transaction processing and information systems activities as well as other computer-related areas. Also often called the *chief information officer (CIO).* **(573)**

Video disk. An optically readable disk on which video images are stored. **(152)**

Virtual storage. An area on disk in which programs are "cut up" into manageable pieces and staged as they are processed. While the computer is processing a program, it fetches the pieces that are needed from virtual storage and places them into main memory. **(264)**

VLSI. See Very-large-scale integration. *(80)*

Voice-grade transmission. Medium-speed transmission characterized by the rates of speed available over ordinary telephone lines. **(224)**

Voice-input device. A device capable of recognizing the human voice. **(192)**

Voice mail. An electronic mail system in which phone messages are digitally recorded and stored in an electronic mailbox. **(511)**

Voice-output device. A device that enables the computer system to produce spoken output. **(197)**

Volatile storage. Storage that loses its contents when the power is shut off. Contrast with nonvolatile storage. **(125)**

WAN. See Wide area network. **(231)**

Wide area network (WAN). A network that covers a wide geographical area. **(231)**

Wideband transmission. High-speed transmission characterized by the rates of speed available over coaxial cable, fiber optic cable, and microwave. **(224)**

Winchester disk. A sealed data module that contains a disk, access arms, and read/write heads. **(137)**

Window. Refers to either (1) using the display screen as a "peek hole" to inspect contiguous portions of a large worksheet or (2) dividing up the display screen into independent boxes of information. **(274)**

Window area. In spreadsheet software, the portion of the screen that contains the window onto the worksheet. Also called the *worksheet area.* **(412)**

Windowing software. Software that enables a user to assemble independent boxes of information on the screen at the same time. **(274)**

Word. A group of bits or characters that are treated by the computer system as a unit and are capable of being stored in a single memory location. **(109)**

Word processing. The use of computer technology to create, manipulate, and print text material such as letters, legal contracts, and manuscripts. **(372, 511)**

Worksheet. In spreadsheet software, the grid that contains the actual labels and values. **(408)**

Worksheet area. See Window area. **(412)**

WYSIWYG. An acronym for "What You See Is What You Get," WYSIWYG shows on the display screen an output image identical or very close to the desired, final hardcopy image. **(375)**

Answers to Fill-in and Matching Review Exercises

CHAPTER 1

Fill-in Questions
1. processing
2. primary, internal, or main
3. information
4. software
5. secondary, external, or auxiliary
6. hardware
7. program
8. computer system

Matching Questions
1. e   2. f   3. a   4. c
5. b   6. d

CHAPTER 2

Fill-in Questions
1. input/output medium
2. auxiliary
3. online
4. Applications
5. Systems
6. field
7. file
8. realtime

Matching Questions
1. b   2. f   3. c   4. e
5. a   6. d

CHAPTER 3

Fill-in Questions
1. ENIAC
2. pascaline
3. difference engine
4. Mark I
5. ABC

6. UNIVAC
7. Digital Equipment
8. Altair 8800

Matching Questions
1. h   2. e   3. f   4. g
5. a   6. c   7. d   8. b

CHAPTER 4

Fill-in Questions
1. millisecond
2. microsecond
3. nanosecond
4. picosecond
5. kilobyte
6. megabyte
7. gigabyte
8. terabyte

Matching Questions
1. b   2. d   3. g   4. e
5. h   6. a   7. f   8. c

CHAPTER 5

Fill-in Questions
1. volatile
2. disk pack
3. cylinder
4. hard card
5. logical, physical
6. tracks
7. file-protection ring
8. mass storage unit

Matching Questions
1. d   2. a   3. c   4. f
5. e   6. b

CHAPTER 6

Fill-in Questions
1. hard copy
2. pixels
3. cursor
4. monochrome
5. near-letter-quality
6. thermal-transfer
7. ink-jet
8. flatbed, drum
9. bit-mapped
10. film recorder

Matching Questions
1. e   2. f   3. g   4. b
5. d   6. a   7. h   8. c

CHAPTER 7

Fill-in Questions
1. twisted-wire pairs
2. Coaxial cable
3. digital
4. Fiber optic cable
5. modem
6. Synchronous
7. Common carriers
8. Asynchronous
9. dedicated
10. star

Matching Questions
1. d   2. e   3. b   4. a
5. f   6. c

CHAPTER 8

Fill-in Questions
1. Systems
2. operating system

3. multiprogramming
4. Time-sharing
5. Multiprocessing
6. language translator
7. Utility

Matching Questions
1. e 2. d 3. a 4. c
5. g 6. b 7. f

CHAPTER 9

Fill-in Questions
1. Systems analysts
2. Maintenance programmers
3. Coding
4. structured walkthrough
5. code generator
6. reusable code
7. debugging
8. desk check

Matching Questions
1. h 2. c 3. e 4. b
5. f 6. g 7. d

CHAPTER 10

Fill-in Questions
1. flowchart
2. conditional
3. unconditional
4. initializing
5. top-down
6. Pseudocode
7. Structure charts, HIPO charts
8. Decision tables

Matching Questions
1. d 2. f 3. a 4. e
5. b 6. c

CHAPTER 11

Fill-in Questions
1. BASIC
2. FORTRAN
3. COBOL
4. Pascal
5. PL/1
6. C
7. LISP
8. fourth-generation

Matching Questions
1. g 2. a 3. c 4. d
5. e 6. f 7. b

CHAPTER 12

Fill-in Questions
1. wordwrap
2. Proportional spacing
3. mailing list
4. dedicated
5. what you see is what you get
6. orphan
7. page description language
8. clip art

Matching Questions
1. e 2. b 3. a 4. f
5. c 6. d

CHAPTER 13

Fill-in Questions
1. window, worksheet
2. cursor, cell pointer (high-light)
3. control panel
4. absolute, relative, mixed
5. template
6. macro facility
7. Add-on
8. dedicated, integrated

Matching Questions
1. d 2. f 3. e 4. a
5. c 6. b

CHAPTER 14

Fill-in Questions
1. file managers, database management systems
2. template
3. database
4. hierarchical, network, relational
5. database administrator
6. concurrent
7. Structured Query Language
8. integrated software package

Matching Questions
1. b 2. e 3. a 4. d
5. f 6. c

CHAPTER 15

Fill-in Questions
1. random access memory
2. read-only memory
3. microprocessor
4. nonvolatile
5. operating systems
6. modem
7. surge suppression
8. multifunction

Matching Questions
1. d 2. e 3. c 4. b
5. a 6. h 7. g 8. f

CHAPTER 16

Fill-in Questions
1. artificial intelligence
2. accounts receivable

3. general ledger
4. computer-aided design
5. electronic mail
6. Teleconferencing
7. robotics

Matching Questions
1. c 2. a 3. f 4. e
5. d 6. b

CHAPTER 17

Fill-in Questions
1. chief information officer (CIO)
2. steering
3. management
4. End-user development
5. system design
6. tangible

7. vendor rating
8. benchmark test

Matching Questions
1. b 2. d 3. e 4. c
5. a

CHAPTER 18

Fill-in Questions
1. Data-entry operators
2. Computer operators
3. System librarians
4. Computer operations managers
5. Systems programmers
6. Applications programmers
7. Systems analysts
8. data processing director

Matching Questions
1. c 2. a 3. b 4. d

CHAPTER 19

Fill-in Questions
1. cyberphobia
2. Ergonomics
3. Computer ethics
4. piracy
5. Fair Credit Reporting
6. Education Privacy

Matching Questions
1. c 2. f 3. a 4. e
5. b 6. d

Credits

Module A opening photos Courtesy of Quantel Ltd.

Chapter 1 opening photo Courtesy of Cathrine Colgan/Wasatch Computer Technology.

Figure 1-2 Courtesy of (a) International Business Machines Corporation, (b) Apple Computer, Inc., (c) Hewlett-Packard Company.

Figure 1-3 Courtesy of Digital Equipment Corporation.

Figure 1-4 Courtesy of International Business Machines Corporation.

Figure 1-5 Photo, Paul Shambroom; Courtesy Cray Research, Inc.

Tomorrow box photos Courtesy of Pontiac Division of General Motors Corporation.

Chapter 2 opening photo Courtesy of Cathrine Colgan/Wasatch Computer Technology.

Figure 2-2 Courtesy of (a) International Business Machines Corporation, (b) Apple Computer, Inc.

Figure 2-3 Courtesy of International Business Machines Corporation.

Figure 2-4 Courtesy of Canon U.S.A., Inc.

Figures 2-5–2-8 Courtesy of International Business Machines Corporation.

Figure 2-9 Courtesy of (a) BASF Corporation, (b) 3M, (c) International Business Machines Corporation, (d) BASF Corporation.

Tomorrow box photo Courtesy of VISA International.

Chapter 3 opening photo Unisys Corporate Archives. Courtesy Unisys Corporation.

Figures 3-1, 3-2, 3-3 Courtesy of International Business Machines Corporation.

Figure 3-4 Courtesy of Unisys Corporation.

Figure 3-5 Courtesy of International Business Machines Corporation.

Figure 3-6 Courtesy of AT&T Archives.

Figure 3-7 Courtesy of International Business Machines Corporation.

Figure 3-8 Courtesy of Digital Equipment Corporation.

Figure 3-9 Courtesy Intel Corporation.

Figure 3-10 Courtesy of Microsoft Corporation.

Figure 3-11 Courtesy of Apple Computer, Inc.

Figure 3-12 Courtesy of International Business Machines Corporation.

Module B opening photo Courtesy of DuPont Design Technologies, Inc.

Chapter 4 opening photo Courtesy of Covia

Figure 4-9 Courtesy of International Business Machines Corporation.

Figure 4-10 Charles S. Parker.

Chapter 5 opening photo Courtesy of Hewlett-Packard Company.

Figure 5-2 Courtesy of International Business Machines Corporation.

Figure 5-7 Courtesy of 3M.

Figure 5-11 Courtesy of Hewlett-Packard Company.

Figures 5-13, 5-14 Courtesy of Plus Development Corporation.

Figure 5-15 Courtesy of BASF Corporation.

Figures 5-16, 5-17 Courtesy of International Business Machines Corporation.

Figure 5-21 Charles S. Parker.

Figures 5-22, 5-23 Courtesy of International Business Machines Corporation.

Figure 5-24 Courtesy of ByVideo Incorporated.

Tomorrow box photo Courtesy of International Business Machines Corporation.

Feature 5A photo Courtesy of International Business Machines Corporation.

Chapter 6 opening photo Courtesy of Intergraph Corporation.

Figure 6-1 Courtesy of (a), (b), (c) International Business Machines Corporation, (d) Moniterm.

Figure 6-3 Courtesy of CalComp Inc.

Figure 6-4 Courtesy of Wang Laboratories Inc., Copyright © 1989.

Figure 6-5 Courtesy of International Business Machines Corporation.

Figure 6-7 Courtesy of International Business Machines Corporation.

Figure 6-8 Courtesy of Qume Corporation.

Figure 6-12 Courtesy of NEC Information Systems.

Figure 6-13 Produced by Pat Coleman on Pixel Paint software from SuperMAC. Courtesy Tektronix, Inc.

Figure 6-14 Courtesy of Qume Corporation.

Figure 6-16 Courtesy of (a) NEC Information Systems, (b) Tektronix, Inc., (c) Hewlett-Packard Company.

Figure 6-17 Courtesy of NEC Information Systems.

Figures 6-18, 6-19 Courtesy of International Business Machines Corporation.

Figure 6-24 Courtesy of NCR Corporation.

Figure 6-25 Courtesy of Hewlett-Packard Company.

Figure 6-28 Courtesy of Apple Computer, Inc.

Figure 6-29 Courtesy of CalComp, Inc.

Figure 6-30 Courtesy of Howtek, Inc.

Figure 19-6 Courtesy of International Business Machines Corporation.
Figure 19-7 Courtesy of Oberon Systems Inc. and C. F. Peters Corporation.
Figure 19-8 Courtesy of Dave Clendenon/Wasatch Computer Technology.
Figure 19-9 Courtesy Ship Analytics, Inc.
Figure 19-10 Courtesy of Apple Computer, Inc.
Feature 19C photo Courtesy of Thumbscan, Inc.
Appendix B Section 3 box photos Courtesy of (a) Microsoft Corporation, (b) True BASIC, Inc.

WINDOW PHOTOGRAPHS

Window 1

1 © 1987 WOB, Advertising Agency/Artist: Walter Hertig. Courtesy Cubicomp Corporation.
2,3 Pacific Data Images/Marks Communications. Produced and animated by Pacific Data Images.
4 © 1987 Contact Video/Tandem Computers. Courtesy Cubicomp Corporation.
5 Genigraphics Corporation.
6 © 1987 Matchframe Computer Graphics. Courtesy Cubicomp Corporation.
7,8 Courtesy Broadcast Television Systems. Produced on FGS-4500.
9 E-Machines Inc.
10 Cathrine Colgan/Wasatch Computer Technology.
11,12 DuPont Design Technologies, Inc.
13 © 1987 Cubicomp Corporation/Artist: Amie Slate.
14 © 1988 Design Vision.

15,16 Courtesy International Business Machines Corporation.
17 Courtesy of NCR Corporation.
18 Courtesy of NCR Corporation.
19 Courtesy of Covia.
20 Courtesy of ByVideo Incorporated.
21 Courtesy of Hewlett-Packard Company.
22–24 Courtesy of International Business Machines Corporation.

Window 2

1 Courtesy of General Motors Corporation.
2 Courtesy of Hewlett-Packard Company
3 Courtesy of National Semiconductor.
4 Courtesy of Digital Equipment Corporation.
5–7 Courtesy of General Motors Corporation.
8 Courtesy of National Semiconductor.
9 Courtesy of Intel Corporation.
10 Courtesy of General Motors Corporation.

Window 3

1 Artist: James Dowlen. Computer systems by: Everex Systems Inc. and Vision Technologies. Software: Color-scheme III by Vision Technologies.
2–4 © Truevision, Inc. 1988.
5 Matrix Instruments Inc.
6 Genigraphics Corporation.
7 Courtesy Show & Tell Systems, Summagraphics.
8 Genigraphics Corporation.
9 Silicon Graphics.
10 Design Vision.
11 Courtesy Aurora Systems.
12 Quantel, Ltd.
13 Produced on Electronic Arts' Studio/8. Courtesy Tektronix.
14 Courtesy Tektronix.
15 Courtesy of CalComp Inc.
16 "Old Cars" by Linda Prosch. Produced with Lumena/32 software. Courtesy Time Arts Inc.

17 "Chardonnay" by Steve Keller. Produced with Lumena/32 software. Courtesy Time Arts Inc.
18 "Eyetech" by Garrett Moore and Terry Grieves. Produced with Lumena/32 software. Courtesy Time Arts Inc.
19 "Chicago 19" by Jim Hillin. Produced with Lumena/32 software. Courtesy Time Arts Inc.
20 Brian Johnson/Wasatch Computer Technology.
21,22 Cathrine Colgan/Wasatch Computer Technology.

Window 4

1 Courtesy of Apple Computer, Inc.
2,3 Brøderbund Software, Inc.
4–9 Mediagenic.
10–14 Owl International, Inc. and Cornell University.

Window 5

1 © 1987 Adobe Systems Incorporated. Art produced using Adobe Illustrator 88™. All rights reserved.
2–5 Adobe Systems Incorporated.
6 Z-Soft.
7,8 Courtesy of Micrographx.
9 Letraset.
10 Z-Soft.
11 Crosfield Lightspeed Inc.
12 Letraset.
13 Z-Soft.
14 Crosfield Lightspeed Inc.
15,16 © 1987 Adobe Systems Incorporated. Art produced using Adobe Illustrator 88™. All rights reserved.

Window 6

1,2 Courtesy Microsoft.
3,4 Courtesy Computer Associates International, Inc.
5 Genigraphics Corporation
6 Courtesy SAS Institute Inc., Cary, N.C.
7 Courtesy of Micrographx.
8 Matrix Instruments Inc.
9 Courtesy SAS Institute Inc., Cary, N.C.

10 David Clendenon/Wasatch Computer Technology.
11 Brian Johnson/Wasatch Computer Technology.
12 Genigraphics Corporation.
13 Nancy Palie, Autographix.
14–16 General Parametrics Corporation.
17 © 1987 Electric Paintbrush/Artist: Eleanor Dixon. Courtesy Cubicomp Corporation.

Window 7

1 GRiD Systems Corporation.
2 Courtesy of International Business Machines Corporation.
3 Zenith Electronics Corporation.
4 Courtesy of Hewlett-Packard Company.
5 Courtesy of International Business Machines Corporation.

6–8 Courtesy of Hewlett-Packard Company.
9 Courtesy of International Business Machines Corporation.
10 GRiD Systems Corporation.

Window 8

1 Courtesy Broadcast Television Systems.
2,3 © 1988 Cubicomp Corporation. Artist: Arianne Dickinson.
4,5 Courtesy of International Business Machines Corporation.
6 Matrix Instruments Inc.
7 "Glasses" Digital Art, Belgium. Courtesy Alias Research Incorporated.
8 DuPont Design Technologies, Inc./ Herb Bossardt, Artist.
9 Data Translation, Inc.

10–13 Data Translation, Inc.
14–18 Scitex America Corporation.
19–22 Contex Graphics Systems, Inc.
23 DuPont Design Technologies, Inc.
24–28 Courtesy Island Graphics Corporation, Erol Otus.
29 Courtesy Island Graphics Corporation, Erol Otus, and PennWell Publishing Company.

Window 9

1 Courtesy Iterated Systems, Inc.
2–10 LDL, Inc.
11–14 Evans & Sutherland.
15 Evans & Sutherland and Bell Helicopter Textron.
16–18 Evans & Sutherland.

INDEX